W9-BUS-069

20°E 40°E 60°E 80°E 100°E 120°E 140°E 160°E 180°

Arctic Ocean 80°N

NORWAY SWEDEN FINLAND

ARCTIC CIRCLE

RUSSIA

Europe-Asia Boundary 60°N

DENMARK ESTONIA LATVIA LITHUANIA (Rus.)
GERMANY POLAND BELARUS
LUX CZECH REP. SLOVAKIA UKRAINE MOLDOVA
FRANCE AUS HUNG ROMANIA
SWITZERLAND ITALY SLOVENIA CROATIA BULGARIA
GREECE GEORGIA ARMENIA AZERBAIJAN

KAZAKHSTAN

MONGOLIA

UZBEKISTAN

KYRGYZSTAN

TURKMENISTAN TAJIKISTAN

Bejing CHINA

NORTH KOREA
SOUTH KOREA

JAPAN 40°N

Istanbul
TURKEY
TUNISIA CYPRUS LEBANON SYRIA
ISRAEL JORDAN IRAQ IRAN
KUWAIT

AFGHANISTAN Islamabad
PAKISTAN

Yarahmadzaï

Shanghai Na

Pacific Ocean

ALGERIA LIBYA EGYPT
BAHRAIN QATAR U.A.E.
SAUDI ARABIA OMAN

Musha

NEPAL BHUTAN
Hijra
BANGLADESH

TAIWAN

TROPIC OF CANCER

NIGER SUDAN YEMEN
ERITREA DJIBOUTI

INDIA

MYANMAR (BURMA) LAOS
Lua

MACAU (Port.)
HONG KONG (U.K.)

20°N

CHAD

ETHIOPIA

THAILAND VIETNAM
CAMBODIA

PHILIPPINES

NORTHERN MARIANA ISLANDS (U.S.)

REPUBLIC OF THE MARSHALL ISLANDS

NIGERIA CENTRAL AFRICAN REP.
CAMEROON

Nuer, Dinka

Mbuti UGANDA SOMALIA

SRI LANKA

Agta

GABON CONGO
SÃO TOMÉ AND PRÍNCIPE
DEMOCRATIC REPUBLIC OF THE CONGO RWANDA BURUNDI

KENYA Maasai, Kikuyu

MALDIVES

Bukittinggi

BRUNEI
MALAYSIA

Sumatra SINGAPORE Borneo

FEDERATED STATES OF MICRONESIA

Arapesh, Enga, Mundugumor, and Tchambuli 0°

CABINDA (Angola)

Mwanza TANZANIA

SEYCHELLES

Diego Garcia

Toraja

INDONESIA
PAPUA NEW GUINEA

SOLOMON ISLANDS

TUVALU

Melanesians

ANGOLA ZAMBIA
MALAWI

COMOROS IS.

Indian Ocean

Trobriand Islanders VANUATU FIJI

Juǀ'hoansi NAMIBIA
ZIMBABWE
MOZAMBIQUE
MADAGASCAR

MAURITIUS

Pintupi

NEW CALEDONIA (Fr.) 20°S

WALVIS BAY (status to be determined)
BOTSWANA SWAZILAND

TROPIC OF CAPRICORN

SOUTH AFRICA LESOTHO

AUSTRALIA

NEW ZEALAND 40°S

Maori

1. SLOVENIA
2. CROATIA
3. BOSNIA AND HERZEGOVINA
4. ALBANIA
5. MACEDONIA

60°S

ANTARCTIC CIRCLE

ANTARCTICA

80°S

20°E 40°E 60°E 80°E 100°E 120°E 140°E 160°E 180°

THIRD EDITION

CULTURE COUNTS

A Concise Introduction to Cultural Anthropology

Serena Nanda
John Jay College of Criminal Justice,
City University of New York

Richard L. Warms
Texas State University

CENGAGE
Learning·

Australia • Brazil • Japan • Korea • Mexico • Singapore • Spain • United Kingdom • United States

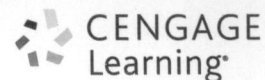
CENGAGE
Learning·

Culture Counts: A Concise Introduction to Cultural Anthropology, Third Edition
Serena Nanda and Richard L. Warms

Product Director: Jon-David Hague

Content Developer: Lin Marshall Gaylord

Content Coordinator: Sean Cronin

Product Assistant: Kyra Kane

Media Developer: John Chell

Brand Manager: Molly Felz

Content Project Manager: Cheri Palmer

Art Director: Caryl Gorska

Manufacturing Planner: Judy Inouye

Rights Acquisitions Specialist: Thomas McDonough

Production Service: Jill Traut, MPS Limited

Photo Researcher: PreMedia Global

Text Researcher: PreMedia Global

Copy Editor: Heather McElwain

Illustrator and Composition: MPS Limited

Maps: Graphic World

Cover and Text Designer: Norman Baugher

Cover Image: Frans Lemmens

For product information and technology assistance, contact us at **Cengage Learning Customer & Sales Support, 1-800-354-9706.**

For permission to use material from this text or product, submit all requests online at **www.cengage.com/permissions**
Further permissions questions can be e-mailed to **permissionrequest@cengage.com**

Library of Congress Control Number: 2013940725

ISBN-13: 978-1-285-73851-2

ISBN-10: 1-285-73851-9

Cengage Learning
200 First Stamford Place, 4th Floor
Stamford, CT 06902
USA

Cengage Learning is a leading provider of customized learning solutions with office locations around the globe, including Singapore, the United Kingdom, Australia, Mexico, Brazil, and Japan. Locate your local office at **www.cengage.com/global**

Cengage Learning products are represented in Canada by Nelson Education, Ltd.

To learn more about Cengage Learning Solutions, visit **www.cengage.com**

Purchase any of our products at your local college store or at our preferred online store **www.cengagebrain.com**

Printed in the United States of America
1 2 3 4 5 6 7 17 16 15 14 13

Dedication

To the grandchildren:
Alexander, Adriana,
Charlotte, Kai, and
Waverly. —SN—

To Karen, Ben, and
Nathan. —RW—

BRIEF CONTENTS

FEATURES CONTENTS

DETAILED CONTENTS

CHAPTER 5

MAKING A LIVING   105

CHAPTER 6

ECONOMICS   131

CHAPTER 7

POLITICAL ORGANIZATION   159

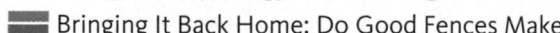

CHAPTER 8

STRATIFICATION: CLASS, CASTE, RACE, AND ETHNICITY   185

CHAPTER 9

MARRIAGE, FAMILY AND KINSHIP   211

CHAPTER 10

SEX AND GENDER   237

CHAPTER 11

RELIGION   263

CHAPTER 12

CREATIVE EXPRESSION: ANTHROPOLOGY
AND THE ARTS 291

PREFACE

ANTHROPOLOGY is the study of all people, in all places and at all times. Students and scholars alike are drawn to anthropology as part of the realization that our lives and experiences are limited, but human possibilities are virtually endless. We are drawn to anthropology by the almost incredible variability of human society and our desire to experience and understand it. We are drawn by the beauty of other lives and sometimes by the horror as well. We write *Culture Counts,* third edition, to transmit some of our sense of wonder at the endless variety of the world and to show how anthropologists have come to understand, analyze, and engage with human culture and society.

Culture Counts, third edition, is a brief introduction to anthropology written particularly for students in their first two years of college but is accessible to and appropriate for other audiences as well. Our goal has been to write in a clean, crisp, jargon-free style that speaks to readers without speaking down to them. Each chapter is relatively brief but is packed with ethnographic examples and discussions that keep readers involved and focused. Although it is written in an extremely accessible style, *Culture Counts* sacrifices none of the intellectual rigor or sophistication of our longer work, *Cultural Anthropology,* now in its 11th edition. Each chapter of *Culture Counts* opens with an ethnographic situation, circumstance, history, or survey designed to engage the readers' interest and focus their attention on the central issues of the chapter. These chapter opening essays raise questions about the anthropological experience, the nature of culture, and the ways in which anthropologists understand society. Much of what follows in each chapter indicates the ways in which the themes of the opening stories are illuminated by anthropological thinking.

Each chapter concludes with a feature entitled "Bringing It Back Home," which contains an example of a current controversy, issue, or debate. Each example is followed by a series of three critical thinking questions entitled "You Decide." The questions encourage students to apply anthropological understandings as well as their own life experiences and studies to the issue under discussion. Through these exercises, students learn to use anthropological ideas to grapple with important issues facing our own and other cultures. They learn to apply anthropology to the realities of the world.

Design is an important feature of *Culture Counts.* One of our goals is to present students with a clear, easy-to-follow text that is uncluttered and that highlights the main source of anthropology—ethnographic data.

To address the visual orientation of contemporary students, we have taken considerable care to choose visually compelling photographs and to include high-quality maps and charts that provide visual cues for content and help students remember what they have read. Each image and its accompanying explanatory caption reflects specific passages

and themes in the text. Extended ethnographic examples are accompanied by maps that provide the specific geographical location of the group under discussion.

PERSPECTIVE AND THEMES

As with *Cultural Anthropology,* our main perspective in *Culture Counts* is ethnographic, and our theoretical approach is eclectic. Ethnography is the fundamental source of anthropological data, and the interest in ethnography is one of the principal reasons students take anthropology courses. Ethnographic examples have the power to engage students and encourage them to analyze and, also of great importance, to question their own culture. Ethnographic examples that illuminate cultures, situations, and histories, both past and present, are used extensively in every chapter. *Culture Counts* describes the major issues and theoretical approaches in anthropology in a balanced manner, drawing analysis, information, and insight from many different perspectives. It takes a broad, optimistic, enthusiastic approach and promotes the idea that debates within the field are signs of anthropology's continued relevance rather than problems it must overcome.

Additionally, we believe that issues of power, stratification, gender, and ethnicity, and globalization and change, are central to understanding contemporary cultures. These topics are given chapters of their own as well as integrated in appropriate places throughout the text.

Culture Counts, third edition, continues the collaboration between Serena Nanda and Richard Warms. Warms's specialties in West Africa, anthropological theory, and social and economic anthropology complement Nanda's in India, gender, law, and cultural anthropology. The results are synergistic. Our experiences, readings, discussions, and debates, as well as feedback from reviewers and professors who have adopted our other books, have led to the production of a book that reflects the energy and passion of anthropology.

Both Nanda and Warms have extensive experience in writing textbooks for university audiences. In addition to *Cultural Anthropology,* now in its 11th edition, Nanda is the author of *American Cultural Pluralism and Law,* now in its third edition, with Jill Norgren, and *Gender Diversity: Cross-cultural Variations.* Warms, with R. Jon McGee, is author of *Anthropological Theory: An Introductory History,* now in its fourth edition, and of *Sacred Realms: Readings in the Anthropology of Religion,* second edition, with James Garber and R. Jon McGee. Collaborative writing continues to be an exciting intellectual adventure for us, and we believe that the ethnographic storytelling approach of this book will promote students' growth as well.

NEW IN THIS EDITION

We have made a number of significant changes and additions to this third edition, based partly on recent developments in the field of anthropology and partly on the valuable feedback we have received from our adopters and reviewers. To begin with, we have added new ethnographic examples, expanding cross-cultural comparisons and trimmed terminology, included in the glossary, while keeping the essential key terms to help guide student understanding.

The number of photographs, maps, tables, charts, and graphs has also been expanded.

We have eliminated the former Chapter 14, "Anthropology Makes a Difference," using some of this material as well as new examples in a section called "Using Anthropology." This section appears in each chapter and emphasizes the many different ways anthropologists today are engaged in applying and using anthropology to solve practical human problems. "Using Anthropology" is designed to bring anthropology into the lives of students and to encourage them to see the ways in which anthropological knowledge and the work of anthropologists is an active force in the social, political, and economic lives of people around the world. In addition to these changes, we have carefully revised and re-edited each chapter to include new references and new examples.

We have added a new chapter, Chapter 12, called "Creative Expression: Anthropology and the Arts," which looks at the arts from cultural, social, global, and political perspectives. In addition, we have slightly revised the book's chapter organization, so that "Political Organization," now Chapter 7 immediately follows the Chapter on "Economics." New chapter opening student "Learning Objectives" replaces the former chapter outlines, and the new end-of-chapter "Summary" is in question-and-answer format, drawing on the "Learning Objectives."

CHAPTER OVERVIEWS

Each chapter is organized so that the main ideas, secondary ideas, important terms and definitions, and ethnographic material stand out clearly. Although we have a deep appreciation for classic ethnography and cite it frequently, each chapter also presents current work in anthropology and includes many references to books and essays published in the past five years.

In Chapter 1, "What is Anthropology and Why Should I Care?", the order in which the subfields are presented is changed, new material is added (and some old material replaced) to make the length of space devoted to each subfield more balanced. The "Using Anthropology" section in this chapter is "Forensic Anthropology," a subject of great practical use and of popular interest. A new section, "Everyday Anthropology," has been added that emphasizes the use of anthropology in daily life, and the section titled "Why Study Anthropology" has more of a focus on how anthropology is useful in future employment. "The Anthropology of Violence" is the new "Bringing It Back Home" essay.

In Chapter 2, "Culture Counts," a new opening story on feral children replaces one on autism, and there is a new table of anthropological theories. The "Using Anthropology" section describes the fascinating case of Lia Lee, describing how culture influences the explanations and treatment of illness among different immigrant groups in the United States. There is also new material on the issue of the legalization of marijuana, and the new "Bringing It Back Home" feature focuses on the question of whether there is an American culture.

Chapter 3, "Doing Cultural Anthropology," incorporates new sections on Boas and Malinowski, in addition to new information and a new table on interview techniques; we have shortened the sections on engaged anthropology (which appear throughout in the "Using Anthropology" features) and also on postmodernism. The "Using Anthropology" section describes how anthropological engagement helped establish food self-sufficiency among the Ju/'hoansi and helped reduce violence in Papua New Guinea. The section on studying one's own society has been updated, featuring the work of the Penobscot Indian anthropologist, Darren Ranco, and the section of anthropology in the military has been somewhat trimmed.

Chapter 4, "Communication," begins with a new chapter opening scenario, "Why Don't You Speak Good?" and we have also added information on deaf communities, while trimming the sections on technical aspects of grammar, such as phonology, and on glottochronology. "Forensic Linguistics" is the subject of the "Using Anthropology" section, and there is an expanded section on language and social stratification, including a discussion of Irish D4 accents. We have also added two charts, one describing the great vowel shift and the second presenting the world's most common languages.

In Chapter 5, "Making a Living," we have rewritten and edited the chapter opening story, the section on industrialization, and given more balanced space to the different subsistence strategies and the beef industry. The "Using Anthropology" section focuses on "Anthropology and Nutrition," and we have added a chart to the "Bringing It Back Home" essay.

Chapter 6, "Economics," incorporates a newly edited opening story, a new chart of the relation of education to salaries, and a re-editing of the section on the potlatch, tying it to information on the United States. The section on resistance to capitalism has been substantially rewritten, and the "Bringing It Back Home" on "Product Anthropology" has been updated. The new "Using Anthropology" section describes "Gifts, Bribes, and Social Networks" in the Ukraine.

Chapter 7, "Political Organization," begins with a new story about the Arab Spring and includes a new feature on the integration of power and wealth in the Asante state. "Using Anthropology: Advocating for the Chagossians" is a new example of the engagement of anthropologists in advocating for indigenous peoples.

Chapter 8, "Stratification: Class, Caste, Race, and Ethnicity" has been rearranged so that caste stratification in India follows a discussion of social class in the United States. The new opening story gives a cross-cultural account of exploited children, while the "Using Anthropology" section describes a successful effort of an anthropologist in changing the lives of homeless people in Massachusetts. The section on race includes a new cross-cultural comparison between race in Brazil and the United States, and the new "Bringing It Back Home" raises the question: Who is an American?

Chapter 9 on "Marriage, Family, and Kinship" incorporates an updated section on the American family, and the "Using Anthropology" section provides an analysis of the family in a global context. The section on arranged marriage has been expanded to incorporate some changes taking place among Indian women garment workers, and the "Bringing It Back Home: Caring for the Elderly" has been greatly expanded.

Chapter 10, "Sex and Gender," has been revised to incorporate material on women bullfighters in Spain and Tongan soccer players in Japan, to highlight the "deep play" of sports in its connection to gender. The "Using Anthropology" section highlights the applied/ethnographic work of Ann Dunham among women in Indonesia, and there is a new section on how market women in Vietnam are incorporated into an economic paradigm of socialism. A new "Bringing It Back Home" features an essay on domestic violence and cultural values.

Chapter 11, "Religion," incorporates organizational revision and new ethnography. The functions of religion are spread throughout the chapter, there is a substantial rewriting of the sections on ritual and witches and sorcerers, and expansion of information on religious narratives and cosmologies. The new "Using Anthropology" section features the use of magic and witchcraft in addressing HIV/AIDS in Tanzania, and the "Bringing It Back Home" feature titled "Religion, Art, and Censorship" has been revised and updated.

Chapter 12, "Creative Expression: Anthropology and the Arts," is a new chapter, reflecting the importance of the great variety of creative expression in all human cultures, dating back to the Paleolithic. Opening with a description of world music, the chapter explores—among other issues—art and cultural and personal identity, deep play, "reality" TV among "primitive peoples," and the impact of the global art market on the art of societies cross-culturally. The "Using Anthropology" section highlights the multiple roles of anthropology museums in today's global society.

Chapter 13, "Power, Conquest, and a World System," contains a substantial rewriting of the relevance of this subject to anthropology. There is also an updating of statistical information. The new "Using Anthropology" section illuminates a connection between anthropology and "unpleasant history," in the work of Scott Joplin, and the section on decolonization and postcolonialism has been substantially revised. The new "Bringing It Back Home" raises the question of Islam and multiculturalism in contemporary Europe.

Chapter 14, "Culture, Change, and Globalization," is the new chapter title, reflective of some new material, most particularly the "Bringing It Back Home: America as a Foreign Culture" section, which describes how others see the culture of the United States. The "Using Anthropology" section is about the ways in which anthropologists are applying their knowledge to help refugees in the United States who have fled from conflict and persecution. The anthropology and development sections have been updated and feature the work of medical anthropologist Jim Yong Kim, the new president of the World Bank. Also new in the chapter is a detailed examination of workers at Foxconn, who make the Apple electronic products, and a new look at global migration.

◪ TEACHING FEATURES AND STUDY AIDS

Each chapter includes outstanding pedagogical features to help students identify, learn, and remember key concepts and data. Several learning aids help students better understand and retain the chapter's information, as follows:

Δ Full-color opening photos with captions are placed at the beginning of each chapter.

Δ New "Student Learning Objectives" replace the chapter outline at the beginning of chapters, providing a road map for reading.

△ Each chapter opens with an essay that focuses on an ethnographic situation, circumstance, or history designed to capture students' interest and launch them into the chapter.

△ Each chapter concludes with a brief essay ("Bringing It Back Home") and questions ("You Decide") that encourage the application of anthropological thinking to a current controversy, issue, or debate. The questions can be used as assignments or to promote classroom discussion.

△ Summaries are now arranged as numbered questions and answers at the end of each chapter; these recap critical ideas and aid study and review.

△ Key terms are listed alphabetically at the end of each chapter, for quick review.

△ A running glossary of key terms is found in the margins of the pages where the terms are introduced.

△ References for every source cited within the text are listed alphabetically at the end of the book.

SUPPLEMENTS

 ## Instructor Resources

△ **Instructor's Edition for *Culture Counts: A Concise Introduction to Cultural Anthropology*, third edition.** Using ethnographic storytelling, Nanda and Warms's concise, engaging text shows students how culture matters in driving and explaining human behavior, and that culture is a dynamic concept that interrelates various cultural systems in adaptive (or maladaptive) ways.

△ **Instructor's Manual and Test Bank for *Culture Counts: A Concise Introduction to Cultural Anthropology*, third edition.** The instructor's manual contains a variety of resources to aid instructors in preparing and presenting text material in a manner that meets their personal preferences and course needs. It presents chapter-by-chapter suggestions and resources to enhance and facilitate learning. For assessment support, the updated test bank includes multiple-choice, true/false, short-answer, and essay questions for each chapter.

△ **Cengage Learning Testing Powered by Cognero for *Culture Counts: A Concise Introduction to Cultural Anthropology*, third edition.** This flexible online system allows you to author, edit, and manage test bank content from multiple Cengage Learning solutions; create multiple test versions in an instant; and deliver tests from your LMS, classroom, or wherever you need.

△ **Online PowerPoint® Slides for *Culture Counts: A Concise Introduction to Cultural Anthropology*, third edition.** These vibrant Microsoft® PowerPoint® lecture slides for each chapter assist you with your lecture by providing concept coverage using images, figures, and tables directly from the textbook.

◥◣ Student Resources

△ **CourseMate with eBook for *Culture Counts: A Concise Introduction to Cultural Anthropology*, third edition.** Interested in a simple way to complement your text and course content with study and practice materials? Cengage Learning's Anthropology CourseMate brings course concepts to life with interactive learning, study, and exam preparation tools that support the printed textbook. Watch student comprehension soar as your class works with the printed textbook and the textbook-specific website. Anthropology CourseMate goes beyond the book to deliver what you need!

△ **Wadsworth Anthropology Video Library.** Qualified adopters can select full-length videos from an extensive library of offerings drawn from such excellent educational video sources as *Films for the Humanities and Sciences.*

△ **AIDS in Africa DVD.** Expand your students' global perspective of human immunodeficiency virus (HIV)/acquired immunodeficiency syndrome (AIDS) with this award-winning documentary series that focuses on controlling HIV/AIDS in southern Africa. Films focus on caregivers in the faith community; how young people share messages of hope through song and dance; the relationship of HIV/AIDS to gender, poverty, stigma, education, and justice; and the story of two HIV-positive women helping others.

△ **Anthropology CourseReader.** Anthropology CourseReader allows you to create a fully customized online reader in minutes. Access a rich collection of thousands of primary and secondary sources, readings, and audio and video selections from multiple disciplines.

△ *Neither Man nor Woman: The Hijras of India,* **second edition, by Serena Nanda.** This ethnography is a cultural study conducted by text author Serena Nanda of the hijras of India, a religious community of men who dress and act like women. It focuses on how hijras can be used in the study of gender categories and sexual variation. (978-0-534-50903-3)

△ *Globalization and Change in Fifteen Cultures: Born in One World, Living in Another,* **edited by George Spindler and Janice E. Stockard.** In this volume, 15 case study authors write about culture change in today's diverse settings around the world. Each original article provides insight into the dynamics and meanings of change, as well as the effects of globalization at the local level. (978-0-534-63648-7)

△ *Classic Readings in Cultural Anthropology,* **third edition, edited by Gary Ferraro.** Brief and accessible, this reader edited by Gary Ferraro features articles and excerpts from works that have proved pivotal in the field of cultural anthropology. Topics include culture, language and communication, ecology and economics, issues of culture change, and many more. (978-1-111-29792-3)

△ *Case Studies in Cultural Anthropology,* **edited by George Spindler and Janice E. Stockard.** Select from more than 60 classic and contemporary ethnographies representing geographic and topical diversity. Newer case studies focus on culture change and culture continuity, reflecting the globalization of the world, and include a legacy edition of Napoleon Chagnon's *Yąnomamö,* and a fourth edition of Richard Lee's *The Dobe Ju/'hoansi*. Recent publications include *Shadowed Lives,* by Leo Chavez.

△ ***Case Studies on Contemporary Social Issues,* edited by John A. Young.** Framed around social issues, these new contemporary case studies are globally comparative and represent the cutting-edge work of anthropologists today. Recent publications include *Slaughterhouse Blues,* by Donald Stull and Michael Broadway, and *Seeking Food Rights: Nation, Inequality and Repression in Uzbekistan,* by Nancy Rosenberger.

ACKNOWLEDGMENTS

It gives us great pleasure to thank the many people who have been associated with this book. We are most appreciative of the helpful comments made by our reviewers:

> Janet Altamirano, Wharton County Community College
>
> Jennifer Basquiat, College of Southern Nevada
>
> Susan Fogarty, Lakeland Community College
>
> Wendy Fonarow, Glendale Community College
>
> Valerie Johnson, Mid South Community College
>
> Hannah Jopling, Fordham University
>
> Sharon Methvin, Mt. Hood Community College/University of Portland
>
> Virginia Ochoa-Winemiller, Auburn University, Montgomery
>
> Jerry Ratcliffe, The College of New Jersey
>
> Anna Tacon, Texas Tech University
>
> Terance Winemiller, Auburn University, Montgomery

We gratefully acknowledge the support of our universities and the help of the staffs of our departments at John Jay College of Criminal Justice and Texas State University. In addition, many of our students have contributed ideas, reflections, and labor to this project. We particularly thank Bita Razavimaleki, graduate student at Texas State University, for her analysis and comments.

Our families continue to form an important cheering section for our work, and we thank them for their patience and endurance and for just plain putting up with us.

We are deeply grateful to the people at Cengage Learning, particularly our Senior Product Manager, Aileen Berg and Senior Content Developer, Lin Marshall Gaylord, for their support, their encouragement, and their insight. In addition, we thank Victor Lu, product assistant; Sean Cronin, content coordinator; Lauren Oliveira, media developer; and Cheri Palmer, content production manager, as well as Molly Felz and Michelle Williams in marketing. We are also grateful to Jill Traut of MPS Limited who shepherded us through the production process.

The knowledge, editing skills, and superb suggestions made by the many people involved in the production of this book have greatly contributed to it.

◢ABOUT THE AUTHORS

Serena Nanda is professor emeritus of anthropology at John Jay College of Criminal Justice, City University of New York. In addition to *Cultural Anthropology,* now in its 11th edition, her published works includes *Neither Man nor Woman: The Hijras of India,* winner of the 1990 Ruth Benedict Prize; *American Cultural Pluralism and Law;* and *Gender Diversity: Cross Cultural Variations.* She is also the author of two anthropological murder mysteries: *The Gift of a Bride: A Tale of Anthropology, Matrimony and Murder,* set in an Indian immigrant community in New York

Courtesy of Serena Nanda

City, and *Assisted Dying: An Ethnographic Murder Mystery on Florida's Gold Coast.* Nanda has also authored many journal and encyclopedia articles on arranged marriage, gender pluralism, and teaching anthropology, and is currently the associate editor for the gender section of the forthcoming *Encyclopedia of Sexuality.* She has always been captivated by the stories people tell and by the tapestry of human diversity. Anthropology was the perfect way for her to immerse herself in these passions, and, through teaching and writing, to spread the word about the importance of understanding both human differences and human similarities. Students and faculty are invited to contact her with their comments, suggestions, and questions at snanda@jjay.cuny.edu.

Courtesy of Rich Warms

Richard L. Warms is professor of anthropology at Texas State University in San Marcos, Texas. In addition to *Cultural Anthropology,* now in its 11th edition, his books include *Anthropological Theory: An Introductory History,* now in its 5th edition, and *Sacred Realms: Essays in Religion, Belief,* and *Society.* Warms is co-editor of the SAGE *Encyclopedia of Theory in Social and Cultural Anthropology* as well as the author of articles in journals and edited volumes on commerce, religion, and ethnic identity in West Africa; African exploration and romanticism; African veterans of the French colonial armed forces; kinship and friendship in Africa; as well as essays on the history of anthropology. Warms's interests in anthropology were kindled by college

courses and by his experiences as a Peace Corps volunteer in West Africa. He has traveled extensively in Africa, Europe, and Japan. He continues to teach Introduction to Cultural Anthropology each year and also teaches classes on the history of anthropological theory, economic anthropology, the anthropology of religion, and the anthropology of film and media at both the graduate and undergraduate levels. Students and faculty are invited to contact him with their comments, suggestions, and questions at r.warms@txstate.edu.

Although most anthropologists study a single problem, together they are interested in the total range of human activity. Here, colorfully dressed women from the Miao ethnic minority pose on a narrow mountain trail in Guizhou, China. What questions would you ask about them?

Source: peace-on-earth.org

CHAPTER 1

WHAT IS ANTHROPOLOGY AND WHY SHOULD I CARE?

LEARNING OBJECTIVES

After you have read this chapter, you will be able to:

△ Define anthropology and explain how it differs from other academic disciplines.

△ List the major subdisciplines of anthropology.

△ Explain some of the ways that anthropology is applied both for careers and for general understanding.

△ Discuss and explain the ideas of cultural relativism and ethnocentrism.

△ Describe anthropology's position on race.

△ Describe some of the key reasons for studying anthropology.

THE NACIREMA

NTHROPOLOGISTS have become so familiar with the diversity of ways different peoples behave in similar situations that they are not apt to be surprised by even the most exotic customs. However, the magical beliefs and practices of the Nacirema present such unusual aspects that it seems desirable to describe them as an example of the extremes to which human behavior can go. The Nacirema are a North American group living in the territory between the Canadian Cree, the Yaqui and Tarahumare of Mexico, and the Carib and Arawak of the Antilles. Little is known of their origin, although tradition states that they came from the east.

Nacirema culture is characterized by a highly developed market economy, but Naciremans spend a considerable portion of the day in ritual activity. The focus of this activity is the human body, the appearance and health of which loom as a dominant concern in the ethos of the people.

The fundamental belief underlying the whole system appears to be that the human body is ugly and has a natural tendency to debility and disease. People's only hope is to avert these through the use of ritual and ceremony, and every household has one or more shrines devoted to this purpose. The rituals associated with the shrine are secret and are discussed with children only when they are being initiated into these mysteries. I was able, however, to establish sufficient rapport with the natives to examine these shrines and to have the rituals described to me.

The focal point of the shrine is a box or chest built into the wall in which are kept the many charms and magical potions no native believes he could live without. Beneath the charm box is a small fountain. Each day, every member of the family, in succession, enters the shrine room, bows his head before the charm box, mingles different sorts of holy water in the fountain, and proceeds with a brief rite of purification. The holy waters are secured from the Water Temple of the community, where the priests conduct elaborate ceremonies to make the liquid ritually pure.

The Nacirema have an almost pathological horror of and fascination with the mouth, the condition of which is believed to have a supernatural influence on all social relationships. Each day, Naciremans perform a complex set of rituals devoted to the mouth. Were it not for these rituals, they believe that their teeth would fall out, their gums bleed, their jaws shrink, their friends desert them, and their lovers reject them.

In addition to daily mouth rites, the people seek out a holy-mouthman once or twice a year. These practitioners have an impressive set of paraphernalia, consisting of a variety of augers, awls, probes, and prods. The use of these objects in the exorcism of the evils of the mouth involves almost unbelievable ritual torture of the client. The holy-mouthman uses these tools to scrape, prod, and cut particularly sensitive areas of the mouth. Magical materials believed to arrest decay and draw friends are inserted in the mouth. The extremely sacred and traditional character of the rite is evident in the fact that the natives return to the holy-mouth-men year after year, despite the fact that their teeth continue to decay. One has but to watch the gleam in the eye of a holy-mouth-man, as he jabs an awl into an exposed nerve, to suspect that a certain amount of sadism is involved in these practices. And indeed much of the population shows definite masochistic tendencies. For example, a portion of the daily body ritual performed only by men involves scraping and lacerating the surface of the face with a sharp instrument.

Nacirema medicine men have an imposing temple, or latipsoh, in every community of any size. The more elaborate ceremonies required to treat very sick patients can be performed only at this temple. These ceremonies involve not only the priests who perform miracles but also a permanent group of vestal maidens who move sedately about the temple chambers in distinctive costume.

The latipsoh ceremonies are so harsh that it is surprising that sick adults are not only willing but also eager to undergo the protracted ritual purification, if they can afford to do so. No matter how ill the supplicant or how grave the emergency, the guardians of the temple will not admit a client if he cannot give a rich gift to the custodian. Even after one has gained admission and survived the ceremonies, the guardians continue to demand gifts, sometimes pursuing clients to their homes and businesses.

Supplicants entering the temple are first stripped of all their clothes. Psychological shock results from the fact that body secrecy is suddenly lost. A man whose own wife has never seen him in an excretory act suddenly finds himself naked and assisted by a vestal maiden while he performs his natural functions into a sacred vessel. Female clients find their naked bodies are subjected to the scrutiny, manipulation, and prodding of the medicine men. The fact that these temple ceremonies may not cure, and may even kill the patients, in no way decreases the people's faith in the medicine men.

In conclusion, mention must be made of certain practices of the Nacirema that have their base in native esthetics but depend on the pervasive aversion to the natural body and its functions. There are ritual fasts to make fat people thin and ceremonial feasts to make thin people fat. Other rites are used to make women's breasts larger if they are small, and smaller if they are large. General dissatisfaction with breast shape is symbolized by the fact that the ideal form is virtually outside the range of human variation. A few women afflicted with almost inhuman hyper-mammary development are so idolized that they make a handsome living by simply going from village to village and permitting the natives to stare at them for a fee.

Our review of the ritual life of the Nacirema has shown them to be a magic-ridden people. It is hard to understand how they have managed to exist so long under the burdens they have imposed upon themselves. But even exotic customs such as these take on real meaning when they are viewed with the insight that Bronislaw Malinowski, one of the most important 20th-century anthropologists, provided when he wrote: "Looking from far and above, from our high places of safety in civilization, it is easy to see all the crudity and irrelevance of magic. But without its power and guidance early man could not have mastered his practical difficulties as he has done, nor could man have advanced to the higher stages of civilization."

The essay you've just read is adapted from a classic piece of American anthropology by Horace Miner. Despite being a half century old, it has lost none of its bite. The essay is good because it plays upon two critical themes that continue to draw people to anthropology: our quest to gain knowledge and to understand people who are vastly different from ourselves, and our desire to know ourselves and our own culture better.

Miner's essay draws you in as you read about the strange and bizarre customs of people who at first appear utterly different from yourself. You're titillated by the details of the exotic practices of the other but also comforted by the scientific writing style that seems to assure you that somehow this all makes sense. At some point in your reading, you may have realized that Miner is, in fact, describing American customs as they might be seen from the point of view of an unknowing but perhaps quite perceptive observer. Your first reaction might be to chuckle at the narrator's misunderstandings and treat the essay as an example of just how deeply an outside observer might be in error about a culture. But if you're a reflective person, you might have also wondered if the narrator hadn't turned up some fairly penetrating insights about the nature of our society. Clearly the narrator has misunderstood some of the ways Americans think about bathrooms, dentists, and hospitals. But is the narrator so far off in describing the American attitude toward disease, decay, and death? Finally, if you caught the joke early enough, you might have pondered the meaning of the quote that ends the essay: Have we really "advanced to the higher stages of civilization?" What does that mean anyway?

Miner's essay deals with some of the critical questions and desires at the heart of anthropology: How do we understand other people and actions that seem different, odd, or strange? Why do people do what they do? And, perhaps more profoundly, how do we go about describing other people's cultural worlds, and how do we know if these descriptions are accurate? We will return to these issues in many places in this book. But first, a brief definition and description of anthropology: **Anthropology** is the scientific and humanistic study of human beings. It encompasses the evolutionary history of humanity, physical variation among humans, the study of past societies, and the comparative study of current-day human societies and cultures.

A **society** is a group of people who depend on one another for survival or well-being. **Culture** is the way members of a society adapt to their environment and give meaning to their lives.

Some critical goals of anthropology are to describe, analyze, and explain different cultures, to show how groups live in different physical, economic, and social environments, and to show how their members give meaning to their lives. Anthropology attempts to comprehend the entire human experience. Through human paleontology, it describes the evolutionary development of our species. Through archaeology, it reaches from current-day societies to those of the distant past. Through primatology, it extends beyond humans to encompass the animals most closely related to us.

Human beings almost everywhere are **ethnocentric** (see Figure 1.1). That is, they consider their own behavior not only right but also natural. We often want other people to behave just like we do, and we feel troubled, insulted, or outraged when they do not. Indeed, part of our reaction to the Nacirema essay stems from the fact that the Naciremans seem to do things that, to us, seem neither right nor natural. However, as the essay suggests, the range of human behavior is truly enormous. For example, should you give your infant bottled formula, or should you breast-feed not only your own child but, like the Efe of Zaire, those of your friends and neighbors as well

Anthropology: The scientific and humanistic study of human beings encompassing the evolutionary history of humanity, physical variation among humans, the study of past societies, and the comparative study of current-day human societies and cultures.

Society: A group of people who depend on one another for survival or well-being as well as the relationships among such people including their statuses and roles.

Culture: The learned behaviors and symbols that allow people to live in groups; the primary means by which humans adapt to their environment; the ways of life characteristic of a particular human society.

Ethnocentrism (ethnocentric): Judging other cultures from the perspective on one's own culture. The notion that one's own culture is more beautiful, rational, and nearer to perfection than any other.

Figure 1.1 Ethnocentrism is the belief that one's own culture is superior to any other.

Margaret Bourke-White/Masters/Time Life Pictures/Getty Images

(Peacock 1991:352)? Is it right that emotional love should precede sexual relations? Or should sexual relations precede love, as is normal for the Mangaian of the Pacific (Marshall 1971)? If a child dies, should we bury it, or, as Wari' elders say was proper, should it be eaten (Conklin 1995)? And what about sex? Are boys naturally made into men through receipt of semen from older men, as the Sambia claim (Herdt 1987)? For anthropologists, these examples suggest that what is right or natural for human beings is not easily determined, and that attempts to understand human nature and theories of human behavior cannot be based simply on our own cultural assumptions. To accurately reflect humanity, they also must be based on studies of human groups whose goals, values, views of reality, and environmental adaptations are very different from our own. We can achieve an accurate understanding of humanity only by realizing that other groups of people who behave differently from us and have different understandings also consider the things they do and the ways they understand the world to be normal and natural.

One job of anthropology is to understand what actions and ideas mean within their contexts and to place these within the broader framework of human society, environment, and history. Anthropologists refer to the practice of attempting to understand cultures within their contexts as **cultural relativism**. It is important to understand that practicing cultural relativism does not mean that anthropologists believe all cultural traditions to be good or to be of equal worth. People around the world, and indeed in our own society, do terrible things. Slavery, human sacrifice, and torture are all cultural practices. Anthropologists do not defend such customs on the basis of cultural relativism. However, anthropologists do try to understand how all cultural practices, even those that horrify us, developed, how they work in society, and how they are experienced by the people who live them. Both ethnocentrism and cultural relativism are examined in greater detail in Chapter 3.

Anthropologists bring a holistic approach to understanding and explaining. To say anthropology is **holistic** means that it combines the study of human biology, history, and the learned and shared patterns of human behavior and thought we call *culture* in order to analyze human groups. Holism separates anthropology from other academic disciplines, which generally focus on one factor—biology, psychology, physiology, or society—as the explanation for human behavior.

Because anthropologists use this holistic approach, they are interested in the total range of human activity. Most anthropologists specialize in a single field and a single problem, but together, they study the small dramas of daily living as well as spectacular social events. They study the ways in which mothers hold their babies or sons address their fathers. They want to know not only how a group gets its food but also the rules for eating it. Anthropologists are interested in how people in human societies think about

Cultural relativism: The idea that cultures should be analysed with reference to their own histories and values rather than according to the values of another culture.

Holism (holistic): In anthropology, an approach that considers the study of culture, history, language, and biology essential to a complete understanding of human society.

time and space and how they see and name colors. They are interested in health and illness and the significance of physical variation as well as many other things. Anthropologists study these things not only in other societies but in our own as well. Anthropologists maintain that culture, social organization, history, and human biology are tightly interrelated. Although we can never know absolutely everything about any group of people, the more we know about the many different facets of a society, the clearer picture we are able to draw and the greater the depth of our understanding.

⧄ SPECIALIZATION IN ANTHROPOLOGY

In the United States, anthropology has traditionally included four separate subdisciplines: biological (or physical) anthropology, cultural anthropology, linguistic anthropology, and archaeology. In this section, we briefly describe each of them.

◧ Biological or Physical Anthropology

People are found under a broad range of ecological and social conditions. Our ability to survive and prosper in many different circumstances is based on the enormous flexibility of cultural behavior. The capacity for culture, however, is grounded in our biological history and physical makeup. Human adaptation is thus biocultural; that is, it involves both biological and cultural dimensions. Therefore, to understand fully what it is to be human, we need a sense of how the biological aspects of this adaptation came about and how they influence human cultural behavior.

Biological (or physical) anthropology is the study of humankind from a biological perspective. It focuses primarily on those aspects of humanity that are genetically inherited. Biological anthropology includes numerous subfields, such as skeletal analysis, or osteology; the study of human nutrition; demography, or the statistical study of human populations; epidemiology, or the study of patterns of disease; and primatology.

Biological anthropology is probably best known for the study of human evolution and the biological processes involved in human adaptation. Paleoanthropologists search for the origins of humanity, using the fossil record to trace the history of human evolution. They study the remains of the earliest human forms, as well as those ancestral to humans and related to humans.

Another subspecialty of biological anthropology, called human variation, is concerned with physiological differences among humans. Anthropologists who study human variation map physiological differences

Biological (or physical) anthropology: The subdiscipline of anthropology that focuses on the study of people from a biological perspective, primarily on aspects of humankind that are genetically inherited.

among modern human groups and attempt to explain the sources of this diversity.

Because the human species evolved through a complex feedback system involving both biological and cultural factors, biological anthropologists are also interested in the origins and evolution of culture. For example, in *Catching Fire* (2009), Richard Wrangham argues that an aspect of culture, the ability to control fire and use it to cook food, led to dramatic biological and social changes in human ancestors. Cooked food was more digestible than raw, and this resulted in changes in human anatomy (far shorter digestive tracts than our closest primate relations). Cooking food required changes in social organization that led to much greater cooperation between males and females than is found among nonhuman primates. Wrangham thus argues that human evolution was both a biological and a cultural process.

Our unique evolutionary history resulted in the development of a biological structure, the human brain, capable of inventing, learning, and using cultural adaptations. Cultural adaptation, in turn, has freed humans from the slow process of biological adaptation: Populations can invent new ways of dealing with problems almost immediately, or adopt solutions from other societies. The study of the complex relationship between biological and cultural evolution links biological anthropology, cultural anthropology, and archaeology.

In addition to studying living human groups, biological anthropologists study living nonhuman primates, members of the order that includes monkeys, apes, and humans. Primates are studied for the clues that their chemistry, physiology, morphology (physical structure), and behavior provide about our own species. At one time, primates were studied mainly in the artificial settings of laboratories and zoos, but now much of the work of biological anthropologists involves studying these animals in the wild. Jane Goodall and Dian Fossey are two well-known anthropologists who studied primates in the wild. Fossey, who died in 1985, worked with gorillas in Rwanda. Goodall works with chimpanzees in Tanzania.

Linguistic Anthropology

Linguistic anthropology: The study of language and its relation to culture.

Language is the primary means by which people communicate with one another. Although most creatures communicate, human speech is more complex, creative, and used more extensively than the communication systems of other animals. Language is an essential part of what it means to be human and a basic part of all cultures. **Linguistic anthropology** is concerned with understanding language and its relation to culture.

Language is an amazing thing we take for granted. When we speak, we use our bodies—our lungs, vocal cords, mouth, tongue, and lips—to produce noise of varying tone and pitch. And, somehow, when we do this, if we speak the same language, we are able to communicate with one another. Linguistic anthropologists want to understand how language is structured, how it is learned, and how this communication takes place.

Language is a complex symbolic system that people use to communicate and to transmit culture. Thus, language provides critical clues for understanding culture. For example, people generally talk about the people, places, and objects that are important to them. Therefore, the vocabularies of spoken language may give us clues to important aspects of culture. Knowing the words that people use for things may help us to glimpse how they understand the world.

Language involves much more than words. When we speak, we perform. If we tell a story, we don't simply recite the words. We emphasize some things. We add inflection that can turn a serious phrase comic or a comic phrase serious. We give our own special tilt to a story, even if we are just reading a book out loud. Linguistic anthropologists are interested in the ways in which people perform language—in the ways they change and modify the meanings of their words.

All languages change. Historical linguists work to discover the ways in which languages have changed and the ways in which languages are related to each other. Understanding linguistic change and the relationships between languages helps us to work out the past of the people who speak them. Knowing, for example, the relationships among various Native American languages give us insight into the histories and migrations of those who speak them.

The technological changes of the past two decades have opened a new world of communications. The widespread use of cell phones, email, texting, and social networking sites such as Facebook create entirely new ways of communicating, changing both the occasions on which people communicate and the language they use. For example, 20 years ago, people who lived at great distance from each other communicated relatively rarely. The mail was often slow, and phone calls were expensive. Now, such people may communicate many times daily, speaking on the phone and visiting each other's websites. Cell phones in particular have become extremely important in poorer nations. For example, in 1998, there were no cell phones in Botswana. But by 2006, there were more than 800,000, enough for half the total population and more than six times the number of landlines. By 2008, virtually the entire population had cell phones (Aker and Mbiti 2010). Studying these changes in communication is an exciting new challenge for linguistic anthropologists.

Understanding language is a critical task for people interested in developing new technology as well. We live in a world where computers talk to us and listen to us. We will only be able to build machines that use language effectively if we understand how humans structure and use language.

◤ Archaeology

Archaeology: The subdiscipline of anthropology that focuses on the study of past cultures based primarily on their material remains.

Archaeologists add a vital time dimension to our understanding of cultures and how they change. **Archaeology** is the study of past cultures through their material remains (archaeologists don't dig up dinosaurs or other ancient fossils: That is the job of paleontologists).

Many archaeologists study prehistoric societies—those for which no written records have been found or no writing systems have been deciphered. However, even when an extensive written record is available, as in the case of ancient Greece or Colonial America, archaeology can help increase our understanding of the cultures and lifeways of those who came before us.

Archaeologists do not observe human behavior and culture directly but rather reconstruct them from material remains or artifacts. An artifact is any object that human beings have made, used, or altered. Artifacts include pottery, tools, garbage, and whatever else a society has left behind.

In the popular media, archaeology is mainly identified with spectacular discoveries of artifacts from prehistoric and ancient cultures, such as the tomb of the Egyptian king Tutankhamun. As a result, people often think of archaeologists primarily as collectors. But contemporary archaeologists are much more interested in understanding and explaining their finds in terms of what they say about the behavior that produced them than in creating collections. Their principal task is to infer the nature of past cultures based on the patterns of the artifacts left behind. Archaeologists work like detectives, slowly sifting and interpreting evidence. The context in which things are found, the location of an archaeological site, and the precise position of an artifact within that site are critical to interpretation. In fact, these may be more important than the artifact itself.

There are many different specialties within archaeology. Urban archaeology is a good example. Urban archaeologists delve into the recent and distant past of current-day cities. In doing so, they uncover knowledge of the people often left out of the history books, making our understanding of the past far richer than it was. For example, Elizabeth Scott's work at Nina Plantation in Louisiana (2001) adds to our understanding of the lives of slaves and free laborers from the 1820s to the 1890s, and the discovery of an African Burial Ground in New York City in 1991 provides us with insight into the lives of free and enslaved Africans in the 17th and 18th centuries.

Another important archeology subfield is cultural resource management, or CRM. Archaeologists working in CRM are concerned with the protection and management of archaeological, archival, and architectural resources. They are often employed by federal, state, and local agencies to develop and implement plans for the protection and management of such cultural resources.

Cultural Anthropology

The study of human society and culture is known as cultural anthropology. Anthropologists define society as a group of people persisting through time and the social relationships among these people: their statuses and roles. Traditionally, societies are thought of as occupying a specific geographic location, but modern transportation and electronic communication have made specific locales less important. Societies are increasingly global rather than local phenomena.

As Chapter 2 will show, culture is an extremely complex phenomenon. Culture is the major way in which human beings adapt to their environments and give meaning to their lives. It includes human behavior and ideas that are learned rather than genetically transmitted, as well as the material objects a group of people produces.

Cultural anthropologists attempt to understand culture both as a universal human phenomenon and as a characteristic of a group of people. They use many different research strategies to search for general principles that underlie all cultures or examine the dynamics of a particular culture. They may explore the ways in which different societies adapt to their environments, how members of cultures understand the world and their place in it, or how members of different cultures interact with and change one another. They are often particularly interested in the effects of differences of power both among cultures and within individual cultures. Research in **cultural anthropology** is almost always based on participant observation, long-term fieldwork gathering data by observing and participating in people's lives.

Ethnography and ethnology are two important aspects of cultural anthropology. **Ethnography** is the description of society or culture. An ethnographer attempts to describe an entire society or a particular set of cultural institutions or practices. Ethnographies may be either emic, or etic, or may combine the two. An **emic** ethnography attempts to capture what ideas and practices mean to members of a culture. It attempts to give readers a sense of what it feels like to be a member of the culture it describes. An **etic** ethnography describes and analyzes culture according to principles and theories drawn from Western scientific traditions such as ecology, economy, or psychology. **Ethnology** is the attempt to find general principles or laws that govern cultural phenomena. Ethnologists compare and contrast practices in different cultures to find regularities.

Cultural anthropology: The study of human thought, behaviour, and lifeways that are learned rather than genetically transmitted and that are typical of groups of people.

Ethnography: The major research tool of cultural anthropology, including both fieldwork among people in a society and the written results of such fieldwork.

Emic: Examination of societies using concepts, categories, and distinctions that are meaningful to members of those societies.

Etic: Examination of societies using concepts, categories, and rules derived from science; an outsider's perspective.

Ethnology: The attempt to find general principles or laws that govern cultural phenomena through the comparison of cultures.

Cultural anthropology is a complex field with many different subfields. One index of this complexity is the more than 50 different sections and interest groups of the American Anthropological Association; the vast majority of these are concerned with cultural anthropology. Some examples include political and legal anthropology, which is concerned with issues of nationalism, citizenship, the state, colonialism, and globalism; humanistic anthropology, which is focused on the personal, ethical, and political choices humans face; and visual anthropology, which is the study of visual representation and the media.

Cultural anthropologists are often particularly interested in documenting and understanding the ways in which cultures change (see Figure 1.2). They examine the roles that power and coercion play in change, as well as humans' ability to invent new technologies and social forms and modify old ones. Studies of culture change are important because rapid shifts in society, economy, and technology are basic characteristics of the contemporary world. Understanding the dynamics of change is critical for individuals, governments, and corporations. One goal of cultural anthropology is to be able to contribute productively to public debate about promotion of and reaction to change, both in our own society and elsewhere.

© Olivier Asselin/Acclaim Images

Figure 1.2 Cultural anthropologists describe and analyze current-day cultures. Their studies often focus on culture change. Here, a Moroccan tribesman gives water to his camel with a disposable plastic bottle.

Applied Anthropology

Although anthropology is mainly concerned with basic research—that is, asking the big questions about the origins of our species, the development of culture and civilization, and the functions of human social institutions—from the start, anthropologists have been interested in the application of their studies. Anthropologists such as Franz Boas contributed to debates on race and foreign policy at the turn of the 20th century. Margaret Mead, Ruth Benedict, and others did studies aimed at helping America's efforts during World War II. However, in the first half of the 20th century, almost all anthropologists worked in universities. In the past 50 years, anthropology has increasingly become a full-time profession for people outside of academe. **Applied anthropology** is the use of cultural anthropology, linguistics, archaeology, and biological anthropology to solve practical problems in business, politics, delivery of services, and land management. There are anthropologists who analyze factory floors and decision-making structures for large corporations. There are those who try to determine the

Applied anthropology: The application of anthropological knowledge to the solution of human problems.

best ways to sell products or deliver services. There are anthropologists who work for hospitals and health care organizations, improving the ability of these agencies to serve their patients. Some anthropologists work in politics, performing foreign and domestic policy analysis for governmental agencies. Some are employed in trying to find effective ways to deliver aid to people in poor nations. Other anthropologists work in museums or on public lands, uncovering our archaeological heritage and both preserving it and making it available to the public.

Using Anthropology: Forensic Anthropology

Every chapter in this book has a section called "Using Anthropology," in which we describe some of the different ways that anthropologists use their skills in effecting action in the world. Among other topics, we explore examples of how engaged anthropologists work for the communities they study, linguistic anthropologists help solve crimes (see Chapter 4), and nutritional anthropologists help stop hunger. Our first section is about forensic anthropologists.

Popularized in television shows such as *Bones* and documentaries such as *The Decrypters*, forensic anthropology is a well-known example of applied biological anthropology. Forensic anthropologists use their anthropological training to identify skeletal or badly decomposed human remains (see Figure 1.3). Their goal is to discover information that can assist in the detection of crime and the prosecution of those responsible.

A case begins when a law enforcement agency or medical examiner's office calls for help in discovering the identity and cause of death of an individual whose remains have recently been found. Sometimes, the remains are nonhuman; at other times, they are very old. However, in many cases, the remains are from a recent violent crime.

The next step is the recovery of the body. Sometimes the law enforcement agency has already done this, but anthropologists are frequently called upon to assist and supervise the procedure. Sometimes bodies are found complete and in good preservation, but often they are found skeletonized, buried, burned, fragmentary, or in various stages of decomposition. Michelle Hamilton, a forensic anthropologist at Texas State University, reports that she has recovered bodies in caves and rock shelters, on mountaintops, in forests, down wells, under water, from burned homes, in submerged vehicles, and in many other environments.

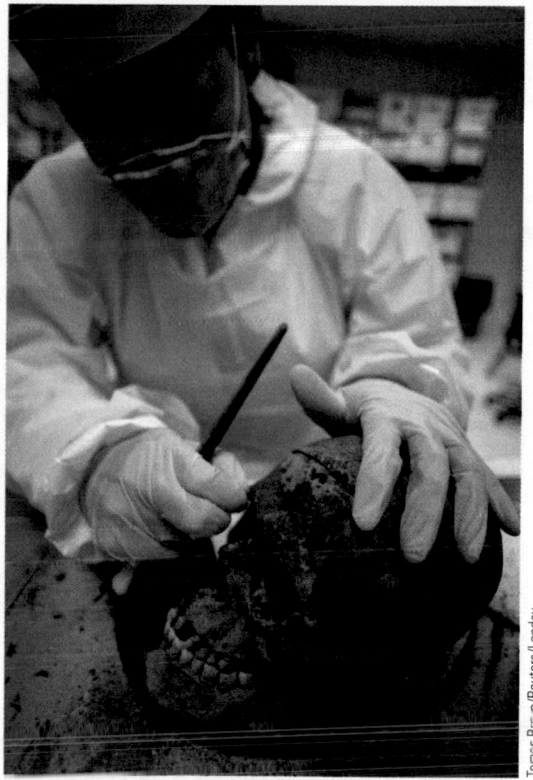

Tomas Bravo/Reuters/Landov

Figure 1.3 Forensic anthropologists advise law enforcement agencies and other organizations about the identity of victims of crime, political violence, and natural disaster. Here, a forensic anthropologist cleans a skull exhumed from a mass grave near Juarez, Mexico.

In one tricky case, Hamilton was called in to excavate underneath a house foundation where a body was reported buried. A family member who lived in this house had disappeared seven years previously. When the body was unearthed, it was still fully fleshed and recognizable. Therefore, Hamilton concluded that it could not have been buried the entire time since the individual first disappeared. The mystery was solved when family members confessed that the individual had been killed seven years ago, but they had stored the body in a freezer and had only buried it that week.

After a body has been recovered, the anthropologist's job is to establish both the individual's identity and to aid in the interpretation of events surrounding death. To do this, the bones and any other remains are analyzed to determine the sex, age, estimated time since death, ancestry, and stature of the individual, as well as any unique identifying marks such as healed fractures or skeletal abnormalities that might be useful in making a positive identification. In some cases, facial reconstructions are made to provide a likeness of the deceased and to further aid in identification. Analysis of trauma and fracture patterns on the bones can provide information about the sequence of events that occurred at the time of death. Cases may show evidence of blunt force trauma, sharp force trauma, gunshot wounds, or fire trauma.

In every case, forensic anthropologists are required to produce a report of their findings. Law enforcement agencies use these reports to match the bodies with missing persons reports and, if foul play is suspected, to prosecute the individuals believed to be responsible. Usually the anthropologist's work ends with the delivery of the report, but on occasion, a forensic anthropologist is required to testify as an expert witness in a criminal trial.

Everyday Anthropology

Although there are many careers in anthropology, it is our conviction that applied anthropology consists of more than just people earning their living with the skills they gained through training in anthropology. Perhaps the most important aspect of anthropology (and the primary justification for its existence) is the way an anthropological perspective demands that we open our eyes and experience the world in new ways. In a sense, anthropology is like teaching fish the meaning of water. How could a fish understand water? Water is all a fish knows, and it knows it so well it cannot distinguish it from the nature of life and reality itself. Similarly, all humans live in cultures, and our experiences are normally bounded by our cultures. We often mistake the realities and truths of our culture for reality and truth itself, thinking that the ways we understand and do things are the only appropriate ways of understanding and doing.

The fish only understands the meaning of water when it's removed from the water (usually with fatal consequences). If anthropology is not exactly about removing people from their culture, it is, in a sense, the conscious attempt to allow people to see beyond its bounds. Through learning about other cultures, we become increasingly aware of the variety of different understandings present in the world and of the social dynamics that underlie culture. This promotes awareness of the meanings and dynamics of our own and other cultures.

Applied anthropology doesn't just mean that you get paid to use your anthropological training. All of us do applied anthropology when we bring anthropological understandings and insight to bear on problems of poverty, education, war, violence, and peace. We don't apply anthropology only when we write a report. We apply anthropology when we go to the voting booth and to the grocery store, when we discuss issues with our friends and, if we're religious, when we pray. Anthropology provides no simple answers. There is no correct anthropological way to vote, shop, or pray. However, anthropology does inform our decisions about these things. Our attempt to understand other cultures and our own lets us look on these things with new eyes.

ANTHROPOLOGY AND "RACE"

One thing that all subdisciplines of anthropology can help us understand is "race." In the United States, most people see humanity as composed of biological "races." Census forms, applications, and other documents ask us to indicate our "race." Although "race" is clearly an important social and historical fact in the United States, most anthropologists believe that "race" is not a scientifically valid system of classification. Despite more than a century of attempts, biological anthropologists have never found an agreed-on, consistent system of "racial" classification. We have put the word *race* in quotation marks in this paragraph to begin to focus your attention on these problems. To make reading easier, we dispense with the quotation marks for the remainder of the book.

There are many problems in developing a scientifically valid racial classification scheme. First, most Americans understand race as a bundle of traits: light skin, light hair, light eyes, and so on. But, if this is so, the races you create are the result of the traits you choose. For example, races based on blood type would be very different than races based on skin color. Skin color strikes most Americans as a "natural" way to identify race but there is no biological reason to think that skin color is more important than blood type. Almost all traits we use to assign people to a race are facial traits. It is hard to imagine a biological reason why the shape of one's eye or nose should be more important than the characteristics of one's gallbladder or liver. However, it is easy to find a social reason: Traits easily visible

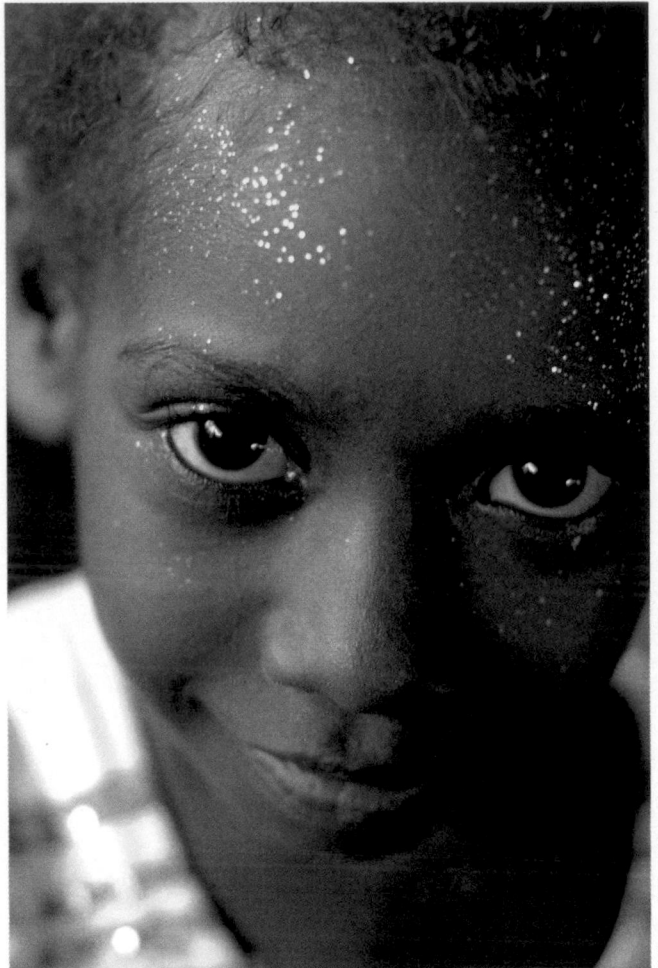

© Thomas Cockrem/Alamy

Figure 1.4 People who appear similar might have very different ancestries. The girl in this photo might look African but is from Vanuatu in the South Pacific Ocean, over 8,000 miles from the closest point on the African continent.

on the face enable us to rapidly assign individuals to a racial group. This is a good clue that race is about society, not biology.

There are many other problems with racial classifications. For example, if race is biological, members of one race should be genetically closer to one another than to members of different races. But measurement reveals that people are as different from others classified in their same race as they are from those in different races. Or consider people from Central Africa, Melanesia (islands in the western Pacific), and France. Most Central Africans and most Melanesians have dark-colored skin (see Figure 1.4). Most French are light. However, Africans are more closely related to the French than either is to Melanesians. This isn't surprising considering the geographical distances involved, but it suggests that traits like skin color have arisen at many times and many places in the past. Furthermore, although the characteristics of our species, *Homo sapiens,* were fully present 35,000 to 40,000 years ago, a 2004 study by Rohde, Olson, and Chang argues that all current-day humans have common ancestors who lived only 2,000 to 5,000 years ago. At a time depth of more than 5,000 years, all people alive today have exactly the same ancestors. Thus, differences among people are very recent and unlikely to be of great biological importance.

Anthropology teaches us that the big differences among human groups result from culture, not biology. Adaptation through culture, the potential for cultural richness, and creativity are universal. They override physical variation among human groups. We explore issues surrounding race and ethnicity many places in this book, particularly in Chapter 8.

WHY STUDY ANTHROPOLOGY

If you're reading this book for a course at a college or university, and particularly if you are considering a major in anthropology, you've probably faced some strong questioning from friends and family members.

Some may have known about anthropology and applauded your wisdom in taking this course. Others may have had no idea what anthropology is. Still others probably asked you what anthropology is good for and what you hope to do with it. You might have told them that you want to work in one of the many aspects of applied anthropology or to become a college professor, but we think there are other good answers as well.

Anthropology is, in most places, part of a liberal arts curriculum, which also generally includes English, geography, history, modern languages, philosophy, political science, psychology, and sociology, as well as other departments and programs. Some liberal arts departments have teacher training programs. If you want to teach middle school English, in most places, you will probably need a degree in English. Some liberal arts programs involve training in highly technical skills that are directly applicable to jobs. For example, geography departments may offer training in remote sensing, the acquisition and analysis of aerial photography, and multispectral and infrared imagery and radar imagery for use by government and business; these are highly complex skills with very specific job applications. However, the vast majority of liberal arts programs produce generalists. An undergraduate degree in psychology does not generally get you a job as a psychologist. Most people who study political science do not go on to be politicians, and few who study sociology go on to work as sociologists. In fact, survey data show that there is often little connection between people's undergraduate major and their eventual career. For example, in a survey of 3,000 alumni from the University of Virginia School of Arts and Sciences, 70 percent reported that there was little such connection. And this survey included many who had majored in subjects that taught very specific technical skills (University of Virginia 2008). Even more surprising, data from the National Science Foundation show that only about a quarter of science and engineering graduates hold jobs that are related to their degrees and that require at least a bachelor's degree to perform (*Science* 2012:275).

The fact is that both job prospects and the careers that people eventually pursue are about the same for students who study anthropology and those who major in other liberal arts disciplines. Many private and public organizations look specifically to hire anthropologists. The U.S. government is probably the largest employer of anthropologists, followed by Microsoft (Wood 2013:51). Companies that have hired anthropologists include Intel, Citicorp, AT&T, Kodak, Disney, and General Mills, and many others. Additionally, there are numerous jobs in the public and nonprofit sectors, including positions in international development, social services, museums, national parks, and governmental organizations concerned with national security. However, like students with other majors, most anthropology graduates go on to more general positions in government, business, and the professions. Some become executives at large corporations, some are restaurateurs, some are lawyers, some are doctors, some are social service workers, some sell insurance, some are government officials, some are diplomats, and yes, no doubt, some still live with their parents and might even ask, "Do you want fries with that?" And you could say the same of the vast majority of majors in most subjects at every university.

To refocus our question, we might ask: What are the particular ways of thought that anthropology courses develop and that are applicable to the very broad range of occupations that anthropologists follow? How is anthropology different from other social science disciplines? Although there are certainly many ways to answer these questions, it seems to us that three are of particular importance.

First, anthropology is the university discipline that focuses on understanding different groups of people. This focus on culture is one of the most valuable contributions anthropology can make to our ability to understand our world. Understanding cultures and approaching cultural differences from the perspective of cultural relativism helps us to develop the critical thinking skills that aid in analyzing and solving problems.

Although the United States has always been an ethnically and culturally diverse place, for most of its history, white Protestant men of northern European ancestry have held the reins of wealth and power. This isn't to say that all such men were rich and powerful. Most certainly were not. However, even if they were poor, they had an advantage: They were members of the dominant culture. If members of other cultural groups wanted to speak to them, do business with them, participate in public and civic affairs with them, they had to learn to speak the proper style of English. They had to learn the forms of address, body language, clothing, and manners appropriate to their role in U.S. culture. Because others had to do the work of changing their behavior, white Protestant men were often unaware of this disparity and accepted it simply as the way things were. *Miami Herald* columnist Leonard Pitts has pointed out that "if affirmative action is defined as giving preferential treatment on the basis of gender or race, then no one in this country has received more than white men" (2007). This is true whether or not such men wanted preference or even realized they were getting it. Many, focusing on their own hard work and very real struggles, bristled at the notion that they were privileged, but this didn't make it any less true.

The white, Protestant, northern European male is hardly an extinct species in the United States (such people still today control most of the nation's wealth). However, by the late 20th century, their virtual monopoly on power had begun to break up. Women and men from a great diversity of religious, ethnic, and racial backgrounds have moved to stronger economic and political positions. Moreover, the United States increasingly exists in a world filled with other powerful nations with very different histories and

Thomas Hawk

Figure 1.5 The United States is once again a nation of immigrants. In 2007, about 12 percent of the U.S. population was foreign born.

traditions. It is less and less a world where everyone wants to do business with the United States and is willing to do so on American terms. Instead, it is a rapidly globalizing world characterized by corporations with headquarters and workforces spread throughout the globe, and by capital and information flows that cross cultural boundaries in milliseconds. Americans who wish to understand and operate effectively in such a world must learn other cultures and other ways; failure to do so puts them at a distinct disadvantage.

At home, the United States is once again a nation of immigrants (see Figure 1.5). Until the late 20th century, most immigrants were cut off from their homelands by politics and by the expense and difficulty of communication. Under these conditions, assimilation to the dominant culture was essential. Although politics will always be an issue, today's immigrants can, in most cases, communicate freely and inexpensively with family and friends in their homelands and may be able to travel back and forth on a regular basis. Thus, complete assimilation is far less necessary or desirable.

Some people may applaud multiculturalism; others may bemoan what they feel is the passing of the "American" way of life. What no one can really dispute is that the world of today is vastly different from the world of 1950. Given the increasing integration of economic systems, declining costs of communication and transportation, and the rising economic power of China and other nations, we can be sure that people of different ethnic, racial, and cultural backgrounds will meet more and more frequently in arenas where none has clear economic and cultural dominance. Thus, an understanding of the nature of culture, and knowledge of the basic tools scholars have devised to analyze it are essential, and anthropology is the place to get them.

In addition to this first, very practical application, there is a second, more philosophical concern of anthropologists. Like scholars in many other disciplines, anthropologists grapple with the question of what it means to be a human being. However, anthropologists bring some unique tools to bear upon this issue. Within anthropology, we can look for the answer to this question in two seemingly mutually exclusive ways. We can look at culture as simply the sum total of everything that humans have done, thought, created, and believed. In a sense, as individual humans, we are heirs to the totality of human cultural practices and experiences. Anthropology is the discipline that attempts to observe, collect, record, and understand the full range of human cultural experience. Through anthropology, we know the great variety of forms that cultures can take. We know the huge variation in social organization, belief systems, production, and family structure that is found in human society. This gives us insight into the plasticity of human society as well as the limits to that plasticity.

Alternatively, we can answer the question by ignoring the variability of human culture and focusing on the characteristics that all cultures share. In the 1940s, George Murdock listed 77 characteristics that he believed were common to all cultures. These included such things as dream interpretation, incest taboos, inheritance rules, and religious ritual. More recent authors (Brown 1991; Cleaveland, Craven, and Danfelser 1979) have developed other lists and analysis. Brown (1991:143) notes that human universals are very diverse, and there is likely no single explanation for them. However, thinking about such commonalities among cultures may guide us in our attempt to understand human nature.

Finally, a third interest of anthropologists is in creating new and useful ways to think about culture. One particularly effective way to understand culture is to think of it as a set of answers to a particular problem: How does a group of human beings survive together in the world? In other words, culture is a set of behaviors, beliefs, understandings, objects, and ways of interacting that enable a group to survive with greater or lesser success and greater or lesser longevity. At some level, all human societies must answer this critical question, and to some degree, each culture is a different answer to it.

In the world today and in our own society, we face extraordinary problems: hunger, poverty, inequality, violence between groups, violence within families, drug addiction, pollution, crime. … The list is long. However, we are not the only people in the world ever to have faced problems. At some level, all of these problems are the result of our attempt to live together as a group on this planet. Learning how other peoples in other places, and other times, solved or failed to solve their problems may give us the insight to solve our own; we might learn lessons, both positive and negative, from their cultural experiences.

In some ways, the cultures of today are unique. Societies have never been as large and interconnected as they are today. They have never had the wealth that many societies have today. They have never had the levels of technology, abilities to communicate, and abilities to destroy that our current society has. These characteristics make it naïve to imagine that we can simply observe a different culture, adopt their ways as our own, and live happily ever after. We can no more recreate tribal culture or ancient culture or even the culture of industrialized nations of 50 years ago than we can walk through walls. But it does not therefore follow that the answers of others are useless to us.

In Greek drama, the notion of hubris is critical. Hubris is probably best understood as excessive pride or confidence that leads to both arrogance and insolence toward others. In Greek tragedy, the hubris of characters is often their fatal flaw and leads to their downfall. Heroes such as Oedipus and Creon were doomed by their hubris.

We surely won't find that the members of other cultures have provided ready-made answers to all the problems that confront us. But to imagine ourselves as totally unique, to imagine that the experiences of other peoples and other cultures have nothing to teach us, is a form of hubris, and as in tragedy, could well lead to our downfall.

The ancient Greeks contrasted hubris with *arete*. This characteristic implies a humble striving for perfection, along with the realization that such perfection cannot be reached. With the notion of arete in mind, we approach the study of anthropology cheerfully and with a degree of optimism. From anthropology, we hope to learn new ways of analyzing, understanding, celebrating, and coming to terms with the enormous variations in human cultural behavior. We hope to be able to think creatively about what it means to be human beings and to use what we learn to provide insight into the issues, problems, and possibilities of our own culture. We hope that, with the help of such understanding, we will leave the world a better place than we found it.

BRINGING IT BACK HOME:
THE ANTHROPOLOGY OF VIOLENCE

The holistic approach of anthropology can help us understand violence. To what extent is violence simply an ineradicable part of human nature and to what extent is it a product of certain kinds of cultures? Have human beings always been violent or was there an age when

people lived in societies without violence? Can we hope for a future without violence or are we condemned to ever-increasing cycles of violence?

There are no simple answers to these questions. Anthropologists, political philosophers, and others have sometimes imagined that people in early human societies led a peaceful, almost utopian existence. At other times, they have imagined such societies as a struggle of all against all: constant battle for survival in which violence against nonfamily and non–group members was the rule rather than the exception. Neither of these ideas seems to hold much validity.

There is no doubt that humans have often lived in societies characterized by high levels of violence. Archaeological remains show evidence of violence in ancient societies, and biological anthropologists analyze the mechanisms of violence and reconciliation that are present among nonhuman primates. Cultural anthropologists have often documented violence, and sometimes warfare in many different societies.

However, anthropologists have documented societies that have extremely low levels of violence as well. Some of these include the Chewong of the Malaysian peninsula (Howell 1989), the G/wi of central Botswana (Silberbauer 1982), and the Yandi of the Indian state of Andhra Pradesh (Kumar 1995). The Semai, a gardening society in the central Malay Peninsula, are one of the best documented peaceful societies. Clayton and Carole Robarchek, anthropologists who have studied the Semai for more than 30 years, report that worldview is a key factor in Semai peacefulness. Semai see themselves as "essentially helpless in a hostile and malevolent universe" and believe that virtually all activities, even the most innocuous, are fraught with danger (1992:201). In this frightening world, they depend vitally on one another, and anything that threatens discord or violence is understood as a threat to their survival itself. Thus, although their society is peaceful, theirs is not a worldview that many would like to share.

More recently, Steven Pinker in *The Better Angels of Our Nature* (2011) argues that humanity as a whole is becoming less violent. He claims that acts of violence, torture, and cruelty of all types that were common in humanity's past are far less present today. Pinker argues that the decline in violence is the result of a combination of factors including the political dominance of large state societies whose governments monopolize the use of force, the emergence of humanitarian thinking in 17th- and 18th-century Europe, and the spread of commerce. Using a phrase from philosopher Peter Singer, Pinker talks of an "escalator of reason" that we use to discover that our interests are similar to those of other people and thus, we develop empathy with them.

Many anthropologists will be deeply skeptical of Pinker's claims. It is probably true that the routine cruelty of the relatively recent Western past has greatly diminished. However, much of this has happened quite recently and clearly the use of torture is still an important political issue in our society. There is little doubt that, in terms of total numbers of people killed, the 20th century was the most violent in the history of humanity. Much of this death occurred in various forms of state-sponsored violence, from warfare to famines caused by political actions. Even when physical violence is not present, state society includes the pervasive violence of inequality and, in many cases, outright oppression.

Anthropology does not provide any easy answers on violence. Instead, it shows that both violence and reconciliation are very basic aspects of human and indeed nonhuman primate behavior. The sources of both peace and violence may ultimately lie in human nature. However, the expression of violence is clearly an aspect of culture. The ways in which our cultures are structured and the worldviews we hold deeply affect the degree to which violence is present in any given society. Humans will probably always have violent thoughts and desires. But we can hope to create societies in which violence is rare or, perhaps, even entirely absent.

YOU DECIDE

1. Do you believe that humankind is getting more or less violent and cruel? What evidence can you bring to support your position?
2. The Robarcheks' analysis of the Semai shows that their peaceful lifestyle is a product of both the way their society is structured and the worldviews they hold. What kind of social structures and worldviews do you think promote peace?
3. Do you believe in the possibility of a society and a world without violence? What do you think is the relationship between physical violence and less obvious forms of violence such as discrimination, inequality, and oppression?

CHAPTER SUMMARY

1. What critical themes presented in Horace Miner's essay "Body Ritual among the Nacirema" continue to draw people to anthropology? Miner's essay encourages us to think about our quest to gain knowledge and understanding of people who are different from ourselves, and our desire to know ourselves and our own culture better.

2. What is anthropology? Anthropology is a comparative study of humankind. Anthropologists study human beings in the past and in the present and in every corner of the world.

3. What does it mean to say that anthropology is holistic? Anthropologists study the entire range of humans' biological, social, political, economic, and religious behavior as well as the relationships among the different aspects of human behavior in the past and present.

4. What are the main subfields of anthropology? Cultural anthropology, linguistic anthropology, archaeology, biological (physical) anthropology, and applied anthropology.

5. Does anthropology stress biological or cultural adaptation? Anthropology stresses the importance of culture in human adaptation. It asserts that critical differences among individuals are cultural rather than biological.

6. What is the anthropological position on race? Anthropology demonstrates that race is not a valid scientific category but rather is a social and cultural construct.

7. What sorts of jobs do anthropology majors usually get? Anthropology is part of the liberal arts curriculum. Both the job prospects and the careers of those who study anthropology are similar to those who study other liberal arts disciplines.

8. What critical problems and ways of thinking do anthropology courses address? Anthropology courses develop three important ways of thought that are applicable to the broad range of occupations followed by anthropologists: (1) Anthropology focuses on understanding other groups of people within their own historical and cultural context; (2) anthropologists grapple with the question of what it means to be human by observing, collecting, recording, and attempting to understand the full range of human cultural experience; and (3) anthropology encourages us to use our understanding of other cultures to think about our own.

KEY TERMS

Anthropology
Applied anthropology
Archaeology
Biological (or physical) anthropology
Cultural anthropology
Cultural relativism
Culture
Emic

Ethnocentrism
Ethnography
Ethnology
Etic
Holism (holistic)
Linguistic anthropology
Society

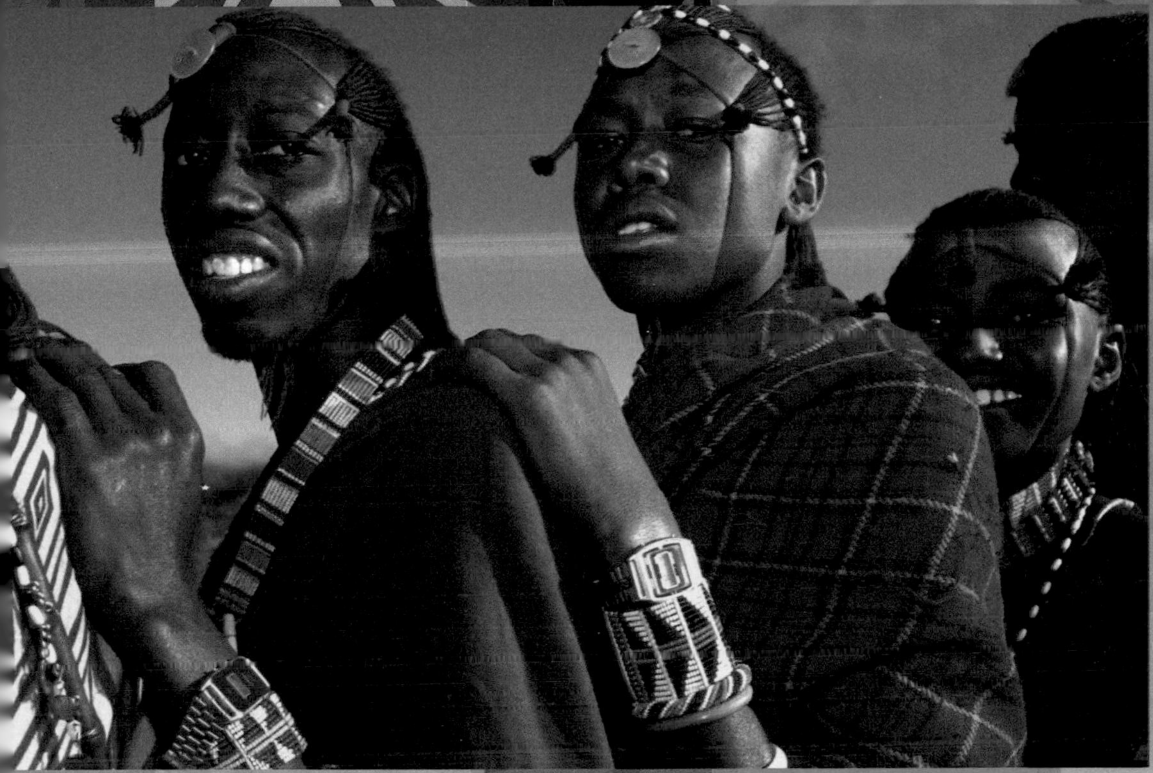

© adrian arbib/Alamy

Many dimensions of culture are expressed in the ritual dress of these Maasai men participating in an initiation ritual. They are dressed in styles and patterns that the Maasai have used for many years, but each wears a wristwatch as well.

CHAPTER 2

CULTURE COUNTS

LEARNING OBJECTIVES

After you have read this chapter, you will be able to:

- List the major characteristics of culture.
- Describe the role that child-rearing practices play in culture.
- Explain the relationship between culture and the ways in which people classify the world.
- Give some examples of the way in which symbols create meaning for people in particular cultures.
- Explain the ways in which culture can be considered a system and the ways in which it is not like a system.
- Tell some of the ways in which culture is and is not shared.
- Compare and contrast cultural and biological adaptation.
- List some of the ways in which culture changes and describe the role of conflict and consensus in change.

FERAL CHILDREN

UROPEANS, as well as members of many other cultures have often been fascinated by tales of feral or wild children, human children who are alleged to have grown up by themselves in the wild, apart from human civilization. Accounts of such children date to antiquity, and a website that appeared in the early 2000s claimed to document more than 80 cases between CE 250 and 2002 (Benzaquén 2006). Frequently, feral children are popularly supposed to have been raised by members of other animal species, often wolves or bears.

There is no reliable evidence that any human child has ever actually been raised by members of another species. Some of the many accounts of feral children seem to be outright fraud, but many others are probably stories about children who were abandoned because of a physical or mental disability and who survived by scavenging and begging around the edges of human settlement. Many of the most famous of these cases would, if they were alive today, probably be diagnosed with autism.

Two of the most famous feral children were Peter the Wild Boy, and Victor the Wild Boy of Aveyron (Newton 2002). Peter was found in 1725, in what is today northern Germany. Brought to the court of King George I in England, he was a well-known curiosity for the rest of his long life. Given to the care of court physician John Arbuthnot who tried to educate him, Peter acquired the ability to use a few simple words and perform a few tasks but made little progress beyond that. He disappeared for more than three months in the summer of 1751 and, after he was found, was forced to wear a brass collar engraved with his name and address.

Victor lived in the forests around Aveyron in southern France in the last years of the 1790s. Like Peter, Victor's inability to speak and his bizarre behavior garnered much attention, first in Aveyron and later in Paris. Like Peter, Victor was given to the care of a physician, Jean Marc Gaspard Itard, who attempted to teach him to speak and to perform rudimentary tasks. And like Arbuthnot, Itard's attempts at instruction were largely ineffective.

Victor and Peter were famous in their own day and to some degree in ours as well. Some of the most important intellectuals of the era wrote about Peter, including Jonathan Swift (author of *Gulliver's Travels*), Daniel Defoe (author of *Robinson Crusoe* and many other works), and the Scottish jurist and early evolutionist James Burnett, Lord Monboddo. Victor was also the subject of extensive commentary during his lifetime, and his fame has continued into modern times. His life in both realistic and fictionalized form appears in many novels and films, particularly Francois Truffaut's 1970 film *L'enfant sauvage* (*The Wild Child*).

So, what is it about feral children that fascinated people in the 17th and 18th centuries and continues to fascinate today? Swift and Defoe provided two different answers: Swift imagined Peter, who in reality was mute, trying to comprehend the alien social customs of the British aristocracy. Thus, through Peter, the culture of his era was made visible...and through his eyes, it was shown to be corrupt and absurd. Swift used what he imagined to be a creature of nature, without culture, to see and critique the culture of his era. Defoe (1726) approached Peter from a more challenging angle. He wondered about the degree to which Peter really was a human being. Did he have a soul? Peter was human in form, but he could neither speak nor participate in human society in any meaningful way. Unable to speak, he was perhaps unable to think as well. Without culture, Peter's existence was a horribly lonely burden. For Monboddo, Peter and other wild children proved that little or nothing was natural to humanity: Speech, upright posture, walking on two feet are all capacities that people had to be taught through a process of civilization. Monboddo used this idea to argue that orangutans were humans too; they had the capacities for human characteristics but had not learned to use them (Benzaquén 2006:131).

Victor was captured and displayed in the era immediately following the French Revolution and the terror. In this context, he too raised important questions. The philosophers of the French Revolution wanted to make humanity over anew. Many, following the philosopher Jean-Jacques Rousseau, believed that humans, in their natural form, free of the constraints of (European) culture, lacked morals but were essentially noble. Was Victor a "noble savage" without culture? Could proper education make him into a new and better type of person? Did Itard's failure to educate Victor mean that humans without society were so degraded that they could not be brought into society?

Because Peter and Victor were almost certainly individuals with profound autism (and in Peter's case, perhaps a rare chromosomal disorder as well [Kennedy 2011]), observations of them could not have answered questions about humanity without culture. However, the writings and questions that surrounded them and the continued interest in cases of feral children today draw our attention to the nature of culture and the relationship between culture and human nature. Cases of wild children seem to make it clear that, without the constraints, assumptions, and patterns imposed by culture, it is extraordinarily difficult to express our human qualities and abilities. But what is culture?

Although coming up with a useful, brief definition of culture is difficult, an anthropologist from Mars observing the many different human cultures might come up with six characteristics shared by all cultures:

1. Cultures are made up of learned behaviors. People are not born knowing their culture. They learn it through a process called enculturation.
2. Cultures all involve classification systems and symbols. A **symbol** is simply something that stands for something else. People use cultural symbols to create meaning.
3. Cultures are patterned and integrated. Thus, changes in one aspect of culture affect other aspects. However, elements of culture do not necessarily work smoothly with one another.
4. Cultures are shared. Although there may be disagreement about many aspects of a culture, there must be considerable consensus as well.
5. Cultures are adaptive and include information about how to survive in the world, but cultures can contain much that is maladaptive.
6. Cultures are subject to change. Whether propelled by their internal dynamics or acted upon by outside forces, cultures are always in flux.

Based on this list, we might define culture as the learned, symbolic, at least partially adaptive, and ever-changing patterns of behavior and meaning shared by members of a group. Although anthropologists agree on the basic characteristics of culture, they disagree on their relative importance, how to study them, and indeed the goals of anthropology itself. For example, some anthropologists are deeply concerned with observable behavior. Other anthropologists wish to comprehend the ways in which other people understand their world. Some anthropologists hope to find general laws of human cultural behavior. Others are more concerned with describing specific aspects of culture. These disagreements reflect different theoretical positions within anthropology. For our purposes, an **anthropological theory** is a set of propositions about which aspects of culture are critical, how they should be studied, and what the goal of studying them should be. Although those who hold different theoretical perspectives may insist that there is a right way and a wrong way to do anthropology, we suggest that theoretical perspectives are more like different windows through which one may view culture (see Table 2.1). Just as two windows may have views that overlap or views that show totally different scenes, perspectives on culture may overlap or reveal totally different aspects. Some of the major theoretical perspectives in anthropology are summarized in Table 2.1. In this chapter, we examine each element of our definition of culture. Each is a common characteristic of all human groups. However, each also raises questions, problems, and contradictions. Through examining these elements, we come to a keener appreciation of the nature of culture and, ultimately, what it means to be human.

Symbol: Something that stands for something else. Central to language and culture.

Anthropological theory: A set of propositions about which aspects of culture are critical, how they should be studied, and what the goal of studying them should be.

Table 2.1 Some Major Anthropological Schools of Thought and Their Understanding of Culture.

Theory Name	Understanding of Culture	Critical Thinkers
Nineteenth-century evolution	A universal human culture is shared, in different degrees, by all societies.	E. B. Taylor (1832–1917) L. H. Morgan (1818–1881)
Turn-of-the-century sociology	Groups of people share sets of symbols and practices that bind them into societies.	Emile Durkheim (1858–1917) Marcel Mauss (1872–1950)
American historical particularism	Cultures are the result of the specific histories of the people who share them.	Franz Boas (1858–1942) A. L. Kroeber (1876–1960)
Functionalism	Social practices support society's structure or fill the needs of individuals.	Bronislaw Malinowski (1884–1942) A. R. Radcliffe Brown (1881–1995)
Culture and personality	Culture is personality writ large. It both shapes and is shaped by the personalities of its members.	Ruth Benedict (1887–1948) Margaret Mead (1901–1978)
Cultural ecology and neo-evolutionism	Culture is the way in which humans adapt to the environment and make their lives secure.	Julian Steward (1902–1972) Leslie White (1900–1975)
Ecological materialism	Physical and economic causes give rise to cultures and explain changes within them.	Morton Fried (1923–1986) Marvin Harris (1927–2001)
Ethnoscience and cognitive anthropology	Culture is a mental template that determines how members of a society understand their world.	Harold Conklin (1926–) Stephen Tyler (1932–)
Structural anthropology	Universal original human culture can be discovered through analysis and comparison of the myths and customs of many cultures.	Claude Lévi-Strauss (1908– 2009)
Sociobiology	Culture is the visible expression of underlying genetic coding.	E. O. Wilson (1929–) Jerome Barkow (1944–)
Anthropology and gender	The roles of women and ways societies understand sexuality are central to understanding culture.	Sherry Ortner (1941–) Michelle Rosaldo (1944–1981)
Symbolic and interpretive anthropology	Culture is the way in which members of a society understand who they are and give lives meaning.	Mary Douglas (1921–2007) Clifford Geertz (1926–2006)
Postmodernism	Because understanding of cultures most reflect the observer's biases, culture can never be completely or accurately described.	Renato Rosaldo (1941–) Vincent Crapanzano (1939–)
Globalization	Culture is best analyzed as the global flow of identity, symbolism, money, and information.	Arjun Appadurai (1949–) David Harvey (1935–)

Note: Theoretical positions in anthropology represent sophisticated thinking and cannot be summed up in a single line. There are many outstanding books about anthropological theory, including McGee and Warms (2004), *Anthropological Theory: An Introductory History.*

◢ CULTURE IS MADE UP OF LEARNED BEHAVIORS

Just about everything that is animate learns. Your dog, your cat, even your fish show some learned behavior. But, as far as we know, no other creature has as much learned behavior as human beings. Almost every aspect of our lives is layered with learning. Our heart beats, our eyes blink, and our knees respond reflexively to a doctor's rubber mallet, but to get much beyond that, we need learning. Food is a good example. Humans must eat; that much is determined biologically. However, we do not just eat; our culture teaches us what is edible and what is not. We decline many things that are nutritious as not being food. Many insects, for example, are perfectly edible. The philosopher Aristotle was particularly fond of eating cicadas, and northern Europeans ate some species of beetles well into the 19th century. Yet, most Americans have learned that insects are not food, and they will go hungry, to the point of starvation, before knowingly eating them (though we are perfectly willing to eat them if we are unaware we are doing so. For example, Natural Red #4, a common food dye is made from cochineal, a type of beetle). Further, we eat particular things at particular times, in particular places, and with particular people. For example, although it is acceptable to eat popcorn at the movies, you would be unlikely to have lamb chops and asparagus, or a nice stir-fry at most movie theaters.

Enculturation: The process of learning to be a member of a particular group.

We sometimes think of learning as an aspect of childhood, but in every society, human beings learn their culture continuously. We are socialized from the moment of our births to the time of our deaths. Although large demands for labor and responsible behavior may be placed on children in many societies, all humans remain physically, emotionally, and intellectually immature well into their teen years and perhaps into their early 20s. This lengthy period of immaturity has profound implications. First, it allows time for an enormous amount of childhood learning. This means that very few specific behaviors need be under direct genetic or biological control. Second, it demands that human cultures be designed to provide relatively stable environments that protect the young for long periods of time. Child-rearing practices in all cultures are designed to produce adults who know the skills, norms, and behavior patterns of their society—the cultural content. But the transmission of this content also involves shaping children's attitudes, motivations, values, perceptions, and beliefs so that they can function in their society. The process of learning to be a member of a particular cultural group is called **enculturation**.

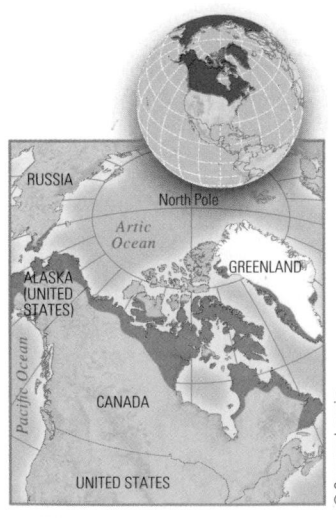

© Cengage Learning

The Inuit.

As an example, we can consider child rearing among the Inuit, a hunting people of the Arctic. The Inuit teach their children to deal with a world that is a dangerously problematic place, in which making wrong decisions might well mean death (Briggs 1991). To survive in this harsh environment, Inuit must learn to maintain a "constant state of alertness" and an "experimental way of living." Therefore, developing skills for solving problems quickly and spontaneously is central to Inuit child rearing. Children are brought up to constantly test their physical skills to extend them and to learn their own capacity for pain and endurance (Stern 1999).

Inuit children learn largely through observing their elders. Children are discouraged from asking questions. Rather, when confronted with a problem situation, they are expected to observe closely, to reason, and to find solutions independently. They watch, practice, and then are tested, frequently by adults asking them questions based on the idea of *isummaksaiyuq*, a northern Baffin Island Inuit term meaning to "cause (or cause to increase) thought." Some questions are very practical. For example, as they travel on the featureless, snow-covered tundra, an adult may ask a child, "Where are we?" or "Have you ever been here before?" Others are existentially challenging. Adults may ask children "Why don't you kill your baby brother?" or "Your mother's going to die—look, she's cut her finger—do you want to come live with me?" Such questions are not considered cruel. Rather, they force children to grapple with issues of grave consequence (Briggs 1999:5).

Play is a critical part of Inuit child rearing. Inuit games prepare children for the rigors of the arctic environment by stressing hand–eye coordination, problem solving, and physical strength and endurance (see Figure 2.1). Some games involve learning by taking objects apart and trying to put them back together. This process develops careful attention to details

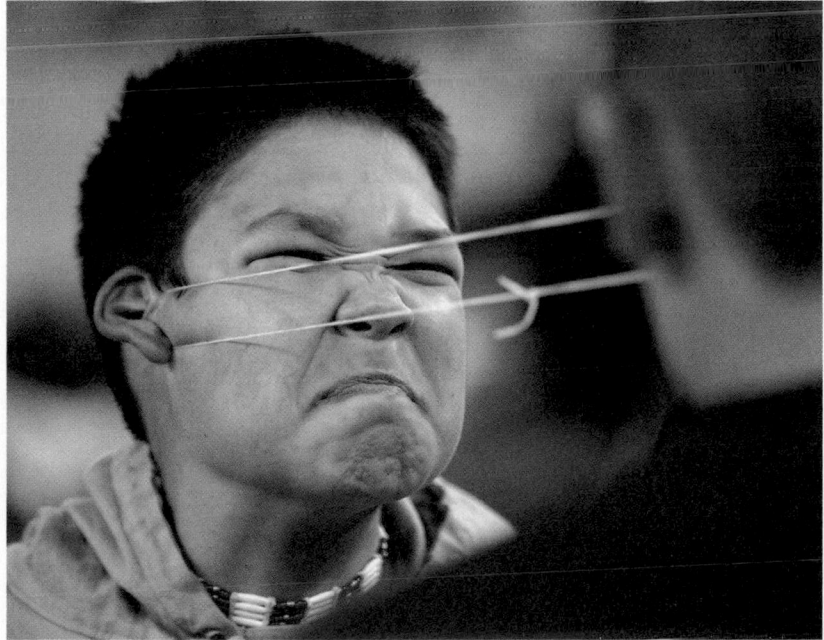

Figure 2.1 The Inuit ear pull game is a harsh test of physical endurance. Contestants pull against one another until one can no longer endure the pain. Here, Jacey Brave Heart, age 12, pulls against Drew Dewberry at the 2007 World Eskimo Indian Olympics in Anchorage, Alaska.

AP Photo/Al Grillo

and relationships, to patient trial and error, and to a mental recording of results for future reference. Many games stress the body and test the limits of the individual's psychological and physical endurance (Nelson 1983). For example, in the ear pull game, a thin loop of leather is positioned behind the ears of each of two competitors, who then pull away from each other until one gives up in pain (Canadian Broadcasting Company 1982).

In addition to being physically adept and independent, Inuit children must learn to be cooperative and emotionally restrained. Under the conditions of their closely knit and often isolated camp life, expressions of anger or aggression are avoided. The Inuit prize reason, judgment, and emotional control, and believe that these characteristics grow naturally as children grow.

The Inuit believe that children have both the ability and the wish to learn. Thus, educating a child consists of providing the necessary information, which the child will remember sooner or later. Scolding is seen as futile. Children will learn when they are ready; there is no point in forcing children to learn something before they are ready to remember it. Inuit elders believe that frequent scolding makes children hostile, rebellious, and impervious to the opinions of others.

The study of enculturation has a central place in the history of anthropology and gave rise to some of its classic works. Margaret Mead's 1928 book, *Coming of Age in Samoa,* was a popular best seller and a landmark work that changed how Americans looked at childhood and culture (Mead 1971/1928). Mead and others who studied childhood learning are known as **culture and personality** theorists. They held that cultures could best be understood by examining the patterns of child rearing and considering their effect on adult lives and social institutions. Culture and personality theory was extremely influential from the 1920s to the 1950s. Although few anthropologists today would call themselves culture and personality theorists, enculturation remains an important topic of anthropological research.

Culture and personality: A theoretical position in anthropology that held that cultures could best be understood by examining the patterns of child rearing and considering their effect on social institutions and adult lives.

◢ CULTURE IS THE WAY HUMANS USE SYMBOLS TO ORGANIZE AND GIVE MEANING TO THE WORLD

Consider this: Can you really see your environment? For example, when you walk into a classroom, you notice some things but not others. You see your friends and other students, the professor, the video equipment, and so on. You might spend an entire semester without ever seeing the cracks in the ceiling, the pattern of the carpeting, or the color of the walls. Yet these things are as physically present as the chairs and your friends.

You see certain things in the classroom and overlook others because you mentally organize the contents of the classroom with respect to your role as a student. It is virtually impossible to see things without organizing and evaluating them in some manner. If you paid as much attention to the cracks in the wall, the patterns on the floor, and the humming of the ventilation system as you did to the professor's lecture, not only would you likely fail the class, but you would also live in a world that was overwhelming and impossibly confusing. Only through fitting our perceptions and experiences into systems of organization and classification can we comprehend our lives and act in the world. A human without this ability would be paralyzed, frozen by an overwhelming bombardment of sensations.

Methods of organizing and classifying are typical of groups. You are not the only one who thinks that the students and professors in a classroom are more important than the ceiling tiles; all students and professors probably share that perception.

Anthropologists have long proposed that culture is a shared mental model that people use to organize, to classify, and ultimately to understand their world. A key way in which this model is expressed is through language, a symbolic system.

Different cultures have different models for understanding and speaking about the world. For instance, in English, the verb *smoke* describes the action of ingesting a cigarette and the verb *drink* describes the action of consuming a liquid. However, in the Bamana language (also known as Bambara), spoken by the Bambara of Mali, the verb *min* is used both for smoking and for drinking. Americans classify rainbows as objects of beauty and frequently point them out to one another. However, Lacandon Maya in southern Mexico classify rainbows as dangerous and frightening, and pointing them out to other people is highly inappropriate. For them, rainbows are unlucky because they hold back the rain. Snakes, rather than a pot of gold, are found under them, and they are associated with particular types of ghosts.

Anthropologists who are particularly interested in describing the systems of organization and classification different cultures use often use a theoretical perspective called **ethnoscience**. Generally, these anthropologists are interested in capturing the understanding of members of a culture. Ethnoscience is one position or technique within a broader perspective called **cognitive anthropology**, which focuses on the relationship between the mind and society.

Using Anthropology: Culturally Specific Diseases: The Case of Lia Lee

Because all human beings are biologically extremely similar, all are subject to the same biologically based diseases. However, the ways in which people classify, experience, and understand health and illness

Ethnoscience: A theoretical position in anthropology that focuses on recording and examining the ways in which members of a culture use language to classify and organize their cognitive world.

Cognitive anthropology: A theoretical position in anthropology that focuses on the relationship between the mind and society.

differ dramatically among cultures. Anthropologists have identified many culturally bound syndromes, illnesses that are identified in only one, or a small number of cultures. Fan death, the commonly held Korean belief that running a fan overnight in a room with the windows and doors closed can lead to the death of those sleeping in the room, is one example (Jennings 2013). *Bangungot*, the name for another culturally specific syndrome, is a term originating from the Tagalog word for "bad dream" and is found in the Philippines and elsewhere in Southeast Asia. Bangungot is diagnosed when young people, particularly adolescent and young adult men, die suddenly in their sleep. Eating disorders such as anorexia nervosa are culturally bound syndromes particular to rapidly industrializing societies, particularly in western Europe, the United States, and Asia.

Different ways of classifying, understanding, and treating illness present enormous challenges to health care around the world and particularly in multicultural societies such as the United States. The case of Lia Lee, described in Anne Fadiman's now classic 1997 *The Sprit Catches You and You Fall Down*, presents a powerful example and a cautionary tale. Lia Lee was the 14th child born to Foua Yang and Nao Kao Lee, Hmong refugees from Laos living in California. When she was three months old she began to experience seizures. However, the Lees were unable to explain Lia's condition to health care workers who spoke no Hmong and had no experience of Hmong culture. For them, the seizures were evidence that Lia's soul was being touched or taken by something from a different realm. Health care workers could not understand this, and it took a long time to diagnose Lia with epilepsy. However, this was the beginning of the problem, not the end. For the doctors, epilepsy was a disease to be treated with medicines, and they demanded that the Lees comply with their prescriptions, some of which were quite difficult and unpleasant to administer to a toddler. For the Lees, Lia's symptoms showed that she had *qaug dab peg*, an illness caused when a person's soul becomes separated from her body. Though Lia's condition needed a cure, it also meant that she could have spiritual powers and might become a shaman.

Doctors, social workers, and the Lee family fought bitterly over Lia's treatment. At one point, she was placed in foster care for a year because her parents refused to administer her medications, treating her instead with herbs and shamanic ritual. In 1986, when she was four years old, Lia suffered a profound seizure, followed by an infection. She lost most brain function, and was expected to die...but didn't. Although doctors and medical personnel at hospitals that treated her often spoke of her as if she were dead, she lived for another 26 years, never regaining consciousness but both cared for by her family and central to their lives. Though Fadiman (2012) acknowledges that it's not a medical explanation, she feels that Lia was kept alive by the constant love of her family.

Fadiman's account of Lia's story and the role of different cultural understandings in health care is required reading in many medical and social work programs. It was one of many cases that led to greater sensitivity regarding issues of language and culture in health care delivery in the United States. In an interview after Lia's death in the summer of 2012, Fadiman said that one of the key lessons of Lia's case was that Western medical personnel must try to understand illness from the point of view of their patients, particularly when they have patients from cultures that have different understandings of health and illness. Doctors must understand that treatment is not something they can dictate but something that must be created through collaboration between patients and health care providers (Fadiman 2012; Fox 2012).

Symbols and Meaning

Human beings not only classify the world, but they also fill it with meaning. A key way that they do this is through the use of symbols. The simplest definition of a symbol is something that stands for something else. Words, both spoken and written, objects, and ideas can all be symbols. Symbols enable us to store information. For example, the book you are currently holding contains a huge amount of information all stored symbolically. Nonhuman animals must learn through experience or imitation and, therefore, the amount they can learn is relatively small. Humans can store information symbolically, as stories and teachings passed from generation to generation or as written words, thus human cultures can be endlessly large.

Symbols also have the ability to condense meaning (see Figure 2.2). People may take a single symbol and make it stand for an entire constellation of ideas and emotions. Religious symbols and national symbols often have this characteristic. The meaning of a national flag or a symbol such as the cross cannot be summed up in a word or two. These symbols stand for vast complexes of history, ideas, and emotions. People are often literally willing to fight and die for them.

Symbolic anthropologists try to understand a culture by discovering and analyzing the symbols that are

Symbolic anthropology: A theoretical position in anthropology that focuses on understanding cultures by discovering and analyzing the symbols that are most important to their members.

VEER Thomas Francisco/Solus/Getty Images

Figure 2.2 Symbols do not have a single meaning but stand for large numbers of ideas and feelings. For many people in the United States, patriotic and military symbols have deep intellectual and emotional content.

most important to its members. These often reflect the deep concerns that are difficult for culture members to articulate. For example, according to Victor Turner (1967), among the Ndembu of East Africa, the mudyi tree is a central symbol and plays an important role in girls' puberty rites. The tree has a white, milky sap that symbolizes breast-feeding, the relationship between mother and child, the inheritance through the mother's family line, and, at the most abstract level, the unity and continuity of Ndembu society itself. It is unlikely that all Ndembu think deeply about all of these meanings during the puberty rites of their girls. However, Turner argues that this complex symbolism helps hold Ndembu society together by reaffirming its central tenants. For anthropologists, to understand the meaning of the mudyi tree and the role it plays in Ndembu society is to have penetrated deeply into the Ndembu view of the world.

Interpretive anthropology: A theoretical position in anthropology that focuses on using humanistic methods, such as those found in the analysis of literature, to analyze cultures and discover the meanings of culture to its participants.

Culture can also be analyzed using the tools of literature, and this is the job of **interpretive anthropology**. Clifford Geertz, one of the best-known interpretive anthropologists, said that, in a sense, culture is like a novel. It is an "ensemble of texts... which the anthropologist strains to read over the shoulders of those to whom they properly belong" (Geertz 2008/1973a:531). He meant that culture is a story people tell themselves about themselves. Like all good stories, culture engrosses us and helps us understand the nature and meaning of life. It comments on who we are and how we should act in the world. Interpretive anthropologists often find these cultural texts in public events, celebrations, and rituals. Analyzing them gives us clues and insights into the meaning of culture for its participants.

Consider the American fascination with football. American football has little appeal outside the United States, but here it draws more fans than any other sport. Football has lots of excitement and action, but so do many less popular sports. Some anthropologists argue that football's popularity is related to its symbolic meanings, that is, the unique ways in which it presents and manipulates important American cultural themes. Football attracts us because, more than other sports, it displays and manipulates ideas about the violence and sexuality underlying competition between men, the relationship of the individual to the group, racial character (Oriard 1993:18), as well as themes of national identity, particularly competitive opportunity and homeland security (Lindquist 2006:445). Football is just a game, but so is checkers. Millions watch football because it is meaningful to them in ways that checkers is not. For interpretive anthropologists, football's meaning derives from the ways in which it explores and comments on critical themes in American culture. Those who wish to understand American culture would do well to consider the meanings of football.

Interpretive and symbolic anthropologists use methods drawn from the humanities rather than from the sciences to uncover and interpret the deep emotional and psychological structure of societies. Their goal is to understand the experience of being a member of a culture and to make that experience available to their readers (Marcus and Fischer 1986).

CULTURE IS AN INTEGRATED SYSTEM—OR IS IT?

Consider a biological organism. The heart pumps blood, the lungs supply the blood with oxygen, the liver purifies the blood, and so on. The various organs work together to create a properly functioning whole. An early insight in anthropology was the usefulness of comparing societies to organisms. The subsistence system provides food, the economic and political systems determine how the food is distributed, religion provides the justification for the distribution system, and so on. Societies, like bodies, are integrated systems.

This **organic analogy** has strengths and weaknesses. It allows us to think about society as composed of different elements (such as kinship, religion, and subsistence), and it implies that anthropologists should describe the shape and role of such elements as well as the ways in which changes in one affect the others. For example, subsistence and social structure are two identifiable social elements and are related to each other. Foraging is an activity most often done in small groups and requires little direction or coordination. People who forage for their food will probably have relatively loosely defined social groups with changing membership. Farming requires more coordination than foraging; therefore, people who farm will likely have a society with a more rigid structure and a more stable membership. If a group were to move from foraging to farming, we would expect it to develop an increasingly well-defined social structure.

Organic analogy: The comparison of cultures to living organisms.

However, the organic analogy also implies that properly functioning societies should be stable and conflict-free. The parts of a biological organism work together to keep the entire being alive and well. The lungs do not declare war on the liver. The result of conflict between the parts of a living thing is usually sickness or death. If such conflict occurs (an autoimmune disease, for example), we understand that the organism is not functioning properly, and steps should be taken to restore the system. Thinking of cultures as systems may similarly suggest that their parts should work in harmony and that conflict and struggle are deviations from normality. But are cultures really like that? Do their elements really fit well together?

Consider, for example, whether the American family system fits well with the demands made by most American jobs. Most Americans want to maintain long-term marriage commitments, raise families, and live middle-class lifestyles. Most jobs in the United States provide inadequate income for this purpose. Many require mobility, long hours, and flexibility, which come at the expense of the family. Americans must negotiate the contradictions between the lifestyle they desire, the demands of their families, and the requirements of their jobs.

Consider that, in socially stratified societies, different groups have different interests, and this creates conflict. For example, in capitalist societies, both workers and owners want their companies to do well, but within this context, the owners hope to maximize their profit and the workers want to maximize their pay. However, increases in workers' pay come at some expense to owners' profits. Therefore, there is a structural conflict between the owners and the workers. This conflict does not occur because society is not working properly. Rather, it is a fundamental condition of a capitalist society.

There is nothing uniquely American or modern about contradiction and conflict within culture. People in nonindustrialized societies must also handle conflicting commitments to their families and other social groups such as secret societies or religious associations. Even in societies that lack social groups beyond the family, the interests of men and women, or those of the old and the young, may differ. Thus, in all societies, social life is characterized by conflict as well as concord. Although culture certainly is patterned and surely is a system, often the parts may rub, chafe, and grind against each other.

Anthropologists who are drawn to the study of the relationships among different aspects of culture have often sought to find laws of cultural behavior. In the first half of the 20th century, **functionalists** such as A. R. Radcliffe-Brown and Bronislaw Malinowski searched for such laws in the mutually supportive relationships among kinship, religion, and politics. For example, Radcliffe-Brown (1965/1952:176) argued that religion supports social structure by giving individuals a sense of dependence on their society.

More recently, **ecological functionalists** have focused on the relationship between environment and society. These anthropologists view social institutions and practices as elements in broader ecological systems. They are particularly concerned with ways in which cultural practices both alter and are altered by the ecosystem in which they occur. For example, Marvin Harris's (1966) classic explanation of the Hindu taboo on eating beef focused on the effect of cattle in the Indian environment rather than on the Hindu belief system. Harris noted that despite widespread poverty and periodic famine in India, Hindus refuse to eat their cattle. Although this seems unreasonable superficially, it makes good ecological

Functionalism: A theoretical position in anthropology that focuses on finding general laws that identify different elements of society, showing how they relate to each other, and demonstrating their role in maintaining social order.

Ecological functionalism: A theoretical position in anthropology that focuses on the relationship between environment and society.

sense. Cows are important in India because they provide dung for fertilizer and cooking fuel, and they give birth to bullocks, the draft animals that pull the plows and carts essential to agriculture. If a family ate its cows during a famine, it would deprive itself of the source of bullocks and could not continue farming. Thus, the Hindu religious taboo on eating beef is part of a larger ecological pattern that includes the subsistence system.

Many anthropologists today, although they accept that culture is a patterned system, choose to focus on conflicts within the system. This often reflects the deep influence of the work of Karl Marx and the early 20th-century sociologist Max Weber. Both Marx and Weber saw conflict in society as a key factor driving social change. For example, Marx understood society to be made up of different social groups, such as factory owners and workers, who had opposing interests. Marx believed that, over time, these opposing interests inevitably would lead to both conflict and social change.

CULTURE IS A SHARED SYSTEM OF NORMS AND VALUES—OR IS IT?

What would a person with his own private culture be like? Perhaps he would be like Peter or Victor in the introduction to this chapter, unable to meaningfully participate in the society around him. Alternatively, such a person might live in a world in which everything has one set of meanings to her but different meanings to everyone else. People with certain forms of schizophrenia seem to have just this problem; they live in a world rich in symbols that have meaning only to them. In either case, it would be very difficult for such people to interact with others; they would probably be isolated and, in some cases, considered insane. Clearly, then, at some level, members of a culture must share ways of thinking and behaving. Often, we refer to these as *norms* and *values*.

Norms are shared ideas about the way things ought to be done—rules of behavior that reflect and enforce culture. **Values** are shared ideas about what is true, right, and beautiful. For example, shaking hands rather than bowing when introduced to a stranger is an American norm. The notion that advances in technology are good is an American value.

Human behavior is not always consistent with cultural norms or values (see Figure 2.3). People do not necessarily do what they say they should do. Norms may be contradictory and manipulated for personal and group ends. For example, people in India believe that women should stay in their homes rather than go out with their friends. They also believe that women should spend a lot of time in religious activities. Modern Indian women use the second of these ideals to get around the first. By

Norms: Shared ideas about the way things ought to be done; rules of behavior that reflect and enforce culture.

Values: Shared ideas about what is true, right, and beautiful.

Steve Skjold/Alamy Limited

Figure 2.3 Not everyone in a culture must conform. Although cultures demand a certain amount of consensus, members often show great variability in knowledge, style, and beliefs. Here, a 24-year-old attends a Bastille Day festival in Minneapolis.

Subculture: A group within a society that shares norms and values significantly different from those of the dominant culture.

Dominant culture: The culture with the greatest wealth and power in a society that consists of many subcultures.

forming clubs whose activities are religious, they have an excuse to get out of the house, to which their elders cannot object too strongly.

This example raises important questions. How do we determine the norms and values of a society? Do all people in society agree on these things? How many people must agree on something before it is considered a norm or a value? Research shows that, even in small societies, norms are not always followed and values are not universal. Individuals differ in their knowledge, understanding, and beliefs. For example, one might expect that all members in a small fishing society would agree on the proper names for different kinds of fish, but on Pukapuka, the small Pacific atoll Robert Borofsky (1994) studied, even experienced fishermen disagreed much of the time.

The degree to which people do not simply share a single culture is even more obvious in large societies. Sometimes the term **subculture** is used to designate groups within a single society that share norms and values significantly different from those of the **dominant culture**. The terms *dominant culture* and *subculture* do not refer to superior and inferior but rather to the idea that the dominant culture, because it controls greater wealth and power, is more able to impose its understanding of the world on subcultures than the reverse.

Dominant cultures retain their power partly through control of institutions, like the legal system, criminalizing practices that conflict with their own (Norgren and Nanda 1996). In contemporary society, public schools help maintain the values of the dominant culture, and the media play an important role in encouraging people to perceive subcultures in stereotypical (and usually negative) ways. For example, in a study that focused on television news and reality shows, Oliver (2003) found that images of race and crime systematically overrepresented African Americans as criminal. Furthermore, such shows tended to portray black men as particularly dangerous and presented information about black suspects that assumed their guilt. By contrast, many portrayals of African Americans in the 1990s and early 2000s focused on the "magical Negro," "a lower-class, uneducated black person who possesses supernatural or magical powers" (Hughey 2009:544). The "magical Negro" appears in films such as *The Green Mile* (1999), *The Legend of Bagger Vance* (2000), and *Bruce Almighty* (2003). Hughey argues that, although such characters are an improvement over earlier stereotypes, they capitalize on traditional stereotypes of African Americans, such as poverty, cultural deficiency, and folk wisdom. They treat whiteness as normal, and glorify black characters, only placing them in racially subservient positions.

Although domination of one group by another is sometimes extreme, rarely is it complete. People contest their subjugation and protect their subcultures through political, economic, and military means. Sometimes, when domination is intense, minorities can protect themselves only through religious faith or by building cultural tales in which they hold positions of power and their oppressors are weak (Scott 1992).

Ideas we sometimes think of as timeless and consensual are constantly changing and being renegotiated. This involves conflict and subjugation as well as consensus. Which norms and values are promoted and which are rejected is particularly important because such cultural ideas influence and are influenced by wealth, power, and status. For example, what are American norms and values about using drugs to alter one's state of consciousness? Should the use of such drugs be legal? Clearly, these are difficult questions. In the past, Americans considered alcohol a dangerous mind-altering substance. Its manufacture, sale, and transport were prohibited in the United States between 1920 and 1933. Even today, substantial numbers of Americans oppose alcohol. In 2006, the Southern Baptist Convention, which represents about 16 million church members, passed a resolution expressing "total opposition to the manufacturing, advertising, distributing, and consuming of alcoholic beverages" (Southern Baptist Convention 2006). Marijuana, on the other hand, has been illegal in the United States since 1937, but a Quinnipiac University (2012) poll in December 2012 showed that about 51 percent of American voters favored its legalization, substantially up from the one-third who favored legalization in the early 2000s (Carroll 2005). This norm is clearly changing rapidly. The second edition of *Culture Counts* noted that 14 states had legal medical marijuana. By spring 2013, 16 states and the District of Columbia had legalized medical marijuana and two additional states, Colorado and Washington, had legalized nonmedical marijuana as well.

Believing that people should consume or not consume either alcohol or marijuana clearly does not make one more or less "American." However, which of these notions is held by those in power is critical. It influences the laws and social policies that shape our lives and history.

The focus on culture as a shared set of norms and values is often associated with the American anthropologists of the first half of the 20th century, particularly Franz Boas and his students, members of a school of thought referred to as **historical particularism**. These anthropologists were interested in presenting objective descriptions of cultures within their historical and environmental context. Their emphasis on

Historical particularism: A theoretical position in anthropology associated with American anthropologists of the early 20th century that focuses on providing objective descriptions of cultures within their historical and environmental contexts.

norms and values was designed to show that, although other cultures were very different from our own, they were coherent, rational, and indeed often beautiful. In contrast to the logical coherence seen by the historical particularists, some contemporary anthropologists, particularly **postmodernists**, believe that culture is a context in which norms and values are contested and negotiated. Rather than assuming a cultural core of shared beliefs and values, these anthropologists see culture and society as battlegrounds where individuals and groups fight for power and the right to determine what is accepted as true.

Postmodernism: A theoretical position in anthropology that focuses on issues of power and voice. Postmodernists hold that anthropological accounts are partial truths reflecting the backgrounds, training, and social positions of their authors.

CULTURE IS THE WAY HUMAN BEINGS ADAPT TO THE WORLD

All animals, including human beings, have biologically based needs. All need habitat and food, and each species must reproduce. All creatures are adapted to meet these needs. **Adaptation** is a change in the biological structure or lifeways of an individual or population by which it becomes better fitted to survive and reproduce in its environment. Nonhuman animals fill their needs primarily through biological adaptation. Lions, for example, have a series of biologically based adaptations that are superbly designed to enable them to feed themselves (and their mates). They have large muscles for speed as well as sharp teeth and claws to capture and eat their prey.

Adaptation: A change in the biological structure or lifeways of an individual or population by which it becomes better fitted to survive and reproduce in its environment.

Humans are different. We lack offensive biological weaponry, and, if left to get our food like the lion, we would surely starve. There is little evidence that we have an instinct to hunt or consume any particular kind of food, to build any particular sort of structure, or to have a single fixed social arrangement. Instead, human beings, in groups, develop forms of knowledge and technologies that enable them to feed themselves and to survive in their environments. They pass this knowledge from generation to generation and from group to group. In other words, human beings develop and use culture to adapt to the world.

Most of a lion's adaptation to the world is set biologically. The growth of its teeth and claws, its instinct to hunt, and the social arrangement of a pride are largely expressions of the lion's genetic code. Humans have a biological adaptation to the world: learning culture. All humans, except those with profound biologically based differences (such as autism) automatically learn the culture of their social group. This strongly suggests that such learning is a manifestation of our genetic code. Thus, our biology compels us to learn culture. But it does not compel us to learn a particular culture. The range of human beliefs and practices is enormous. However, people everywhere learn to fill their basic needs, such as

Jacques Langevin/Sygma/Corbi

Figure 2.4 In many societies, housing is well adapted to the environment. The Dolgon of Siberia build houses on runners that allow them to move the house from place to place using reindeer teams.

food and shelter, through cultural practices. Culture everywhere must, to some extent, be adaptive.

Cultural adaptation has some distinct advantages over biological adaptation. Because humans adapt through learned behavior, they can change their approach to solving problems quickly and more easily than creatures whose adaptations are primarily biological (Figure 2.4). Lions hunt and eat today in much the same way as they have for tens of thousands of years. The vast majority of human beings today do not live like humans of even three or four generations ago, let alone like our distant ancestors. Our means of feeding ourselves, our culture, have changed. **Plasticity**—the ability to change behavior—has allowed human beings to thrive under a wide variety of social and ecological conditions.

Cultural adaptation has some disadvantages too. Misinformation, leading to cultural practices that hinder rather than aid survival, may creep into human behavior. Cultural practices, such as unrestrained logging, mining, or fishing that encourage destruction of the environment, may lead to short-term success but long-term disaster. Furthermore, many human practices are clearly not adaptive, even in the short run. Political policies of ethnic cleansing and genocide that urge people to murder their neighbors may benefit the leaders of a society, but it is hard to see any meaningful way in which these practices are adaptive. A normal lion will always inherit the muscle, tooth, and claw that, given a relatively stable environment, let it survive. Normal humans, on the other hand, may inherit a great deal of cultural misinformation that hinders their survival.

Historically, a focus on the adaptive aspect of culture is associated with a theoretical position called **cultural ecology**, first proposed in the

Plasticity (in anthropology): The ability of humans to change their behavior in response to a wide range of environmental and social demands.

Cultural ecology: A theoretical position in anthropology that focuses on the adaptive dimensions of culture.

1930s. Although many of our ideas have changed since then, investigating the adaptive (and maladaptive) aspects of culture continues to be an important aspect of anthropology. Anthropologists who view culture as an adaptation tend to be concerned with people's behavior, particularly as it relates to their physical well-being or the relationship of cultural practices to ecosystems. They investigate the ways in which cultures adapt to specific environments and the ways in which cultures have changed in response to new physical and social conditions.

◪ CULTURE IS CONSTANTLY CHANGING

Did you ever want to visit a culture where people were untouched by the outside world, living just the same way they have been living for thousands of years? Well, you are out of luck. One of the most romantic notions of anthropology presented in the media is that there are "Stone Age" cultures waiting to be discovered. But this is false. No culture has ever been stuck in time or isolated from others for very long. Cultures are constantly changing. They change because of conflict among different elements within them. They change because of contact with outsiders. Population growth, disease, climate change, and natural disaster all drive culture change. However, cultures do not always change at the same speed. Cultural change may happen in small increments, or it may happen in revolutionary bursts. Historically, in most places and at most times, culture change has been a relatively slow process. However, the pace of change has been increasing for the past several hundred years and has become extremely rapid in the past century.

Since the 16th century, the most important source of culture change has been the development of a world economic system based primarily in the wealthy nations of Europe and Asia. This has involved invasions, revolutions, and epidemic diseases. These historic processes and the resultant global economic system are the primary foci of Chapters 13 and 14. Here, we focus on some of the more traditional ways in which anthropologists have examined culture change.

Anthropologists sometimes discuss cultural change in terms of innovation and diffusion. An **innovation** is an object, a way of thinking, or a way of behaving that is new because it is qualitatively different from existing forms (Barnett 1953:7). Although we often think of innovations as technological, they are not limited to the material aspects of culture. New art forms and new ideas are also innovations.

Innovation: An object or way of thinking that is based upon but is qualitatively different from existing forms.

New practices, tools, or principles may emerge from within a society and gain wide acceptance. Anthropologists sometimes call these *primary innovations,* and they are frequently chance discoveries and accidents. In our own society, some examples of accidental discovery include penicillin, found when British researcher Alexander Fleming noticed that bacteria samples he had left by a window were contaminated by mold spores, and Teflon, discovered by Roy Plunkett, who was trying to find new substances to use in refrigeration. All such innovations are based on building blocks provided by culture. For example, although Fleming is justly famous for the discovery of penicillin, this innovation also illustrates the importance of context and incremental discovery. Fleming was not a random person who woke up one morning thinking about mold and bacteria. He was a trained bacteriologist who had been looking for a substance to fight infection for more than a decade. He was very aware of the work of other scientists studying the problem of infection. It does not diminish his achievement to point out that he, like every other inventor or discoverer, did not create something totally new. He realized the critical importance of new combinations of things that already existed. His culture provided him with the training, tools, and context in which his discovery could be made.

Innovations tend to move from one culture to another, a process known as **diffusion**. Diffusion can happen in many ways; trade, travel, and warfare all promote it. Direct contact among cultures generally results in the most far-reaching changes, and cultures located on major trade routes tend to change more rapidly than do those in more isolated places. However, because no human society has ever been isolated for a long time, diffusion has always been an important factor in culture. This implies that "pure" cultures, free from outside influences, have never existed.

Diffusion: The spread of cultural elements from one society to another.

MARKA/Alamy

Figure 2.5 Innovation often involves repurposing materials to create something new. Here children in a refugee camp in Kakuma, Kenya play with an airplane they have crafted from scraps of wood and metal.

Innovation and diffusion are not simple processes. People do not "naturally" realize that one way of doing things is better than another or that one style of dress, religion, or behavior is superior. For innovation and diffusion to occur, new ideas must be accepted, and even when the desirability of an innovation seems clear, gaining acceptance is a very complex process. Again, the discovery of penicillin provides a good example. Although Fleming understood some of the importance of his discovery in 1928, human trials did not take place until World War II, and the drug was not widely prescribed until the mid- to late 1950s (Sheehan 1982; Williams 1984).

People may not accept an idea because they do not fully understand it, but other factors are usually involved as well. For psychological reasons, individuals may vary in their willingness to adopt change. Far more importantly, changes rarely provide equal benefits to everyone. For example, new agricultural techniques were introduced in Latin America and Asia from the 1940s to the 1960s (an era known as the "Green Revolution"). The new techniques did radically improve crop yields, but large landowners received the greater part of the benefit. Laborers, many of whom were landless, were often impoverished by the change and, as a result, were very resistant to it (Das 1998).

Change is often promoted or resisted by powerful interests. Innovations that have strong political, economic, or moral forces behind them may be rapidly accepted. But, when those forces are arrayed against an innovation, acceptance can be delayed. New technologies may face resistance from those who have invested heavily in older ones. For example, FM radio broadcasting is clearly superior to AM broadcasting; it has greater fidelity and is much less susceptible to static and interference. Although it was invented in 1933, the opposition of CBS, NBC, and RCA, powerful corporations heavily invested in AM technology, prevented FM from gaining popularity until the late 1960s (Lewis 1991).

Like innovation, diffusion is often accompanied by conflict. People who are colonized or captured by others are often forced to assume new cultural practices. New rulers may require that older traditions be abandoned. Economic demands by governments or creditors often compel the adoption of new technologies and practices. Although these processes happen in most places where cultures have confronted one another, they have been particularly important in the past 500 years. During this time, cultures have been increasingly tied together in an economic system controlled largely in northern Europe, North America, and Japan, a process we explore further in Chapters 13 and 14.

The rapid pace of cultural change and diffusion, particularly in the past 100 years, raises the question of cultural homogenization. Are cultural differences being erased? Are we all being submerged in a single global culture? There are no simple answers to these questions. On the one hand, modern technological culture now penetrates virtually every place on earth. On the other hand, this penetration is uneven. The wealthy have far greater access to and ability to control technology than the poor.

The world dominance of industrialized nations has affected cultures everywhere, but rather than annihilating local culture, cultural traits are transformed as they are adopted, and new cultural forms result. Radio, television, and video recording are good examples. Developed by industrialized societies, these technologies have spread around the world. However, they do not necessarily promote the values and practices of the societies that created them. Insurgents and revolutionaries around the world use cell phones, Twitter accounts, and other technologies to pursue political and social goals vastly different than those of most members of the societies that created these products.

Anthropologists have traditionally worked in tribal and peasant societies. Because such cultures have been profoundly affected by their contact with industrial societies, most anthropologists today, whatever their theoretical orientations, are interested in change. The study of cultural change has special interest for applied anthropologists, particularly those who investigate issues related to the economic development of poor nations.

CULTURE COUNTS

Culture is many different things. It is learning, symbolism and meaning, patterns of thought and behavior, the things we share with those around us, the ways in which we survive in our world, and dynamism and change. It is both consensus and conflict. Culture makes us human and ties us to others everywhere. Ultimately, because all societies are based around fundamental patterns of culture, no society can be utterly incomprehensible to members of another. On the other hand, enormous variability is built into these patterns. The fact that human lifeways are shared, learned, and symbolic, the fact that we don't simply adapt to our environment but fill it with meaning, results in extraordinary differences in human cultures.

Naked mole rats are a highly social species found in the Horn of Africa. Their behavior is extremely complex, but they lack culture in a human sense. Each colony is more or less identical to every other. Imaginary mole rat explorers visiting each colony would understand everything they saw or heard. But the history of human exploration is one of miscomprehension. Because cultures are so different and count for so much in human life, we need tools to help us understand them. One job of anthropology is to provide these tools. In Chapter 3, we examine the methods anthropologists have used to investigate culture.

BRINGING IT BACK HOME: IS THERE AN AMERICAN CULTURE?

Throughout this chapter, we have identified culture as something shared by a group of people. And, indeed, we believe that this is a necessary aspect of culture. However, it is also problematic. We often think of groups as neat, bounded collections of individuals or families. But, think for a moment: How many groups do you belong to? You almost certainly have a nationality, a place where you grew up, a school (or perhaps more than one), perhaps an ethnic identity, perhaps a religious identity, maybe you were a member of a group like the military, and, of course, you certainly had some kind of family identity. These identities overlap, but are different. All of them have characteristics of culture such as processes of enculturation and symbolism. Now, which of them is your culture? In fact, if we investigate this level by level, we will find that there is no one on the planet who shares precisely your cultural experience. Even identical twins don't end up with identical lives. So, are you then a culture of one?

The problem of culture is particularly acute when we talk about very large and complex groups. The United States is a nation of more than 310 million people. They have different geographical origins, ethnicities, beliefs, sexualities, and so on. In a vast, diverse country, can there really be anything such as American culture?

If the question is "Are there things upon which 100 percent of Americans agree?," then the answer is almost certainly no. It's difficult if not impossible to find that kind of consensus even in a very small community. However, as we have seen in this chapter, discord, argument, even violence are not aberrations; they are common parts of all cultures. To have a culture, we don't need to agree but we do need to in some way share some things, not in the sense that we all partake of them equally, but rather that, overwhelmingly, we have some significant connection with them.

So what kinds of things do Americans share? There's no definitive list but here are some ideas. We share and are shaped to some degree by the critical institutions of our society: the federal government, court system, and education system. Although many languages are spoken in the United States, we are overwhelmingly an English-speaking nation, and historically, virtually all grandchildren of non-English-speaking immigrants are monolingual English speakers.

Anthropologists and other social scientists have proposed a variety of other American characteristics. Anthropologist Clyde Kluckhohn (1947) described American culture as characterized by "effort optimism": the belief that if a person tries hard enough at anything, he or she will succeed. Sociologist Robert Bellah and his colleagues (1985) say that the dominant elements of American culture are utilitarian and expressive individualism. Utilitarian individualism is the claim that humans have a right to behave in their self-interest, pursuing the satisfaction of their goals, appetites, and fears. Bellah sees this as countered and moderated by expressive individualism, the belief that each person has the right to express a unique core of creativity and individuality. Bellah and others have also noted that ideas such as utilitarian and expressive individualism are reinforced constantly in schools, films, and television. They also articulate well with American capitalism.

Numerous other attributes have been proposed. A typical list includes things such as the belief that the environment can and should be controlled for the benefit of people, belief that progress is good and that things in the future will probably be better, a strong sense of good and bad (combined with a belief that we can know what is morally good and we should act upon it), the notion that there should be a schedule and that people should stick rigorously to it, a fundamental belief in human equality (often combined with a deep prejudice toward particular groups of people), and the idea that people should be friendly and open. However, we're sure that you can think of many cases where you and people you know do not behave in ways this list suggests they should. Does this mean that American culture is a fiction, or that American culture contains much friction?

YOU DECIDE:

1. Do you believe there is such a thing as American culture? Support your position with at least three examples.
2. Briefly explain the connections between values such as effort optimism, utilitarian individualism, and the American economic system.
3. To how many cultures do you think you belong? Describe some of the critical differences between different cultures to which you belong.

CHAPTER SUMMARY

1. Give a definition of culture. Culture is the learned, symbolic, at least partially adaptive, and ever-changing patterns of behavior and meaning shared by members of a group. Humans are vitally dependent on culture for their existence.
2. Describe the importance of learning in culture. Almost all human behavior is learned. Humans learn throughout their entire life span. The example of the Inuit shows how children are taught to survive in a harsh environment.

3. Describe the importance of symbols in culture. Humans understand the world by classifying it and using symbols to give it meaning. Different cultures use different systems of classification. People use symbols to give meaning to their lives. Anthropologists analyze and interpret symbols and rituals to understand cultural meanings.

4. In what ways are cultures like biological organisms, and what are the problems with this organic analogy? Like biological organisms, cultures are systems of related elements working together. However, unlike biological organisms, cultural systems include contradictions that lead to conflict.

5. What are norms and values? Do people within a culture agree on them? Norms are shared ideas about the way things ought to be done. Values are shared ideas about what is true, right, and beautiful. Typically, people within a culture do not fully agree on norms and values. Some amount of conflict is the rule, not the exception.

6. How is culture similar to the biological adaptations of nonhuman animals? Culture is the way that humans adapt to their world. Unlike other species, humans adapt primarily through cultural learning. This enables people to respond to change rapidly but can, in some cases, also be maladaptive.

7. Are cultures typically static, or do they change? All cultures change. Innovation and diffusion are two sources of change. Many factors determine the acceptance or rejection of a culture change.

8. What role does anthropology play in coping with cultural differences? Culture makes humans unique, but the vast differences between human cultures make cultural understanding a challenge. Anthropology supplies tools to meet that challenge.

KEY TERMS

Adaptation	Historical particularism
Anthropological theory	Innovation
Cognitive anthropology	Interpretive anthropology
Cultural ecology	Norms
Culture and personality	Organic analogy
Diffusion	Plasticity
Dominant culture	Postmodernism
Ecological functionalism	Subculture
Enculturation	Symbol
Ethnoscience	Symbolic anthropology
Functionalism	Values

courtesy of Greg Simon

Anthropologist Gregory Simon, whose work is described in the opening of this chapter, joins friends at a Minangkabou wedding feast in Bukittinggi, West Sumatra. Simon notes that if had he known he was going to the feast when he left home, he would have dressed differently. However, he also points out that anthropologists are often cultural participants who may be a bit out of place.

CHAPTER **3**

DOING CULTURAL ANTHROPOLOGY

LEARNING OBJECTIVES

After you have read this chapter, you will be able to:

Δ Explain who Boas and Malinowski were, and their importance to the development of anthropology.

Δ Define participant observation and explain its importance in anthropology.

Δ Describe some of the techniques that anthropologists use during their fieldwork.

Δ Analyze the role of cross-cultural research in anthropology and describe some of the tools used to conduct it.

Δ Summarize the importance of feminism and postmodernism in the development of anthropology.

Δ Describe collaborative and engaged anthropology and give examples of them.

Δ Discuss the advantages and difficulties of doing fieldwork in one's own society.

Δ Give some examples of ethical dilemmas facing anthropologists.

ANGER MANAGEMENT IN INDONESIA

DOING fieldwork is a fundamental part of anthropology, but is often a deeply challenging experience as well. In this passage from an essay in *Dispatches from the Field* (2006), Greg Simon describes some of his fieldwork experiences in Bukittinggi, Indonesia:

> When I picture myself moving through the streets of Bukittinggi during my first months of fieldwork, I picture myself angry.
>
> After living several months in this small mountain city, I have found myself thinking: I am being abused. I am like an animal at the local zoo; people stare at me, point, make jokes about me. They comment to each other—as if I were not present—on my skin, my nose, my height, my movements. I tense whenever I go to use the local dialect, knowing that every time I do, they will be sure to laugh and parrot me. Sometimes they greet me, in barely audible tones, only after we have passed each other moving in opposite directions. Or they zoom by in pairs on motorcycles, screaming at me then laughing as they speed away.
>
> When I remember myself during those first months here, I remember myself bracing for attack....
>
> Day after day, I saw red when faced with an enthusiastically smiling visage; I was prone to feel my blood pressure rise when greeted with a hearty, "Hello, Mister!" and I was vulnerable to feeling a prick of irritation at the curious probe of a stranger's questions. Seeing a stranger looking towards me, perhaps about to speak to me, I might find myself turning away as if frightened, or directing a steely stare in their direction as if hardening myself for their approach. It was all done in an effort to protect myself. But it also made what I needed to do—meet people, interact, have conversations—all that much more difficult. So I would despair at my prospects for carrying out successful research, and I would lay blame: Minang people are hostile, unwelcoming, mean-spirited, and indifferent to making any genuine connection with me.
>
> I felt horribly guilty for these thoughts. Wasn't this, after all, exactly the kind of bigotry that anthropology is supposed to confront and defuse? I also knew, rationally, that this characterization of Minang people was not true. Not only did it brush broadly over the behavior of the thousands of people around me, each with a different personality and attitude, but so often it seemed to be exactly the opposite of what I have experienced here from the beginning. In between these failed encounters, I was also spending hours enjoying people's hospitality and conversation and developing genuine friendships. I receive frequent invitations to visit people in their homes, or to attend weddings and parties, and at gatherings I am always an extraspecial guest, given the most careful attention and deference. (2006:105–108)

© Cengage Learning 2015

Indonesia.

Greg Simon is challenged by his emotional reaction to fieldwork. On the one hand, he finds that he is often treated extremely well. People tell him that he is "like their very own child." However, he also has many uncomfortable experiences. People laugh at him, treat him as a child, and accuse him of being a spy. Simon finds it difficult to escape the feelings of anger and hostility that these encounters cause. He knows that such feelings will get in the way of being an anthropologist, but, anthropologists are humans too, and fieldwork cannot be divorced from individual emotions the way an experiment in chemistry or biology might be. Instead, anthropologists must reconcile their own emotional responses with the skills of data collection they need to perform their jobs. Eventually, Simon finds that his experiences of being treated as "less than completely human" gave him some insight into the lives of many Indonesians who themselves "often feel that they live in a world that is liable to dismiss them as less than fully human." Through the course of his fieldwork, Simon learns to control his anger and learn from it; however, he still has occasional experiences that leave him feeling lost and confused (Simon 2006:105–106, 108, 114, 118).

Although Simon's particular experiences are unique, almost all anthropologists must face the confusion and disorientation of immersion in a different culture and the intense learning and reflection that ensue.

If you have any picture of anthropologists at all, you probably think of men and women who share the lives of people who are different than themselves. Indeed, although anthropologists also work in their own cultures, a topic we will discuss in some detail in this chapter, one of the fundamental ways in which anthropologists work is by spending time in other cultures. Psychologists or sociologists may be able to do research without leaving the college campus. They conduct surveys using the telephone, the Internet, or the postal service, or they may bring students into a laboratory and ask them questions or observe their reactions. Philosophers or scholars of literature may work by reading, observing, and pondering. Anthropologists do these things too, but, in addition, must go into the field.

For more than 100 years, anthropologists have gone into other cultures. They have lived among small isolated groups that forage for their food, have joined with societies that travel with their herds, and have spent time in agricultural villages and in bustling modern cities. They have lived among farmers, craftsmen, thieves, and crack cocaine dealers. If you enjoy anthropology, fieldwork is probably one of the key reasons you are attracted to it. There is something profoundly romantic about the idea of living with members of another culture, learning their way of life, and attempting to understand the world in a new and different manner. However, as Simon's description of his experiences show, there is also confusion, strangeness, alienation, and a host of challenges and dilemmas. Fieldwork is a wonderful experience. It is essential to the ways in which anthropology is done. However, it can also be intensely lonely and disturbing. In this chapter, we explore some of the history and practice of fieldwork. We examine fieldwork techniques and different trends in anthropological data collection and discuss some of the ethical issues raised by the practice of anthropology.

A LITTLE HISTORY

Anthropology was not always based around fieldwork. The first scholars who called themselves anthropologists worked in the second half of the 19th century. Among the most famous of them were Sir Edward Burnett Tylor and Lewis Henry Morgan. Both saw themselves as compilers and analysts of ethnographic accounts rather than as field researchers. They relied largely upon the writings of amateurs—travelers, explorers, missionaries, and colonial officers—who had recorded their experiences in remote areas of the world. Because of this, critics of Tylor and Morgan sometimes referred to them as "armchair anthropologists."

Morgan and Tylor were deeply influenced by the evolutionary theories of their era. They assumed that such theories could be applied to human society. Thus, as they analyzed societies, they used type of technology and social institutions, such as family and religion, to place each society on an evolutionary scale of increasing complexity. Their scale began with simple, small-scale societies (classified as "savages"), passed through various chiefdoms (usually classified as "barbarians"), and ended with societies such as their own (classified as "civilization"). Although Morgan and Tylor were deeply critical of many aspects of their own societies, they were also convinced that they lived in the most highly evolved society that had ever existed.

There were numerous problems with Morgan and Tylor's evolutionary anthropology. Explorers, colonial officials, and missionaries had particular interests in playing up the most exotic aspects of the societies they described. Doing so increased the fame of explorers (and the number of books they were able to sell). It made the natives more in need of the "good government" or salvation that colonial officials and missionaries claimed they could provide. Perhaps more importantly, the evolutionists were so sure that they had properly formulated the general evolutionary history of society that they twisted and contorted their data to fit their theories.

Franz Boas and American Anthropology

The problems implicit in Morgan and Tylor's evolutionary approach led to a radical reappraisal of evolutionary anthropology at the end of the 19th century. The most important critic of evolutionism was Franz Boas (see Figure 3.1). Born in Minden, Germany, Boas came to the United States after completing his doctorate in geography and living among the Inuit on Baffin Island. In the late 1890s, he became the first professor of anthropology at Columbia University in New York City. From there, he trained many students who became the leading anthropologists of the first half of the 20th century. As a result, Boas's ideas had a profound impact on the development of anthropology in the United States.

Boas's studies and his experiences among the Inuit convinced him that evolutionary anthropology was both intellectually flawed and, because it treated other people and other societies as inferior to Europeans, morally defective. Boas argued that anthropologists should not be collectors of tales and spinners of theories but should devote themselves to objective data collection through fieldwork. Anthropologists must live among the people they study, both observing their activities and collecting stories and information from the most knowledgeable members of society. They should record as much information about the group's culture as possible. This was particularly important because Boas believed that many of the lifeways of the societies he and his students studied (most often Native American societies) were disappearing.

One of Boas's core beliefs was that cultures are the products of their own histories. He argued that a culture's standards of beauty and morality as well as many other aspects of behavior could be understood only in light of that culture's historical development. Because our own ideas are also the products of history, they should not be used as standards to judge other cultures. Evolutionists failed partly because they assumed, incorrectly, that the most evolved cultures are those that have values most similar to their own. In other words, the evolutionists failed because of their own ethnocentrism. In one sense, **ethnocentrism** is simply the belief that one's own culture is better than any other. In a deeper sense, it is precisely the application of the historical standards of beauty, worth, and morality developed in one culture to all other cultures.

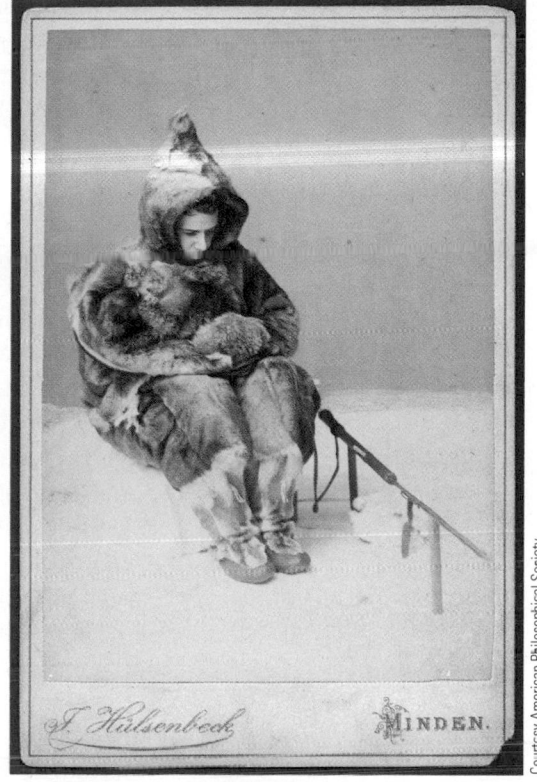

Courtesy American Philosophical Society

Figure 3.1 In the early 20th century, Franz Boas was the most influential anthropologist in the United States. He emphasized fieldwork, cultural relativism, and participant observation. In this picture, he dresses in Inuit clothing.

Ethnocentrism: Judging other cultures from the perspective on one's own culture. The notion that one's own culture is more beautiful, rational, and nearer to perfection than any other.

An American tourist who asks "How much is this in real money?" when presented with a handful of Mexican pesos is being ethnocentric. He or she thinks of the money of their own country as real but that of others as "play money." But there is nothing uniquely American or Western about ethnocentrism. People all over the world tend to see things from their own culturally patterned point of view. For example, when the people living in Highland New Guinea first saw European outsiders in the 1930s, they believed them to be the ghosts of their ancestors. It was the only way they could initially make sense of what they were seeing (Connolly and Anderson 1987).

Although most people are ethnocentric, the ethnocentrism of Western societies has had greater consequences than that of smaller, less technologically advanced and more geographically isolated peoples. Wealth and military technology have given Westerners the ability to impose their beliefs and practices on others. It may matter little, for example, to the average Frenchman if the Dogon (an ethnic group in Mali) believe their way of life to be superior. The Dogon have little ability to affect events in France. However, French ethnocentrism mattered a great deal to the Dogon. The French colonized Mali and imposed their beliefs and institutions on its people.

Some ethnocentrism seems necessary. A group's belief in the superiority of its own way of life binds its members together and helps them to perpetuate their values. However, to the extent that ethnocentrism prevents building bridges between cultures and leads members of one culture to force their ways of life on another, it is maladaptive. It is but a short step from this kind of ethnocentrism to **racism**—beliefs, actions, and patterns of social organization that exclude individuals and groups from the equal exercise of human rights and fundamental freedoms.

Boas insisted that anthropologists free themselves, as much as possible, from ethnocentrism and approach each culture on its own terms. This position came to be known as **cultural relativism** and is one of the hallmarks of anthropology. Boas and his followers maintained that anthropologists must suspend judgment to understand the logic and dynamics of other cultures. Researchers who view the actions of other people simply in terms of the degree to which they correspond to their own notions of the ways people should behave systematically distort the cultures they study.

Boas was a tireless campaigner for human rights and justice. He argued that all human beings have equal capacities for culture and that although human actions might be considered morally right or wrong, no culture was more evolved or of greater value than another. He was an unwavering supporter of racial equality. His work and that of his students, notably Ruth Benedict and Margaret Mead, were widely used by Americans who argued for the equality of men and women and for the rights of African Americans, immigrants, and Native Americans. Today, virtually all anthropologists rely on Boas's basic insights.

Racism: The belief that some human populations are superior to others because of inherited, genetically transmitted characteristics.

Cultural relativism: The idea that cultures should be analysed with reference to their own histories and values rather than according to the values of another culture.

 From Haddon to Malinowski in England and the Commonwealth

While Boas was forming his ideas in the United States, a separate fieldwork tradition was developing in Britain. In the late 19th century, Alfred Cort Haddon mounted two expeditions to the Torres Straits (between New Guinea and Australia). Haddon originally was a biologist, but his travels turned his interest to **ethnography**, the gathering and interpretation of information based on intensive firsthand study. Haddon and his colleagues became professors at Cambridge and the London School of Economics, where they trained the next generation of British Commonwealth anthropologists. Like Boas, their understandings were based in fieldwork, and they made it a basic part of their students' training.

Bronislaw Malinowski was one of the most prominent students of the Torres Straits scholars. Malinowski grew up in Krakow, then part of the Austro-Hungarian Empire (now in Poland). He came to England to study ethnography, and his mentor, Charles Seligman, sent him to do fieldwork on the Trobriand Islands (in the Torres Straits) (see Figure 3.2). Malinowski arrived in the Trobriands in 1914, as World War I broke out. Because Australia governed the Trobriands and Malinowski was a subject of the Austro-Hungarian Empire, he was considered an enemy national. As a result, he was unable to leave the islands until the end of the war. Thus, what he had intended as a relatively short fieldwork expedition became an extremely long one.

Malinowski's time on the Trobriands was a signal moment in British Commonwealth anthropology. A diary he kept during those years shows that, like Greg Simon many years later, he was frequently lonely, frustrated, and angry. Despite his problems, he revolutionized fieldwork. The Torres Straits scholars had studied culture at a distance, observing and describing it for a short time. Malinowski spent years with native Trobrianders, learning their language, their patterns of thought, and their cultural ways. He not only observed the culture, to the extent that it was possible he participated in it, joining in many Trobriand activities. Malinowski's style of fieldwork became known as **participant observation** and has become central to the practice of anthropology. Malinowski also centered his research on empathic understandings of native lifeways and on analyzing culture by describing social institutions and showing the cultural and psychological functions they performed.

In an era when non-Europeans were often considered incomprehensible and illogical, Malinowski forcefully promoted the idea that native cultural

Figure 3.2 Bronislaw Malinowski, one of the pioneers of participant observation, worked in the Trobriand Islands between 1915 and 1918.

Ethnography: The major research tool of cultural anthropology, including both fieldwork among people in a society and the written results of such fieldwork.

Participant observation: The fieldwork technique that involves gathering cultural data by observing people's behavior and participating in their lives.

London School of Economics Archives, Malinowski/3/18/2

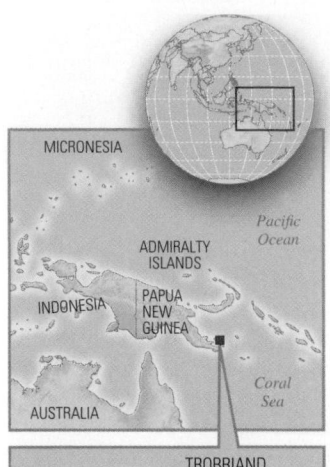

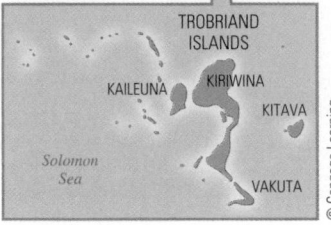

The Trobriand Islands.

ways were logical. For example, in a famous essay on science and magic, he argued that natives used magic only for goals they were unable to attain by more rational means (such as controlling the weather) (Malinowski 1948).

The anthropologies of Malinowski and Boas were quite different. Boas and his students focused on understanding cultures with respect to their context and histories. Malinowski and his students emphasized the notion of function: the contribution made by social practices and institutions to the maintenance and stability of society. However, both developed traditions of fieldwork and participant observation. Both traditions have strong histories of opposition to racism. Both see other cultures as fully rational and as neither superior nor inferior to their own. Despite the great many new approaches in anthropology since the days of Boas and Malinowski, their fundamental insights remain basic to the discipline.

ANTHROPOLOGICAL TECHNIQUES

Today, anthropologists work in a wide variety of settings. They work for universities, for businesses, for government, and for nongovernmental organizations. They work on a variety of projects from investigating the relations among kin to researching topics such as shopping behavior and the ways in which people relate to their computers. Because of the multiplicity of anthropologies, it would be impossible to describe all of the different ways that anthropologists go about their work. Therefore, we will focus on the ways in which fieldwork is done in such communities.

Most anthropologists begin to do fieldwork as part of their graduate training and continue fieldwork as a basic element of their careers. Fieldwork is often funded by grants given by universities, government agencies, and nonprofit organizations that promote social science research. Decisions about which communities anthropologists investigate are based on factors including personal history, geographical preferences, political stability, cost, physical danger, and connections their professors and other mentors may have. However, the most critical aspect of choosing a location has to do with the particular research questions that anthropologists wish to answer.

In the early 20th century, anthropologists studying relatively small groups often attempted to write complete descriptions of societies. Their books, with titles such as *The Tiwi of North Australia* (Hart and Pilling 1960), *The Sebei* (Goldschmidt 1986), and *The Cheyennes* (Hoebel 1960), had chapters on subjects such as family, religion, farming, and legal affairs. In a sense, it did not matter much where anthropologists chose to work; any small-scale community or society could be described.

Today, few anthropologists attempt to write such descriptions. This is partly because most feel that societies are so complex that they cannot be adequately described in a single work. But, more importantly, although societies never were really isolated, they are so interconnected today and so changed by these connections that they must be seen in regional and global contexts. Current ethnographies focus on specific situations, individuals, events, and, frequently, on culture change. For example, recent ethnographies describe the ways in which people in Jamaica use cell phones (Horst and Miller 2006), the survival techniques of drug addicts on the streets of San Francisco (Bourgois and Schonberg 2009), and sexuality, femininity, and black magic in Brazil (Hays 2011). As research has narrowed, both the questions anthropologists ask and the conditions and locations where they can be answered have become more specific.

After they have identified an area of interest, anthropologists spend time reading the existing research on their subject. It is no exaggeration to say that most researchers spend several hours reading for each hour they spend doing active field research. From their studies, they gain an understanding of the geography, history, and culture of their chosen area. They find out what is known and what remains to be learned about the subjects of their interest. They then try to design projects that help close the gaps in existing knowledge. It is a bit like filling in pieces of a jigsaw puzzle, with one important exception: You can finish a puzzle, but good research leads to posing interesting questions and, thus, more research.

Arriving at a field location can be a disorienting experience. For most people, living in another culture and trying to learn its ways are difficult. Most anthropologists probably have at least some experiences like those Greg Simon describes in the passage that opens this chapter. Anthropologists are objects of curiosity and sometimes hostility. Perhaps more importantly, culture is learned behavior, and we have been learning our culture since the moment of our births. When we move to a radically different culture, much of that learning is no longer relevant.

Anthropologists arriving in new cultures are in many ways like children. Their language skills are often weak, and their speech is sometimes babyish. Their social skills are undeveloped. They are ignorant of many aspects of their environment and their new culture. One almost universal result of this situation is the syndrome called **culture shock**—the feelings of alienation, loneliness, and isolation common to one who has been placed in a new culture. For graduate students, sometimes the journey stops there. You can be an outstanding scholar—well versed in literature and able to think and write creatively—yet unable to do fieldwork.

Culture shock: Feelings of alienation and helplessness that result from rapid immersion in a new and different culture.

Getting past culture shock is a process of learning the language, customs, and social organization, of gaining the fundamental grounding knowledge that it takes to be an adult in a different culture. Most anthropologists never truly become members of the cultures they study. They are separated from their subjects by their backgrounds, educations, and sometimes by the color of their skin. Anthropologists are also separated by the knowledge that their time in the field is temporary and that they will leave to rejoin their other lives. However, in our best moments, anthropologists do come close to acting and feeling like members of the cultures they study.

In most cases, as anthropologists begin to adapt to new cultures, they develop networks of friends and contacts who both guide them in their new surroundings and offer insights into the culture. Traditionally in anthropology, these people are called **informants**. They may also be called **respondents, interlocutors, consultants,** and sometimes **partners**. These terms emphasize the collaborative nature of fieldwork and suggest that the people who work with anthropologists are active and empowered. Much of what anthropologists know they learn from such people, who frequently become enduring friends. In some cases, anthropologists work with a few individuals whom they believe to be well informed and eager to talk with them (called "key informants") (see Figure 3.3). Alternatively, they may construct statistical models and use techniques such as random sampling to choose their consultants. Sometimes, they are able to interview all members of a community.

Working with consultants is often informal, but anthropologists also use an arsenal of more formal tools, depending on their theoretical

Informant: See consultant.

Respondents: See consultant.

Consultant/informant/ interlocutor/respondent/ partner: A person from whom anthropologists gather data.

Partner: See consultant.

Figure 3.3 In fieldwork, anthropologists both observe culture and participate in it, as with this anthropologist living with the Mentawai in Sumatra, Indonesia. Such tattoos are usually incised with needles and vegetable dye, but these are being done with washable pigments.

Judith Pearson

Table 3.1 Interviewing Techniques

Informal Interviews	Researchers engage in, overhear, remember, and write down conversations from their daily experience.
Unstructured Interviews	Researchers engage with another in a scheduled conversation. Researchers may have a plan but informants are allowed to express themselves as they choose.
Semistructured Interviews	Similar to an unstructured interview but based on the use of a written list of questions or topics that the researchers intend to cover in a specific order.
Structured Interview	Researchers ask different subjects to respond to a set of questions as nearly identical as possible; often involves the use of very explicit instructions.

interests. Much of anthropology is done by interviewing, using many different interview techniques. Some anthropologists prepare exhaustive inventories and questionnaires; however, more frequently, they design a series of open-ended questions that allow their subjects to talk freely and extensively on a topic. Sometimes they use interview techniques drawn from ethnoscience and designed to help identify the objects and ideas their consultants think are important. Because kinship structures are important in many societies, anthropologists become adept at gathering genealogical information. Table 3.1 details some specific types of interviews. Almost all anthropologists use informal, unstructured, and semistructured interviews. Structured interviews are less common.

In addition to interviewing, anthropological data gathering includes participating in activities with culture members, mapping, photographing, carefully observing activities, measuring various kinds of production, and, occasionally, serving apprenticeships. It all depends on the nature of the problem the anthropologists are investigating. For example, an anthropologist studying nutrition might need to observe food gathering and preparation techniques, weigh and measure all food consumed, and analyze it for nutritional value. An anthropologist studying pottery production would be unlikely to use any of these techniques.

As with the techniques used, analysis of data also depends on the questions asked and the theoretical perspective of the researcher. Anthropological data generally come in the form of extensive field notes, tape recordings, and photographs. In most cases, organizing data presents substantial challenges. Notes have to be indexed, recordings transcribed, and data entered in spreadsheets. Successful anthropologists often spend more time working with their data than they did collecting it in the first place. Recording an interview may take only an hour or two. Transcribing and indexing that recording may take several days.

◥ Ethnographic Data and Cross-Cultural Comparisons

Boas and his students were interested in describing cultures in their contexts. Because they understood each culture as the product of its unique history, they did not attempt systematic comparison of one culture to another, and they were not very interested in discovering laws or principles of cultural behavior. However, some comparison has always been implicit in anthropology. For example, one goal of the Boasians was to use their research to cause Europeans and Americans to see their own societies in a new light.

British and European anthropologists were more explicitly interested in **ethnology**, the attempt to find general principles or laws that govern cultural phenomena. They compared societies in the hope of finding such laws and principles. Starting in the 1860s, Herbert Spencer began to develop a systematic way of organizing, tabulating, and correlating information on a large number of societies, a project he called *Descriptive Sociology*. The American scholar William Graham Sumner, his student Albert Keller, and Keller's student George Murdock brought this idea to the United States. In the late 1930s, Murdock and Keller created a large, indexed ethnographic database at Yale University. First called the "Cross Cultural Survey," in the late 1940s, the project was expanded and its name was changed to the **Human Relations Area Files** (HRAF).

The HRAF is an attempt to facilitate cross-cultural analysis. It provides a single index to ethnographic reports and other sources on 710 numbered subject categories. Some examples of categories are 294 (techniques of clothing manufacture) and 628 (traditional friendships and rivalries within communities). Using the HRAF, researchers can find information on these and many other topics for a wide range of current and historic societies.

The HRAF frequently comes under fire as critics charge that the project takes cultural data out of context and therefore corrupts it. They correctly note that the works indexed in the HRAF were written from different perspectives, for different purposes, and in different eras. In consequence, the indexing is often inconsistent and analyses based on it are suspect. Despite these problems, work based on the HRAF is often both interesting and insightful. For example, back in the 1950s, the rising divorce rate in the United States was causing alarm. Was divorce truly something new and different, a product of modernity? Murdock used the HRAF to show that almost all societies had some form of divorce and that the divorce rate in the United States (in the 1950s) was lower than average. Thus, his use of the HRAF allowed people to think about divorce in a comparative context. In recent years, the HRAF, now available online, has been used to consider a wide variety of issues including family violence (Levinson 1989), corporal punishment of children (Ember

Ethnology: The attempt to find general principles or laws that govern cultural phenomena through the comparison of cultures.

Human Relations Area Files: An ethnographic database that includes cultural descriptions of more than 300 societies.

and Ember 2005), patterns of cultural evolution (Peregrine, Ember, and Ember 2004), and the relationship between production and beliefs about the afterlife (Dickson et al. 2005).

CHANGING DIRECTIONS AND CRITICAL ISSUES IN ETHNOGRAPHY

In the past several decades, new trends and issues in anthropological research have emerged. These include anthropology and gender, postmodernism, engaged and collaborative anthropology, and issues surrounding studying one's own culture.

Anthropology and Gender

By the 1960s, the role of fieldwork in anthropology was extremely well established. Additionally, the position of women within academic anthropology was relatively good, particularly in comparison to other areas of the university. Franz Boas had trained several female anthropologists who had gone on to become well known within the discipline. One, Margaret Mead, had become a household name outside of anthropology as well. Despite this (or perhaps because of it), the political movements of the 1960s, particularly the civil rights movement and the feminist movement, caused anthropologists to begin thinking about gender and their discipline in new ways. Feminists soon discovered that the presence of some very high-profile women within anthropology did little to counteract the fact that the overwhelming majority of anthropologists were men and that their areas of interest tended to focus on the social roles, activities, and beliefs of men in the societies they studied. There were several reasons why anthropologists had focused on men. First, in many societies, men and women live quite segregated lives. Because they were men, most anthropologists had little access to the lives of women. Second, anthropologists tended to assume that men's activities were political and therefore important, whereas women's activities were domestic and therefore of less importance. Third, in most societies, men's activities were far more public than women's activities. Anthropologists tended to assume that what was public and visible was more important than what was more behind the scenes and less visible. However, this clearly is not always (or even often) the case.

The result of taking men more seriously than women was a systematic bias in anthropological data and understandings. Anthropologists had often reported with great detail and accuracy about men's social and cultural worlds, but they had barely scratched the surface of women's

Figure 3.4 Anthropologist Narumon Hinshiranan of Chulalongkorn University, Bangkok, interviews a Moken woman in Kuraburi, Thailand. The Moken are a nomadic people who depend on ocean resources for their livelihood. Their way of life is threatened by economic changes and development in Thailand.

Aroon Thaewchatturat/Alamy

worlds. Furthermore, the assumption that men spoke for all of society that is frequently implicit in ethnographies often made cultures appear more harmonious and homogeneous than they actually were.

Starting in the 1970s, increasing numbers of women joined university anthropology faculties. By the late 1990s, more than 50 percent of new anthropology PhDs and more than 40 percent of all anthropology professors were women (Levine and Wright 1999). They began paying greater attention to women's lives (see Figure 3.4). By the 2000s, lesbian, gay, bisexual, transgender, and questioning (LGBTQ) people also found increasing representation on university faculties, leading to the emergence of LGBTQ studies as an academic field. As this happened, anthropologists turned from the study of women to more general considerations of the nature and role of gender in our own and other societies. We will address these issues more fully in Chapter 9.

▧ Postmodernism

Postmodernism: A theoretical position in anthropology that focuses on issues of power and voice. Postmodernists hold that anthropological accounts are partial truths reflecting the backgrounds, training, and social positions of their authors.

Ultimately, the issue of gender in anthropology focused on ways of knowing. Feminists argued persuasively that male anthropologists had missed vital dimensions of society because their gender and their academic interests predisposed them to see certain things and not others. These ideas dovetailed well with **postmodernism**, a critique of both natural and social sciences that gained prominence in the 1980s. Postmodernists hold that all knowledge is influenced by the observer's culture and social position. They claim fieldworkers cannot discover and describe an objective reality because such a thing does not exist (or exists but cannot be discovered or comprehended by human beings). Instead, postmodernists propose that there are many partial truths or cultural constructions, which depend on frame of reference, power, and history.

Postmodernists urged anthropologists to examine the ways they understood both fieldwork and writing. They demanded that anthropology become sensitive to issues of history and power. Some postmodernists challenged the ethnographer's role in interpreting culture, claiming that anthropological ethnographies were just one story about experienced reality and the ethnographer's voice was only one of many possible representations.

During the 1990s, reflection on the nature of fieldwork and the anthropological enterprise became a central focus of writing in anthropology. Work such as Edward Said's *Orientalism* (1978), an analysis of the problematic ways Westerners had viewed and written about the Middle East, encouraged anthropologists to think about the ways in which their own status, personality, and culture shape their view of others and to consider how ethnographers interact with members of other cultures to produce data. In many cases, anthropologists turned from writing about culture to writing about anthropology itself, and critical analyses of earlier anthropological literature became common. In other cases, rather than trying to describe culture or to find principles underlying cultural practices, anthropologists wrote about their own experience of living in other cultures.

The claims of postmodernists have been a subject of intense debate in anthropology. Few anthropologists accept the postmodern critique in its entirety. To do so would be to understand anthropology as a rather peculiar sort of travel writing or a school of literary criticism. However, some of the ideas of postmodernism have become part of the mainstream. For example, almost all anthropologists today agree that ethnographers need to reflect critically on their positions as observers and be aware of the moral and political consequences of their work. Most ethnographies now include information about the conditions under which the fieldwork was carried out and the nature of the relationships between anthropologists and their consultants. Most are sensitive to issues of voice and power and the ways anthropology is written.

Engaged and Collaborative Ethnography

Engaged and **collaborative ethnography** reflect some of the concerns just noted. Collaboration is the process of working closely with other people and in a sense describes all anthropological research. Collaborative anthropologists highlight this aspect of their work. They consult

Collaborative ethnography: Anthropological work that gives priority to desires and interests of cultural consultants on the topic, methodology, and written results of fieldwork.

with their subjects about shaping their studies and writing their reports. They attempt to displace the anthropologist as the sole author representing a group, turning research into a joint process between researcher and subject. The work of James Spradley (1934–1982) is an important contribution to collaborative, engaged anthropology. His classic ethnography, *You Owe Yourself a Drunk* (1970), was aimed at getting the public to understand and help the homeless alcoholics who were the subject of the book.

Eric Lassiter, an anthropologist inspired by Spradley, has done collaborative work with the Kiowa Indians in Oklahoma. The Kiowa were particularly interested in an ethnography of Kiowa song. They stipulated that it be written so that it could be read and understood by the Kiowa people themselves and that they would be acknowledged for their contributions. Lassiter emphasizes that a critical aspect of his collaboration with the Kiowa was to give the highest priority to representing the Kiowa cultural consultants as they wished to be represented, even if this meant adding or changing information or changing his interpretations. For Lassiter (2004), collaborative ethnography is not just eliciting the comments of the cultural consultants but, even more importantly, integrating these comments back into the text.

Although many anthropologists practice some elements of collaborative anthropology, there are deep problems with the notion that anthropologists' primary job is to write and say what their consultants want. First, most probably would agree that anthropologists have an obligation to accurately report what people say and do to the best of their ability. They may have an additional obligation to not knowingly falsify information. Furthermore, communities are rarely so homogeneous that they speak with a single voice. Collaborative anthropology may give voice and legitimacy to one element of a community over another. Often, writing what consultants want really means choosing their side in a political contest.

Using Anthropology: A Life in Engaged Anthropology

Anthropology has a long history of engagement with the societies that anthropologists study and political activism in anthropologists' own societies. Franz Boas, for example, wrote and spoke frequently on the major political and social issues of his day. He was deeply involved with the National Association for the Advancement of Colored People (NAACP) and contributed to its journal, *The Crisis* (Lewis 2001). His work was fundamental to the Supreme Court's *Brown v. Board of Education* decision ending legal segregation (Baker 2000). Many other anthropologists have followed Boas's example of engagement.

Pauline Wiessner has been a working anthropologist since the early 1970s. Though she trained in archaeology, her interests shifted to working with current-day people during research for her doctoral thesis among the Ju/'hoansi bushmen in Botswana and Namibia. In Botswana, she documented the gift giving and exchange patterns that tied people together and helped them survive in difficult times by giving them broad access to resources. However, Wiessner's academic interests soon led to deeper and more active engagement in the community. As the Ju/'hoansi lost access to their historic lands and were forced to move from nomadic to sedentary lifestyles, Wiessner became concerned with their ability to feed themselves. She established a nonprofit organization, the Tradition and Transition Fund, to help the Ju/'hoansi protect their water sources and gardens from animals and develop new sources of food (see Figure 3.5).

Wiessner's involvement with the Enga of Papua New Guinea (PNG) has been even more dramatic. She began working with the Enga in the 1980s. As with the Ju/'hoansi, her initial interest was in documenting exchange patterns and social networks across both space and time. However, by the 1990s, it turned to warfare. The Enga, like many PNG groups, had a long history of warfare. Though these wars were serious, they were fought with bow, arrow, and spear, and the number of people killed was small, usually less than five. This changed in the 1990s. Then, young Enga men became increasingly impoverished and hopeless, but had increasing access to weaponry such as M16 rifles. Previously small, contained wars erupted in large-scale violence that claimed hundreds of lives and turned large areas of Enga territory into wastelands.

Wiessner's studies have shown that the violence came to an end after more than a decade as the result of three factors: the exhaustion of the majority of the population, the influence of the Christian church that provided an alternative ideology of peace to the Enga ideology of war, and the presence of a traditional justice system that could be used to mediate disputes (Wiessner and Pupu 2012; Culotta 2012). Wiessner used the results of her research to lobby with both Enga leaders and local government officials to gain support for the use of the traditional justice system. Beginning in 2005, Wiessner used her own funds along with money she and her Enga colleagues raised to open the Enga Take Anda, a community center and museum located in the capital of Enga Province that both preserves Enga culture and provides a neutral place where members of different groups could come together (Balter 2010).

© adrian arbib/Alamy

Figure 3.5 A Ju/'hoansi boy fills a Coke bottle with water at a pump in Tchumkwe, Namibia.

Studying One's Own Society

When most people think of anthropologists, they imagine researchers who study others in exotic locations, but, since the early 20th century, anthropologists have also studied their own societies. W. Lloyd Warner, Solon T. Kimball, Margaret Mead, Zora Neale Hurston, and Hortense Powdermaker were all American anthropologists who wrote about American culture. Kenyan anthropologist (as well as freedom fighter and first president of Kenya) Jomo Kenyatta wrote about the Gikuyu of Kenya in 1936, and Chinese anthropologist Francis Hsu wrote extensively on Chinese society. In recent years, writing about one's own culture has become even more common. This trend is driven by many factors, including the training of more anthropologists from more different cultures, the increasing total number of anthropologists, the rise of interest in ethnicity in the United States and Europe, as well as the dangers of violence in some areas where anthropologists have studied in the past.

The emphasis on more reflective fieldwork and ethnography affects all anthropologists but particularly those who study their own societies. Traditionally, anthropologists doing fieldwork try hard to learn the culture of the people with whom they are working. In a sense, anthropologists working in their own culture have the opposite problem: They must attempt to see their culture as an outsider might. This is challenging because it is easy to take cultural knowledge for granted. In addition, it may be as difficult to maintain a neutral stand in one's own culture as it is in a different one. As Margaret Mead once noted, it may be easier to remain culturally relativistic when we confront patterns, such as cannibalism or infanticide, in other cultures than when we confront problematic situations such as child neglect, corporate greed, or armed conflict in our own.

Some of the problems and the rewards of studying one's own culture can be seen in Barbara Myerhoff's books and films. Myerhoff contrasted her work with the Huichol of northern Mexico (1974) with her work among elderly Jewish people in California (1978). She notes that, in the first case, doing anthropology was "an act of imagination, a means for discovering what one is not and will never be." In the second case, fieldwork was a glimpse into her possible future, as she knew that someday she would be a "little old Jewish lady." Her work was a personal way to understand that condition and to contemplate her own future. Tragically, it was a future that never arrived. Myerhoff died of cancer when she was only 49.

More recently, Darren Ranco (2006), an anthropologist and member of the Penobscot American Indian Nation, has considered the problems and issues native anthropologists face. Ranco notes that in his earliest anthropological projects, he had trouble trying to do work that seemed anthropological to him and at the same time treat his family and friends in respectful ways. For Ranco, one way out of this dilemma was to try to do work that the Penobscots themselves would find interesting and important. He decided that the criteria for such work included empowering people, involving members of the community, making the finished products of research available to the community, and focusing on research that provides direct benefits to the community. Ranco writes that when he considers a project, he asks himself how the project will "endorse, elaborate, or enhance tribal sovereignty," and he will not undertake the research if he cannot answer the question.

We can all empathize with Ranco's desire to benefit our community. However, we can also see the complications it may create. How can one be sure of the outcome of a project at its beginning? What should anthropologists do if project results turn out not to enhance tribal sovereignty? Should any anthropologist refrain from asking questions for fear that the answer might be displeasing? Is enhanced tribal sovereignty always beneficial to all members of the Penobscot Nation?

Anthropologists should certainly investigate groups to which they belong and may indeed have particularly useful insights into those groups. However, the very concept of a native anthropologist is problematic. Groups are almost never homogenous, and individuals have many identities. Being a native in one identity does not make one a native in all one's identities (Cerroni-Long 1995; Narayan 1993).

ETHICAL CONSIDERATIONS IN FIELDWORK

As questions about native anthropologists show, ethical issues frequently arise in anthropological research. Anthropologists have obligations to the standards of their discipline, to their sponsors, to their own and their host governments, and to the public. However, their first ethical obligations are usually to the people they study and to the people with whom they work. These obligations can supersede the goal of seeking new knowledge. According to the American Anthropological Association *Code of Ethics* (2009), "Anthropological researchers must ensure that they do not harm the safety, dignity, or privacy of the people with whom they work. ..." This includes safeguarding the rights, interests, and sensitivities of those studied, explaining the aims of the investigation as clearly as possible to the people involved; respecting anonymity of informants; not exploiting individual informants for personal gain; and giving "fair return" for all services. It also includes the responsibility to communicate the results of the research to the individuals and groups likely to be affected, as well as the general public.

Informed consent is a critical aspect of anthropological ethics. Generally, this requires anthropologists to take part in ongoing discussion with their consultants about the nature of study as well as the risks and benefits of participation in it (Clark and Kingsolver n.d.). In particular, informed consent means that study participants should understand the ways in which release of the research data are likely to affect them and that they must be free to decide whether or not they will participate in the study (and, if they begin to participate, they must always be free to stop).

Anthropologists also have obligations to the discipline of anthropology. Two of these seem both particularly important and particularly problematic. First, anthropologists should conduct themselves in ways that do not endanger the research prospects or lives of other anthropologists. Anthropologists who violate the mores and ethics of the communities where they work make it unlikely that those communities will accept other anthropologists in the future. Anthropologists who become involved with and identified with governments, military forces, or political platforms may endanger not only their own safety but also the work and lives of others. People may come to believe that because some anthropologists are identified with specific political actors, all are.

Most anthropologists also believe that the primary purpose of research is to add to the general store of anthropological knowledge. Thus, they have an obligation to publish their findings in forms that are available to other anthropologists and to the general public. Publishing usually involves review of the work by other anthropologists to help assure the validity and quality of research. Anthropologists acknowledge that certain forms of secrecy are acceptable, and, on occasion, even required. For example, to protect both the communities where they work and the individuals with whom they work, anthropologists may decide to not reveal the precise location of their research or the actual names of the individuals they discuss. However, research in which the methods and findings are secret is a far greater problem. Not only does such research not contribute to general anthropological knowledge, but the scientific community also has no way of assessing its validity.

The obligations to protect other anthropologists and to publish research findings both pose dilemmas. The engaged anthropologists described in this chapter believe that anthropologists must work for the communities they study. However, this may make it impossible for future anthropologists to work at all. For example, governments may not grant anthropologists research visas, and organizations may not allow research if they believe anthropologists will promote political action against them. Applied anthropologists wish to work for businesses and governments. Often anthropological findings have greatest value for these entities when they are not shared with other businesses or the general public. There may be very few jobs available for applied anthropologists who insist on the right to publish all of the results of their research.

Numerous projects have tested the boundaries of ethics in anthropology, both in regard to the people anthropologists study and to the discipline itself. One of the best known of these was "Project Camelot," a mid-1960s attempt by the U.S. Army and Department of Defense to enlist anthropologists and other social scientists in achieving American foreign policy goals. Project Camelot's purpose was to create a model for predicting civil wars but it was also implicated in using military and cultural means to fight insurgency movements and prop up friendly governments (Horowitz 1967). When Project Camelot was made public in 1965, the United States had recently invaded the Dominican Republic and was escalating the war in Vietnam.

Project Camelot created controversy both inside and outside of anthropology. In countries where anthropologists worked, people began to see them as spies whose presence presaged a U.S. invasion. At the American Anthropological Association, Project Camelot led to vitriolic debate, where members raised concerns for the integrity of research, the safety of anthropologists in the field, and the purposes to which anthropological knowledge might be put. These concerns eventually led to the issuing of the first official statement on anthropological ethics in 1971.

Anthropology and the Military

In the past decade, concerns similar to those raised by Project Camelot have reemerged over the engagement of some anthropologists with the U.S. military (see Figure 3.6). Anthropologists have worked at

Figure 3.6 Anthropologists and other social scientists working for the military raise important ethical concerns. Here, Ted Callahan talks to Afghan villagers in 2009. Callahan spent 18 months working for the U.S. Army's Human Terrain System program.

Marco Di Lauro/Getty Images

military colleges and bases, providing anthropological training for officers or analyses of the culture of the military itself. They and other social scientists have also worked on the ground collecting data in zones of active conflict as part of a program called Human Terrain System (HTS).

Starting in early 2007, the Pentagon employed HTS teams to help its combat brigades. According to some, this program has been very successful. For example, the obituary of Michael Bhatia, an HTS member killed in active duty, reports that his work helped save the lives of both U.S. soldiers and Afghan civilians. Colonel Martin Schweitzer testified before Congress that HTS very substantially reduced the number of lethal army operations, increased support for the Afghan government, and reduced Afghan civilian deaths (Fondacaro and McFate 2008). However, the use of anthropologists in such circumstances is extremely problematic.

It is indeed difficult to see how many of anthropology's ethical requirements can be met under conditions of warfare. How, for example, are participants to give coercion-free consent while subject to military occupation? How can anthropologists honestly inform participants about the ways the research data will be used and are likely to affect them? Are individuals in a conflict ever really free to decide whether or not they will participate in a study? Can anthropologists working under such circumstances assure, within reason, that the information they supply will not harm the safety, dignity, or privacy of the people with whom they work? Isn't the point of their work sometimes just the opposite of that? What about anthropologists' obligation to publish their research? Aren't the results of this sort of research necessarily secret? Historically, anthropologists have been concerned with protecting the rights and safety of the people they study. The primary concern of anthropologists working in HTS must be the safety, security, and goals of their employers instead.

Given all of the problems with HTS, it is probably safe to say that a strong majority of anthropologists oppose this use of anthropology. In fact, the American Anthropological Association has issued an official statement disapproving of it (AAA 2007). However, ultimately, ethical behavior is the responsibility of each individual anthropologist. The members of the American Anthropological Association are supposed to subscribe to its code of ethics. Universities and some other research organizations have institutional review boards (IRBs) that examine all research involving human subjects for ethical violations. However, not all anthropologists are subject to the AAA or to IRBs. Lawyers who behave unethically can be disbarred. Doctors can have their medical licenses revoked. In both cases, they violate laws and can be punished if they continue to practice. There is no comparable sanction for anthropologists (and, indeed, for members of most disciplines). Therefore, there will always be a great diversity of anthropological practice.

⬛ NEW ROLES FOR ETHNOGRAPHERS

Although there have been native anthropologists for a long time, until the 1970s, the prevailing model of fieldwork was a European or North American ethnographer visiting a relatively isolated and bounded society and then reporting on that society to other Europeans and North Americans. In some cases, anthropologists may have overstated the degree to which the societies they studied were isolated. Societies have always been connected with each other. However, in the past several decades, inexpensive communication, relatively cheap airfare, and immigration have greatly increased the scale of these connections.

Today, whether they work in cities, villages, or with tribal groups, anthropologists have to take regional and global connections into account. Research may mean following consultants from villages to their workplaces in cities, collecting genealogies that spread over countries or even continents, and following cash and information flows around the world. In addition to expanding the research site, contemporary ethnographers must often use techniques such as questionnaires, social surveys, archival material, government documents, and court records in addition to participant observation. The deep connections among cultures and the global movement of individuals mean that we must constantly reevaluate the nature of the cultures we are studying, their geographical spread, their economic and political position, and their relation to one another.

Today, not only are native anthropologists much more common, but the people anthropologists study also generally have far greater knowledge of the world than they did in earlier times. They are likely to understand what anthropology is and what anthropologists do, something not true in the past. In some cases, this has led to difficulties as people struggle over the question of who has the right to speak for a group. In other cases, people from the groups that anthropologists have described have publicly taken issue with their analysis. For example, in the early 2000s, a fierce controversy broke out over anthropological descriptions of the Yanomamo, an often studied Amazonian group. Had their primary ethnographer, Napoleon Chagnon, portrayed them accurately? Was the research team that he was part of responsible for spreading disease and decimating Yanomamo villages? Anthropologists, journalists, and Yanomamo tribe members debated these questions at meetings and in the popular press (for a review of the debate, see Borofsky 2005).

Despite controversies, for the most part, natives' increased knowledge of the outside has resulted in closer relations among anthropologists and the people they study as well as more accurate ethnography. Ethnographic data are often useful to a society. Sometimes they serve as the basis for the revitalization of cultural identities that have been nearly effaced by

Western impact (Feinberg 1994). Sometimes they play important roles in establishing group claims to "authenticity" and are useful in local political and economic contexts. For example, when Kathleen Adams (1995) carried out her fieldwork among the Toraja of Sulawesi, Indonesia, she became a featured event on tourist itineraries in the region. Toraja tour guides led their groups to the home of her host, both validating his importance in the village and bolstering the tourists' experience of the Toraja as a group sufficiently "authentic" and important to be studied by anthropologists.

In the past, anthropologists sometimes worried about their subject disappearing. They argued that the main thing anthropology was designed to study was small-scale, relatively isolated "primitive" societies. They worried that, as economic development spread around the world, such societies would go out of existence and anthropology would essentially be done. In a small sense they were right, but in the larger sense they were wrong. Any anthropologist today looking to study a society untouched by the outside world would be out of luck. No such societies have existed for a long time. On the other hand, the forces of globalization have been as productive of diversity as they have been of homogeneity. Economic, political, and social forces bring groups of people together in new ways, in conflict and in cooperation. New cultural forms are created and old ones modified. Human cultural diversity, imagination, and adaptability show no signs of dying out, so anthropologists will always have material to study. Wherever human cultures exist and however they change, anthropologists will be there, devising means to study, understand, and think about them.

BRINGING IT BACK HOME:
ANTHROPOLOGISTS AND HUMAN RIGHTS

What could be more obvious than that anthropologists should support human rights and be actively engaged in their promotion? For most Americans, doubting the value of human rights is unthinkable, like arguing against freedom of speech or claiming that children are not important. Yet, human rights pose ethical dilemmas for anthropologists. Almost all anthropologists believe firmly in their duty to promote human rights in our own society. Many also believe that they have an obligation to promote the interests of those they study. For example, Laura R. Graham (2006:5) writes that "[o]ur privileged position, specialized training, and unique skills . . . carry with them specific ethical obligations to promote the well-being of the people who are collaborators in our anthropological research and in the production of anthropological knowledge." Ida Nicolaisen points out that standing for human rights is often a matter of life and death. For example, she notes that in the Philippines between 2005 and late summer 2006, at least 73 indigenous people were "subjected to extra-judicial killings" and concludes that "[w]e owe it to indigenous peoples and other marginalized groups to stand up for their basic human rights when needed" (Nicolaisen 2006:6).

But there often are difficulties determining what the rights are and whether or not we should stand up for them. Laura Nader (2006:6) writes that ideas about human rights were developed in a largely western European context and are often conceived of as "something Euro-Americans take to others." Promoting Western notions of human rights may mean denying people in other societies what they consider to be their rights to pursue individual and cultural choices. Consider Islamic hadd ("to the limit") punishments, such as stoning for adultery, amputation of limbs for theft, and flogging for moral offenses like consumption of alcohol. Hadd punishments deeply offend many people (including many Muslims), yet they form a core component of ethical belief and practice for many people in some Islamic nations. The organization Human Rights Watch reports that courts in Saudi Arabia continue to impose punishments such as amputations of hands and feet for robbery and floggings for lesser crimes such as "sexual deviance" and drunkenness (Human Rights Watch 2001:14). In northern Nigeria, between 2000 and 2004, courts passed more than 60 amputation sentences (Human Rights Watch 2004:38). Anthropologist Carolyn Fluehr-Lobban (2005) interviewed attorneys, judges, social scientists, and journalists in Sudan, a country that has practiced hadd punishments. She notes that most Sudanese Muslims oppose the use of hadd, and see it as an abuse of religion by the state. However, they also think that Western interest in eliminating such punishment is unwarranted interference in their right to determine their own culture. They point to a double standard: Westerners, particularly Americans, see hadd punishments as "barbaric" while they ignore their own abuses of human rights, such as the death penalty, waterboarding, the torture and abuse of prisoners that took place at the Abu Ghraib prison during the Iraq War, and the detention of prisoners without trial at Guantanamo Bay.

■ YOU DECIDE:

1. Given the diversity of culture and the anthropological importance of cultural relativism, can there be such a thing as universal human rights?
2. If anthropologists have moral obligations to the people with whom they work, should they ever work with people whose beliefs and

practices they disapprove of? If yes, then what obligations do they have to such people? If no, how are we to accurately represent such people?
3. What sorts of things do you consider to be universal human rights? How good is our society at assuring the rights you have identified? Do you think there is a core set of universal rights upon which most people could or should agree?

■ CHAPTER SUMMARY

1. Describe the research style and goals of early anthropologists. Anthropology began in the 19th century. In that era, anthropologists did not go into the field. They were compilers of data, and their goal was to describe and document the evolutionary history of human society. There were numerous problems with their data and methods.
2. Explain Franz Boas's role in founding modern American anthropology. In the United States, Franz Boas established a style of anthropology that rejected evolutionism. Boas insisted that anthropologists collect data through fieldwork. He argued that cultures were the result of their own history and could not be compared to one another, a position now called *cultural relativism*.
3. How did modern anthropology develop in Britain? Bronislaw Malinowski and others in Britain developed a tradition of fieldwork that emphasized participant observation. Although their focus was different than Boas's, they also saw members of other cultures as fully rational and worthy of respect.
4. Where do current-day anthropologists work and what are their techniques? Almost all anthropologists today do fieldwork. Although many continue to work in small communities, others work in large industrial and postindustrial societies. Most focus on answering specific questions rather than describing entire societies. Anthropological techniques include participant observation, interviews, questionnaires, and mapping.
5. What is the role of cross-cultural comparison in anthropology? Cross-cultural comparison has always been an aspect of anthropology. The Human Relations Area File (HRAF) is a large database that facilitates cross-cultural research.
6. How has the role of women as anthropologists and anthropological subjects changed over the past century? Despite the presence of important women in early 20th-century anthropology, women were historically underrepresented in anthropological writing. This situation began to be redressed in the late 1960s, as increasing

numbers of women became anthropologists and as anthropologists increasingly studied women.

7. What was the influence of postmodernism on anthropology? In the 1980s, postmodernists urged anthropologists to become more sensitive to issues of voice, history, and power. Postmodernists' insistence that the objective world was unknowable and that the anthropologist's voice was uncertain created intense debate but ultimately enriched ethnography.

8. What are collaborative and engaged anthropology? One response to postmodernism was collaborative and engaged anthropology. Some anthropologists placed special emphasis on the political dimensions of their work. They often took great pains to involve members of the group being studied in the production of ethnographic knowledge. Engaged anthropologists also promote social change in the communities where they work.

9. What are native anthropologists and what advantages and disadvantages do they face? Native anthropologists are those who study their own society. Although native anthropologists may have advantages of access and rapport in some cases, they also experience special burdens more intensely, such as whether to expose aspects of the culture that outsiders may receive unfavorably.

10. What ethical issues are raised by anthropology and how are they addressed? Anthropological ethics require protecting the dignity, privacy, and often the anonymity of the people who anthropologists study. However, anthropological ethics are rarely simple. The use of anthropologists in pursuit of foreign relations goals is sometimes extremely problematic.

11. How has globalization changed anthropological practice? Anthropologists are increasingly enmeshed in a global society. Those they study are rarely isolated and are often quite knowledgeable about anthropology. Anthropological knowledge is often important in the ways people understand their identity and, as such, is increasingly political.

KEY TERMS

Collaborative ethnography
Consultant
Cultural relativism
Culture shock
Ethnocentrism
Ethnography
Ethnology

Human Relations Area Files
Informant
Participant observation
Partner
Postmodernism
Racism
Respondents

AP Photo/Sergei Grits

Human language consists of words and gestures as illustrated by this interaction between two Tajik men in a square on the outskirts of Dushanbe, the capital of Tajikistan.

CHAPTER 4

COMMUNICATION

LEARNING OBJECTIVES

After you have read this chapter, you will be able to:

△ List some of the characteristics of human languages, and explain how humans learn language.

△ Summarize the meanings of phonology, morphology, syntax, and semantics.

△ Illustrate the relationship between language and culture.

△ Explain the ways in which language is related to social structure, and give examples.

△ Summarize the Sapir-Whorf hypothesis, and debate the relationship between language and thought.

△ List several forms of nonverbal communication.

△ Compare different ways in which language changes, and discuss the implications of globalization for language change.

WHY DON'T YOU SPEAK GOOD?

IN'T ain't a word.... Or is it? Language is full of different styles of speaking. Different individuals and different communities express themselves in different ways. Are any of these ways of speaking better or worse than any others? Do any of them have important implications for the ability of their speakers to think logically? For example, is it better, more logical, more beautiful to ask "Why don't you speak well?" instead of "Why don't you speak good?"?

It has certainly often been proposed that speaking "properly" and thinking logically are linked. For example, from the 1950s to the 1970s, a group of linguists, psychologists, and educators called *cultural deficit theorists* argued that children who spoke African American Vernacular English (AAVE), a variety of English common in many (but not all) African American communities, did poorly in school because of the way they spoke English. The theorists argued that the poor speech of these children, which they characterized as coarse, simple, and irrational, was due to a culturally deprived home environment (Ammon and Ammon 1971). They proposed that if children could be taught to speak "proper" English, they would be able to think more logically, and this would help lift them from poverty (Bereiter and Engelmann 1966; Engelmann and Engelmann 1966).

The work of linguists such as William Labov has disproved these ideas. Labov and his colleagues analyzed the speech of African American teens and demonstrated that it was neither logically nor structurally inferior to any other sort of speech; it just used rules that were somewhat different than the language of most white upper-middle-class Americans (called Standard American English or SAE). For example, whereas speakers of SAE use words such as *usually* and *always* to express habitual action (I am usually in my office by 7:30), speakers of AAVE use the verb *be* to express the same thing (I be in my office by 7:30) (Green 2002:48). The AAVE usage is concise, logical, and consistent. AAVE is just a different way of speaking and, from a linguistic point of view, neither better nor worse than any other.

So, what is good English? Consider the double negative. Almost everyone reading this book has heard someone (perhaps a teacher) claim that a double negative is really a positive. Thus, saying "I don't want no" is really saying "I want some." This is simply incorrect. When Mick Jagger sings, "I can't get no satisfaction," no native English speaker believes he is saying how satisfied he is. And no one imagines that the kids singing in Pink Floyd's "The Wall" are telling us how much they want to go to school.

But sometimes, two negatives do make a positive, as when a child who refuses to do her homework says: "I won't not do my homework if you buy me some ice cream." And two or more positives can sometimes make a negative, as in:

Speaker A: "Yes, I will do it."

Speaker B: "Yeah, yeah, yeah, sure you will."

The point is that, from a linguistic perspective, one way of speaking is as good as the next. There is no reason to prefer "I don't have any money" to "I ain't got no money," and there is no reason that saying "I'm about to go get lunch" is better than saying "I'm fixin' to get me some lunch." All the statements are fully logical, comprehensible, and communicate the information the speaker desires.

So why does society act as if one statement is good and the other bad? Because speech often identifies the speakers' ethnic background, social class, geographical location, and other aspects of their life. Our judgments are really about people, particularly their ethnic backgrounds and social class, not about the speech itself.

Communication in general and language in particular are great examples of the ways in which human biology and human culture are intimately entangled. Language is a biological aspect of human beings. All humans who are physically able to do so communicate through language. Deaf communities create sign languages that are as complex and sophisticated as spoken languages. However, speech is not just an aspect of biology. The language we speak, the style of our speaking, to whom we speak, and how we speak to them are all aspects of culture. In this chapter, we briefly explore some of the biological and structural elements of language and communication and then turn to their social and cultural aspects.

◪ THE ORIGINS AND CHARACTERISTICS OF HUMAN LANGUAGE

Although passing information is critical to the survival of most living things, members of other species communicate very differently than humans. No member of any other species can make up a story and tell it to another, understand a piece of poetry, or discuss what it would like to eat tomorrow, yet these are things that people in all human cultures do regularly.

Animal vocalizations are referred to as *calls,* and animal **call systems** may be very sophisticated. However, even large call systems are restricted to a fixed number of signals generally uttered in response to specific events

Call system: The form of communication among nonhuman primates composed of a limited number of sounds that are tied to specific stimuli in the environment.

Figure 4.1 Some nonhuman animals show surprising linguistic abilities. One research tactic has been to teach very simplified American Sign Language to chimpanzees. Here, Joyce Butler signs "drink" to "Nim Chimpsky" (1973–2000), a famous subject of these experiments.

Susan Kuklin/Science Source

(see Figure 4.1). Human language, on the other hand, is capable of re-creating complex thought patterns and experiences in words.

So, when did humans first begin to speak? Anthropologists offer several answers to this question. Certainly our distant ancestors communicated, but they probably used call systems similar to modern-day primates. Some believe that language might have begun as early as two million years ago, when the genus *Homo* emerged (Schepartz 1993:119), but most anthropologists think that language like our own has been limited to members of our own species. The earliest *Homo sapiens* date from about 200,000 years ago, so language may well have emerged at that time. A third position (Bickerton 1998) holds that modern human language emerged about 50,000 years ago, in connection with a big jump in the sophistication of human toolmaking and symbolic expression. Work in biology suggests a relationship between language and a gene called FOXP2. Although the ability to acquire and use language is controlled by many genes, FOXP2 is the only one that has been clearly identified (Dominguez and Rakic 2009). Interestingly, the human form of FOXP2 has also been found in Neanderthals (Krause et al. 2007).

Regardless of the date at which humans acquired language, anthropologists generally agree that language is part of our biological adaptation. Although in any culture, some people talk with greater or lesser artistry than others, all physiologically normal individuals in all cultures develop adequate language skills.

Language is more than simply a human capacity or ability. For example, people have the capacity to learn algebra or ice-skating. They may or may not do it as their culture and their individual choices dictate. Language is different. Unless prevented by total social isolation or physical incapacity, all humans learn a first language as part of the developmental process of childhood. All go through the same stages of language learning in the same sequence and at roughly the same speed regardless of the language being learned. Language is an innate property of the mind.

Humans have what Steven Pinker (1994) calls a "language instinct." Pinker points out that the language instinct in humans is very different from instinctive communication in other animals. Among animals, the instinct for communication means that dogs do not *learn* to wag their tails when they are content and growl when they are angry: They do these things as an expression of their underlying genetic code. Dog behavior is species-wide. A growl means the same thing to a dog in Vladivostok as it does to a dog in Manhattan. But language is not instinctual in this way. The human instinct is to learn the language of the group into which the individual is socialized. There is no biological basis for learning one language over another. For example, an infant born to French-speaking parents but raised in an English-speaking family has no predisposition to speak French.

The universality of the process of learning a first language as well as the underlying similarities that unite all human languages led Noam Chomsky (1975) and many others to propose that there is a **universal grammar**—a basic set of principles, conditions, and rules that form the foundation of all languages. Children learn language by applying this unconscious universal grammar to the sounds they hear.

The social element of language learning is critical. To learn language, we must be able to interact verbally with others. There is a particularly important period from our birth until about 6 years of age. Children deprived of contact during these years never learn to speak like other members of their community. This is illustrated by the case of Genie, a child discovered by social workers in the 1970s in California. Genie had been locked in an attic for the first 12 years of her life. With training and good living conditions, she acquired a large vocabulary, but she was never able to master English syntax; she created sentences like "Genie have momma have baby grow up" (Pinker 1994:292). Children like Genie demonstrate that although language is a biological capacity, it can only be activated within a social group. Thus, language provides an outstanding example of the interrelation of biology and culture.

Human language is first and foremost a system of symbols. A **symbol** is just something that stands for something else. Words are symbols, and they stand for things, actions, and ideas because speakers of a language agree that they do, a feature of human language called **conventionality**. An animal is no more a dog than it is a *chien* (French), a *perro* (Spanish), or a *kutta* (Hindi).

This seemingly trivial fact is critical for two reasons. First, because the relationship between a series of sounds (a word) and their meaning is symbolic, relatively few sounds can be used to refer to an infinitely large number of meanings. For nonhuman animals, there is a direct connection between a sound and its meaning; 60 sounds equals 60 meanings. Most human languages have only 30 to 40 sounds. However, used in combination, these sounds can produce an endless variety of words and meanings. There is no maximum number of words or sentences in any human language. People constantly create new ones, a characteristic known as **productivity**.

Second, symbols enable humans to transmit and store information, a capacity that makes our cultures possible. If humans had to learn everything they know by trial and error or by watching others, our lives would

Universal grammar: A basic set of principles, conditions, and rules that form the foundation of all languages.

Symbol: Something that stands for something else. Central to language and culture.

Conventionality: The notion that, in human language, words are only arbitrarily or conventionally connected to the things for which they stand.

Productivity (linguistics): The idea that humans can combine words and sounds into new, meaningful utterances they have never before heard.

be vastly different and much simpler than they are. Human beings do learn by these methods, but they also learn by talking. We tell each other our experiences and the stories passed down to us. We discuss the past and plan for the future using words. This human ability to speak about different times and places is called **displacement**.

The ability of humans to use symbols allows us to store information. In cultures with writing, such stored information is vast. Consider, for example, that no one individual could possibly know everything written in the books in even a relatively small university library. However, because we can store our knowledge symbolically as words, we can have access to everything that is there. And with the Internet... well, you get the point!

Displacement: The capacity of all human languages to describe things not happening in the present.

THE STRUCTURE OF LANGUAGE

Although there are enormous differences among languages, there are also some compelling similarities. Every language has a structure: an internal logic and a particular relationship among its parts. Descriptive, or structural, linguistics is the study of the internal workings of language. A basic insight of structural linguistics is that all languages are composed of four subsystems: **phonology** (a system of sounds), **morphology** (a system for creating words from sounds), **semantics** (a system that relates words to meanings), and **syntax** (a system of rules for combining words into meaningful sentences).

Phonology: The sound system of a language.

Morphology: A system for creating words from sounds.

Semantics: The subsystem of a language that relates words to meaning.

Syntax: A system of rules for combining words into meaningful sentences.

Phone: Smallest identifiable unit of sound made by humans and used in any language.

Phoneme: The smallest unit of sound that serves to distinguish between meanings of words within a language.

At a very basic level, all language is made up of sounds. Humans use a vast array of sounds in their languages. For example, the International Phonetic Alphabet (IPA), a system designed to represent the sounds of all human languages in writing, has more than 100 base symbols, which can be altered by about 55 modifiers. A sound found in human language is called a **phone** of language. No individual language uses more than a small subset of this huge number of possible sounds. A sound that is used in any individual language is called a **phoneme** of that language.

At some level, almost everyone is aware of the phonemic differences among languages. For example, the "rolled r" common in Spanish is not found in most varieties of English, and many English speakers find the sound difficult to make. On the other hand, the "/th/" sound (as in the word *the*) is common in most varieties of English but does not exist in French or Japanese (as well as many other languages). Different languages have different phonemes, and within a language, different geographical, ethnic, and social groups use somewhat different sets of phonemes. We experience these different sets of phonemes as accents (though accents may also include word choice). Because everyone speaks their own language with a particular set of phonemes not shared by all speakers, everyone always speaks with an accent!

All languages are made up of units that have meaning called **morphemes**. Morphemes can be composed of any number of phonemes. Some are as simple as a single phoneme (the English morphemes "a" and " s" for example), and most are relatively brief. Words are composed of any number of morphemes. Some are extremely simple: "A" is a phoneme, a morpheme, and a word. The word *teacher* has two morphemes: "teach" and " er" (here, "-er" refers to someone who does what came before it). Long words, such as antidisestablishmentarianism, for example, are simply strings of morphemes.

Morpheme: The smallest unit of language that has a meaning.

The total stock of words in a language is known as its **lexicon**. A lexicon often provides clues to culture because it tends to reflect the objects and ideas that members of that culture consider important. For example, the average American can name 50 to 100 types of plants, but members of foraging societies can often name 500 to 1,000 types (Harris 1989:72). Germans in Munich have a vocabulary of more than 70 words to describe the strength, color, fizziness, clarity, and age of beer because it is so central to their culture (Hage 1972, cited in Salzmann 1993:256) (see Figure 4.2). Americans have large numbers of words to describe cars or money but have far fewer to describe bicycles.

Lexicon: The total stock of words in a language.

Anthropologists sometimes use vocabulary as a clue to understanding different cultures. For example, the words people use for their kin tell us something of the nature of their families. In English, a woman uses the term *brother-in-law* to speak about her sister's husband, her husband's brother, and the husbands of all her husband's sisters. The use of a single term for all of these relations reflects the similarity of a woman's behavior toward the men in these kinship statuses. In Hindi, a language of North India, a woman uses separate terms for her sister's husband (*behnoi*), her husband's elder brother (*jait*), her husband's younger brother (*deva*), and her husband's sisters' husbands (*nandoya*). The variety of words in Hindi reflects the fact that a woman treats the members of each of these categories differently.

Figure 4.2 Languages build vocabularies around ideas and things important to their speakers. Germans in Munich have more than 70 words to describe beer.

Michael Dalder/Reuters/Corbis Wire/Corbis

Sounds and words alone do not make up a language. To convey meaning, every language has syntax, rules that structure the combination of words into meaningful utterances. Languages differ in their syntactic structures. In English, word order is a basic element of syntax, so statements such as "The dog bit the man" and "The man bit the dog" have very different meanings. Word order is not equally important in all languages. In Japanese, the subject and object of a sentence are indicated by word endings, and order is less important. For example, John gave Mary the book is translated *John-san ga Mary-san ni hon o ageta.* The same word order, with the word endings "ga" and "ni" reversed *(John-san ni Mary-san ga hon o ageta)* would be "Mary gave John the book."

Parts of speech (nouns, verbs, and so on) are a critical aspect of syntax. All languages have a word class of nouns, but different languages have different subclasses of nouns, frequently referred to as *genders.* (Although masculine and feminine are common linguistic genders, the word *gender* in linguistics refers to the category or "class of a word," not its sex-related connotation or characteristics.) For example, Papago, a Native American language, divides all the features of the world into two genders: "living things" and "growing things." Living things include all animated objects; growing things refer to inanimate objects. Some languages have many more subclasses. Kivunjo, a language spoken in East Africa, has 16 of them (Pinker 1994:27; Corbett 2008).

Applying the rules of grammar turns meaningless sequences of words into meaningful utterances, but we can recognize a sentence as grammatical even if it makes no sense. To use a now classic example (Chomsky 1965), consider the following sentences: "Colorless green ideas sleep furiously," and "Furiously sleep ideas green colorless." Both sentences are meaningless in English, but English speakers easily recognize the first as grammatical, whereas the second is both meaningless and ungrammatical.

Using Anthropology: Forensic Linguistics

Everyone speaks with an accent. That is, they speak their language with a particular set of phonemes. Most native speakers of American English can use these accents to guess at some of the characteristics of the speaker: their geographical origin, perhaps their ethnic background. In addition to marking group membership, our speech and our writing contain mannerisms that are particular to ourselves alone. We may favor certain words or combinations of words. We may even use particular forms of punctuation. Forensic anthropologists use the details of speech and writing to provide legal evidence in a wide variety of situations.

Immigration and customs officials often make use of linguistics experts to find out if the accent, slang, and idiomatic expressions used by asylum seekers are the same as those of the countries they claim to be from. Information identifying the regional origin of an individual can play an important role in criminal investigation as well. For example, forensic linguist Roger Shuy helped solve a kidnapping in Illinois. In this case, the kidnapper had left a ransom note that instructed that money be left in a trash can on the "devil's strip" at a particular street corner. Shuy knew that there is only one place in the United States where the term *devil's strip* is used to identify the small grass area sometimes found between a sidewalk and the street: Akron, Ohio. There was only one suspect from Akron and, when confronted with this evidence, he confessed (Hitt 2012; Dahl 2008).

In some cases, forensic linguists may be able to identify a particular individual rather than just the region a person comes from. For example, in 2006, Garry Weddell, a police inspector who lived near London, claimed he came home to find that his wife Sandra, a nurse, had committed suicide, leaving a typed suicide note. However, police were suspicious about the cause of death. A forensic linguist examined the suicide note and compared the wording and, in particular, the sentence structure, to diaries and other writings by Sandra and Garry Weddell. The linguist concluded that it was extremely unlikely that Sandra Weddell could have written the suicide note but that the writing was a good match for her husband (Wright 2008; Narayanaswami 2010), and he was arrested for the murder of his wife.

Attempts at detection based on writing can sometimes fail spectacularly. For example, in 2003, English professor Donald Foster, who had used a literary forensics technique to reveal the author of the anonymously published *Primary Colors*, a popular book of the era, published an article claiming to use the same technique to discover the person who perpetrated the anthrax attacks of 2001 (Foster 2003). However, the man he identified was innocent and later sued both Foster and the magazines that published the article (Freed 2010).

Forensic linguistics is often extremely important in determining what is said in voice recordings. Such recordings are problematic because a lot of meaning in conversation is carried in visual expression, hand gestures, and other nonverbal aspects of communication. These are missing in such recordings. Additionally, we tend to hear what we want to hear: Our existing ideas and prejudices can deeply affect how we interpret what is said. In this circumstance, forensic linguists' close attention to the specifics of phonetics can often clarify meaning, sometimes reversing what people think they hear (Hitt 2012).

Forensic linguistics is a powerful tool, but needs to be used cautiously. It may be fine for amateurs to speculate on the authorship of literary works, but court cases really demand careful work by highly trained professionals.

◢ LANGUAGE AND CULTURE

Phonemes, morphemes, syntax...these are essentially elements of the biology of language, but language is much more than just its structure. Consider the following exchange:

Scene: It's a clear, hot evening in July. J and K have finished their meal. The children are sitting nearby. There is a knock at the door. J rises, answers the knock, and finds L standing outside.

J: Hello, my friend! How're you doing? How are you feeling, L? You feeling good? *(J now turns in the direction of K and addresses her.)*

J: Look who here, everybody! Look who just come in. Sure, it's my Indian friend, L. Pretty good, all right. *(J slaps L on the shoulder and, looking him directly in the eyes, seizes his hand and pumps it wildly up and down.).*

J: Come right in, my friend! Don't stay outside in the rain. Better you come in right now. *(J now drapes his arm around L's shoulder and moves him in the direction of a chair.)*

J: Sit down! Sit right down! Take your loads off you ass. You hungry? You want crackers? Maybe you want some beer? You want some wine? Bread? You want some sandwich? How about it? You hungry? I don't know. Maybe you sick. Maybe you don't eat again long time. *(K has now stopped what she is doing and is looking on with amusement. L has seated himself and has a look of bemused resignation on his face.)*

J: You sure looking good to me, L. You looking pretty fat! Pretty good all right! You got new boots? Where you buy them? Sure pretty good boots! I glad.... *(At this point, J breaks into laughter. K joins in. L shakes his head and smiles. The joke is over).*

The Western Apache.

The joke is over....So what was the joke? This joke, from the Western Apache, recorded by Keith Basso (1979), is about how the Apache see white people as communicating with them and with each other. In the joke, *J* pretends he is a white man. The joke is that white speech, as *J* presents it, is highly inappropriate and offensive. For starters, you do not publicly call someone a friend or ask how he or she is feeling. For the Western Apache, these are very personal statements and questions. To use them in a highly public way as *J* does here conveys insincerity. The Apache believe that one should enter and leave a room as unobtrusively as possible, so *J* making a big to-do about *L* coming into the room is inappropriate as well. Actions such as putting an arm around another man's shoulder or asking repeatedly if he wants something to eat are understood as both violations of individual dignity and overwhelming bossiness. To the Apache, such actions suggest that the speaker thinks the person he or she is talking to is of no account and that his wishes can be safely ignored. Perhaps worst of all is suggesting that another might be sick. Not only is this a violation of privacy, the Apache fear that talking about misfortune may well bring it on.

Knowing only the technical grammatical aspects of language would not help much in understanding J's and L's speech. Their speech embeds critical cultural concepts and values. Without understanding their culture, an observer cannot possibly get the joke.

Language is so heavily freighted with culture that understanding one is almost always a key to understanding the other. One way anthropologists analyze this relationship is to think in terms of speech performance. Such performance includes what people are saying as well as what they are communicating beyond the actual words. **Sociolinguistics** is the study of the relationship between language and culture. Sociolinguists study speech performances and attempt to identify, describe, and understand the ways in which language is used in different social contexts.

Sociolinguistics: The study of the relationship between language and culture and the ways language is used in varying social contexts.

The ways in which people actually speak are highly dependent on the context of their speech as well as issues such as class, ethnicity, and geography. For example, a public political speech has different purposes and is limited by different norms than a political discussion among friends. And different cultures have different norms regarding political speeches: who can participate as speaker and audience, the appropriate topics and cultural themes for such a speech, where such speeches can take place, the relationship between the speaker and hearer, the language used in a multilingual community, and so forth.

Speech is critical in the construction of identity. Penelope Eckert (2000) has studied the way children and adolescents in American schools use language to create and enforce social roles and identities. This process starts with teasing in elementary and junior high schools. It continues for girls in the form of both true and false compliments that "establish and enforce social hierarchies and boundaries" (Eckert 2004), and for boys with increased use of language styles specifically opposed by teachers and other powerful adults, including sexual references and obscenities. In high schools, verbal labels indicate social terrain and frequently physical location within the school. In the Detroit high school Eckert studied, the critical labels were jocks and burnouts. Jocks identified with the institution, with adolescence, and with the white suburban middle class. Burnouts saw themselves as opposed to the institution, wanting to be adults, and identified with the urban working class. Jock and burnout groups used language differently: Jock girls were the most standard speakers, and burnout girls used the most vernacular language. Boys' language was between these two groups. Burnout girls made frequent use of multiple negatives and other stigmatized speech forms. These differences involved not only the use of different vocabularies but changes in the sounds of the languages they used as well (Eckert 1989).

In some cultures, different speech forms are used depending on whether the speaker and hearer are intimate friends, acquaintances on equal footing, or people of distinctly different social statuses. French, German, and Yoruba, among many other languages, have formal and informal pronouns that are not found in English. The rules for their use vary among cultures. In France, parents use the informal term to address their children, but children use the formal term to address their parents. In the Spanish spoken in Costa Rica, many people use three forms: the informal *tú* is used by an adult speaking to a child (or lover), the formal *usted* is used among strangers, and the intermediate term *vos* can be used among friends. In India, the status of a husband is higher than that of a wife, and among most Hindi speakers, a wife never addresses her husband by his name (certainly not in public) but uses a roundabout expression that would translate into English as something like "I am speaking to you, sir."

Language and Social Stratification

From a linguistic perspective, all languages are equally sophisticated and serve the needs of their speakers equally well, and every human being speaks with equal grammatical sophistication. Despite this, as we saw in the opening of this chapter, in complex stratified societies such as the United States, some speech is considered "correct" and other speech is judged inferior.

In hierarchical societies, the most powerful group generally determines what is "proper" in language. Indeed, the grammatical constructions used by the social elites are considered *language,* whereas deviations from them are often called *dialects.* Because the power of the speaker rather than any inherent qualities of a speech form determines its acceptability, linguist Max Weinreich has defined a language as "a dialect with an army and a navy" (quoted in Pinker 1994:28).

The relation of language usage to social class and power is reflected in the speech of different social classes in the United States. In a classic study, sociolinguist William Labov (1972) noted that elites and working-class people have different vocabularies and pronounce words differently. The forms associated with higher socioeconomic status are considered "proper," whereas forms spoken by those in lower socioeconomic statuses are considered incorrect and stigmatized.

Labov found that speakers often vary their vocabulary and pronunciation in different contexts and that the degree of such variation is related to their social class. At the bottom and top of the social hierarchy, there is little variation. Elites use privileged forms of speech, and the poor use stigmatized forms. However, members of the lower middle class often use stigmatized forms in casual speech but privileged forms in careful speech. One interpretation is that people at the bottom and top of the social hierarchy do not vary their speech because their social position is stable. The very poor do not believe they have much chance to rise, and the wealthy are secure in their positions. Members of the lower middle class, however, are concerned with raising their social position and, in consequence, copy the speech patterns of the wealthy in some social situations. However, they are also concerned with maintaining connections to family and friends and therefore use stigmatized speech with them. Labov's study makes clear what many of us know but do not like to admit: We do judge a person's social status by the way he or she speaks. What we say and how we say it are ways of telling people who we are socially or, perhaps, who we would like to be.

The development of D4 accents in Ireland (Moore 2011) shows an interesting parallel to Labov's observations and shows the complexity of the relationship between language and social stratification. D4 is the postal code of a prosperous area of Dublin. In the 1990s, as the economy of Ireland grew, D4 became associated with a way of speaking that differentiated those who used it from Irish who spoke with rural or Dublin working-class accents. D4, sometimes called "DORTspeak" after the way its users pronounce DART, the name of the Dublin public transportation system, identified its users with the rising, globalized, urbanized elite. It rapidly spread from Dublin to other areas of the country. However, D4 also came under brutal criticism as pretentious and inauthentic. Authors of newspaper editorials tied the use of D4 to what they imagined was the rejection of Irish identity. Moore (2011:59) notes that for many, D4 became associated with the worst excesses of the era of Irish growth and the (supposed) disintegration of Irish society. This changed its meaning and led to a decline in its use.

Although there are many stigmatized variants of American English, including Appalachian English, Dutchified Pennsylvania English, Hawaiian Creole, Gullah, and emergent Hispanic Englishes, the most stigmatized is African American Vernacular English (AAVE). As we noted earlier, AAVE is simply a variant of Standard English, neither better nor worse than any other. Further, from Mark Twain and William Faulkner to Toni Morrison and Maya Angelou, from George Gershwin to Public Enemy and Run DMC, AAVE has had deep influences on American art, speech, fiction, and music.

Individuals who speak only AAVE are at a disadvantage in the larger society, and most realize that AAVE is stigmatized as symbolizing ignorance whereas Standard American English (SAE) is considered "normal" and symbolizes intelligence. Fordham (1999) found that successful students at a predominantly black high school in Washington, DC learned to switch rapidly between using SAE in the classroom and AAVE

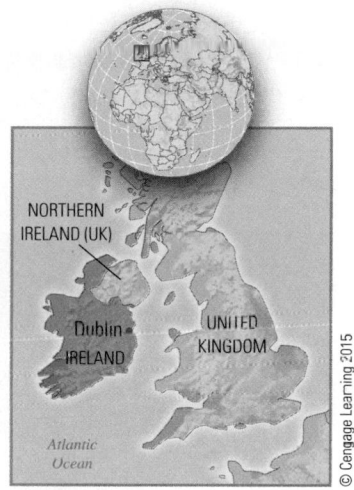

Dublin, Ireland.

with friends and in social settings. Often, they attempted to hide their proficiency in SAE from their friends. In fact, most AAVE speakers do become effective speakers of several varieties of English. AAVE and SAE have similar capacities to deliver both "formal and informal knowledge as well as local knowledge and wisdom" (Morgan 2004), but speakers of AAVE, like others who are bilingual, must learn **code-switching**, to move seamlessly between two languages, and this ability is often central to their identities and their interactions inside and outside of their communities.

Code-switching: Moving seamlessly and appropriately between two different languages.

Sapir-Whorf hypothesis: The hypothesis that perceptions and understandings of time, space, and matter are conditioned by the structure of a language.

The Sapir-Whorf Hypothesis

The close relationship between culture and language raises interesting questions about the connections between language and thought (see Figure 4.3). At the opening of the chapter, we pointed out that some social scientists in the 1950s and 1960s believed, incorrectly, that AAVE was less logical than SAE and that, as a result, AAVE speakers thought illogically. In so doing, they assumed a strong relationship between speaking and thinking. The existence of such a relationship is an old and controversial idea in anthropology. It is often associated with the work of Boas's student Edward Sapir and Sapir's student Benjamin Lee Whorf.

In the early 20th century, Sapir and Whorf argued that, because language played a critical role in determining the way people understand the world, then people who spoke different languages must understand the world in different ways. They proposed that people's ability to think about things such as time, space, and matter are conditioned by the structure of the languages they speak. They argued that we perceive the world in certain ways because we talk about the world in certain ways. This idea has come to be known as the **Sapir-Whorf hypothesis**.

Buyenlarge/Archive Photos/Getty Images

Figure 4.3 Edward Sapir and Benjamin Lee Whorf argued that Native American languages such as Hopi compelled their speakers to understand the world in a way different from native English speakers. Above, a Hopi snake priest photographed by Edward Curtis around 1910.

We clearly choose our words to guide and direct the thoughts of others. Politicians, for example, routinely search for derogatory words and phrases to characterize their opponents. Or consider the term *side effect*. A side effect is an unwanted consequence of something such as a drug. However, the phrase *side effect* encourages us to think of it as off to the side and therefore less important than the *"central" effect* of the drug. But is it less important? In the late 1950s and early 1960s, thalidomide was prescribed to calm the stomachs of pregnant mothers. The drug was effective but had the horrible "side effect" of causing severe malformations in babies born to those mothers. Calling the deformities *side effects* did not prevent people from thinking that they were more important than the drug's effect. In fact, the thalidomide case led to special testing of drugs prescribed during pregnancy. This makes an important point: Word choice can encourage people to think certain ways. However, words cannot force people to think in one way or another. Even a government that controlled all the words people used could not control their thoughts. People merely invent new words or give the old ones new and ironic meanings.

Sapir and Whorf also argued that the grammatical structure of languages compelled their speakers to think and behave in certain ways. For example, Whorf (1941) claimed that because tenses in the Hopi language were very different from tenses in English, Hopi speakers necessarily understood time in ways very different from English speakers. This position is sometimes called "strong determinism," and it has some deep problems. For example, consider the differences in the way we speak about missing a person in English and in French. In English, we say "I miss you." "I," the person doing the missing, is the subject; "you," the person being missed, is the object. In French, however, the order is reversed: You say "Tu me manques." The person being missed is the subject, and the person doing the missing is the object. Literally translated, the French sentence appears to mean "you miss me." A strong determinist would expect this structural difference to indicate that speakers of French and English have different understandings of missing a person. However, no evidence suggests that this is so.

This is not to say that language structure and thought are completely unrelated. Bowerman (1996) argues that space is understood differently in English and Korean, and Gordon (2004) reports that members of the Piraha, a Brazilian tribe he studied, have difficulty understanding and recalling numbers for which they have no words. Other interesting work argues that some kinds of perception are partially universal and partially mediated by specific languages. Experiments done by Gilbert et al. (2005) suggest that language affects color perception in the right visual field, but not the left. This corresponds to the fact that language processing is located primarily on the left side of the brain. Casasanto (2008) conducted studies on the way that Greek and English speakers estimate time. He argues that the association of time with distance or with quantity is given by people's experience of the physical world. All humans experience the fact that it takes a certain amount of time to move a certain distance and the fact that material such as rain or snow accumulates over time. All languages use space and material as metaphors for time. For example, in English we talk about a long time, or visualize time as sand in an hourglass. However, languages use these metaphors unequally. English uses mostly distance metaphors whereas Greek uses mostly material metaphors. Casasanto showed that, in an experimental situation, Greek and English speakers estimated time differently because of this. However, a brief training session caused these differences to disappear. Casasanto's work, like that of Gilbert et al., shows the complexity of the relationship between language and perception. It shows both universal and language-specific elements. But, it also shows that the relationship of language to perception is fairly weak.

◤ NONVERBAL COMMUNICATION

Before returning to our discussion of spoken language, it is important to note that anthropologists also study the nonverbal ways in which humans communicate (see Figure 4.4). Our use of our bodies, interpersonal space, physical objects, and even time can communicate worlds of information: "Time talks" and "space speaks" (Hall 1959). Nonverbal communication includes artifacts, haptics, chronemics, proxemics, and kinesics.

Artifacts (in communications studies): Communication by clothing, jewelry, tattoos, piercings, and other visible body modifications.

Haptics: The analysis and study of touch.

In the context of nonverbal communication, **artifacts** such as clothing, jewelry, tattoos, piercings, and other visible body modifications send messages. For example, among the Tuareg, a people of the Sahara, men often wear veils and use their position as an important part of nonverbal communication (Murphy 1964). A Tuareg man lowers his veil only among intimates and people of lower social status. He raises it high when he wishes to appear noncommittal. The use of artifacts to send messages is familiar to every American. Tattoos, piercings, and jewelry all provide information about those who wear them.

Haptics refers to the study and analysis of touch. Handshakes, pats on the back or head, kisses, and hugs are all ways we communicate by touch. Many American males, for example, believe that the quality of a handshake communicates important

Jeff Greenberg / PhotoEdit

Figure 4.4 In addition to speaking, people use hands and facial expressions as well as interpersonal space to communicate.

information. Firm handshakes are taken to indicate self-confidence and strength of character, whereas limp handshakes often suggest indecisiveness or effeminacy.

Some anthropologists suggest that societies can be divided into "contact" cultures, where people tend to interact at close distances and touch one another frequently, and "noncontact" cultures, where people interact at greater distance and avoid touching (Hall 1966; Montagu 1978). Contact cultures are common in the Middle East, India, and Latin America. Noncontact cultures include those of northern Europe, North America, and Japan. But this dichotomy is simplistic. In India, for example, social equals may touch, but nonequals almost never do. In the United States, equality and inequality also play an important role in touch. Your boss may pat you on the back, but you will rarely pat your boss (Leathers 1997:126).

Chronemics refers to the study of cultural understandings of time. For example, in North American culture, what does it say when a person shows up for an appointment 40 minutes late? Does it mean something different if he or she shows up 10 minutes early? Is a Latin American who shows up late for an appointment saying the same thing?

Chronemics: The study of the different ways that cultures understand time and use it to communicate.

Edward Hall (1983) divided cultures into those with monochronic time (M-time), such as the United States and northern European countries, and those with polychronic time (P-time) such as Brazil and India. Hall argued that in M-time cultures, time is perceived as inflexible and people organize their lives according to schedules. In P-time cultures, time is understood as fluid. The emphasis is on social interaction, and activities are not expected to proceed like clockwork. Thus, being late for a meeting in P-time cultures does not convey the unspoken messages that it conveys in an M-time culture (Victor 1992).

Like the contact/noncontact dichotomy, M-time and P-time seem to capture a basic truth about cultural variation but fail to account for the enormous variability within cultures. How long an individual is kept waiting for an appointment may have more to do with power than with cultural perceptions of time. People are likely to be on time for their superiors but may keep their subordinates waiting.

Proxemics is the social use of space. Hall (1968) identified three different ranges of personal communicative space. *Intimate distance,* from 1 to 18 inches, is typical among intimates. Personal distance, from 18 inches to 4 feet, characterizes relationships among friends. *Social distance,* from 4 to 12 feet, is common among relative strangers. These distances are affected by circumstances, culture, gender, and individual personality. We speak to strangers at a much closer distance in a movie or a classroom than in an unconfined space. In the United States, women and mixed-gender pairs talk at closer distances than do men. In Turkey, on the other hand, men and women talk at close distances with members of their own sex but at very large distances with members of the opposite sex (Leathers 1997).

Proxemics: The study of the cultural use of interpersonal space.

Kinesics: The study of body position, movement, facial expressions, and gaze.

Finally, **kinesics** refers to body position, movement, facial expressions, and gaze. We use our posture, visual expression, eye contact, and other body movements to communicate interest, boredom, and much else. Smiling and some other facial expressions likely are biologically based human universals. There are no societies in which people do not smile. In all societies, social interactions are more likely to have a positive outcome if people are smiling than if they are frowning or scowling. Smiling is also found in chimpanzees and gorillas, our nearest nonhuman relations.

Smiling also shows the powerful effects of culture on biology. A smile does not mean the same thing in all cultures. Americans generally equate smiling with happiness, but people in many cultures smile when they experience surprise, wonder, or embarrassment (Ferraro 1994). A guidebook on international business advises American managers that the Japanese often smile to make their guests feel comfortable rather than because they are happy (Lewis 1996:267). Despite this, Japanese and Americans agree that smiling faces are more sociable than neutral faces (Matsumoto and Kudoh 1993), and that they most often interpret smiles in the same way (Nagashima and Schellenberg 1997).

LANGUAGE CHANGE

> Fæder ure þu þe eart on heofonum
>
> Si þin nama gehalgod
>
> to becume þin rice
>
> gewurþe ðin willa
>
> on eorðan swa swa on heofonum.
>
> urne gedæghwamlican hlaf syle us todæg
>
> and forgyf us ure gyltas
>
> swa swa we forgyfað urum gyltendum
>
> and ne gelæd þu us on costnunge
>
> ac alys us of yfele soþlice[1]

This 11th-century version of the Lord's Prayer shows how much English has changed in the past thousand years. The sounds, structures, and

---

[1]In Modern English, the Lord's Prayer is: "Our father who art in heaven, hallowed be thy name. Thy kingdom come, thy will be done on earth as is in heaven. Give us this day our daily bread and forgive us our trespasses as we forgive those who trespass against us; and lead us not into temptation but deliver us from evil, amen." The nonstandard symbols are from the International Phonetic Alphabet mentioned on page 84. You can find additional information on the IPA at www.omniglot.com.

vocabulary of all languages are constantly changing, and some of this change happens in patterned ways.

Consider sound. When we imagine people speaking English hundreds of years ago, we often think of them using different words than we do but otherwise sounding pretty much like us. But English spoken in the 14th century sounded very different from the English of today. Between 1400 and 1600, there was a change in sound of English called the **great vowel shift**. A correct reading aloud of the Lord's Prayer at the beginning of this section would involve speaking the words using the sounds of 11th-century English. For example, the fifth word of the last line, *yfele*, gives us the modern English word *evil*. The medieval pronunciation is close to "oo-vah-la." Shifting sounds are not just something out of the past. Language sounds are constantly changing. For example, since about 1950, some vowel sounds in U.S. cities around the Great Lakes have been changing, a process linguists call the "northern cities shift" (Labov, Ash, and Boburg 2005) (see Table 4.1).

The grammatical structures of a language (its syntax) also change. For example, as we have seen, meaning in modern English is tightly tied to word order. But in Old English, as in Latin, the endings of nouns indicated whether they were subjects or objects, making word order within sentences less important. Thus, in Old English, "The dog bit the child" and "The dog the child bit" would have the same meaning and be equally grammatical.

Vocabulary, particularly slang, is the most noticeable aspect of language change. Consider slang terms from the 1950s and 1960s, such as *boss* to mean "great" (as in "The new Little Richard album is really boss") or *bag* to mean something that an individual likes (as in "What's your bag?"). We may still understand slang from the 1960s, but terms from the 19th century and early 20th century are almost entirely lost: Would you know what *ramstuginous* or *kafooster* mean?

Great vowel shift: A change in the pronunciation of English language that took place between 1400 and 1600.

Table 4.1 The Great Vowel Shift

Middle English Vowel	Shifts to	Modern English Vowel	Middle English Word	*Is Pronounced to Rhyme with*	Modern Word	Becomes	Modern Word
i		aj	mis	piece			mice
u		aw	mus	moose			mouse
e		i	ges	place			geese
o		u	gos	close			goose
ɛ		e	brɛk	trek			break
ɔ		o	brɔk	squawk			broke
a		e	name	comma			name

New words are constantly added to language. In the past 10 to 20 years, an entire vocabulary has grown up around computers and the Internet. Words such as *software, dot-com, disk drive, gigabyte,* and *email* would have been unintelligible to most people in 1980. *Wi-Fi, spyware, domain name, texting,* and many others would have been meaningless to people in the mid-1990s.

Language and Culture Contact

The meeting of cultures through travel, trade, war, and conquest is a fundamental force in linguistic change. Languages thus reflect the histories of their speakers. Current-day English has French words such as *reason, joy, mutton,* and *liberty,* which came into the language after the Norman Conquest of England in the 11th century. Other words speak of more recent political events. For example, *cot, pajamas, avatar,* and *jungle* come from Hindi and reflect the British colonization of India. *Gumbo, funky, goober,* and *zebra* come from Kongo and reflect the slave trade. Nahuatl, a language spoken in Mexico and Central America, gives us *tomato, coyote, shack,* and *avocado.* Most Americans in 1970 probably did not know the meanings of words such as *Sunni, jihad,* or *ayatollah.* Today, we do.

When people from societies where different languages are spoken meet, they often develop a new language that combines features of each of the original languages. Such languages are called *pidgins* (see Figure 4.5). No one speaks a pidgin as a first language, and the vocabulary of pidgin languages is often limited to the words appropriate to the sorts of interactions shared by the people speaking it.

As culture contact deepens and time passes, pidgins are sometimes lost, and people speak only the language of the dominant power. Or pidgin languages may become creoles. A *creole* is a language composed of elements of two or more different languages. But people do speak creoles as their first languages, unlike with pidgins, and the vocabulary of these languages is as complex and rich as any others.

Many creoles were formed as Europeans expanded into Asia and the Americas. Often, in countries that

Frederick Atwood

Figure 4.5 Pidgin languages develop when people who speak different languages come together. This church banner in Papua New Guinea, where people speak more than 750 different languages, means "Jesus is Lord."

were colonized, upper classes speak the language of the colonizing power, while the lower classes speak creoles. For example, in Haiti, 70 to 90 percent of the population speaks only Creole, but almost all governmental and administrative functions are performed in French, the language of the elite.

Tracing Relationships among Languages

Comparative linguistics is a field of study that traces the relationships of different languages by searching for similarities among them. When such similarities are numerous, regular, and basic, it is likely that the languages are derived from the same ancestral language. Linguists use a statistical technique called glottochronology to estimate the date of separation of related languages, to discover historic relationships among languages, and to group languages into families.

> **Comparative linguistics:** The science of documenting the relationships between languages and grouping them into language families.

Considering the history of language raises two interesting questions. First, at any point, was there a single original human language? Second, in the future, will there be a world with one language? Neither of these questions is fully answerable, but we can speculate about each of them.

We do not know if there was a single original human language. However, the development of language almost certainly involved specific genetic changes. Such changes probably happened in a single small group. If this is the case, an original language probably did exist. What might it have been like? Well, again, we cannot say with any confidence. There are no established techniques for discovering the patterns and content of language that can reach back tens of thousands of years.

The question of whether a single world language is emerging is provocative. We are certainly moving toward a world of linguistic homogenization. The number of languages in the world has clearly declined. About 10,000 years ago, there may have been as many as 15,000 different languages. Today, there are only about 6,500, and half of these are under threat of extinction in the next 50 to 100 years (Krauss 1992). Today, 95 percent of the world's languages are spoken by only 5 percent of the world's population. Almost one-third of the world's languages are spoken by fewer than 1,000 people. At the same time, more than half of the world's population speaks one of the 20 most common languages (Gibbs 2002).

Languages may disappear for various reasons: All their speakers may be killed by disease or genocide. Government policies may deliberately seek to eliminate certain languages. For example, in 1885, the U.S. government explicitly forbade the use of Indian languages in Bureau of Indian Affairs schools. Children were beaten and otherwise punished for speaking their tribal languages (Coleman 1999).

Table 4.2 Most Common Languages by Country

Number	Language	Primary Country	Number of First-Language Speakers in Millions
0	Chinese (all types)	China	1,213
1	Chinese (Mandarin)	China	845
2	Spanish	Spain	329
3	English	United Kingdom	328
4	Arabic (all types)	Saudi Arabia	221
5	Hindi	India	182
6	Bengali	Bangladesh	181
7	Portuguese	Portugal	178
8	Russian	Russian Federation	144
9	Japanese	Japan	122
10	German	Germany	90.3

Source: Ethnologue, Web version, Statistical Summaries. Retrieved on March 23, 2012, from www.ethnologue.com/ethno_docs/distribution .asp?by=size.

Nation-states often try to suppress linguistic diversity within their borders, insisting that government, the court system, and other aspects of public life be conducted in the language of the most numerous and politically powerful groups. Global trade favors people who speak the languages of the wealthiest and most populous nations. Similarly, the vast majority of television and radio broadcasts, as well as the Internet, are in a very few languages. In the face of such forces, people who are members of linguistic minorities often abandon their languages because they find it more convenient, prestigious, or profitable to speak the languages of wealth and power.

In some ways, linguistic homogenization is a positive development. Today, more people are able to speak to one another than ever before. In the future, this may be true to an even greater extent. However, the global movement toward fewer languages is troubling. There is generally a strong connection between language and ethnic identity. Language often is rooted in culture and is entwined with it. As language is lost, so are important elements of cultural identity. Additionally, the disappearance of languages reduces our ability to understand the underlying structures of language and the range of variability they enable.

Not all global forces lead toward language homogenization. First, there is no language spoken by the majority of the world's people. Mandarin Chinese, with more than a billion speakers, is by far the most commonly spoken language, while hundreds of millions of people speak

English, Spanish, Russian, French, Hindi/Urdu, Arabic, Portuguese, and several other languages. None of these languages seems likely to disappear in the foreseeable future. Second, although the number of languages spoken in the world has diminished, the diversity within each language has increased. People in New York City; Kingston, Jamaica; Glasgow, Scotland; and Mumbai, India may all speak English, but that does not necessarily mean they can understand what each other says. Perhaps more importantly, the nature of language, the human ability to create new meanings, new words, and new grammatical structures, means that language adapts to the needs, interests, and environments of its speakers. Thus, even as globalizing forces move humans toward cultural and linguistic homogeneity, spaces are created in which diversity can flourish.

BRINGING IT BACK HOME:
ENGLISH ONLY

Language has become an important political issue in the United States. As of spring 2013, 31 states have enacted legislation to make English their state's official language. No federal bill making English the national language has yet passed both chambers of Congress, but the House and the Senate have, at different times, both voted to make English the national language or to require the federal government to conduct all of its official business in English. A recent survey suggests that 87 percent of Americans believe English should be the official national language (Rasmussen Reports 2010).

U.S. English, Inc., a lobbying group that promotes legislation to make English the official language of every state, claims to have 1.8 million members. According to U.S. English, Inc., "Official English benefits every resident of this wonderful melting pot called America. The melting pot works—because we have a common language. English is the key to opportunity in this country. It empowers immigrants and makes us truly united as a people. Common sense says that the government should teach people English rather than provide services in multiple languages. What would happen if our government had to provide services in all 325 languages spoken in the United States? Without a common language, how long would we remain the 'United' States?" (U.S. English 2012).

U.S. English says it promotes official English rather than English only; however, most anthropologists see little difference between these positions, and most believe that the legislative program of groups like U.S. English is misguided and their claims inaccurate. Graham et al.

(2007), for example, say that when people talk about language, they really are talking about race: "People in positions of social advantage feel free to say things about the language of stigmatized groups that they would never say about race or ethnicity." Furthermore, Graham et al. claim that promoters of English-only efforts assume that difficulties in communication are caused by people speaking many languages, ignoring the simple fact that sharing the same language does not create effective communication. Finally, critics of English-only efforts say that the idea that requiring official English will unify the nation and help provide answers to the problems of racism is backward. The underlying problem is not language; it is inequality. Official English, in the name of promoting unity and opportunity, actually disadvantages the poor and the powerless, making it harder for them to gain access to education and public services.

▇ YOU DECIDE:

1. Do you speak a language other than English as a first language? If so, do you want your children and grandchildren to speak that language? If English is your first language, did your parents or grandparents speak a different first language? How do you feel about your abilities (or lack of ability) in that language?
2. In the United States, how closely is language linked both to American identity and to ethnic identity? To what degree can a person be a full citizen of the United States without speaking English as a primary language?
3. Multiple languages are great assets in the global economy. Should the United States mandate increased training in second languages rather than mandate the use of English?

▇ CHAPTER SUMMARY

1. Are some ways of speaking a language better than others? Is there any correct way of speaking a language? From a scientific point of view, no way of speaking is better or worse than any other.
2. How does human language differ from animal communication? Human language is far more complex than animal call systems. It is symbolic, and it is able to describe abstract times, places, and ideas in ways that animal communications are not.
3. What are the principal components of all human language? Despite great variability, all human languages are based around similar patterns and show deep similarities. All are composed of a

phonology (a system of sounds), morphology (a system for creating words from sounds), semantics (a system that relates words to meanings), and syntax (a system of rules for combining words into meaningful sentences).

4. What is the relationship between the rules of language and the performance of language? Language can be described by rules, but actually speaking and understanding language requires a deep understanding of culture. Environment, cultural ideas, values, and beliefs are encoded in the way people speak. The meaning of conversation is usually much more than simply the words that are spoken.

5. What is the relationship between language and social stratification? Cultural aspects of language are heavily influenced by wealth and identity. Privileged and stigmatized ways of speaking reflect the power dynamics of different groups. Individuals who move between social groups must often learn multiple forms of speech and the correct times and places to use them.

6. What is the relationship between speech and thought? Speakers choose words to encourage others to think in certain ways. Early 20th-century theorists Sapir and Whorf believed that the structure of language had a critical influence on culture, but this does not seem to be the case. Because language can be changed rapidly, it can neither force people to think in one way nor prevent them from thinking in others.

7. What forms of nonverbal communication are used in human societies? In addition to speaking, people communicate in many different ways. Some of these ways are through touch, the use of time, the use of space, and the use of body position. There is substantial variability in nonverbal aspects of communication, both within and between cultures.

8. Does language change? The sounds, words, and structures of language all are subject to change. Comparative linguists study the ways language changes and are able to describe the historical relationships among different languages. However, no agreed-upon technique has been found to determine or describe very early human language.

9. Are we moving toward a world with only a single language? Linguistic diversity has decreased dramatically, and many languages face extinction. However, many languages also have millions of speakers and are unlikely to disappear. Additionally, as languages expand, the diversity within them increases; people who speak the same language may not understand one another.

KEY TERMS

Artifacts	Morphology
Call system	Phone
Code-switching	Phoneme
Chronemics	Phonology
Comparative linguistics	Productivity
Conventionality	Proxemics
Displacement	Sapir-Whorf hypothesis
Great vowel shift	Semantics
Haptics	Sociolinguistics
Kinesics	Symbol
Lexicon	Syntax
Morpheme	Universal grammar

Frans Lemmens/Photographer's Choice/Getty Images

People in different societies use many different strategies to make their livelihoods. Subsistence patterns develop in response to seasonal variation, long-term environmental changes, demographic changes, and the presence of other groups. Here, a man herds llama in Peru.

CHAPTER 5

MAKING A LIVING

LEARNING OBJECTIVES

After you have read this chapter, you will be able to:

△ Explain the relationship between environment and subsistence strategy.

△ Summarize the major characteristics of foraging, pastoralism, and horticulture, and give an example of each.

△ Analyze the differences between horticulture and agriculture, and discuss the environmental impact of each.

△ Explain the role of landlords, peasants, and the state in agricultural systems.

△ Differentiate between agriculture and industrialism, and assess the advantages and disadvantages of each.

WHERE HAVE ALL THE ICEBERGS GONE?

WICH'IN elders long ago predicted that a day would come when the world would warm and things would not be the same with the animals. That time is now..." says Matthew Gilbert of the Gwich'in, an Athabascan people of northeastern Alaska and northwest Canada. "The lakes, the rivers, the waterfowl and, most of all, the caribou that we depend on are under threat" (Gilbert 2007).

The subsistence strategies of Arctic populations such as the Gwich'in are well adapted to their harsh environment. Their knowledge and ingenious technology enabled them to be successful hunters. For thousands of years, the Gwich'in, the Inuit, and other peoples of the Arctic hunted large land and sea animals including caribou, polar bear, seal, walrus, and whales. They devised technologies that effectively utilized the materials of their environment for survival, building shelters of snow, which hold the heat and keep out the wind, and expertly fashioning layered clothing that keeps out the cold yet prevents overheating.

Their culture and social organization are also adapted to their environment and foraging strategy. Their values emphasize cooperation and mutual aid; their religious rituals provide effective outlets for the isolation and tension of the long dark winters; and their flexible kinship organization allows local populations to expand and contract in response to the seasonal variation in resources. For the Inuit of Baffin Island, this involves a set of economic practices called *ningiqtuq*, best translated as "sharing." *Ningiqtuq* orders the flow of goods and food across individuals, families, and entire communities. Among the Inuit, no one need go without food or shelter. Inuit subsistence isn't just about food. It is also about practices that provide individuals with security (Wenzel 2009:92–93).

As with many other foragers, however, the Arctic peoples and their subsistence strategies have been significantly changed by 20th century and the global economy (Chance 1990; Condon et al. 1996). Most now base their livelihoods on a combination of cash income and foraging. Commercial trapping and fur sales became dependable sources of income, providing cash, which they used to buy guns and ammunition, food, tobacco, tea, canvas tents, and clothing. Other sources of income today are handicrafts, tourism, work for oil corporations, various kinds of government subsidies, and, for the Alaska natives, payments from the Alaska Native Claims Settlement Act.

Subsistence hunting and use of wild foods still provide at least half of the diet for Arctic peoples, and current-day foraging techniques make use of modern technology, such as snowmobiles, gasoline, fishing nets, and sleeping bags. Many Arctic households also enjoy modern conveniences, and this requires that household members work full time or seasonally in the cash economy (Kofinas 2007).

However, Arctic lifestyles are threatened by global warming (see Figure 5.1). Hunting is dependent on the transformation of water areas into ice during the long, cold winters. Sea ice is used as a highway, formerly for dog sleds and now for snowmobiles, as building materials, and as hunting platforms. As the climate warms, this ice is less and less available, making hunting more difficult and the cultural patterns it sustains more fragile. Warmer weather also affects the animals on which the people prey. The shrinking ice makes it harder for polar bears to fatten up on seals, and the bears are becoming emaciated. Alaskan whale hunters in the open seas have seen walruses try to climb onto their white boats, mistaking them for ice floes. The pelts of fox, marten, and other game are thinning, and even seasoned hunters are falling into water that used to be ice.

Figure 5.1 A polar bear crosses from one ice floe to another in summer pack ice. The warmer water due to climate change has led to the starvation of many polar bears.

In addition to climatic changes, Arctic peoples also face challenges to their subsistence from drilling for oil in the Arctic. Some (but not all) of them have become locally active in resisting the exploitation of oil reserves in the Arctic National Wildlife Refuge and other areas where oil companies now have access to offshore energy resources revealed by global warming (Matthiessen 2007).

It is not clear how Arctic peoples will cope with the challenges that confront them. On the one hand, people regret the changes in hunting patterns that will inevitably happen as the earth warms. One Canadian Inuit said: "The next generation . . . is not going to experience what we did. . . . We can't pass the traditions on as our ancestors passed on to us" (Myers et al. 2005). On the other, Arctic peoples have faced climate changes before and it is worth remembering that they collectively have thousands of years of experience adapting to an extremely difficult environment. Arctic peoples have shown great flexibility in the past. Although global warming will lead to the disappearance of some species, it is also likely to lead to abundance in others, and Arctic hunters will likely adapt (Ford, Smit, and Wandel 2006).

Anthropologists seek to understand the interactions between humans and their physical environments, both the effects of the environment on culture and the effects of culture on the environment. All societies must

Subsistence strategies: The pattern of behavior used by a society to obtain food in a particular environment.

utilize the physical environment to provide their people with the basic material requirements of life: food, clothing, and shelter. Different societies have different **subsistence strategies**, or ways of transforming the material resources of the environment into food. These subsistence strategies may be stable for hundreds, even thousands, of years, but they must change in response to new challenges in the environment.

HUMAN ADAPTATION AND THE ENVIRONMENT

Unlike most other animals, humans live in an extremely broad range of environments. Some, such as the Arctic or the Great Australian Desert, present extreme challenges to human existence and are relatively limited in the numbers of people and types of subsistence strategies they can support. The productivity of any particular environment, however, is related to the type of technology used to exploit it. For example, the Arctic can sustain only a relatively small population with the traditional Inuit technology. With modern technology and transportation, however, the circumpolar Arctic supports more than four million people, engaged in indigenous hunting and herding strategies as well as modern industrial pursuits (UNEP/GRID-Arendal 2008).

Technology enables humans to transform a wide range of materials into sources of usable energy. As a result, humans have built many environments, such as farms and cities, and developed many different economic systems and forms of social organization. These human cultural adaptations have resulted in great increases in population that, in turn, have further altered the environment, frequently in unintentional ways.

Foraging (hunting and gathering): Fishing, hunting, and collecting vegetable food.

For most of the history of our species, humans and our ancestors lived by **foraging**—fishing, hunting, and collecting vegetable food. As populations increased, foragers spread out into many environments, created new tools, and developed diverse cultures. By 16,000 to 12,500 years ago, humans had spread to every continent except Antarctica (see Stanyon, Sazzini, and Luiselli 2009). About 11,000 to 10,000 years ago, human groups in the Old World began to domesticate plants and animals, a change that occurred about 1,000 years later in the New World (Bryant 2003; Temple University 2009). Called the agricultural "revolution," the transition to food production was really more like a gradual evolution, although it was revolutionary in the possibilities it opened up for the development of complex social organization.

Foraging sets significant limits on population growth and density and, consequently, on the complexity of social organization. The domestication of plants and animals supported increased populations, and

sedentary village life became widespread. Over time, more intensive means of cultivation and animal management developed, and human labor was more closely coordinated and controlled, leading eventually to complex social forms such as the state. Thus, in general, humans have historically gained increasing levels of control over the environment, and human population has increased. However, only specific environmental, cultural, and historical conditions can explain the exact sequence of events in any particular place (Diamond 1998).

Sedentary: Settled, living in one place.

Why cultivation did not arise everywhere—and why some populations, such as the aboriginal peoples of Australia or the Inuit, never made the transition from foraging to food production—has several answers. It is important to understand that, under many conditions, foraging is far less work than agriculture and the benefits of agriculture are not always apparent. In the Arctic, climate and soil composition precluded agriculture, whereas in the fertile valleys of California, aboriginal foraging was so productive that there was little pressure to make the transition to food production. Sometimes foraging strategies actually were more dependable than cultivation or animal husbandry. For example, with the introduction of the horse by the Spaniards in the 16th century, some Native American Plains cultures, such as the Cheyenne, did so well with bison hunting that they gave up their traditional cultivation strategy. Even today, many foraging and pastoral populations resist abandoning these occupations for cultivation. In many places, cultivation is simply less dependable than foraging or pastoralism. But it is also true that subsistence strategies are usually intimately connected to a people's cultural identity: In these societies, foraging and pastoralism are highly valued in their own right.

Another dramatic change in human subsistence strategies was the Industrial Revolution, which involved the replacement of human and animal energy by machines. Industrialism greatly increased human productivity: In a typical nonindustrial society, more than 80 percent of the population is directly involved in food production; in industrial societies, this number declines dramatically. Additionally, industrialization has produced a relatively high standard of living for enormous numbers of people.

However, the price of industrialization has been high. Industrial societies have high levels of inequality, and industry itself is a major source of environmental degradation and climate change. The energy and production needs of business and the consumer desires of the world's people have had a devastating effect on the environment. The U.S. Environmental Protection Agency controls over 180 hazardous air pollutants alone (U.S. EPA n.d.). Oil and gas exploration, logging, mining, dams, and many other large-scale projects fundamentally change the environment. Although consumers in wealthy nations are responsible for most of the world's pollution, populations in China, India, and many other nations contribute increasing amounts and will contribute even more in the future. In mid-January 2013, the Air Quality Index for Beijing climbed to 755. Any reading over 400 is considered hazardous (*Economist* 2013).

The environmental problems resulting from industrial and postindustrial society have reawakened interest in and respect for the subsistence adaptations of nonindustrial people. Through detailed knowledge of their environment and using ingenious, if simple, technology, many nonindustrial societies live in ways that are sustainable and that create fewer environmental problems than industrialization.

MAJOR TYPES OF SUBSISTENCE STRATEGIES

Pastoralism: A food-getting strategy that depends on the care of domesticated herd animals.

Horticulture: Production of plants using a simple, nonmechanized technology and where the fertility of gardens and fields is maintained through long periods of fallow.

Agriculture: A form of food production in which fields are in permanent cultivation using plows, animals, and techniques of soil and water control.

Industrialism: The process of the mechanization of production.

Population density: The number of people inhabiting a unit of land (usually given as people per square mile or kilometer).

Productivity (food production): Yield per person per unit of land.

Efficiency (in food production): Yield per person per hour of labor invested.

Anthropologists identify five basic types of subsistence strategies: foraging, pastoralism, horticulture, agriculture, and industrialism (Cohen 1971). Foraging depends on the use of plant and animal resources naturally available in the environment. **Pastoralism** primarily involves the care of domesticated herd animals, whose dairy and meat products are a major part of the pastoralist diet. **Horticulture** is the production of plants using a simple, nonmechanized technology. **Agriculture** involves the production of food using the plow, draft animals, and more complex techniques of water and soil control so that land is permanently cultivated and usually needs no fallow period. Finally, **industrialism** involves the use of machine technology and chemical processes for the production of food and other goods. Within these basic types of subsistence strategies, however, there is much diversity. Furthermore, whereas any society normally uses one dominant strategy, many societies combine strategies to meet their material needs. Today, no society, however seemingly remote, remains unaffected by industrialism and the global economy.

Each subsistence strategy generally supports a characteristic level of **population density** (number of people per unit of land) and has a different level of **productivity** (yield per person per unit of land) and **efficiency** (yield per person per hour of labor invested). These criteria, in turn, tend to be associated with characteristic forms of social organization and certain cultural patterns. For example, where local technology allows only limited exploitation of the environment and where safe and reliable methods of artificial contraception are unknown, cultural practices such as sexual abstinence, abortion, infanticide, late weaning, and prohibitions on sexual intercourse after the birth of a child may be used to limit population growth.

In addition to limiting population, a society can extend its resource base through exchange. Trade occurs in all types of societies and forms the basis of historical and contemporary globalization. People throughout the world are incorporated into wide-ranging food, manufacturing, and financial exchanges.

Foraging

Foraging is a diverse strategy that includes hunting large and small game, fishing, and collecting various plant foods. Foragers do not produce food, either directly by planting or indirectly by keeping domestic animals. In most cases, foragers use simple tools including digging sticks, spatulas, spears, and bows and arrows. However, in some places, such as the Arctic, foraging technology can be quite complex. Because foragers do not consciously alter their surroundings to produce food, they have little impact on the environment in most cases.

Foragers use a variety of strategies. In some extreme environments, like the Arctic peoples described in the chapter opening, they may depend almost solely on hunting. However, in most cases, they rely primarily on gathered vegetable foods, and women are responsible for gathering. Successful foraging requires extensive and highly detailed knowledge of the environment. Studies among Ju/'hoansi foragers of Botswana and Namibia show that women can identify over 150 species of edible plants, and men recognize over 40 species of edible animals (Lee 2003).

In most cases, foraging can only support a low population density. Foragers generally live in communities of between 20 and 50 individuals. Even at this low density, few of the marginal areas where current-day foragers are found can support a year-round human population. Therefore, foraging almost always involves seasonal movement to gain access to water or food. Thus, foraging requires independence and mobility. For this reason, foraging bands tend to have highly flexible social arrangements, and values like *ningiqtuq* (see the chapter opening) are common. Seasonal movement is also a strong disincentive for the accumulation of material goods. Because they must frequently transport everything they own, their material possessions tend to be limited to items essential to their survival.

In some environments, foraging is unquestionably a harsh and dangerous way of life. However, in less demanding places, foragers often live in relative abundance. Further, the extreme flexibility of forager social arrangements means that there is very little hierarchy in foraging societies.

At one time, all human beings lived by foraging, and foragers occupied fertile plains and river valleys. However, as other forms of production developed, the number of foragers declined. Today, they constitute only a very small proportion of the world's population and are mostly found in marginal areas such as deserts and arctic tundra into which they have been pushed by the expansion of militarily superior agricultural peoples and states.

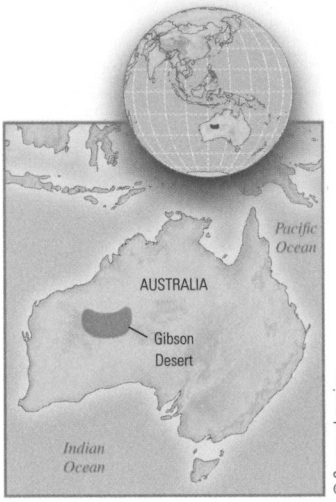

Gibson Desert, Australia.

The Pintupi, A Foraging Society in Australia

The Pintupi people of the Gibson Desert of Australia were more typical of foraging than the Inuit described in the opening of this chapter. The key to their adaptation was the use of a wide variety of seasonally available plant and animal foods and their detailed knowledge of their environment. Even with simple technology, this made foraging a reliable strategy, though a very difficult way of life in certain seasons.

The Pintupi recognize and can name 126 plants serving 138 different social, economic, and medicinal functions. They use more than 75 different plants for edible seeds. Their diet also includes tubers, fruits, nectars, sap, and edible insects, as well as birds, bird eggs, lizards, and small mammals (see Figure 5.2). The main constraint on them is the scarcity of water during the driest and hottest months, which influences the distance they travel, the places they stay, and how much time they spend in each place. Thus, the Western Desert societies consist of small, isolated family groups, and have population densities as low as one person per 150 to 200 square miles.

Climatic changes are extreme. Summer temperatures reach 120 degrees, and winter temperatures average around 72 degrees. Rainfall is very low, unpredictable, and evaporates quickly. In the wet season, December through February, water is available but food is scarce, limited mainly to that left over from the previous year's growing season. Men and women gather lizards and edible toads, which are relatively easy to collect. Families spread across the desert, moving great distances to search for food and to attend ceremonies.

At the end of the wet season, when temperatures moderate, families move near the large surface water holes. June and July bring the greatest material prosperity, as tubers, fruits, and grass seeds are all abundantly available. Edible fruits are collected from 12 different plants and stored for the "hungry time" in November, when temperatures will rise to reach 120 degrees. People live around the water holes until August, when food availability decreases and temperatures rise. The landscape begins to dry out and people fall back to large rock holes where there is water. They set fires on the plains to attract game and to stimulate the growth of new grass seeds and tubers for the following year. Both men and women spend most of the day in the food quest, hunting

Figure 5.2 A wide variety of plant foods and small animals allow people to survive in the harsh environment of the Gibson Desert. Here, Pintupi women hold goanna lizards.

monitor lizards and kangaroos and gathering fruits, bulbs, tubers, and grass seeds, which are both eaten and stored.

November is the harshest time of year. The heat is intense and families travel to the largest rock holes for water, but even these occasionally run dry. Food becomes less available, and many seeds and tubers run out completely. If the rain has not come by December, foraging ceases almost entirely. People try to take it easy to conserve food and water. Women remain in camp, looking after the children and the elderly while the men search for food, sometimes traveling as far as 12 miles a day from camp. Average daily intake may be reduced to 800 calories per person. Heat stress and the shortage of water prevent the whole camp from moving to areas where food might be more available, and people are thus "trapped" in the areas around the larger water holes. Under these conditions, weak individuals may be fed blood from healthier people to get them through the worst times.

The Pintupi and other Australian foragers demonstrate the extraordinary ability of human beings to adapt to the most extreme environments. Though constrained by their simple technology, foragers' detailed knowledge of their environment has permitted them to survive for thousands of years, as well as to develop highly complex ceremonial, religious, kinship, and artistic cultural patterns. These Australian tribes survived using traditional foraging strategies until the mid-20th century. Beginning in the 1920s, because of prolonged drought, the Pintupi began moving to mission stations, cattle stations, government settlements, and towns around the desert fringe. The last Pintupi left the Western Desert in 1984 (Adam 2007; Myers 1986). Though they often visit the desert and continue to do some foraging, they no longer depend on it for all their needs. From their point of view, food was easier to get elsewhere.

The Pintupi subsistence strategy demonstrates that foraging in extreme environments can be a harsh existence with periods of desperation. However, in less extreme environments where predictable vegetal foods can be supplemented by hunting, foragers may experience abundant leisure time and generally good health. For example, Richard Lee estimated that an adult Dobe Ju/'hoansi of the Kalahari Desert in southern Africa spends an average of only two and a half six-hour days per week in subsistence activities, and a woman can gather enough in one day to feed her family for three days (1984:50–53).

Today, like the Pintupi, most foragers have moved to permanent settlements, either by choice or as the result of government pressure. Old trading relationships between foragers and nonforaging people have, in most places, disappeared or become greatly diminished. Although people throughout the world continue to forage when they can, members of contemporary foraging bands rely on the market for much of their food.

◥ Pastoralism

Pastoralists depend primarily on the products of domesticated herd animals. Theirs is a specialized adaptation to an environment that, because of hilly terrain, dry climate, or unsuitable soil, cannot support a large human population through agriculture but can support enough native vegetation for animals if they are allowed to range over a large area. Because human beings cannot digest grass, raising animals that can live on grasses makes pastoralism an efficient way to exploit semiarid natural grasslands. Unlike ranching (commercial animal husbandry), in which livestock are fed grain that could be used to feed humans, pastoralism does not require that animals and humans compete for the same resources (Barfield 1993:13).

Pastoralists may herd cattle, sheep, goats, yaks, or camels, all of which produce both meat and milk (see Figure 5.3). The major areas of pastoralism are found in East Africa (cattle), North Africa (camels), southwestern Asia (sheep and goats), central Asia (yaks), and the subarctic (caribou and reindeer). Because the herd animals of the New World, except for the llama and alpaca, could not be herded, pastoralism was much less common there.

Pastoralism is either transhumant or nomadic. In **transhumant pastoralism**, found mostly in East Africa, men and boys move the animals regularly throughout the year to different areas as pastures become available at different altitudes or in different climatic zones, while women and children and some men remain at a permanent village site.

Transhumant pastoralism: A form of pastoralism in which herd animals are moved regularly throughout the year to different areas as pasture becomes available.

Nomadic pastoralism: A form of pastoralism in which the whole social group (men, women, children) and their animals move in search of pasture.

In **nomadic pastoralism**, the whole population—men, women, and children—moves with the herds throughout the year, and there are no permanent villages.

Pastoralism involves a complex interaction among animals, land, and people. With domestication, animals became dependent on their human keepers for pasture, water, breeding, shelter, salt, and protection from predators. Pastoralists must be highly knowledgeable about the needs of their animals, the carrying capacity of the land, and the subsistence demands of the human population.

The key to the pastoralist economy is herd growth. The number of animals needed to support a family is a constant concern for pastoralists. Eating or selling too many animals in a single year may lead to insolvency, so pastoralists must always balance their present needs against future herd production. However, animals are also a source of wealth and prestige among pastoralists

Jane Hoffer

Figure 5.3 In East African cattle cultures, like the Maasai, the blood and milk of cattle are the major dietary elements. Cattle are killed for meat only on very special ceremonial occasions.

so they may also keep herd sizes well above any immediate need. Pastoralism is a risky business; weather disasters such as drought or storms, disease, or theft can easily decimate a herd.

Many pastoral nomads engage in mixed subsistence strategies, rarely existing solely on the products of their herds. The survival of pastoralists depends on their relationships with their sedentary neighbors, with whom they trade meat, animals, wool, milk products, and hides for manufactured goods and grain.

The Yarahmadzai: A Nomadic Pastoralist Society in Iran

The Yarahmadzai, who live in the southeastern corner of Iran known as Baluchistan, are an example of a mixed pastoralist adaptation that has undergone changes due to both a global economy and the restraints of adapting to the control of the national state (Salzman 2000). Yarahmadzai territory occupies a plateau at 5,000 feet high, where their chief problem is finding adequate water and pasture year-round. They solve this by moving to seek pasture according to the seasons. The Yarahmadzai live in small camps of between 5 and 20 families. When information about good pasture becomes available, the whole Yarahmadzai camp migrates. Because even good pasturage can be quickly exhausted, the camp migrates constantly, anywhere from 5 to 25 miles in each move.

Most of the maximum six-inch annual rainfall occurs in winter. This means that there is good pasturage on the Yarahmadzai's high plateau in the spring. However, by June or July, the animals have eaten all of the spring's growth and the season has turned very dry and hot. In response, the Yarahmadzai migrate to areas served by government irrigation projects to earn money by harvesting grain. They remain there until the harvest ends in early autumn. Then they migrate to the lowland desert where there are groves of date palms, leaving their tents, as well as their goats and sheep on the plateau in the care of young boys. They harvest dates and prepare date preserves for the return journey to their winter camps. At this time, the Yarahmadzai plateau is almost completely barren with very little for the animals to eat. Animals must live on their accumulated fat and the small quantities of roots, grains, dates, and processed date pits their keepers provide. The people depend on food stores from the previous year, but because winter is the rainy season, water is normally available.

Milk is the staple food of the Yarahmadzai and is consumed in many different forms and preserved as dried milk solids and butter. Milk and milk products are also sold and exchanged for grain. Milk is the main source of protein, fat, calcium, and other nutrients; the Yarahmadzai, like most other pastoral peoples, do not eat much meat. Their flocks are their capital, and the Yarahmadzai hope to increase their size. Because killing animals for food works against this objective, the Yarahmadzai rarely do it (Salzman 1999:24).

Baluchistan, Iran.

© Cengage Learning

Like most contemporary pastoralists, the Yarahmadzai combine herding with other subsistence strategies to earn a living. Many pastoralists now depend less than before on consuming the direct products of their herds. Instead, they are often successful in adapting their products to local and even global markets. Nomads in Afghanistan and Iran, for example, are highly integrated into national and international trade networks. They specialize in selling meat animals to local markets, lambskin to international buyers, and sheep intestines to meet the huge German demand for natural sausage casings (Barfield 1993:211). Thus, they are becoming ranchers: pastoral specialists in a cash economy.

Pastoralism cannot support an indefinitely increasing population, and many pastoralists have already become sedentary. With their knowledge of their environment, their creative use of multiple resources, and the global demand for their products, however, pastoralism as a subsistence strategy has a strong future in exploiting the planet's large arid and semiarid zones.

Horticulture

Horticultural societies depend primarily on the production of plants using simple, nonmechanized technology such as hoes or digging sticks, but not draft animals, irrigation techniques, or plows. Fields are not used year after year but remain fallow for some time after being cultivated.

Horticulturalists usually grow enough food in their fields or gardens to support the local group, but they do not produce surpluses that involve the group in a wider market system. Population densities among horticultural peoples are generally low, usually not exceeding 150 people per square mile (Netting 1977). Despite this, horticultural villages may be quite large, ranging from 100 to 1,000 people.

Horticulture may be practiced in dry lands, such as among the Hopi Indians of northeastern Arizona, who cultivate maize, beans, and squash, but is typically a tropical forest adaptation. In these environments, people practice **swidden** (slash-and-burn) cultivation, clearing fields by felling the trees and burning the brush. The burned vegetation is allowed to remain on the soil, which prevents it from drying out. The resulting bed of ash also acts as a fertilizer, returning nutrients to the soil. Fields are used for a few (1 to 5) years and then allowed to lie fallow for a longer period (up to 20 years) so that the forest cover can be rebuilt and soil fertility restored. Swidden cultivators require five to six times as much fallow land as they are actually cultivating.

Swidden cultivation *can* have a debilitating effect on the environment if fields are cultivated before they have lain fallow long enough to recover their forest growth. Eventually, the forest will not grow back, and grasslands will replace the tree cover. Because of this, governments often consider swidden cultivation both inefficient and destructive. However,

Swidden (slash and burn) cultivation: A form of cultivation in which a field is cleared by felling the trees and burning the brush.

modern industrial strategies such as logging and agribusiness, not swidden cultivation, are mainly responsible for the deterioration and disappearance of tropical forests (Sponsel 1995). New studies report that soil fertility is better preserved using long-fallow swidden agriculture than under annual cropping or tree plantations (Bruun et al. 2009), and that replacing swidden with intensified agriculture can lead to swift environmental deterioration (Ziegler et al. 2009).

Horticulture is also a mixed subsistence strategy. Most swidden cultivators grow several crops. They may also hunt, fish, or raise some domestic animals. In New Guinea, for example, domestic pigs are an important source of protein, and the Yanomamo of the Amazon rain forest hunt monkeys and other forest animals. The Kofyar of Nigeria practice a wide range of strategies including swidden, agriculture, keeping domesticated animals, and participating in the global economy (Stone 1998).

The Lua': A Horticultural Society in Southeast Asia

The Lua' of northern Thailand are swidden cultivators (see Figure 5.4). Swidden gardens are cultivated in a regular rotational sequence. After using a block of land for one or two years, villagers allow it to lie fallow for about nine years before planting again.

Figure 5.4 Swidden, or slash-and-burn, horticulture, as practiced traditionally in northern Thailand, is based on a deep understanding of the forest environment. All the features of the landscape are taken into account as Lua' build their houses and plant their fields with a variety of crops used for subsistence, for cash, and for animal fodder.

F. Jack Jackson/Bruce Coleman Inc./PhotoShot

In January, village elders inspect the gardens they expect to use the following year to confirm that the forest regrowth is adequate for cultivation. Using long steel-bladed knives, the men clear their fields by felling small trees. They leave strips of trees along watercourses and at the tops of ridges to prevent erosion and provide seed sources for forest regrowth during the fallow period. They leave taller trees standing, but trim their branches so they will not shade the crops. Such Lua' practices encourage ecosystem diversity (Rerkasem et al. 2009).

The fields cleared in January and February dry until the end of March when a day is chosen to burn them. First, a firebreak is cleared around the field so that fire does not accidentally spread into the forest. Then the swidden is burned.

The cultivators then plant cotton and corn on the slopes of the fields, and yams on the lower, wetter portions. By mid-April, they begin to plant the main subsistence crop, upland rice, jabbing the earth loose with ten-foot iron-tipped planting poles. They hope the rice will take root and sprout before the heavy monsoon rains come. Different types of rice are sown in different areas of the field. Quick-ripening rice is planted near the field shelter, where it can be easily watched. Drought-resistant varieties are planted on the drier, sandier tops of the slopes, along with millet. In addition, there are gardens with mustard greens, peppers, beans, and other vegetables. Vine plants are grown in places particularly susceptible to erosion.

By May, weeding begins, with mainly women and older children using a short-handled tool to scrape and hack at the weeds on the surface; weeds are not dug or pulled out by the roots.

Both men and women harvest the rice, using small, handheld sickles, cutting the stems of each bunch of rice close to the ground. The stalks are spread out to dry for a few days, and then young men beat them against a threshing mat to knock the rice grains loose, separating them as completely as possible. After a second winnowing, the cleaned rice is loaded into baskets and kept in a temporary barn near the field shelter.

After the harvest, swiddens are allowed to lie fallow. However, villagers use the plants that grow on fallow fields for grazing, as traditional medicines, and for other purposes. Such plants are also particularly important during food shortages. The Lua' also keep pigs, water buffalo, cattle, and chickens, which they may sell at local markets. In earlier times, the Lua' hunted and fished, but environmental changes and increased population in the last 50 years has greatly reduced these activities.

By the mid-20th century, many newcomers had begun to settle in Lua' territory. They were less careful about their swidden practices than the Lua', and the quality of the land began to deteriorate. Additionally, through environmental regulations and the promotion of development projects, the government pressured the Lua' to limit their use of swiddens

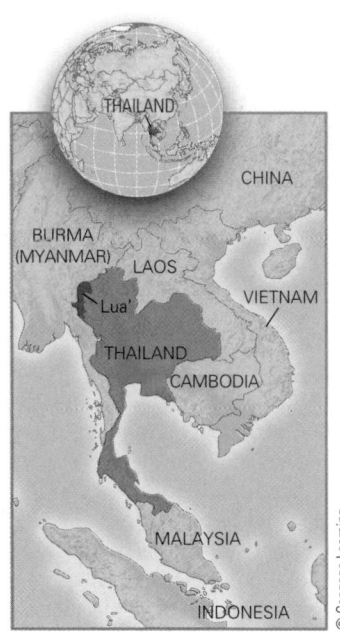

The Lua' of northwestern Thailand.

© Cengage Learning

(Delcore 2007:96). The result has been an increase in intensive agriculture and cattle herding. Many crops such as sorghum and cotton have been severely reduced or eliminated. Cattle now graze the fallow swiddens, leaving few plants for human use. The increase of cash cropping in soybeans has transformed the previously clear and free-flowing streams to muddy, polluted pools, which the Lua' consider too dirty to wash their clothes in, and year-round irrigation has brought in year-round mosquitoes.

The changes in swidden practices among the Lua' are typical of trends in Southeast Asia, and perhaps, worldwide. Rising population, pressure toward industrial agriculture from governments and corporations, and the desire of farmers to raise and sell cash crops all work against swidden agriculture. A recent analysis shows that other agricultural systems are replacing swidden farming in Southeast Asia, and that fallow times are growing shorter where it is still being practiced. The authors note, however, that farmers maintain short fallow swidden farming alongside other agricultural practices so it is unlikely to disappear entirely (Schmidt-Vogt et al. 2009). Despite this, the move away from swidden farming will have profound cultural consequences for the Lua' and other groups.

▨ Using Anthropology: Anthropologists and Nutrition

Anthropologists have long been involved in trying to understand the foods that people eat and their effect on health and nutrition. Some nutritional anthropologists are concerned with trying to improve the nutritional status of people. Others are more concerned to discover what we can or cannot learn from the diets of various groups.

The work of the husband and wife team of Nevin Scrimshaw and Mary Goodrich is a good example of the first. Scrimshaw, one of the world's most important nutrition scientists, was trained in biology, physiology, medicine, and public health. Goodrich, his wife, was trained in nutritional anthropology. As a doctor working in Central America after World War II, he was struck by the large number of young children who suffered from protein malnutrition. He designed a cheap protein source based on cottonseed meal that was both culturally acceptable and extremely inexpensive. He did the same with a peanut-based product in India in the 1960s. He also worked to find ways to add goiter-preventing iodine to the types of salt available in Central America. Scrimshaw traveled with his wife, who introduced anthropological data into his studies. They worked together in Guatemala, Indonesia, and many other places (Martin 2013; Scrimshaw 2012). When he helped found the Institute of Nutrition of Central America and Panama, a direct aid and research organization that works to provide food security in seven Central American countries, he sought advice from well-known anthropologists including Margaret Mead. As the institute's first director, he brought in anthropologists, including Richard Adams and Nancy Solien de Gonzalez, to help guide the institute's policies, particularly toward native Mayan populations (Scrimshaw 2012).

James Howe's work among the Kuna is an example of the second. The Kuna are a large ethnic group living mostly in Panama. In the past decade, they have received a lot of attention because of claims that their high level of cocoa consumption was linked to lower rates of cardiovascular disease. Norman Hollenberg, the lead researcher of many of the studies, claimed that the high consumption of locally grown chocolate by rural Kuna explained the fact that they had far lower levels of hypertension and heart disease than Kuna living in urban areas such as Panama City. According to Hollenberg, the rural Kuna consumed a minimum of 35 cups of chocolate drink a week and that this was associated with their good health (2006). Unfortunately for the chocolate lovers among us, Howe's work shows that Hollenberg's assertions about Kuna chocolate consumption are simply incorrect (2012:45). Although the Kuna do drink chocolate, they consume very much less than Hollenberg states, and much of that is commercial powdered chocolate. They do use cacao beans in religious ceremonies...but by burning them rather than drinking chocolate. Howe notes that the rural Kuna diet is low in fat and higher in fruit and fish than that of urban dwellers in general and that this is far more likely to explain their better health than is chocolate consumption. He argues that Hollenberg makes the mistake of basing health claims for chocolate on the Kuna because he neither spent sufficient time with the Kuna nor devoted effort to examining the rich anthropological literature about them (2012:50).

Agriculture

In agriculture, the same piece of land is permanently cultivated with use of the plow, draft animals, and more complex techniques of water and soil control than horticulturalists use. Plows are more efficient at loosening the soil than are digging sticks or hoes, and turning the soil brings nutrients to the surface. Irrigation is often important in agriculture. Irrigation may require elaborate terracing in hilly areas and sophisticated systems of water control. Preindustrial agriculture also uses techniques of natural fertilization, selective breeding of livestock and crops, and crop rotation, all of which increase productivity.

Intensive cultivation generally supports higher population densities than horticulture. In Indonesia, for example, the island of Java, with 9 percent of the nation's land area, is able to support more than two-thirds of the Indonesian population through intensive wet rice cultivation using elaborate irrigation terraces. The Javanese population density of well over 2,000 people per square mile (Republic of Indonesia 1997) contrasts sharply with the maximum population density of swidden areas in Indonesia, which is about 145 people per square mile.

The greater productivity of agriculture also results from more intensive use of labor. Farmers must work long and hard to make the land productive. For example, growing rice in an irrigated paddy requires about 233 person days of labor per year for each hectare (a hectare is about 2.5 acres) (Barker, Herdt, and Rose 1985:128). In addition to human labor, agriculture requires more capital investment than horticulture. Plows must be bought and draft animals raised and cared for. Although agriculturalists may have more control over food production than horticulturalists, they are more vulnerable to the environment. When people depend on the intensive cultivation of one or two crops, one crop failure or a disease that strikes draft animals may become an economic disaster.

Agriculture is generally associated with sedentary villages, the rise of cities and states, occupational diversity, social stratification, and other complex forms of social organization. In contrast to horticulturalists, who grow food mainly for the subsistence of their households, agriculturalists are enmeshed within larger complex societies. Part of their food production is used to support non-food-producing occupational specialists, such as religious or ruling elites. Rural cultivators who produce for the subsistence of their households but are also integrated into larger, complex state societies are called **peasants**.

Peasants: Rural cultivators who produce for the subsistence of their households but are also integrated into larger, complex state societies.

Musha: A Peasant Agricultural Village in Egypt

Musha is an agricultural village about 250 miles south of Cairo in the Nile Valley. Musha's farmers practice a two-year crop rotation system based on both summer and winter crops (see Figure 5.5). The cycle begins with cotton in the first summer, followed by wheat in the winter. Maize or sorghum follows in the second summer, or the land may be left fallow. The cycle is completed in the second winter with millet, lentils, and chickpeas. In addition, farmers grow grapes and pomegranates and raise a variety of vegetables for home consumption. They also depend on the milk, cheese, and butter from water buffalo, cows, sheep, and goats. Only water buffalo are regularly eaten and sold.

Historically, Musha farmers relied on either animal power or human effort and a few basic wooden tools. Shallow

Robert Caputo/ Aurora Photos

Figure 5.5 In peasant villages in Egypt, farmers make important decisions about allocating labor, buying products for home and farm, scheduling machinery, and dealing with the government.

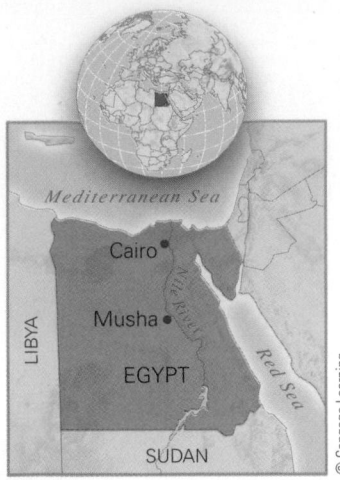

Egypt.

plows and threshing sleds were pulled by cows. Winnowing relied on the wind and a winnowing fork and sieves for the final cleaning. Donkeys and camels were also used to haul crops, people, and equipment.

Many changes occurred in Musha starting in the 1950s. By 1980, almost all farmers used machines at least some of the time. They also came to depend on chemical fertilizers and pesticides as well as animal manure.

In the 1960s, when the completion of the Aswan High Dam brought an end to the flooding of the Nile, the government constructed feed canals and these became the main source of water for the fields. The government is responsible for maintaining these canals and cleans them once a year. However, the farmers must raise water from the canals to the level of the fields. Pumps that perform this task are generally owned by several people, who share the work involved in their maintenance and operation. After arranging for the distribution of water to his fields, the farmer must hire a driver and tractor to plow the fields if he, like many small farmers, does not own one. Fertilizer and seed are hauled from the village bank to his home and from his home to the field. The fertilizer is then spread by hand.

Wheat is one of the most important crops in Musha. It is planted in November and harvested in May and June, and is used for both grain and straw. Hired laborers usually harvest wheat using a small sickle. The reaped wheat is bundled into sheaves, which are transported by camel or wagon to the threshing ground where it is fed into a threshing machine. The threshed grain is winnowed and sifted by specialists who are paid piece rates. Finally, the grain and straw are hauled from the threshing ground back to the farmer's storeroom.

The household is central in Musha cultivation, with extra laborers hired as needed. Women do not work in the fields, but keep house, care for animals, and make cheese. Children, recruited by labor contractors, cut clover for animals and help harvest cotton. The household head plays a key managerial role supervising others, making agricultural purchases, hiring labor, scheduling the use of machinery, and arranging for the water flow into his fields.

In deciding on their strategies for making a living, Musha farmers must adapt to government policies. At one time, the government controlled prices for key crops such as wheat and cotton. However, direct government intervention was greatly reduced or eliminated in the 1980s and 1990s. Despite this, the government is still heavily involved in agriculture. Indeed, through investments in irrigation systems and other infrastructure, the government has remodeled the very landscape on which the farmer works. Government organizations make loans to farmers, distribute agricultural inputs such as seed and fertilizer, subsidize the production of particular agricultural products, and buy some of the farmers' crops. State policies such as importing wheat from the United States affect the prices farmers receive.

The state sets land ownership laws, makes rules governing land tenancy, and affects the labor market through policies that encourage migration.

Profits from farming are uncertain, and most families have several sources of income. Sales of animals, fruits and vegetables, and handicrafts supplement household income. In fact, 70 percent of village households derive their major income from activities other than farming: day labor, government jobs, craft trades, specialist agricultural work, as well as remittances from family members who have migrated, or from rents and pensions.

Farmers today must know the skills of farming as well as how to manage a wide range of other activities. They must interact with family members and government officials and negotiate with the owners of tractors, day laborers, and many others. They supervise agricultural work and manage a wide range of activities, making important decisions at every step. Farmers are affected by global prices for the commodities they produce as well as the policies of their own national government and foreign governments. All over the world, farmers are increasingly part of a globalized, industrialized economy.

Industrialism

In industrialism, the focus of production moves away from food to the production of other goods and services. Investments in machinery and technologies of communication and information become increasingly important. In foraging, pastoralism, horticulture, and agriculture, most of the population is involved in producing food. Although the food industry is very large in industrial societies, only a very small percentage of the population is directly involved in food production. In the United States, in the early 1900s, more than one-third of families lived on farms (Lobao and Meyer 2001). In 2005, fewer than one million people, less than one-half of one percent of the population, listed farming as their primary occupation (U.S. Census Bureau 2008, Statistical Abstract).

Industrialism has an explosive effect on many aspects of economy, society, and culture. It has led to vastly increased population growth, expanded consumption of resources (especially energy), increased occupational specialization, and a shift from working for subsistence and selling the products of one's labor to selling the labor itself for hourly or yearly wages. In every industrialized society, most people work for wages that they use to purchase food, goods, and services. Although cash transactions are found in other production systems, almost all transactions in industrial economies are mediated by money.

Industrial economics are based on the principles that consumption must constantly expand, and material standards of living must always rise. This contrasts with economies created by the production systems previously discussed, which put various limits on both production and consumption and thus make lighter demands on their environments. Industrialism today has vastly outgrown national boundaries. The result has been great movement of resources, capital, and labor, as the whole world has gradually been drawn into the global economy, a process we call **globalization**.

Contemporary industrial and postindustrial societies are characterized by well-coordinated specialized labor forces that produce goods and services and by much smaller elite and managerial classes that oversee the day-to-day operations of the workplace and control what is produced and how it is distributed. Government bureaucracies become important economic and social strata. Increasingly, mobility, skill, and education are required for success.

Because industrialized societies generate much higher levels of inequality than societies based on foraging, pastoralism, or horticulture and because industrial systems require continued expansion, wealth and poverty become critical social issues. Unequal distributions of opportunity, economic failure, illness, and misfortune limit the life chances of vast numbers of people in industrialized societies. Conversely, economic success creates lifestyles well above poverty for large numbers, and conditions of truly extraordinary wealth for a very small number. Inequalities characterize relations among as well as within nations. The creation of complex global systems of exchange between those who supply raw materials and those who use them in manufacturing, as well as between manufacturers and consumers, has resulted in increasing disparities of wealth around the world.

The Beef Industry: Industrialized Agriculture in the United States

The American beef industry is a good if disturbing example of industrialism. Americans have long had a love affair with beef. Because meat was expensive for the average family during much of America's past, beef became both the symbol and the substance of having made it into the middle class. For Americans, steak is symbolic of manliness, and "meat and potatoes" make up the iconic American meal.

As the standard of living in the United States rose after World War II, so did the demand for inexpensive beef. The postwar era brought the rise of the suburbs and the entry of large numbers of women into the workforce. This increased the complexity of American family life and reduced the amount of time available for cooking and dining together, thus favoring packaged convenience foods and meat that could be rapidly prepared. Additionally, beginning in the 1960s, the expansion of the fast food industries greatly increased American consumption of hamburgers and the demand for beef. In 2007, McDonald's purchased close to one billion pounds of beef in the United States alone (Roybal 2007).

American dinner tables had been supplied with meat that came through a production chain that started on a family farm and ended in the neighborhood retail butcher shop. However, this system of production could not generate the levels of supply that families and fast food chains now demanded. Only large corporations employing mass production technologies could meet this high level of demand (see Figure 5.6). By the late 1980s, most family farms were no longer economically viable and many small farmers lost their land. Rural America became dominated by large farming operations, tied to multinational corporations. Looking to preserve jobs and stem the flow of people leaving the countryside, local governments recruited agribusinesses with free land and tax breaks, but this put greater revenue burdens on those who remained and did not stop the downward economic spiral.

The cost of labor is a significant factor in the production of meat. Through the 1970s and 1980s, meat processors succeeded in driving down the wages paid to workers. The key to this was their use of nonunion workers, frequently immigrants from Latin America and Southeast Asia. In many cases, these workers were undocumented. For example, when Immigration and Customs agents raided Agriprocessors in Postville, Iowa in 2008, more than a third of its workers were found to be undocumented (Jones 2012). Such workers were not easily (or very willingly) absorbed into tightly knit farm communities and small towns. As the rural economy declined, resentment of immigrants and social problems increased. There were strains on health care, schools, and social services (Artz, Orazem, and Otto 2007).

In many cases, large-scale meatpacking had disastrous environmental impacts. U.S. livestock production creates about 900 million tons of waste annually (see Figure 5.7). In Iowa, hog farming alone produces 50 million tons of manure annually. This waste often seeps into local streams and groundwater supplies, polluting critical resources (Bittman 2008). Although some rural regions experienced short-term job increases from the meatpacking

Figure 5.6 In Industrial agriculture, food is processed using techniques similar to other manufacturing processes.

Kevin Moloney/Aurora Photos/Corbis

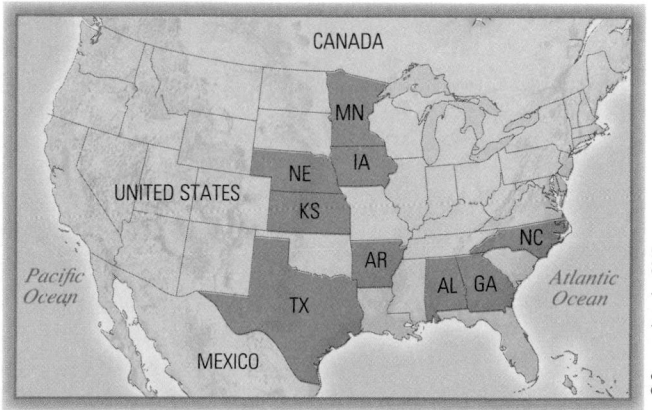

Figure 5.7 Top livestock and poultry slaughtering states (American Meat Institute 2011).

© Cengage Learning 2015

industries, this pollution created a hidden cost and a long-term downside for rural communities (Stull and Broadway 2004).

The efficiency of assembly line beef processing has high human costs as well. The meatpacking industry has a long history of horrific working conditions. In 1906, Upton Sinclair described the deeply impoverished lives, terrible working conditions, and hopelessness of workers in Chicago's slaughterhouses. Although the meatpacking industry today is vastly different from the industry of 100 years ago, working conditions at America's 6,278 meat and poultry slaughtering and processing plants are still deeply disturbing in many cases. The low costs and high availability of American meat is made possible by cheap labor and getting the maximum product out the door. "On the floor," this translates into a large proportion of unskilled, poorly trained, low-paid hourly workers; a sped-up "disassembly" line; and few break periods for workers.

Work in the meatpacking industry is difficult and dangerous even in the best plants. The processing operations involve thousands of moving animals being stun-gunned by a "knocker," axed in half by "splitters" on a moving platform, and deboned and cut up with sharp knives wielded by an assortment of specialists such as "stickers," "gutters," "tail rippers," and "head droppers." The working conditions of this sector of American agribusiness are so severe that Human Rights Watch has deemed them in violation of international standards and basic human rights. These conditions affect not only the health of the workers, but also the quality of the product. This was dramatically demonstrated in early 2008, when the Westland/Hallmark Meat Packing Company recalled 143 million pounds of contaminated meat, some of which was used in school lunch programs and the largest meat recall in U.S. history. Smaller recalls are frequent; for example, there were 82 meat recalls in 2012, together totaling 3.4 million pounds (USDA 2013b). Despite this, demand for inexpensive beef remains high, and meaningful reform of the industry does not seem likely in the near future.

The Global Marketplace

The contemporary world is characterized by connectedness and change of a magnitude greater than anything seen earlier. For some people, the expansion of the global economy has meant new and more satisfying means of making a living. However, these opportunities are not equally available to all peoples or to all individuals within a culture. For many people, the promise of prosperity offered by the global economy has yet to be fulfilled.

Anthropology is particularly sensitive to the complex linkages among local, regional, national, and global contexts that structure the modern world. Anthropologists today can play an important role in shaping government and global economic policies that take into account the environmental impact of different ways of making a living, the values and practices of local cultures, international plant and animal conservation efforts, and corporate- and state-driven efforts to participate in global markets. In the postindustrial globalized society, individuals, governments, and businesses must find new ways to adapt to significant changes in the production and distribution of goods. We explore some of these changes in Chapter 6 on economics.

■ BRINGING IT BACK HOME:
GLOBALIZATION AND FOOD CHOICE

In the recent past, much of the food on American tables was locally produced and seasonally available. Today, our food is produced on large farms located in rich agricultural regions thousands of miles away from the populations they serve. For example, more than half of all fruit produced in the United States comes from California, which, together with Washington and Florida, accounts for 80 percent of U.S. fruit production (USDA 2012). However, our culinary net spreads far wider than the United States. In the fiscal year 2012, the United States imported $105.9 billion worth of agricultural products (USDA 2013a).

The presence of so much food from distant places is one of the great triumphs of globalization. Fruits and vegetables are available all year long. We dine on frozen Indian meals actually prepared in India and accompany them with water from Fiji and fruit from Chile. However, this global food network also extracts a high price. Although determining the carbon footprint of individual products is extremely difficult (*Economist* 2008), moving food around the world may have high environmental costs. For example, the average tomato imported into Canada has traveled almost 3,000 miles and, in so doing, produces more than three times more carbon dioxide than a locally grown tomato (Brandt 2008:26). As our dependence on imported food increases, so does our reliance on the fuel necessary to move it. This means that changes in the price of oil can result in large jumps in the price of food, making our food supply more vulnerable than ever to global economics and politics (Figure 5.8).

Dependence on food shipped long distances also favors foods that look pretty and are easy to ship. Along with this comes the loss of indigenous and traditional varieties. Although estimates about the percentage of plant species that have disappeared vary, one study found that 97 percent of the vegetable varieties on a U.S. Department of Agriculture (USDA) list from the early 20th century are extinct today (Brandt 2008:56).

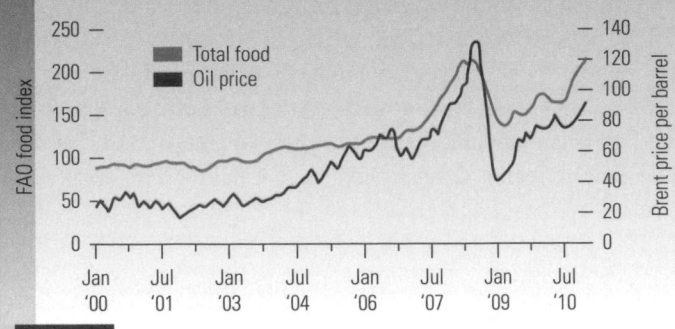

Figure 5.8 World food index versus Brent oil prices.
Source: United Nations Food and Agriculture Organization (FAO) and U.S. Energy Information Agency (EIA).

The varieties that are extensively grown, along with the fertilizers and pesticides necessary to grow them, are produced by large multinational corporations such as Monsanto, ADM, Cargill, DuPont, and Bayer. These companies make huge profits, sometimes at the expense of workers. According to the World Health Organization (2004), there are about three million cases of pesticide poisoning each year, resulting in a quarter million deaths. Poor nations account for only 25 percent of the world's pesticide use but 99 percent of the deaths from pesticide poisoning (World Health Organization 2008). Buying globally does provide jobs for agricultural workers around the world, but working conditions in such jobs are often very harsh and the key beneficiaries are the corporations that organize food production and transportation.

In recent years, food alternatives have become more mainstream. These include vegetarianism, the slow food movement, and community-supported and local agriculture. All of these are probably healthier for both individuals and the environment than large-scale globalized food production (Wilk 2006). However, thus far, they affect relatively few people in wealthy nations, often cost more than alternatives, and increasing their use involves the difficult task of changing culturally ingrained food habits.

YOU DECIDE:

1. What are the cultural patterns and values that underlie food choices in the United States, and how do they affect what you eat?
2. Locavores are people who eat only food grown within a relatively short distance of their home. Would you become a locavore? Why, or why not?
3. Do you believe movements in favor of local agriculture, organic foods, and slow foods are likely to have success in the United States? What factors might favor or retard their success?

CHAPTER SUMMARY

1. What is the relationship between the environment and subsistence (food-getting) pattern of a society? All societies must adapt to their physical environments, which present different problems, opportunities, and limitations to human populations. The subsistence pattern of a society develops in response to seasonal variations in the environment and environmental variations over the long run, such as drought, flood, animal diseases, climate, demographic changes, and the presence of other groups.

2. What are the five major subsistence strategies of human populations? The five major patterns of using the environment to support human populations are foraging (gathering, fishing, hunting), pastoralism, horticulture, agriculture, and industrialism.

3. What is foraging? Give an example of a foraging society and explain how foraging has been affected by climate change? In foraging, people rely on food, most often plants, naturally available in the environment. Climate change threatens forager livelihood, particularly in the Arctic. The Pintupi people of the Gibson Desert of Australia were a foraging culture.

4. What is pastoralism? Give an example of a pastoralist society and comment on the relationship between pastoralism and more sedentary lifestyles? Pastoralism is subsistence based primarily on care of domesticated herd animals. Because it is difficult to live on animal products alone, pastoralism either is found along with cultivation (transhumance) or involves trading relations with food cultivators. The Yarahmadzai are an example of a nomadic mixed pastoralist economy.

5. What is horticulture? Give an example of a horticulturalist society. Horticulture typically is a tropical forest adaptation based around planting gardens or small fields. It uses simple technology and requires the cutting and burning of jungle to clear fields for cultivation. Fields are not used permanently but are allowed to lie fallow after several years of productivity. The Lua' are swidden cultivators in Thailand.

6. What is agriculture and how is it related to larger societies and states? Agriculture is the use of large areas that are permanently cultivated, usually in grain. It often involves more complex technology than horticulture, often including plows and irrigation. Agriculture generally supports high population densities and is associated with sedentary village life. Agricultural societies are stratified and farmers constitute only one element of them.

Governments often intervene in agriculture. Musha, an Egyptian village, is an example of peasant agriculture.

7. What is industrialism and how is it related to wealth and environment? In industrialism, machines and chemical processes are used for the production of goods. Food production constitutes only a small percentage of total production and occupies little of the population. Industrialism creates great material prosperity of many people, but at a cost of high levels of inequality and environmental destruction.

KEY TERMS

Agriculture

Efficiency

Foraging (hunting and gathering)

Globalization

Horticulture

Industrialism

Nomadic pastoralism

Pastoralism

Peasants

Population density

Productivity

Sedentary

Subsistence strategies

Swidden (slash-and-burn) cultivation

Transhumant pastoralism

Specialization and the creation of markets is a critical aspect of the development of large-scale economies. In earlier times, cheeses were made and consumed locally. Now they enter a network of international trade. The Alkmaar cheese market in the Netherlands, pictured here, is an important node in that network.

CHAPTER **6**

ECONOMICS

LEARNING OBJECTIVES

After you have read this chapter, you will be able to:

△ Define economic behavior, and give examples of situations when people use it and when they do not.

△ Summarize the ways in which people in foraging, pastoral, horticultural, and agricultural societies generally allocate resources.

△ Differentiate between generalized, balanced, and negative reciprocity, and give an example of each.

△ Discuss the differences between redistribution and reciprocity using examples of the potlatch and kula trade.

△ Define market exchange, and analyze the ways in which it differs from other systems of distribution.

△ Summarize the key characteristics of capitalism.

△ Describe the ways in which people in wealthy nations both participate in and resist capitalism. Debate the advantages of each.

ULTIMATE DICTATOR

HE notion that human beings are rational, individual economic actors underlies much of Western economic theory. Economists assume that people are capable of assessing the economic choices facing them, and, when they do so, they make decisions that maximize their wealth and minimize their labor. There is certainly some truth to this idea, and all of us can think of cases where we behave precisely this way. But, economic choices do not occur in a vacuum. Real economic decisions are made in a cultural context and are influenced by ideas about what is right, valuable, and moral, not just about how much we can profit. However, as we have seen in the previous chapters of this book, what is right, valuable, and moral are not the same for everyone.

Economists and anthropologists have developed interesting tools to test the degree to which people in different cultures really behave the way that theories say they are supposed to. Two examples are the dictator game and the ultimatum game.

In the dictator game, there are two individuals: a "proposer" and a "responder." The proposer is given a sum of money, say the equivalent of one day of wages, and is told to split it with the responder. The proposer and the responder are unknown to each other and they play the game only once, so there is no chance that generosity will be reciprocated. If people simply try to maximize their wealth and minimize their work, we would expect that the proposer would keep the entire sum, offering nothing to the responder. In fact, that doesn't always happen. In the United States and other wealthy nations, about 30 to 40 percent of the players take the whole pot. However, most proposers leave between 20 and 30 percent for the responders. Jean Ensminger (2002) found that among the Orma, a group of cattle pastoralists living in Kenya, only 9 percent took the whole pot; the others gave an average of 31 percent to the responders.

The ultimatum game is also played with a proposer and a responder. However, in this case, the proposer offers to split a sum of money, and the responder may either accept or reject the split. If the responder accepts the split, the money is divided and the game is over. If the responder rejects the split, neither player receives any money and the game ends. As in the dictator game, players are anonymous and play only once, so generosity cannot be returned. In the ultimatum game, respondents who behaved simply as rational maximizers would always accept the proposer's offer because accepting the offer involves no financial cost, and even a very low offer is greater than nothing. But, real people do not play this way.

In the past 15 years, anthropologists and economists have played the ultimatum game with members of many different cultures. The results show that there are no cultures where everyone is willing to accept whatever is offered...and they show a great deal of variation in how much people are willing to offer. For example, among the Machiguenga of the Peruvian Amazon, proposers rarely offered more than 15 percent, and offers were almost never rejected (Henrich et al. 2004). American college students, on the other hand, offered 42 to 48 percent of the pot to their responders, and responders tended to reject offers of less than 30 percent.

Some of the results may seem counterintuitive. For example, in foraging groups, there is a high degree of equality, but foragers were not generous game players. The Hadza, foragers who live in Tanzania, made some of the lowest proposals of any groups tested. On the other hand, industrialized economies are highly stratified and unequal, but their members are likely to offer almost half the pot to responders. In fact, the results show an interesting trend. The greater the degree to which a group is involved in a market economy, the more likely proposers were to give a larger share of the money to responders. Later in this chapter, we will explore some of the reasons why this is the case.

The results of the dictator and ultimatum games demonstrate the social and cultural dimensions of economic decision making. The fact that, cross-culturally, a strong majority of proposers give responders something may show that all people have a bias toward at least a little generosity. However, the systematic differences among cultures demonstrate that decisions are set in cultural contexts that determine moral and appropriate behavior, and that these are different in different economic systems.

Economics is the study of the ways in which the choices people make as individuals and as members of societies combine to determine how their society uses its resources to produce and distribute goods and services. But, as our example shows, this process is always set within a cultural context. How we make these decisions depends on the values we give to both goods and ideas. And that depends upon culture.

Every society must have an **economic system** in the sense that each group of people must produce, distribute, and consume. However, cultural context determines the ways in which goods and services are produced and distributed as well as the meanings of consumption.

Economics: The study of the ways in which the choices people make combine to determine how their society uses its scarce resources to produce and distribute goods and services.

Economic system: The norms governing production, distribution, and consumption of goods and services within a society.

ECONOMIC BEHAVIOR

Economists assume that because human wants are unlimited and the means for achieving them are not, organizations and individuals must make decisions about the best way to apply their limited means to meet

Figure 6.1 Decisions these traders at the Chicago Board of Trade make are based almost entirely on profit and loss. However, most of the time, our decisions are motivated by other considerations as well. We may prefer relaxation and free time to financial return.

their unlimited desires. As we saw in the opening story, one way of understanding economic decisions is to assume that decision makers will always maximize their financial benefit and minimize their work. Will a business firm cut down or expand its production? Will it purchase a new machine or hire more laborers? Such decisions are assumed to be motivated by the desire to maximize profit (see Figure 6.1).

However, the opening story also shows us that this understanding misses critical factors. As human beings, we only have so much time and energy to expend in meeting our desires. But, we do not always allocate these to maximize our financial wealth. Consider a choice you may make today. After you finish reading this chapter, you might confront a series of decisions: Should you reread it for better comprehension? Should you study for another course? Call and get a pizza delivered? Play with your kids? Socialize with your friends? You will make your choice based on some calculation of benefit. However, that benefit probably cannot be reduced to financial profit. You may believe that you will make more money if you study and get higher grades. However, your choice is set in a context in which money is unlikely to be the most important element of value; we value our friends, our children, our leisure time, and many other things as well. If you choose to socialize instead of hitting the books, your choice is not irrational, but it does not necessarily lead to greater profit. We cannot assume that you will always act to increase your material well-being. Rather, we need to find out what motivates you.

Just as you might value an evening spent with friends over an "A" in this class, members of other cultures might value family connections, cultural tradition, social prestige, leisure time, or other things over monetary profit. For example, the Hadza, mentioned earlier, live in an area of Tanzania with an abundance of animal and vegetable food. They have considerable leisure time but make no attempt to use it to increase their wealth. Although they know how to farm, they don't do it because it would require too much work (Woodburn 1968).

Leisure time is only one of the ends toward which people expend effort. They may also direct their energies toward increasing social status or respect. In Western society, **prestige** is primarily tied to increased consumption and display of goods and services, but this is not universal. In many societies, prestige is associated with giving goods away. Conspicuous consumers and stingy people become objects of scorn and may be shunned or accused of witchcraft (see Danfulani 1999; Offiong 1983, for examples). The notion that prestige can be gained through giving is well established in our own society. Universities have buildings bearing the names of their most generous donors. Bill Gates is not only the chairman of Microsoft, but, with his wife and father, he also co-chairs the world's largest charitable foundation. The Bill and Melinda Gates Foundation had over $36 billion in assets in 2012, and in 2011, gave more than $3.4 billion in grants (Bill and Melinda Gates Foundation n.d.).

Prestige: Social honor or respect.

To understand the economies of various cultures, anthropologists face two related problems. First, they must analyze the broad institutional and social contexts within which people make decisions, and second, they must determine and evaluate the factors that motivate individual decision making.

One way we can think about any given economic system is to consider a series of fundamental issues that all societies must face. Because all societies must acquire the food and other materials necessary to their lives, all must engage in production. To do so, all societies must acquire resources, such as land and water, and all must have some system through which the rights to use such resources are allocated.

However, resources in and of themselves do nothing. Rather, people must be organized in specific ways to use resources in the production of goods and services. Thus, each society has a **division of labor**: a pattern by which different tasks are given to different members of a society. For example, foragers rely on the plants and animals in their environment. But, foragers never simply gather and eat the plants and animals randomly. In each group, specific groups of people do specific tasks. Most often, men hunt and women gather. Thus, they are organized to produce.

Division of labor: The pattern of apportioning different tasks to different members of a society.

Additionally, people in all societies exchange and consume the products of production. Thus, each society has a system of distribution, and in each, there are distinct styles and patterns of consumption. In the remainder of this chapter, we will explore how different societies tackle the problems of allocating resources, organizing labor, and distributing and consuming the results of production.

◢◤ ALLOCATING RESOURCES

Productive resources: Material goods, natural resources, or information used to create other goods or information.

Productive resources are the things that members of a society need to create goods and services and to participate in the economy. How people access these is basic to every culture. The most obvious productive resources are tools, labor, and in some economic systems, money. However, knowledge is a critical productive resource. We can see the effects of access to knowledge in current-day society by looking at the relationship between university degrees and income. According to the U.S. Bureau of Labor Statistics (2013), the median income for high school graduates in 2011 was about $33,176. The median income for those with a bachelor degree was almost $54,756. The median for those with master's and doctoral degrees was substantially higher (see Figure 6.2). Of course, the university is not the only source of knowledge in our society.

An important point of contrast between economic systems is the extent to which the members of a society have access to productive resources. In general, differential access to resources develops as population and social complexity increase. Small societies generally have a limited number of productive resources, and most everyone has access to them. Large-scale societies have a great many more resources, but access to them is limited. Again, considering differential access to knowledge in the United States, we see that only 3 percent of the students at most selective U.S. universities come from households in the lowest 25 percent of the income scale, and only 10 percent come from the bottom 50 percent (Lexington 2005). Thus, family wealth plays a critical role in accessing knowledge and is a powerful predictor of future wealth and social position.

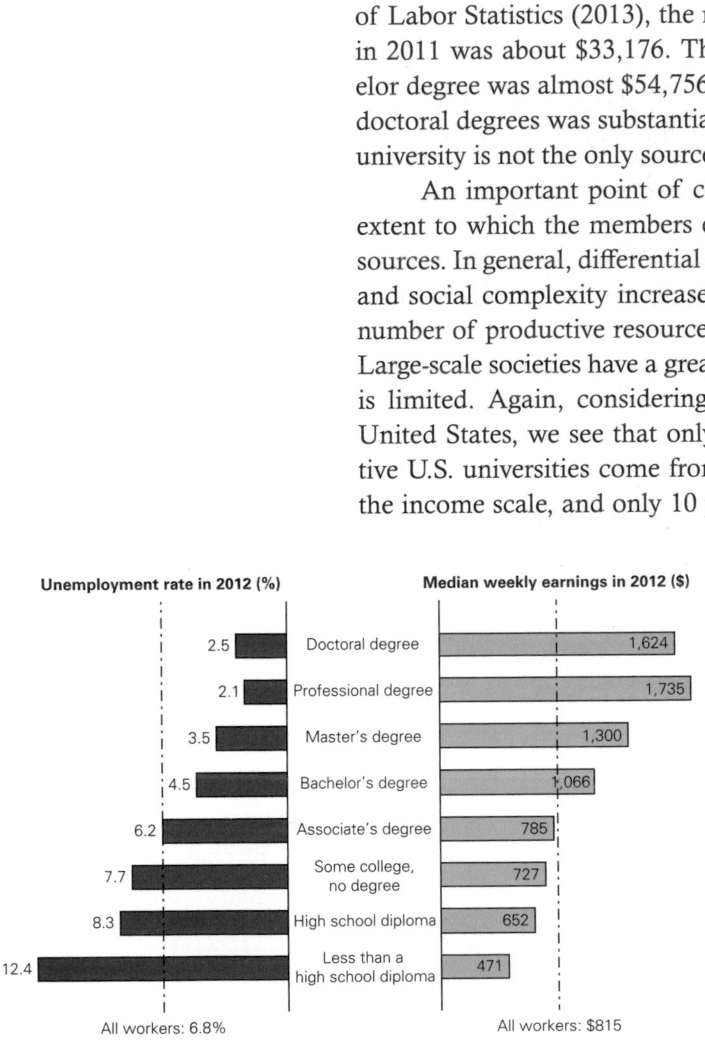

Access to the knowledge that allows one to make and use tools plays an important role in all societies. There may be additional important forms of knowledge that can be controlled as well, such as the knowledge of healing or of religious rituals. In preindustrial societies, however, the most basic resources are land and sometimes water. Examining the ways in which people access these particular resources can give us insight into the social organization and other aspects of a culture.

The requirements of a foraging lifestyle generally mean that a group of

Unemployment rate in 2012 (%)		Median weekly earnings in 2012 ($)
2.5	Doctoral degree	1,624
2.1	Professional degree	1,735
3.5	Master's degree	1,300
4.5	Bachelor's degree	1,066
6.2	Associate's degree	785
7.7	Some college, no degree	727
8.3	High school diploma	652
12.4	Less than a high school diploma	471
All workers: 6.8%		All workers: $815

Figure 6.2 The relationship between education and earnings in the United States.

Source: U.S. Bureau of Labor Statistics, 2013.

people must spread out over a large area. Boundaries are generally flexible so that they can be adjusted as the availability of resources change. Abundance and scarcity shape people's relationship to land. Where resources are scarce and large areas are needed to support the population, boundaries usually are not defended. Where resources are more abundant and people move less, groups may be more inclined to defend their territory (Cashdan 1989:42).

Among pastoralists, the most critical resources are livestock and land. Livestock are owned and managed by individual heads of households. Animals, in turn, produce goods that are directly consumed, such as milk. They are also kept as a form of wealth, to produce other animals and to exchange goods and services. Land and water are generally not owned. In many cases, during the summer or the rainy season, cattle graze in deserts and highland areas unsuitable for farming. In the winter or dry season, they move to areas that are occupied by settled farmers. There, agreements with landowners and village leaders allow animals to graze on crop waste and the stubble from harvested fields. Most such agreements specify rights, payments, and schedules for all parties.

In most societies characterized by horticulture, land is communally owned by an extended kin group. Designated elders or officials of the group allocate the rights to use land to individuals or heads of households. But such land may not be sold. Because almost everyone belongs to some land-controlling kin group, few people are deprived of access to this basic resource. Thus, control over land is not a means by which one group can exploit or exert permanent control over another.

Horticulture often involves investing a great deal of labor in clearing, cultivating, and maintaining land. Generally, the rights to cleared land and its products are vested in those who work it. Because such individuals may die while the land is still productive, some system of inheritance of use rights is usually provided. Among the Lacandon Maya, for example, individuals can farm any unused piece of land. However, clearing virgin land is difficult, so people retain rights to land they have cleared even if it is not currently in production. Maya who migrate may lose their land rights, but their families retain ownership of any fruit trees that they have planted. Should a man die after investing time and labor in clearing and planting land, his wife and children retain rights to use the land (McGee 1990).

In more politically and technologically complex societies, agriculture dominates production. Enormous amounts of labor are invested in the land and very large quantities of food produced. When this happens, control of the land becomes an important source of wealth and power (see Figure 6.3). Land ownership moves from the kin group to the individual or family. Within the limits of law or custom, an owner has the right to keep others off the land and to dispose of it as he or she wishes.

Figure 6.3 In complex societies, enormous amounts of labor are often invested in land. This results in high levels of production, and land ownership becomes an important source of wealth and power. This picture shows a farmer walking through rice paddies in Bali.

In agricultural societies, land and other productive resources are often owned by an elite group. Landowners usually do not work their fields themselves. Most fieldwork is done by laborers who often are referred to as *peasants*. Today, peasants typically pay cash rent to their landlords, but in the past, they also provided goods and services, including a portion of their agricultural production, labor, finished craft goods such as cloth, and raw material such as lumber. As a result, landowners enjoy relatively high standards of living but peasants do not.

Many current-day societies rely on industrialized agriculture. But in these cases, as we saw in Chapter 5, only a miniscule percentage of the population is directly involved in farming. Therefore, access to productive land is not important for most people in these societies. In industrialized economies, most people earn their livelihood by working for wages for businesses and other organizations that provide goods and services. These usually are organized as capitalist enterprises. We will discuss capitalism at some length later in this chapter.

ORGANIZING LABOR

In small-scale preindustrial and peasant economies, the household or some extended kin group is the basic unit of production and of consumption (White 1980). The **household** is an economic unit—a group of people united by kinship or other links who share a residence and organize production, consumption, and distribution of goods among themselves. A household is different from a family because it may include

Household: A group of people united by kinship or other links who share a residence and organize production, consumption, and distribution among themselves.

lodgers, servants, and others. Household members use most of the goods they produce themselves.

Households and kin groups do seek financial gain, but this is not their primary purpose. Their goals are often social or religious rather than monetary. Labor is not a commodity bought and sold in the market; rather, it is an important aspect of membership in a social group. The labor that people both perform and receive situates them with respect to others in their family and gives them both a sense of identity and a sense of meaning.

In economies where households are the units of production, there can be little economic growth. Households cannot easily expand or contract as the economy fluctuates. They cannot easily fire their members or acquire new ones. Thus, large-scale production and distribution systems tend not to develop under such conditions. However, as we will see in the ethnography of Turkey later in this chapter, household social relations can play an important role in an industrialized economy.

In Western society, work also has very important social implications. Of course, people work to put food on their table and a roof over their head. But, as anthropologist Pamela Crespin notes, an individual's self-image and social status is bound up with work in our society. Joblessness or the inability to earn a living wage diminishes an adult's identity and status (Crespin 2005:20). This is a particularly important issue in a nation such as the United States, where in 2011, about one-third of working families earned less than twice the official poverty rate (Fletcher 2013)

Gender also plays an important role in organizing labor. In all human societies, some tasks are considered appropriate for women and others appropriate for men. At some level, the sexual division of labor is biological because only women can bear and nurse children. However, beyond this, the specific tasks defined as men's or women's work vary widely from group to group. For example, in Aztec Mexico, weaving was a female task. Newborn girls were presented with tools for weaving, and weaving equipment was placed with women when they died (Brumfiel 1991, 2006:866). However, in most West African societies, weaving is considered men's work. The tight connections between gender and the organization of society are explored at length in Chapter 9.

Specialization in Complex Societies

The division of labor in society becomes more specialized and complex as the population increases and agricultural production intensifies. This is particularly the case where a society is dependent on grain agriculture. Grains are hard, durable, and storable. Those who are able to control them have access to wealth and power in new and important ways. Landowners and rulers are able to support many people. Occupational specialization spreads through society as individuals are able to exchange their services or the products they produce for food and wealth. Specialists are likely to include soldiers, government officials, and members of the priesthood as well as artisans, craftsmen, and merchants.

Traditional areas of contemporary India provide an excellent example of occupational specialization. There, only people belonging to particular hereditary kinship groups can perform certain services or produce certain kinds of goods. Literally thousands of specialized activities—washing clothes, drumming at festivals, presiding over religious ceremonies, making pots, painting pictures—are performed by specific named hereditary groups.

Much of the world's population today lives in industrial or postindustrial societies, and almost everyone is a specialist of one kind or another. In the United States, the Department of Labor recognizes 840 numbered occupational categories and divides each of these into many subspecialties (SOCPC 2010).

Although specialization undoubtedly has advantages in terms of efficiency and the ability to produce large quantities of goods, it can take a physical and emotional toll on members of a society. Since the beginnings of the industrial age, many factory jobs involved repetitious and mind-numbing labor often performed under hazardous conditions (see Figure 6.4). In the American automobile plants of the early 20th century, for example, almost all skilled tasks were mechanized. Workers simply inserted pieces into machines, turned a switch and waited until the machine completed its task, removed the finished pieces, and passed them on to the next worker. The machinery determined the pace of work and the tasks performed. In the 1920s, one worker said simply, "The machine is my boss" (Meyer 2004).

Figure 6.4 In the past 200 years, jobs have become increasingly specialized. Repetitive monotonous factory labor, such as work at this electronic appliance factory in Taizhou, China, has altered people's lives and led to new understandings of identity.

Factory labor often led to new notions of identity. For example, in the 19th century, many American workers associated masculinity with skilled labor, independence, and decision-making power at work. On the assembly lines in early 20th century United States, labor was boring and monotonous, and workers had little decision-making ability. Companies such as Ford Motors, through public speeches, company policies, and employment practices, sought to redefine masculinity, associating it with "working hard in the company of other men, on a useful product, and being paid well for it" (Lewchuk 1993:852), rather than with skill and independence.

DISTRIBUTION: SYSTEMS OF EXCHANGE AND CONSUMPTION

In all societies, goods and services are exchanged. In fact, some anthropologists have long theorized that the exchange of goods is one of the fundamental bases of culture. The great French anthropologist Marcel Mauss (1990/1924) theorized that societies were held together by patterns of giving and receiving. He pointed out that, because gifts invariably must be repaid, we are obligated to each other through exchange. And in many situations, it is better to give than to receive.

The three main patterns of exchange are reciprocity, redistribution, and the market. Although more than one kind of exchange system exists in most societies, each system is predominantly associated with a certain kind of political and social organization (Polyani 1944). Let us look first at reciprocity.

Reciprocity

Reciprocity is the mutual give-and-take among people of similar status. Three types of reciprocity can be distinguished from one another by the degree of social distance between the exchanging partners (Sahlins 1972).

Generalized reciprocity usually is carried out among close kin and carries a high moral obligation. It involves a distribution of goods in which no overt account is kept of what is given, and no immediate or specific return is expected. In our culture, the relationship between mother and child is usually a good example. Ideally, such transactions are without any thought of self-interest.

Generalized reciprocity involving food is an important social mechanism among foraging peoples. In these societies, hunters distribute meat among members of the kin group or camp. Each person or family gets an equal share or a share dependent on its kinship relationship to the hunter. We might wonder what the hunter gets out of this arrangement. Aren't

Reciprocity: A mutual give-and-take among people of equal status.

Generalized reciprocity: Giving and receiving goods with no immediate or specific return expected.

some people always in the position of providing and others always receiving? Part of the answer is that hunters gain satisfaction from accomplishing a highly skilled and difficult task (Woodburn 1998), and that this is accompanied by a degree of prestige. Additionally, because all people in the society are bound by the same rules, the system provides everyone with the opportunity to give and receive, although this does not necessarily mean that people do so equally.

Balanced reciprocity involves greater social distance than generalized reciprocity and entails a clear obligation to return, within a reasonable time limit, goods of nearly equal value to those given. In the United States, we participate in balanced reciprocity when we give gifts at weddings or birthdays, exchange invitations, or buy a round of drinks for friends. The economic aspect of these exchanges is repressed; we say it is the spirit of the gift that is important. However, we also know that accepting a gift involves the obligation to return a gift of approximately the same value. If we fail to do so, our relationship with the gift giver is unlikely to last very long.

Balanced reciprocity is often characteristic of trading relations among nonindustrialized peoples without market economies. Such trade is frequently carried out over long distances and between different tribes or villages. It is often in the hands of trading partners, men or women who have a long-standing and personalized relationship with one another.

Bronislaw Malinowski's (1984/1922) analysis of the **kula ring**, an extensive system of intertribal trade among the inhabitants of a ring of islands off New Guinea, is one of the most famous anthropological studies of reciprocal trading. The kula trade moves two types of prestige goods from island to island around the kula circle. *Soulava*, long necklaces of red shell, always move in a clockwise direction. *Mwali*, bracelets of white shell, move counterclockwise (see Figures 6.5). Participants receive the necklaces or bracelets from their trading partners. Although kula items can be permanently owned and can be taken out of circulation (Weiner 1976), people generally hold them for a while and then pass them on. Kula valuables are not simple objects. Each item is known by its history and associations, and some are much more valuable and important (and famous) than others. The gift or receipt of an important *soulava* or *mwali* is an action heavily loaded with prestige and politics. Kula exchanges can carry a deep emotional importance, and issues of jealousy, anger, sickness, and witchcraft are sometimes involved (Munn 1990).

Balanced reciprocity: The giving and receiving of goods of nearly equal value with a clear obligation of a return gift within a specified time limit.

Kula ring: A pattern of exchange among trading partners in the South Pacific Islands.

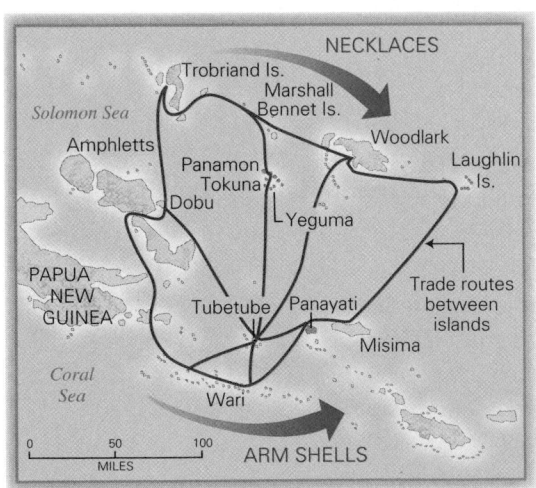

Figure 6.5 The kula trade binds people in the South Pacific in a network of reciprocal trading relationships.

Although the central drama of trading involves the gift or receipt of a kula valuable, *mwali* are never simply exchanged for *soulava*. A visiting trader hoping to receive an important kula valuable instead brings goods that may include canoes, axe blades, pottery, and pigs, as well as other items. Traders are likely to bring things not found on the island where the trading is taking place, because these are likely to be particularly valuable to their recipients. The presentation of goods by a visiting trader, as well as declarations of alliance and support, encourages a kula partner to give a *mwali* or *soulava* to the visitor. Such a gift (especially if it is an important or famous valuable) demonstrates and confirms the political importance and allegiances of both giver and recipient. Critically, the receipt of such a gift also implies the obligation to present gifts of equal or greater importance to the kula partner when he or she comes as a visiting trader.

Kula exchanges thus have economic, social, and political functions. They bring kula partners into systems of balanced reciprocity and, in so doing, create alliances that are critical in settling disputes and maintaining peace. This is particularly important because there is no formal government incorporating the different groups that take active roles in the kula. In addition, by moving products from island to island, kula exchanges increase the islanders' consumption of a wide range of goods, particularly those they do not produce, thus raising their standard of living.

Negative reciprocity is the unsociable extreme in exchange. It happens when trade is conducted for the purpose of material advantage and is based on the desire to get the better of a bargain. Negative reciprocity is characteristic of both impersonal and unfriendly transactions. Tribal and peasant societies often distinguish between the insider, whom it is morally wrong to cheat, and the outsider, from whom every advantage may be gained. Anthropologist Clyde Kluckhohn did important studies of the Navajo in the 1940s and 1950s. He reported that, among the Navajo, the rules for interaction vary with the situation; to deceive when trading with outsiders is a morally accepted practice. Even witchcraft techniques are considered permissible in trading with members of foreign tribes (Kluckhohn 1959).

Negative reciprocity helps explain some of the findings from the ultimatum game described in the opening of this chapter. Recall that in ultimatum, one person splits a quantity of money, offering a portion to another. If the second person accepts the split, they divide the money. If the second person rejects the offer, neither gets any money. Researchers found that the results of the game varied from society to society. In many kin-based societies, the first person was likely to offer only a small percentage of the money and the second person usually accepted it, whereas in market-based societies, the first person offered much larger percentages and the second was likely to reject small offers (Chibnik 2005; Henrich et al. 2004).

Negative reciprocity: Exchange conducted for the purpose of material advantage or the desire to get something for nothing.

A key aspect of the ultimatum game is that the players are anonymous. In kin-based societies, negative reciprocity often characterizes anonymous transactions. For players from such societies, offering little or nothing to an anonymous partner is both expected and proper. Because the second player does not expect to receive much from an anonymous person, he or she is likely to accept very small offers.

Using Anthropology: Gifts, Bribes, and Social Networks

Many classic anthropological studies have focused on gift exchange in relatively small societies without money. However, using gifts to build social networks that may serve instrumental purposes may be part of large, current-day monetized societies as well. When this happens, it raises important questions about the line between a gift and a bribe. Good examples of this come from the countries of the former Soviet Union (though they certainly exist in our own society as well). In Soviet times (1917–1991), having at least some money was relatively common, but goods that could be bought with the money were scarce. In this condition, a system called *blat* pervaded many aspects of life. *Blat* referred to social connections, reinforced by gift giving, that allowed people to gain access to goods, services, employment, and often admission to universities. A proverb of the era said "better 100 friends than 100 rubles."

In the post-Soviet Union era, *blat* and other arrangements persist but they are increasingly complicated. Now, goods are widely available in most places in the former Soviet Union, but money to buy them is not. Abel Polese (2008) examines gift giving and corruption in post-Soviet Ukraine and finds a wide gray area between the two. The Ukrainian government is unable to adequately provide many services to its citizens. Salaries paid to government workers including doctors and teachers are inadequate to cover their living expenses. In this context, money and goods received by doctors and teachers from their patients and students are extremely important to their economic survival. However, are these gifts or bribes? From a U.S. perspective, they are bribes and evidence of corruption. Receiving gifts of any kind is illegal in Ukraine but the government permits these practices to avoid paying higher wages. The perspective of the participants themselves is nuanced. In at least some cases, people giving gifts and payments see these as signs of gratitude rather than bribes. For many, the sequence of events is important: A payment received before taking an exam or undergoing surgery is a bribe, payment afterwards, a gift. The specific actions of the service provider also make a difference. Teachers may allow students to pass exams and doctors might provide services in expectation of receiving a gift, but they believe that is

Ukraine.

© Cengage Learning 2015

different from requiring an up-front payment. As one of Polese's informants expressed it: "If I receive it, it's a gift. If I demand it, then it is a bribe" (Polese 2008:53).

Neither gift givers nor gift receivers understand their actions as simple corruption. But neither do these transactions create the ongoing social ties typical of most gift giving. Such transactions are not exactly gifts and not exactly bribes, and Polese proposes the term *brift,* halfway between gift and bribe to describe them. He argues that brifting is a fundamental aspect of Ukrainian social life and that although brifts in some cases do harm Ukraine's social and economic structures, they are "complementary to an economic system that does not guarantee even distribution of welfare and needs to be somehow 'helped'" in many other cases (2008:57). The government, he suggests, needs to narrow its understanding of corruption to concentrate its energies on those things worth fighting for and avoid "going against the socioeconomic structures of the country" (2008:58).

Redistribution

In **redistribution**, goods are collected from or contributed by members of a group and then given out to the group in a new pattern. Thus, redistribution involves a social center to which goods are brought and from which they are distributed. Redistribution occurs in many different contexts. In household food sharing, pooled resources are reallocated among family members. In state societies, redistribution is achieved through taxation.

Redistribution can be especially important in societies where political organization includes bigmen, self-made leaders who gain power and authority through personal achievement. Such individuals collect goods and food from their supporters. Often these items are redistributed back in communal feasts, which the bigman sponsors to sustain his political power and raise his prestige. Redistribution also occurred in some chiefdoms. In these cases, however, a distinct hierarchy was involved. Chiefs collected goods and staple foods from many communities to support their households and attendants as well as to finance large public feasts that helped solidify their power (Earle 1987).

Potlatch feasting among Native American groups of the Pacific Northwest, including the Kwakwaka'wakw (Kwakiutl), Haida, and Tlingit, is a good example of redistribution. In these groups, potlatches were held to honor and to validate the rank of chiefs and other notables, usually in connection with births, deaths, and marriages (Rosman and Rubel 1971). A leader holding a potlatch called on his followers to supply food and other goods to be consumed and distributed during a feast to which he invited group members and rivals. The number of guests present and

Redistribution: Exchange in which goods are collected and then distributed to members of a group.

Potlatch: A form of redistribution involving competitive feasting practiced among Northwest Coast Native Americans.

Figure 6.6 Potlatches were competitive feasts held among Native Americans of the Northwest Pacific coast. Here, Tlingit chiefs at a potlatch pose for a photo in 1904, in Sitka, Alaska.

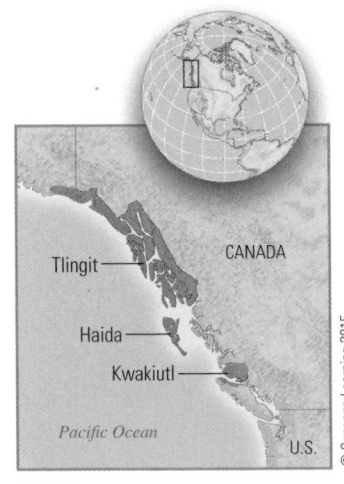

The Tlingit, Haida, and Kwakiutl of the Pacific Northwest Coast.

the amount of goods given away or destroyed revealed the wealth and prestige of the host chief. At a potlatch, the host publicly traced his line of descent and claimed the right to certain titles and privileges. Each of these claims was accompanied by giving away, and sometimes destroying, large quantities of food and goods, such as blankets and carved wooden boxes. As these goods were given or destroyed, the individual and his supporters boasted of their wealth and power.

The feasting and gifts given at a potlatch demonstrated the host's right to the titles and rights he claimed, and created prestige for him and his followers (see Figure 6.6). Guests either acknowledged the host's claims or refuted them by staging an even larger potlatch. Thus, potlatching involved friendship but also competition and rivalry.

From an economic perspective, the drive for prestige encouraged people to produce much more than they would otherwise. This increased the amount of work they did but also the amount of food and goods they produced and consumed. Because this wealth was given to people who traveled substantial distances to come to a potlatch, it was distributed to a fairly large population and ecological area.

Between 1884 and 1951, the Canadian government authorities outlawed potlatch, which they believed was wasteful and irrational (Bracken 1997). Since the 1950s, the potlatch has been revived as a symbol of tribal identity and cooperation rather than a major element in tribal economy.

Although the term *potlatch* (a Chinook word meaning "to give away") refers specifically to the feasting of Northwest Coast people, feasting is a widespread phenomenon. In many places, it plays an important role in establishing social identities, creating political power and inequalities as well as in accomplishing work and creating gender identities (Hayden and Villeneuve 2011). We see some elements of competitive feasting in our own society. There may be competition within families or within communities to throw the largest and most elaborate holiday parties, weddings, or coming-of-age celebrations (such as confirmations, bar or bat mitzvahs, and quinceañeras). A poll of nearly 18,000 brides who got married in 2011 put the average cost of a wedding in the United States at more than $27,000 (Reaney 2012), an extraordinary amount in a nation where the average family income that year was just slightly over $50,000. However, high-prestige weddings in many cases cost very much more. When Chelsea Clinton married hedge fund manager Marc Mezvinsky in 2010, ABC News estimated the price tag at more than $2 million with more than a quarter million spent on flowers alone (Mayerowitz 2010). And the 2004 wedding of Vanisha Mittal, Indian billionaire Lakshmi Mittal cost an estimated $60 million (Barlow 2011). A couple married in a brief, low-cost wedding and a couple married in a lavish ceremony have the same legal standing, but the weddings make different statements about power and prestige.

Redistribution may either increase or decrease inequality within a society. A **leveling mechanism** is a form of redistribution that tends to decrease social inequality. Leveling mechanisms force accumulated resources or capital to be used in ways that ensure social goals are considered along with economic ones. Leveling mechanisms take many different forms. For example, if generosity rather than the accumulation of wealth is the basis for prestige, those who desire power and prestige will distribute much of their wealth. Sometimes, as with the potlatch, this is accomplished through feasting. However, there are numerous other possibilities.

Leveling mechanism: A practice, value, or form of social organization that evens out wealth within a society.

Manning Nash (1961) and June Nash (1970) described a number of leveling mechanisms that operate in the village of Amatenango, in the Chiapas district of Mexico. One is the organization of production by households. As mentioned earlier, economic expansion and accumulation of wealth are limited where households, rather than business firms, are the productive units. A second is inheritance. Because all children share equally in the estate of a parent, large estates rarely persist over generations. Accusations of witchcraft are a third mechanism. People who accumulate more wealth than their neighbors or have wealth but are not generous may face such accusations, and those believed guilty of witchcraft may be killed.

Finally, in Amatenango, prosperous community members must hold religious and secular offices, called "cargos." Cargos are held for a year at a time and require their holders to perform civic duties and to pay for feasts and celebrations. Cargos are ranked, and those held by older, wealthier community members are more prestigious and more expensive. Such customs are common in southern Mexico and Central America and are referred to as **cargo systems**.

Cargo system: A ritual system common in Central and South America in which wealthy people are required to hold a series of costly ceremonial offices.

Anthropologists have shown that community obligations such as cargos help limit the economic gap between the relatively rich and the poor, but they do not eliminate it. In fact, they may help preserve social hierarchies (Chance and Taylor 1985). Wealthy individuals take expensive cargos that increase their prestige but do not severely impact their total wealth. They remain rich throughout their lives. The poor are generally unable to take cargos and remain poor throughout their lives. Thus, although some wealth is redistributed, economic differences are reinforced rather than equalized (Cancian 1989:147).

Market Exchange

Market exchange is the principal distribution mechanism in most of the world's societies today. Goods and services are bought and sold at a monetary price determined, at least in theory, by impersonal market forces and, in most cases, buyers and sellers are not connected by webs of kinship, association, or, in many cases, even community residence.

The market involves cultural and moral assumptions that are well illustrated by the results of the ultimatum game. As we noted earlier, ultimatum players from market economies tended to offer relatively large shares of their money to their partners, and these partners tended to reject low offers, even though this penalized both players. They played this way because they shared a culturally based understanding of the market. For an impersonal market to run smoothly, most participants must believe that they will usually be treated fairly by people they do not know. People who take advantage of anonymity to enrich themselves at others' expense spoil the market and must be punished. Thus, ultimatum players from market economies are often willing to reject low offers, taking a loss to show the other player that anonymous partners must bargain and exchange fairly.

Of course, the ideal of fair and impersonal exchange is just that— an ideal. Real markets are full of conflicts, inequities, and outright cheats. In our own society, there are clearly areas of commerce where people anticipate a certain amount of deceit. For example, merchants of used goods, particularly cars and machinery, often have reputations for shady practice. The continued importance of social connections among market participants is well illustrated by electronic marketplaces such as eBay, where buyers and sellers come close to true anonymity. In these cases, a sophisticated system of ratings simulates social connections and knowledge. This gives trading partners a degree of certainty that the terms of trade will be fair. But, eBay participants know that the fewer and worse the ratings of their trading partners, the greater the risk of a hostile exchange. The phrase *caveat emptor* (let the buyer beware) neatly captures the notion that the rules of even trade are not always in force.

In principle, the primary factors that set prices and wages in a market are related to supply and demand, and individuals participate freely in a market, choosing what they buy and sell. However, the market is almost never truly free. Most markets occur in social and cultural contexts that limit or forbid certain kinds of transactions. As we have seen, people in many societies gain access to land, labor, and some goods through ties of kinship or obligations of reciprocity and redistribution. In such places, markets, if they exist at all, are limited to a small number of goods. In theory, in a society dominated by the market, everything can be bought or sold. In practice, however, all societies limit what can be purchased legally. For example, we live in a market-dominated society but, for moral, social, and political reasons, there are restrictions on the sale of drugs, guns, children, and college degrees.

Many other factors interfere with the market in almost all societies. In some cases, wealthy and powerful individuals, organizations, and industries fix prices or wages, forcing people into wage labor or the market at disadvantageous terms. In other cases, monopolies, secret knowledge, private deals, and hidden connections may distort the market. In yet other cases, cultural ideas about the proper or "just" price of a good or service are more important than supply and demand. Sometimes, governments control or influence the prices of commodities such as grain, setting them either high (to encourage farmers) or low (to feed often rebellious city dwellers cheaply).

Capitalism

In the past 300 years, capitalism has become the world's predominant economic system. Capitalism expanded from northern Europe, North America, and Japan and has transformed economies worldwide, connecting them in a complex integrated international economy (Wallerstein 1995). We describe this historic process in Chapter 13, and we examine and analyze the problems and promises of the global economy in Chapter 14. Here we focus on describing capitalism and pointing out some of its most salient features.

In noncapitalist societies, most people produce goods to consume them, to trade them for other goods, or to pay rents and taxes. In capitalist societies, **firms** produce goods as a means to create wealth. For example, General Motors is not really in business to make cars. General Motors (GM) is in business to increase the wealth of its shareholders. Manufacturing automobiles is one (but only one) of the ways it achieves that end. GM is also heavily involved in banking and was historically involved in aviation, military contracting, and the production of consumer products such as refrigerators.

Productive resources become **capital** when they are used with the primary goal of increasing their owner's financial wealth. In capitalism, this becomes the most common (but not the only) use of such resources. **Capitalism** is further characterized by three fundamental attributes: First, most productive resources are owned by a small portion of the population. Banks, corporations, and wealthy individuals own the vast majority of farms, factories, and business of all kinds. Although many Americans invest in business through ownership of stocks, mutual funds, and retirement plans, ownership of substantial wealth is highly concentrated. For example, in the United States in 2002, almost half of all households owned some stocks or mutual funds (and thus owned some share of a

Firm: An institution composed of kin and/or nonkin that is organized primarily for financial gain.

Capital: Productive resources that are used with the primary goal of increasing their owner's financial wealth.

Capitalism: An economic system in which people work for wages, land and capital goods are privately owned, and capital is invested for profit.

business). However, the median value of these investments was $65,000 (Investment Company Institute 2005). According to G. William Domhoff (2013), in 2010, the wealthiest 10 percent of American households held over 90 percent of all stocks and mutual funds owned in the United States. Thus, although a great many people held some ownership of business, the vast majority was held by comparatively few.

The second attribute of capitalism is that most individuals' primary resource is their labor. To survive, people sell their labor for a salary or an hourly wage.

The third attribute is that the value of workers' contribution to production is always intended to be greater than the wages they receive. The difference between these two is the profit that accrues to those who own the productive resources, generally the shareholders of a corporation (Plattner 1989:382–384). The extremely high wages of some professional athletes and entertainers provide a good illustration of this principle. For example, Los Angeles Lakers player Kobe Bryant earned $23 million in the 2009–2010 season. For the team owners, his high salary was easily justified. They believed that his presence would enable them to earn substantially more than they paid him. This proved a good guess. With Bryant, the team won 92 percent more games than the average NBA team per dollar spent on player salary. Team owners Jerry Buss and Philip Anschutz saw the value of their investment rise from $288 million to over $600 million (Forbes 2009a). Because a good deal of this appreciation was due to Byrant's skill and popularity, the value of his labor was substantially greater than the wages he received. Because of his success, Bryant has been able to supplement his Lakers income with another $25 million in product endorsements (Forbes 2010). Although Bryant is undoubtedly very rich, his wealth pales before that of team owners Buss and Anschutz, whose combined wealth is well over $7 billion (most belonging to Anschutz, America's 37th richest person) (Forbes 2009b).

We should note here that in a capitalist society, the amount a person is paid has little to do with the value of their labor to society (a very difficult quantity to measure). Although we may be fans of Mr. Bryant, we will not suffer terribly when he eventually retires. And life continued unchanged for most of us during the 161-day NBA lockout of 2011. However, if sanitation workers were to strike or be locked out and we had no trash pickup for more than five months, almost all of us would be deeply affected, and our lives would be far more difficult. By this measure, sanitation workers are much more socially useful than professional basketball players, but they shouldn't expect to make millions any time soon.

Modern capitalist economies are dominated by market exchange, but this does not mean that people always experience their economy in terms of buying and selling at whatever price the market will bear. Capitalism always occurs within the context of other social relationships, and sometimes these provide a mask behind which it can hide. In other words, capitalist relationships are sometimes camouflaged by family ties or social obligations. When this happens, entrepreneurs may be able to extract extra profits. The production of knitted sweaters in Turkey is a good example of this.

Turkey produces many goods and services used in wealthy capitalist nations. Most of the inhabitants of Istanbul, its largest city, are part of a capitalist economy selling their labor in enterprises aimed at generating a profit. However, as Jenny B. White (1994) reports, many of them, particularly women, understand their work in terms of reciprocity and kin obligations rather than capitalism and the marketplace.

Turkey is a patrilineal and patriarchal society. Turkish women live in complex social networks characterized by social obligations and relations of reciprocity. To a great degree, they measure their worth by the work they do for family members, including parents, in-laws, husbands, and children. Being a good woman means laboring for relatives.

Married women live with their husband's family and are expected to manage the household and to keep their hands busy with knitting and other skilled tasks (see Figure 6.7). Such tasks are not considered work (in the sense of work outside of the home) but are rather understood as necessary obligations of married life.

Business in Turkey is often patterned on social life, and this can be seen clearly in women's piecework. Women produce garments that are sold in the United States and other Western nations. The materials they use are generally supplied to them by an organizer, who also finds a buyer for the finished product. The organizers often are relatives, neighbors, and friends of the women who do the work.

In the neighborhood White (1994:13) investigated, almost everyone believed that women should not work for money, yet about two-thirds of women are involved in piecework. How is this contradiction explained? The women who do it see piecework as a way for them to keep their hands busy and thus part of their duty as wives rather than a form of paid labor. Their work forms part of their obligation to their husband's family and to organizers with whom they have social connections, and they consider it a gift of labor. They understand the payments they receive as gifts from someone with whom they have an established social relationship.

Yaacov Dagan/Alamy

Figure 6.7 For many Turkish women, knitting is a social obligation. This is one factor that leads them to accept very low wages for sweaters they knit. However, these sweaters enter a capitalist trade system and are sold for high prices in wealthy nations.

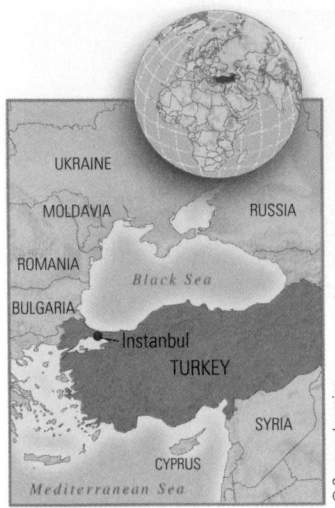

Turkey.

Because the women's work is set within a context of global capitalism, work organizers may be friends and neighbors, but they are also capitalist entrepreneurs hoping to make money. In the end, women produce goods for the capitalist marketplace, and their wages ultimately derive from that market. However, these capitalist relationships are masked by social relations of balanced or generalized reciprocity with the labor organizer. Because they understand their work in terms of a social obligation, they rarely think about how much they are earning per hour or how they might use their time and talents to make more money. Thus, they are willing to accept far lower wages than might otherwise be the case.

In some ways, the system serves the women well. They are able to fill their roles as wives and in-laws, and their social connections with labor organizers may give them some degree of security from the ravages of the marketplace. This is important in a country such as Turkey, where most people have little money and social services are few. However, it is clear that the greatest beneficiaries of this system are firms and consumers in wealthy nations. The fact that reciprocity masks capitalism for poor women in Turkey allows rich consumers in Europe and the United States to buy hand-knitted sweaters at very low prices, and the firms based in these nations to make windfall profits.

It would be difficult to find any people in the world today not affected by capitalist markets. For the most part, members of traditional societies enter the market as low-wage laborers. The wealth they produce accrues to elites within poor nations as well as to owners and consumers in wealthy nations (Wolf 1982). The case of the Turkish women illustrates some of the ways in which this process takes place. Not all societies are able to make such accommodations, however, and the expansion of capitalism and political power has been accompanied by the wide-scale destruction of traditional societies. Chapter 13 examines this process in some detail.

Resistance to Capitalism

Capitalism is a powerful economic system. It undoubtedly provides a greater number of goods and services to larger populations than do other ways of organizing an economy, but at a cost. When some individuals or groups own or control basic resources, others must inevitably be denied access to them. This results in permanently differentiated economic and social classes. Capitalism dictates that there will always be rich and poor. Often, part of the population lives in extreme poverty, without access to basic resources. In American society, this includes the homeless, the landless rural poor, and the permanently unemployed.

Although some individuals probably act as capitalists in most monetized economies, societies organized primarily by capitalism are a late development in the history of humankind. Such societies were not a natural and inevitable outcome of economic evolution. Rather, they owe their origin to the specific conditions of the Industrial Revolution in Europe in the 18th and 19th centuries and have become increasingly prevalent in the world in the past 150 years.

Although the capitalist economy has expanded in every part of the world, there probably are no countries where all of the population is directly involved in it. Noncapitalist groups, often indigenous people, remain. These people are often pushed to areas such as the jungles of Brazil or the border between Pakistan and Afghanistan where the terrain or climate make agriculture unprofitable and military control expensive and difficult. However, mass-produced goods, media, and fashions from capitalist societies are easily found, even in these locations. In other places, issues of race, gender, and ethnicity prevent people from fully participating in the capitalist economy.

Despite the international success of capitalism, it has from its origins encountered frequent and sometimes violent resistance. In the early 19th century, Luddites smashed the weaving machines of early capitalists in an attempt to preserve skilled labor and cottage industry. By the late 19th and early 20th centuries, radical unions such as the Industrial Workers of the World (IWW) campaigned for the abolition of capitalism and wage labor. In the United States by the mid-20th century, unions they had largely become bulwarks of capitalism, arguing for better wages and working conditions but fully supporting the fundamental ideas of wage labor and capitalist ownership. However, anticapitalist union activity continued elsewhere in the Western world, and by the 1960s, protest against capitalism had, in some places, moved to the streets. A good example of this is the wave of student protests that broke out across Europe, Japan, and the United States in 1967 and 1968. Protests in France were particularly widespread with workers joining student protesters and bringing the nation to the brink of revolution. More recently, protests at the meetings of the World Bank, International Monetary Fund, and World Trade Organization in Seattle (1999), Washington (2000), Prague (2000), Oslo (2002), and numerous other places have resulted in vandalism, clashes with police, mass arrests, and occasional deaths. In the wake of the 2008 financial crisis, protests broke out again in many places. The best known of these was the Occupy movement of 2011, which began in New York but rapidly became global with rallies held in more than 900 cities throughout the world (Adam 2011). Although support for the movement eventually diminished, in October 2011, a CBS News/*New York Times* poll showed that 43 percent of Americans agreed with the

Figure 6.8 Garage sales, gardening, raising livestock, and doing odd jobs help many Americans avoid full participation in the capitalist economy.

views of the Occupy movement and two-thirds thought that money and wealth were unfairly distributed in the United States (Montopoli 2011).

In addition to taking to the street in protest, people resist capitalism in other, more subtle ways. The fundamental social arrangement of capitalism is that most people sell their labor for wages to capitalists who reinvest profit to create greater wealth. However, many people in the United States and throughout the world neither work for wages nor hire workers and make investments to increase their wealth. Many people throughout the United States get by using a combination of techniques that include subsistence gardening, garage sales, and trading their labor with others (see Figure 6.8). They work for others only when they absolutely must, taking part-time jobs or leaving employment as soon as they have enough cash for an immediate need (Halperin 1990; Hansen 1995). And this is not only an American phenomenon: Wilson found that people who drove horse carriages (jarveys) in Ireland were often fleeing wage labor. Other members of their families worked in factories and they had previous experience of wage labor themselves but had given it up. One said that even if they paid him twice as much to work in a factory, he'd rather drive a carriage (2003:303).

In the United States, individuals are often very proud of their ability to support themselves outside the boundaries of wage labor. However, the fact that they resist principal elements of capitalism (perhaps unknowingly) in so doing reminds us that economic systems are not natural and inevitable. The ways in which we organize our economy are the result of history, politics, economics, and individual choices—a creation of culture, not natural law.

BRINGING IT BACK HOME:
PRODUCT ANTHROPOLOGY

In *Creating Breakthrough Products,* Jonathan Cagan and Craig M. Vogel (2002) write that the most promising area of research is "new product ethnography." They argue that anthropologists can offer vital services to business, turning the techniques and theoretical perspectives of anthropology into a resource for the corporate world. Those who promote it argue that anthropologists can and should provide vital information that helps corporations design and market products in ways that maximize their profits. New companies such as ReD Associates focus specifically on anthropological consulting. ReD's clients include Adidas, Carlsberg, Intel, Lego, and Samsung. Technology companies are among the biggest consumers of anthropology, and Microsoft is among the world's largest employers of anthropologists (Wood 2013).

One of the most successful examples of new product ethnography was the creation of Yoplait's Go-Gurt. In focus groups, mothers reported that they always wanted to provide complex, healthy breakfasts for their children. However, what mothers said was quite different from what they did. Ethnographic fieldwork by anthropologist Susan Squires and Bryan Byrne (2002) showed that working parents, complicated schedules, and different notions about what constitutes a "good" breakfast meant that mothers had difficulties producing breakfasts and kids frequently did not eat them. The solution, Go-Gurt, was portable, sweet, brightly colored, and made claims to be nutritious.

In many ways, product anthropology and other uses of anthropology in business and government are promising breakthroughs. Since the founding days of the discipline, anthropologists have wanted their voices heard by people outside the university. Now they are increasingly employed in different capacities in consumer research, product design, and marketing. On the one hand, this results in a better fit between products and consumers as well as higher profits for corporations. From the PT Cruiser (partially designed by French anthropologist G. Clotaire Rapaille) to computer software, toothbrushes, cookware, and ethnobanking (developing banking services for ethnic target groups), anthropologists have made products more friendly and businesses more money. As companies create products for markets around the globe, anthropologists have valuable contributions to make to design, production, and marketing. On the other hand, the involvement of anthropologists in these fields raises difficult ethical problems. For example, anthropologists mine information

from their informants. If corporations then profit from this information, is payment owed to the informants? Key consumers of anthropological research are beverage and packaged food companies, but should anthropologists be promoting the sale of sugary drinks and junk food? Should anthropology be a way to help corporations make more money?

◼ YOU DECIDE:

1. Historically, the introduction of cheap, mass-produced manufactured goods has undercut existing economies and drawn people into the capitalist economy, generally as consumers of low-quality merchandise and low-paid wage earners. Given this, should anthropologists be involved in the design and marketing of products to groups about which they have expertise?
2. The advance of capitalism into all areas of the world has been relentless. With the aid of anthropologists, corporations can produce products that meet local needs and are marketed in culturally appropriate ways. The alternative often is inappropriate, poorly designed, and poorly marketed products. Given this, can anthropologists justifiably refuse to work with corporations?
3. Perhaps the previous two questions present a false dichotomy. What are some positions that anthropologists might take between these two? Are they practicable in the real world without the security of a university appointment?

◼ CHAPTER SUMMARY

1. What cultural economic principles are demonstrated by the dictator and ultimatum games? The games show that people's economic behavior differs from culture to culture. Some of this variation is systematic. People from market-oriented societies tend to play differently than those from societies with other forms of economic organization.
2. What is economics, and how is it related to culture? Economics is the study of the ways people make choices within the value systems of their societies. These choices then determine how those societies use their scarce resources to produce and distribute goods and services. Hence, people in different societies are motivated by different principles and different goods.
3. Give examples of productive resources and how access to them changes at different levels of social complexity. In every society,

certain goods are productive resources. Such resources generally include land, labor, and knowledge. Societies have systems by which such resources are allocated to their members. As social complexity increases, access to productive resources becomes increasingly more restricted.

4. How is labor organized in most preindustrial and peasant societies? Labor must be organized in specific ways to produce goods. In most preindustrial and peasant economies, labor is organized by the household or kin group. Work that people both perform and receive locates them with respect to their social network and often is integral to their identity.

5. What is the relationship between population and social complexity? As societies become more populous, the number of specialized jobs found in them increases. Current-day wealthy societies have extremely high degrees of specialization. This creates great efficiency but involves changing notions of identity and often has heavy human costs.

6. What three general mechanisms for the distribution of goods and services are described in this chapter? In all societies, there are systems for distributing and consuming goods and services. Every society uses some combination of reciprocity, redistribution, and the market to redistribute goods and services and to provide patterns and standards for their consumption.

7. What is reciprocity and what are three different types of reciprocity? Exchange among people of similar status is characterized by reciprocity. As social distance among individuals increases, the characteristic form of reciprocity tends to change from generalized, to balanced, and, sometimes, to negative. The kula trade in the South Pacific provides an example of balanced reciprocity.

8. What is redistribution, and in what kinds of societies is it commonly found? In redistribution, goods are collected by a central individual or office and then distributed in a new pattern. Redistribution is characteristic of exchange in chiefdoms as well as parts of state-level economy. Potlatch among Pacific Northwest coastal Native Americans provides an example of redistribution.

9. What are the chief characteristics of market exchange, and where is it found? In market exchange, goods and services are bought and sold at a money price determined, at least in theory, by the impersonal forces of supply and demand. Market change is found in most societies but is the main economic mechanism of current-day states.

10. What are the defining characteristics of capitalism? In capitalism, the owners of productive resources use them to increase their financial wealth. In capitalist societies, a small percentage of the population primarily hold productive resources, most people sell their labor for wages, and the value of people's labor is always more than the wages they receive. Capitalism can be masked by other relationships such as reciprocity.

11. Where is resistance to capitalism found, and what forms does it take? Although capitalism is ubiquitous around the world, many people resist it, sometimes protesting violently against it. People also resist capitalism by avoiding wage labor and, to some degree, participation in the market.

KEY TERMS

Balanced reciprocity
Capital
Capitalism
Cargo system
Division of labor
Economic system
Economics
Firm
Generalized reciprocity
Household

Kula ring
Leveling mechanism
Market exchange
Negative reciprocity
Potlatch
Prestige
Productive resources
Reciprocity
Redistribution

Courtesy of Joan Gregg

The rise of the state is a key event in human political organization. This photograph illustrates the view of the Sun Gate in Machu Picchu, the center of the Inca Empire, which emerged as a result of specific ecological conditions. It was destroyed by the Spanish conquistadors and is now a global destination for archeologists, tourists, and students.

CHAPTER 7

POLITICAL ORGANIZATION

LEARNING OBJECTIVES

After you have read this chapter, you will be able to:

△ Define the different aspects of political process, and apply these to the Arab Spring.

△ Contrast egalitarian, rank, and stratified societies, illustrating the key features of each.

△ List the major features of leadership in band, tribal, chiefdom, and state-level societies.

△ Assess the role that warfare plays in different forms of political organization.

△ Compare the Asante and the United States to explain how political ideology helps maintain social stratification in state-level societies.

△ Describe some factors that support nationalism in nation-states.

△ Explain how anthropology contributes to our understanding of the roles of ethnic and indigenous groups in the maintenance of nation-states.

THE ARAB SPRING

O N December 17, 2010, Mohamed Bouazizi, a young man who lived in a remote town in Tunisia, burned himself to death to protest against police corruption and brutality after the police confiscated his unlicensed vegetable cart, which was his only source of income. This act led to widespread, initially peaceful protests and also riots throughout Tunisia; by April 2011, the "Arab Spring" in which protesters had successfully overthrown the police states of Tunisia, Egypt, and Libya, among others, as well as the leaders who ruled them, was well under way. Ironically, the military and monarchial dictatorships in the Arab world were themselves a result of mass political movements in the 1950s and 1960s, when these nations overthrew colonial control. What partly invigorated the protests, once they were started, was the somewhat surprising realization that these "old, rotten regimes" could be brought down by popular protests (Lynch 2012).

The wake of the Arab Spring provokes analysis of the many and complicated political processes involved in political organization and political change. The most common word used by those actually engaged in the Arab liberation struggle is *revolution,* although the terms *intifada* (uprising) and *awakening* are also used. For some, the Arab Spring is a successful revolution because it deposed totalitarian governments and instituted the writing of new, more democratically influenced constitutions. Others despair at what they see as waste, destruction, and death in the wake of these protests, which began as a fight for a better life, but seem to have resulted in conflict, often violent, between ethnic, religious, and tribal groups, as well as conflict between different Islamic religious factions, and between Islamists and secularists (Agha and Malley 2012). The mostly young protestors who initially organized the protests, experiencing poverty and unemployment, and using social media like Twitter, Facebook, and YouTube, have been superseded by more well-organized groups, like the Muslim Brotherhood in Egypt, which has been operating underground in Egypt for decades.

The Arab uprisings, which now includes the civil war in Syria, are also influenced by the global political context, for example, the alliance between Syria, Russia, and China; an alliance between the United States and Saudi Arabia, which funds extreme Islamism that inspires anti-American jihadists; the links between the Shiite government in Syria with the Shiite-dominated government in Iraq, liberated by the United States, who have a natural alliance with the Shiite-dominated government of Iran, a nation with very hostile relations with the United States; and the importance of international military assistance in the overthrow of Muammar Qaddafi in Libya. Central to the uprisings of the Arab Spring were demands for democracy, open government, and an end to corruption, but for these demands to succeed, poverty and unemployment, especially in countries like Egypt and Tunisia, would have to be addressed. Where it will all end is still uncertain, and will be for many years to come.

The Arab Spring—and other protest movements, such as Occupy Wall Street and its spin-offs—demonstrate the fine line between rebellion and revolution; how rebellions and uprisings may end up as revolutions; why some revolutions fail or succeed—history demonstrates the importance of "outside help" in this regard, much as the success of the American Revolution was aided by France; and the role of violence or nonviolence in the outcomes (Roberts and Ash 2009).

Rebellion, which is the attempt of one group to reallocate power and resources within an existing political structure, and **revolution**, which is an attempt to overthrow the existing political structure and put another type of political structure in its place, are both examples of political process. The Arab Spring emphasizes a major theme in this chapter: Political organization and political process can only be understood in their wider cultural, historical, economic, and political contexts. Political organization and the uses of power grow out of specific situations and change as these situations also change.

The Arab Spring exemplifies the complexity of political process— the ways in which groups and individuals organize to use power and authority to achieve various public goals. These goals may benefit the larger society or they may benefit only smaller groups or individuals. Decisions and activities by groups and individuals may be motivated by material profit, prestige, altruism, survival, or any combination of motives, but are usually justified by reference to the public good.

The study of political processes illustrates how new kinds of political organization and ideologies develop and how power changes hands, as well as how political structures and political organization may be used to stabilize a social order, avoid or resolve conflicts, and promote the general welfare, but they may also be used to contest prevailing political ideologies and change or even destroy existing political systems. Factions, which are informal alliances within a group or society, as well as governments, use diverse means to gain their ends. These may include violence and terror, behind-the-scenes manipulation, peaceful protest, the ballot box, and political lobbying, propaganda, or bribery.

Rebellion: The attempt of a group within society to force a redistribution of resources and power.

Revolution: An attempt to overthrow an existing form of political organization and put another type of political structure in its place.

◢ POLITICAL ORGANIZATION

political organization: The patterned ways in which power is legitimately used in a society to regulate behavior, maintain social order, make collective decisions, and deal with social disorder.

Political organization is about how societies use power to address the universal problem of how to maintain themselves over time with a minimum of social disorder and social discontent. This means that every society must make and implement decisions affecting the whole society; provide a means of managing conflicts, dissent, and deviance; and generally regulate behavior so that it is consistent with social order.

◣ Power and Authority

power: The ability to impose one's will on others.

Power is the ability to exercise one's will over others: Sources of power are ultimately based on the control of resources that people need or desire. Anthropologists examine the sources and uses of power and analyze how political organization is related to other cultural patterns and social institutions. Power differs from **authority**, which is the socially approved, or legitimate, use of power. An individual's authority may be based on personal characteristics, such as knowledge, ability, social status, and respect. Political leaders have authority based on their legitimate occupation of public office, but they may also wield power through their control of resources and/or control over the use of force or knowledge. Power can exist without authority: An armed robber has power, but no authority.

Authority: The ability to cause others to act based on characteristics such as honor, status, knowledge, ability, respect, or the holding of formal public office.

Political ideology: The shared beliefs and values that legitimize the distribution and use of power in a particular society.

The shared values and beliefs that legitimate the distribution and uses of power and authority in a particular society are called its **political ideology**. A political ideology may be widely, though not universally shared; the sources of power may be coercive, based on force or the threat of force rather than consensual, or more likely, both. Types of political organizations differ in the degree to which they use coercion or consensus—a generally agreed-upon political ideology—to achieve and maintain social order.

◣ Social Control and Conflict Management

Because all societies contain conflict, all societies must manage conflict and persuade individuals to conform to (at least most of) society's norms if they are to survive. In small-scale societies, organized through kinship, conformity mainly results from the internalization of norms and values as part of enculturation and from many informal processes and sanctions. Internalization of norms also regulates behavior in complex, socially stratified state societies, but the control of the state over many social institutions and regulatory processes, including the mobilization of force, is also crucial.

Those who transgress society's rules are handled differently in different types of societies (see Figure 7.1). In small-scale societies, informal mechanisms of social interaction such as ridicule, avoidance, or gossip are effective means of social control because most people value the esteem of (at least some) others, and because marginalized people may also be restricted from access to resources. These mechanisms may also be effective when used against society's leaders (Besnier 2009).

Informal sanctions, such as gossip or ridicule, are also effective in small groups in complex and industrialized societies. Bullying, which combines gossip and ridicule, in both face-to-face encounters and on social media, has become an important sanction among teenagers in U.S. schools, leading some of those "picked on" even to commit suicide. In some small-scale societies, fear of witchcraft accusations or other supernatural interventions is widely used to ensure social control of "deviants," those who try to stand above the group, are malicious, have a nasty temper, or refuse to share according to group norms (Evans-Prichard 1958/1937). Avoidance works in small-scale groups and societies because where cooperative action is necessary to succeed or even to survive, a person shunned by others is at a great psychological and economic disadvantage.

Law: A means of social control and dispute management through the systematic application of force by a politically constituted authority.

Law refers to the systematic application of force by a constituted authority in society (S. Moore 1978:220). Law is applied when a social norm is so important that its violation authorizes the community, or some part of it, to punish an offender, resolve a conflict, or redress a wrong. In every society, some offenses are considered so disruptive that force or the threat of force is applied. In this sense, law is universal, although in small-scale societies it is most often embedded in other social institutions, like kinship relations or religion, and is most often directed at maintaining existing social relationships. In more complex, stratified societies, law's functions belong to separate legal institutions, such as a police force, courts, and a prison system, and punishment is aimed at asserting society's control over the individual, rather than repairing damaged social relationships (see p. 168).

Courtesy of Andrew Arno

Figure 7.1 This informal kava drinking circle is an important means of resolving disputes in Fiji and other Pacific Islands. Unlike the adversary process of law, informal processes attempt to reconcile the disputants.

⬛ TYPES OF POLITICAL ORGANIZATION

Band: A small group of people related by blood or marriage, who live together and are loosely associated with a territory in which they forage.

Tribe: A culturally distinct population whose members consider themselves descended from the same ancestor.

Chiefdom: A society with social ranking in which political integration is achieved through an office of centralized leadership called the chief.

State: A hierarchical, centralized form of political organization in which a central government has a legal monopoly over the use of force.

social differentiation: The relative access individuals and groups have to basic material resources, wealth, power, and prestige.

Leadership: The ability to direct an enterprise or action.

egalitarian society: A society in which no individual or group has more privileged access to resources, power, or prestige than any other.

rank society: A society characterized by institutionalized differences in prestige but no important restrictions on access to basic resources.

stratified society: A society characterized by formal, permanent social and economic inequality in which some people are denied access to basic resources.

elites: The social strata that has differential access to all culturally valued resources, whether power, wealth, or prestige, and possessively protects its control over these resources.

Systems of political organization are related to social complexity, the degree to which political roles, institutions, and processes are centralized and differentiated from other aspects of social organization or embedded within other social institutions. Anthropologists identify four main types of social complexity: **bands**, **tribes**, **chiefdoms**, and **states**. Each of these types of societies is associated with a characteristic way in which people make a living; a dominant principle of economic exchange (see Chapter 6); characteristic forms of leadership and social control; and different systems of **social differentiation**, or social hierarchy (Service 1962). Inequalities exist in all societies, but not all societies formally recognize these differences, nor do these inequalities necessarily affect access to important resources.

In smaller-scale nonindustrial societies such as bands, tribes, and chiefdoms, the uses of power and authority, decision making, and the coordination and regulation of human behavior are highly integrated. Power and authority do not operate independently but are embedded in other social institutions such as kinship, economics, and religion. In these societies, **leadership**, the ability to direct an enterprise, may be based in political office or individual authority, but it may also be based on an individual's position as the head of a kinship group; on supernatural connections and interventions; or on the relative access and control individuals and groups have over basic material resources, wealth, power, and prestige.

Anthropologists define three ideal types of social differentiation: *egalitarian societies, rank societies,* and *stratified societies.* In **egalitarian societies**, individual (as well as age and gender) distinctions are recognized, but no individual or group is barred from access to material resources or has power over others. There are no rules of inheritance by which some individuals accumulate material goods or prestige passed down over generations. Unlike egalitarian societies, **rank societies** recognize formal differences among individuals and groups in prestige and symbolic resources, and these may be passed on through inheritance. However, there are no important restrictions on access to basic resources, and all individuals can obtain the material necessities for survival through their membership in kinship groups.

In **stratified societies**, there are formal and permanent social and economic inequalities. Wealth, prestige, and office are frequently passed down over generations, establishing relatively permanent elites. **Elites** are those who have maximum access to all culturally valued resources, whether power, wealth, or prestige, and possessively protect their control over these resources. In stratified societies, some individuals and groups are also systemically denied access to the basic material resources needed to survive. Thus, stratified societies are characterized by permanent and wide differences among groups and individuals in their standard of living, security, prestige, political power, and the opportunity to fulfill one's potential. All contemporary industrialized nations are stratified societies, even those such as the United States or socialist societies like Cuba, which proclaim equality as a dominant value.

Political organization, social differentiation, and social complexity can be analyzed separately, but in reality, these intersect with each other in significant ways. The following types of societies described are ideal types; the reality is much more complex as history, geography, culture, and other factors all affect the specific characteristics of any particular society. Although many anthropologists reject the evolutionary implications of these typologies (the idea that societies develop on a single trajectory from simpler bands to more complex states), the typologies are useful in grasping some of the varieties of political organization.

Band Societies

A band is a small group of people (usually 20 to 50) belonging to extended families who live together and are loosely associated to a territory in which they make a living. Foragers generally live in bands, which tend to be egalitarian and mainly use generalized or balanced reciprocity as mechanisms of exchange. Band societies have minimal role specialization or differences of wealth, prestige, or power. Bands are fairly independent of one another, with few higher levels of social integration or centralized mechanisms of leadership. Ties between bands are mainly established by marriage and kinship, and also by trading relations. Band membership is flexible, with individuals easily changing residence from one band to another. The flexibility of band organization is particularly adaptive for a foraging way of life and low population density.

Band societies have no formal leadership; decision making is by consensus. Leaders in foraging bands are usually the elders, whose experience, knowledge of group traditions, special skills or success in foraging, and generosity are sources of prestige. Leaders cannot enforce their decisions; they can only persuade, attracting others to their leadership based on the basis of past performance. Among some Inuit, for example, a local leader is called "The One to Whom All Listen," "He Who Thinks," or "He Who Knows Everything Best." Social order in band societies is primarily maintained through gossip, ridicule, and avoidance, or by supernatural interventions and sanctions, such as the public confessions directed by a shaman among the Inuit (Balikci 1970), a practice that may not serve them well in contemporary U.S. courts, where they may too freely admit guilt, which penalizes them in the adversarial legal system of the United States. Inuit bands sometimes resolve disputes through public contests that involve physical action, such as head butting or boxing, or verbal contests, like song duels, where the weapons are words—"little, sharp words like the wooden splinters which I hack off with my ax" (Hoebel 1974:93); these contests are publicly performed as part of the annual World Eskimo-Indian Olympic Games as a way of maintaining traditional Inuit culture.

Individual violence, such as the frequent fights over women among the Ju/'hoansi hunters of the Kalahari Desert in Africa, does occur in band societies, but because of the low level of technology, lack of formal leadership, and other ecological factors, organized warfare is largely absent. Bands have no warriors and no cultural or social support for sustained armed conflict (R. Lee 2003). When conflict gets too disruptive, bands may break up into smaller units, which separates people in extended conflict and prevents prolonged hostilities (Turnbull 1968).

Tribal Societies

A tribe is a culturally distinct population whose members view themselves as descended from the same ancestor. Tribes are mainly found among pastoralists and horticulturalists; they are generally egalitarian and exchange goods through reciprocity and redistribution. Like bands, most tribes do not have distinct or centralized political institutions or roles, and power and social control are embedded in other institutions, such as kinship or religion. Tribes are usually organized into unilineal kin groups (see pp. 227), who "own" the basic economic resources and are the units of political activity. These large unilineal kin groups are consistent with the larger populations in horticultural and pastoral societies, relative to foraging band societies.

The effective political unit in tribal societies may shift from independently operating local units of a tribe, who may even be in a state of ongoing violent conflict among themselves, to occasional higher-level unity, which most often occurs in response to the threat of attack from another society or the opportunity to attack another society. Among the Nuer of East Africa, lineages at different levels join each other to attack a common enemy (Evans-Pritchard 1968/1940), a process that steers competition away from close kin and helps stronger tribes who want to expand into nearby territories held by weaker tribes.

Another type of group that helps integrate tribal societies beyond kinship ties are those organized on the basis of age, in which individuals move through life's stages together in an organized progression. Age-based groups are mainly male, and have political and military functions. Because their members come from different kinship groups, they are an important basis for wider social integration throughout a tribal society. Other kinds of associations, such as the military societies among some Plains Indian tribes in North America, and the secret societies found in West Africa, such as the male Poro society and female Sande society, also help integrate tribal societies.

Tribal societies have leaders but no centralized government and few formal positions of authority. In New Guinea, for example, the typical leader is a "bigman"—a self-made man who gains power and authority through personal achievements rather than through holding office. A bigman begins as the leader of a small, localized kin group. He builds up his capital, mainly in the form of pigs, and attracts followers through generous loans, sponsoring feasts, purchasing high ranks in secret societies, helping his military allies, paying bridewealth for young men seeking wives, and other initiatives. These actions increase his reputation and put other people under obligation to him, thus further extending his alliances and influence.

The bigman is a fragile mechanism of tribal integration above the local level, however, because it does not create a permanent office but rather depends on the constant striving of an individual. Bigmen rise and fall, and their support disperses when they die. Big men are vulnerable because they must spur their local group on to ever greater production if they are to hold their own against other bigmen in the tribe. To maintain prestige, a bigman must give his competitors more than they can give him. Excessive giving to competitors means a bigman must begin to withhold gifts to his followers. The resulting discontent may lead to defection among his followers, or even murder of the bigman. Bigman status cannot be inherited so each aspiring bigman must begin anew to amass the wealth and forge the internal and external social relationships on which bigman status depends (Sahlins 1971) (see Figure 7.2).

Tribes mainly use informal mechanisms for controlling deviant behavior and settling conflicts. Compensation—a payment demanded by an aggrieved party to compensate for damage—is important in New Guinea, among other places. The amount of compensation is based on the severity of the act that precipitated the dispute, and the individual's kin group shares in the payment. Payment of compensation implies acceptance of responsibility by the donors and acceptance of compensation

© Irven devore/AnthroPohoto

Figure 7.2 This New Guinea man is a bigman, an informal leader in Melanesian tribal societies. His influence mainly depends on his ability to distribute resources, among which pigs are the most important.

implies a willingness to terminate the dispute by the recipients (Scaglion 1981). Demands for excessive compensation, however, may not resolve conflicts, but rather become the basis for further disputes (Ottley and Zorn 1983).

Mediation: A form of managing disputes that uses the offices of a third party to achieve voluntary agreement between the disputing parties.

Mediation, a common form of tribal conflict management, aims to resolve disputes through consensus rather than adversarial interactions so that the prior social relationship between the disputants is maintained and harmony is restored to the social order. Mediation involves a third party, either a go-between, or even the whole community, in resolving conflict between the disputants. Among the Kpelle of Liberia, a moot, or form of mediation, takes place before an assembled group of kinsmen and neighbors (Gibbs l988). After an opening ritual, the mediator reminds the audience of its common interests and close ties. The two disputing parties can question each other directly and the audience may also ask questions. After everyone has been heard, the mediator proposes a solution that expresses the consensus between the audience and the disputing parties. The party found to be at fault apologizes to the other, food and drink are ritually distributed, and reconciliation is achieved. Through the work of anthropologist James Gibbs, Kpelle mediation became a model for the emerging mediation movement now widely used in the United States to help settle conflict ranging from labor disputes to divorce proceedings (Fry and Bjorkqvist 1997).

War (warfare): A formally organized and culturally recognized pattern of collective violence directed toward other societies, or between segments within a larger society.

Warfare in Tribal Societies

Despite mainly using nonviolent methods of conflict resolution, tribal societies seem prone to a high degree of **warfare (war)**. Perhaps, in the absence of strong mechanisms for tribal integration through peaceful means, and few strong motivations to produce food beyond immediate needs, warfare may help regulate the balance between population and resources. With slash-and-burn horticulture, for example, it is much harder to clear forest for cultivation than to work land that has already been used. Thus, a local group may prefer to take land from other groups, by force if necessary, rather than expand into virgin forest (Vayda 1976).

The Yanomamo of Brazil.

Tribal warfare may also be linked to patrilineality and patrilocality, which promote male solidarity. This enables the use of force to resolve both local conflicts and warfare carried out over long distances, as occurred among the Iroquois of North America (Ember and Ember 1971). Most anthropologists generally agree that warfare is grounded in historical, material, cultural, social, and ecological conditions, and not in any biologically based human instinct for aggression.

The classic ethnography of intratribal violence and warfare describes the Yanomamo of the Amazon areas of Venezuela and Brazil, known as the "fierce people" (Chagnon 2013). According to their ethnographer, Napoleon Chagnon, the frequent and intense warfare among the Yanomamo is motivated mainly by revenge, which then becomes part of an ongoing cycle of intervillage hostility. Each village tries to preserve its autonomy by defeating its enemies in warfare, or in warlike aggressive raids and rituals such as chest pounding or club fighting. The cycle of hostility may initially grow out of sorcery accusations in a village where a death has occurred, or revenge for the abductions or rape of women, which then perpetuate more violence.

There is an ongoing debate in anthropology about the best way to explain Yanamamo warfare: Chagnon (2013) himself has most recently suggested a biological theory rejected by many anthropologists, who rather emphasize functional or historical factors. For example, Yanomamo warfare may function as a means of population control—not due to deaths in battle, but indirectly through female infanticide in this warlike society where aggressive males are more highly valued than females. The shortage of women resulting from female infanticide becomes a motivation for war as villages compete for women (Divale and Harris 1976).

Extreme intervillage Yanomamo violence may also have resulted from European contact, which caused severe depopulation due to European disease epidemics, fatal malnutrition, and intensified competition over European goods. Metal machetes, axes, and knives are very useful for horticulturalists, and the introduction of firearms substantially increased warfare fatalities. By the 1960s, Yanomamo increasingly settled around European outposts such as missionary stations to more easily acquire these goods, and this population concentration led to the depletion of game. The decline of the availability of meat undermined cultural norms of reciprocity, and this also increased conflict within and between villages. These historical factors complement other explanations of Yanomamo "fierceness" and raise questions about how fierce the Yanomamo actually are (Ferguson 1992).

Chiefdoms

Although there is a great diversity among chiefdoms (Earle 1987), a chiefdom may be defined as "an autonomous political unit comprising a number of villages or communities under the permanent control of a paramount chief" (Carneiro 1981:45). Chiefdoms are different from tribes because, unlike tribes in which all social segments are structurally and functionally similar, chiefdoms are made up of social parts that are structurally and functionally different from one another. Chiefdoms may be the first step in integrating villages as units within multilevel forms of political organization (Carneiro 1981).

Chiefdoms vary greatly in their social complexity (Peoples 1990), ranging from simpler tribal structures to those with elaborate systems of social stratification. They may consist of large settlements that function as administrative centers, surrounded by smaller villages. Each geographical unit within a chiefdom may also have its own chief or council. Chiefdoms, like tribes, are also organized through kinship; unlike tribes, however, chiefdoms have centralized leadership vested in the political office of the chief. Chiefs are born to the office and are often sustained in it by religious authority and genealogical records.

Chiefdoms are rank societies, generally based on highly productive horticulture or pastoralism (highly productive foragers on the northwest coast of North America are exceptions), which permit sufficient accumulation of food so that chiefs can appropriate a surplus and redistribute it throughout the society. Redistribution is the main mode of exchange in rank societies, though balanced reciprocity is also important.

Anthropologists generally agree that the rise of chiefdoms is related to redistributive exchange and the ability to deploy labor. Goods are appropriated by the chief and then redistributed to the rest of society in feasts and rituals. Although redistribution is a primary support of the chief's power and prestige, chiefs may also control their communities by coercion or despotism (Earle 1987). Internal violence within chiefdoms is lower than in tribes because the chief has authority to resolve conflict and punish deviant individuals.

Complex chiefdoms are characteristic of Polynesia. Tahitian society was divided into the ariki, or chiefly families and important lineages; the raatira, who were the heads of less important families and lineages; and the manahune, the rest of the population. Social rank in Tahiti had economic, political, and religious aspects. Mana, a spiritual power, was possessed by all people, but in different degrees depending on rank (see Chapter 11, pp. 269). The ariki had the most mana because they were closest to the ancestral gods who are the source of mana. Elaborate taboos separated those with more mana from those with less and also regulated social relations among the three ranks. Higher-ranked people could not eat with those of lower rank; because men had higher rank than women and children, they could not eat with them. The highest-ranking ariki was so sacred that anything he touched became poison for those below him. In some Polynesian islands, the highest chief was kept completely away from other people and even used a special vocabulary that no one else was allowed to use.

Although a chief's authority is backed by his control of symbolic, supernatural, administrative, economic, and military power, violent competition for the office of chief does sometimes occur. Chiefdoms may also be rendered unstable if the burdens the chief imposes on the people greatly exceed the services they receive from him. Chiefs generally suppress any attempt at rebellion or threats from competitors and deal harshly with those who try to take their power. To emphasize the importance of this office for the society, offenses against a chief are often punished by death.

State Societies

A state is a socially stratified, centralized form of political organization in which a central government has a legal monopoly over the use of force. Generally speaking, states are based on agriculture and industrialism, but some, like the Asante state, described later, were also based on horticulture. In states, citizenship rather than kinship regulates social relations between the different social strata and defines a person's rights and duties. Units based on territory are central to state organization, and individuals belong to states through virtue of being born in a specific locale (or of parents from that locale). The state can incorporate a variety of political units, classes, and ethnic groups without disintegrating, making states more populous, heterogeneous, and powerful than any other kind of political organization.

States are characterized by **government**, an interrelated set of status roles that become separate from other aspects of social organization, such as kinship. **Bureaucracy**, an administrative hierarchy characterized by specialization of function and fixed rules, is essential to state functioning. The administrative divisions of a state are territorial units, like cities or districts. Each unit has its own government specifically concerned with making and enforcing public policy, although these governments are not independent of the central government.

State organization helps maintain a society in many ways. Through taxation, the state redistributes wealth and can stimulate or discourage various sorts of production. The state can order people to work on roads and buildings and to serve in armies, thus affecting the workforce available for other occupations. The state protects the exchange and distribution of goods by making travel safe for traders as they move from one place to another, by keeping peace in the marketplace, and by backing contracts. The many economic, coordinating, and controlling functions of states, in peace and war, require extensive record keeping, which gave rise to writing and systems of weights and measures. Urbanization developed in states, where cities arose as administrative, religious, and economic centers. These centers then stimulated important cultural achievements in science, art, architecture, and philosophy.

A key characteristic of state societies is the government's monopoly over the use of force. Most modern states use a code of law to make clear how and when force will be used and forbid individuals or groups to use

Government: An interrelated set of status roles that become separate from other aspects of social organization, such as kinship, in exercising control over a population.

Bureaucracy: Administrative hierarchy characterized by specialization of function and fixed rules.

force except under its authorization. Laws (usually written) are passed by authorized legislative bodies and enforced by formal and specialized institutions. Courts and police forces have the authority to punish deviants through fines, confiscation of property, imprisonment, and even death. In practice, in authoritarian states, rulers may "become the law," implementing and enforcing those laws that suit their own purposes. States frequently engage in warfare, which both increases and centralizes their power. Warfare enables states to extend the regulation of daily life; resolve internal conflict; and more stringently control information and communication channels.

Anthropologists explain the origin of the state in several ways. As historical and ecological situations change, a state may change its political structures, subdue a competing group, or establish regional dominance through trade. These initial shifts set off a chain reaction that may lead eventually to state formation. Ecological factors appear to have been dominant in the emergence of the Inca Empire in what is now Peru (Carneiro 1970). In this area, independent, dispersed farming villages were confined to narrow valleys bounded by the sea, the desert, or mountains. As the population grew, villages split and populations dispersed until all the available land was used up. At this point, more intensive methods of agriculture were applied to land already being farmed, and previously unusable land was brought under cultivation by terracing and irrigation. As population continued to increase, pressure for land intensified, resulting in war.

Because of the constraints of the environment, villages that lost wars had nowhere to go. To remain on their land, they had to accept a politically subordinate role. As more villages were defeated, the political organization of the area became more complex and chiefdoms developed. The warring units were now larger, and as conquest of larger areas continued, centralization of authority increased. Finally, the entire area was brought under the control of one chief. The next step was the conquest of weaker valley chiefdoms by stronger ones until powerful empires emerged, most notably that of the Inca. States may also emerge out of violent rivalry between kinship groups, where the "winners become the rulers," leading to early state formation as perhaps occurred in Mesopotamia, China, and Mexico (Otterbein 2010). The rulers controlled the population by repressive sanctions and waged war through their control of elite military organizations. As war between mature states declined, these states may have waged defensive war against other, early state aggressors.

The State and Social Stratification

Intensive cultivation enables a state's government to appropriate an economic surplus through taxation. This surplus supports the development of cities, economic and occupational specialization, and extensive trade. As specialized, non-food-producing elites emerge, economic and social inequalities become a key element in social structure. In state societies, unlike most chiefdoms, only a part of the surplus goes back to the people directly. The rest supports the activities of the state itself: maintaining administrative bureaucracies, standing armies, artists and craftworkers, and a priesthood, as well as supporting a ruling class in a luxurious lifestyle.

In state societies, elites are almost always a numerical minority, so the question arises of how they manage to dominate. One means is through **hegemony** (Gramsci 1971), a process whereby the state succeeds in promoting elite values among ordinary people in the larger society (Durrenberger and Doukas 2008:214). Although primarily serving elite interests, hegemonic cultural ideologies explain the existing social order as benefitting the society as a whole, repressing the greater benefits to the elite, a process we can see in the Asante state, described in the following, as well as in the contemporary United States.

Hegemony: The dominance of a political elite based on a close identification between their own goals and those of the larger society.

Hegemony, however, must be constantly reinforced, and elite interests cannot count on permanent stability; inequalities inherent in state societies continually pose substantial challenges to the status quo. Political and economic elites thus use many and varied economic, political, and symbolic means to ward off efforts to depose the government or to disrupt the privileges of vested interests. To the extent that elites provide reasonably effective protection of some basic economic and political rights, hegemony works to maintain the state, and the constant use of force may not be necessary. In totalitarian and authoritarian states, it is always there in the background, however, as a potential instrument of social control (Nagengast 1994:116).

Anthropological theories of the rise of the state tend to emphasize either conflict (Fried 1967) or integration (Service 1971). Integration, or functional theories, emphasize the benefits of the state to its members: its ability to provide the stability needed for growth and technological development, protection of the rights of its citizens, effective mechanisms for the peaceful settlement of disputes, protection of trade and financial arrangements, defense against external enemies, and an ability to expand. Conflict theories emphasize the emergence of the state as centrally related to protecting the power and privileges of an elite class through management of political ideology and force, when necessary.

The precolonial Asante state in West Africa is a good example of how hegemony established through the integration of power and wealth operates (McCaskie 1995) (see Figure 7.3). The highly productive Asante economy supported a complex social hierarchy ruled by the Asantehene, or king. The urban elite mainly transacted government business, performed elaborate state ceremonies, and produced luxury goods for

Jake KY Anderson/Alamy

Figure 7.3 This photo of an Asante chief of Ghana illustrates the point that as societies become more complex, specialized positions of authority, such as kings and chiefs, develop as centers of power and control.

the wealthy. The Asantehene's household daily consumed large quantities of locally grown food, along with imported delicacies such as mutton, turkey, duck, wild game, rice, European biscuits, tea, sugar, and wine, reflecting the association between elite status and material well-being.

Precolonial Asante society was composed of slaves, peasant commoners, urban specialists, and government officials, with the Asantehene and his royal family at the top of the hierarchy. Social stratification was based on achievement, competition, and accumulation of wealth, with many opportunities for social competition and social mobility. Though the state did use coercive force—espionage, detention, fines, confiscation of property, exile, and execution—a key factor in its stability for over 150 years was the government's success in promoting a core Asante value: that wealth and power went hand in hand, and that the accumulation of wealth by an individual was of benefit to the whole society. Accumulating wealth resulted in high office, and holding high office was justified by the accumulation and display of wealth, especially gold, and control of the rituals in which wealth was displayed.

The state accepted only gold for payment of fines, tributes, taxes, and levies. Those who could not pay had to provide land and laborers instead, enriching the state coffers. The state also permitted an individual to buy himself out of a mandatory death sentence with a payment of gold to the state and enacted various "estate taxes," which prevented the emergence of a class of hereditary property owners that might be a threat to its own power. The state controlled the opportunities to accumulate wealth on the largest scale: Commanding the state's armies, conducting the state's trade, holding state office, or being a favored beneficiary of the state's laws were themselves a gift of the state.

The state also controlled "symbolic capital." Only the state could bestow titles or other symbols of high status, or organize the complex rituals and ceremonies that glorified the state, emphasizing the role of public officials as providers and protectors of the people. Although the Asante state became a British colony in the late 19th century and an ethnic group within the Republic of Ghana when the British left in 1957, the Asantehene today retains his high traditional position as a ritual, spiritual, and cultural leader of the Asante people.

THE EMERGENCE OF THE NATION-STATE

Although empires are states that expand to incorporate a wide variety of ethnic groups and cultures, **nation-states** are governments and territories that are identified with (relatively) culturally homogeneous populations and national histories (see Figure 7.4). A nation is popularly felt by its members to be a natural entity based on bonds of common descent, language, culture, history, and territory. In fact, all modern nation-states are composed of many ethnic (and other) groups; Benedict Anderson (1991) calls nation-states "imagined communities" because an act of imagination is needed to weld the many disparate groups that actually make up the state into a coherent national community.

In addition to constructing national identities by drawing boundaries between spatially defined insiders and outsiders, nation-states are constructed by attaching people to time as well as to space. A common interpretation of the past is essential in creating national identities. As different groups within a nation may have different interpretations of its history, the creation of national histories often is marked by struggles over which version of history will prevail (Deák 2002; Friedman 1992). "Tradition," "the past," "history," and "social memory" all are actively invented and reinvented in accordance with contemporary national

Nation-state: A sovereign, geographically based state that identifies itself as having a distinctive national culture and historical experience.

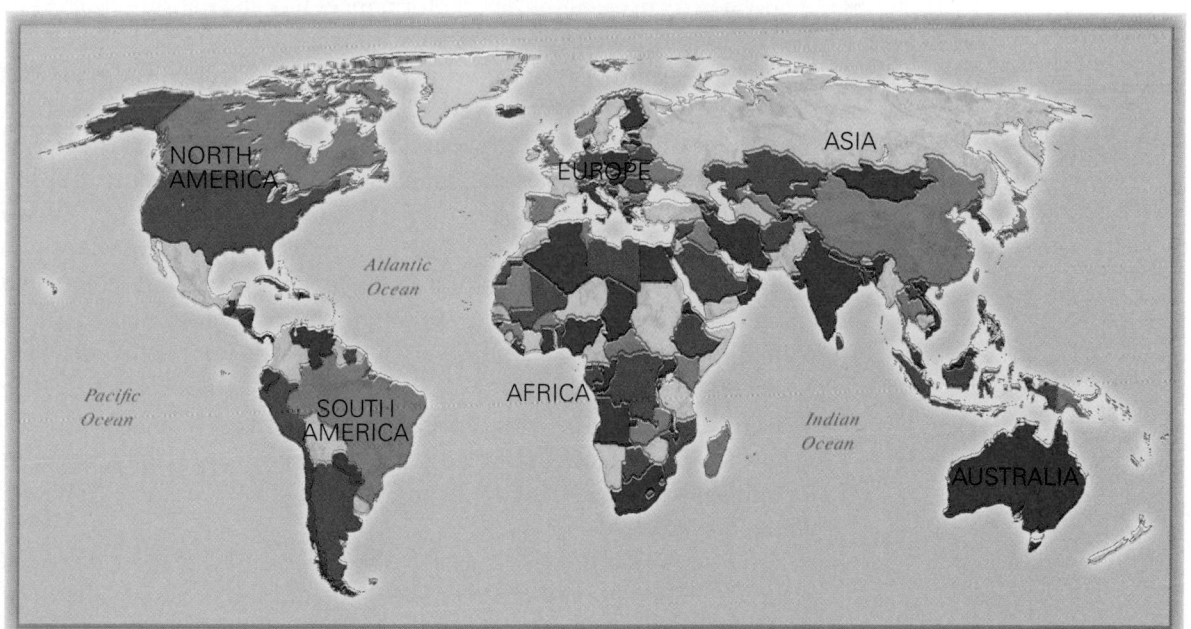

© Cengage Learning

Figure 7.4 Contemporary world maps reinforce the importance of the nation-state as a territorial unit.

Figure 7.5 This reenactment of a battle of the Revolutionary War in New York State typifies the ways in which nation-states intensify national identities by presenting history in emotionally intense ways.

Courtesy of Joan Gregg

interests and reproduced through rituals, symbols, ceremonies, memorials, and representations in museums and other cultural institutions (Hobsbawm and Ranger 1983; Nanda 2004; White 1997) (see Figure 7.5).

These constructions and performances link the nation's dead to its living and thus the past to the present; all these are essential to maintaining a nation-state. Nation-states may also outlaw public presentations of alternative histories, as currently being done in Turkey. Constructing national identities has been particularly problematic for postcolonial states, whose artificial colonial boundaries encompassed many different ethnic groups, but it also holds true for older nations. After World War I and World War II, the ethnic homogeneity of many nation-states was achieved by the coerced migration of ethnic minorities (Judt 2005), and ethnic cleansing and genocide were both widely used to make nations culturally homogenous (Kaufman 2001; Levine and Roberts 1999; Naimark 2001). In Canada, because of the dual influence of English and French culture, the search for Canadian national identity is ongoing, occasionally flaring up in demands for French-speaking Quebecois separatism (Handler 1988); in 2006, Quebec officially became "a nation within Canada."

The nation-state always seeks to repress the invented or imagined nature of national unity (Foster 1991:238), and it has many sources of power in fostering some group identities and marginalizing or disparaging others. States use media, politics, educational institutions, and the law, among other things, to create a national culture and identity that becomes the only authorized representations of society and suppresses subcultural variations.

The Nation-State and Ethnicity

Ethnicity, like nationality, is an imagined identity, which is based on the *perceived* "natural" ties—such as culture, religion, language, and national origin largely unchanged from generation to generation (Geertz 1973b:277)—by which groups of people distinguish themselves and are distinguished from others in the same social environment. Ethnic groups view themselves as sharing an ethnic identity that differentiates them from other groups or from the larger society as a whole. Ethnic boundaries are the claimed cultural attributes by which ethnic groups distinguish themselves from others. But although ethnicity does have cultural content, ethnic group identity is constructed: The perception that one belongs to a particular ethnic group and the emergence of particular ethnic groups and identities evolves from the *interaction* of a group with other groups and with the larger society, significantly shaped by competition and conflict over resources (Barth 1998/1969). This view of ethnicity leads anthropologists to ask questions about how ethnic groups and ethnic identities emerge, change, and disappear in responses to economic and social environments, especially as related to political and economic inequality (De Vos and Romanucci-Ross 1995).

Although the popular media often explain ethnic conflict and violence, including genocide, as natural eruptions of age-old ethnic hatreds and culture clashes between different ethnic groups within nation-states— for example, between Hutus and Tutsis in Rwanda, between Hindus and Muslims in India, between Kurds, Shi'a, and Sunni Muslims in Iraq, between Basques and Spanish in Spain, between the Luo and the Kikuyu in Kenya, among many others. Many of these conflicts may be better explained as contemporary struggles for political and economic power, now finding its main expression in nationalism (Stolcke 1995). Ambitious politicians may promote ethnic identities in opposition to the state, building constituencies from groups that hope to gain increased access to economic and political power. Such individuals mobilize a rhetoric of historical abuses and inequities, arousing fears of victimization among members of different groups who then become openly in conflict with each other or with their governments, as happened in the former Yugoslavia. Authoritarian governments may also repress ethnic groups as disruptive to government, as in the case of China's conflicts with Tibetans and its Muslim Uighur minority, or even repress historical memory of certain ethnic groups in the interest of fostering national solidarity, which helps explain contemporary Turkey's repression of media references to the Armenian genocide.

Ethnicity: Perceived differences in culture, national origin, and historical experience by which groups of people are distinguished from others in the same social environment.

▨ The Nation-State and Indigenous Peoples

Indigenous people: Small-scale societies designated as bands, tribes, or chiefdoms that occupied their land prior to European contact.

In much of the world today, particularly in North and South America, Africa, and parts of Asia, indigenous peoples are an important part of the multicultural landscape in nation-states. **Indigenous peoples** are those small-scale societies designated as bands, tribes, and chiefdoms that occupied their land prior to European contact. Generally, indigenous people are closely identified with their land, are relatively egalitarian, manage resources at the community level, and (previously) had high levels of economic self-sufficiency. They consider themselves distinct from other sectors of society now living in their territories and today function as nondominant sectors of the larger nation-states of which they are a part. Indigenous societies today are determined to preserve and transmit their lands and culture to future generations in order to continue their existence as a people, which frequently brings them into conflict with the nation-state (Lee 2000).

As a result of European expansion to Asia, Africa, and the New World, beginning in the 15th century, many indigenous societies completely disappeared, or survived only as remnants in marginal geographic areas (see Chapter 12). The destruction of indigenous peoples intensified rapidly by the mid-19th century as new frontiers were opened up in nations such as the United States, Australia, and Brazil. Although there was much resistance, indigenous peoples in most places were no match for the military and economic power of nation-states. After World War II, many indigenous peoples were incorporated into new postcolonial states, such as in Indonesia, Malaysia, and India, and few independent, self-sufficient indigenous societies remained (Maybury-Lewis 1997).

National policies of neglect or hostility toward indigenous peoples were often based on the expectation that indigenous peoples eventually would disappear as they were assimilated into national cultures and participated in national and global economic programs. International financial organizations, such as the World Bank and the International Monetary Fund—whose lending practices supported economic "development" programs that adversely affected the subsistence economies of indigenous peoples (Bodley 2000:378)—were also based on this assumption.

Policies of cultural assimilation, designed to foster a national identity, also contributed to the cultural loss among indigenous peoples, as in the United States. In many Central and South Americans, indigenous Indian cultures may not be totally repressed, but Indians may be identified with a fossilized past as a folkloric irrelevance, a tourist commodity, or a backward culture standing in the way of national development (Alonso 1994:398). Only a few nations have raised indigenous Indian ethnicity to a central place in national identity and political leadership (Guillermoprieto 2006), most recently Bolivia with the election of Evo Morales as its president.

The incorporation of indigenous peoples into modern nation-states involved at least partial destruction of their political and economic autonomy. Because indigenous peoples must maintain control over their land base and subsistence resources to remain self-sufficient and politically autonomous, their political defeat was usually accompanied by their economic marginalization. Europeans appropriated their land, and, without their land base, indigenous peoples were forced into participation in the global market economy and forced to give up their traditional livelihoods, or were pulled into national economies by their desire for Western goods. The colonial agenda was also imposed on indigenous peoples through the imposition and enforcement of Western law.

After World War II, the United Nations provided an international framework within which the concept of human rights and self-determination was expanded to include indigenous peoples. Because the United Nations policy worked within the framework of the nation state, however, it did little to support indigenous rights in any substantial way. Some of this changed with the passage of the Declaration on the Rights of Indigenous Peoples in 2007, although several industrialized societies such as Canada, fearful of indigenous land claims, did not sign the declaration.

USING ANTHROPOLOGY: ADVOCATING FOR THE CHAGOSSIANS

Forty years ago, 1,500 Chagossians, an indigenous group on the island of Diego Garcia, an island in the Chagossian Archipelago in the Indian Ocean, were forcibly removed from their homes when this small island became a military base for the United States during the Cold War. The island continues its military role today both as a storehouse for military weaponry and as a takeoff point for United States military bombing aircraft in the Gulf War and the invasions of Iraq and Afghanistan.

In the late 18th century, the French created coconut plantations on the previously uninhabited islands, using imported slave and indentured laborers from Madagascar, Mozambique, and India. Called Ilois, these people created a distinct culture and society, almost totally isolated from the rest of the world. They constructed a viable subsistence economy based on vegetable gardens, fishing, chickens, and ducks. Not a luxurious life, but one that provided security, with universal employment and free housing, education, pensions, and basic health care, as well as small salaries the plantation owners and the Mauritian government provided. Later, the French colonial government added schools, refuse removal, small dirt roads, and some modern technology like motorbikes, trucks, and tractors to the island.

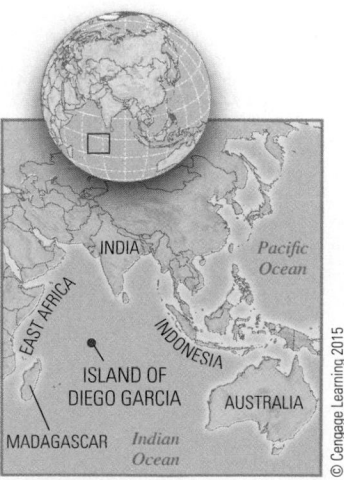

The Chagossians of Diego Garcia.

In 1965, through secret arrangements, the American and British governments took complete military and political control of the islands, deciding that "the Chagossians must go." Government benefits began winding down, mail service was suspended, and hundreds of Chagossians found themselves stranded in Mauritius. "Life turned completely upside down," one Chagossian told anthropologist David Vine, "[we were] in the fire with our feet burning." Most Chagossians were sent to Mauritius where they were promised compensation in the form of land, housing, employment, and money.

Vine's ethnography of the Chagossians, *Island of Shame* (2009), is based on archival research of British and American documents, fieldwork among the displaced Chagossians on Mauritius, and interviews with military and congressional representatives instrumental in the island's transformation. The Chagossians, as a displaced people, are entitled to compensation under United Nations laws protecting the rights of indigenous cultures. After their eviction, they formed the Chagos Refugees Group, which is waging an ongoing struggle both to receive just compensation and to return to their island; they seek, in fact, to work for the U.S. military, not to remove it. By 1997, the group had brought lawsuits against the British government and planned one against the United States.

Vine, in collaboration with several lawyers, documented the Chagossians' status as indigenous peoples and how they have been harmed as a result of their displacement. He helped calculate the compensation they were due as a result of these damages. Vine's work with the Chagossians is just one of the many ways that engaged anthropology makes a difference for indigenous peoples.

BRINGING IT BACK HOME:
DO GOOD FENCES MAKE GOOD NEIGHBORS?

Contemporary states view a fixed and secure border as essential to sovereignty and national security (see Figure 7.6). They accept the notion that states have a right and responsibity to restrict and control immigration. The most passionate debate about immigration today concerns the U.S. border with Mexico, which has become increasingly militarized in an effort to keep out undocumented workers.

Politicians often justify the militarization of the border though the rhetoric of protecting domestic labor markets, and since 9/11, protecting the nation from terrorism. In spite of fencing, lighting, the use of infrared scopes, underground sensors, increased law enforcement, and vigilante groups, hundreds of thousands of undocumented Mexicans continue to cross the border in search of work. They are encouraged by employers who use them as a source of cheap labor. Although there are supposedly penalties for employers who exploit undocumented workers in this way, in fact, there are far too few law enforcement officers to make such penalties meaningful. And so, although the debate over undocumented immigration generates much heat, most of it is aimed at the undocumented immigrants themselves, rather than the employers of such workers who are subject to much less vigilance.

Another aspect of border crossing that is aligned with law enforcement is the process of human smuggling, which according to government officials enables unathorized immigration, victimizes vulnerable migrants, threatens national security, and may be associated with drug smuggling or sex trafficking. Anthropologist David Spener (2009) ethnographically unpacks this aspect of border crossing, based on a decade of ethnographic research, using both anthropological analysis and the stories of individual migrants to make his point. Spener questions the exclusive American narrative that all human smuggling is "bad," and illustrates that not only are the *coyotes* who facilitate the smuggling an aspect of Mexican culture, but that the smuggling is a multifaceted process that may work as a service provider aiding in consensual international migration of Mexican workers. Like many anthropological studies of political issues, Spener's views are contentious but require us to rethink some of our cherished ideologies about crossing borders.

ZUMA Press, Inc./Alamy

Figure 7.6 Protecting borders is an urgent concern for nation-states as they try to hold back refugees, undocumented immigrants, and terrorists who are increasingly crossing borders for economic and political purposes.

The latest proposal to control undocumented migration is the erection of a double-layered 700-mile-long border fence. Thus far, measures such as the fence have only succeeded in directing immigration to more difficult and dangerous terrain, making the immigrants even more vulnerable to exploitation (Chavez 1998:196; Holthouse 2005).

The border fence is a controversial project and highlights the clash of economic interests and cultures in the American Southwest. Seventy-five miles of the border, at one of its most vulnerable points, is located on the Tohono O'odham (Indian) Reservation, not far from Tucson, Arizona. The Tohono O'odham oppose the wall, claiming a need to freely cross the border to visit friends and relatives in Mexico, take their children to school, gather traditional foods, and visit religious sites to perform rituals, all of which they have been doing for years. Their cultural concerns also focus on how the wall will restrict the free range of deer, wild horses, coyotes, jackrabbits, and other animals they revere and regard as kin. "In our tradition, we are taught to be concerned about every living thing as if they were people. We don't want that wall," said one tribal council member.

The Tohono O'odham cooperate extensively with the U.S. border patrol and the Department of Homeland Security in patrolling the border. Because the federal government is the trustee of all Indian lands, it could build the fence through the reservation without tribal permission, but that would jeopardize the valuable help the Tohono O'odham now gives the government (Archibold 2006).

YOU DECIDE:

1. Do you think human movement between states should be free and unrestricted? Why or why not? If you believe that there should be restriction of immigration, what criteria would you use for admitting immigrants?

2. What kinds of solutions would you suggest to the problem of undocumented immigration? Do you think that the construction of the border fence will make a substantial contribution in addressing this problem? Why or why not?

3. Decisions made by states often pit groups in society against each other. In this case, do you think the need to prevent undocumented immigrants crossing the border justifies overriding the cultural values of the Tohono O'odham? How would you mediate the conflict between the U.S. government and the Tohono O'odham over the building of a wall on their reservation?

■ CHAPTER SUMMARY

1. How does political organization relate to power? Anthropologists try to understand political organization by focusing on power: Who has it? What are its sources? How is it related to other aspects of culture, especially political ideology? And how is it used in achieving public goals?

2. How is social control maintained in different kinds of societies? In all societies, social control is effected through formal sanctions such as exile, death, and punishments meted out by courts, judges, police, and other institutionalized forms of regulation. Conformity is also achieved through informal means such as gossip, ridicule, and ostracism.

3. What is the relationship between political organization and social differentiation? Political organization is closely related to social differentiation, which is in turn related to the dominant pattern of making a living and exchanging goods and services. Band societies, which are characteristic of foragers, are egalitarian and dominated by generalized reciprocity.

4. What are the main characteristics of tribal societies? Tribal societies, found among pastoralists and horticulturalists, also tend to be egalitarian and operate through generalized reciprocity as well as balanced reciprocity. Though tribal societies have many different nonviolent means of resolving conflicts within the society, they also have a high degree of warfare.

5. What are the main characteristics of chiefdoms? Chiefdoms, which are found in highly productive horticultural societies and among pastoralists, are called rank societies. Though kinship integrates the society, social units are socially ranked, and social position may be inherited. The chief is a central office, supported by his position as one who redistributes goods within the society.

6. What are the main characteristics of state societies? The most complex form of political organization is the state, found mainly in agricultural and industrial societies, and associated with social stratification. Social, political, and economic inequality are institutionalized and maintained through a combination of internalized controls (hegemony) and force. Kinship ties between the upper and lower classes no longer serve to integrate the society, and there is a wide gap in standards of living.

7. What are the main characteristics of a nation-state, and what role does ethnicity play in the construction of nationalism? The nation-state is a state that identifies itself with a culturally homogenous

group and a shared history and geographic territory, and uses various social and cultural institutions to foster nationalism. Many nation-states are in fact multicultural, incorporating ethnic groups who also define themselves as culturally homogenous. Sometimes ethnic conflict occurs between various ethnic groups within a nation or between ethnic groups and the nation iself.

8. What are indigenous groups and how do they relate to the construction of nation-states? Many nation-states today incorporate indigenous peoples, whose cultures, economies, and social institutions are constrained by the need to live within these complex societies and their regulatory systems.

9. How are national borders implicated in contemporary political issues? With the large numbers of migrants across borders, many borders are now militantly policed and guarded by walls or fences, both of which often promote protests and violent conflict.

KEY TERMS

Authority	Nation-state
Bureaucracy	Political ideology
Band	Political organization
Chiefdom	Power
Egalitarian society	Rank society
Elites	Rebellion
Ethnicity	Revolution
Hegemony	Social differentiation
Indigenous people	State
Law	Stratified society
Leadership	Tribe
Mediation	War (warfare)

The first African American president, Barack Obama, and his appointment of the first Hispanic Supreme Court Justice, Sonia Sotomayor, represent a historic moment in the intersection of race, class, ethnicity, and gender in the United States.

CHAPTER 8

STRATIFICATION: CLASS, CASTE, RACE, AND ETHNICITY

LEARNING OBJECTIVES

After you have read this chapter, you will be able to:

△ Summarize the differences between functionalist and conflict approaches to inequality, and list some of the strengths and weaknesses of each approach.

△ Discuss the relationship between wealth, power, and prestige.

△ Explain the differences between a class and a caste system, giving examples of each.

△ Analyze, with statistics, income inequality in the United States.

△ Explain the intersection of race and class in the United States with examples.

△ Compare the construction of race in the United States with that in Brazil.

△ Describe the American narrative of immigration and how it relates to ethnically based stratification in the United States.

Exploited Children: Victims and Survivors

ID you see the film *Slumdog Millionaire?* Were you shocked by its portrayal of childhood in Mumbai, India? And more shocked by its "happy ending?" A culturally universalist view of childhood, enshrined in the United Nations Convention on the Rights of the Child, is that childhood should be a time of life separate from adulthood, in which children should be "...protected from economic exploitation and from performing any work that is likely to be hazardous or to interfere with the child's education, or to be harmful to...[their] development." Most of us would agree. But, in fact, perhaps as many as a billion children worldwide live in just these conditions, and 100 million of these children live on the streets.

In Olinda, Brazil, a deeply impoverished town, 60 percent of its population lives in shantytowns. Its wood, paper, and tin homes house an average of ten people (Kenny 1997). Available work is low paid and difficult to find: People do day labor, wash cars, or sell peanuts and ice pops; women work as laundresses, hairdressers, or seamstresses. These jobs cannot support even a small family, and child labor is essential for survival. Children guard cars, carry goods, wash dishes, hawk small items like gum and candy, and beg. They, along with adults, also pick up garbage, an occupation that exposes them to disease, infections, parasites, and rodents, but is an essential source of edible food. Using their children's labor, a family of garbage pickers can earn enough to survive. Children also beg, targeting the tourists in the town's historic district. "If I don't work, my family will go hungry...[but] I can take it. It's my fate," says 12-year-old Dalva, whose income-generating abilities make her a household head.

In Nairobi, Kenya, as in Olinda, street children are part of the powerless "hot sun" workers in the informal economic sector: They sell newspapers and flowers, shine shoes, and hawk radios, watches, flashlights, telephones, dust pans, magazines, fruits and vegetables, and used clothes. "Street boys" earn money by guarding or washing parked cars, carrying packages for store patrons, begging, or collecting and selling garbage, which is recycled into school exercise books and toilet paper. For girls, selling sex on the street is a major means of economic survival (Kilbride 2010).

Nairobi street children, though marginal and stigmatized by the larger society, share in Kenya's core cultural values: They may organize to beg funds for a friend's proper burial; participate in street food-sharing networks; and girls desire to have children. Concerns about sleeping on the street and the frequent police harassment are secondary to children's concerns about food: As one street girl put it, "You cannot sleep if you eat nothing." But Nairobi street children are smart survivors and know how to get food from charities and nongovernmental organizations (NGOs) that supply food regularly. Street children not only survive but also sometimes even move up, from "poking" garbage dumps to becoming middlemen who buy paper from street collectors and sell it to recyclers. Girls on the street have been less lucky. They are at the bottom of a gendered class system: Having a child is no longer a guarantee of receiving charity, and sex work without condoms has caused a substantial rise in HIV/AIDS.

The hard lives of the children described result from the extreme poverty and economic inequality in socially stratified, complex societies. Although some become vulnerable, psychologically traumatized victims, ethnographic studies of street children conducted by Mary Kenny in Brazil (2007), Philip Kilbride in Kenya (2010), and Ric Curtis et al. in New York City (2008) provide an important alternative perspective: Street children may be desperately poor, but they are also survivors, making the most of their very limited opportunities. What they want most are jobs that pay decent wages, because most nations, unlike societies like Sweden, do not have a strong social safety net that permits these children to leave their life on the streets (Hinman 2011; Thrupkaew 2012).

EXPLAINING SOCIAL STRATIFICATION

Social stratification is the structure that results from unequal access to and distribution of goods and services in state societies. No society has ever successfully organized a large and diverse population without stratification and economic inequalities.

Functionalism and conflict theory are two major explanations of social stratification. **Functionalism** holds that social stratification generally benefits the whole society, by rewarding people socially and economically for working harder, taking risks, doing difficult jobs, or spending more time in school or occupational training. Medical doctors, for example, whose work is essential to society, are rewarded for their long years in school, by both high income and high prestige.

Although functionalism explains some aspects of contemporary social stratification, it does not explain everything: Many of society's most difficult or dirty jobs are not highly paid. Schoolteachers, nurses, and fireman who are essential to society, at best, make it into the middle class. Social stratification also does not necessarily recruit the best people to the most demanding positions. In addition, though getting rich is a powerful motivator, other considerations also count in people's life choices. And even in the most open class systems, resentment of economic and social inequality may eventually explode into open conflict and even violence, especially

Social stratification: A social hierarchy resulting from the relatively permanent unequal distribution of goods and services in a society.

Functionalism (functionalist perspective): A theoretical position in anthropology that focuses on finding general laws that identify different elements of society, showing how they relate to each other, and demonstrating their role in maintaining social order.

when based on factors that an individual is born with and cannot change, such as family background, social connections, gender, ethnicity, race, and inherited wealth (Berreman 1988; Stiglitz 2012).

Conflict theory: A perspective on social stratification that focuses on economic inequality as a source of conflict and change.

In contrast to functionalism, **conflict theory** holds that social stratification results from the constant struggle for scarce goods and services in stratified societies. Inequalities exist because the elites use their wealth, power, and prestige to maintain control over the system of production and the apparatus of the state. When political ideologies falter and elite dominance is challenged, elites may fall back on the threat or use of force to maintain the status quo. Conflict and change are thus inherent in systems of social stratification.

Conflict theory is associated with Karl Marx and his followers, who focus on the economic aspect of social stratification. For Marxists, the relationship of individuals to the means of production is critical in determining their power and prestige. Marx differentiated two main social classes in capitalist society: the capitalists, who own the means of production, and the workers, who must sell their labor to survive. Marx predicted that the inherent conflict between the workers and the owners of the means of production would eventually lead to capitalism's downfall. Although Marxist predictions have not been fully realized, conflict theory is useful in explaining some aspects of social stratification. However, just as functional theorists may ignore structural conflict, conflict theorists may sometimes ignore the solidarity across class, caste, racial, ethnic, and gender lines, which also brings about change.

Criteria of Stratification: Power, Wealth and Prestige

All social stratification systems depend on the complex interaction of the three main dimensions of stratification: power, wealth, and prestige. Anthropologists analyze **power** by examining its sources, the channels through which it is exercised, and the goals it is deployed to achieve. For example, in the United States, we might analyze the different sources, uses, and goals of power among corporate CEOs, elected public officials, entertainment celebrities, heads of organized crime families, or information technology (IT) entrepreneurs. Cross-culturally, we might compare the sources, uses, and goals of power among an American president, the prime minister in a parliamentary system of government such as France, the chairman of the Communist Party in the People's Republic of China, the supreme leader (Ayatollah) in the Islamic Republic of Iran, or the king of Jordan.

Power: The ability to impose one's will on others.

Wealth: The accumulation of material resources or access to the means of producing these resources.

Wealth is the accumulation of material resources or access to the means of producing these resources. Although wealth is not the sole criterion of social status even in capitalist societies, it can eventually translate into high social position and power. Wealth enables people to send their children to the most prestigious schools, buy homes in the best residential locations, and join the right social clubs. It enables access to political power through large campaign contributions to politicians or permits people to run for political office themselves.

The bases of **prestige**, or social honor, vary cross-culturally: Prestige may be based on race and ethnicity; income; accumulated wealth; power; personal characteristics such as integrity or charisma; family history; and/or the display of material goods. Not all wealth is a source of prestige; illegally earned incomes generally carry less prestige than legitimate enterprises. Compare the prestige, for example, between a drug czar making billions of dollars and winners of Nobel Prizes, or between leaders who lived austerely simple lives like Mahatma Gandhi or who languished in prison for decades, like Nelson Mandela of South Africa.

Prestige: Social honor or respect.

Occupation is a key source of prestige in all societies, both for its relation to income and the cultural values attached to it, though different societies rank occupations differently (see the section on the Hindu caste system). As political and economic conditions change, cultural rankings of occupations may also change. In 18th-century Europe, surgery was a lower-class occupation performed by barbers; in contemporary North America, surgeons rank very high in prestige because of both their very high income and their prodigious skills and training.

China is a culture in which the evaluation of occupations has changed radically. Before the Communist revolution, a Confucian value system dominated and scholars had the highest prestige. After the revolution, workers were honored and scholars often explicitly ridiculed and despised. Today, with China's increasing economic role in globalization, free-market enterprises are now valued, and businesspeople, previously a target of socialist contempt and even violence, are highly regarded, or at least highly rewarded financially. As a result, a large and growing middle class has emerged, but inequality has also increased, particularly between rural and urban areas. Even as the new economy has benefitted the Chinese in general, millions of urban migrants remain poverty stricken and exploited; this suggests that rapidly increased prosperity tends to result in increased class stratification (Wong 2008).

There has long been a debate over whether prestige or economic factors explain behavior and identity in stratified societies. In contrast to Marx's argument for the primacy of economic or class interests, Max Weber, a late 19th-century German sociologist, argued for the dominance of social status, dress, speech, and other external behavior patterns; indeed, it is sometimes argued that anxiety about social status is the animating force in modern societies. Weber argued that even political action can be motivated by a group's desire to defend its social position, sometimes in opposition to its economic self-interest, a position Marx called "false consciousness." In the American South, whites were more committed to the prestige based on race than to allying with blacks to improve their economic conditions.

CLASS SYSTEMS

Two main types of social stratification systems are "open class systems," where social position is based on **achieved status**, that is, a person's individual efforts, and "closed class systems," where social position is based on **ascribed status**, or birth, using criteria such as race, ethnicity, family heritage, or biological sex. In fact, in modern complex societies, both achievement and ascription play a role in the social stratification system, though to different degrees.

A **class** is a category of people who generally share similar economic resources, power, and prestige and who are ranked high and low in relation to other class categories. A **class system** has possibilities for **social mobility**, or movement between the classes that is (ideally) based on individual achievement rather than ascribed status. Even in the most open class systems, however, ascribed statuses always play a role in moving from one class to another. Closed stratification systems, or caste systems, where there is little or no possibility of social mobility, are discussed later.

Achieved status: A social position that a person chooses or achieves on his or her own.

Ascribed status: A social position into which a person is born.

Class: A category of people who all have about the same opportunity to obtain economic resources, power, and prestige and who are ranked relative to other categories.

Class system: A form of social stratification in which the different strata form a continuum and social mobility is possible.

Social mobility: Movement from one social strata to another.

The American Class System

The United States is culturally defined as an open class system, based on upward social mobility from one class to another through education, hard work, self-reliance, and taking risks—a system called the American Dream. Although this belief is strong among almost all Americans, in fact, achieving the dream is significantly correlated with race, ethnicity, gender, and class (Bialostok 2009; DeParle 2012; Haskins, Isaacs, and Sawhill 2008).

In 2006, Gloria Castillo, 22, a child of undocumented immigrants, married, with two children, lived in a tough neighborhood in Dallas, Texas. She worked the night shift at a fast food chain store, 10:30 p.m. to 6:30 a.m., for $252 a week before taxes, and received no health care benefits. To help make ends meet, she worked a second job, earning $150 a night for the hour and a half it took her to clean three bathrooms in a local bar. Her husband worked at an auto parts shop during the day, so Gloria took the children, age 7 and 8, for a fast food breakfast before dropping them at school, returned home, slept until 2, picked up the kids, prepared their frozen food dinners, put them to bed at 7, spent a few hours with her husband, and left for work. On Saturdays she attended a community college, working toward a degree as a paralegal. "I got dreams," she said (LeDuff 2006).

One corollary of the American Dream is that economic failure and downward social mobility are seen as resulting from individual failings as well as from a lower-class culture, rather than as a systemic aspect of social stratification. Until the recent recession, downward mobility was almost invisible in the media and in American culture, as it did "not fit into our cultural universe" (Newman 1999).

With the current recession, downward mobility has become increasingly visible. Instead of media stories about Gloria Castillo, we read about David Loechner. In 2007, Loechner earned $65,000 a year managing a truck rental company, and his wife earned $24,000 working two part-time jobs. They lived in a $1,000-a-month furnished apartment and thought of themselves as solid, middle-class citizens. Then the Great Recession hit: Loechner lost his job, and it took over a year to find another—working as a janitor in a supermarket, earning $8.60 an hour. His wife became too depressed to work so she gets Social Security disability insurance. The Loechners eat a lot of soup, shop online at free thrift sites, and their son only made it to a technical college through scholarships, loans, and by taking a job. "We're no longer middle class," Brenda says (Brubaker 2012).

The Material Basis of Class in the United States: Growing Inequalities

There is no definitive consensus in the United States on the criteria of social class, which since the economic growth after World War II, was viewed as a ladder with lots of rungs that could be climbed with ingenuity and hard work. Most Americans considered themselves "middle class" (Durrenburger 2001), but no longer. Now one-third of Americans define themselves as lower class, including growing numbers of people under 30, Hispanics, and whites (Morin and Motel 2012).

Statistical and ethnographic evidence challenges the image of contemporary United States as a middle-class and upwardly mobile society. Many Americans now experience widespread and long-term unemployment or part-time employment, loss of wealth in the form of stocks and pensions, lack of access to medical care, an inability to pay the mortgage and subsequent home foreclosures, rising costs of college tuition and student loans, and rising food prices. Affording these items once defined middle-class status. The main prospective job growth is overwhelmingly in low-wage sectors like service and retail.

In addition, there is rapidly growing income disparity between the huge incomes of the very rich and declining opportunities and stagnant

Figure 8.1 Occupy Wall Street, a resistance movement that raised questions about the concentration of wealth and power in the United States, soon spread globally. Its motto, distinguishing the "99 percent" of ordinary people from the I percent of the elite, was created by anthropologist David Graeber, and brought economic inequality into the center of political debate.

or declining incomes of ordinary people (see Table 8.1). Extreme poverty, which affects millions of Americans in places ranging from Appalachia to Indian reservations to the Florida tomato fields and to inner cities, has also increased throughout the United States (Hedges and Sacco 2012), but remains almost invisible in the media (Haharidge 2011).

Table 8.1 U.S. Class Structure

Class	Annual Income	Education	Occupation	Approx. %
Privileged Classes				
Capitalist	$1,000,000 +	Prestigious universities	CEOs, investors, heirs	1
Upper-middle	$100,000 +	Top colleges/ postgraduate	Upper managers, professionals	14
Majority Classes				
Middle	$55,000	High school/some college	Lower managers, teachers, civil servants	30
Working class	$35,000	High school	Clerical, sales, factory	30
Lower Classes				
Working poor	$22,000	Some high school	Service jobs, laborers	13
Underclass	$10,000 or less	Some high school	Unemployed	12

Adapted from Dennis Gilbert (2011:244).

Social classes differ in lifestyle, occupational roles, values, educational backgrounds, social affiliations, leisure activities, religious belief and practice, and political views, but most importantly, in income and wealth (see Table 8.2). When outsourcing manufacturing to low-wage countries and easy credit made cheaper fashionable consumer goods (even if they were fake) available to ordinary people, a surface similarity with the upper classes masked the actual increasing differences in income, wealth, and homeownership among Americans. But income does affect lifestyle: Although imitation luxury goods went down market, the ever-more expensive luxury goods and services available only to the one percent sold briskly: $4,000 handbags, $130,000 Hummer automobiles (Rolls Royces now preferred), $12,000 mother/baby diamond bracelet sets, personal chefs and personal trainers, face lifts and other cosmetic surgery, private school for children, and exotic travel tours costing upward of $50,000 (Newman and Chen 2006). The most important—and permanent—lifestyle differences continue to be class segregation of residence, thus increasing personal safety and availability of high-quality schools, and avoiding environmental pollution and natural disasters (Checker 2005; Brown 2012).

The extraordinary jump in inequalities in income and wealth over the past 30 years, primarily caused by the political power of the richest Americans over the legislative and regulatory process, makes the perception of the United States as an egalitarian society a fantasy divorced from reality (Hacker 2012; Stiglitz 2012; Greenhouse 2013). Wages are the lowest percentage of the national income in 50 years, while corporate profits have climbed to their highest share during this same period. During the past 30 years, the after-tax income of the top 1 percent of American households

Table 8.2 Total Net Worth of U.S. Households, 2007

	Percentage Share of Wealth Held By:
Top 1 percent	34.6
Next 4 percent	27.3
Next 5 percent	11.2
Next 10 percent	12.0
Highest quintile combined	85.0
Fourth quintile	10.9
Third quintile	4.0
Lowest two quintiles combined	0.2

From Wolff, 2010:44.

jumped 139 percent to more than $700,000; the income of the middle fifth of households rose only 17 percent, to $43,700, and the income of the poorest fifth rose only 9 percent. In 2004, the chief executives at the 100 largest companies in California took home a collective $1.1 billion, an increase of nearly 20 percent, while wages are a record low of the gross domestic product. Reductions in pensions have also increased the prospect of financial insecurity in retirement. In spite of an American ideology of progressive taxes, in fact, state tax policies favor the rich and middle class with the poorest Americans, primarily in the South and Southwest, paying the most in relation to their income (Newman 2013).

Under President Bush's tax cuts for the wealthy, the 400 taxpayers with the highest incomes—over $87 million a year each—now pay income, Medicare, and Social Security taxes amounting to the same percentage of their incomes as people making $50,000 to $75,000 a year. Warren Buffett, one of the world's richest men, repeatedly emphasizes that his 2006 tax rate was almost half that of his secretary (Brown 2009). Ninety-three percent of the income gains from the 2009/2010 stimulus and other government measures went to the top 1 percent of taxpayers, who also gain most from tax deductions and tax loopholes (Freeland 2012). This income inequality affects not only middle-class families but also has a negative effect on the nation's economic growth as a whole.

Income and wealth inequalities are correlated with health and longevity. People with higher education and income are less likely to have and die of heart disease, strokes, diabetes, and many types of cancer (J. Scott 2005). They are also more likely to have more information about and benefit from advances in medicine; be covered by health insurance; are less likely to smoke, are less obese, exercise more, and eat healthier food than people in the lower classes. Sufficient, steady family income is essential for upward mobility, and insufficient and irregular income negatively affects both one's own life chances and those of one's children (Bowles et al. 2005; Lareau 2003; Neckerman 2004).

Class differences also significantly affect family structure and educational achievement. The upper classes are more likely to be married before they have children, have fewer children, and have them later in life, all factors that positively affect children's achievements. Family income and stability are critical for upward mobility, and single women with children are the most likely not to succeed.

Using Anthropology: Homelessness and Social Action

One of the results of growing economic inequality, which perhaps most shamefully is affecting American veterans of the Iraq War, is the tremendous increase in homelessness, among both males and females. In the absence of much media attention, an important contribution of cultural anthropology is to give people living on the margins of society, like homeless people, a voice that reaches the wider public, illustrated in anthropologist Elliot Liebow's classic ethnography about the "street corner society" of black men in Washington, DC (1967). But contemporary engaged cultural anthropologists want to go further: Vincent Lyon-Callo (2004) stresses the necessity of both educating the public about the causes of homelessness and also engaging in political action to change their lives. Lyon-Callo holds that most homelessness in the United States results from neoliberalism, a cultural and political philosophy that embraces the free market and private initiative as the solution to social problems. He argues that the American "social services" orientation to homelessness, which views the problem as one that can be solved through charity or services aimed at reforming homeless people, obscures the importance of unemployment, declining wages, the exploitation of workers, and the lack of affordable housing, which he sees as the root of the problem. He argues that without political efforts to transform the economy, caring social services cannot in themselves end homelessness. While promoting profound political and social change is slow and discouraging work, it is, for Lyon-Callo, a necessary beginning. And it can bring some solutions as well: Working in collaboration with community members and homeless people in Northampton, Massachusetts, Lyon-Callo helped create a winter cot program in community churches, a living-wage campaign, and new job opportunities for homeless people, efforts that helped improve "life on the ground" for homeless people in this one small American community.

◢◤ CASTE

In contrast to open class systems, a **caste system** is based on birth, or ascribed status. Individual movement between castes or marriage between individuals from different castes is theoretically not possible. Castes are socially ranked and characteristically associated with traditional occupations, which carry different degrees of purity or spiritual pollution and may exhibit subcultural differences. A caste system, then, consists of ranked, culturally distinct, interdependent, endogamous groups, with rigidly maintained boundaries between the castes. Caste-like systems exist in several cultures, but caste is mainly identified with India, where it is deeply culturally and historically embedded and plays a central role in social stratification.

Caste system: Social stratification based on birth in which social mobility between castes is not possible.

The Caste System in India

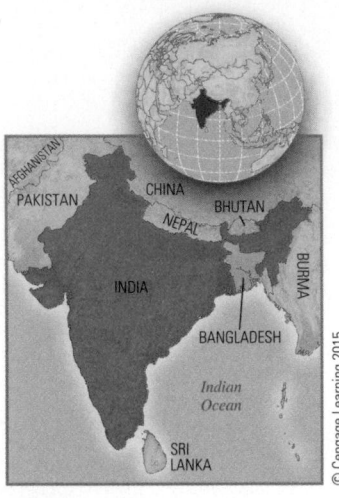

India.

The Indian caste system is unique in its complexity, its relation to Hindu religious beliefs and rituals, and the degree to which the castes (or, more accurately, subcastes) are cohesive and self-regulating groups. The four main castes (*varnas*), ranked according to the ritual purity of their traditional occupations, are the Brahmins, who are priests and scholars; the Kshatriyas, who are rulers and warriors; the Vaisyas, or merchants; and the Shudras, or menial workers and artisans. Below these four varnas is a fifth group, previously called untouchables, now called Dalits, who perform spiritually polluting work such as cleaning latrines or tanning leather. Traditionally, the mere touch, or even shadow, of a Dalit, contaminated higher caste purity (hence the term, untouchables).

Caste boundaries are maintained by rules against intercaste marriage, eating together, and spatial segregation: Traditionally, the lowest castes in Indian villages were prohibited from using high-caste wells and temples. In its rural setting, the caste system involved traditional exchanges of goods and services between higher and lower castes. Families of artisan and serving castes—carpenters, potters, blacksmiths, water carriers, and leather workers—performed services for high-caste landowning families, and in return received, among other things, grain, clothing, animal fodder, animal products, or small amounts of cash. These relationships, which continued over several generations, were viewed by the higher castes as the benefits of the caste system: Landowners gained a steady supply of available workers while the serving castes gained a relatively reliable source of subsistence. The lower castes, however, viewed themselves as exploited; these different perceptions are examples of the ongoing debate over functional versus conflict explanations of social stratification.

Although Indian castes are ranked on the basis of prestige rather than wealth, higher castes benefit materially—and politically—as well as symbolically from their higher status. They use their considerable political power to maintain these material benefits and resist any efforts at lower castes' attempts to change the system. Although the lower castes *appear* to accept their position, their conformity often hinges on their awareness that economic sanctions and physical force often results from resistance; indeed, violent intercaste conflict occurs frequently in rural India. Traditional Hindu religious belief holds that individuals occupy their social position based on the virtue of their actions in a previous life, a convenient justification for elite caste hegemony, which functions like the dominant American ideology that holds that one's class status is a result only of individual effort.

© Cengage Learning 2015

Changes in the Caste System

The caste system in India, like any social stratification system, continues to change. When India became independent of British rule, untouchability was outlawed and affirmative action programs in education and government jobs for lower castes, tribal peoples, and untouchables were incorporated into the constitution, a process that generates political conflicts, much as affirmative action does in the United States. A low caste may also try to raise its social position by requiring its members to follow the rules and rituals of higher castes and constructing a new story of high-caste origin for itself. Dr. R. R. Ambedkar, a follower of Mahatma Gandhi, urged those of lower caste to convert to Buddhism, to put them outside the caste system altogether.

Today, partly as a result of increasing differentiation of wealth and power *within* castes, caste ranking appears less sharply defined than formerly, both in rural and urban areas, and especially among those in higher castes. In cities and in public spaces, caste boundaries such as interdining have also weakened, though many caste-related boundaries, particularly regarding marriage, remain in intimate settings and rural areas. The traditional connection between caste and occupation is also weakening, as new occupations, such as factory work and information technology, which are not caste related, open up opportunities for those in both lower and middle castes (Kapur 2012) (see Figure 8.2). Even people who live in slums have improved their lives through such occupations as recycling trash (Boo 2012). Still, people in higher castes continue to be the primary beneficiaries of India's recent economic growth, through their previous

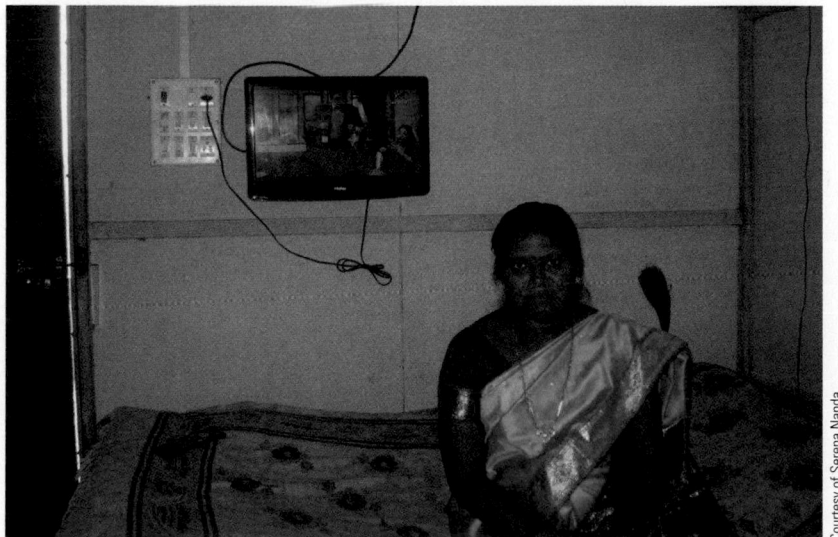

Courtesy of Serena Nanda

Figure 8.2 Sonu, a low-caste village woman who moved to the city for better economic opportunities and now works as a maid for an upper-class family, proudly poses for the anthropologist in her best sari, in front of her flat-screen television set.

accumulation of capital, their higher education, their business and social contacts, and their ability to speak English (Beteille 1998).

▨ RACE: A CULTURAL CONSTRUCTION

When traveling in Malaysia, Nanda asked a friend to explain this exceptionally diverse society. He began by saying, "The Indians are the black people," referring to the dark skin color of the Indians in Malaysia who are mainly from South India. Joking with him a little, Nanda asked, "If the Indians are the black people, who are the white people?" "Oh," he answered, without missing a beat, "the Portuguese used to be the white people but now the Chinese are the white people."

This conversation emphasizes the anthropological view that "race" is a cultural construction, based on specific histories and social structures. This conversation makes sense in terms of Malaysia's economic history, where its main ethnic groups—the Chinese, Indians, indigenous Malays, and the small population of Portuguese descended from 16th-century traders who politically dominated Malay society for 100 years—occupied different economic niches. The Portuguese were later defeated by the British, who colonized Malaysia (then called Malaya), and replaced the Portuguese in the most important political and economic positions. After Malaysia's independence, the British left, and the Chinese moved into many commercial and professional positions and now dominate the Malaysian economy. Having taken over the economic position formerly occupied by the Portuguese and then the British, the Chinese are now defined as having taken over their racial category as well.

Race: A culturally constructed category based on *perceived* physical differences.

The term **race** is used to define people based on *perceived* physical differences that imply hereditary differences. Anthropologists emphasize that race is not a natural category, but it is a significant cultural and social fact used to justify differential treatment of racial majorities and racial minorities. Even in the absence of physical differences among groups of people, class, ethnicity, and caste are often conceptualized in racial terms. The 19th-century English theologian Charles Kingsley described the Irish as "human chimpanzees...a race of utter savages, truly barbarous and brutish...," noting unhappily, that "[their] skins are as white as ours" (in Curtis 1968:84). The British used the idea of a "degenerate Irish race" to justify their control over Ireland, just as people in the United States used racist stereotypes of Africans to justify slavery.

Conceptualizing group differences as "racial" implies differences in culture, character, morality, intelligence, personality, and purity that are seen as natural, inherited, and unalterable, in a word, ascribed. Differences in outward physical appearance make it easier to distinguish "races" socially, but as the English perceptions of the Irish indicate, a lack of observable physical differences does not prohibit the implementation of racial stratification.

Racial Classification in Brazil

In much of Brazil, as in the American South, a plantation system whose core was African slave labor formed an important part of the economy, especially in the Northeast. After 1888, when Brazil abolished slavery, government policy attempted to "whiten" its population by encouraging European immigration and teaching only Euro-Brazilian history and culture. At the same time, however, unlike the United States, where interracial marriages were outlawed in many states, racial distinctions and racial discrimination in Brazil were not encoded in law, and interracial marriage and sexual relations were not illegal (Goldstein 1999; Sheriff 2001).

In contemporary Brazil, individuals of African descent account for about 45 percent of the total population, yet only about 15 percent of these people identify themselves as *preta* (black) on the census forms. The rest mainly self-identify as *parda* (brown, of partial African ancestry), although claims to indigenous Indian ancestry are growing, both as a way to secure material gains, such as land rights, and as a way to avoid the stigma of blackness (French 2010) (see Figure 8.3).

But while Brazilian understandings of race may be flexible, race is implicated in a profoundly unequal class system: whites at the top, blacks at the bottom, and *parda* somewhere in between. Brazilian racial classification is extremely complex, particularly within communities of those who self-identify as of African descent. In one village studied by anthropologist Conrad Kottak (1992:67), while all villagers were of African slave ancestry, almost half identified themselves as *mulatto,* a commonly used intermediate category between black and white. Brothers and sisters were often classified as belonging to different races, depending on multiple criteria such as skin color, nose length and shape, eye color and shape, hair type and color, and shape of the lips. The villagers used more than ten different racial terms to describe people, such as mulatto, *mulatto claro* (light mulatto), or *sarara,* meaning a person with reddish skin and light curly hair. These terms were applied inconsistently, and there was wide disagreement among villagers in placing individuals into racially defined categories, with such placement

Figure 8.3 These girls represent a small part of the great racial diversity in Brazil. Unlike the United States, which encoded a black/white dichotomy into its laws, racial differences in Brazil have no legal standing.

frequently mediated by class and social status. Indeed, as many as 133 shades of blackness have been identified in Brazil (Gates 2011; Bailey 2009).

In Brazil, as throughout much of Latin America, multiracialism is viewed as central to a positive national identity (see Daniel 2006). In the 1940s, influential Brazilian anthropologist and politician Gilberto Freyre promoted the idea that "Brazilianness" resulted from mixing among people of European, African, and indigenous ancestry (Bailey and Telles 2006; Freyre 1946). A student of Franz Boas at Columbia University, Freyre adopted many of Boas's understandings of race and racial equality, and his work supported other trends in Brazilian society that gave race mixing a positive connotation (Sánchez-Eppler 1992).

Brazilian politicians and some social scientists used Freyre's work to promote the notion that Brazil was a racial democracy. In the 1970 census, the military government declined to ask people's race, based on the argument that there was no race issue in Brazil (Bailey and Telles 2006:77). The official denial of race in Brazil has had both positive and negative effects. On the one hand, the linkage between Brazilian identity and multiracialism makes it easier for Brazilians to negotiate their own identity. It has also resulted in a society where, in theory, opportunity is open to people of diverse physical characteristics. On the other hand, the persistent denial that race is a social issue has led to a widespread refusal to take discrimination and racial stratification seriously until recently (Reichman 1995), in spite of the fact that racial inequality exacts a high toll. On every measure of social and economic well-being, Brazilians who self-identify as having African ancestry are far worse off than are those who self-identify as white. Their illiteracy rates are far higher and their wages are far lower. Higher education is almost exclusively the domain of white Brazilians. The United Nations Human Development Index (HDI), which measures national quality of life, ranks Brazil 74th in the world; if white and African-descended populations were measured separately, the white population would rank 48th and the African-descended population would rank 108th (Roland 2001).

The educational disparities between whites and nonwhites are much greater in Brazil than in the United States. This difference is based partly on the commitment of the U.S. government to provide public education to all its citizens, a responsibility of government in Brazil only since World War II. Thus, the general level of education in Brazil for both whites and nonwhites is much lower than in the United States. Brazil has a high rate of illiteracy, and higher education is almost entirely the province of white elites (Berman, in Danaher and Shellenberger 1995:91). In attempting to deal with this inequality, the Brazilian government recently passed a new law requiring public universities to reserve one-half their seats for the mostly poor students in Brazil's public schools; this will considerably raise the number of Brazilians of African descent in higher education (Romero 2012). A comparison of Brazilian and American racial stratification systems thus indicates that racial inequality exists in societies with very different cultural constructions of race.

Race and Racial Stratification in the United States

The major criteria of the cultural construction of race in the United States is presumed ancestry. Except for some regional variations—for example, the Anglo-Hispanic distinction in the American Southwest, the complex racial/ethnic system in Hawai'i, and the legal designations of Native Americans—the North American system of racial stratification primarily divides people into blacks and whites. This dichotomy ignores the reality that widespread racial mixing occurred historically and continues into the present (Basson 2008). An American cultural view of race that includes a mixed-racial identity is increasing, however. For the first time, the 2000 U.S. Census permitted people to self-identify as more than one race, and seven million people—almost half of whom were under 18—chose to do so (Boynton 2006; Nobles 2000). Indeed, some scholars suggest that as multiraciality undermines the American "binary race" construction (Daniel 2006), the cultural construction of race in the United States may be becoming a continuum more like Brazil than a dichotomy of discrete racial categories.

Although we think of race as "minority" races in the United States, anthropologists note that white is also a racial identity. But because "white" has been the cultural norm, the privileges and advantages that go with it are unconsciously assumed and largely invisible (T. Allen 1997; Frankenburg 1993; Hartigan 1997; J. Hill 1998; McIntosh 1999). For whites, ordinary experiences such as shopping, buying or renting a place to live, finding a hairdresser, or using a credit card do not generally involve a reflection on their racial identity, as is still true for "minority" races, in spite of the election of a black president in 2008.

The binary form of racial classification—black and white—and its accompanying system of racial stratification grew out of historical conditions of slavery in the United States. The racial stereotypes used to justify slavery and later segregation were, shamefully, supported by the then emerging biological and social sciences, including anthropology, with which few exceptions such as Franz Boas legitimized races as hierarchically arranged natural categories characterized by physical, cultural, intellectual, and moral differences (Smedley 1998); anthropologists roundly critique this view today (Nisbett 2007).

In the United States, race, class, and ethnicity interact in complex ways to produce a culturally unique social stratification system, which impacts every aspect of life, indeed, the very potential of life itself. African Americans have a higher mortality rate for both infants and mothers (Stolberg 1999), unequal access to health care, and unequal health care outcomes. Cancer survival rates, death rates for heart disease and HIV/AIDS, and complications from diseases like diabetes, such as loss of a limb or kidney disease, are all substantially higher for African Americans than for whites. As Gerald Markowitz and David Rosner (2013) demonstrate in their new book on the politics of lead poisoning, black children are six times more likely to be adversely impacted by elevated lead poisoning, which has both physical and psychological effects, than are white children, a fact partially a result of substandard housing. Racial health disparities are also linked to unequal access to medical insurance, though this may be somewhat ameliorated by the new health care law passed in the Obama administration. In New York City, for example, 30 percent of African Americans, Latinos, and members of other minority groups are uninsured, compared to 17 percent whites. Where people are covered by Medicaid, they are also treated differently by health care institutions, for example, more likely to be seen by rotating medical students and interns and thus less likely to receive coordinated medical care (Calman et al. 2005, p. 25).

Race and racism are also highly correlated with industrial pollution (Akom 2008; Checker 2005) and negative impacts of natural disasters, as tragically demonstrated by Hurricane Katrina, where death came most often for the poor—those who had no private transportation, no credit cards, no wealthy relatives to rely on, no home insurance, and no resources to evacuate the young and the aged. Not just the effect of the hurricane, but the government's response to it, deepened the social grooves—of class and race—already built into New Orleans society (Paredes 2006; Smith 2005:9) (see Figure 8.4).

Racial stratification affects job and educational opportunities open to racial minorities, as well as access to fair credit, salary levels, and accumulation of wealth, all of which affect social mobility and have been exacerbated by the 2007 recession. These include home ownership, mortgage rates, and housing foreclosures—black and Latino homeowners were nearly twice as likely to lose their houses to foreclosure than their white counterparts; use of public spaces; levels and types of violence; and interactions with law enforcement and the criminal justice system (Bajaj and Nixon 2006; Harrison 2009; Reed, Jr. 2006). Although African Americans and Latinos comprise only 25 percent of the national population, they are more than 60 percent of those in prison. Black women are also overrepresented in prison, convicted at rates 10 to 35 times higher than white women, while child abuse, sexual abuse, and murder have grown to disastrous proportions on Indian reservations, partly because of the lack of both social services and law enforcement.

Courtesy of Jean Gregg

Figure 8.4 Volunteering: It's the American way. Volunteers reach out to help the victims of Hurricane Sandy. Unlike Hurricane Katrina, the storm damage significantly affected all social classes and drew volunteers from across the social spectrum.

The intersection of race and class is also indicated by long-standing inequalities in income and wealth between blacks and whites: In 2005, the median per capita income for blacks was $16,629 and $28,946 for whites. This economic gap—made worse by the meltdown in the Detroit auto industry, where employment was an important route to African American mobility (Chapman 2008)—is even more obvious in asset accumulation: In 2004, African American families' median net worth was $20,600, and that of Latinos was $18,600, only 14.6 percent and 13.2 percent, respectively, of the $140,700 median net worth for whites (Muhammad 2008).

Although most Americans, white and black, are literate, and most are high school graduates, in contrast to Brazilians, educational disparities between blacks and whites are still a major aspect of our social stratification system, which led to affirmative action laws in the United States. Educational achievement reflects the stratified nature of class, race, ethnicity, and indigenous status in the United States. Though some social scientists (e.g., Patterson 2006) argue that this variation reflects cultural differences among racial and ethnic minorities, most anthropologists reject the "culture of poverty" explanation for an emphasis on systemic aspects of social stratification. Anthropologist John Ogbu, for example, argues that immigration status is key: He emphasizes that "involuntary minorities" such as African Americans, Mexican Americans, and Native Americans perceive social stratification in the United States as unfair, permanent, and systemically discriminatory, and develop cultural traits that hinder their success, while "voluntary minorities," or immigrants, emphasize education as the main route to economic success and accordingly exhibit higher degrees of educational achievement (Gibson and Ogbu 1991). Asian Americans, for example, largely credit their traditional cultural values of family support and educational achievement for their success in American society (Spencer 2012).

Other anthropologists, while acknowledging the negative effect of the "oppositional cultures" of involuntary minorities, hold that these cultural patterns have their source in the poverty of inner-city neighborhoods: discriminatory educational policies such as low expectations of minority students; overcrowded and underfunded schools; and less qualified teachers (Gibson 1997; Mateu-Gelabert and Lune 2007). Studies also show that most involuntary minorities do view educational achievement as a major route to upward social mobility (Anderson 1999), and that the problem of educational inequity is not a problem of culture, but rather needs to be addressed by a fairer distribution of resources, more equitable educational policies, and the transformation of schools into safer, more disciplined environments.

ETHNICITY AND STRATIFICATION

Ethnicity, like the nation, is a constructed narrative that focuses primarily on cultural differences, though it may incorporate racial differences as well. Many nation-states are characterized by ethnic stratification, as different ethnic groups have differential access to political and economic resources, and different symbolic roles in the national narrative.

Ethnic Stratification in the United States

In the United States, the dominant narrative of ethnicity is that the United States is a nation of immigrants who are welcomed into this country to pursue freedom from fear and the American Dream. In fact, the American immigrant narrative is laden with contradictions and conflicts with the ongoing project of creating an American national identity based on a common culture and language. Indeed, historically, the vision of the United States as a land of immigrants was largely restricted to immigrants from northern and western Europe: The Constitution originally limited citizenship to those who were "free and white (and male)," excluding Native Americans, Mexican Americans, and African Americans. In spite of, or perhaps because of, increasing immigration from southern and eastern Europe in the late 19th century, by the 1920s, immigration was restricted for Asians, Latin Americans, southern and eastern Europeans, and people from the Middle East. These restrictions were based on a widely shared view that these people were "undesirable elements"—racially inferior and from cultures that would prevent their assimilation into the larger American society.

By the 1950s, concerns over immigrant assimilation abated, and the United States celebrated itself as a "melting pot," like a stew, in which all ethnicities were blended to produce a unique American identity (Glazer and Moynihan 1970). Although many important ethnic cultural patterns, like language, had in fact disappeared or faded for groups of European descent by this time, more subtle ethnic patterns, such as food preferences; verbal and nonverbal means of communication; the experience of health, illness, and pain; occupational choices; and voting patterns continued (Cerroni-Long 1993; Schensul 1997). But in any case, the melting pot analogy, like earlier American immigration narratives, excluded Mexican Americans, African Americans, and Native Americans, and people from Asia and the Middle East.

By the 1960s, a new model of ethnic relations, called multiculturalism, emerged. Supported by the civil rights movement, multiculturalism embraced cultural diversity as a positive value. In 1965, a new Immigration and Nationality Act was passed that explicitly aimed at reversing the discriminatory basis of earlier immigration laws. This greatly expanded the cultural backgrounds of people permitted to immigrate from previously discriminated-against nations and resulted in substantially increased immigration from the Middle East, the Indian subcontinent, China, Korea, the Caribbean, parts of Central and South America, including Mexico, and Africa (Abdo 2006; Ewing 2008a; Pew Research 2007; Wong 2008). This resulted in increasing ethnic diversity: The latest U.S. Census (2012) documents that no single ethnic group will be big enough to be a majority by 2042.

Anthropologists studying these new immigrants take into account the changing contexts of immigration as these are shaped by changes in local, national, and global economies and political conditions (Brettell 2003; Lamphere 1992). These include the rise of international terrorism; the cyclical nature of global, national, and regional economies; the increase of illegal immigration; transnationalism; the events of 9/11; and global political instability.

Muslim Immigrants after 9/11 in the United States

For more than 200 years, Muslims lived in almost near invisibility in the United States, blending into an ethnically diverse landscape. From 1870 to World War I, there was an increase in Christian immigration from Muslim-dominated countries like Syria and Lebanon. In an effort to establish national organizations to facilitate their integration into

American society, however, these immigrants constructed a common ethnic identity as Arab (Ewing 2008a). As the 1965 immigration laws opened the United States to skilled, highly educated Muslim immigrants from South Asia as well as from the Middle East, the increasing numbers and diverse origins of Muslims increased and the new immigrants began organizing as Muslims, focusing on maintaining Islamic religious practices rather than identifying themselves with their distinctive nationally based ethnicities. In the United States, this is reflected in a more public presence for Islam, with expanded construction of mosques and Islamic schools (Abdo 2006); the expansion of a Koranically acceptable banking system that rejects charging interest on loans; a renewed emphasis on Muslim identity such as wearing the hijab, especially among the younger generation and particularly after 9/11; and the emergence of Muslim institutions providing information about Islam to the American public (Goodstein 2009).

After 9/11, ethnographic and social science research on immigrant Muslim communities increased, not surprisingly, perhaps indicating increasing American hostility toward Muslims (see Abdo 2006; Ewing 2008a; see also Bayoumi 2012; Strum and Tarantolo 2003). In spite of this hostility, American Muslims express almost as much satisfaction with their lives as other Americans, and on many socioeconomic indicators, such as annual income, compare favorably with non-Muslims (Pew Research 2007). Fifty percent of American foreign-born Muslims have attended college, and most believe that they can fulfill their American Dream with hard work; this is a higher percentage than among African American Muslims. Sixty-three percent of American foreign-born Muslims see no conflict between being a devout Muslim and living in a modern society, although some younger Muslims do identify with extreme fundamentalism. Compared with Europe, however, the Muslim presence in the United States has engendered little extreme conflict and violence.

Latino Immigrants and Social Stratification in the United States

Latinos in the United States are a large and diverse ethnic group, sharing a common cultural heritage of the Spanish language. The approximately 21 million Latino immigrants and their descendants include approximately 13 million Mexican Americans; 3 million Puerto Ricans; 1 million Cuban Americans; and 4 million other Latin Americans, mostly from Central America. Legal immigration of Latinos sharply increased subsequent to the 1965 immigration law, so a larger proportion of Latinos, particularly Mexican Americans, are first-generation immigrants. As of 2002,

Mexicans accounted for about 20 percent of the total legal immigration to the United States. It is also estimated that they constitute approximately three-fifths of the almost 12 million undocumented immigrant population (Strum and Selee 2004).

Much of the Mexican American population of the United States originated in the populations of the Southwest and California, whose settlement predated the 1846–1848 Mexican–American War. Originally rural agricultural workers, since the 1950s, Mexican Americans have become about 90 percent urban, concentrated in California, Texas, New Mexico, and Arizona. Puerto Ricans and Cubans, in contrast, initially migrated to urban areas, especially East Coast cities, with Cubans mainly concentrated in South Florida. Political upheavals in Central America led to increasing numbers of both documented and undocumented immigrants from Guatemala, Nicaragua, and El Salvador, and since the 1960s, there has been large-scale immigration from the Dominican Republic.

Although Mexican immigrants are still largely concentrated in the Southwest, since 1990, they have been drawn, primarily by low-wage meatpacking factory and construction employment, to other parts of the country that had not previously experienced Latino immigration, such as Arkansas, Georgia, Colorado, and North Carolina. Much of the work Latino immigrants perform, as in the meat-processing plants in the Midwest, is difficult, dirty, and hazardous, with few health benefits (Preston 2009). With the current downturn in the economy and a crackdown on undocumented immigrants through raids on their places of employment, stricter scrutiny of Social Security cards, the withdrawal of social services, local laws prohibiting driving licenses, and greater cooperation between local police forces and federal immigration agents, the already low economic position of Latinos is under increasing threat. And although many Americans losing their jobs can turn to the government for a safety net of unemployment insurance and job assistance, this is not available to undocumented immigrants, who are working longer hours for less pay, at any job they can get (see Figure 8.5). As one sociologist pointed out, many factories in rural parts of the country are only able to hang on because of immigrant workers taking jobs other Americans won't take. As wages fall, employers tend to move from white employees, to black employees, to Latino employees, and in many cases, ultimately to closing their doors (Preston 2009).

Courtesy of Beth Pacheco

Figure 8.5 Latinos, who make up the largest number of immigrants in the United States, are often economically exploited by employers. In recent years, they have become more active in pressing for immigration reform and for fair labor practices for workers.

BRINGING IT BACK HOME:
THE VOICES OF NEW IMMIGRANTS

In addition to the economic motivations of many immigrants, the spread of near starvation, ethnic conflict, civil wars, and human rights abuses in many contemporary societies has increased the number of migrants to the United States. Many of these new migrants are from places like Sudan, Somalia, El Salvador, Kurdistan, Vietnam, or Iraq: These places are familiar to Americans only because of U.S. political or military interventions, but most Americans have little knowledge of these cultures. In addition, unlike migrants from the late 19th and early 20th centuries, these contemporary migrants are as—or more—likely to be found in rural Wisconsin or Georgia, in small cities in the Southwest, or the far reaches of Maine or Minneapolis than in ethnically diverse urban centers.

Putting a human face on the lives of different ethnic groups helps us understand how the lives of these migrants have been shaped by the difficulties they face in trying to understand and fit into American society. Ping Chong, director of a brilliant and innovative theater company, uses anthropological techniques of individuals telling their own stories to introduce these migrants to diverse American audiences. In using the title "Undesirable Elements" for his theater pieces on migrants, Ping (2012) plays on the term used in the American political culture of the 19th and early 20th centuries about non-European immigrants.

Like an anthropologist, Ping Chong has the double vision of an insider/outsider. He was born into a family of Chinese opera stars who were forced to migrate from China because of their dissident political beliefs, and he grew up in the ethnic enclave of New York City's Chinatown. He describes himself as a "young man sitting on a cultural fence."

The stories told by the migrants in Ping's plays frequently emphasize the comparisons they see between the diverse ethnic and racial stratification system in the United States and their own societies, as well as the contrast between American ideals and the reality of ethnic and racial stratification.

One migrant from Kurdistan says, "everyone we watched on American TV shows was blond-haired and blue-eyed, but when we arrive in America, they are not. This [diversity] is the *real* America." Another Kurdish migrant says, "I don't speak English. It's hard. I look different. I have black eyes and black hair. The kids in my class think I'm weird." Another migrant teenager, fleeing the violence accompanying the fall of the shah in Iran, who was a strong American ally, couldn't understand the anti-Iranian bumper stickers she saw on cars or the restaurant signs saying Iranians would not be served. "I am very confused," she said, "I thought I was an American." Saul, a teenaged Mexican immigrant, is shopping in a mall in Atlanta, Georgia. He sees there is a white salesperson following him. Now, when Saul enters a shop he tells the salesperson, "Yeah, I'm Mexican, but don't worry. I'm not going to steal anything. I have money."

Perhaps the most telling comment on American stratification comes from a migrant now applying for college: "I had to check a box. Caucasian, black, Hispanic, Asian, other. I don't know which one to check. The administrator tells me, you are from Venezuela, check Hispanic. I say, but Hispanic is someone from Spain. I'm half Lebanese, half Venezuelan, half Catholic, half Druze from the Middle East. People here talk about race and color, but that doesn't happen in Venezuela or Lebanon. What does it have to do with what people are?" What indeed? That is a major question in this chapter.

YOU DECIDE:

1. How have you experienced American class, race, and ethnic stratification in the United States? How does your experience relate to the ideal of the American Dream?
2. The historical narrative in the United States emphasizes both the assimilation of American immigrants and multiculturalism, a respect for cultural differences. Which narrative do you think best describes the contemporary United States and why?
3. How would you check the box on your racial and ethnic identity? What does this "have to do with what people are?" Or with "being American?"

CHAPTER SUMMARY

1. What are the differences between functionalist and conflict theories of social stratification? Functionalist theory holds that social stratification benefits the whole society because it motivates people to undertake all the jobs necessary for the society to survive. Conflict theory emphasizes the conflicts within stratified societies as different social strata, with opposing interests, clash with one another over goals and resources.
2. What are the major dimensions of social stratification, and how do they relate to other aspects of culture and society? The major dimensions of social stratification are power, wealth, and prestige, which are

closely tied to occupation, which is closely tied to income. The particular value system of a culture shapes how these factors interact to determine where a person is placed in the stratification system.

3. What are the main features of the class system in the United States? The culture of the United States emphasizes "the American Dream," the idea that one can and should improve one's life chances and material wealth. Although many Americans dismiss the importance of class in the United States, there are important material and life change differences in the different social classes. Inequality between social classes is increasing, as is downward mobility.

4. What are the main differences between a class system and a caste system? In a class system, social position is ideally achieved, rather than ascribed, although class status in reality is also ascribed. People can move between the social classes. Classes are largely based on differences of income and wealth, but also characterized by different lifestyles and cultural differences. In the Indian caste system, based on Hindu ideas of ritual purity, social position (caste) is largely ascribed (based on birth), and caste boundaries are sharply defined by prohibitions on intercaste marriage and intercaste food sharing, which tend to reinforce class as well as caste differences.

5. How do the Brazilian and American racial stratification systems differ from each other? In the United States, race is mainly conceived as a dichotomy between white and black and is based on presumed ancestry. In Brazil, race is constructed as a continuum, though race and class in both societies interact and benefit members of the racial elites.

6. What is the major narrative of ethnicity in the United States? The cultural diversity of the United States has largely been framed in terms of ethnicity based on the national origins of immigrants who came seeking the American Dream. African Americans, Native Americans, and Mexican Americans were ignored in this narrative, but today's migrants come from a wider historical and geographical background than previously.

KEY TERMS

Achieved status	Power
Ascribed status	Prestige
Caste system	Race
Class	Social mobility
Class system	Social stratification
Conflict theory	Wealth
Functionalism	

Chander Dembla

Marriage rituals in India, as elsewhere, contain many symbolic elements. The color red symbolizes fertility and the bride's gold jewelry indicates her family's social status and is considered auspicious for a long married life.

CHAPTER 9

MARRIAGE, FAMILY AND KINSHIP

LEARNING OBJECTIVES

After you have read this chapter, you will be able to:

△ Describe some of the roles and functions that marriage and family have in society.

△ Define the incest taboo and present two different explanations for it.

△ Define endogamy and exogamy with examples of each.

△ Summarize the differences between polygyny, polyandry, and monogamy, and some of their important functions in different societies.

△ Explain the difference between bride service, bridewealth, and dowry, and their different functions in different social contexts.

△ Discuss how the American family has changed in the last half century and some reasons for these changes.

△ Explain how extended families differ from nuclear families and how patrilineal families differ from matrilineal families.

A Society Without Marriage: the Na of China

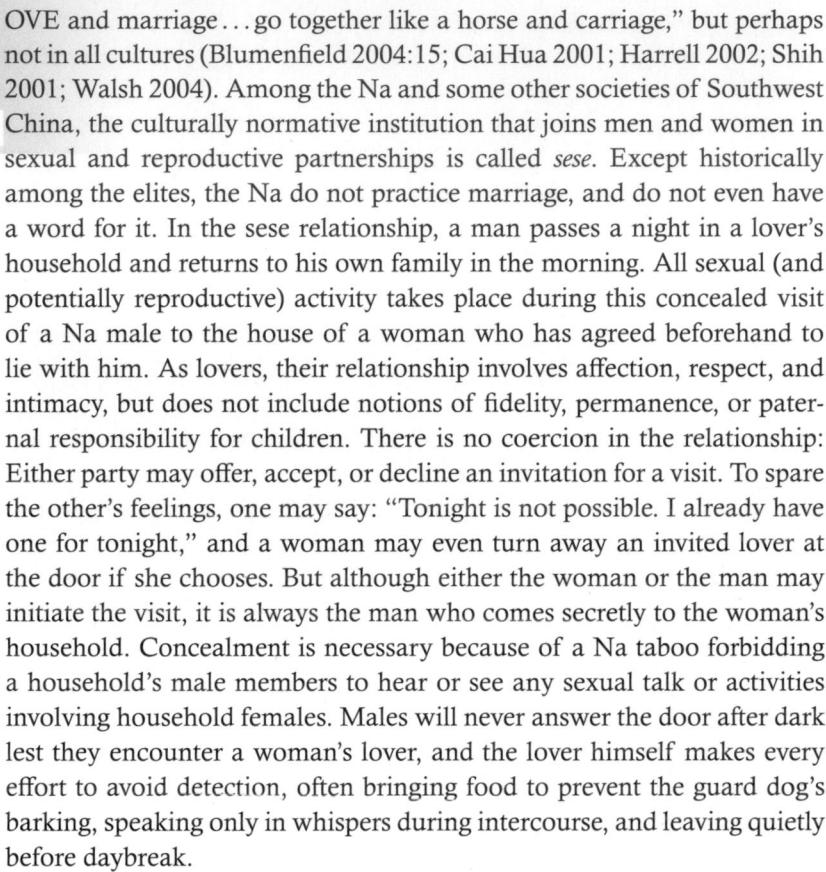

"Love and marriage...go together like a horse and carriage," but perhaps not in all cultures (Blumenfield 2004:15; Cai Hua 2001; Harrell 2002; Shih 2001; Walsh 2004). Among the Na and some other societies of Southwest China, the culturally normative institution that joins men and women in sexual and reproductive partnerships is called *sese*. Except historically among the elites, the Na do not practice marriage, and do not even have a word for it. In the sese relationship, a man passes a night in a lover's household and returns to his own family in the morning. All sexual (and potentially reproductive) activity takes place during this concealed visit of a Na male to the house of a woman who has agreed beforehand to lie with him. As lovers, their relationship involves affection, respect, and intimacy, but does not include notions of fidelity, permanence, or paternal responsibility for children. There is no coercion in the relationship: Either party may offer, accept, or decline an invitation for a visit. To spare the other's feelings, one may say: "Tonight is not possible. I already have one for tonight," and a woman may even turn away an invited lover at the door if she chooses. But although either the woman or the man may initiate the visit, it is always the man who comes secretly to the woman's household. Concealment is necessary because of a Na taboo forbidding a household's male members to hear or see any sexual talk or activities involving household females. Males will never answer the door after dark lest they encounter a woman's lover, and the lover himself makes every effort to avoid detection, often bringing food to prevent the guard dog's barking, speaking only in whispers during intercourse, and leaving quietly before daybreak.

Both women and men have multiple partners, serially or simultaneously, and no records are kept of visits to ascertain the paternity of children. The Na do not have a word for incest, illegitimate child, infidelity, or promiscuity. The Na are matrilineal, and children by a variety of fathers stay with the mother's household for their entire lives. When a generation lacks females, a household may adopt a relative's child or encourage a son to bring his lover into the household. The only males in a Na household are relatives of different generations, who are brothers, uncles, and granduncles. There are no husbands or fathers. Where males are in short supply in a family, a woman may bring her lover home.

The Na visit, which has been part of Na culture for more than a thousand years, is treated as a mutually enjoyable but singular occurrence that entails no future conditions. The Chinese state has periodically tried to change what they call this "barbarous practice," but without success so far. But as the Na adapt to the new conditions of the nation-state and the

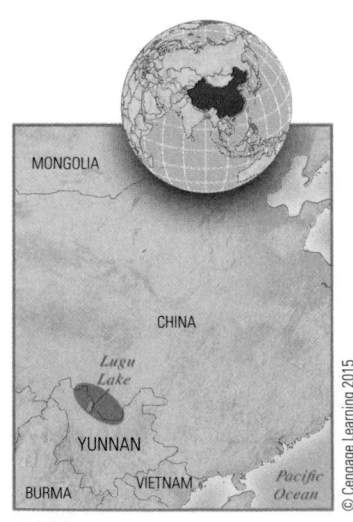

Location of the Na.

© Cengage Learning 2015

globalizing economy, they are increasingly subjected to state-sponsored public school education and media, which reflect mainstream Han mores and lifestyles and stigmatize Na practices. This, as well as their inability to name a father on official documents, may spell the end of Na visits, eliminating yet one more example of the rich diversity of human adaptive strategies.

All human societies face certain problems for which marriage, the creation of families, and kinship systems offer solutions. Every society must regulate sexual access between males and females, find satisfactory ways to organize labor, assign responsibility for child care, provide a clear framework for organizing an individual's rights and responsibilities, and provide for the transfer of property and social position between generations. The many human solutions to these challenges are guided by cultural rules, accounting for a wide variety of kinship and family systems. These systems tend to be adaptive to subsistence patterns and other realities: When these change, rules about kinship and family also tend to change.

▨ FORMS AND FUNCTIONS OF MARRIAGE

The need to regulate sexual access stems from the potentially continuous receptivity of human males and females to sexual activity. If sexual competition was not regulated and channeled into stable relationships that were given social approval, it could cause societal conflict. These relationships need not be permanent, though in most societies—though not all—they are relatively stable; we refer to these relationships as marriage. **Marriage**, which refers to the customs, rules, and obligations that establish a socially endorsed relationship between adults and children, and between the married couple's kin groups, is a very widespread, though not a universal social institution, as the Na illustrate. But in the absence of safe and dependable contraception throughout most of human history and with the near certainty that children would be born, marriage, as a relatively stable union between a male and female that involves responsibility for children as well as economic exchange, became the basis for most human adaptations.

In addition to forming bonds between a couple, marriage extends social alliances by linking together different families and kin groups, leading to cooperation among groups of people larger than the married couple. This expansion of the social group within which people can work

marriage: The customs, rules, and obligations that establish a special relationship between sexually cohabiting adults, between them and any children they take responsibility for, and between the kin of the married couple.

together and share resources is of great advantage for the survival of the human species.

Although marriage and the subsequent formation of families in most societies rests on the biological complementarity of males and females in reproduction, both marriage and family are cultural patterns. Thus, they differ in form and function both among and within human societies and change over time with changing political and economic circumstances and the life stages of individuals.

Heterosexual, monogamous marriage, dominant in the United States, is only one of many culturally acceptable kinds of marriages worldwide. Marriages involving plural spouses or same-sex relationships also fulfill the functions of marriage in satisfactory ways. This cultural variation makes it difficult to give one universally applicable definition of marriage.

Among some African societies, woman-woman marriage is an alternative to heterosexual marriages. This allows a barren woman to divorce her husband, take another woman as her wife, and arrange for a surrogate to impregnate this woman. Children born from this arrangement become members of the barren woman's natal lineage and refer to her as their father. A similar pattern is found among the Azande, where royal power is sustained by multiple wives. Where there was a shortage of marriageable women, a man might take a young man for his wife and the couple would be recognized as a married couple (Kilbride 2004).

Like marriage, the concept of the family also varies among cultures. In many societies, the most important family bond is between lineal blood relations (father and children or mother and children) or between brothers and sisters rather than between husband and wife. In these societies, the lineage or the clan rather than the immediate family confers legitimacy on children.

MARRIAGE RULES

Every society has culturally defined rules concerning sexual relations and marriage. These rules may determine how spouses are chosen, limit marriage to certain groups, dictate the number of spouses and how they are chosen, allow for dissolving marriages, determine rules for remarriage, specify the kinds of exchanges and rituals that legitimate marriage, and determine the rights and obligations established by marriage. Among the most universal of these rules is the incest taboo.

Incest Taboos

incest taboo: A prohibition on sexual relations between relatives.

Incest taboos are rules that prohibit sexual relationships with specific categories of kin. Incest taboos are universal, though they apply to different categories of kin in different societies. Because sexual access is a key right of marriage, incest taboos restrict who are considered acceptable marriage partners.

Except for brother-sister marriage in some ancient empires like Egypt, Peru, Rome, and Hawai'i, probably to keep power and wealth within royal families, incest taboos banning sex between parents and their children and between brothers and sisters, is universal. In many societies, people beyond the immediate family, such as lineage or clan members, or certain categories of cousins may be covered by the incest taboo. These rules demonstrate that kinship, although based on biological relationships, is in fact, culturally constructed. For example, although an individual's parallel and cross-cousins both stand in the same biological relationship to an individual (see Figure 9.1) in some societies, the incest taboo may cover one category but not the other.

Different explanations have been proposed for the universality of the incest taboo. Biologically based theories argue that the incest taboo prevents inbreeding that would have a deleterious effect on humanity. Although sex between close biological relatives does lead to increased birth defects, it is questionable whether this connection would be perceived in premodern societies, which have extremely high infant mortality rates. And, as we noted, the incest taboo may apply to people who are not close biological relatives.

Psychologically based theories argue either that humans have an innate aversion to those with whom they are raised, or that sexual competition among siblings or parents and children would create disruption and kin role confusion in the family. However, these theories do not account for all the incest taboos and avoidance patterns in different societies. In addition, if aversion to intimate kin is innate, what is the need for a rule against it?

endogamy: A rule prescribing that a person must marry within a particular group.

Alliance theory argues that incest taboos force people to marry outside of their group, creating wider social bonds that are useful in helping these groups survive. When Margaret Mead asked a man in New Guinea if he was allowed to marry his sister, he was astonished. If a man married his sister, he replied, he would have no brother-in-law with whom to hunt, to garden, or to visit (in Levi Strauss 1969/1949:485). Creating wider alliances is a very powerful argument for the incest taboo.

Endogamy rules require people to marry within their own group, however

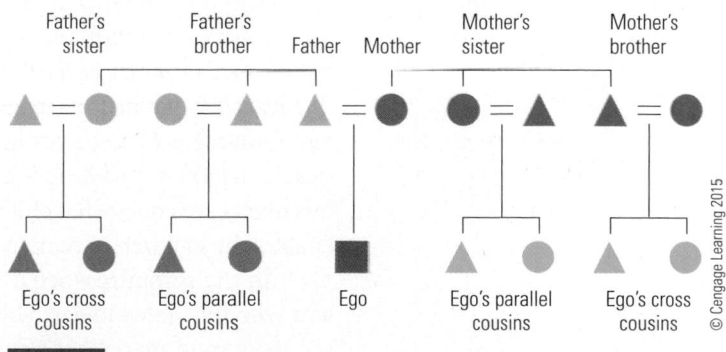

Figure 9.1 This diagram indicates the relationships of cross-cousins and parallel cousins. In many cultures, these relationships determine rules of exogamy.

Father's sister — Father's brother — Father — Mother — Mother's sister — Mother's brother

Ego's cross cousins — Ego's parallel cousins — Ego — Ego's parallel cousins — Ego's cross cousins

© Cengage Learning 2015

that group is defined. As noted previously, blood relations among royalty may be encouraged or required to marry each other. In India, castes and subcastes are endogamous; in the United States, although there are no named endogamous groups, so-called racial groups, religious groups, and social classes tend to be endogamous, based on opportunities to meet, cultural norms, and similarities in lifestyle.

Preferential Marriages

Some societies have preferential marriage rules, usually involving cousin marriage. In **cross-cousin marriage** the preferred partners are the children of one's parents' siblings of the opposite sex—mother's brother or father's sister. Preferred cross-cousin marriage reinforces ties between kin groups established in the preceding generation, preserving the relationship between two intermarrying kin groups across generations.

Parallel-cousin marriage involves children of the parents' same-sex siblings—mother's sister or father's brother—and is found in some Arab and North African Muslim societies. Because descent and inheritance are in the male line in Muslim Arab societies, parallel-cousin marriage helps prevent the fragmentation of family property and keeps economic resources within the family. Parallel-cousin marriage reinforces the solidarity of brothers, but by socially isolating groups of brothers from each other, it adds to factional disputes and disunity within the larger social system. This illustrates that although different kinship and family structures may contribute to solidarity and stability at one level of society, they may be socially disruptive at another level. Again, because cross-cousin and parallel-cousin marriage differentiate kin who are equally biologically close (see Figure 9.1), preferred cousin marriage rules demonstrate the important cultural dimension of kinship systems.

The **levirate** and the **sororate** are two types of marriage rules that demonstrate the importance of marriage as an alliance between two groups rather than between individuals. These rules allow a marriage to survive the death of one of the partners with the continuance of group alliances and fulfillment of the marriage contract. Under the levirate, a man marries the widow of his dead brother, and in some cases the children born to this union are considered children of the deceased man. Thus, the levirate enables the children to remain within the dead husband's descent group.

In the sororate, when a woman dies, her kin group supplies a sister as a wife for the widower. The sororate also allows the husband of a barren woman to marry her sister, and at least some of the children of this marriage are considered those of the first wife. If no qualifying relative is available to fulfill the levirate or the sororate, other appropriately classified kin may be substituted, or these marriages may not take place.

cross-cousin marriage: Marriage between an individual and the child of his or her mother's brother or father's sister.

parallel-cousin marriage: Marriage between the children of a parent's same-sex siblings (mother's sisters, father's brothers).

levirate: The custom whereby a man marries the widow of a deceased brother.

sororate: The custom whereby, when a man's wife dies, her sister is given to him as a wife.

Number of Spouses

All societies have rules about how many spouses a person may have at one time. **Monogamy**, which permits each individual to have only one spouse at any given time, is the rule in Europe and North America, but not in most of the world's cultures. **Polygamy**, or plural marriage, includes **polygyny**, the marriage of one man to several women, and **polyandry**, the marriage of one woman to several men. About 75 percent of the world's cultures permit (and prefer) polygyny (Murdock 1949:28), but even in these cultures, the male/female ratio and the requirements of a bride-price, which many men cannot afford, inhibit its actual occurrence.

Polygyny

Polygyny has important economic and political functions in some societies. Where women are economically important, polygyny increases a man's wealth and therefore his social position. Because marriage links groups together, having several wives from different groups within a society also extends a man's alliances. Thus, chiefs, headmen, and state leaders may take wives from many different groups or villages to increase their political power.

Polygyny is found primarily in societies where plural wives—and their children—increase both a family's labor supply and its productivity. For example, among the Tiwi of Australia, a foraging group, women's food collecting makes a very important contribution to the food supply. Thus, the more wives a man has, the better his family's standard of living (Goodale 1971). Although Western cultural stereotypes criticize polygyny as oppressing women, the status of females in polygynous societies is not uniformly low and may even, as among the Tiwi, be relatively high and accord women a high degree of sexual and economic freedom. Where women's work is hard and monotonous, as it often is, women may welcome the addition of a co-wife because it eases their own workload and provides daily companionship. Conflict among co-wives does occur in polygynous societies and is sometimes mitigated by sororal polygyny, a preference for a man to marry sisters. In many polygynous societies, co-wives live in separate dwellings, and cultural norms requiring a man to distribute his economic resources and sexual attentions evenly among his wives also mitigate family conflict. Like all other cultural patterns, marriage rules adapt to changing economic and social circumstances. Thus, with declining amounts of available agricultural land, increasing expenses in educating children, and the social pressures of Western and Christian condemnation of polygyny, this form of marriage has to

monogamy: A rule that permits a person to be married to only one spouse at a time.

polygamy: A rule allowing more than one spouse.

polygyny: A rule permitting a man to have more than one wife at a time.

polyandry: A rule permitting a woman to have more than one husband at a time.

some extent declined or been driven underground in parts of Africa (Kilbride 2006).

Polyandry

Polyandry is relatively rare, found mainly in Tibet, Nepal, and some indigenous groups in India, like the Toda. In Tibet, as in other polyandrous societies, polyandry is related to a shortage of land. If brothers marry a single wife, their father's land can be kept intact within the family rather than fragmented over the generations. Polyandry is also functional in societies where men are away from home for long periods of time, in that a woman has more than one husband to provide for her. Among the Toda, polyandry was related to a shortage of women, but because they no longer practice female infanticide, and under the influence of Christian missionaries, the Toda today are largely monogamous (Queen and Haberstein 1974).

Choosing a Mate

The cultural context of marriage includes how mates are chosen. In most societies, kin group interests—rather than individual desires—are the bases of mate selection, and the families of the bride and groom take an important, even determinative, role in selecting their children's spouses, often through a go-between. This practice of arranged marriage strongly contrasts with marriage in the United States, where individuals ideally select their own mates on the basis of sexual compatibility, emotional needs, physical attractiveness, and personality, a cluster of patterns called "romantic love."

Arranged marriage is related to other cultural patterns. In India, for example, its dominance is aligned with the patrilineal, patriarchal, and patrilocal ideals of Indian society. Even in contemporary India, where women are increasingly working outside the home, most people prefer arranged marriage, although patterns are changing. Among the urban middle-class, the bride and groom are more likely to meet, perhaps even outside family visits, before they marry; traditionally, potential spouses did not see each other before the wedding ceremony (Nanda 2000a). Economic and cultural globalization has also had an impact. In South India, young, lower-class women are working in garment factories, earning salaries that are becoming essential to family subsistence. In the past, these families paid the dowries of their daughters in arranged marriages (even if they had to borrow much of it), but now many of these women save for their own dowries. This has led to greater independence for young, unmarried women who now demand greater rights to choose their own mates rather than accepting the matches their families arrange. These "love matches" have, however, disrupted the kin support networks that traditionally accompany arranged marriages and put these women at greater risk for abuse and infidelity (Lessinger 2013).

◪ THE EXCHANGE OF GOODS AND RIGHTS IN MARRIAGE

Almost everywhere, the public rituals and ceremonies that accompany marriage distinguish it from other, similar kinds of unions. Marriage involves the transfer of certain rights and obligations, primarily involving sexual access of the partners to each other, rights over any children born to the marriage, obligations by one or both parents to care for children born to the union, and rights of the marriage partners to the economic services of the other.

Almost universally, marriage requires an exchange of goods or services between the families of the bride and groom (see Figure 9.2). Although sometimes called "gifts," these exchanges are obligatory for the transfer of marital rights, and if the exchanges are not completed, the rights in marriage can be forfeited. Although certain exchanges are dominant in a society, any particular society may have several legitimate forms of exchange (Huber et al. 2011).

Figure 9.2 Displaying bride-price in Africa. Bridewealth often includes the presentation of goods from the family of the husband to the family of the wife, as depicted here among the Fulani of Guinea-Bissau in West Africa.

Ami Vitale/Alamy

Bride Service and Bridewealth

Bride service, bridewealth, and dowry are three main kinds of marriage exchanges. In addition, other less-common forms include groom service, where a potential bride spends a week or two at the groom's house to demonstrate her domestic skills (Huber et al. 2011).

In bride service, most commonly found in foraging societies where few material goods are accumulated, the husband must work for a specified number of years for his wife's family in exchange for his marital rights (Marlowe 2004). Among the Ju/'hoansi of the Kalahari Desert in Africa, this may be as long as 15 years or until the birth of the third child.

bridewealth: Goods presented by the groom's kin to the bride's kin to legitimize a marriage (formerly called "bride-price").

The most common form of marriage exchange is **bridewealth**, where cash or goods are given by the groom's kin to the bride's kin to seal the marriage. Bridewealth previously was called *bride-price,* but this falsely conveys the idea that the marriage is merely an economic exchange (Ogbu 1978) and that women's status in such societies is devalued. In fact, in these societies, daughters are valuable to their families because their bridewealth finances males' marriages.

In societies with bridewealth, a person can claim compensation for a violation of conjugal rights only if the bridewealth has been paid. Furthermore, bridewealth paid at marriage is returned (subject to specified conditions) if a marriage is terminated. Although many studies of bridewealth emphasize its role in entitling a husband to domestic, economic, sexual, and reproductive rights, bridewealth also confers rights on the wife, as it allows wives to hold their husbands accountable for violations of conjugal rights. In sanctioning these mutual rights and obligations, bridewealth helps stabilize marriage by giving both families a vested interest in keeping the couple together.

Although globally widespread, bridewealth transactions are particularly characteristic of Africa. Among the Kipsigis, a pastoralist/horticultural society of East Africa, the traditional bridewealth payment was livestock, but it now includes cash (Borgerhoff Mulder 1995:576). Formerly, when agricultural land was available and crop prices were high, bridewealth was high because of the importance of women's agricultural labor. Now, however, land is scarce, crop prices are low, and women's agricultural labor has lost its value, so bridewealth has declined. On the other hand, Kipsigis parents of educated girls often demand high bridewealth as compensation for their daughters' school fees because their daughters' education will both increase their earning potential and benefit their marital home.

Dowry

dowry: Presentation of goods by the bride's kin to the family of the groom or to the couple.

Dowry, which is less widespread than bridewealth, refers to goods given by a bride's family to the groom's family, and is associated with private ownership of property. Today, dowry is mainly associated with India, and although it is illegal, it remains central to arranged marriage. One explanation of Indian dowry is that it is a voluntary gift, symbolizing affection for a daughter leaving home and compensating her for her traditional exclusion from the inheritance of land or property. Dowry is also sometimes explained as a source of a married woman's security because it always includes jewelry, which is—theoretically—her property (in practice, her husband's family usually keeps control of it). Dowry is also sometimes explained as compensation to the groom's family, who must now take on the economic burden of a wife, who traditionally did not work outside the home. In contemporary India, with its new emphasis on consumerism and social class mobility, dowry is increasingly perceived by the husband's family as a way to improve their financial and social standing. As such, insufficient dowry is sometimes used as emotional blackmail of a woman's family and is linked to wife abuse and even wife murder (Nanda and Gregg 2009; Stone and James 2005).

◪ FAMILY STRUCTURES, HOUSEHOLDS, AND RULES OF RESIDENCE

Two basic types of families are the elementary, or nuclear, family and the extended family. **Nuclear families** are organized around the relationship between husband and wife (the conjugal tie). The **extended family** is based on **consanguinity**, or blood ties between relations extending over three or more generations.

A household, or domestic group, is different from a family. Although most households contain people related by blood or marriage, nonkin may be included; conversely, members of a family may be spread out over several households. Household composition is affected by the cultural rules about residence after marriage. Under neolocal residence rules, married couples create their own households. Under patrilocal residence rules, a newly married couple lives with the husband's family, whereas under matrilocal residence rules, the couple lives with the wife's family. Under avunculocal residence rules, the couple lives with the wife's uncle's family (usually the husband's mother's brother); this rule permits the geographical concentration of male lineage mates and the preservation of male control of lineage wealth in a matrilineal system. Bilocal residence rules permit a couple to choose between living with the wife's family or the husband's family. Each of these residence rules is associated with a different type of kinship system.

nuclear families: Organized around the relationship between husband and wife (conjugal tie).

extended family: Family based on blood relations extending over three or more generations.

consanguinity: Blood ties between people.

Nuclear Families

A nuclear family, consisting of a married couple and their children, is mainly associated with independent households. Only 5 percent of the world's societies are traditionally neolocal. The nuclear, neolocal family is adapted to industrialized capitalism, where jobs are not generally dependant on family connections and where employment and promotion often require geographical mobility. Independence and flexibility are also requirements in foraging societies, and nuclear families predominate in more than 75 percent of all foraging groups.

The Changing American Family

American culture still generally extols the independent, nuclear, neolocal family, although the diversity of American family structures is far from this ideal. This is a result of the high divorce rate; increasing same-sex commitments and domestic partnerships (see Figure 9.3), and in some states, legal same-sex marriage; the increasing number of working mothers and single-parent households; the growing number of unmarried couples living together in long-term relationships; surrogate reproduction; the growing number of childless couples; the greater number of people who never marry; the increasing number of people who remarry after divorce or widowhood; and the increasing number of three-generation households.

The high rates of divorce and remarriage enmesh nuclear families in larger and more complicated kinship networks. Sometimes called "blended families," these networks include previously divorced spouses and their new marriage partners; sometimes children from previous marriages; or multiple sets of grandparents and other similar relations. Although blended families may function in some ways like traditional two-parent families, in fact, only one child in six averages a weekly visit with a divorced father, and only one in four sees him once a month. Almost half of the children of divorced parents have not seen their biological fathers for more than a year, and more than two-thirds have lost contact with him ten years later (Hacker 2002:22). Another change in the American family is the growing

© Billie L. Porter

Figure 9.3 Families based on gay and lesbian relationships are increasingly a part of the American family culture. Here, the two fathers of the boy and girl have been together for over 20 years. Their mothers have been in a relationship for over 15 years. Together, they form a happy and successful family unit. The children divide their time between their mothers' home and their fathers' home, which are very near to each other.

number of multigenerational families, which has increased substantially since 1970, caused both by the increase of immigrants who live in such families (Kramer 2011) and an increase in the number of adult children moving back to their parental home because they cannot find employment. At the same time, the number of Americans living alone is also rising, including young people, middle-aged people, and even the elderly (Klinenberg 2012a; 2012b).

Single-parent households are also increasing (DeParle 2012). In 2009, single-parent households, mainly single-mother households, accounted for about 27 percent of all households with children, and 3.1 million American children lived with neither of their parents (Kreider and Ellis 2011). One study estimates that about half the children in the United States will spend at least some of their childhood in a single-parent family, either as the result of divorce or separation, or because their mothers never married (Luker 1996).

The number of children born to unmarried mothers is an important, and increasing trend in the United States; today, that figure is over 40 percent, reaching to over 50 percent for children born to women under 30. This trend occurs in other wealthy countries as well: In Sweden, over 55 percent of births are to unmarried mothers, and France and the United Kingdom both have higher rates than the United States (Ventura 2009). While unmarried mothers giving birth was associated with teenagers in the past, most unmarried mothers today are between ages 20 and 30. Although rates of birth to unmarried mothers are up for all ethnic groups in the United States, they have risen particularly sharply among Hispanic and black women where they account for 53 percent and 73 percent of all births, respectively (Wildsmith Steward-Streng and Manlove 2011; see also Banks 2011). As a group, single-mother families are far poorer than other families (DeParle 2012; Mather 2010). One exception to the trend of single motherhood are college graduates, for whom marriage makes more sense economically than it does for poor women whose mates are less likely to have well-paying jobs, or even to be employed (Furstenberg in Tavernise 2012).

Composite Families

Composite (compound) families are aggregates of nuclear families linked by a common spouse, most often the husband. The typical composite family is a polygynist household, consisting of one man with several wives and their respective children, with each wife and her children normally occupying a separate residence. In composite families, the tie between a mother and her children is particularly strong. The dynamics of the composite family typically involves the interaction of the husband

composite (compound) family: An aggregate of nuclear families linked by a common spouse.

with several wives, interaction between co-wives, and competition among the children of different wives over inheritance and succession.

Extended Families

The extended (consanguineal) family consists of two or more generations of male or female kin and their spouses and offspring, occupying a single household under the authority of a household head. An extended family is not just a collection of nuclear families; in an extended family system, lineal ties—the blood ties between generations (such as father and son)—are more important than the ties of marriage.

Extended families are particularly adaptive among cultivators as they provide more workers than in nuclear families, which is adaptive both in food production and in the production and marketing of handicrafts. In peasant agricultural societies where land ownership is important for both prestige and power, the extended family helps keep land intact over generations rather than parceling it out into ever smaller and more unproductive pieces among male descendants. Although the extended family is the ideal in more than half of the world's societies, it is found most often among the landlord and prosperous merchant classes.

The patrilineal extended family is organized around the male line: a man, his sons, and the sons' wives and children. Societies with patrilineal extended families also tend to have patrilocal residence rules. A matrilineal family is organized around the female line: a woman, her daughters, and the daughters' husbands and children. Matrilineal families may have matrilocal residence rules or avunculocal residence rules.

Using Anthropology: Families Adapting to Globalization

The functional, cross-cultural and holistic perspectives of anthropology help us understand the impact of globalization on social institutions such as the family. Residence rules and family type are economically and politically adaptive. Thus, patrilocality is functional in traditional hunting and agricultural societies where men work cooperatively, and is also functional where males cooperate in warfare (Ember and Ember 1971).

But family structures adapted to traditional subsistence patterns or forms of political organization may no longer be adaptive under the emerging industrial and postindustrial economies of the 21st century. New economies, along with population increase, the spread of global capitalism, changing technology, and women's new economic roles, have greatly affected family patterns. As more women enter the paid workforce, the value of marriage has declined. People everywhere marry later, and more people remain unmarried. In Japan, Taiwan, South Korea, and Hong Kong, the average age for marriage is now between 29 and 30 for women, and between 31 and 33 for men. In 2010, a third of Japanese women entering their 30s were unmarried, and many of these will never marry (*Economist* 2011).

Childbearing is also decreasing. In agricultural and herding societies, children are a good economic investment: The cost of raising them is relatively low and they provide a strong economic boost to the family. But both these subsistence patterns are shrinking: In urban settings based on an information and service economy, economic benefits go to those who have technical training. The costs of raising and educating children become very high and the economic benefit of children to their families shrinks. In the United States, for example, a middle-income family will spend almost $300,000 to raise a child from birth to age 18, not including college expenses (USDA 2011). Costs in other wealthy countries are comparable. Families in wealthy nations derive many benefits from their children, but these are only rarely economic.

Costs of raising children in poor nations are lower, but in the urban areas in which people increasingly live, they are still high, and this has driven family size down dramatically. For example, in Ethiopia, families in the capital city have, on average, four fewer children than families in rural areas (Mace 2008).

To replace the population, women must have between 2.1 and 2.5 children on average. However, in the European Union, women average only 1.6 children and, in some countries, less than this (Eurostat 2012). The number is comparable for wealthy Asian nations. In the United States, the number hovers near 2.1, the replacement value. Even in poor countries, fertility is declining rapidly. Government policies and technological changes also affect family size. Since the late 1970s, China has used a variety of incentives and punishments to encourage families to have only a single child, and many other countries now also promote family planning. In countries such as China and India, where male children are more prestigious than female children, the combination of policies promoting family planning, the high cost of child rearing, and the increasing availability of ultrasound technology that allows people to determine the sex of their children, have resulted in many more boys than girls being born, a figure strengthened by abortion, infanticide, and neglect of girls. This, in turn, affects the availability of marriage partners for men and has resulted in recruitment of brides across national boundaries. The holistic approach of anthropology highlights the interconnectedness between political, economic, technological, and cultural factors in analyzing globalization and cultural change.

KINSHIP SYSTEMS: RELATIONSHIPS THROUGH BLOOD AND MARRIAGE

kinship: A culturally defined relationship established on the basis of blood ties or through marriage.

Kinship includes relationships established through blood, described through the idiom of blood, and relationships through marriage. Kinship determines the formation of social groups (like families), is the basis for classification of people in relation to each other, structures individual rights and obligations, and regulates behavior. Because all of these elements of social life are entwined, anthropologists refer to kinship as a system. Although a **kinship system** always rests on some kind of biological relationship, kinship systems are cultural phenomena, as indicated earlier by the differential classification of parallel and cross-cousins. Kinship classification may or may not reflect a scientifically accurate assessment of biological ties.

kinship system: The totality of kin relations, kin groups, and terms for classifying kin in a society.

In small-scale, nonindustrial societies, kinship is the most important social bond. It is the basis of group formation and norms of kinship govern the most important relationships, rights, and responsibilities between individuals and groups. The extension of kinship ties is the main way of linking groups to one another and of incorporating strangers into a group. Even in modern industrialized societies, where citizenship is an important basis of rights and obligations, kinship has many important functions. It is the major context within which wealth is inherited. Kinship is important on many ritual occasions, and there is a strong sentiment that "blood is thicker than water."

Kinship systems have several functions necessary to the continuation of a society: They provide continuity between generations and provide for the orderly transmission of property and social position between generations. Kinship systems define a universe of others on whom a person can depend for aid. The adaptiveness of social groups larger than the nuclear family accounts for the fact that expanded kin groups are found in so many human societies.

Kinship systems grow out of a group's history as well as its relationship to the environment and its subsistence strategies. Once in place, however, kinship systems take on a life of their own, although as economic and historical circumstances change, kinship ideologies may be manipulated and negotiated to fit the new realities.

Rules of Descent and the Formation of Descent Groups

descent: The culturally established affiliation between a child and one or both parents.

descent group: A group of kin who are descendants of a common ancestor, extending beyond two generations.

In anthropological terminology, **descent** is a culturally established affiliation with one or both parents. Descent is an important basis of social group formation in many societies. A **descent group** is a group of consanguineal (blood-related) kin who are lineal descendants of a common ancestor extending beyond two generations. In nonindustrial societies, descent groups organize domestic life, enculturate children, determine the use and transfer of property and political and ritual offices, carry out religious ritual, settle disputes, engage in warfare, and structure the use of political power.

Unilineal Descent

The rules for establishing descent may be unilineal or bilateral. Under **unilineal descent**, descent group membership is based on links through *either* the paternal line or the maternal line, but not both. Unilineal descent rules are either patrilineal, where a person belongs to the descent group of the father, or matrilineal, where a person belongs to the descent group of the mother. One important adaptive advantage of unilineal descent systems is that kin groups do not overlap, thus binding their members more tightly to one another. Also, unilineal descent rules provide a clearly defined group membership for everyone in the society. This allows people to more easily understand their rights of ownership, social duties, and social roles, and allows them to relate to a large number of known and unknown people in the society.

unilineal descent: Descent group membership based on links through either the maternal or the paternal line, but not both.

Unilineal descent groups can perpetuate themselves over time even though their membership changes. Like modern corporations, corporate descent groups are permanent units that have an existence beyond the individuals who are members at any given time. Old members die and new ones are admitted through birth, but the integrity of the corporate group persists. Such groups can own property and manage resources, also like modern corporations.

Types of Unilineal Descent Groups

A **lineage** is a kin group whose members trace descent from a common ancestor and who can demonstrate those genealogical links among themselves. **Patrilineages** are lineages formed by descent through the male line; **matrilineages** are formed by descent through the female line. Lineages may vary in size, from three generations upward. Related lineages may form clans. The common clan ancestor may be a mythological figure; sometimes, no specific ancestor is known or named.

lineage: A group of kin whose members trace descent from a known common ancestor.

patrilineage: A lineage formed by descent in the male line.

matrilineage: A lineage formed by descent in the female line.

Clans and lineages have different functions in different societies. The lineage often is a local residential or domestic group whose members cooperate on a daily basis. Clans are generally not residential units but tend to spread out over many villages. Therefore, clans often have political and religious functions rather than primarily domestic and economic ones. Clans are important in regulating marriage. In most societies, clans are exogamous, which strengthens their unilineal character. **Exogamy** is a rule specifying that a person must marry outside a particular group. If

exogamy: A rule specifying that a person must marry outside a particular group.

a person married within the clan, his or her children would find it difficult to make sharp distinctions between maternal and paternal relatives. This person would not know how to act toward others, and others would not know how to act toward him or her. Clan exogamy also extends the network of peaceful social relations within a society as different clans are allied through marriage.

Patrilineal Descent Groups: The Nuer

patrilineal descent: A rule that affiliates a person to kin of both sexes related through males only.

In societies with **patrilineal descent** groups, both males and females belong to the descent group of the father, the father's father, and so on (see Figure 9.4). Thus, a man, his sisters and brothers, his own children, his brother's children (but not his sister's children), and his son's children (but not his daughter's children) all belong to the same descent group. Inheritance and succession to office move from father to son.

Although the status of women varies in patrilineal systems, in general, the husband is guaranteed rights and control over his wife (or wives) and children because the continuity of the descent group depends on this. Patrilineal systems most often have patrilocal rules of residence, so a wife may find herself living among strangers, which tends to undermine female solidarity and support.

The Nuer, an East African pastoral people, are a patrilineal society. All rights, privileges, obligations, and interpersonal relationships are regulated by kinship. A man, his father, his brothers, and their children are considered the closest kin. Patrilineal membership confers rights to land, requires participation in certain religious ceremonies, and determines political and judicial obligations, such as making alliances in feuds and warfare.

Lineage membership may spread over several villages, helping to create alliances between members of otherwise independent villages that contain members of several different lineages. Each Nuer clan, which is viewed as composed of related lineages, not individuals, is also spread over several villages. Because one's own lineage or clan, and one's mother's lineage and clan are exogamous, kinship relations are widely extended throughout the tribe. In the absence of a centralized system of political control, these kinship-based alliances are an important mechanism of governance. The Nuer believe that close kin should not fight with one another, so interlineage or interclan disputes are kept small and are settled rapidly (Evans-Pritchard 1968/1940). But nonkin are perceived as potential enemies, so an attack

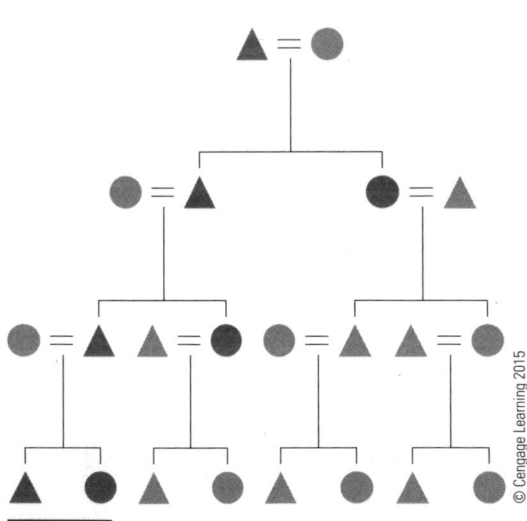

© Cengage Learning 2015

Figure 9.4 Membership in a patrilineal descent group is based on links through the father only. Sons and daughters belong to their father's descent group (shown in dark green), as do the children of sons but not of daughters.

by outsiders on one lineage segment may cause all clan members to join in warfare against a common enemy and their clan brothers (Sahlins 1961).

Matrilineal Descent Groups: The Hopi

In matrilineal societies like the Hopi of the American Southwest, the most important ties are between a woman, her mother, and her siblings. Because children belong to the mother's descent group, the membership of a **matrilineal descent** group (see Figure 9.5) consists of a woman, her brothers and sisters, her sisters' (but not her brothers') children, her own children, and the children of her daughters (but not of her sons).

In matrilineal societies, the rights and responsibilities of the father in a patrilineal society fall to a woman's brother, not her husband. Marriage gives a man sexual and economic rights over his wife, but not rights over their children. After marriage, a man usually goes to live with or near his wife's kin; he is thus an outsider in his wife's household, while she is surrounded by her kin. Because a husband's role in a matrilineal society is less important than in a patrilineal one, marriages in matrilineal societies tend to be less stable.

In matrilineal societies, like the Hopi, the rights and responsibilities vested in male elders fall to a woman's brother rather than her husband. This decreases conflict between fathers and sons, but also means that a man must pass on his knowledge, property, and offices to the sons of his sister, not his own sons. This may engender conflicts between a man and his nephews, who are subject to his control. Thus, in a matrilineal system, a man's loyalties are split between his own sons and his sisters' sons, a tension that does not occur in patrilineal systems.

Among the Hopi, the strongest tie is between sisters, who, with their mother, form the foundation of the household group (see Figure 9.6). If one sister dies, another looks after her children; sisters cooperate in all domestic tasks, and the few quarrels that arise are settled by the mother's brother or by their own brothers.

Husbands are peripheral in their wife's household. Their mother's place is their home, to which they return for rituals and ceremonials and upon separation or divorce. A son belongs to his mother's lineage, keeps his personal and ritual property in her home, and consults his mother for all important decisions.

A boy's relationship with his maternal uncle is characterized by reserve, respect, and even fear, while his relationship with his father is affectionate and involves little discipline. He has a few ritual and

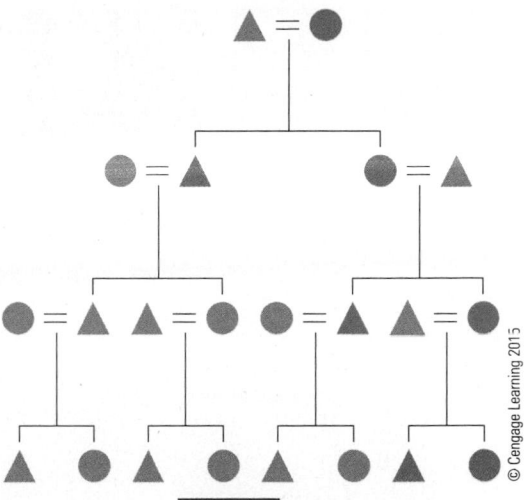

© Cengage Learning 2015

Figure 9.5 Membership in a matrilineal descent group is defined by links through the mother. Sons and daughters are members of their mother's descent group (shown in dark green), as are the children of daughters but not of sons.

matrilineal descent: A rule that affiliates a person to kin of both sexes related through females only.

© Cengage Learning

Location of the Hopi.

Figure 9.6 The Hopi matrilineal family revolves around a core of women. The most important male role in Hopi society is a man's relation to his sister's son, and a man retains authority in the household of his birth even after he marries and moves to his wife's house.

double descent: The tracing of descent through both matrilineal and patrilineal links, each of which is used for different purposes.

bilateral descent: Both maternal and paternal lines are used as a basis for reckoning descent.

economic obligations to his father's family but engages in little direct cooperation and does not come under their authority. A Hopi man teaches his sons the subsistence tasks of farming and sheepherding, and sons support their father in his old age. A man's relationship with his daughters is affectionate but not close, and he has few specific duties regarding her upbringing.

Hopi matrilineal clans extend over many villages, as both his own clan, his father's clan, and his mother's father's clan are exogamous. Through matrilineal clan membership and through marriage, a Hopi man acquires a wide range of relatives, all of whom are called by kinship terms. This relates a Hopi man to almost everyone in his village, in other villages, and to similar clans in other Pueblo societies (Eggan 1950).

Double Descent

About 5 percent of the world's cultures practice **double descent**. In this system, a person belongs both to the patrilineal group of the father and to the matrilineal group of the mother. However, these descent groups operate in different areas of life. Among the Yako of Nigeria, for example, rights to farmland, forest products, as well as some religious offices derive from membership in a patrilineal group, while matrilineal relations govern the transfer of accumulated wealth, such as currency, livestock, tools, weapons, and household goods.

Bilateral Kinship Systems

About 40 percent of the world's societies do not have lineages, and are bilateral (some are ambilineal, as discussed later). Under rules of **bilateral descent**, both maternal and paternal lines are used equally as the basis for reckoning descent and for establishing the rights and obligations of kinship. Bilateral systems do not have clear-cut descent groups. Rather, they have networks of kin, called kindreds, that are defined only in their relation to a particular individual. Except for brothers and sisters,

Courtesy of Tom Curtin

Figure 9.7 Kinship ties through descent and marriage are important, even in societies like the United States. This family reunion of the Tracys, with nuclear families wearing shirts of the same color, indicates the importance of both the nuclear family and the kindred.

every individual's kindred is unique. Kindreds are actually overlapping categories of kin rather than social groups, and thus are more difficult to organize as cooperative, kin-based collectivities. For example, because a kindred is not a group, it cannot own land or have continuity over time.

Bilateral kinship systems seem particularly adaptive in societies where mobility and independence are important. They are basic to Western culture, including the United States, and predominate among foraging societies as well (see Figure 9.7).

In some Pacific Island societies, the kinship system is ambilineal: Individuals may choose to affiliate with either their mother's or with their father's descent group, but not simultaneously with both. Upon marriage, the new couple can live with either spouse's descent group, a decision most often based on access to land, although friendship and politics also play a role.

THE CLASSIFICATION OF KIN

In all societies, kin are referred to by special terms. The total system of kinship terms and the rules for using these terms make up a kinship classification system. Every kinship classification system classes some relatives together (referred to by the same kinship term) and differentiates them from other relatives (called by different terms). Some kinship systems have only a small number of kinship terms, whereas others have a different term for almost every relative.

The classification of kin is related to the roles they play in society. In a kinship diagram, ego is the person from whose perspective the chart is drawn and viewed. If, for example, ego refers to his father and his father's brothers by the same term, his relationship with them tends to be similar. By the same token, if ego's father and father's brothers are referred to by different terms, it is expected that ego will act differently toward each of them and that they will act differently toward him. These ideals are modified (within limits) by the relationships and personalities of particular individuals.

Kinship classification is one of the most important regulators of behavior in most societies. It defines how each person must act toward others and how others must act toward him or her. Kinship classification systems are related to other aspects of culture, such as the types of social groups that are formed and the systems of marriage and inheritance.

Understanding the variety of kinship systems makes the crucial anthropological point that although each society considers its own kinship classification system natural and normal, the logic underlying all kinship systems is cultural, not biological. For example, in the United States, the brothers and sisters of one's parents and their spouses are called "aunt" and "uncle," and the children of these relatives are called "cousin." Have you ever asked yourself why the same term is used for mother's sister, a relative by blood, and mother's brother's wife, a relative by marriage? Or why there are no separate terms for male and female cousins, but gender does differentiate nieces from nephews?

Principles for the Classification of Kin

Societies use a combination of some, but not all, of seven important principles of kinship classification in their kinship terminology: (1) *generation,* which distinguishes ascending and descending generations from ego; (2) *relative age,* where seniority counts, for example, in distinguishing an older and younger brother; (3) *lineality* versus *collaterality,* where **lineal kin** are related in a single line, such as grandfather–father–son, whereas collateral kin are descended from a common ancestor with ego but are not ego's direct ascendants or descendants, for example, siblings or cousins; (4) *gender,* which differentiates relatives according to whether they are male or female (in English, for example, gender distinguishes between aunt and uncle, but not cousins); (5) *consanguineal* versus *affinal* kin, which differentiates relatives by blood in contrast to relatives by marriage; whereas the principle of (6) *sex of linking relative* operates, for example, to differentiate cross-cousins from parallel cousins; and (7) *bifurcation,* which distinguishes relatives from the mother's side of the family from those

lineal kin: Blood relations linked through descent, such as Ego, Ego's mother, Ego's grandmother, and Ego's daughter.

of the father's side, and is used by societies that distinguish the mother's brother from the father's brother. These seven principles combine in different ways to form different types of kinship systems.

In making sense out of kinship systems, anthropologists attempt to understand the relationship of terminologies, rules of descent, and kinship groups to the ecological, economic, and political conditions under which different kinship systems emerge.

BRINGING IT BACK HOME:
CARING FOR THE ELDERLY

Aging is a universal biological aspect of being human that must be understood within a cultural context (Sokolofsky 2009). One essential question every society must address is who will care for the aged. This question is particularly important today: With the advent of modern medicine, particularly in wealthy Western nations, old age has become associated with a long dying process and such potentially incapacitating diseases as hypertension, cancer, coronary heart disease, and Alzheimer's, resulting in the emergence of many forms of institutionalized care, such as assisted living facilities, nursing homes, home care, and hospices (Nanda and Gregg 2011).

Even in societies with extended family systems, like India and China, where family care for the aged at home is embedded in traditional cultural values, such institutions now have an expanded role in elder care (Lamb 2009). In China, as the young migrate to cities, old people are left in the villages and the traditional obligations for a son to provide for his parents in their old age are breaking down (French 2006; Jacobs and Century 2012). Indeed, girls may now be favored over boys as they are emotionally closer to their families and take their family care obligations more assiduously (Greenhalgh 2007). Still, some urban communities, in an effort to shame people who neglect their elderly parents, post their names on public bulletin boards; in others, local homes for the elderly fine children who miss weekend parental visits.

Even in societies like Japan, where integration and group harmony are valued over competitive independence, the Japanese elderly are frequently anxious about becoming a burden to their children, and anxious about their inability to ever pay back the obligations they incur toward family members who care for them (Traphagan 1998). With Japan's smaller families, new death rituals have been constructed so that those

left behind will be less burdened by elaborate—and expensive—mortuary rites (Kawano 2010).

American Muslims are also finding that the realities of modern life may conflict with the Koranic interpretation to care for one's elderly relatives at home. For many American Muslims, the idea of nursing homes is unthinkable, but some working Muslim families have no other options. In response, some Muslims are designing institutions for the elderly that make these more acceptable—by adjoining the nursing homes to mosques or providing communal prayer rooms; serving halal food; providing same-sex medical and nursing care; and adding multilingual staff (Clemetson 2006).

In the United States, the importance of independence as a cultural value and the anxiety surrounding "becoming a burden" help explain the increasing numbers of elderly people who prefer to live alone if financially able to do so. This varies by gender: Elderly widowed or divorced males are twice as interested in dating and remarriage than elderly women (Klinenberg 2012). There is also variation among subcultures: Among Italian Americans, there is a high expectation that elderly parents will be taken care of by their children, and will often expect to live with them. Unlike the Indian diaspora, where sons are mainly responsible for elder care, this responsibility among Italian Americans tends to fall more on daughters than on sons, and can become fraught with difficulties, especially if the parent is widowed or in poor health, if family finances are tight, or if daughters are working professionals as is increasingly the case. As in other aspects of family structure, economics, culture, public policy, and personal family factors all play a role in who cares for the elderly.

YOU DECIDE:

1. Who do you think should bear the major burden for caring for the elderly in American society? How do various options reinforce or conflict with important American values, such as individualism, economic success, or privacy?
2. What options would you choose for caring for the elders in your own family? How are these choices shaped by your own current life situation or the future you envision for yourself? What private or government services do you think could ease this responsibility for elder care in a way consistent with American values?
3. How does gender affect the experience of elder care, for example, the differences between caring for a widowed father or a widowed mother, or whether this responsibility should fall more on sons or daughters? Explain your response.

■ CHAPTER SUMMARY

1. What are some major functions of marriage and the family? Three major functions of marriage and the family are regulating sexual access between males and females, arranging for the exchange of services between males and females, and assigning responsibility for child care.

2. Define the incest taboo and give some explanations for its universality. Incest taboos are prohibitions on mating between people classified as relatives. It may function to prevent disruption based on sexual competition within the family and force people to marry out of their immediate families, thus extending their social alliances.

3. What are some universal or widespread marriage rules? Exogamy and endogamy are almost universal. Cousin marriage, the number of spouses, the exchange of goods and services, the degree of control a kin group has over spousal choice, and the responsibilities for elders are all embedded in marriage rules.

4. What are the two basic types of families, and how are these related to other social or economic conditions? The *nuclear* family is found mainly in contemporary industrial and foraging societies, and the *extended* family is found predominantly in agricultural societies.

5. What defines a household, and how does household composition relate to other rules about marriage and family? A household is usually made up of family members, but may include others. Household composition is shaped by postmarital residence rules, which are most commonly patrilocal, but may also be matrilocal, or least frequently, neolocal, as in the United States.

6. What are kinship systems, and what are their functions in society? Kinship systems are cultural creations that define and organize relatives by blood and marriage. They include groups formed by kinship and the terms used to classify different kin. Kinship systems provide continuity between generations and define a group of people who can depend on one another for mutual aid.

7. How are lineages different from clans in structure and functions? Lineage members can trace their descent from a common ancestor while clan members believe they have a common ancestor but cannot trace the relationship genealogically. Lineages mainly have domestic functions, while clans mainly have political and religious functions. Both lineages and clans are important in regulating marriage.

8. What is the difference between patrilineal and matrilineal systems? In patrilineal systems, a man's children and his sons' children, but not his daughters' children, belong to his lineage. In matrilineal systems, a woman's children belong to her lineage, not their father's lineage. In matrilineal systems, the mother's brother has authority over his sisters' children, and relations between husband and wife are more fragile than in patrilineal systems.

9. What are some of the important categories of kinship terminology? Kinship terminology categorizes people according to generation, relative age, lineality or collaterality, gender, consanguinity or affinity, bifurcation, and sex of the linking relative.

KEY TERMS

Bilateral descent
Bridewealth
Composite (compound) family
Consanguinity
Cross-cousin marriage
Descent
Descent group
Double descent
Dowry
Endogamy
Exogamy
Extended family
Incest taboos
Kinship
Kinship system
Levirate

Lineal kin
Lineage
Marriage
Matrilineage
Matrilineal descent
Monogamy
Nuclear family
Parallel-cousin marriage
Patrilineage
Patrilineal descent
Polyandry
Polygamy
Polygyny
Sororate
Unilineal descent

The hijras of India are an alternative gender, neither men nor women. They exhibit exaggerated female gestures, wear women's clothing, keep their hair long, and perform at weddings and childbirth.

CHAPTER 10

SEX AND GENDER

LEARNING OBJECTIVES

After you have read this chapter, you will be able to:

△ Differentiate between sex and gender.

△ Illustrate the ways in which gender is culturally constructed, and provide at least two examples.

△ Explain alternative gender roles using examples from different cultures.

△ Compare sexuality practices in different societies.

△ Describe the functions of gender-related initiation rites for males and females.

△ Summarize different theories that attempt to explain gender hierarchy.

△ Compare gender relations typical of foraging, horticultural, pastoral, agricultural, and industrial societies.

THE HIJRAS: AN ALTERNATIVE GENDER IN INDIA

HE **hijras** are an ambiguous gender role in India. Although born male, they are considered neither man nor woman. Hijras undergo an operation in which their genitals are surgically removed. This "operation" accounts for the popular designation of hijras as eunuchs. Hijras consider this operation a rebirth, and it is carried out as an act of devotion to the Hindu mother goddess. After the operation, hijras are believed to incorporate the goddess's powers of procreation. Thus, their presence is required at weddings and at the birth of a child.

Hijra performances involve clapping, drumming, and the tinkle of ankle bells, which announce their arrival. Tossing their spangled scarves, flashing their heavy jewelry, and beating their drums, the hijras sing and dance, making comic, ribald gestures and striking sexually suggestive feminine poses, causing men to laugh and women to hide discreet, embarrassed giggling behind their hands. In celebrating childbirth, the dancers take the infant from his mother's arms and bless him with wishes for prosperity and virility, meanwhile examining his genitals to confirm that he is a fully formed male infant. At the end of their performance, the hijras are given their traditional payment of money, cloth, and sweets, satisfied with having once again confirmed their importance in Indian society.

Because they are born male, hijras are mainly perceived as "not man," but they are also thought of as "man plus woman." They adopt women's clothing, gestures, and behaviors. They must wear their hair long, like women, and they have a special language that includes feminine expressions, intonations, and female kinship terms. But hijras are also "not woman" mainly because they cannot bear children.

As neither man nor woman, hijras identify with the many ambiguous **gender roles** and figures in Hindu mythology and Indian culture: male deities who change into or disguise themselves as females temporarily, deities who have both male and female characteristics, male religious devotees who dress and act as women in religious ceremonies, eunuchs who serve in the Muslim courts, and the ascetics, or holy men of India, whose renunciation of all sexuality paradoxically becomes the source of their power to bless others with fertility. Indian culture thus not only accommodates such androgynous figures as the hijras but views them as meaningful, sacred, and even powerful (Nanda 1999; 2013).

hijra: An alternative gender role in India conceptualized as neither man nor woman.

gender role: The cultural expectations of men and women in a particular society, including the division of labor.

India is only one of the many societies throughout the world where cultural support is given to individuals who transcend or bridge the differences between male and female (Herdt 1996; Nanda 2000b). Among these are the *mahu* of Polynesia (Besnier 1996; Matzner 2001), the *xanith* of Oman on the Saudi Arabian peninsula (Wikan 1977), the *two-spirit* found in many Native American tribes (Roscoe 1995; 1991; Whitehead 1981; Williams 1986), the *travesti* of Brazil (Kulick 1998), the *kathoey* of Thailand (Costa and Matzner 2007), the *bakla* of the Philippines, the *waria* of Indonesia (Boellstorff 2004; Graham 2006), the *yan daudo* of Nigeria (Gaudio 2009), and the many gender alternatives in Malaysia (Peletz 2009). Most of these roles involve males who adopt women's work, dress, and behavior, but there are female alternative gender roles as well (Blackwood 1998).

Among some subarctic groups, for example, people depended on sons to feed the family through big game hunting. A family that had daughters and no sons would select a daughter to "be like a man." When the youngest daughter was about 5 years old, the parents performed a transformation ceremony that was aimed at preventing menstruation and pregnancy, and bring luck in hunting. From then on, she dressed like a male, trained like a male, and often developed great strength and became an outstanding hunter (Williams 1996:202).

Why do anthropologists study such esoteric subjects as alternative genders, and what we can learn from them? After all, the division of humans into two opposite sexes—male and female—appears to be natural and a basic aspect of human biology. Sex assignment, which takes place at birth, is assumed to be permanent over a person's lifetime. Most of us take for granted that sex is the same as gender and that people come in two opposing and unchangeable categories. But, although every culture acknowledges the biological differences between male and female, there is great cultural variety in the number of sexes and genders a society constructs and how sex and gender are defined. As Alexeyeff and Besnier (2013) point out in their study of alternative genders in Pacific Island societies, understanding "marginal" gender roles helps us explore the gender "norm," as well as the relationships between gender and sexuality, local and global dynamics, and historical change, and how those considered marginal subvert or reinforce larger cultural and social structures.

◪ SEX AND GENDER AS CULTURAL CONSTRUCTIONS

A basic anthropological concept is the distinction between the biological and cultural aspects of being male or female. **Sex** refers to the biological differences between male and female, particularly the visible

sex: The biological difference between male and female.

gender: A cultural construction that makes biological and physical differences into socially meaningful categories.

differences in external genitalia and the related difference in the role each sex plays in the reproductive process. **Gender** is the cultural and social classification of masculine and feminine. In other words, gender refers to the social, cultural, and psychological constructs that different societies superimpose on the biological differences of sex (Worthman 1995:598). Every culture recognizes distinctions between male and female, but cultures differ in the meanings attached to these categories, the supposed sources of the differences between them, and the relationship of these categories to other cultural and social facts. As noted previously, gender is not limited to masculine and feminine; neither in fact, is sex. In the United States in the 20th century, the parents of infants born biologically intersexed were persuaded by medical and psychological professionals to "fix" their sex through surgery and socialize such infants into the gender consistent with their new, altered sex. But more recent research indicates that there are many different kinds of biological intersex conditions and that this "mixture," like sex and gender itself, is culturally constructed (Karkazis 2008).

Gender and gender relations are among the basic building blocks of culture and society, central to social relations of power; individual and group identities; formation of kinship and other groups; and attribution of meaning and value. This makes gender a central interest of contemporary anthropology. Understanding that gender roles are not biologically determined but rather are culturally constructed raises new questions about the culturally patterned nature of women's and men's lives in all cultures, including our own.

Cross-cultural ethnography demonstrates that not only do different cultures incorporate different genders beyond those of man and woman, but that concepts of masculine and feminine also vary among cultures. Thus, to grasp the potential and the limits of diversity in human life, we must look at the full range of human societies—particularly those outside Western historical, cultural, and economic traditions. When we broaden our perspective on sex and gender beyond our own society, we see that culture counts. Both sex and gender are culturally constructed and extraordinarily diverse, as are the relationships between sex and gender.

The work of anthropologist Margaret Mead was essential in developing the now central anthropological principle that gender is a cultural construction. In the 1930s, Mead (1935/1963) began to question the biologically determined nature of gender. She organized her ethnographic research around the question of whether the characteristics defined as masculine and feminine in Western culture, specifically the United States, were universal. In her studies of three groups in New Guinea—the Arapesh, the Mundugamor, and the Tchambuli—Mead found that the whole repertoire of behaviors, emotions, and roles that go into being masculine and feminine is patterned by culture. Among the Arapesh, men and women both were expected to act in ways that Americans considered "naturally" feminine. Both sexes were concerned with taking care of children and nurturing. Neither sex was expected to be aggressive. In Mundugamor society, both sexes were what American culture would call "masculine": aggressive, violent, and with little interest in children. Among the Tchambuli, the personalities of men and women were different from each other but opposite to American conceptions of masculine and feminine. Women had the major economic role and showed common sense and business shrewdness. Men were more interested in esthetics. They spent much time decorating themselves and gossiping. Their feelings were easily hurt, and they sulked a lot.

Although Mead's ethnographic descriptions of these societies were later criticized and superseded (di Leonardo 1998:213–215; 2003; Roscoe 2003), her work made a lasting contribution by raising the issue of the great diversity in cultural definitions of masculine and feminine and by calling attention to the ways in which gender and gender relations are cultural constructions. A society's **gender ideology**, that is, its totality of ideas about sex, gender, the natures of men and women, including their sexuality, and the relations between the genders, is significant not only in its own right but because it is a core element in a society's stratification system, which is also gendered.

Location of the Arapesh, the Mundugamor, and the Tchambuli.

gender ideology: The totality of ideas about sex, gender, the natures of men and women, including their sexuality, and the relations between the genders.

▨ CREATIVE EXPRESSIONS OF GENDER: DEEP PLAY AND MASCULINE IDENTITY

Every society includes many and varied cultural dimensions of gender ideology and gender identity. Games and sports such as football in the United States, cockfighting in Bali, rugby in Tonga, or bullfighting in Spain are all ways of both learning and reinforcing culturally constructed gender values. Clifford Geertz calls these activities "deep play" (Geertz 1973a), because they heighten emotions, display compelling aspects of social structure and culture, and reinforce culturally constructed gender identities.

A prime example of deep play in the construction of masculinity is the Spanish bullfight (see Figure 10.1). Although bullfighting is a cruel assault on animals for cultural outsiders, and even a growing number of Spaniards, bullfighting is traditionally an aesthetic ritual central in gender ideology, and is not viewed as a form of violence or cruelty (Eller 2006:104). Despite their violent acts, bullfighters are culturally compelled to restrain any sign of anger or aggression; indeed, such signs contradict the essence of bullfighting as an art. In Spanish

Figure 10.1 The Spanish bull-fight is one of the many diverse ways in which masculine gender identity and roles are expressed in the deep play of sports.

© Imagesofanthropology.com

culture, bullfights involve a complex and elaborate process of ritualized violence that makes it not only acceptable, but also beautiful. The point of a bullfight is not simply to kill a bull; that would be easy and would lack any cultural meaning. Rather, it is the skill, grace, and courage of the bullfighter that is essential to the performance. The bullfight embodies the values of male competition in defense of the male self-image of honor. For the audience, the maximum vindication of honor is in the physical showdown, in public, between two men. The matador symbolizes the role of the honorable male; he is not a fighter or a man with a reputation for violence, nor is he an athlete, nor personally aggressive, nor necessarily big or muscular. In a bullfight, the matador does not initiate violence, nor does he act against the bull in self-defense. It is the bull that is the angry and ferocious male, whereas the matador is skilled, self-controlled, and calm—he is able to master the violent situation without becoming violent himself.

For the matador and the spectators, it is not the suffering of the bull but the style and aesthetic performance of the matador that is central. At the kill, the most dangerous part of the performance for the matador, the matador cannot use his sword to weaken the bull or defend himself. Any prolonged suffering of the bull is strongly disapproved of by the spectators, and a matador who performs a "sloppy" kill is called a "murderer." For the Spanish, a bullfight is not an example of indulging in man's animal nature (which is how they view a North American boxing match), but a performance that allows man to transcend his animal nature as it distinguishes a man of honor from a man of anger. Honor is a central concept in Spanish masculine identity—and indeed in much of Mediterranean culture (Gilmore 1996). The art of the bullfight is one of the ways in which this cultural value is expressed, both for the performers and the audience.

In spite of the well-established connection between bullfighting and masculinity in Spain, this **cultural construction of gender** is slowly changing. Over the last century, women in Andalusia, in southern Spain, have been fighting to enter the bullring. Many Andalusians, however, including male bullfighters, reject this attempt to overturn traditional gender roles. Some male bullfighters refuse to fight in the ring with women; parents discourage their daughters from pursuing a bullfighting career, trainers refuse to train women bullfighters, and some spectators refuse to attend bullfights where female bullfighters participate. But the women bullfighters themselves, and their supporters, are persisting. And some Andalusians even support the women's efforts: In contrast to those who reject women participating in this most masculine example of Spanish "deep play," some male Andalusians view the women as supremely courageous and professional, and find them, in their tight costumes, supremely sexy. But, however one views women bullfighters, they certainly stretch the traditional notion of what it means to be a woman in Spain (Gottlieb 2002:167–189).

In the Pacific Island of Tonga, rugby is the form of deep play central to the construction of masculinity (Besnier 2012). Of English origin, introduced to Tonga in the early 20th century, today almost all Tongan boys play rugby from early childhood. Girls, in contrast, play netball, a watered-down version of basketball, which is of practically no public interest. Rugby is essential in male socialization: All Tongan villages and boys' schools have rugby clubs, and boys and many men play rugby informally almost every day. Rugby gives boys the chance to learn resourcefulness and skills to confound opponents, central to the male gender role. For Tongans, rugby expresses ideals of virility, fortitude, and controlled aggression, and it favors the large, heavily muscular bodies of Tongan men, also central to masculine identity and pride.

Ironically, because of a shortage of outstanding rugby players in Japan, where rugby is an elite and marginal sport, Tongan players have been recruited to beef up organized rugby teams. The Tongan players are viewed as both physically and socially unattractive, however. Their corpulence, hairiness, crude manners, hard drinking, and chain smoking are identified as "gorilla macho," the very antithesis of the contemporary Japanese masculine ideal of "slim macho," which incorporates a slim and well-groomed look. Such is the diversity of constructions of masculinity from a cross-cultural perspective!

cultural construction of gender: The idea that gender characteristics are the result of historical, economic, and political forces acting within each culture.

◪ CULTURAL VARIATION IN SEXUAL BEHAVIOR

Understanding gender systems as culturally constructed also helps explain the cultural variations in definitions of appropriate sexual behavior. Although sexual activity is most often—and for most people—viewed as "doing what comes naturally," a cross-cultural perspective demonstrates that human sexual activity is patterned by a culture's gender ideology and influenced by learning.

Culture patterns the habitual responses of different peoples to different parts of the body. What is erotic in some cultures is considered disgusting in others. Kissing, for example, is not universal. The Tahitians learned to kiss from the Europeans; before this cultural contact, Tahitians began sexual intimacy by sniffing. Among the Alaskan Inuit, sniffing the hollow in another's cheek can be both a pattern of sexual as well as nonsexual behavior. When an adult asks a child to do this, it is affectionate and innocent, whereas among adults it is considered quite erotic. Like a kiss in our own culture, it is the social construction of behavior that counts.

Sexual foreplay is also culturally diverse. In the Trobriand Islands, a couple expresses affection by inspecting each other's hair for lice, a practice Westerners may find disgusting. To the Trobrianders, however, the European habit of a couple going on a picnic with a knapsack of prepared food is equally disgusting, although it is perfectly acceptable for a Trobriand boy and girl to gather wild foods together as a prelude to sexual activity (Malinowski 1929b:327, 335).

Who is considered an appropriate sexual partner also differs among cultures. In some societies, like the United States, same-sex practices stigmatize men as homosexual, but same-sex intimacy may be a matter of indifference or even approval in other cultures. Among the Sambia of New Guinea, what Americans call homosexual practice is culturally central in the sex/gender system as a core ritual in male initiation. In Sambian culture, women are viewed as dangerous creatures that pollute men and deplete them of their masculinity substance. The Sambia believe that males do not naturally mature as fast or as competently as females. The Sambia believe that males cannot achieve reproductive competence without semen, which is not naturally produced but must be externally and artificially introduced into the body. Thus, an essential part of Sambia male initiation is for boys to consume semen from adult men through repeated homosexual fellatio. Only in this way can boys become "strong men" capable of becoming fathers and vigorous warriors (Herdt 1981; 1996:431–436).

Among ancient Greeks, homosexual relationships were considered superior to heterosexual relations, and in many contemporary cultures, such as India (Seabrook 1999) or Brazil (Kulick 1998), the male who takes the dominant (inserter) role in same-sex relationships is not considered homosexual and his behavior is not stigmatized. In Thailand, as long as a man fulfills his family obligations to marry, his homosexual practice does not become a source of discrimination or dishonor (Jackson 1999). The many cultures in which same-sex relationships are viewed as normal variants of human sexuality strongly contrast with the varied and constantly changing ways that homosexuality is viewed in modern Europe and the United States, where consistent male heterosexuality has been considered essential to masculine identity.

The ages at which sexual response is believed to begin and end, the ways in which people make themselves attractive, the importance of sexual activity in human life, and its variation according to gender—all these are patterned and regulated by culture and affect sexual response and behavior. Two classic ethnographies that highlight the role of culture in impacting sexuality are that of the Irish of Inis Beag and that of the Polynesians of Mangaia.

Anthropologist John Messenger (1971:15) describes Inis Beag as "one of the most sexually naive of the world's societies." Sex is never discussed at home when children are near, and parents provide practically no sexual instruction to children. Adults believe that "after marriage nature takes its course." (As we shall see, "nature" takes a very different course in Inis Beag than it does in Polynesia!) Women are expected to endure but not enjoy sexual relations; to refuse to have intercourse is considered a mortal sin among these Roman Catholic people. There appears to be widespread ignorance in Inis Beag of the female capacity for orgasm, which is considered deviant behavior in any case. Nudity is abhorred, and there is no tradition of "dirty jokes." The main style of dancing allows little bodily contact among the participants; even so, some girls refuse to dance because it means touching a boy. The separation of the sexes begins very early in Inis Beag and lasts into adulthood. In sexual relations, there is a virtual absence of sexual foreplay, almost no premarital sex, and a high percentage of celibate males. In explaining the extraordinarily late age of marriage, one female informant told the anthropologist, "Men can wait a long time before wanting 'it' but we [women] can wait a lot longer" (Messenger 1971:16).

The extreme sexual repression in Inis Beag is usefully compared to sexual ideology in Mangaia, in Polynesia, described by Donald Marshall (1971). Fantasies of complete sexual freedom in the "South Seas" have long been a part of Western culture. In fact, no society has complete sexual freedom, but compared to the traditional Puritan culture of the

West, Polynesia comes perhaps closest. In Mangaia, sexual intercourse is one of life's major interests. Sex is not discussed at home, but Mangaia elders teach sexual information to boys and girls at puberty. For adolescent boys, this formal instruction about the techniques of intercourse is followed by a culturally approved experience with a mature woman in the village. After this, the boy is considered a man. This contrasts with Inis Beag, where a man is considered a "lad" until he is about 40. In Mangaia, there is continual public reference to sexual activity: Sexual jokes, expressions, and references are expected as part of the preliminaries to public meetings. And yet, in public, sex segregation is the norm. Boys and girls should not be seen together in public, but practically every girl and boy has had intercourse before marriage. The act of sexual intercourse itself is the focus of sexual activity. Both men and women are expected to take pleasure in the sexual act and to reach orgasm. Celibacy is practically unknown. The contrast between Inis Beag and Mangaia indicates clearly that societies' different attitudes pattern the sexual responsiveness of males and females in each society.

Gender Ideology and Women's Sexuality

A culture's gender ideology always includes ideas about sexuality, and most societies view males and females as different in this respect. In societies where women are considered more sexually voracious than men, such as both Muslim and Hindu India—a clear contrast with the traditionally dominant Western view—this ideology is often used to justify men's control over women. This control becomes a basis for gender stratification, constraints on women's lives, and discrimination against women who work, go to school, or appear outside their homes without a male escort. It also may include control over women's dress, marriage, divorce, and laws regarding adultery and abortion. Male control over women in many societies ranging from the horticultural Yanamamo to contemporary postindustrial societies is often expressed in widespread violence against women, including beatings, rape, forced suicide, and even murder. Society's control of female sexuality may also be inscribed on female bodies, as in female circumcision (Barnes-Dean 1989); Chinese foot binding (Anagnost 1989); and in the West, anorexia and eating disorders motivated by the cultural ideal of model-like slimness (Rhode 2010).

In many cultures, male control of female sexuality is central to notions of honor and shame, and thus to cultural understandings of masculinity (Gilmore 1996; Wikan 2008). This pattern, central in many circum-Mediterranean cultures, may have its roots in medieval Catholic religious beliefs or in Islam (Brandes 1981), but violence against women today is also a political tool, illustrated by widespread rape in warfare in the Congo, Bosnia, and the Sudan, among other places; as an expression of social stratification, as in the recent gang rape of a lower-caste young woman by the high-caste men in a north Indian village (Yardley 2012); or part of the male culture at a high-status college like Amherst, in the United States, where college administrators look the other way and try to persuade rape victims not to bring charges (Perez-Pena 2012:A15). This may have political implications. During the military rule period in Myanmar (formerly Burma), for example, the state demonized revered political activist and opposition leader, Aung San Suu Kyi, in gendered and sexualized terms, holding that like all women, she used female guile and manipulation to achieve her political goals. The government's propaganda held that, also like other women, she was driven by lust and thus was unfit for any leadership roles (Peletz 2012).

Although some cultural anthropologists emphasize the universality of certain gender ideologies, anthropology also emphasizes the significant diversity regarding women's sexuality both within and among cultures, as affected by history, geography, economics, politics, and the impact of globalization. The issue of female modesty and control of sexuality in Islam provides a useful example (El-Feki 2013). Although Islam is a global religion, Muslim gender ideologies and practices regarding women's sexuality and requirements for modest dress, vary in different Islamic societies. This is illustrated by the debates over the wearing of the hijab, or headscarf (see Figure 10.2). For some Muslims as well as for many non-Muslim Westerners, the hijab is a sign of the oppression of women, making them invisible and restricting their freedom of choice. But some young Muslim women in Europe and the United States view the hijab as a liberating garment that forces the world to see them as more than sexual objects, and establishes their identity as Muslims (Bowen 2007).

The Qur'anic injunction requiring modest dress for Muslim women (Qur'an 24:30-31) does not command any specific styles, nor specifically mention hijab, making room for much local variation and interpretation. The varying practices regarding female modesty are shaped by history, culture, religious politics, and the degree of male dominance in a society. Factors influencing

© Joan Gregg

Figure 10.2 The hijab, or headscarf, worn by these Malaysian girls, is one means by which some Muslims accommodate the Islamic requirement for women to dress modestly. Wearing the hijab has become a political issue in some Muslim and European societies.

modest female dress vary among religious sects, social classes, between rural and urban populations, and among the generations, ranging from the total restrictions on women's autonomy in Saudi Arabia, to the "split personality" of cosmopolitan Dubai. In some societies, most Muslim women only wear a hijab that loosely covers their hair and neck; in others, like Yemen, women wear full head and body coverings as well as a face veil. In the airlines of the United Arab Emirates, a compromise is reached between fashion and religion as air hostesses wear "jaunty little caps with attached gauzy scarves that hint at hijab" (Zoepf 2008). In Afghanistan, under Taliban rule, women were required to wear a burqa, or full body and face covering; these restrictions weakened with the defeat of the Taliban.

In all of these countries, some women resist these laws and customs (Ali 2006; Manji 2003), with varying responses from both the public and public officials. In Afghanistan, some brave women persist in playing football, in spite of being subject to government harassment and death threats, while in Egypt, the postrevolutionary government sponsors a highly successful television show featuring El Set Ghalia, a working-class woman who has become "the Egyptian Oprah." On her cooking show, she demonstrates recipes that will especially appeal to the ordinary, lower-class Egyptian, and also discusses social and marital issues and women's rights (Todras-Whitehill 2012).

In Tunisia, also, with the support of international nongovernmental organizations (NGOs), the great increase in women working outside the home, and important socioeconomic changes impacted by globalization, particularly the tourist industry, wearing the veil and various religiously based laws regarding polygyny, child custody, divorce, and unequal inheritance have become issues for debate in this still patriarchal society. And in Turkey, although women commonly wear the headscarf in public, until recently, they were previously not permitted to wear it in government offices or universities. Wearing the hijab is part of a heated public debate about what should be the secular versus religious character of this largely Muslim state (Tavernise 2008).

Cultural anthropologist Pardis Mahdavi makes an important contribution to this discussion through her ethnography in the Islamic Republic of Iran. In Iran, women are required to wear the hijab, and wearing a chador (outer garment or cloak) is increasingly common due to government and some public pressure. Mahdavi's ethnography of sexuality in Iran (2009), however, describes the widespread breach of many Muslim sexual restrictions, such as premarital chastity, marital fidelity, and the wearing of modest dress among educated, upper-class Iranians. Dating, fashion, nail polish, makeup, and immodest dress are outlawed in Iran, but the formerly widespread policing of these practices in public places has diminished greatly, and girls wear layers of makeup in private. Women's more modern headscarfs are often so transparent and fashionable that they actually look sexy.

The relation between gender practice and culture particularly impacts men in the Muslim diaspora. As anthropologist Katherine Ewing (2008b) demonstrates, German society demonizes Turkish Muslim men as the "other," bearers of Islamic "barbarism," who are associated with the repression and abuse of women as victims of patriarchal oppression. These German assumptions about Turkish masculinity play a central role in the construction of German national identity, reinforced by the popular media, films, social work policies, and public policy, assumptions that Ewing points out are based on long-standing European fantasies about Middle Eastern gender relations that are contrasted with European enlightenment. This deep study of cross-cultural variation is one of anthropology's most important contributions, and it also helps us reflect more deeply on our own cultural values in the intensely emotional area of gender.

▨ MALE AND FEMALE RITES OF PASSAGE

In all cultures, the role expectations of individuals change at different points in life, and the individual must learn what is necessary for these new roles. In many societies, the transition from one social status to another is formalized by special **rites of passage**, which move individuals publicly and ceremonially from one stage of life to the next. One widespread rite of passage signals the transition from childhood to adult gender roles (van Gennep 1960/1909).

rite of passage: A ritual that moves an individual from one social status to another.

Male rites of passage have important psychological and sociological functions. They reinforce the social order by dramatizing cultural values in a public context; they express and affirm male relationships, male solidarity, and, sometimes, male dominance; they publicly validate a change of status from child to adult; and they transmit the cultural knowledge necessary to being a responsible adult male in the society.

These initiation rites often involve an extended period during which boys are separated from the larger society, which emphasizes the importance of an individual's responsibility to his kinship group as well as the larger community (Hart 1967). The rites often include painful practices such as scarification or circumcision that symbolize the formal transition from child to adult. Such rites may also include difficult and dangerous tasks, such as killing a large animal, which test a boy's preparation for the obligations of male adulthood.

Among the Maasai, a herding society in Kenya, male initiation rites are part of an age-graded social system. Males follow a well-ordered progression through a series of age grades, entry into which requires a formalized rite of passage. After childhood, boys are initiated as warriors, and remain in that stage for about 15 years. Warriorhood is a period of training in social, political, and military skills, and traditionally geared to warfare and cattle raiding. The warriors then graduate ceremonially to a less active stage, during which they can marry, and then finally, to elderhood in a great ceremony.

Male rites of passage have been interpreted as a means of psychologically separating boys from identification with their mothers (Whiting, Kluckhohn, and Anthony 1967); as the symbolic appropriation of the fertility related to female reproductive capacities; and as a fertility cult in which men celebrate and ritually reproduce their control over the fertility of crops, animals, and humans. These rites also have important social functions. They bring together boys from different parts of the tribe and serve as a lifetime source of solidarity and political integration in social systems that have little formal or central government.

Although masculinity does take different forms in different cultures (Conway-Long 1994; Gutmann 1996; Kimmel 1996), a very widespread cultural pattern is one in which men must *prove* themselves to be virile, successful in competition with other men, daring, heroic, and aggressive, "proving their manhood" in formal rites, or more informally, on the streets, in bars, or in warfare (Gilmore 1990). In Chuuk, Micronesia (formerly the U.S. territory of Truk), for example, male adolescents engage in excessive drinking and violent brawling as an expression of a cultural concept of masculinity that is defined by competitiveness, assertiveness, risk taking in the face of danger, physical strength, and physical violence (Marshall 1979).

Anthropologist David Gilmore calls this widespread male need to publicly test and prove one's manhood the "manhood puzzle." To the question of why manhood needs to be proved, why it is regarded as so uncertain or precarious that manhood requires trials of skill, endurance, or special rituals (see Figure 10.3), Gilmore suggests that cultural patterns of "proving

© Imagesofanthropology.com

Figure 10.3 In the Jewish religion, the bar mitzvah of a boy, at age 13, is a key ritual in the public acceptance of the obligations and responsibilities of manhood.

manhood" help ensure that men will fulfill their roles as procreators, providers, and protectors of their families. This essential contribution to society, he argues, is at the heart of the *"macho"* masculine role and accounts for its intensity, near universality, and persistence.

Female Rites of Passage

Female rites of passage are more widespread than male rites, although generally less spectacular and intense. Female initiation into adulthood is often performed at *menarche* (first menstruation), but there is much cross-cultural variability (Lutkehaus and Roscoe 1995). Sometimes the initiate is isolated from society; sometimes she is the center of attention. Some rituals are elaborate and take years to perform; others are performed with little ceremony.

As with male rites, female initiation rites also have multiple interpretations. In matrilocal societies where the young girl continues her childhood tasks in her mother's home, an important function of the rite is to publicly announce a girl's status change, as she will now carry out these tasks as a responsible adult (Brown 1965), and to teach girls what they need to know to be effective adults. Female rites of passage also channel sexuality into adult reproduction, and in some rituals, the rites emphasize the connections between beauty, sexuality, and power. These rites, in New Guinea, for example, motivate girls to bear and rear children, strengthen their fortitude, and provide them with the capacity for the hard work necessary to assist their husbands in gathering wealth.

POWER AND PRESTIGE: GENDER STRATIFICATION

A central concern in anthropology is **gender stratification**. Anthropologists have long debated whether male dominance is universal and, if so, why it is so. In the interest of addressing these questions, anthropologists look at the social and cultural significance of women's roles as mothers, sisters, wives, and daughters; women's economic contributions in different types of societies; informal as well as formal sources of women's power and influence; development of women's identities; and changes in all these dimensions as a result of historical factors, particularly colonialism, technological and economic change, and globalization.

One early anthropological theory that addresses the widespread, some say universal, subordination of women to men is called the **private/public dichotomy**. This theory holds that female subordination is based on women's universal role as mothers and homemakers, occupying a domestic

gender stratification: The ways in which gendered activities and attributes are differentially valued and related to the distribution of resources, prestige, and power in a society.

private/public dichotomy: A gender system in which women's status is lowered by their almost exclusive cultural identification with the home and children, whereas men are identified with public, prestigious, economic, and political roles.

(private) world that is less prestigious than the public world dominated by men (Rosaldo and Lamphere 1974). But a closer look indicates that the private/public dichotomy is not universal but rather characterizes the highly gender-stratified 19th-century capitalist societies, such as those of Victorian Europe and the United States: In these societies, productive relationships moved out of the household, and middle-class women (but not working-class women) retreated into the home, where they were supposed to concern themselves solely with domestic affairs, repress their sexuality, bear children, and accept a subordinate and dependent role (Martin 1987; see also Lamphere 2005 for a reevaluation of this theory). The private/public dichotomy seems less applicable to smaller-scale, non-Western societies where home, family, economics, and politics were not so easily separated, and where women played an important though perhaps not as easily observable role in economic production and distribution (Friedl 1975). With increasing Western influence on these societies, through capitalism, Christian missionaries, and colonialism, the public/private dichotomy became a more relevant context for gender stratification (Leacock 1981; Lockwood 2005:504).

Other anthropologists have used controlled cross-cultural comparisons to understand male dominance. Peggy Sanday (1981), for example, concluded that male dominance was *not* universal but occurred in connection with ecological stress and warfare: Where the survival of the group rests more on male actions, such as warfare, women accept male dominance for the sake of social and cultural survival.

Gender Relations: Complex and Variable

Anthropological debates in earlier gender studies focused on which gender dominated a society. Male dominance, called **patriarchy**, was considered universal, or nearly so, although matriarchy, or female dominance, was held to exist in some societies. Although anthropologists generally do not find matriarchies where women hold power equal to that of men in patriarchies, there is more recognition today that female power does find a place in many societies. With a greater understanding of the complexity and variability in gender stratification systems, anthropologists today have moved from the question of whether male dominance is universal to explanations of gender stratification in particular societies. This has led to a closer examination of the sexual division of labor in different types of societies and an examination of the informal as well as formal bases of female power.

patriarchy: A male-dominated society in which most important public and private power is held by men.

Gender Relations in Foraging Societies

Earlier anthropological descriptions of foraging societies viewed male hunting as the major source of the food supply, providing the basis of male dominance in these societies. Contemporary ethnographic studies have modified this view. In many foraging societies, such as the Tiwi of Australia and the Ju/'hoansi of the Kalahari Desert in Namibia (Africa), women make very significant contributions to the food supply by gathering vegetable foods (Hart and Pilling 1960; Lee 2003). In other societies, like the Agta of the Philippines, women also substantially contributed to the food supply by hunting (Estioko-Griffin 1986), although in different ways and for different kinds of animals than men hunted. These contributions by women to the society's food supply were an important source of female power.

The Tlingit of the northwest coast of North America is a foraging society in which women traditionally had equal power and prestige with men. Important Tlingit social roles are based on individual ability, training, and personality rather than on gender (Klein 1995). Both Tlingit women and men achieve prestige through their own efforts and their own kin relationships. Women may be heads of clans or tribes, and Tlingit aristocrats are both male and female. Titles of high rank are used for both men and women, and the ideal marriage is between a man and woman of equal rank. The prestige the Tlingit achieved through extensive trade with other coastal societies is open to both men and women. Although long-distance trade centered on men in the past, women often accompanied the men, acting as negotiators and handling the money, and both girls and boys were—and are today—expected to "work, save, get wealth and goods" (Klein 1995:35).

Gender egalitarianism continues to be a core Tlingit cultural value. Today, women occupy the highest offices of the native corporations administering Tlingit land and are employed in government, social action groups, business and cultural organizations, and voluntary associations (Klein 1976). Tlingit women take advantage of educational opportunities and easily enter modern professions. Unlike many non-Western societies where European contact diminished women's economic roles and influence, modernization expanded Tlingit women's roles, and modern gender egalitarianism is not experienced as diminishing men, who encourage their wives and daughters to go into public life.

Gender Relations in Horticultural Societies

Generally speaking, women have more autonomy and power in egalitarian foraging societies than in horticultural, pastoral, or agricultural societies, but again, there is great cross-cultural variation (see Figure 10.4). For example, the Iroquois of the eastern United States are highly egalitarian (Brown 1975), whereas the Yanomamo of Venezuela and Brazil are highly sex segregated and male dominated (Chagnon 1997), as are most societies in highland New Guinea (Strathern 1995, but see Lepowsky 1993).

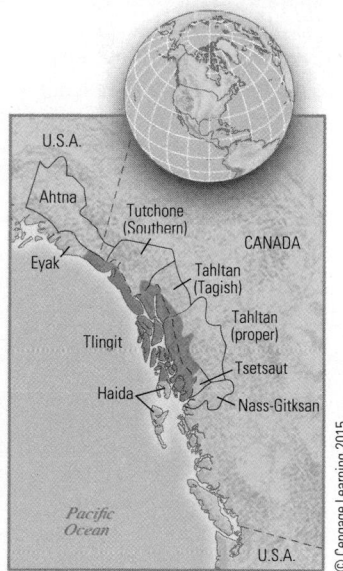

The Tlingit, on the Northwest Coast of North America.

© Judith Pearson

Figure 10.4 The emphasis on male dominance and aggression in horticultural societies overlooks the elements of affection and nurturance that males play as fathers, as in the Iban society of Indonesia.

A high degree of sex segregation, paralleled by the importance of males in ritual, is associated with male dominance in some horticultural societies. Among the Mundurucu of South America, for example, adolescent boys are initiated into the men's cult and thereafter spend most of their lives in the men's house, only visiting their wives, who live with the children in their own huts in the village. The men's cults exclude women and are surrounded by great secrecy. The men's house itself usually is the most imposing structure in the village and houses the cult paraphernalia and sacred musical instruments, which are flutelike in shape (like male genitals) and are the symbolic expressions of male dominance, just as the men's house is an institution of male solidarity (Murphy and Murphy 1974).

The solidarity of women in horticultural societies usually is not formalized in cults or associations but is based on the cooperation of domestic life and strong interpersonal bonds among female kin. In sub-Saharan Africa, for example, the most important economic and emotional ties for both men and women are more likely to be between generations (consanguineal ties) than between spouses (conjugal ties). Women's most important ties are with their children, particularly their sons, on whom women depend for emotional support and security in old age (Potash 1989:199). Women, like men, also use kinship ties with their natal groups to gain access to land, gain support in marital disputes, and participate in ritual activities (Sacks 1982). In many parts of West Africa, women's power is expressed through political office (Kaplan 1997) and also through formally organized secret societies, such as the Sande society of Sierra Leone (MacCormack 1974). Contemporary ethnography demonstrates that women's power and influence sometimes go beyond their economic contributions, their significant roles within households and families, and even beyond formal political offices sometimes occupied by women. An important dimension of female power may rest on female alliances and participation in networks and groups outside the household that provide arenas for entertainment, prestige, influence, and self-esteem. Anthropologist Annette Weiner (1976), for example, demonstrated the important exchanges among women in the Trobriand Islands, where the emphasis on male kula exchanges had excluded any anthropological attention to women's participation in exchange networks.

In some societies, like the Yoruba of West Africa, power is conceptualized as a vital force present in all living things. Personal power may be projected through certain body parts, for example, the eyes, mouth, hands and fingers, and genitals. Power associated with sexuality and reproduction is especially strong and potentially dangerous and polluting, especially female genital power. Indeed, the universal covering of the female genitals may well be related to the power of these body parts (Stevens 2006).

The impact of European expansion on women in horticultural societies varied. Generally, women's roles declined as indigenous economies shifted from subsistence horticulture to cash crops sold in the world market. Among the Nukumanu, a Pacific island society, women's primary responsibilities were domestic, whereas men contributed food acquired at longer distances from the home through fishing, collecting shellfish, and collecting and husking coconuts. Men also made canoes and constructed new buildings, whereas women cooked food and collected and prepared leaves for thatch. Both women's and men's roles were highly valued in traditional Nukumanu society. Women exclusively controlled and cultivated swamp taro lands, which were inherited matrilineally. Matrilocality added to women's status, whereas men's power came from their economic contribution and their exclusive occupation of formal positions of power in the chiefly hierarchy.

With the advent of German colonial occupation in the 1880s, most of Nukumanu was turned over to the production of copra (dried coconut meat). Wage laborers were brought in from nearby islands, commercially marketed foods such as wheat flour and rice supplanted taro, and men's wages were needed to buy coffee, tea, and sugar (once luxury items). As a result, women's traditional sphere of influence and their status declined, while men's spheres of power expanded (Feinberg 1986). The traditional segregation of men's and women's activities also intensified. Kareve (a potent alcoholic beverage made from fermented coconut sap) was introduced in the 1950s, and men's economic activities, such as canoe building, took on a social aspect involving drinking. Because kareve production and consumption takes up much of men's leisure time and excludes women, sexual segregation increased.

As taro declined in importance, women's collective activities became more individualized, leaving them more isolated and dependent on their husbands and brothers than previously. Male–female tensions also increase partly as a result of kareve drinking, which many women vehemently oppose. The traditional tendency for men to travel off the island more than women also lowered women's status, and even today men primarily go overseas for wage labor and higher education. More recently, however, more women are leaving the island to take advantage of opening educational and career opportunities, and the prestige, money, and social influence of such women may move Nukumanu back toward its tradition of sexual egalitarianism.

Gender Relations in Pastoral and Agricultural Societies

Pastoral and agricultural societies tend to be male dominated, although there is some variation. In pastoral societies, women's status depends on the degree to which the society combines herding with cultivation, its specific historical situation, and the diffusion of cultural ideas, such as Islam. Generally speaking, women's contribution to the food supply in pastoral societies is small (Martin and Voorhies 1975). Men do almost all the herding and most of the dairy work as well. Male dominance in pastoral society is partly based on the required strength to handle large animals, but females sometimes do handle smaller animals, engage in dairy work, carry water, and process animal by-products such as milk, wool, and hides (O'Kelly and Carney 1986). Pastoral societies generally do not have the rigid distinction between public and domestic roles of agricultural societies. Herders' camps typically are divided into male and female spaces, but both men and women work in public, somewhat blurring the private/public dichotomy.

In pastoral societies, men predominantly own and have control over the disposition of livestock, which is an important source of power and prestige. However, the disposition of herds is always subject to kinship rules and responsibilities, and men and women may jointly hold animals. Still, the male economic dominance in pastoral societies seems to give rise to general social and cultural male dominance, reinforced by patricentric kinship systems and the need for defense through warfare (Sanday 1981).

Again, this generalization is subject to variation. Among the Tuareg of the central Sahara, for example, which is a matrilineal society, women generally have high prestige and substantial influence (Rasmussen 2005). Tuareg women do not veil their faces, they have social and economic independence and can own property, including herd animals, and they have freedom of movement. There is minimal sex segregation, and women organize many social events as singers and musicians. Although the traditionally high status of Tuareg women, and matrilineality itself, is undermined today by the migration of men to cities, where they work for wages, and by the incorporation of the Tuareg into larger nation-states, with their patrilineal cultures, cities may also provide increasing opportunities and freedom for Tuareg women.

In agricultural societies, with the use of plows, the direct female contribution in food production generally drops drastically, though this varies. Women, for example, play important productive roles in wet rice agriculture. As women's economic contribution declines, they lose status, and this is also generally accompanied by their increasing isolation in domestic work in the home and increasing numbers of children (Ember 1983). Machine technology reduces the overall labor force, and this also particularly affects women, who are disproportionately excluded from mechanized agriculture. Women are also paid less, and remain in traditional labor, and are concentrated in such labor-intensive agricultural tasks as weeding, transplanting, and harvesting. Also, as men more easily enter a cash economy, selling crops and animals, transition to this economic system in most cases also lowers women's status and makes them more dependent on men.

Women's status in modern stratified societies varies greatly and is affected by economic development, political ideology, and globalization. Women have been highly involved in the global economy, primarily through the expansion of industrial production by multinational corporations in Latin America, Asia, and Africa. As urban lifestyles and industrial production replace rural lifestyles and agriculture, women may even benefit relative to men. For example, in Mata Chico, Peru, in the 1930s, the only way for women to get land, a critical resource, was to marry. But by the 1980s, as Peru became increasingly urban, many occupations were available to both men and women. Because women could support themselves and their children through employment in urban areas, they began to remain single longer and in some cases chose to not marry at all (Vincent 1998).

Using Anthropology: Economic Development for Women

As with colonialism, foreign aid and development programs often fail because while they increase male productivity, they neglect the economic role of women (Kristoff and Wudunn 2009). Indeed, development programs may actually increase gender inequality (Moser 1993; Warren and Bourque 1989). Where anthropologists are involved in development projects, however, more attention may be paid to women's roles. Ann Dunham*, an anthropologist, craftsperson, and weaver, did her fieldwork in Indonesia, and was particularly interested in craft marketing, an important potential source of income for village Indonesians (Dunham et al. 2009). Dunham became particularly interested in the economic possibilities of marketing and later worked for the Ford Foundation and USAID development projects in Indonesia and Pakistan. Her fieldwork findings challenged the then common notion that the culture of the poor themselves created the roots of poverty, a view portrayed by one of anthropology's most prominent anthropologists, Clifford Geertz, who worked in Indonesia 25 years before Dunham. In contrast to Geertz,

---

*Ann Dunham Soetoro is the mother of President Barak Obama.

Dunham observed that underdevelopment in these village communities largely resulted from a scarcity of capital. As a development anthropologist, Dunham—who also worked with international organizations like the World Bank and the Ford Foundation—set up credit cooperatives for Indonesian women street food sellers, factory workers, hand-loom weavers, shop girls, and scavengers. As Dunham pointed out, with the exception of iron tools, which have a religious connection to blacksmithing and are only handled by men, women mainly work in Indonesian markets and form an essential part of the economy and the family. The success of the Grameen Bank project of microlending for women, which results in their increasing prestige, income, and autonomy, confirmed Dunham's anthropological insights about the potential of village woman. The global marketing of women's textiles and pottery from Mexico and Guatemala has also proven economically successful, although here it has sometimes led to greater tension and even violence between men and women (Nash 1993; 1994:15). As anthropologists increasingly point out, the impact of development projects on women is a result of the interplay of specific economic and cultural conditions in a particular society (Lockwood 2005).

In spite of its gender egalitarian ideology, even in the developed nations of Europe, Japan, and the United States, the status of women is not equal to men. In the United States, for example, the view that women should be excluded from all but domestic and child-rearing roles has historically been culturally dominant and remains so among many Americans today. Although American women have made great strides in professions such as law, medicine, and academe, there is still much stereotyping and discrimination. More women than men may go to medical school, but they tend to take on less prestigious medical specializations after graduation. Even in academic anthropology, where women like Margaret Mead and Ruth Benedict are among our most influential and celebrated elders, women's rates of promotion to full professor lag behind the rates of men.

Although legal restrictions on public roles for women, such as jury duty, no longer apply today, the numbers of women in Congress are decidedly small, and, as of this writing, there has yet to be a female president or vice president. Domestic violence, sexual harassment, and continued attempts to constrain women's reproductive rights are other significant problems still being fought over in the United States. Gender identities and gender stratification are taught from infancy (last week, I agonized over buying a blue baby suit for a friend's new baby girl and settled for yellow!). In some progressive societies like Sweden, a real effort is made to blur gender differences. Teachers avoid the pronouns "him" and "her" and avoid gender nouns like boy and girl. The library contains few classic fairy tales, such as Cinderella or Snow White, which are laden with gender stereotypes. Boys as well as girls are allowed to cry, and neither sex is admonished for engaging in activities typically associated with the other gender, though there appears to be less opposition to girls taking on boys' roles than the opposite. The Swedish government and the public realize that erasing gender stratification must begin early (Tagliabue 2012).

Contemporary socialist societies, such as Vietnam, for example, are also transforming gender ideology and practice in the transition from state socialism to partly neoliberal market economies (Leshkowich 2011). Early socialist ideology proudly announced its support for gender equality, but today has tweaked that notion, as it encourages women to participate in the new economy (see Figure 10.5). Previously, socialism had denigrated petty traders, most of whom were women, as part of an unpatriotic and antirevolutionary class motivated by personal monetary gain. But to capitalize on the growing economic importance of these markets, especially for the increasing international tourist trade since the end of the Vietnam War, the Vietnamese government currently emphasizes how market trade is particularly suited to women's innate gendered personalities. Women realize the advantage of this gender construction themselves and encourage it by denigrating their status in relation to their customers, engaging in flattery and "sweet talk" with their customers, and perhaps most importantly, defining men as innately incapable of successfully engaging in such trade. For the government, this new feminine gender construction also turns women into a productive class in the socialist system. Thus do economics, politics, and gender construction interact in the contemporary world.

Joan Young Gregg

Figure 10.5 In socialist Vietnam, both culture and state ideology have constructed women's gender identity as especially suitable for managing small-scale markets. Men are considered too impatient and lazy for this work, preferring to sit around smoking cigarettes or playing cards.

BRINGING IT BACK HOME:
VIOLENCE AGAINST WOMEN AND THE CULTURAL DEFENSE

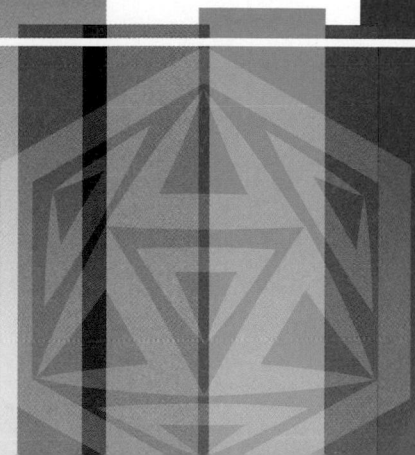

Violence against women is an international problem, and domestic violence is considered acceptable in many patriarchal societies. When the government of Kazakhstan invited anthropologist Edward Snajdr (2007) to analyze and

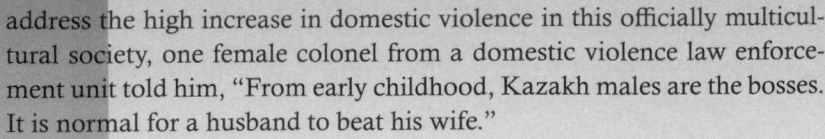

address the high increase in domestic violence in this officially multicultural society, one female colonel from a domestic violence law enforcement unit told him, "From early childhood, Kazakh males are the bosses. It is normal for a husband to beat his wife."

It may be "normal," but in the United States and many other societies, including Kazakhstan, it is illegal. Although some multicultural societies like Kazakhstan will consider "culture" in responding to domestic violence, courts in the United States do not generally recognize culture as a defense. The "cultural defense" of domestic violence in court has mainly been used to defend men who come from immigrant cultures where domestic violence is "normal." These cases have sometimes even involved anthropologists as expert witnesses, testifying to violence as a culturally appropriate response to a wife who has dishonored her family through sexual "transgressions" (Norgren and Nanda 2006; Renteln 2004). In many of these cases, courts have cited the cultural defense in not holding a husband fully accountable for his actions, or considered culture as a mitigating circumstance, and reducing the sentence (Winkelman 1996). As a result of the use of the cultural defense in mitigating sentences for assault and even murder, many women's groups and legal scholars protest that "there should be only one standard of justice," which should not be affected by a defendant's cultural background. In this view, a court's decision to allow a cultural defense sends out the dangerous message that immigrant women cannot be fully protected by U.S. law.

In addition to raising ethical issues about anthropological participation, the cultural defense also distorts the anthropological concept of culture as varied and changing; lawyers, judges, and the popular media tend to have a static and generalizing perspective on culture, which is inaccurate (Demian 2008). Anthropology does not accept the idea that "culture made me do it," but anthropology has been helpful in raising awareness of the need for culturally and linguistically sensitive responses to victims of domestic violence. Ethnographies that illuminate the diverse cultural contexts of domestic violence (Nanda and Gregg 2009) and groups like Sakhi, which helps defend immigrant women from the Indian subcontinent, show how culturally relevant interventions make an important difference in serving victims of domestic violence in both our own and other societies.

YOU DECIDE:

1. Given the dominant anthropological view that culture is diverse, dynamic, multifaceted, and shapes but does not determine behavior, what role, if any, do you think the cultural defense should be permitted to play in criminal cases involving domestic violence?

2. What in your view would be the most effective local and/or national responses to domestic violence in the United States: social services, laws and law enforcement, counselling, mediation? What might be some consequences of each of these responses?

3. What might be the most effective way of using anthropological expertise to decrease the rate of domestic violence in our own society or in other cultures?

■ CHAPTER SUMMARY

1. What is the difference between sex and gender? *Sex* refers to biological differences between male and female; *gender* refers to the social classification of masculine and feminine and the roles that people assume.

2. What is the evidence that gender is culturally constructed? An important anthropological principle is that gender, including sexuality, is not biologically determined but is culturally constructed. This is demonstrated by the presence of alternative genders in different societies and by the culturally variable definitions of femininity and masculinity in different cultures.

3. Are sexual behavior and sexual desire "doing what comes naturally"? Views about the nature of male and female sexuality are part of gender ideologies. Attempts to control female sexuality, for example, in constraints on women's dress in Islam, are embedded in gender hierarchies and culture.

4. How do gender-based initiation rites function in different societies? Many societies have rites of passage for males and females, in which boys and girls are transformed into adult men and women. These rites have many social and psychological functions, such as the transmission of cultural knowledge, the public acceptance of the obligations of adulthood, and the reaffirmation of cultural values, including gender hierarchies.

5. What are some of the theories anthropologists have developed to explain the universality or near universality of male dominance? A male-dominated gender stratification system is one in which men are dominant, reap most of the social and material rewards of society, and control the autonomy of women. Two important theories used to explain male dominance are male control over economic resources and women's association with the domestic rather than the public sphere.

6. What are some of the differences in gender stratification systems in foraging, horticultural, agricultural, and industrial societies?

Gender stratification is interrelated with the economy. Foraging societies appear to be mostly egalitarian, but women also have sources of power—through marketing or specialized economic niches in more complex societies. There is great variety, however; European colonialism and contemporary globalization, including development projects, have brought both positive and negative changes to gender stratification systems.

KEY TERMS

Cultural construction of gender
Gender
Gender ideology
Gender role
Gender stratification

Hijra
Patriarchy
Private/public dichotomy
Rite of passage
Sex

On Vanuatu, the John Frum movement is a classic example of what anthropologists call a cargo cult. Here, John Frum worshippers celebrate by marching in military formation. The letters USA are painted in red on their chests.

CHAPTER 11

RELIGION

LEARNING OBJECTIVES

After you have read this chapter, you will be able to:

△ Summarize the critical characteristics all religions share.

△ Analyze the roles of sacred narratives and symbols in religion.

△ Discuss the types of ritual commonly found in religion, and give examples of rites of passage and rites of intensification.

△ Explain the differences between priests and shamans, and give examples of the kinds of societies in which each is found.

△ Define prayer, magic, and sacrifice, and give examples of their uses.

△ Examine the roles that accusations of witchcraft or sorcery play in society.

△ Summarize the role of religion in social change, and assess the conditions under which it is likely to be an important factor in speeding or slowing change.

Thierry Falise/LightRocket/Getty Images

CARGO CULTS

IGH on a mountaintop in New Guinea, a group of men are performing a ritual around the body of a small plane that crashed there years ago. Their ritual is aimed at ensuring the arrival of *cargo*, their word for the trade goods of Western culture that are the focus of their desires, stimulated by the encounters with Europeans, Americans, and Japanese over the past hundred years. Outsiders frequently promised wealth and political equality, but members of these groups soon realized that their words did not match reality. Not only did Melanesians fail to gain riches and power, but, in many cases, they grew poorer and were more deeply oppressed under colonial rule.

Melanesians observed that these outsiders did not seem to work but instead made "secret signs" on scraps of paper, built strange structures, and behaved in odd ways. For example, they built airports and seaports with towers and wires, and they drilled soldiers to march in formation. When they did these things, planes and ships arrived, disgorging a seemingly endless supply of material goods. Melanesians, who did so much hard physical labor, got nothing.

In Melanesian culture, secret knowledge was the source of power and wealth. Plainly, the outsiders knew the secrets of cargo and were keeping them from the islanders. Many Melanesians believed that if they could learn the hidden knowledge and rituals of cargo, they could rid their societies of oppressive colonial governments and gain access to immense wealth for themselves.

In this context, Melanesians made numerous attempts to discover the knowledge and rituals of cargo. Cargo cults usually began with a local prophet who claimed such knowledge and announced that the world was about to end in a terrible catastrophe, after which God (or the ancestors, or a local culture hero) would appear, and a paradise on earth would begin. The end of the world could be caused or hastened by the performance of rituals that copied what Melanesians had observed the outsiders doing. In some places, the faithful sat around tables dressed in European clothes, making signs on paper. In others, they drilled with wooden rifles and built wharves, storehouses, airfields, and lookout towers in the hope that such ritual would cause planes to land or ships to dock and disgorge cargo.

Cargo cults are not limited to Melanesia. In the United States and Latin America, millions of followers of prosperity theology and the Word-Faith movement believe that God wants Christians to be wealthy (Van Biema and Chu 2006). Promoted by Oral Roberts and other televangelists, the movement teaches their adherents that if they give money (the more, the better) to movement churches and pray with sincerity, devotion, and frequency, God will reward them with cash and other material wealth, such as cars and houses. In other words, if they perform the correct rituals, they will receive cargo. If they remain poor, it is because they failed to properly ask God for wealth.

But perhaps cargo is not merely a cult in the United States but is central to our culture. Westerners do seem obsessed with cargo: An endless desire for consumer goods and the belief that buying specific brands of cars, drinks, or clothing will make them forever young, sexy, and powerful (Lindstrom 1993). Some might say that this is as likely to happen as it is for cargo to descend from the skies in Melanesia.

Recent research links religious experience to specific capacities of the right temporal and right parietal lobes of the brain (Chan et al. 2009; Johnstone and Glass 2008). Because religiosity is a biologically based capacity of humans, it is unsurprising that all societies have spiritual beliefs and practices that anthropologists refer to as *religion*. Yet because of the great diversity of these beliefs and practices, defining religion is surprisingly difficult. Most definitions focus on the supernatural. However, for most Westerners, the natural is easily equated with the normal, logical, and rational, and the supernatural with the unusual, illogical, and irrational. However, religious believers generally understand their own beliefs and experiences as normal, logical, and rational.

CHARACTERISTICS OF RELIGION

From an anthropological perspective, all religions share five common characteristics. First, religions are composed of sacred stories that members believe are important. Second, religions make extensive use of symbols and symbolism. Third, religions propose the existence of beings, powers, states, places, and qualities that cannot be measured by any agreed-upon scientific means—they are nonempirical (for convenience, we refer to the nonempirical as supernatural, even though, as previously noted, this term is problematic). Fourth, religions include rituals and specific means of addressing the supernatural. Fifth, all societies include individuals who are particularly expert in the practice of religion. Thus, we might define **religion** as a social institution characterized by sacred stories; symbols and symbolism; the proposed existence of supernatural beings, powers, states, places, and qualities; rituals and means of addressing the supernatural; and specific practitioners.

Early anthropologists were primarily interested in the development of religion. They argued that religion had evolved from **animism**, the

Religion: A social institution characterized by sacred stories, symbols, and symbolism; the proposed existence of immeasurable beings, powers, states, places, and qualities; rituals and means of addressing the supernatural; specific practitioners; and change.

Animism: The notion that all objects, living and nonliving, are imbued with spirits.

Figure 11.1 Religions provide a sense of order and meaning in a world that often seems chaotic. Here in the village of Kościelisko, Poland, a priest leads a procession on the Feast of Corpus Christi.

belief that all living and nonliving objects are imbued with spirits passed through a stage of polytheism and finally arrived at monotheism. They held that this evolutionary process was characterized by increasing levels of logic and rationality. However, this view has been discredited. Today, anthropologists understand that there is no orderly process of religious evolution and that no religion can be considered any more logical or evolved than any other. Anthropologists today are interested in exploring religion in terms of its functions, its symbolism, and its relation to both social stability and change.

Religion may provide meaning and order in people's lives (see Figure 11.1). It may reduce social anxiety and give people a sense of control over their destinies. It may promote and reinforce the status quo. But, it does not always do these things. In some cases, religion may make people profoundly disquiet or fearful. It may be an important force resisting the status quo, and it may catalyze radical politics and, on occasion, even murderous violence.

In the following sections, we provide descriptions and examples of the ways in which each of the defining characteristics of religion works in society and in the lives of individual society members. We then turn to an examination of religion and social change.

Sacred Narratives

Sacred narratives (myths): Stories of historical events, heroes, gods, spirits, and creation that members of a religious tradition hold to be holy and true.

At a fundamental level, all religions consist of a series of stories told by members of a group. These **sacred narratives** are powerful ways of communicating ideas. Sometimes, such stories are held to have a sacred power that is evoked when they are told. Sacred narratives may recall historic events, although these are often clothed in poetic language.

Sacred narratives are often called myths and, in some ways, this is appropriate as they often include stories of heroes, explanations of origins, and distortions of reality. However, we frequently use the word *myth* to denote a false belief (or one we do not share). It is worth remembering that ancient Greeks were just as convinced of the truths of their stories of Zeus and Hera as current-day people are convinced of the truths of the central stories of their own religions. Clearly, we should apply the same terminology to others' religious beliefs that we apply to our own.

By explaining that things came to be the way they are through the activities of sacred beings, sacred narratives legitimize beliefs, values, and customs. The origin narrative of the Hopi, an agricultural people of Arizona, provides a clear example. The Hopi subsist mainly on blue corn, a variety that is more difficult to grow than other varieties of corn but is stronger and more resistant to damage. According to Hopi belief, before their ancestors appeared on the earth's surface, they were given their choice of subsistence activities. The ancestors chose blue corn and were taught the techniques for growing it by the god Maasaw. The Hopi believe that in growing blue corn, they re-create the feelings of humility and harmony their ancestors experienced when they first chose this form of agriculture. Thus, the Hopi live their religious understanding of the world as they grow blue corn. The stories that accompany this action reinforce social customs and enhance solidarity.

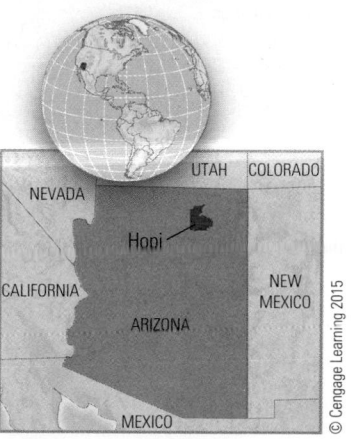

The Hopi.

Religious narratives provide **cosmologies** or frameworks for interpreting events and experiences. These are visible in religious symbols and rituals as well. A cosmology may include principles or beliefs about the nature of life and death, the creation of the universe, the origin of society, the relationship of individuals and groups to one another, and the relationship of humankind to nature.

Cosmology: A system of beliefs that deals with fundamental questions in the religious and social order.

Cosmologies give meaning to the lives of believers. By defining the place of the individual in society and establishing moral codes, they provide people with a sense of personal identity, a sense of belonging, and a standard of behavior. When people suffer a profound personal loss or when life loses meaning because of radically changed circumstances or catastrophic events, religion can supply a new identity or new responses that become the basis for personal and cultural survival.

Symbols and Symbolism

Religious stories depend on symbolism, which may be expressed in words, in material objects such as masks and statues, in body decorations, by objects in the physical environment, or through performance. Some religious symbols may be understood to have power in and of themselves, such as the masks used in African ceremonies or the wafers used in Catholic communion.

Part of the power of religious symbols is that they pack many different and sometimes contradictory meanings into a single word, idea, object, or performance. Consider the Christian cross. Among its meanings are death, love, sacrifice, identity, history, power, weakness, wealth, poverty, and many more.

Because they carry so many meanings, religious symbols often have great emotional and intellectual power. As a result, they can be used in leadership. For example, since the first centuries of Christianity, the cross has been used as a military symbol and to rally people to political causes. Desecration of the cross may inflame passions and provoke very strong reactions as well.

Symbolic representation allows people to grasp the often complex and abstract ideas of a religion without much concern or knowledge of the underlying theology. The Christian ritual of communion, for example, symbolizes the New Testament story of the Last Supper, which communicates the abstract idea of communion with God. In Hinduism, this idea is represented in plays, paintings, and sculptures as the love between the divine Krishna, in the form of a cowherd, and the milkmaids, particularly Radha, who are devoted to him. Dramatic reenactments, songs, and artwork about the love of Krishna and Radha offer paths to communion with God that ordinary people can understand and participate in.

Supernatural Beings, Powers, States, and Qualities

Although many religions do not separate the natural from the supernatural, all religions propose that there are important beings, powers, emotional states, or qualities that exist apart from human beings. These are nonempirical in that there is no scientifically agreed-upon way to measure them. For example, although many people claim to see proof of God's existence, there is nothing that members of all religions, as well as those who do not believe in any religion, could agree to measure that would demonstrate the existence of God. Thus, science, which depends upon such empirical measurement, can neither prove nor disprove the existence of God.

Most religions populate the world with nonempirical beings and spirits (see Figure 11.2). These can be happy or unhappy, stingy or generous, or experience any other emotion. The understanding of spirits and souls of animals among the Netsilik Inuit provides a good example. The Netsilik depend upon hunting and believe that if the soul of an animal they kill receives the proper religious attention, it will be pleased. Such an animal will reincarnate in another animal body and let itself be killed again. An animal soul that does not receive the proper attention, however, will be angered and will not let itself be killed a second time and the hunter may go hungry. Particularly offended animal souls might become blood-thirsty monsters and terrorize people (Balikci 1970:200–201).

The term **god** (or **deity**) is generally used for a named spirit believed to have created or to have control of some aspect of the world. Gods, who are the creators of the world and the ultimate powers in it, are present in only about half of all societies (Levinson 1996:229).

Polytheism refers to belief in many gods, and **monotheism** to a belief in a single god. However, the difference between these two is sometimes small. In polytheistic religions, the many gods may be different aspects of one god. For example, India has millions of gods, yet Indians understand these are all aspects of one divine essence. Conversely, in monotheistic religions, the one god may have several aspects. For most Christians, God the Father, God the Son, and God the Holy Spirit are all part of a single, unitary God.

In addition to supernatural beings, religions posit the existence of supernatural states, qualities, or powers, such as the enlightenment of Buddhist tradition, the saintliness of Catholicism, or the nirvana of the Hindus. Religious beliefs often include the notion of an impersonal spiritual force that anthropologists call **mana** (a term of Polynesian origin). Specific places, or objects or individuals (such as the Tahitian chiefs discussed in Chapter 7), may have a lot of mana. Mana is like electricity: It is uniform but may be concentrated in particular places, and it is powerful but dangerous if not approached with caution. That is why a belief in mana is often associated with an elaborate system of taboos, or prohibitions.

Bob Burch/Bruce Coleman Inc.

Figure 11.2 In religious ritual, humans may be transformed into supernatural beings. This masked dancer from Cote d'Ivoire is not just a person wearing a mask, but a person who has become a supernatural being.

God (deity): A named spirit who is believed to have created or to have control of some aspect of the world.

Polytheism: Belief in many gods.

Monotheism: Belief in a single god.

Mana: Religious power or energy that is concentrated in individuals or objects.

Ritual: A ceremonial act or a repeated stylized gesture used for specific occasions involving the use of religious symbols.

Rituals and Ways of Addressing the Supernatural

People enact their religion through **ritual**, a ceremonial act or a repeated stylized gesture used for specific occasions involving the use of religious symbols (Cunningham et al. 1995). Religious rituals may involve the telling or acting out of sacred stories; the repetition of words considered to be sacred; the use of music, dance, drugs, or pain that sometimes moves worshippers to a state of trance; and the use of ritual objects to convey religious messages.

The stories, symbols, and objects of worship that make up the content of religious rituals are exceedingly diverse, yet there are commonalities. Many religious practices are aimed at ensuring success in human activities. Prayers, sacrifice, and magic are often used in the hope that they will aid a particular person or community. Further, despite great diversity, some types of rituals, including rites of passage and rites of intensification, are extremely widespread, if not universal.

The Power of the Liminal

Liminal: The stage of a ritual, particularly a rite of passage, in which one has passed out of an old status but has not yet entered a new one.

The word **liminal** refers to those objects, places, people, and statuses that are understood as existing in an indeterminate state, between clear-cut categories. Objects that are liminal often play important roles in religious ritual.

Anthropologist Victor Turner (1969) wrote that rituals frequently generate liminal states in which the structured and hierarchical classifications that normally separate people into groups such as castes or classes are dissolved. Thus, in ritual, people can behave in ways that would be clearly unacceptable under other circumstances. In some cases, this includes role reversals. For example, many Japanese festivals included ritual transvestism, where community members dance in the clothing of the opposite sex (Norbeck 1974:51). In the Wubwang'u ritual among the Ndembu of Zambia, men and women publicly insult each other's sexual abilities and extol their own, but no one is allowed to take offense (Turner 1969:78–79). Ritual role reversals include class as well as gender. In Holi, the Hindu harvest festival, members of the lower class and castes throw colored powder (and in the old days, excrement and urine) at males of the middle and upper classes.

Communitas: A state of perceived solidarity, equality, and unity among people sharing a religious ritual, often characterized by intense emotion.

More controversially, Turner argued that in liminal states people experienced a state of equality and oneness he called **communitas**. The sense that people sometimes get after great natural or man-made disasters is one example. In the wake of events such as Hurricanes Sandy and Katrina, or the attacks of 9/11, social distinctions are, for a time forgotten. The wealthy and the poor, the powerful and the powerless may have strong experiences of unity and community identity.

Turner's ideas are provocative, but controversial. It may be fine for the wealthy and powerful to talk about the unity they feel with the poor and powerless. However, the reverse is not necessarily true. Poor people who claim that they have the same status as the rich are likely to face harsh penalties. The powerless may also use liminal symbols and rituals of reversal to subvert the social order (even if temporarily), expressing feelings not of oneness, but of conflict with the powerful.

In state-level societies, institutionalized liminal statuses sometimes emerge. Organizations such as monasteries and convents where people live permanently as members of a religious community are examples of liminality. Other examples include members of particular occupational groups, those who have certain diseases, and those of ambiguous social status. In many cases, liminal groups have low status. However, paradoxically, this is the source of their power. The hijras of India (see p. 238) are good examples. Their sexual ambiguity contains the power both to bless and to curse.

Anthropologists often refer the status reversals and carnival atmosphere of some rituals involving liminality as **antistructure**. Although all societies must have structure to provide order and meaning, according to Turner (1969:131), antistructure—the temporary ritual dissolution of the established order—is also important, helping people to more fully realize the oneness of the self and the other.

Antistructure: The socially sanctioned use of behavior that radically violates social norms; frequently found in religious ritual.

Rites of Passage

Rites of passage are public events that mark the transition of a person from one social status to another. Rites of passage almost always mark birth, puberty, marriage, and death, and may include many other transitions as well. Rites of passage involve three phases (van Gennep 1960/1909). The first phase is separation, in which the person or group is detached from a former status. The second phase is transition and is often characterized by liminality. The individuals in this phase have been detached from their old statuses but not yet attached to a new one. The third stage is reincorporation, in which the passage from one status to another is symbolically completed. After reincorporation, the person takes on the rights and obligations of his or her new social status.

Rite of passage: A ritual that moves an individual from one social status to another.

The rites of initiation for boys and girls described in Chapter 9 are good examples of rites of passage. Before these rituals, the boys and girls have the public status of children. Afterward, they have the public status of grown men and women. Other rites of passage affect similar changes of status. Baptisms and other ceremonies around birth transition a new child from the status of none–community member to a member. Quinceañeras mediate between the status of childhood and that of young womanhood, eligible for dating. Marriages mediate between single and couple status. Funerals mediate between the living and the dead.

Basic training for military service is an example of a rite of passage with which many Americans are familiar. In basic training, recruits are separated from their friends and families and are taken to military posts where they are given identical haircuts and identical uniforms. All signs of differences among them are minimized; no matter their position in life before joining the military, ideally they are treated identically during training. Training itself involves a wide variety of rigorous exercises and tasks designed to impart knowledge and build trust and camaraderie. In this state, they experience communitas, a shared identity along with the breaking down of barriers between individuals. Training ends with a large ceremony that reintegrates the recruits, now soldiers, into society with a new identity.

Rites of Intensification

Rite of intensification: A ritual structured to reinforce the values and norms of a community and to strengthen group identity.

Rites of intensification are rituals directed toward reinforcing the values and norms of the community and strengthening group identity and well-being. Through these rituals, the community maintains continuity with the past, enhances the feeling of social unity in the present, and renews the sentiments on which social cohesion depends (Elkin 1967).

In some groups, rites of intensification are connected with totems. A **totem** is an object, an animal species, or a feature of the natural world that is associated with a particular descent group.

Totem: An object, an animal species, or a feature of the natural world that is associated with a particular descent group.

Totemism is a prominent feature of the religions of the Australian aborigines. Groups of related individuals are linked with particular totemic species that they are usually prohibited from eating (see Verdon and Jorion 1981). In their religious rituals, members of each group assemble to celebrate their totem. The ceremonies explain the origin of the totem (and hence, of the group) and reenact the time of the ancestors. Through singing and dancing, both performers and onlookers are transported to an ecstatic state in which they no longer recognize themselves and feel as though they are being carried away to a special world (Durkheim 1961/1915:247–251).

Emile Durkheim, a pioneer in the anthropological study of religion, believed that totems were symbols of common social identity. When people worshipped totems, they were worshipping that common identity and at the same time reinforcing the moral and social order of their society. The ecstatic religious experience of their shared identity helped to bind them together.

The religious rituals of the Australian aborigines may seem exotic, but Americans participate in similar observances, some religious but many secular, to the same effect. The rallies associated with college football games are a good example. If the game is "good" or the school has "spirit," these gatherings produce enormous excitement among their fans and transport them to "a special world," increasing collective identity and intensifying loyalty to the school (and hopefully motivating financial donations from them as alumni). Schools, like Australian descent groups, also have totems, usually in the form of animal mascots.

Prayer, Sacrifice, and Magic

Prayer, sacrifices, and magic are found in most religious traditions. Although theoretically differentiated by the degree of control that humans believe they exert over the spirit world, the distinctions between them are more a matter of degree than of exclusive classification.

Prayer is any conversation held with spirits and gods in which people petition, invoke, praise, give thanks, dedicate, supplicate, intercede, confess, repent, and bless (Levinson 1996). A defining feature of prayer is that people believe the results depend on the will of the spirit world rather than on actions humans perform. When prayer involves requests, the failure of a spirit to respond to a request is understood as resulting from its disinclination rather than from improper human action. Prayer may be done without any expectation of a particular response from the beings or forces prayed to. There are many forms of prayer. In the West, prayer mainly involves words recited aloud or silently, but in Buddhist tradition, people may pray by hoisting flags or spinning wheels with prayers written inside them (see Figure 11.3).

Sacrifice occurs when people make offerings to gods or spirits to increase their spiritual purity or the efficacy of their prayers. People may sacrifice the first fruits of a harvest, animal lives, or, on occasion, human lives. Changes in behavior are often offered as sacrifices, as in the Muslim practice of fasting for Ramadan or the Christian practice of giving up something for Lent, a sacrifice intended to help the worshipper identify with Jesus, show devotion, and increase purity. In many religions, people make a vow to carry out a certain kind of behavior, such as going on a pilgrimage or building a place of worship, if a prayer is answered.

Prayer: Any conversation held with spirits and gods in which people petition, invoke, praise, give thanks, dedicate, supplicate, intercede, confess, repent, and bless.

Sacrifice: An offering made to increase the efficacy of a prayer or the religious purity of an individual.

Figure 11.3 Monks pray by turning prayer wheels outside a temple in Lhasa, Tibet.

©iStockPhoto.com/KeithSzafranski

Magic: A religious ritual believed to produce a mechanical effect by supernatural means.

Magic is an attempt to mechanistically control supernatural forces. When people do magic, they believe that their words and actions *compel* the spirit world to behave in certain ways. Failure of a magical request is understood to result from incorrect performance of the ritual rather than the refusal of spirits to act, as in prayer.

Imitation and contagion are two of the most common magical practices. In **imitative magic**, the procedure performed resembles the result desired. Most people are familiar with voodoo dolls (actually an aspect of magical practices called hoodoo that originated in African American communities rather than of vodou, a Caribbean and African religion). These are based on a form of imitative magic centered on the principle that mistreatment of a doll-like image of a person will cause injury to that person. **Contagious magic** is based on the idea that an object that has been in contact with a person retains a magical connection with that person. For example, one might attempt to increase the effectiveness of a voodoo doll by attaching a piece of clothing, hair, or other object belonging to the person he or she wishes to injure. People in the United States often attribute special power and meaning to objects that have come in contact with famous or notorious people. Signed baseballs, bits of costumes movie stars wore, pens used to sign famous documents and, sometimes, bits of the stars themselves all become collectors' items and are imbued with special power and importance. For example, in 2011, a lock of pop star Justin Bieber's hair in a plastic box that he signed sold for $40,668 (the money went to an animal rescue charity) (*Los Angeles Times* 2011).

Imitative magic: The belief that imitating an action in a religious ritual will cause the action to happen in the material world.

Contagious magic: The belief that things once in contact with a person or object retain an invisible connection with that person or object.

In many cultures, magical practices accompany most human activities. Among the people who live along the upper Asaro River in Papua New Guinea, when a child is born, its umbilical cord is buried so that it cannot later be used by a sorcerer to cause harm. To prevent an infant from crying at night, a bundle of sweet-smelling grass is placed on the mother's head, and her wish for uninterrupted sleep is blown into the grass. The grass then is crushed over the head of the child who, in breathing its aroma, also breathes in the mother's command not to cry (Newman 1977:413).

Divination: A religious ritual performed to find hidden objects or information.

Divination is a widespread ritual practice directed toward obtaining useful, hidden, or unknown information from a supernatural authority. Divination may be used to predict the future, diagnose disease, find hidden objects, or discover something about the past. In many cultures, divination is used to discover who committed a crime. Many Americans are familiar with divination techniques such as tarot cards, palmistry, flipping coins, reading auras, and the Magic 8 Ball.

Divination makes people more confident in their choices when they do not have all the information they need or when several alternative courses of action appear equal. It may be practiced when a group must decide on something about which there is disagreement. If the choice is made by divination, no member of the group feels rejected.

Prayer, sacrifice, magic, and divination are frequently related to risk. The less predictable an outcome is, the greater the likelihood they will be used. For example, professional baseball players in the United States rarely use magical practices in outfielding where there is little uncertainty, but often use magic for hitting and pitching, the least predictable aspects of the game. Detroit Tigers infielder Tim Maring wore the same clothes and put them on exactly in the same order each day during a batting streak (Gmelch 2000). Many of us do similar things. If you have studied for a test and know the material well, you are unlikely to spend much time praying for success. You are more likely to pray if you have not studied, and you may even bring your lucky pencil or another charm to the test.

Experimental studies show that praying or doing magic to help or hurt an individual has no effect, if that person does not know about your prayers or magical activities (see Flamm 2002; Tessman and Tessman 2000). However, when such attempts are known, they may have profound effect, altering the emotional state of the individuals involved. Bringing your lucky pencil to an exam may give you added confidence and improve your performance. Anthropologists in many parts of the world have observed cases in which sorcery is used to attack people and even cause death. In a study of such reports, Walter Cannon (1942) argued that an individual who was aware that he or she was being attacked by sorcery could exhibit increased anxiety and sometimes an extreme stress reaction that might lead to death. Much work in biomedicine in the past 60 years confirms Cannon's ideas and details the specific biochemical pathways through which such reactions may occur (Sternberg 2002).

Religious Practitioners

Every society includes people who are believed to have a special relationship with the religious world, who organize and lead major ritual events, or who engage in supernatural practice to heal, to gain power, or pursue other objectives for themselves or others. Anthropologists identify shamans, priests, witches, sorcerers, and many other religious practitioners. Although these classifications are useful, each has characteristics that overlap.

Shamans

A **shaman** is a part-time religious practitioner who otherwise works like an average member of his or her community. Learning to be a shaman may involve arduous training, and many are deeply learned in ritual,

Shaman: An individual socially recognized as being able to mediate between the world of humanity and the world of gods or spirits but who is not a recognized official of any religious organization.

© Judith Pearson

Figure 11.4 Among the Mentawai of Indonesia, shamans practice divination by reading the entrails of chickens and pigs to diagnose and cure illness.

herbalism, and magical technique, but such study is never sufficient. The distinctive characteristic of shamans is direct personal experiences of the supernatural that other members of the community accept as authentic. Shamans use prayer, meditation, song, dance, pain, drugs, or any combination of techniques to achieve trance states in which they understand themselves (and are understood by their followers) as entering the real world of the supernatural. They may use such contact to search for guidance for themselves or for their group, to heal the sick, or to divine the future (see Figure 11.4). Almost all societies have some shamans, but in foraging and tribal societies, shamans are likely to be the only religious practitioners.

In some cultures, almost every adult is expected to achieve direct contact with the supernatural. In some Native American societies, this is achieved through a vision quest in which individuals develop a special relationship with a particular spirit from whom they receive special kinds of power and knowledge, and who act as a personal protector or guardian. The vision seeker might fast, might isolate himself or herself at a lonely spot, or might use self-mutilation to intensify his or her emotional state to receive the vision.

Particularly before the advent of modern medicine, many societies treated illness by means that today would be considered primarily spiritual rather than medical. Illnesses were thought to be caused by broken taboos, sorcery, witchcraft, or spiritual imbalance, and shamans had an important role in curing. The shaman, usually in a trance, would travel into the supernatural world to discover the source of illness and how to cure it.

In the modern world, shamanic curing often exists alongside modern technological medicine. People go to shamans for healing when they have diseases that are not recognized by modern medicine, they lack money to pay for modern medical treatment, or they have tried such treatment and it has failed. Shamanistic curing can have important therapeutic effects. Shamans frequently treat their patients with drugs from the culture's traditional pharmacopoeia, and some (but not all) of these have been shown to be scientifically effective (Fábrega 1997:144). Shamanic curing ritual also uses symbolism and dramatic action to bring together cultural beliefs and religious practices in a way that enables patients to understand the source of their illness. Such rituals present a coherent model of sickness and health, explaining how patients got ill and how they may become well again, and these models can exert a powerful curative force (Roberts et al. 1993).

 **Priests**

In most state societies, religion is a formally established institution consisting of a series of ranked offices that exist independently of the people who fill them (a *bureaucracy*). Anthropologically, a **priest** is a person who is formally elected, appointed, or hired to a full-time religious office. Priests are responsible for performing certain rituals on behalf of individuals, groups, or the entire community. Jewish rabbis, Muslim imams, Christian ministers, and Hindu *purohits* all fit the definition of priests. Priests are most often associated with powerful gods and, where they exist, there is a division between the lay and priestly roles. Laypeople participate in ritual largely as passive respondents or as an audience rather than as managers or performers.

People generally become priests through training and apprenticeship and are certified by their religious hierarchy. Although priests need not have ecstatic religious experiences in mainstream religious denominations in the United States, this is not the case in all priestly religions. Ultimately, the priest's authority derives from a priestly office. However, in some cultures, like the ancient Maya, such office may also give a person the right to seek direct ecstatic contact with gods and spirits.

State societies generally attempt to suppress independent shamans or bring them under bureaucratic control. Shamans claim the ability to directly contact the supernatural without certification by any institutionalized religion, and this challenges the authority of church and state.

Priest: One who is formally elected, appointed, or hired to a full-time religious office.

 Witches and Sorcerers

In the 20th century, authors such as Gerald Gardner and Margot Adler created (and sometimes claimed to have "discovered") a new religion usually called Wicca and based on their reading of religious texts and European folklore. Practitioners of Wicca and other associated religions such as neo-paganism often call themselves witches or sorcerers. They usually claim to practice a religion of nature worship. Many follow Gardner's (1949) idea that whatever good or ill people do in the world returns to them threefold (this is sometimes called the threefold law, the rule of three, or the law of return). There is no evidence that Wiccans are more likely to commit evil acts than are members of more mainstream religious groups. They understand witchcraft as a positive, helpful thing. Additionally, the idea of witchcraft in our society is complicated by movies, cartoons, and other media that portray witches in a wide variety of imaginative ways. Given this, it is important to understand that, although there are some exceptions, throughout the world and throughout history, belief in the existence of witches and sorcerers is widespread, and they are usually viewed as evil and a source of social problems. Even when people go to witches or sorcerers for healing or to solve problems, their attitude is at best ambivalent: The person who can magically heal or resolve a problem can also magically cause illness and create a problem.

Although most of us (including anthropologists) use the words *witch* and *sorcerer* interchangeably (or to indicate gender), some societies make a clear distinction between the two. In these cases, **witchcraft** is understood as a physical aspect of a person. People are witches because their bodies contain a magical witchcraft substance, generally acquired through inheritance. If a person's body contains the witchcraft substance, his or her malevolent thoughts will result in misfortune among those around him or her. Sorcerers, on the other hand, are those who do physical magic by the manipulation of words and objects.

The Azande of East Africa, a classic example, believe that witches' bodies contain a substance called *mangu,* which allows them to cause misfortune and death to others (Evans-Pritchard 1958/1937). People who have the witchcraft substance may not be aware that they are witches and are believed to be unable to prevent themselves from causing evil. However, the Azande believe that when witches experience jealousy, anger, envy, or other negative feelings, they cause evil to befall those around them, particularly family members. They also believe in the existence of sorcerers who manipulate magical poisons to cause illness and misfortune. Similar beliefs about the unconscious or involuntary practice of magic are found in many places. For example, in northern Mexican and Mexican American tradition, mal ojo (evil eye) directed at children can be intentional, but often it is not. The envy and jealousy that an adult might consciously or unconsciously feel while looking at a child can harm the child.

Belief in the kind of witches described previously is common. However, the idea that some people can perform magical acts through the conscious manipulation of words and ritual objects with the intent of magically causing either harm or good is even more so. Accounts of the use of imitative and contagious magic as well as other magical forms are extremely widespread. People who believe in a witchcraft substance almost always also believe in the ability of certain people to do physical magic as well.

Although people practice magic, a principal social effect of witchcraft comes through people accusing others of witchcraft. Leveling witchcraft accusations against friends and neighbors is common in many cultures and serves various purposes. The most common form of witchcraft accusation serves to stigmatize differences. People who do not fit into conventional social categories are often suspected of witchcraft. Although men were sometimes accused of witchcraft, women were far more frequently accused. Often, these accusations were related to the

Witchcraft: The ability to harm others by harboring malevolent thoughts about them; the practice of sorcery.

failure of such women to subscribe to the social and sexual mores of their communities. For example, in a study of a community in Spain, Heidi Kelley (1991) found that although many women were occasionally accused of using witchcraft, villagers agreed that two must be witches. These were a pair of sisters living together without husbands but with the illegitimate child of one. Although such witches were sometimes killed, they were usually allowed to remain in a community, serving as negative role models, examples of what not to be.

Witchcraft and sorcery accusations may be used to scapegoat. In times of great social change when war, disease, calamity, or technological change undermines the social order, people's lives lose meaning. Under such circumstances, a community may turn to witchcraft accusations, blaming their misfortunes on the presence of evildoers—witches and sorcerers who must be found and destroyed to reassert normality.

In Europe, for example, the witch craze, which resulted in the death of thousands of men and women, occurred primarily in the 16th and 17th centuries, a time of great artistic and technological achievement but also of great social disasters (Hester 1988). Plague swept repeatedly through Europe, and the medieval social and religious order collapsed in war and chaos. Where governments and religious institutions remained strong, witchcraft accusations were relatively scarce. However, where these institutions collapsed, accusations were frequent (Behringer 2004). Under these circumstances, people were willing to believe that witches were the cause of their misery and to pursue reprisals against people they suspected of witchcraft (see Figure 11.5). Much more recently, between 1992 and 1994, 57 alleged witches were killed in Gusii, in southwestern

Figure 11.5 The European witch craze of the 16th and 17th centuries led to thousands of deaths, particularly in areas where government and church authority had collapsed. This woodcut shows the burning of three witches in Derneburg, Germany in October 1555.

German School/The Bridgeman Art Library/Getty Images

Kenya. This included three incidents in which sons killed their mothers and were exonerated by their communities. Ogembo (2001) relates these killings to economic stress, political upheaval including ethnic attacks, and the specifics of Gusii kinship and ideology.

Using Anthropology: Magic, Witchcraft, and HIV/AIDS

Health is one of the key domains of religious rituals and understandings throughout the world. Although scientific medicine has made great advances in the past 100 years, magical beliefs about health are still common throughout the world. For example, in European and North American medicine, the "doctrine of signatures," the idea that plants that look like human organs or body parts have an effect on those organs or body parts dates from ancient times and is still found among some practitioners of homeopathy and new age medicine today (Morton 2009).

As the HIV/AIDS epidemic swept through parts of Africa in the 1990s and 2000s, a wide variety of beliefs about the causes and cures for the disease emerged, and many of these involved witchcraft or the violation of taboos. For example, Rödlach (2006) documents beliefs in Zimbabwe that associate HIV/AIDS with *ondofa*, spirit beings employed by sorcerers, and with the use of *isidliso* and *ulunyoka*, magical substances used to control both male and female sexuality. Hansjörg Dilger (2008) reports that among the Luo in Tanzania, people often think that the violation of the religious regulations that cover many aspects of social and sexual life results in *chira,* a disease with symptoms similar to AIDS.

Gerry Mshana and colleagues (2006) studied HIV/AIDS beliefs and treatments in Mwanza in northeastern Tanzania. They found that although people there almost always understood the medical causes of sexually transmitted diseases such as syphilis or gonorrhea and usually considered these to have natural, biological causes, there was much more diversity of belief about HIV/AIDS. People accepted that AIDS was a biological, naturally caused disease. However, they also believed that many, perhaps most, people who were alleged to have AIDS were actually victims of a form of witchcraft called *lusumbo*. The specific course of HIV/AIDS favored this interpretation. HIV can have a very long period of latency during which infected people show no symptoms. When AIDS sufferers in Mwanza showed symptoms but those around them such as spouses or other sexual partners did not, others reasoned that the cause was witchcraft rather than a virus. Additionally, even if people suspected that they had AIDS, it was less stigmatizing to suffer from witchcraft than

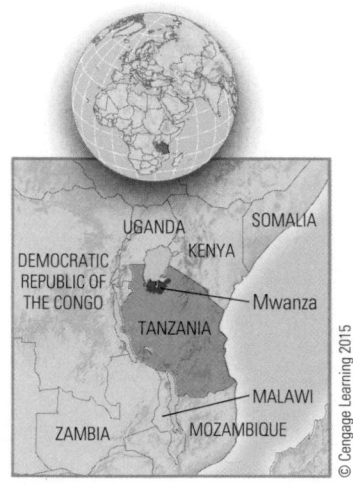

Mwanza Region, Tanzania.

© Cengage Learning 2015

from AIDS. And although people believed that AIDS could not be cured, witchcraft could be successfully treated by traditional healers. However, this sometimes led to violence against those accused of witchcraft. Yamba (1997) reports that witchcraft accusations related to HIV/AIDS in Zimbabwe led to the deaths of 16 accused witches in a four-month period between 1995 and 1996.

Mshana's findings have important implications for AIDS education and treatment in Tanzania. Critically, for the people studied by Mshana as well as those studied by Dilger and probably many others as well, HIV/AIDS is not one disease with two possible causes: biology or witchcraft. Rather, there are two diseases with similar symptoms, one caused by a virus, and the other caused by witchcraft. People believe that HIV/AIDS is infectious and may refrain from sexual intercourse or use condoms to avoid the disease. However, people do not believe that diseases caused by witchcraft or taboo violation are infectious nor do they necessarily refrain from having sex with people afflicted by them. People might go to Western trained doctors to treat AIDS, but they are far more likely to go to traditional healers to treat diseases they believe to be caused by witchcraft. Mshana and colleagues advise that rather than seeing this as a problem, health workers should focus their efforts on working with these healers to provide a first line of defense against the illness as well as treatment for it.

RELIGION AND CHANGE

As we have seen, religion is generally a force that preserves the social order. This may be particularly evident in stratified societies where the elite invoke religious authority to control the poor. In such situations, religion acts as a way of maintaining social, economic, and political inequality. However, even when religion does not support oppression, it is usually a conservative force, promoting the idea that the way that society has historically been ordered is right and proper.

Most religions contain implicit or explicit visions of the ideal society—images of the way a correct, just social order should look. No society actually achieves its vision; people never live exactly the way they are supposed to. However, most of the time, religion validates society. As a result, most people feel that the society they live in is reasonably good.

However, if societies change very rapidly (as a result of colonization, disease, or technological change) or if groups are systematically enslaved and oppressed, the vision of the ideal world painted by people's religious beliefs may move far from their daily experience. People may feel that they are lost, that their vision of the ideal cannot be attained, or that it is simply wrong. Under these conditions, prophets may emerge, and new religions may be created. Religious movements vary in the effectiveness with which they bring social and political change. Even those that fail in these respects may create powerful new identities among their members.

Religion offers a series of principles, encapsulated in story, symbol, and interpretation. These can serve as a charter for political action. Thus, religion can be a powerful force for social change, providing people with the rationale and motivation for political involvement and personal renewal. From the U.S. civil rights movement to the Iranian Revolution, the Taliban and the Tea Party, religious leaders can have a powerful political impact. However, prophets may also give their followers convincing models that cannot exist in our material, social, and political world. When that happens, the results may be explosive.

Varieties of Religious Prophecy

To begin a new religion or substantially modify an existing one, prophets must identify what is wrong with the world, present a vision of what a better world looks like, and describe a method of transition from the existing world to the better world. Religious movements can, to some degree, be characterized by what they believe about this better world and the ways to achieve it.

Many religious movements are either nativistic or vitalistic. A nativistic movement aims to restore what its followers believe is a golden age of the past. The nativistic message is generally that things in the past were far better than at present. The reason things have degenerated is because the people have fallen away from the ways of the ancestors. The glorious past may be regained if certain practices are followed.

The Ghost Dance is a good example of a nativistic religious movement. It arose in the late 19th century among the Plains Indians of the United States and was a response to the disastrous effects of European invasion. As disease, warfare, and technological change undermined native cultures, prophets emerged who taught that a past golden age would re-emerge if Indians returned to traditional practices and performed specific rituals including the Ghost Dance. The prophecy spread widely among Native Americans, especially the Sioux, for whom the conditions of conquest and reservation life were particularly oppressive. U.S. government agents, frightened that the Ghost Dance movement would lead to new war against the whites, ordered the Sioux to stop the dance. Some Sioux did, but others fled and continued to perform the Ghost Dance. In December 1890, the 7th Cavalry captured the last remaining band of Ghost

Dancers at Wounded Knee. In the ensuing battle, about 350 Sioux Ghost Dancers, including many women and children, were killed. This battle effectively ended the Ghost Dance, although it continued among small groups up until the 1960s.

A vitalistic prophecy looks to the future rather than the past. For vitalists, the past is either evil or neutral. The golden age is in the future and can be achieved following the teachings of the prophet. Though it is not specifically religious, an example of a vitalism with which most Americans are familiar is Martin Luther King Jr.'s "I Have a Dream" speech. In that speech, King describes a future where "the sons of former slaves and the sons of former slave owners will be able to sit down together at the table of brotherhood" and where children "will not be judged by the color of their skin but by the content of their character." King thus looked ahead to a future then unprecedented in American history.

Often, the poor and powerless in a society create religions that challenge those of the mainstream. Such religions may rationalize their lower social position and emphasize an afterlife in which their suffering will be rewarded. In some cases, these religions have a **messianic** outlook; they focus on the coming of a special individual who will usher in a utopian world. Other religions are **millenarian**; they look to a future disaster that will destroy the current world and establish a world characterized by their version of justice. In many messianic and millenarian religions, members participate in rituals that give individuals direct access to supernatural power.

The holiness churches common among coal miners and the rural poor in Appalachia are a good example of a religion that has emerged in response to poverty and hardship. In church services, loud music, singing, and dancing cause some members to experience "being filled with the Holy Spirit." In this ecstatic state, they handle poisonous snakes. Snake handlers are frequently bit and sometimes die (see Figure 11.6). However, for members, snake handling proves that "Jesus has the power to deliver them from death here and now" (Daugherty 1976:234). For them, such ecstatic practices demonstrate their

Messianic: Focusing on the coming of an individual who will usher in a utopian world.

Millenarian: Belief that a coming catastrophe will signal the beginning of a new age and the eventual establishment of paradise.

JIM LO SCALZO/epa/Corbis Wire/Corbis

Figure 11.6 In states of religious ecstasy, members of holiness churches in Appalachia handle poisonous snakes. For church members, such practices demonstrate their ability to gain access to God's power, but may also be fatal. Pastor Mack Wolford, seen here, died of a rattlesnake bite received during a service in 2012.

ability to gain access to God's power. The fact that social elites are rarely members of such groups is proof that holiness members have access to forms of power that social elites lack (Burton 1993; Covington 1995).

Syncretism: The merging of elements of two or more religious traditions to produce a new religion.

Religious **syncretism** is often found among deeply oppressed people. In syncretism, people merge two or more religious traditions, hiding the beliefs, symbols, and practices of one behind similar attributes of the other. Santeria, an African-based religion originating in Cuba, is a good example (Murphy 1989). Santeria emerged from slave society. Europeans attempted to suppress African religions, but the slaves resisted by combining African religion, Catholicism, and French spiritualism to create a new religion (Lefever 1996). They identified African deities, called orichas, with Catholic saints and used them for traditional purposes such as curing and casting spells, and influencing other aspects of the worshipper's life. In this way, they could appear to practice Catholicism as they continued to practice their own religions.

Fundamentalism and Religious Change

As the pace of social change has increased, it has been accompanied by an increase in religious **fundamentalism**. Islamic fundamentalism is implicated in numerous conflicts around the world. Membership in American Christian denominations that describe themselves as fundamentalist has ballooned. Jewish ultraorthodox groups such as Lubavitch Hasidim have also grown, as have groups like the Hindu nationalist Bharatiya Janata Party in India. Fundamentalism is now an international phenomenon found on every continent.

Fundamentalism: A proclamation of reclaimed authority over a sacred tradition that is to be reinstated as an antidote for a society that is believed to have strayed from its cultural moorings.

Although members of fundamentalist groups sometimes see their religious beliefs as unchanging, the rise of fundamentalism is an important religious change. Further, fundamentalist movements tend to have specific founders and locations of origin. For example, much of the American fundamentalist movement began with *The Fundamentals: A Testimony to the Truth,* a series of books published between 1910 and 1915. Modern Islamic fundamentalism is associated with the work of Sayyid Qutb (born in the Egyptian village of Musha described in Chapter 5) and the Muslim Brotherhood.

The rise of fundamentalism raises important questions for anthropologists. First, clearly, the people we call fundamentalist have greatly varying beliefs, but are there commonalities despite these differences? Second, what local and global forces have encouraged the development of fundamentalism in so many different locations? Finally, is fundamentalism a problem and, if so, what should be done about it? None of these questions can be answered easily or definitively, but we can propose some partial explanations.

Scholars have shown that fundamentalisms have similar properties. Fundamentalists tend to see religion as the basis for both personal and communal identity. They tend to believe that there is a single unified truth that they can possess and understand. They tend to envision themselves as fighting in a cosmic struggle of good against evil. Fundamentalists tend to perceive themselves as a persecuted minority even when this is not the case. They are selective about which parts of their tradition they emphasize and which parts of modernity they accept and reject (Almond, Sivan, and Appleby 1995; Hadden and Shupe 1989).

The pattern of the emergence of fundamentalism largely fits the model of religious change described in this chapter. In the past century, the world has faced truly revolutionary changes. The forces of technology and global capitalism have permeated societies and brought people of disparate cultures together in a vast global network. However, this process has not been peaceful and has not produced equity. Traditional livelihoods have been undermined, and the gap between the wealthy and the poor has grown. Governments have been discredited. Faced with profound change, people look for stability and certainty. For some, fundamentalism seems to offer a solution. Much (but not all) fundamentalism is nativistic, calling for a return to the society and values of an earlier time, a time that believers understand as better than the current era. However, specific local histories also play an extremely important role in the emergence of fundamentalisms. It would be impossible, for example, to explain the appearance of the fundamentalist group Hamas without reference to the Israeli-Palestinian conflict. Similarly, the development of the Taliban is directly related to the events surrounding the Russian invasion of Afghanistan.

The forces that create rich ground for fundamentalism do not seem likely to abate any time soon. Because rapid political, technological, and economic change is likely to continue, fundamentalisms will probably continue to experience strong growth. This poses an extraordinarily difficult problem. On the one hand, people are surely entitled to their religious beliefs. The vast majority of people who might be classified as fundamentalist are innocent of any wrongdoing; they neither promote nor condone violence. They live peacefully with neighbors of different religious beliefs. On the other hand, fundamentalist beliefs have been repeatedly implicated in murderous violence: from the bombings of abortion clinics and the Olympic Games in Atlanta to the 9/11 attacks on the United States to the repeated anti-Muslim and anti-Sikh violence perpetrated by Hindu fundamentalists in India.

There is no doubt that much violence is enflamed by the harsh political and economic conditions of life and by the subversion of long-standing cultural practices. Promoting prosperity, more equitable distribution of resources, greater cultural sensitivity, and more responsive and honest government will certainly reduce popular support for violence. However, a small percentage of believers in all fundamentalist traditions understand the world in absolutist terms and see violence as a divinely ordained response. For these, nothing short of the total victory of their ideas is acceptable.

BRINGING IT BACK HOME:
RELIGION, ART, AND CENSORSHIP

"... [T]his show is disgusting," said New York City's then Mayor Rudolph Giuliani, commenting on *Sensation*, a 1999 art exhibit at the Brooklyn Museum of Art. He was referring specifically to a painting by the African artist Chris Ofili called "The Holy Virgin Mary." The painting depicted a black Madonna in a colorful flowing robe, dabbed with a clump of elephant dung and surrounded with images of women's buttocks and genitals clipped from pornographic magazines (Steiner 2002). The Giuliani administration attempted to cut the museum's funding and evict it from its building unless it removed the offending works. They were prevented from doing so by a court decision (*The Brooklyn Institute of Arts and Sciences v. the City of New York and Rudolph W. Giuliani*, 64 F.Supp2d 184 [F.D.N.Y. 1999], Opinion and Order 99 CV 6071), which argued that these actions violated freedom of speech.

In 2009, Sony released the video game *Hanuman: Boy Warrior* to worldwide protest by Hindu groups (Hanuman is a Hindu deity and a central figure in one of the epics of Hinduism). Rajan Zed, a leader of the protest and president of the Nevada-based Universal Society of Hinduism, said that controlling Hanuman with a joystick was denigrating. "Lord Hanuman was not meant to be reduced to such a 'character' in a video game and be in the company of *America's 10 Most Wanted, Bad Boys, Jackass,* and *Killer7*" (Das 2009).

In spring 2010, an episode of *South Park* depicted Muhammad as being inside a bear suit (presumably to avoid showing his image). Following the airing of the episode, a radical Islamic website warned the show's creators that they could be killed. In the following episode, Muhammad was replaced by Santa Claus, and Comedy Central, which airs the show, censored numerous scenes (Pilkington 2010).

Of course, incidents such as this are not limited to the United States. In 2001, the Taliban government of Afghanistan destroyed the

1,500-year-old Buddhas of Bamiyan, the largest Buddha sculptures in the world at the time. The Buddhas and artwork in the caves associated with them had been the object of numerous earlier attacks, some dating back to the Genghis Kahn (Higuchi and Barnes 1995). In 2012, rebel forces destroyed ancient tombs in the city of Timbuktu, and when forced from the city by French troops in 2013, they attempted, largely unsuccessfully, to burn manuscripts and artifacts they considered un-Islamic (Balter 2013).

In the United States, religious freedom and freedom of speech are both deeply held cultural values. Yet, Americans also believe, as Supreme Court Justice Oliver Wendell Holmes Jr. (1841–1935) said, "the right to swing my fist ends where the other man's nose begins" (Trachtman 2009:87). In an age of complexity, diversity, and instant global communication, someone's nose seems always to be in the way.

YOU DECIDE:

1. Have you experienced portrayals of your own beliefs that you found offensive? If so, did you think they should be censored? What role did your culture play in your opinion?
2. If the majority in a community finds a religious representation offensive, should it be censored? Why or why not? Does it make a difference if censorship comes from the government or from a corporation like Sony or Viacom (the company that owns Comedy Central)?
3. Art offensive to religion has sometimes led to violence and death (consider deaths resulting from protests over the Danish cartoon depictions of Muhammad or the Nazi's use of anti-Semitic art). Is fear of violence sufficient justification for censorship?

CHAPTER SUMMARY

1. What characteristics do all religions have in common? The great diversity in beliefs and practices worldwide makes religion difficult to define. However, all religions include sacred stories, ideas about the supernatural (or nonempirical), rituals, symbols, and specialized practitioners.
2. What are sacred narratives, and what roles do they play in religion? Sacred narratives, sometimes called myths, are stories that express religious ideas. Sacred narratives explain and validate beliefs, values, and customs.
3. What is the importance of symbols in religion? Religious ideas are often expressed in symbols that have multiple meanings and

frequently great emotional power. Symbols allow people to grasp the complexities of religion without much knowledge of the underlying theology.

4. What roles do supernatural beings and powers play in religion? Religions assume that there are nonmeasurable beings, powers, emotional states, and qualities that exist apart from humans but are important to them. Frequently people, objects, and places are understood as imbued with spiritual power or mana.

5. What is ritual, and how is it related to liminality? Ritual is behavior that enacts religion. Many rituals involve liminality or "betweenness." In states of liminality, normal social rules may be overturned and people may experience temporary states of equality and oneness or communitas.

6. What are rites of passage and rites of intensification? Rites of passage are public rituals that mark a person's transition from one status to another. Examples include marriage and funerals. Rites of intensification are rituals that strengthen group identity.

7. What are prayer, sacrifice, and magic? What are critical differences among them? Prayer, sacrifice, and magic are rituals individuals and groups use to interact with the world of the supernatural. Most religions include examples of all three. The key difference between them is the degree to which people believe their own actions determine outcomes. Also common is the use of divination, a religious technique to discover the hidden.

8. What are shamans and priests, and what is the difference between them? Shamans and priests are two kinds of religions practitioners. Shamans receive power through claims of direct contact with the supernatural and are found in almost all societies. Priests are members of bureaucracies and are appointed, elected, or hired to their positions. They are most common in state-level societies.

9. What are witches and sorcerers, and how do accusations of witchcraft usually operate in society? In most societies, witches and sorcerers are people who are considered to use nonempirical means to harm those around them (modern-day Wiccans are an exception to this). Accusations of witchcraft stigmatize certain kinds of behavior or scapegoat individuals for social or medical problems. In some parts of Africa, AIDS symptoms are understood as evidence of witchcraft.

10. When is religious prophecy likely to be heard, and what are common types of prophecy? Religious prophecy is generally heard when there is rapid social, economic, technological, and political change. Prophecy may be nativistic, calling for a return to a past

golden age, or vitalistic, looking to a future golden age. It may emphasize the coming of a savior or a period of destruction after which a new world will emerge.

11. Under what conditions does fundamentalism occur, and what are its characteristics? Fundamentalism tends to occur in times of rapid change. Fundamentalists often view religion as a basis of identity, believe in a single truth, understand life as a battle between good and evil, and believe they are a persecuted minority. They are selective in their acceptance of modernity.

KEY TERMS

Animism

Antistructure

Communitas

Contagious magic

Cosmology

Divination

Fundamentalism

God (or deity)

Imitative magic

Liminal

Magic

Mana

Messianic

Millenarian

Monotheism

Polytheism

Prayer

Priest

Religion

Rite of intensification

Rite of passage

Ritual

Sacred narratives (myths)

Sacrifice

Shaman

Syncretism

Totem

Witchcraft

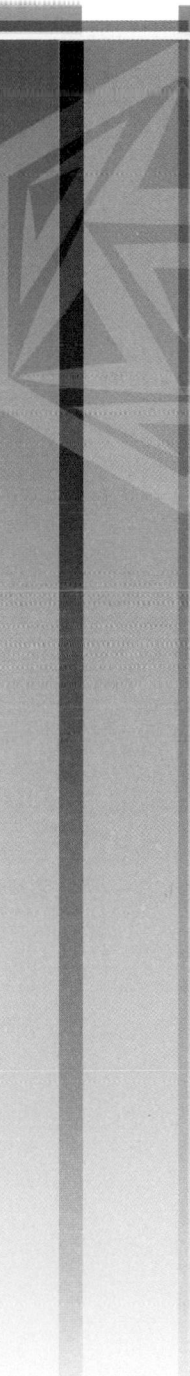

Jeff Morgan 01 /Alamy

World music combines elements of the local and the global. Africa is an especially important source of world music, incorporating elements from local cultures combined with music from the West.

CHAPTER 12

CREATIVE EXPRESSION: ANTHROPOLOGY AND THE ARTS

LEARNING OBJECTIVES

After you have read this chapter, you will be able to:

Δ Summarize some of the functions of art in political and ritual contexts.

Δ Describe the ways art can symbolize key cultural concepts and themes using examples.

Δ Explain "deep play" with examples.

Δ Analyze the roles that art can play in politics. Give examples of the use of art to promote political ends.

Δ Discus how art is used to express cultural and personal identity, using examples from different societies.

Δ Describe the relationship between art made for use within a particular culture and the international art market.

WORLD MUSIC: THE LOCAL GOES GLOBAL

DESPITE the close connection between the arts and particular cultural themes, the arts today have a global reach. One of the fastest-growing global phenomena is the emergence of world music. **World music** incorporates different musical styles from cultures throughout the world. It includes Caribbean music like reggae and salsa but also Celtic folk songs, Louisiana blues and Cajun, and songs from Africa, the Middle East, and Asia.

World music is based on local musical traditions, produced for local occasions, in local languages. Communications technology and migrations have spread these musical traditions around the world. Reggae, a Jamaican musical style linked to religion and resistance, widely popularized by Bob Marley (Jelly-Schapiro 2009), is today performed by Africans, Asians, and Europeans as well as Jamaicans. World music combines Western styles with local instruments. For example, Mory Kanté, an African musician who plays traditional African instruments like the balafon and the kora, is backed by a band of Western drums, guitars, basses, and keyboards. The reverse is also true. The recordings of Paul Simon, Sting, and David Byrne have all been influenced by indigenous musical traditions.

The influence of Africa and African-derived music stands out in world music, for example, creating endless variations from shared foundations in call-and-response and polyrhythm. The music of African religious ceremonies was preserved by slaves and adapted into the sacred and secular music of the New World (Pareles 1996). From the polyrhythmic basis of North American ragtime and early New Orleans jazz, through the African-Cuban percussionist influence of Mongo Santamaria, to the performance combination of Youssou N'Dour of Senegal, to the contemporary albums of griots from West Africa such as Salif Keita, Africa has influenced world music. The music of African Americans also has worldwide popularity: Hip-hop music of urban African American culture is popular in Japan, Cambodia (Mydans 2008; Sterling 2010), and China (Wang 2009), as well as in Europe. In Marseille, in Southern France, hip-hop helps transcend differences between its diverse populations of Muslims, Jews, and other migrants, helping to prevent the interethnic violence found in other French cities (Kimmelman 2007).

Bhangra, which originated in the folk music of Punjab, India and eastern Pakistan, originally performed in harvest festivals, today mixes bhangra beats with British pop music and reggae. The amalgam of contemporary **bhangra** with rock, pop, reggae, and hip-hop styles has spread from London, where it particularly involves members of the South Asian diaspora, to the urban United States, Canada, and other nations with substantial South Asian populations. It is also now popular in India and Pakistan as well.

World music: World music incorporates different musical styles from cultures throughout the world.

Bhangra: A musical form originating in the folk music of Punjab in northern India and eastern Pakistan that is mixing with British pop music and reggae to become a popular form of world music.

Bhangra means different things to different people. To the young, urban, British-born South Asians who created it, bhangra was a music of resistance, with its lyrics—in Punjabi and English—articulating the problems of racism and the balancing of tradition and modernity among this South Asian diaspora (Lipsitz 1994). In smaller British towns, South Asians understood bhangra as a traditional art form, using bhangra parties as occasions to dress in traditional Indian clothing and bring back their traditional cultural memories (Bennett 1997). Many South Asian elders, however, consider modern bhangra a Western pollution of tradition and particularly object to its dance styles that involve close contact between men and women (Katrak 2002). Like all music, bhangra retains its links with its local identities but has also changed as it has diffused around the world.

THE ARTS

Creative expression, like religion, is universal; the arts serve many of the same functions as religion and are similar in using symbols to convey their meanings. **Art** refers to the ways people in every society express themselves using characteristic forms of creativity that are guided by aesthetic principles involving imagination, beauty, skill, and style. Through art, people interpret the world with images and symbols that express the basic themes, values, and perceptions of reality in ways that are culturally meaningful.

Art: Forms of creative expression that are guided by aesthetic principles and involve imagination, skill, and style.

Each culture has specific artistic symbols that stand for things or events in nature and human society or are associated with particular emotions. Because these symbols are culturally specific, art must be understood in its cultural context. Anthropologists are interested in both the more obvious meanings and the deeper meanings of symbols, and the ways in which they are connected to other elements in a culture. But in some cultures, the power of art is not merely symbolic: Artistic creations may be viewed as reality itself. For example, mask dancing in many African cultures is both symbolic and real. The costumes and their different elements have symbolic meanings, but mask dancing is also real in the sense that the masked dancer does not just *represent* the supernatural being but has *become* the supernatural being. In our own culture, the original of a famous artwork also carries the kind of power that a replica does not have.

Cultures differ in their artistic emphases: Some cultures use visual media, others use verbal skills, such as storytelling, and still others use dance and music to convey their central aesthetic values. Calligraphy, for example, is an important art form in both China and the Islamic Middle East, but for different reasons. In China, written language is a central defining attribute of Chinese civilization and a key source of Chinese cultural identity and unity. In Islam, calligraphy is the most respected of the graphic arts because it is the visual representation of the Koran. Because of the Muslim prohibition on the visual representation of graven human images (often extended to animal representations), calligraphy and representations of flowers and geometric designs have an important place in Islamic aesthetics.

Art embodies an artistic style, which refers to a characteristic manner of expression. Different cultures as well as different artists have different artistic styles. Although artistic styles do change, they are often very stable, lasting hundreds, in some cases, thousands of years. Where art is closely tied to religion, artistic styles tend to be more stable than where art and religion are independent of each other.

◪ THE FUNCTIONS OF ART

Art has many functions: It is a vehicle for the display of cultural themes; it validates social hierarchies by making visible the power of the state or a ruling elite; and it is an important way to express personal, social, and individual identities. Art, whether in artifact, movement, or sound, is often central to ritual. Art can be used to support a society's social structure and the importance of its elites. Artistic displays may express the divine source of the ruler's power; the social and ethnic divisions of society, as in totemic symbols; and the political structure through which the society is governed, for example, in the building of temples and monuments. Both the totem poles and the artistic products and performances associated with the potlatch of the Northwest coast of North America are art forms that reflect and send powerful messages about the importance of social hierarchy in these societies (Jonaitis 1991). Art can also be used to resist social hierarchy, providing powerful ways to express disunity and conflict, to resist state authority, and to give voice to members of oppressed or marginalized groups. The Br'er Rabbit folktales of the American South illustrate how stories can undercut the powerful: The trickster, a weak but clever hero resists those in power through wit rather than force. These African American folktales, which ridicule and question social order, have an obvious relationship to slavery and oppression (Friedheim and Jackson 1996:24).

But as society changes, so does art. As possibilities of open protest against the racial caste system increased in the United States, African American oral traditions also changed. The "badman," who openly displays his arrogance and virility, came to supplant the trickster as hero (Abrahams 1970), an image diffused into the blaxploitation films of the 1970s and into the gangsta figure in hip-hop and gangsta rap.

Creative expression is also important in constructing and intensifying personal and group identities, generating intense emotions that foster cultural and social unity. Thus, art forms do not merely reflect a society and its culture, but also heighten cultural integration by displaying and confirming the values a society holds in common. The powerful artistic symbols of a society express universal themes—death, pride, gender relations, aggression, solidarity, and identity—in ways that are culturally particular and therefore culturally compelling, even when (some might say particularly when) their content is not consciously articulated. The arts make dominant cultural themes visible, tangible, and thus more real. In Western music, for example, the use of the minor scale conveys the emotion of sadness. Various other musical forms are traditionally associated with other emotions. These artistic conventions can be used to evoke emotions because people in that culture have been taught the association. Similarly, in the United States, a story that begins "Once upon a time" signals that it is not about real events and people. This knowledge sets the stage for the audience to respond to the story emotionally in certain ways.

The arts are particularly useful in expressing the more unconscious, repressed aspects of a culture, as described later for the Japanese popular arts of manga and anime. Broadly understood, games, sports, and performance, or what Clifford Geertz calls "deep play" (1973a), like the Balinese cockfight described later, are also art forms that express unconscious cultural themes. Like other creative forms, they intensify emotions, display compelling aspects of social structure and culture, and reinforce cultural and personal identities.

In the West, some media art, for example, so-called reality shows or TV travelogues, are sometimes used to dramatically represent outsiders in either negative or fantastical ways. An example of this is the TV show that appeared on both the Travel Channel and BBC, *Mark & Olly: Living with the Machigenga* (sic), in which several Indiana Jones–type Westerners travel to remote locales to "get accepted" by exotic tribes. In this case, not only did these shows totally misrepresent the several Amazonian tribes that they filmed as mean and savage people, mistranslate, and script inauthentic cultural rituals, but they were also alleged to be responsible for a respiratory disease epidemic that resulted in several deaths (Shepard 2011). Western media representations of indigenous people, which through global connections, now reach wide audiences, and often breach ethical principles that are central to anthropological representations of indigenous peoples and other non-Western societies.

Franz Boaz called "the seeing eye...an organ of tradition," and Marshall Sahlins once quipped that "There is no such thing as an immaculate perception" (Price 1989:19, 22). Both these anthropologists were emphasizing that art is not only produced, but viewed, through the lens of culture, which shapes the response of audiences to specific artistic products. The high value that the modern West places on art for art's sake is not universal: In most societies, art is not produced or performed to express an artist's individuality, to provide pleasure, or provide social commentary but rather is inseparable from other activities such as religious or political ritual or the production of utilitarian objects. Although some people in all societies are recognized as more competent in these skills than others, this competence does not necessarily translate into the specialized role of artist.

Furthermore, although producing art in all cultures is recognized as a creative process, it is not necessarily an innovative one (Price 1989). Many cultures do not prize originality—the creation of something entirely new—in their arts, but rather value improvisation, that is, creating interesting and endless variations on already established artistic themes (Vogel 1991:20). Where the arts are allied with religion, as in Navajo songs, there is only one right way to sing a song, with no improvisation permitted. The Navajo believe that "foreign music is dangerous and not for Navajo" (McAllester 1954). Though anthropologists primarily view art through the lens of specific local cultures, globalization—which integrates the arts of many cultures (as in world music)—complicates the relationships between art and culture.

Art and Ritual: Paleolithic Cave Art

The spectacular Paleolithic cave art made by early Homo sapiens in Europe, which is about 32,000 to 10,000 years old, demonstrates the connection between art and ritual. The Altamira caves in Spain, and the Lascaux and Grotte Chauvet caves in France, contain elaborate and realistic images of the abundant and diverse plants and animals that existed in these areas (see Figure 12.1). In addition to painting, these early humans also made jewelry, carved and engraved human figures, made ritual and ceremonial objects, placed elaborate grave goods in burial sites, and made patterned notations that may indicate some form of record keeping.

Many of the images indicate the sexual and seasonal characteristics or behavior of various animal species, for example, stags baying in the autumn rut, a bellowing bison bull and butting mammoth bulls in the autumn, a bison licking a summer

Courtesy of the Peabody Museum of Archeology and Ethnology, Harvard University, 2005.16.351.2

Figure 12.1 The spots and handprints seen in this 15,000-year-old painting of a horse, found in Pech Merle Cave in France, support the argument that these prehistoric paintings had ritual significance for their creators.

insect bite, and a bison with molting fur in the summer. Archeologists speculate that these images played a role in ritual, religion, and storytelling, and were possibly used in curing ceremonies or rites of passage.

Because many of the images are of animals that were commonly eaten, some anthropologists argue that they were drawn as part of ceremonies intended to magically increase the chances of a successful hunt and that they contain encoded information about hunting techniques and other information useful for survival in the harsh conditions of the Ice Age (Strauss 1991). But the paintings also include images of animals, such as lions, that were not commonly eaten, but were associated with varying signs and symbols such as handprints or abstract signs. This suggests that many of the images were made for ritual use. Because these paintings were made over 20,000 years in different places, they are likely to have had diverse functions, and no one theory explains them all.

ART AND THE REPRESENTATION OF CULTURAL THEMES

A characteristic of all art is the expression—whether conscious or unconscious—of cultural themes, as we will see with the importance of World War II in the art of Japan, the theme of prestige in the Balinese cockfight, the theme of contemporary Native American identity in the art of Fritz Scholder, or the theme of gender fantasies in European orientalist art.

Manga and Anime in Japan

Important aspects of post–World War II popular culture in Japan are **anime** (animation) and **manga** (comic book art). Anime, the animation of manga, is now familiar throughout the world, displayed in animation films, video games, children's toys, the Internet, commercial products, and museum and art gallery displays in Japan and abroad. They have also spawned a subculture in Japan, called *otaku* (the closest translation is "nerd" or "geek"), whose darker side includes an obsession with themes of war and violence, including nuclear catastrophes, mutant monsters, robots, and science fiction. On the apocalyptic side of this popular culture are monsters like Godzilla, who was awakened from eons of submarine sleep by a hydrogen bomb explosion. Godzilla exhibits radiation-induced physical deformities and engages in nightly attacks on Tokyo, which reduce the city and its screaming population to ashes.

Takashi Murakami, a successful designer for Louis Vuitton, curated a manga and anime museum show in the United States in 2005 called "Little Boy: The Arts of Japan's Exploding Subculture," after the

Anime: Animation, as in the popular culture of Japan; usually refers to animation of manga, or comic book graphic art.

Manga: Japanese comic book art.

name given to the atomic bomb dropped by the United States on Hiroshima. Murakami interprets anime and manga, and its otaku subculture, as growing out of the repercussions of the Japanese defeat by the United States in World War II, the dropping of the atomic bomb, and the democratization and demilitarization the American military imposed on postwar Japan. In Murakami's view, Japan has not really examined its responsibility for these traumatic historical events. He claims that denying these traumas created repressed emotions such as anxiety, shame, and a pervasive sense of impotence, which find their outlets in the popular culture of manga and anime (Smith 2005). In calling his museum show "Little Boy," Murakami asserts that Japan's postwar dependence on the United States has kept it from growing up. This infantilism is reflected in the popular fascination in Japan with fantasies of violence and power, such as the Godzilla-like monsters and mushroom-cloud explosions that are so frequently used in Japanese animation.

Paradoxically, these anime and manga themes are sometimes joined with another major pop culture theme, an obsession with *kawaii*, or "cuteness." Cuteness is particularly displayed in images of Lolita-like preadolescent, seemingly innocent, schoolgirls, who nevertheless also convey a sexual knowingness that belies their appearance. One major cuteness image is Hello Kitty, a big-eyed, beribboned, expressionless pussycat character (without a mouth to express emotion), whose images—on clocks, stuffed toys, purses, music boxes, and wallpaper—fuel more than a billion dollars a year in domestic and international sales.

Although anime and manga display cultural and psychological themes that are particularly Japanese, they have huge worldwide popularity, and there has been a rich cross-fertilization between American and Japanese manga and anime in popular culture. In the United States, Japanese-style cartoons are represented in the widely popular Genndy Tartakovsky's *Samurai Jack* and Craig McCracken's *Powerpuff Girls*. In Japan, Takashi Okazaki's *Afro Samurai* manga relies heavily on elements of hip-hop and other aspects of American culture, leading to an anime series, a TV movie, and a video game. *Tenjho Tenge, Infinite Ryvius*, and *Samurai Champloo* also include American elements, particularly hip-hop dance and music. As Condry (2005) notes, the intense interchange between Japanese and American youth culture is often ahead of commercialization. The Internet, television, and other media allow almost instant access to events and fashion in New York, Los Angeles, and Tokyo. Members of different cultures pick up styles and statements that appeal to them, recasting culture to give it meaning within their own context. The deep roots of hip-hop culture in the African American urban experience has not prevented Japanese artists from making it their own as well.

◥ Deep Play

The Balinese cockfight is a performance that illustrates the characteristics of deep play, defined by Clifford Geertz. Cockfights are a consuming passion of the Balinese that reveal much of Balinese culture, particularly the competition for prestige among men of different families and social groups. Balinese men have an intense identification with their fighting animals and spend much time caring for them, discussing them, and looking at them. The cocks (the pun works both in English and Balinese) embody two opposing Balinese cultural themes. They are both a magnification of the owner's masculine self and an expression of animality, which in Bali is the direct inversion of what it means to be human. Thus, in identifying with his animal, the Balinese man is identifying with his ideal masculine self but also with what he most fears, hates, and is fascinated by: the powers of darkness that the animals represent. The cockfight embodies the opposition of man and beast, good and evil, the creative power of aroused masculinity, and the destructive power of loosened animality, fused in a bloody drama of violence as cocks with razor-sharp, 5-inch-long steel spurs attached to their legs fight to the death.

Gambling is central to Balinese cockfighting and bets on the cockfight are a basic part of the competition for prestige that forms its deep play aspect. Cocks represent men, families, and social groups. When the individuals and groups represented have little connection with each other, the betting is likely to be light. However, when the individuals or groups are closely related, in status competition, or closely linked in the social hierarchy, bets are likely to be large. A man (only men bet in cockfights) does not bet on the bird that he believes has the greatest chance of victory but on the cock that represents his group. These matches are likely to be deeply emotional.

The Balinese cockfight is a symbolic contest between male egos, but it is also a symbolic expression of Balinese social hierarchy. Prestige is the driving force in Balinese society and the central driving force of the cockfight, transforming the fight into a "status bloodbath." The more nearly a match involves men of equal status, especially high-status men or men who are personal enemies, the deeper and more emotional the match is felt to be.

The Balinese are aware of the deep status concerns involved in cockfighting, which they refer to as "playing with fire without getting burned." Cockfighting activates village and kin group rivalries and hostilities in "play" form. It comes dangerously and entrancingly close to the expression of open interpersonal and intergroup aggression, something that almost never actually happens in the course of ordinary Balinese life. But then, the Balinese say, cockfights are not quite the same as real aggression because, after all, it is only a cockfight. That is, although people at the cockfight can experience changes in prestige, the thrill of victory and the agony of defeat, cockfights change nothing. People's position in the Balinese status hierarchy is set by larger social and economic forces. Winning or losing a cockfight can never really change anything. In a way, this is similar to college (and other) sports. If you are a college basketball fan, you might get to savor that one perfect moment in late March as your school defeats its rival for a national title. However, the game doesn't really change anything about either school. The prestige of universities is set by large social forces and cannot be changed by a basketball game.

ART AND POLITICS

One important function of creative expression is to legitimate social hierarchy and power in many ways, thus contributing to political stability. This is particularly important in times of political transition. After the Spanish conquest of the Inca Empire in Peru, Inca royalty commissioned indigenous artists to paint portraits of their kings to keep alive the memory of Inca rulers for those claiming royal descent and noble status. The native elite of Peru thus asserted their claims to high status and power in the colonial hierarchy by depicting their own illustrious forebears in paintings, the visual language of European culture. In imperial China, also, the arts were central in legitimizing the ruling class, especially the emperor (Hearn 1996).

The Chinese believed that only those with knowledge of the past could have a vision of the future. Thus, it was essential for the imperial courts to possess historical writings and paintings in order to display that knowledge. Throughout Chinese imperial history, figure painting was directed toward commemorating the emperor. Life-size portraits of the emperor had to incorporate the two main Chinese ideals of imperial rule: moral authority and the power of the emperor's central role in a controlled bureaucratic administration. Thus, paintings of the emperor had to show him with individualized features representing the humanistic Confucian values of compassion and virtue while conveying the imposing demeanor of the absolute ruler, the Son of Heaven. Another artistic representation that conveyed imperial power was a series of almost life-size portraits of Chinese cultural heroes, commissioned by some emperors in the 12th century. By displaying these paintings in the court, the emperor demonstrated his identification with a mythologized past and his rightful place in the lineage of Confucian rulers.

At the same time that the arts can help stabilize a society by validating its social hierarchy and expressing its common cultural elements, the arts also provide powerful ways to express disunity and conflict within a society, to resist state authority, to give voice to members of oppressed or marginalized classes or social groups, and to send political messages (see Figure 12.2). Resistance to prevailing social structure is often an important dimension in folktales and other oral traditions. These oral traditions may reverse, ridicule, or question the social order and, in doing so, may provide satisfactory solutions to the conflicts that arise out of domination and control.

Using Anthropology: The Multiple Roles of Museums

Museums are central institutions in connecting cultures. Particularly in Europe and the United States, museums are a major point of contact between Westerners and indigenous peoples. One of the most famous museums in the world is the American Museum of Natural History (AMNH) in New York City. Originally created in the late 19th century for the entertainment and education of schoolchildren and the city's "working classes," the AMNH began mainly with exhibits in natural history, such as paleontology and archaeology, which play such important roles in understanding evolution and the human past.

Gradually, the museum incorporated ethnographic exhibits, sending expeditions around the world, from the northwest coast of British Columbia, to Siberia, Peru, and other remote places, where it was feared that indigenous peoples would soon disappear under the impact of a changing world. By the turn of the 20th century, the AMNH began its own anthropology program, and hired Franz Boas to direct it. From that point on, cultural anthropology exhibits became a central feature in the museum, which became a major attraction for New Yorkers and tourists alike. Under Boas, scientific research was added to entertainment and education as a central goal of museum anthropology.

In a recent fascinating history of the AMNH anthropology department, Stanley Freed—its director for 40 years—illuminates the importance of the relationship between anthropology and museums (Freed 2012). Many of the most famous U.S. anthropologists, like Clark Wissler, Margaret Mead, and Colin Turnbull, were associated with the AMNH, and Freed's stories provide a more personal look at anthropological history, as well as the ways in which international and urban politics affected both museums and museum anthropology.

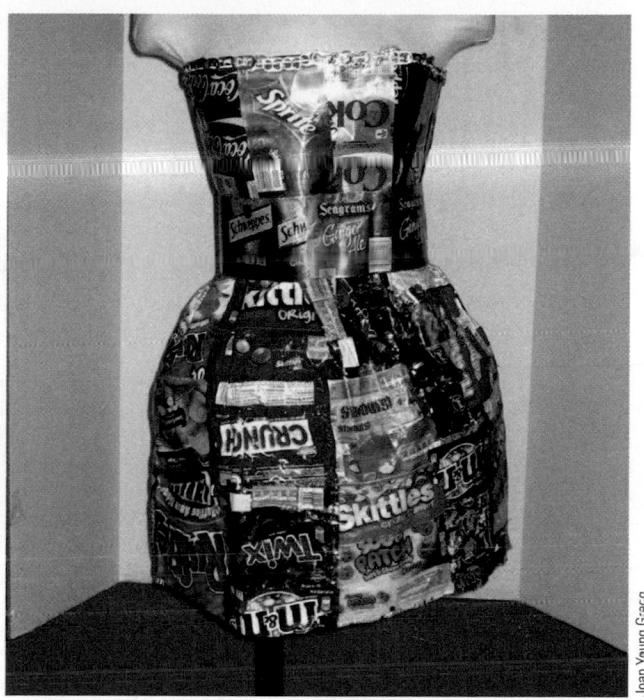

Joan Young Gregg

Figure 12.2 Creative expression can be used to send political messages. The dress pictured here, created by a middle school student, is made of candy wrappers and bottle caps to emphasize how Americans eat unhealthy food and pollute the environment.

One of the most important anthropological roles of museums is exhibiting non-Western art, which, before the expansion of world tourism, were the major way Westerners learned about indigenous peoples. In the 19th century, indigenous arts, particularly the arts of Africa, were mainly exhibited as anonymous ethnographic artifacts in connection with colonialism. In the early 20th century, however, Western fine art underwent a modernist revolution; Pablo Picasso and other European artists began to incorporate features of African and Oceanic art—much of which had a modernist and abstract look—into their own artistic creations. African art especially became an inspiration for the European avant-garde. This alliance of African art with modernism also influenced some African American artists of the Harlem Renaissance, such as Malvin Gray Johnson's self-portraits and paintings of African masks. These artists and the art historians of the time had almost no interest in understanding the meanings of this art, however, then called "primitive art," in its original cultural context, or indeed in discovering the actual artists. Rather, consistent with their own view of art, European artists and art historians mainly responded to the art in terms of its universal aesthetic principles.

Cultural anthropology, in contrast, emphasizes that art must be understood in its cultural context, and this understanding of art, including attempts to discover the identity of the individual artists, now predominates in the exhibit of indigenous arts both in art and ethnographic/natural history museums (Cotter 2009; 2012; Price 1989; 2007; Steiner 1995; 2002). For anthropologists, cultural and functionalist perspectives on this art are central. In analyzing the way the arts contribute to the functioning of society, anthropologists are particularly interested in the social or symbolic worlds in which indigenous art was originally seen or used, such as religious ritual or social relationships. Though it took almost a half century for anthropological approach to be widely adopted, it has made a real difference in enriching Western understandings of indigenous art and indigenous peoples. The anthropological perspective on indigenous art includes indigenous narratives framing the exhibition of this art; labeling objects to emphasize ethnographic context; and collaborating with indigenous peoples in curating exhibits of their arts.

Native Americans, for example, have long contested museum exhibits of their material culture, claiming that such exhibits misleadingly represent their societies as timeless rather than dynamic; excluded Native American voices, consultation, or collaboration; neglected contemporary Native American artists; displayed sacred objects that should not be seen by the nonnative public; and ignored any representation of contemporary political issues involving Native Americans. This has changed significantly: Native American cultural revitalization, remembrance, and political struggle are now prominent in exhibitions of Native American art, for example, in an exhibit on the Kwakiutl potlatch at the American Museum of Natural History in New York (Jonaitis 1991), which involved Kwakiutl Indians in all aspects of the exhibition's curation. Native American perspectives and involvement have also importantly shaped the new Smithsonian National Museum of the American Indian in our nation's capital

As these anthropological perspectives gained influence, many art and ethnographic museums began to consider how both culture and power are implicated in displays of indigenous art (Hochschild 2005); indeed, today, museum exhibits themselves have become the subject of ethnographic inquiry, for what they tell us about the indigenous arts they exhibit, the culture of the people who arrange and promote such exhibits, and that of the people who visit them (Price 2007; 2009).

Art and Historical Narratives

One important and widespread function of creative expression is to construct, display, and sustain narratives of a people's cultural identity, or create new national narratives, such as in the case of South Africa, through depictions of the past (Nanda 2005). Museums play an important role in this goal, aimed at both local and international audiences. Because they display cultural identity and history in ways that are visible, tangible, and emotionally compelling, the arts are an important way of recording, interpreting, and remembering both an actual and a legendary past.

These records, whether material or oral, embody the effort of a people to define, explain, and amuse themselves and to keep alive their cultural identity. Many of the old stories told by Native American groups incorporate jokes and demonstrate the resilience of people who have experienced great hardship. The ledger drawings of some Native American groups are an example of the use of art to record history and preserve cultural identity (Berlo 1996; Greene 2001; Powers 2005). Native American ledger drawings also provide a readable historical record, a way for people to anchor themselves in the real world and locate themselves in history beyond myths and legends.

Ledger drawings got their name from the ledger books obtained from trading posts in which the Native Americans drew their records. The ledger drawings were made only by men, and initially served mainly to record the lost life of warfare, hunting, and tribal identity. At the turn of the 19th century, Native Americans were already using drawings, on skin shirts, robes, and teepee covers, to record personal histories. By the 1860s, these drawings had become more elaborate, colored, and carefully composed, and the original material of war deeds had expanded to include social customs and communal history. Ledger drawing flourished as an art form from about the 1870s to about the 1920s, during the early reservation period, a time of profound cultural change. It expanded when about 70 Native Americans, mostly southern Cheyenne, were imprisoned for a time at Fort Marion, in St. Augustine, Florida. They produced scores of ledger drawings, for personal pleasure, for sale to tourists, and as gifts for the whites with whom they interacted. This period was a time of profound cultural trauma as Native Americans left the old free life of the buffalo-hunting days for a new life as semiprisoners living on government rations, under official pressure to abandon their religion, traditional ceremonies, and the old ways of communal living. Ledger drawings serve not only as an important expression of Native American arts, but also as important documents in the recording of actual events that can be used to expand knowledge about the past.

ART AND THE EXPRESSION OF IDENTITIES

In all cultures, the creative process is used to express both individual and cultural identity.

Body Art and Cultural Identity

For thousands of years, people all over the world have been marking and adorning their bodies. Almost all cultures alter their members' bodies. Circumcision and other genital operations, scarification, piercing, and tattooing are common throughout the world's cultures. These are used to announce identification with particular groups and to mark social position. Tattooing, scarification, and genital operations are ways of permanently engraving group membership on the body. Applying tattoos or facial scars marks one as a member of a group in a visible way that cannot be easily denied. Such body changes may carry elements of particular status as well as membership. For example, body marking has been used in western Europe since ancient times; tattoos and body painting have been used to mark outlaw status, nobility, soldiers, slaves, and various kinds of religious observance and status (Schildkrout 2004). In a study of tattooing in Polynesia, Gell (1993) argues that tattooing both creates and reinforces status hierarchy differences among people but also is critical in the relationship of humans to the sacred. But Gell's work also shows enormous variation in the meanings of tattoos in different Polynesian island societies.

In many cultures, body art is associated with enhancing beauty, and thus related to gender. In India and the Middle East, henna, an orange-red dye made from the leaves of a small shrub, is used to dye fingernails and other parts of the hands and feet to enhance a woman's beauty, especially on ceremonial occasions such as religious holidays or marriage (Messina 1988). In Morocco, where anthropologist Maria Messina studied the body art of henna application, a young girl is first decorated with henna at age 3 or 4, in preparation for the important Muslim holiday of Ramadan. But the cultural importance of henna is primarily related to marriage, and marks the transition of a girl to a woman. The "night of henna" is the first night in the three-day marriage celebration; a girl is also decorated with henna at a "henna party" toward the end of her pregnancy. The month of Muharram, which marks the Muslim New Year, is another occasion for decorating married women with henna.

Henna parties are also viewed as a way of preventing illness or misfortune by placating malevolent spirits, called jinn. Sometimes women hire a specialist in applying henna designs on the skin, but a member of the woman's family may also do this. Although certain designs are traditional in certain regions, henna specialists also innovate in styles, and designs change according to the occasion and also according to fashion. Most of the designs have no explicit meaning, as representational art (art depicting any figures or forms found in nature or culture) is forbidden in Islam.

In addition to the cosmetic function of henna, and the prevention of illness, henna parties are celebrations during which friends visit and possibly sing and dance. They also provide occasions where women are the center of attention. The application of henna designs has diffused from its original home (probably in India), and is now common also among non-Indians in the United States, functioning less as a display of a group identity than as an expression of an individual's assertion of choice and personal preference.

Art and Personal Identity: Fritz Scholder, Indian and Not Indian

For people in European-based cultures, one of the more obvious functions of the arts is the expression of personal identity. Indeed, in these cultures, personal identity is assumed to be deeply connected to an artist's body of work. However, such art must also deal with and reflect broader cultural themes. Fritz Scholder (1937–2005) is a controversial artist whose work reflects both deep issues of individual and cultural identity. Scholder's father was half Indian and half German and his family did not live on an Indian reservation. Although enrolled in his father's tribe (the Luiseño), he often said he was not Indian. Until Scholder's work in the 1960s, much Native American painting, by both native and nonnative artists, romanticized native life and the natural world and reflected popular clichés about the lives of native peoples. In contrast, Scholder's works combined historical images with abstract expressionism and pop art and presented a provocative challenge to these clichés. He directly addressed some uncomfortable truths about contemporary Native American life, such as alcoholism, poverty, and injustice. Scholder's painting, "Indian with Beer Can," generated especially outraged responses among both native and nonnative viewers because it broke the taboo on talking about the ways that alcoholism devastated so many Indian lives. Another of his powerful and controversial paintings is that of a Buffalo Dancer with an ice cream cone. While many viewers found this image disrespectful, for Scholder it cast a realistic look at the contact between the traditional and the modern in contemporary native life.

Scholder's ambivalence about his Indian identity, reflected in his art, and his frequent statements that he was not Indian, led other native artists to criticize what they saw as his denial of the very source of his artistic success. Scholder's powerful art, recently exhibited at the National Museum of the American Indian, illustrates both his own shifting identities and new perspectives on his culture and how the two are intertwined (Ringlero 2008).

ART AND REPRESENTATIONS OF THE OTHER

In representing cultural identities, art depicts not only the "we"—that is, the cultural in-group—but also the "other"—the alien, the foreigner, the outsider. Indeed, artistic forms are important aspects of cultural ideologies of difference, communicating in subtle but significant ways the nature of we/they distinctions.

The rendering of the other appears in art all over the world. Artistic products may reflect the subjects of the art, but they are also a source of insight into the mind-set of the artist, reflecting, perhaps, the cultural fantasies one group of people entertains about another (Bassani and Fagg 1988). Artistic images of outsiders may be useful as historical documents, portraying details of behavior and costume, but the unknown aspects of foreigners also act as an invitation to the imagination in which the reality of the observed becomes subordinate to the fantasies of the observers (Tsuruta 1989).

Orientalism in European Art: Picturing the Middle East

One result of the encounters between Europeans and other peoples was a profound rethinking of European cultural identity (S. Schwartz 1994). Although these encounters were experienced differently in different times and places, Europeans most often responded by creating opposite categories of "them" and "us" (Bitterli 1986). These dichotomies take many forms: East and West; primitive, or barbarian, and civilized; traditional and modern; developed and undeveloped. As we noted earlier, the differences in museum exhibits of Western and non-Western art implicitly distinguished between the "civilized" us of the West and the non-Western "primitive" other.

In the 19th century, Europeans explored, conquered, and then wrote about and painted North Africa, Arabia, the Levant, and the Ottoman Empire. This region, today called the Middle East, was then called the Orient. European artists of the 19th and 20th centuries offered armchair travelers a vividly graphic image of the Islamic, largely Arabic cultures inhabiting this world. One important impetus for these representations, particularly in France, was the Napoleonic campaigns in Egypt (1798 to 1799). By the mid-19th century, the Egyptian experience had become part of the French cultural spirit and was found in a wide range of artistic representations in a style called **Orientalism** (Hauptman 1985:48).

Creative expressions representing the Middle East are particularly interesting. In the 19th century, Middle East was depicted in European art as an enchanting land of mystery, fairy tales, and exotic beauty, yet also threatening in its opposition to European culture. Artists sought out the picturesque and the awesome (fabled ruins, biblical sites, deserts, and mountains). They emphasized the exoticism and glamour of Oriental markets, camel caravans, and snake charmers. Above all, European artists depicted their fantasies of "Oriental" women, hidden behind the veil or revealed in a harem or slave markets (Alloula 1986; Thornton 1994). Such images were more a reflection of European romanticism than an accurate depiction of Middle Eastern culture. However, they have helped shape our understandings of the Middle East (particularly of gender relations) and, as a result, have had important political ramifications (Said 1978). In European-based cultures, a highly significant function of art is the expression of the artist's personal identity. Europeans saw the Oriental "other" as threatening because they perceived it as the opposite of European civilization. They viewed Europe as democratic, dynamic, and rational but viewed the Orient as despotic, static, and irrational. This perception of the Orient was reflected in and reinforced by European paintings (see Figure 12.3). Islam was captured not in its religious experience (to which Europeans were generally hostile) but in the architecture of its mosques and its practice of prayer, all portrayed in lavish, opulent detail. Although many Europeans traveled to the Orient, painters generally worked from secondhand sources or, in some cases, purely from imagination. However, their works were rendered in exquisite detail, which gave viewers a sense of historical accuracy.

Orientalism: Scholarship and art generated by Europeans, representing their views of the Middle East.

Figure 12.3 The enigma of the Middle Eastern woman, whether hidden behind a veil or revealed in a harem, was a core image of Orientalist painting. In many cases, these were purely works of the imagination as in this painting, Juan Gimenez Martin's "In the Harem," painted in the artist's studio in Rome.

Juan Gimenez-Martin/Dahesh Museum of Art

Gender roles and relationships were a central theme in Orientalist painting. Men were shown as clearly dominant and pictured in public places, where women were mostly absent. The Arab warrior was the most common symbol of Oriental masculinity, but men were also painted in more relaxed poses, drinking coffee or smoking a hookah. But Oriental women were central to European fantasies of the period (Thornton 1994). The difficulty of finding women to pose in no way inhibited their depiction. Indeed, this gave free rein to artists' imaginations.

Harems and slave markets, painted for male patrons by male artists, offered a convenient way of feeding European lust by displaying the dominant men and vulnerable women of another culture, far removed from home. Pornographic scenes disguised as either documentation or art were integral to the European market for Orientalist painting (Thubron 2009). These images were not confined to fine art but found frequent expression in other elements of culture such as the picture postcard, a genre that the poet Malek Alloula calls the "comic strip of colonial morality." The postcards reveal the preoccupation of Europeans with the veiled female body. The native models for these postcards were photographed in studios re-enacting exotic rituals in costumes photographers provided. The models represent the French fantasy of the inaccessible Oriental female, more tempting because she is behind the veil in the forbidden harem.

Alloula connects these Orientalist fantasies to colonial reality, noting that the raiding of women has always been the dream and the obsession of the total victor: "These raided bodies are the spoils of victory, the warrior's reward." The postcards are an "enterprise in seduction directed to the troops, the leering wink in the encampment" (1986:122).

Orientalist representations of women also reflected the long-standing conflict between Christian Europeans and Middle Eastern Muslims. Since the Middle Ages, Europeans had criticized Muslims for their practice of polygyny, which Europeans associate with promiscuity. Thus, popular images of slave girls, harems, and concubines provided a continual source of horror and titillation for Western critics of the Muslim world. Even today, much Western thinking about the contemporary Middle East is concerned with the veiling, segregation, and oppression of women (Hale 1989).

◪ WORLD ART

The diffusion of the art of indigenous peoples has today become an important part of a global economy. For Western tourists, the art of traditional and authentic indigenous peoples is a deep and unchanging aspect of their cultures, and purchasing this art is an important part of their experience. In fact, however, traditional art changes as do other aspects of culture, under the impact of globalization, the emergence of art markets, and the expansion of global tourism. Ritually and socially significant creative expressions in indigenous societies are transformed as they become part of a global market. Anthropologists are particularly interested in examining how art becomes functionally and stylistically re-conceptualized to meet a global demand and how this "traffic in culture" affects both the art and the cultural identities of the people who create it (Cotter 2012; 2006; Price 1989; Steiner 1994; Venbrux et al. 2006). In addition to providing new sources of income, objects and performances that originated in traditional indigenous ritual and social life become artistic *products* around which modern cultural identities are constructed, both by outsiders and by members of the societies themselves. As a result of this global context, anthropologists and art historians now speak of **world art**, in which the arts of indigenous peoples are increasingly circulated, and in which the role of the artist is no longer anonymous, but increasingly known, as is typical of Western society. Previously, even when an individual artist could be tracked down, dealers and collectors were generally not interested in doing so; anonymity was often exploited by art middlemen who learned that objects were worth more to buyers from Europe and the United States if they were portrayed as coming from unknown, preferably long deceased artists in remote villages. The middlemen are quite willing to manipulate both the art objects and the information about their production to meet these demands (Steiner 1995:157). Today, however, this is changing and the identification of tribal artists has now become an important factor in both understanding and marketing their arts.

World art: The contemporary visual arts and cultural performances of non-Western peoples.

Outsider interest in developing and marketing indigenous arts in the United States helped create the status of artist where it did not previously exist, as happened in the life and work of the Pueblo Indian potter Maria Martinez (1887–1980) of San Ildefonso (Babcock 1995). In 1908 and 1909, archaeologist and museum director Edgar Lee Hewett asked Martinez to make pottery modeled on the ancient designs he had uncovered near her village. Martinez, with her husband Julian, elaborated their techniques and designs, producing a new black on black pottery style. Maria and Julian actively popularized and promoted their work outside their community, demonstrating their technique and wares at several world fairs and expositions. By the 1930s, the profile of northern New Mexico, in which San Ildefonso is located, was substantially raised among art collectors as well-known artists like Georgia O'Keeffe and Ansel Adams, among others, came to work and live in the area. After Julian's death in 1943, Maria began to work with younger family members; her son Popovi Da was not only a talented artist but also a talented promoter and toured nationally promoting Martinez pottery.

The community of San Ildefonso now became identified with fine pottery, and Maria Martinez became a star of the art world, her signed pottery now selling for thousands of dollars. Ironically, because of her connections to the national and global art market, she also became a romanticized image of the authentic Native American woman potter.

Tourism and World Art

The arts have always been important in marking cultural boundaries. They retain that importance in the contemporary world, particularly with regard to the construction of ethnic identities of indigenous peoples and their relation to tourism (Graburn 1976). The linking of the arts to cultural identity is promoted by popular television shows about non-Western cultures, the worldwide sale of ethnic arts (including on the Internet), traveling museum shows in which indigenous peoples are represented through their arts, the circulation of tribal arts among Western art collectors, and particularly, tourism. Artistic objects and performances that have their origin in ritual and social life may become, through tourism, a core around which modern cultural identities are constructed and an important source of income as well (see Figure 12.4).

Tourism can transform indigenous, culturally authentic, and creative art into mass-produced souvenirs and performances lacking any cultural meaning. On the other hand, it can also support and reaffirm cultural identities by reviving respect for traditional art forms. These are not necessarily mutually exclusive results. In the American Southwest, as we have seen, the 20th century brought a resurgence of wide interest in Native American arts, and this has resulted in the production of a

Figure 12.4 Many traditional arts have been given new life by the tourist industry. Here an artist in Bali paints traditional designs on a cloth hanging designed for sale to tourists.

© Joan Gregg

great deal of outstanding art in both traditional and new media. This continues today, and both older and more recent native art works fetch high prices on the international market. But, as anyone who has traveled in the area knows, the Southwest is also awash with cheap bric-a-brac often mass-produced in Asia. Also, in Bali, the interest of tourists in cultural performances has given such events an economic boost and allowed local troupes to buy new instruments for their musical ensembles and new costumes. It also has encouraged the opening of schools and institutes throughout Indonesia for training people in creating traditional art forms. An expert and professional group of Indonesian artists has maintained tight control over performances to conserve the quality of the arts. Similarly, interest in the Inuit arts and their sale to tourists has been an extremely important alternative source of income for them, especially as hunting declines. The connection between art, tourism, and the strengthening of cultural identity is also seen in the weaving of Native American women in Guatemala and Mexico (J. Nash 1986).

Ritually and socially significant cultural elements change meaning as they become part of staged performances for tourists or move from their original cultural contexts into the world art market. This is part of a larger process in which culture itself has become a marketable commodity, reshaped and packaged in part in response to the demands of globalization. Among the more recent anthropological interests in art are the ways in which the artworks of nonindustrial societies have become commodities in the process of globalization and the ways in which they have been reconceptualized functionally and stylistically to meet a worldwide demand. It is still unclear whether this marketing of culture will move the world inevitably toward cultural homogenization or whether the global economy and the global village will always leave room for the emergence of meaningful local artistic expressions of cultural identity.

BRINGING IT BACK HOME:
MARKETING INDIGENOUS ARTS

Anthropologist Kathleen Adams describes how indigenous arts and identities change under the impact of global tourism and commodification (Adams 2006). Among the Toraja, subsistence cultivators in South Sulawesi, Indonesia, two spiritually important artistic productions are tongkonan, spectacularly carved ancestral houses, and tau taus, wooden effigies of nobles carved in connection with mortuary ritual (see Figure 12.5). Although the Toraja today are predominantly Christian, their traditional art and elaborate rituals connected with the tongkonan and the tau taus are still a major component of contemporary Toraja cultural identity. Tourism has been essential in the maintenance of these traditional aspects of Toraja culture.

By the late 1960s, the expansion of organized tourism to the Toraja area was focused on viewing Toraja mortuary rituals of animal sacrifice; the tongkonan and the tau tau became important parts of Indonesia's tourist development program, aimed at increasing the flow of Western capital (Volkman 1984:162). Tourist interest in the tongkonan led to the Indonesian government banning altering them. The question was even raised as to whether the Toraja should be permitted to live in them, lest they damage these "tourist objects" (Adams 1990:33). Reflecting the worldwide tourist demand for "portable art," the Toraja soon began carving miniature tongkonan and selling them in souvenir shops.

The tau taus also changed under the tourist gaze and the global art market. Traditionally, tau taus, commissioned by the family, represented the spirit of a dead person, considered the vessel of the Torajan soul. When the mortuary rites are completed, the tau tau is placed with its relatives on platforms chiseled into limestone cliffs, where it becomes a visual link between the community of the living and the community of the dead.

Today, tau taus may incorporate Western cultural elements, such as digital watches, eyeglasses, Western clothing, Bibles, and crosses. And while tau taus were traditionally carved only for the wealthiest nobility and were therefore a symbol of aristocratic status among the Toraja, the tau taus are symbolic of a generalized Torajan identity for tourists today. Miniature

© Cengage Learning 2015

The Toraja.

Judith Pearson

Figure 12.5 Iau taus, effigies of the spirit of a recently deceased noble person, have taken on new identities, both for the Toraja and for outsiders, as they have been transformed into artistic commodities in the global art market.

tau taus are sold in tourist markets, along with large carvings of the burial cliffs. Thus, tourism began a process by which ritually significant objects have been transformed into art objects of economic significance.

As traditional tau taus were transformed into artistic commodities in a global art market, hundreds of them were stolen and sold to American, European, and Asian art collectors. Redesignated by Western curators and collectors as archaic Indonesian art, some effigies have also found a home in Western museums. A stolen tau tau is irreplaceable; its theft is tantamount to the abduction of an ancestor, and the loss must be redressed by ritual propitiation. However, legal, political, and economic obstacles stand in the way of repatriation, and tau taus today are openly sold for thousands of dollars in international galleries. The Toraja realize that without the tau taus, tourism will decline, depriving them of an important source of income and prestige. The Indonesian government, more to maintain tourist interest than address Torajan concerns, has replaced stolen tau taus with newly made ones, but the Torajans reject these as not only clumsily made but as having no spiritual significance because they were not made under ritual conditions.

Paradox and pathos thus attend the tau tau today. Their meaning has changed from ritual object to art commodity: Whereas the tau tau once served as a protection for the family of the deceased, today the family of the deceased must protect the tau tau.

■ YOU DECIDE:

1. What are some of the relationships between art and tourism?
2. How has the marketing of indigenous art brought both benefits and problems for its creators?
3. Have you ever bought indigenous art? In a museum shop? On a tourist jaunt? From an upscale art gallery? Describe the artifact and what prompted you to buy it. What meanings does it have for you?

■ CHAPTER SUMMARY

1. What are the basic differences between the anthropology of art and art history? Anthropologists examine the cultural and functional contexts of art, local standards of beauty, and the relation of art to ritual and social relations. Art historians, in contrast, emphasize what they call the intrinsic aesthetic value of art objects with little attention to function and cultural contexts.

2. In what ways do the arts of various cultures differ from each other? The forms of creative expression differ in different societies, as do the rules by which art is created, the importance of originality in art, the interactions of the artist with the audience, the purposes for which art is made, the roles of the artist, and the relation of art to other aspects of culture.

3. What are some aspects of the power of art? The power of art may lie in its emotional expression of important cultural themes, or the art itself may be regarded as inherently powerful, as when art is performed as part of a ritual, as among prehistoric hunters who painted pictures of animals to achieve control over hunting.

4. Using one example, describe the relationship between art and cultural themes. The symbolic nature of art, with multilayered levels of meaning, functions to communicate cultural themes. In Japan, for example, anime and manga display the repressed themes of Japanese militarism in World War II, the trauma of the atomic bombing of Hiroshima and Nagasaki, and the postwar dependence of the Japanese on the United States and resulting feelings of powerlessness.

5. What is deep play? Give examples of art forms that are deep play. Deep play expresses the idea that certain art forms manipulate profound cultural themes. These performances, such as the Balinese cockfight, are "texts" that can be used to interpret cultural values.

6. What are some of the relationships between art and history, art and social structure, art and social justice? The arts may be used to validate a political structure, as in memorials to ruling powers; challenge existing social and political structures by mocking those in power or questioning society's rules; or to record history and commemorate past events.

7. What are some of the connections between the arts and personal identities? Body art can express a cultural identity, a social status, or a personal identity. In Morocco, for example, henna painting of women's hands is intimately related to celebrating a marriage. Native American artist Fritz Scholder uses his paintings to question his own Indian/not Indian identity.

8. How does art express boundaries between the cultural in-group and the cultural other? Art can express the cultural identity of an in-group, but also reinforce that identity by depicting the "other," as in European Orientalism, which represented European fantasies of the Middle East.

9. How does art become an important factor in the cultural identities of indigenous peoples as they interact with others in a globalized context? Today, many indigenous societies, such as the Toraja of Indonesia, are known throughout the world because of their art forms. The global context for indigenous art around the world includes the Internet, international art collections, museum exhibits, and particularly, tourism. Although tourism may confer economic benefits, it also sometimes results in artistic objects, performances, and rituals that had spiritual meanings becoming transformed into staged displays or commodities in international art markets.

KEY TERMS

Anime
Art
Bhangra
Manga

Orientalism
World art
World music

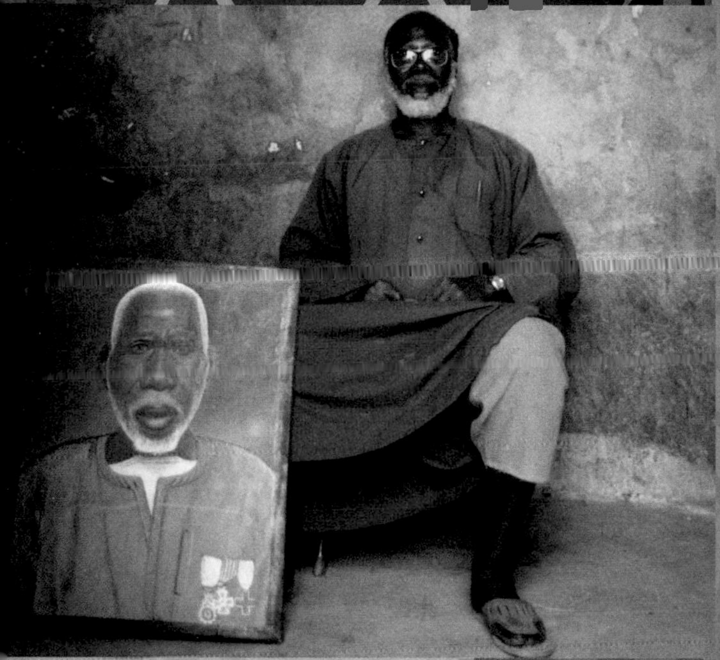

© Richard Warms

Man with a painting of his father, a veteran of the Tirailleurs Sénégalais. The Tirailleurs Sénégalais was an army the French drafted and recruited from their colonial possessions in West Africa between 1857 and 1960.

CHAPTER 13

POWER, CONQUEST, AND A WORLD SYSTEM

LEARNING OBJECTIVES

After you have read this chapter, you will be able to:

- Δ Identify some of the critical reasons for the European expansion of the 16th century.
- Δ Summarize the key methods Europeans used to gain wealth from their global expansion.
- Δ Assess the roles of joint stock companies and monoculture plantations in creating European wealth.
- Δ Compare and contrast the era of colonization between 1500 and 1800 with colonizing in the 19th century.
- Δ Outline the role of disease in European expansion and compare its effects in the Americas and in Africa and Asia.
- Δ Analyze the ways in which Europeans attempted to extract wealth from their colonies in the 19th and 20th centuries.
- Δ Discuss the reasons why almost all colonies achieved independence by the end of the 1960s.

VETERANS OF COLONIAL ARMIES

HEN I (Rich Warms) was young, I was a Peace Corps volunteer. I lived in a town called Ouahigouya in a country that was then called Upper Volta (now Burkina Faso) in West Africa. I spent most of my time working in small villages, but I'd also wander around the town. Frequently on my wanderings, I'd be stopped by a grizzled-looking old man who would start yelling at me in German. Then in French (the language of government and education in Upper Volta), he'd inform me that he'd been a prisoner of the Germans in World War II. At first I took him to be a drunk and a crazy person (the place where he always stopped me was near a bar). But, as I got to know him and other residents of the town better, I learned that what he told me was true. He had been a German prisoner. That, of course, left me wondering how it was possible. After all, I didn't think that this particular individual could have been visiting Europe when the war broke out.

As I spoke to him and to many others like him over the 15 years that followed, I learned a story that had been left out of my high school and college history lessons. I learned that, starting in the second half of the 19th century, France began to create a black African army called the *Tirailleurs Senegalais* or Senegalese Riflemen. In the early years, the French bought slaves to fill the army ranks. But as time progressed, they turned to levying a draft on their colonies and then, finally, after World War II, to a volunteer force. First, they used this army to conquer the areas that became French colonies in Africa. Later, they used these troops to fight in the trenches in World War I and to suppress rebellion in various colonial possessions. In World War II, African troops were essential to the conquest of North Africa and Italy and to taking back France itself. When people think of Charles De Gaulle's Free French forces of that war, they generally summon up a Hollywood image of a white guy in a beret. In fact, before the last phase of the liberation of France in 1944, most Free French forces were black Africans and were more likely to be called Mahamadou than Pierre. In the late years of French colonialism, it was African troops, among others, who fought at the Battle of Dien Bien Phu that ended the French colonial venture in Vietnam in 1954.

In the 1990s, I interviewed more than 50 surviving members of the **Tirailleurs Senegalais**. The stories they told were fantastic, even unbelievable. Dragged out of small African villages and sent to fight in Europe and elsewhere around the globe, they faced horrors and culture shock that nothing could have prepared them for. Some cracked under the strain, responding with violent outbursts and, when they made it home, with drunkenness and insanity. However, most learned to adapt. When they got home, they sometimes put their language skills, organizational skills,

Burkina Faso & Mali.

Tirailleurs Senegalais: Senegalese riflemen. An army that existed from 1857 to 1960, composed largely of soldiers from French African colonies led by officers from metropolitan France.

and bravery to new uses, playing important roles in their communities. But many are also deeply aggrieved. They feel neglected by history and by France. In 1991, Mory Samake, a veteran of World War II, told me:

> Look, when you work for someone, he's got to recognize your efforts. They treat us like their dogs. They are white, we are black but we are all equal. If someone cuts my hand and someone cuts one of their hands, the blood is just the same. When we were there fighting the war, no one said "this one is white, this one is black." We didn't go to fight with ill will. We gave our blood and our bodies so that France could be liberated. But now, since they have their freedom, they have thrown us away, forgotten us. If you eat the meat, you throw away the bone. France has done just that to us.

The story of the Tirailleurs Senegalais and Mory Samake's anger with the French remind us of several extremely important points. A cliché has it that history is written by the winners. It might be more accurate to say that history is written by the powerful and usually presented as a narrative of their inevitable triumph. But such a history ignores inconvenient truths or relegates them to footnotes and appendices. The relation between wealth and poverty and between the powerful and the powerless, or, in this case, between the colonized and the colonizer, are among the most important of these truths.

We tend to assume that the social arrangements we see today, the distribution of wealth and poverty, of power and powerlessness, are of great historical depth. However, our world is the current result of large-scale historic processes that involved the ebb and flow of wealth and power, among nations and among different areas of the world. These processes have had a particularly important impact on the kinds of small-scale societies that anthropologists often study.

The patterns of political, social, and economic change over the past several centuries are complex and diverse. They are characterized by contact among cultures. A significant part of this story concerns the expansion of the affluence and power of places that are now wealthy. This expansion of power occurred in thousands of locations and had many different effects. Sometimes cultural contact was accidentally genocidal, sometimes intentionally so. Many traditional cultures have been destroyed, but others have prospered, although in altered forms. Members of different cultures often confronted each other through a veil of ignorance, suspicion, and accusations of savagery. But sometimes, common interests, common enemies, mutual curiosity, and occasional friendships among people overrode their differences.

In this chapter, we describe the overall pattern of change during the past several hundred years. In the broadest sense, this involved the incorporation of relatively separate cultures and economies into a vast, chaotic, yet integrated world economic system. Understanding this history is critical for anthropologists. People often think of the cultures anthropologists have historically studied as small, isolated groups relatively unaffected by outside political, economic, and technological forces. In fact, anthologists themselves have sometimes made this assumption. However, work in the past several decades has shown that the changing patterns of global trade, politics, information, and technology have had deep impacts on seemingly isolated groups for hundreds of years. These patterns have helped shape their cultures, influencing critical practices such as family and political structure, the conditions under which people labor, and what they produce. To understand the ways in which individual cultures throughout the world have developed, anthropologists need to understand the larger patterns of history that have affected them.

These historical patterns have resulted in enormous inequality both within and among societies and nations as wealth and labor flowed from one area of the world to another. They created the financial accumulation necessary for the Industrial Revolution and the development of capitalism. The Ottoman Empire as well as Russia and Japan played critical roles in the story. However, the expanding influence and power of western European states and the colonies settled by their subjects and citizens probably had the greatest impact worldwide. For that reason, we begin with a bird's-eye view of Europe and the rest of the world as it might have appeared in 1400.

MAKING THE MODERN WORLD

As surprising as it may seem now, a visitor touring the world on the eve of European expansion in 1400 might well have been amused by the notion that European societies would soon become enormously wealthy and powerful. Other areas of the globe would have seemed much more likely prospects for power. Europeans had devised oceangoing vessels, but Arab and Chinese ships regularly made much longer voyages. The cities of India and China made those of Europe look like mere villages. Almost no European states could effectively administer more than a few hundred square kilometers. Certainly, there was nothing that could compare to China's vast wealth and centralized bureaucracy. Europeans were masters of cathedral and castle construction, but other than that, their technology was backward. War, plague, and economic depression were the order of the day (Scammell 1989). Moreover, other areas of the world seemed to be growing in wealth and power. Despite occasional setbacks, the Islamic powers had expanded steadily in the five centuries leading up to 1400, and Muslim societies stretched from Spain to Indonesia. Not only had these empires preserved the scholarship of India and the ancient Mediterranean civilizations, but they also had greatly increased knowledge in astronomy, mathematics, medicine, chemistry, zoology, mineralogy, and meteorology (Lapidus 1988:96, 241–52).

China had an extraordinarily ancient and powerful civilization. As late as 1793, Emperor Ch'ien Lung, believing China to be the most powerful state in the world (or perhaps showing bravado in the face of foreign traders), responded to a British delegation's attempt to open trade by writing to King George III: "Our dynasty's majestic virtue has penetrated into every country under heaven and kings of all nations have offered their costly tribute by land and sea. As your Ambassador can see for himself, we possess all things. . . . [W]e have never valued ingenious articles, nor do we have the slightest need of your country's manufacturers" (Peyrefitte 1992:288–92). Unfortunately for the Chinese, by the time the emperor wrote this letter, it was no longer accurate. Within a half century, at the end of the First Opium War, Britain virtually controlled China.

▨ EUROPEAN EXPANSION: MOTIVES AND METHODS

From slow beginnings in the 15th century, European power grew rapidly from the 16th to the 20th centuries. Many theories have been suggested to account for the causes and motives of European expansion. Although it was often a cover for more worldly aims, the desire of the pious to Christianize the world was certainly a motivating factor. The archives of the Jesuit order include more than 15,000 letters, written between 1550 and 1771, from people who wanted to be missionaries (Scammell 1989:60). The desire to find a wide variety of wonders, both real and imagined, was also important. The Portuguese looked for routes to the very real wealth of Eastern empires, such as China, and also for the mythical kingdom of Prester John, a powerful but hidden Christian monarch, the fountain of youth, and the Seven Cities of Cibola.

Beyond this, there was always the desire for wealth. Nations and nobles quickly invested in exploration as gold and diamonds were discovered. The poor and oppressed of Europe saw opportunities for wealth and respect in the colonies. There, they sometimes fulfilled their dreams of wealth by re-creating the very social order they had fled.

Various social and technological developments aided European expansion. These included the rise of a banking and merchant class, a

Monoculture plantation: An agricultural plantation specializing in the large-scale production of a single crop to be sold on the market.

Joint stock company: A firm that is managed by a centralized board of directors but is owned by shareholders.

growing population, and the development of the caravel, a new ship that was better at sailing into the wind. Two other developments, the **monoculture plantation** and the **joint stock company**, were to have critical impacts on the world's people.

In many cases, however, the key advantage Europeans had over other people was the diseases they carried. Almost every time Europeans encountered populations in the Americas or on islands, they brought death and cultural destruction in the form of microbes.

The European search for wealth depended on tactics that, in their basic form, were ancient. Two of the quickest ways to accumulate wealth are to steal it from others and to get other people to work for you for free. State societies have always practiced these methods. War, slavery, exploitation, and inequality had been present in most of the world since ancient times, so there was nothing fundamentally new about their use by Europeans. However, no earlier empire had been able to practice these tactics on the scale that the European nations would. All previous empires, however large, were regional affairs. European expansion, for the first time in history, linked the entire world into an economic system. This system created much wealth but made impoverishment and slavery possible on a scale never seen before.

Pillage

Pillage: To strip an area of money, goods, or raw materials through the threat or use of physical violence.

One of the most important means of wealth transfer was **pillage**. In the early years of expansion, Europeans were driven by the search for precious metals, particularly gold and silver. When they found such valuables, they moved quickly to seize them. Metals belonging to indigenous peoples were soon dispatched back to Europe, and mines were placed under European control. The profits of these enterprises were enormous. For example, in 1531, Pizarro captured the Inca Emperor Atahuallpa and received between 11 and 24 tons of silver and gold as his ransom. A gang of Indian smiths worked nine forges day and night to melt down this treasure, which was then shipped back to Spain (Duncan 1995:158). In the early 17th century, 58,000 Indian workers were forced into silver mining in the town of Potosi in the Peruvian Andes (Wolf 1982:136). Between 1500 and 1660, Spanish colonies in the Americas exported 300 tons of gold and 25,000 tons of silver (Scammell 1989:133).

Such looting was not limited to the New World. After the British East India Company came to power in India, it plundered the treasury of Bengal, sending wealth back to investors in England (Wolf 1982:244). In addition, art, artifacts, curiosities, and occasionally human bodies were stolen around the world and sent to museums and private collections in Europe (see Figure 13.1).

Forced Labor

Forced labor was another key element of European expansion. Although Europeans acquired forced laborers through debt servitude as well as by requiring labor from the people they governed, the most notorious example of forced labor was African slavery. Europeans did not invent slavery in general or African slavery in particular. Slavery had long been practiced in both Europe and Africa. Non-Europeans probably exported more than seven million African slaves to the Islamic world between 650 and 1600 (Lovejoy 1983). However, Europeans did practice African slavery on a larger scale than any people before them. Between the end of the 15th century and the end of the 19th century, approximately 11.7 million slaves were exported from Africa to the Americas. More than six million left Africa in the 19th century alone (Coquery-Vidrovitch 1988). No one really knows how many died in the process of capturing and transferring slaves within Africa. Estimates vary from one to five individuals dead for every slave successfully landed in the Americas.

The massive transport of people had two important economic effects: First, the use of slave labor was extremely profitable for both slave shippers and plantation owners. Second, slave labor created continuous warfare and impoverishment in the areas from which slaves were drawn. In these places, some undoubtedly grew rich on the profits of slavery but the loss of so many people and the violence and political instability resulting from the capture and transport of slaves radically altered African societies (Coquery-Vidrovitch 1988).

The demand for slaves was created by monoculture plantations—farms devoted to the production of a single crop for sale to distant consumers. Sugar, tobacco, and cotton produced this way in the Americas and spices produced on monoculture plantations in Asia were sold to consumers located primarily in Europe. Through the 19th century, sugar was the most important monoculture crop. British consumption of sugar increased some 2,500 percent between 1650 and 1800. Between 1800 and 1890, sugar production grew another 2,500 percent, from 245,000 tons to more than six million tons per year (Mintz 1985:73). Today, the world consumes about 182 million tons of sugar each year, about 52 pounds for every person on the planet (SUCDEN 2011). Until the 19th century, slaves largely provided the massive amount of labor required for growing and processing sugar. Between 1701 and 1810, for example, Barbados, a small island given

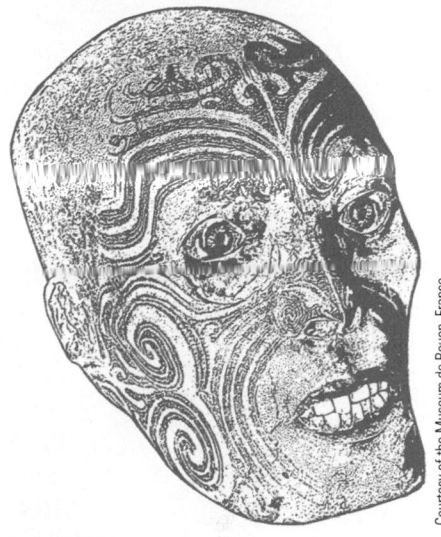

Courtesy of the Museum de Rouen, France

Figure 13.1 Drawing of a mummified Maori head. This head has been in the collection of the Museum of Natural History at Rouen, France. In 2007, the mayor of Rouen offered to return the head to New Zealand in "atonement" for the trafficking of human remains that occurred in the colonial era. However, the French government prevented the return of the head.

over almost entirely to sugar production, imported 252,500 slaves, almost all of whom were involved in growing and processing sugar (Mintz 1985:53).

Joint Stock Companies

The joint stock company was another innovation that allowed extremely rapid European expansion and led to enormous abuses of power. Most early European exploration was financed and supported by aristocratic governments or small private firms. By the turn of the 17th century, however, the British and Dutch had established joint stock companies. The French, Swedes, Danes, Germans, and Portuguese followed by midcentury. The best known of these companies include the Dutch East India Company (founded 1602), the British East India Company (founded 1600), the Massachusetts Bay Company (founded 1628), and the Hudson's Bay Company (founded in 1670).

Joint stock companies were the predecessors of today's publicly held corporations. The idea was simple. To raise the capital necessary for large-scale ventures, companies would sell shares. Each share gave its purchaser a small percentage of the ownership of the company and entitled him or her to a portion of the profits (or losses) from the company's business. Exploration and trade by joint stock companies had critical advantages over earlier forms. First, a great deal of capital could be raised rapidly, so business ventures could be much larger than previously possible. Second, although the motives of aristocratic governments often included the search for prestige and missionary zeal, joint stock companies existed to provide profits to their shareholders and were relatively single-minded in pursuit of that goal. Because they were frequently empowered to raise armies and conduct wars, they could have devastating effects on the societies they penetrated.

Dutch East India Company (VOC): A joint stock company chartered by the Dutch government to control all Dutch trade in the Indian and Pacific oceans. Also known by its Dutch initials VOC for Verenigde Oostendische Compagnie.

Heeren XVII: The Lords Seventeen, members of the board of directors of the Dutch East India Company.

The **Dutch East India Company** (**VOC**, after its initials in Dutch) is an example of a joint stock company. Based on money raised from the sale of shares, the VOC was chartered by the Dutch government to hold the monopoly on all Dutch trade with the societies of the Indian and Pacific Oceans. Shares in the VOC were available on reasonable terms and were held by a wide cross-section of Dutch society (Scammell 1989:101). In many ways, the company functioned as a government in the places in which it was chartered to operate. Led by a board of directors called the **Heeren XVII** (the Lords Seventeen), it was empowered to make treaties with local rulers in the name of the Dutch Republic, occupy lands, levy taxes, raise armies, and declare war. However, although governments are to some degree beholden to those they govern, the VOC was interested solely in returning dividends to its shareholders. This it did very successfully.

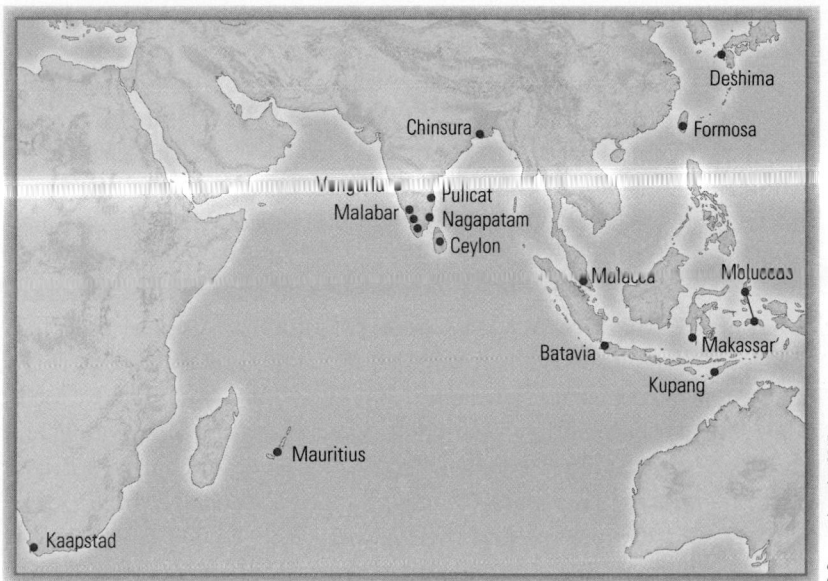

Figure 13.2 Principal holdings of the Dutch East India Company in the Pacific in the 1660s.

Through the 17th and early 18th centuries, the VOC distributed annual dividends of 15.5 to 50 percent. It returned dividends of 40 percent per year for six consecutive years from 1715 to 1720 (Boxer 1965:46). By comparison, the average annual dividend paid by a Standard and Poor's 500 stock index between 1960 and 2007 was between 2 and 5 percent.

Through the 17th century, the VOC used its powers to seize control of many of the Indian Ocean islands. Among these were Java, including the port of Jakarta (which became their headquarters, renamed Batavia), Sri Lanka (Ceylon), and Malacca (see Figure 13.2). In addition, the VOC acquired the right to control the production and trade of the most valuable spices of the area (cloves, nutmeg, and mace) and took brutal steps to maintain this monopoly. For example, during the 1620s, virtually the entire population of the nutmeg-producing island of Banda was deported, driven away, starved to death, or massacred. They were replaced with Dutch colonists using slave labor (Ricklefs 1993:30). By the 1670s, the Dutch had gained complete control of all spice production in what is now Indonesia (Wolf 1982).

Natives did not submit passively to VOC control, and the company did not have a clear-cut military advantage. Instead, the VOC rapidly (and ultimately, disastrously) became embroiled in the area's wars. For example, in the 17th century, the Mataram dynasty controlled most of central Java. In 1677, when the dynasty faced rebellion, the VOC intervened on its behalf in hopes of cash payments and trade concessions. In a bloody campaign, the combined VOC and dynasty forces crushed the rebellion and established Emperor Amangkurat II on the throne. Trouble ensued when the VOC received neither payments nor concessions. An armed force that the VOC sent to make its demands was defeated by Amangkurat II in 1686. The company was unable to recoup its losses or to claim its trading privileges (Ricklefs 1990). This was just the beginning of a series of extremely brutal wars pitting different factions of Javanese kingdoms against each other and against the VOC. Kingdoms alternately allied with and fought against the VOC as their interests dictated. These conflicts lasted until 1757.

The company often acted with extraordinary violence. The treatment of the Chinese in Batavia is a good example. The Chinese had come to Batavia as traders, skilled artisans, sugar millers, and shopkeepers. Despite harsh measures against them, roughly 15,000 lived there by 1740. VOC officials believed they were plotting rebellion, and after an incident in which several Europeans were killed, VOC Governor General Adriaan Valckenier hinted that a massacre would not be unwelcome. In the melee that followed, Europeans and their slaves killed 10,000 Chinese. The Chinese quarter of the city burned for several days, and the VOC was able to stop the looting only by paying its soldiers a premium to return to duty (Ricklefs 1993:90).

The burden of continual warfare, as well as corruption and inefficiency, forced the VOC into serious financial difficulties. By the last quarter of the 18th century, large areas of coastal Java had been depopulated by years of warfare, but the VOC had not succeeded in controlling the principal kingdoms of the island. The Heeren XVII were dismissed by the Netherlands government in 1796, after an investigation revealed corruption and mismanagement in all quarters. On December 31, 1799, the VOC was formally dissolved, and its possessions were turned over to the Batavian Republic, a Dutch client state of France.

The story of the VOC was, in large measure, repeated by other mercantilist trading firms organized by the British, French, Germans, Portuguese, Danes, and Swedes. In each case, companies generated enormous profits but eventually fell into disarray and either were dissolved or were taken over by their national governments. Despite their eventual failure, the trading companies placed fantastic riches in the hands of European elites. Europeans invested this wealth in many different ways: in the arts, in luxury goods, in architecture, but also in science and industry. This supply of wealth became one of the sources for the Industrial Revolution and the rise of capitalism itself.

The effects were far less pleasant for the regions in which the trading companies operated. The VOC and other trading companies left poverty and chaos in their wakes. In every case, Europeans fundamentally altered the communities with which they came into contact. Frequently, brutal policies and disease destroyed entire cultures. However, in most cases, societies were not simply overrun. Before the 19th century, Europeans did not have a truly decisive technological advantage over others. Instead, Europeans collaborated with local elites, which often were able to use their contact with the foreigners to increase their own wealth and power. However, as a whole, their societies suffered.

◤ THE ERA OF COLONIALISM

Colonialism differs in important ways from the earlier expansion of European power. Whereas much of the initial phase of European expansion was carried out by private companies and often took the form of raid and pillage, colonialism involved the active possession of foreign territory by European governments. **Colonies** were created when nations established and maintained political domination over geographically separate areas and political units (Kohn 1958).

There were several different types of European colonies. Some, as in Africa, existed primarily to exploit native people and resources. In other areas, such as North America and Australia, the key goal was the settlement of surplus European population. Still other locales, such as Yemen, which borders on the Red Sea and thus controlled shipping through the Suez Canal, were seized because they occupied strategic locations.

At one time or another, much of the world came under direct European colonization, but the timing of colonialism varied from place to place. The Americas were colonized in the 1500s and 1600s, but most other areas of the world did not come under colonial control until the 19th century. As long as Europeans confronted others with broadly similar weaponry and military tactics, the result was indecisive, and local governments were able to retain autonomy and power. By the 19th century, however, the Industrial Revolution gave Europeans (and their North American descendants) decisive advantages in both technological sophistication and quantity of arms. Although European colonizers faced frequent rebellions and proved unable to entirely subdue guerrilla activity in all places, no non-European government or army could defeat them.

Colonialism: The active possession of a foreign territory and the maintenance of political domination over that territory.

Colony: A foreign territory under the immediate political control of a nation-state.

◤ Colonization, 1500 to 1800

As we have seen, before the 1800s, very little of Africa or Asia was colonized. In these places, Europeans established small coastal settlements, but these existed largely because they were profitable for both Europeans and at least some local elites. In most cases, local powers had the ability to expel Europeans or to strictly limit their activities. Relatively few Europeans settled permanently in such colonies.

In the Americas, the situation was radically different. There, Europeans quickly established colonies and immigrated in large numbers. For example, between 1492 and 1600, more than 55,000 Spaniards immigrated to the New World. In the 50 years that followed, another quarter million joined them (Boyd-Bowman 1975). By comparison, in the first half of the 19th century, the total Dutch population of Indonesia, Holland's most important colonial possession, was about 2,100 (Zeegers et al. 2004).

Although there was stiff resistance to European expansion in the Americas, and Indian wars continued until the late 19th century, Europeans were victorious almost everywhere they wanted to expand. Technology aided European expansion, but the main reason for rapid European success was probably disease. In the wake of contact, up to 95 percent of the total population of the New World died (see Figure 13.3). Although Europeans also died of diseases, they did so in far smaller numbers (Diamond 1997; Karlen 1995; Newson 1999; Palkovich 1994).

Although epidemics may have occasionally been caused intentionally, neither Europeans nor natives had any knowledge of contagion or germs. The vast majority of deaths were not premeditated. However, Europeans came to see the handiwork of God in the epidemics that decimated Native Americans. God, they believed, clearly intended them to populate the Americas and was removing others to make that possible.

New World natives lacked immunity to European diseases for two principal reasons: First, the key diseases that killed indigenous populations, such as smallpox, influenza, and tuberculosis, require large reservoirs of population, in some cases up to a half million individuals

Figure 13.3 In the wake of conquest, up to 95 percent of the population of the Americas died. This colonial-era woodcut shows the Wampanoags of what is now Massachusetts grieving for smallpox deaths.

North Wind/North Wind Picture Archives

(Diamond 1992). Many North American groups were too small to sustain such crowd diseases and therefore lacked immunity to them. Second, although some Central and South American groups did have large populations, most crowd diseases originate in domesticated animals, which were largely absent from the Americas.

Cortés's conquest of Mexico is a good example of the effects of disease. When Cortés first appeared in 1519, the Aztec leader Montezuma, following his tradition, gave Cortés gifts and opened the city of Tenochtitlán to the Spanish. When it became clear that the Spanish were their enemies, the Aztecs expelled them from the city in a fierce battle that cost the Spanish and their allies perhaps two-thirds of their total army. By the time Cortés returned in 1521, a smallpox epidemic had killed up to half the Aztecs. Even after such crushing losses to disease, the Spanish conquest of Tenochtitlán took more than four months to accomplish (Berdan 1982; Clendinnen 1991; Karlen 1995). Had the Aztecs not been devastated by disease, they might have again defeated Cortés.

The die-off of Native Americans had dire effects throughout the Americas. The increasing population of Europeans and the diminishing population of natives assured that resistance to European domination could not be very effective. When John Winthrop, the first governor of Massachusetts, declared that the settlers had fair title to the land because it was *vacuum domicilium* (empty land), he was creating a legal fiction (he was well aware of the natives and their need for agricultural and hunting land), but he also knew that the native population was declining sharply.

If not for disease, the European experience in the Americas probably would have been very similar to its experience in Asia and Africa. Rather than establishing control over vast amounts of territory, Europeans probably would have been confined to small coastal settlements and would have been involved in protracted battles with powerful local kingdoms.

Colonizing in the 19th Century

By the beginning of the 19th century, the Industrial Revolution was underway in Europe and North America. This had two immediate consequences. First, it enabled Europeans and Americans to produce weapons in greater quantity and quality than any other people. Second, it created an enormous demand for raw materials that could not be satisfied in Europe. In addition, discoveries in medicine, particularly vaccines and antimalarial drugs, improved the odds of survival for Europeans in places previously considered pestilential. Thus, Europeans had both motives and means to colonize (see Figure 13.4).

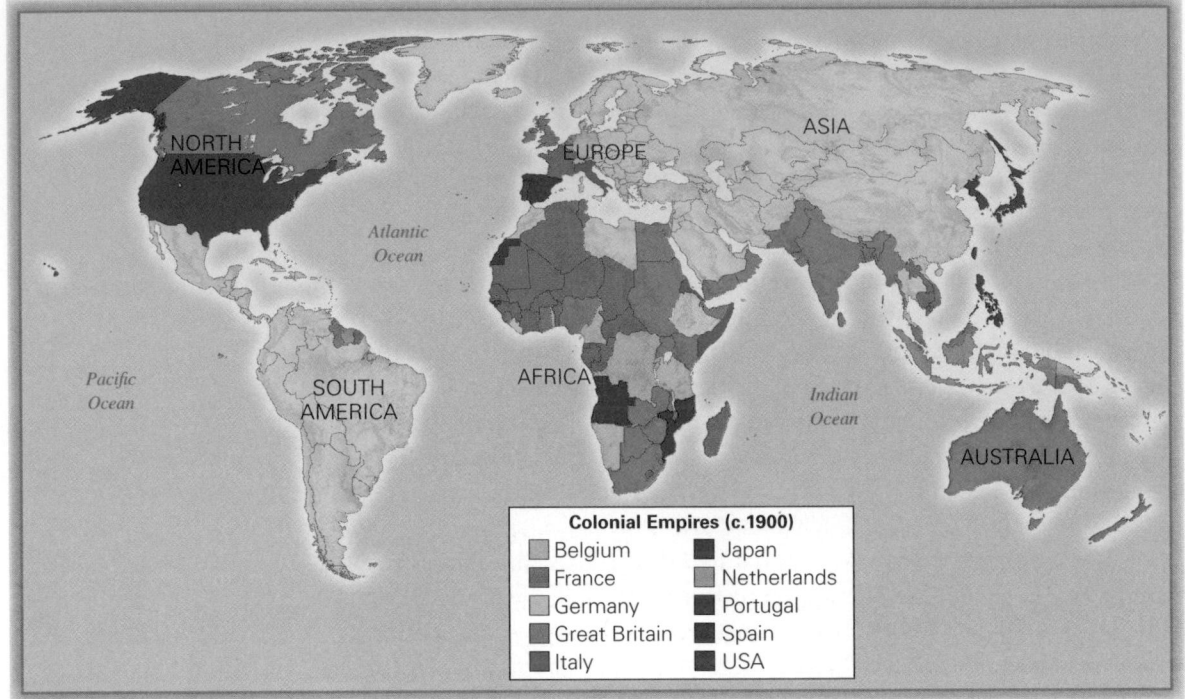

Figure 13.4 By 1900, most nations in the Americas had achieved independence. However, much of the rest of the world was under colonial rule. Many areas not formally colonized, such as China, were dominated by European powers.

Acting in their own self-interest, Europeans and Americans generally did not move rapidly to place other areas under their colonial control. The primary goal of European expansion was the pursuit of wealth and plunder. Mercantilist firms were rapid cost-effective ways to get them. The financial burden of establishing companies such as the VOC was borne by their shareholders. However, colonizing an area required some level of government expenditure. At the very least, this included administrative officials and the troops to back them, all of whom had to be equipped and paid out of the national treasury. In most cases, infrastructure such as roads, bridges, and railways had to be built. These were expensive undertakings, and European taxpayers and governments were generally not enthusiastic about funding them.

Most often, European governments felt forced to assume colonial control either because of the scandals surrounding the collapse of mercantile companies or out of fear that their national commercial interests were threatened, generally by other European nations. This fear led to the Berlin conference partitioning Africa among European powers in the late 19th century.

After European governments had established colonies, they had to convince both their own populations and those they colonized that this action was proper. They defended colonization by cloaking it in the ideology of social betterment. In Britain, citizens were encouraged, in the words of the poet Rudyard Kipling, "to take up the white man's burden" of bringing civilization to the "savage." In France, the population was told that it had a "*mission civilisatrice*," a civilizing mission that would both help the "savages" in the colonized areas and increase French political and cultural power throughout the world. The government portrayed its colonial practices as "*rayonnement*," lighting the way for others (Cole and Raymond 2006:158–59). In the colonies, as we will see next, subjects were taught that they were colonized for their own good and that their societies would advance as a result.

Making Colonialism Pay

Once colonies were seized, they had to be administered and they had to be made profitable. Colonizing powers hoped that tax revenues from colonial subjects would support the cost of colonial government as well as the construction of various public works. However, in many cases, taxes were insufficient, and taxpayers in the colonizing country were required to make up the difference between colonial income and expenses. Despite this situation, colonies were extremely profitable (see Bagchi 2002, for example).

Colonies gave businesses based in the colonizing country places in which they could operate free of competition. This was particularly important for Britain and France, two of the most important colonial powers. In the late 1700s, the Industrial Revolution began in Britain, but by the end of the 19th century, its factories were aging. New, more efficient industrial processes developed in the United States and Germany enabled these countries to produce cheaper manufactured goods (Allitt 2002). France came to industrialization relatively late and had a relatively weak road and rail network. As a result, it had difficulty competing with the United States, Germany, and Britain. Colonies created a zone of protection for older British industry and newer French manufacturers, thus enabling high profits for firms in these nations.

The costs of the colonies were borne (unequally) by subject colonial populations and by colonizing country taxpayers. The windfall profits from colonialism went to shareholders of companies operating in the colonies.

Finding ways to extract taxes and create the conditions in which corporations could make money often meant the systematic undermining of indigenous ways of life. Although the newly colonized societies had for centuries traded with others, frequently including Europeans, external trade usually accounted for only a small percentage of their economy. For the most part, their economic relations were drawn along kinship lines, and most of their production was for their own consumption. For colonialism to be profitable, these patterns had to change. Colonial subjects had to produce the goods that colonizing societies wanted and to labor in ways that would be profitable to the colonizers. From the colonizers' perspective, the key problem was finding ways to cause these changes. Some of the methods they used were control of local leaders, forced labor, forced production of particular commodities, taxation, and direct propaganda through education.

Sometimes colonial powers seized direct control of the political leadership, placing their own nationals in most powerful positions, but this was expensive, and foreign colonial leaders often lacked sufficient knowledge of local language and culture. More often, colonialists ruled indirectly through native leaders. These were recruited through promises of power and wealth as well as their realization that colonial governments held the reins of power and were unlikely to lose them any time soon. In some cases, colonial powers offered education, employment, and improved status to people who were oppressed or outcast in precolonial society, and these individuals were particularly attracted to support the colonizers.

A well-organized chain of command was needed for colonial powers to rule effectively. In hierarchical societies where kings or chiefs already existed, this did not pose a difficult problem. Most often, local elites sympathetic to the colonizers were able to retain a degree of power, although they became answerable to the colonial authorities. Those elites who resisted colonial rule were rapidly replaced. Regions where precolonial relationships were largely egalitarian posed a more difficult problem. If there was no chief or there were many co-reigning chiefs, establishing colonial authority was far more difficult. Colonizers tried to solve this problem by creating new chiefly offices. Sometimes colonialists and missionaries forged entire new ethnic groups, lumping together people with different traditions and even different languages (Harries 1987). For example, the Bété, an ethnic group of the central Ivory Coast in Africa, did not exist before the era of colonialism but was created by the actions of colonial and postcolonial governments (Dozon 1985).

In the long run, policies of indirect rule created the preconditions for instability and violence. Political leaders were compromised by their close connections with colonial authorities, and often lost the confidence and respect of those they purported to lead. Ethnic groups created for the purposes of colonial rule tended to fragment when that rule diminished.

One of the most direct ways that European governments tried to make their colonies profitable was by requiring **corvée labor**—unpaid work demanded of native populations. Until World War II, most colonial

Corvée labor: Unpaid labor required by a governing authority.

governments insisted on substantial labor from their subjects. The British often compelled subjects to work for up to one month a year, two months for the Dutch. In 1926, the French enacted a law that permitted an annual draft of labor for their West African colonies. Conscripts were compelled to work for three years on bridge and road building, irrigation projects, and other public works. Mortality rates during the three years of forced labor often were very high, making it one of the most hated institutions of colonialism. Natives resisted colonial demands by concealing workers or by fleeing from authorities when such work was demanded (Evans 2000; Ishemo 1995).

Even when subject populations were not forced into labor gangs, economic and social policies of colonial regimes required them to radically alter their cultures. For example, Portuguese colonial policy in Mozambique forced almost one million peasants to grow cotton. The colonial government controlled what these growers produced, where they lived, with whom they traded, and how they organized their labor. Although a few growers prospered, the great majority became impoverished and struggled to survive against famine and hardship (Isaacman 1996). By the 1960s, the brutality and terror the colonial regime used resulted in a civil war that continued into the 1990s.

Conditions were perhaps worst in the Congo, ruled between 1885 and 1908, as the personal property of King Leopold II of Belgium. There, each native owed the government 40 hours of labor each month in exchange for a token wage (Bodley 1999:116). Failure to work sufficiently or to produce the proper quantities of goods (particularly rubber) was met with extreme measures. Leopold's subjects were held hostage, were beaten or whipped, had their hands cut off, and, in many cases, were killed outright (see Figure 13.5). By the time the Belgian government stripped Leopold of his control of Congo, between four and eight million Congolese had been killed or had starved to death (Hochschild 1998).

In addition to forced labor and forced production, the British and French both drafted natives into their armed forces. They used these armies to capture and control their colonies, fight colonial wars, and augment their regular armies wherever needed. The *Tirailleurs Senegalais* were described at the opening of this chapter. Additional *Tirailleurs* units included groups from Algeria, Morocco, Madagascar, Vietnam, Cambodia, and other French colonial possessions. In East Africa, the British drafted and

Figure 13.5 From 1885 to 1908, Congo was the property of King Leopold II of Belgium. Atrocities committed during that era cost the lives of four to eight million Congolese. Punishments for disobedience or failure to meet payment quotas included chopping off children's hands.

Universal Images Group/SuperStock

recruited the King's African Rifles. In India, the British created an entire army led by British officers but consisting almost entirely of colonial subjects drawn primarily from ethnic groups the British considered particularly warlike. About 1.3 million members of the Indian Army served in World War I, primarily on the western front and also in the Middle East (Nayar and Paul 2003:66).

Although particular projects might use forced labor, to make a colony truly profitable, colonial masters also used other methods to encourage the population to work for them voluntarily or to produce the goods they desired. Taxation was a critical one of these. Taxation was needed to support the colonial government, but because colonizers knew that colonial economies were small and their tax receipts low, they rarely expected taxes to provide the full cost of governing. However, taxing colonial subjects had another purpose: to force them into the market system. Taxes generally had to be paid in colonial money, which native subjects could obtain only by working for a colonist or by producing something that the colonists wanted to buy. This participation in the market and wage labor was viewed as the essential precondition for "civilizing" the natives.

Taxation often forced colonial subjects into a vicious cycle of dependency on the market system. To raise money for taxes, subjects had to work directly for the colonizers or produce things that colonizers desired. But spending time on these tasks meant that less time could be spent making goods or raising crops for one's own consumption. This in turn meant that food and goods increasingly had to be purchased from the market, which was dominated by companies colonialists owned.

In addition to policies aimed at forcing subjects to take part in an economy centered in the industrial world, colonial governments took more direct aim at cultures through educational policies. Colonial education was often designed to convince subjects that they were the cultural, moral, and intellectual inferiors of those who ruled them. For example, education in 19th-century India encouraged children to aspire to be like the ideal Englishman (Viswanathan 1988). In France's African colonies, children were directly taught to obey their colonial masters, as illustrated in this passage from a turn-of-the-century reader designed to teach French to schoolchildren and used in the colonies:

> It is . . . an advantage for a native to work for a white man, because the Whites are better educated, more advanced in civilization than the natives, and because, thanks to them, the natives will make more rapid progress . . . and become one day really useful men. . . . You who are intelligent and industrious, my children, always help the Whites in their task. (cited in Bodley 1999:104)

Education was often aimed at the children of elites. These children were taught that, although they might never reach the level of the colonists, they were considerably more advanced than their uneducated countrymen. In France's African colonies, individuals who were educated and assimilated to French culture were known both by the French and by themselves as *evolues*, or evolved people. This increased the perception of the uneducated and unassimilated as being backward and primitive. Thus, schooling both reinforced the colonizers' position and created a subservient educated class convinced that it was superior to other colonial subjects (Kelly 1986).

St. Louis, MO.

Using Anthropology: Unpleasant History

Students are often taught history in ways that celebrate unity and the triumph of local, regional, or national causes. Museums and historic sites frequently gloss over unpleasant aspects of history. For example, the Jefferson National Expansion National Memorial in St. Louis is best known for Gateway Arch but also includes the Old Courthouse, the site of litigation in the Dred Scott case of 1847. That case, eventually decided by the Supreme Court in 1857, denied U.S. citizenship to African Americans, prevented the U.S. Congress from regulating slavery, and was a critical step leading to the Civil War. It's probably the most famous thing that happened at the courthouse. However, although the courthouse became a national monument in 1935, it did not devote an exhibit to Dred Scott until 2007! (Baumann et al. 2011:41).

Telling unhappy stories is often deeply problematic. People usually want their history and their heroes portrayed in the best possible light, especially when negative information might reinforce stereotypes. Many issues of community representation were evident in the interactions between the Scott Joplin House State Historic Site in St. Louis, Missouri, and its surrounding community.

Scott Joplin (1867–1917) is probably the best known ragtime composer (see Figure 13.6). Joplin was profoundly gifted and driven to succeed but he was also an African American living in a deeply racist United States. Many aspects of his life reflected this. Joplin moved to St. Louis in 1901, at a time when large numbers of African Americans were migrating from the rural South to northern and midwestern cities. In St. Louis, blacks faced hard conditions of segregation and discrimination. Joplin's neighborhood

Figure 13.6 Ragtime composer Scott Joplin lived in St. Louis, Missouri, between 1901 and 1903.

included the highest density of African American population in the city as well as some of the city's deepest poverty and worst living conditions. Although Joplin's first successful music publication "Maple Leaf Rag" appeared in 1899 and would eventually sell millions of copies, he made very little from it in these years, and his living conditions were similar to those of other impoverished African Americans. You can hear a recording of "Maple Leaf Rag" at http://bit.ly/Yt8BZ2.

The Joplin House Historic Site includes the apartment block where Joplin lived from 1901 to 1903 as well as other surrounding buildings and open spaces. Anthropologists and historians Timothy Baumann, Andrew Hurley, and Valerie Altizer, and site administrator Victoria Love worked with local residents including businesspeople, religious leaders, and educators to increase community involvement with the historic site and decide how to represent some less pleasant aspects of Joplin's life.

Bauman and his colleagues discovered three areas of community sensitivity: the facts that Joplin's apartment lacked an indoor toilet, that there were almost certainly numerous brothels nearby, and that Joplin died of syphilis. Community members feared that exhibits that mentioned these aspects of Joplin's life would encourage negative stereotypes about their neighborhood and St. Louis's African American community. The anthropologists helped historic site officials and local community members find ways to address these concerns. In each case, the solution was to place Joplin's life in broader social and economic context. In the case of sanitation, it was important to note that many of St. Louis's older neighborhoods lacked indoor plumbing in this era and that failures to modernize plumbing were the result of poverty and segregation, not the desires of people living in the neighborhood. A discussion of brothels led to an understanding of the very limited wage earning options open to women in the early 20th century and the extremely low wages they were paid. And this led to a movement to open a women's shelter and a children's safe house on the grounds of the historic site. The issue of Joplin's syphilis death was sensitive but committee members thought it was critical because syphilis was common in Joplin's era and, today, St. Louis has one of the highest syphilis rates in the nation. The response was to set age-appropriate guidelines for how and when tour guides and docents should discuss Joplin's death.

Work on the Joplin House Historic Site shows how careful attention to context, community concerns, and historical research can help us explore, understand, and come to terms with difficult aspects of our own history.

◤ Colonialism and Anthropology

The origins and practice of modern anthropology are bound up with the colonial era. Both anthropology and 19th-century colonialism are products of the 18th-century age of European enlightenment, the Industrial Revolution, the birth of modern science, and other historical and philosophical forces. For example, the evolutionary theories of 19th-century anthropologists described a world in which all societies were evolving toward perfection. This idea shows elements of enlightenment rationality (they were systematizing knowledge and trying to discover laws of social development) and 19th-century romanticism (nations were moving toward perfection). It was very clearly influenced by the scientific theories of Charles Darwin and the social Darwinism of Herbert Spencer. It was also a convenient philosophy that could be pressed into service as a rationale for colonization: Colonization could help "primitive" societies evolve (Ghosh 1991; Godelier 1993).

One of the most important impacts colonialism had on anthropology was in determining the locations of fieldwork. British Commonwealth anthropologists tended to work in British colonies, French anthropologists in their colonies, and Americans within U.S. borders, in areas "protected" by the Monroe Doctrine or in areas of American influence and control in the Pacific. In some cases, colonialism may have played a role in determining the topics of anthropological research. Studies of indigenous political systems or law were of particular interest to colonial governments. Colonialism and, more importantly, the discourse of rationalism and science also tended to promote a kind of anthropology where the anthropologist speaks as an active authority claiming to objectively describe essentially passive subjects.

In the first half of the 20th century, colonial governments faced with the practical problems of governing their possessions sometimes relied on information anthropologists provided. Anthropologists, anxious to find funding for their research, argued that their studies had practical value to colonial administrators (Malinowski 1929a, for example). However, anthropology did not come into being to promote or enable colonialism, which would have gone on with or without it (Burton 1992).

Anthropologists did not generally question the political reality of colonialism, but they often self-consciously tried to advance the interests of the people they studied. Most anthropological research was financed by private charitable organizations with reformist agendas and not by governments (Goody 1995). The result was that colonial officials generally mistrusted anthropologists, believing they were much too sympathetic to colonial subjects (Prah 1990).

▨ DECOLONIZATION, NEOCOLONIALISM, AND POSTCOLONIALISM

The eras of Western expansion and colonization radically and permanently changed the world. By the time of World War II, all peoples had been affected by Western expansion and their cultures altered by this experience. Some, attempting to resist foreign influences and protect their ways of life, had moved as far away from outsiders as possible (for example, see Breusers 1999). However, most people lived in societies where the presence and influence of outsiders, their demands for goods and labor, and their attempts to change culture were fundamental facts of life.

Most of the nations of the Americas had gained their independence in the 18th and 19th centuries. In Africa and Asia, independence from European colonialism was not achieved until after World War II (see Figure 13.7). Many nations that were part of the Soviet Union only received their independence in the late 1980s and early 1990s. Some colonies persist today, although usually with the consent of the majority of their residents. For example, Britain has some 14 "overseas territories," including Bermuda, Gibraltar, and the Pitcairn Islands. French "overseas departments" include Martinique and French Guiana. U.S. "organized unincorporated territories" include American Samoa and Guam. Many consider the U.S. relationship with Puerto Rico colonial as well (Grosfoguel 2003; Melendez 1993).

Figure 13.7 Kwame Nkrumah, Ghana's first president, proclaims independence on March 6, 1957.

National Archives Photo No. 306-RNT-57-18116

There were as many reasons for granting independence as there were for exploration and colonialism, but three are of particular importance: civil disobedience, changing political alignments, and changing economic structures.

Governing colonies was never a simple affair, and from the beginning, there was rebellion against colonial rule. Strikes, acts of terrorism, and guerrilla warfare were common throughout the colonial era. However, there was a substantial upsurge in these following World War II. One reason for this was the return of combat veterans. Veterans knew how to fight European-style warfare. Moreover, they and their supporters felt that colonizing countries owed them a deep debt for their service, a debt to be paid partially by increased political liberties.

In some places, resistance took the form of agitation and demonstrations, but in others, bitter anticolonial wars broke out. In Madagascar, for example, almost 90,000 died in a rebellion between 1947 and 1948. In Algeria, between 1954 and 1962, France fought a protracted war that left at least one-quarter of a million dead (Kepel 2005). Anticolonial wars also broke out in Vietnam, Mozambique, Angola, and numerous other places.

The end of World War II also created a fundamentally different balance of world power. European nations, which held the largest number of colonies, were greatly weakened, which left the United States and the Soviet Union as the dominant superpowers. They quickly engaged in a cold war that was to last for more than four decades, but neither nation had a strong interest in preserving the colonial status quo. Based on the belief that they could bring former colonies into their own economic and political orbit, both promoted rapid independence for colonial possessions and supplied money and weaponry to their supporters within the colonies.

Finally, international economics was also changing. In many cases, colonies had been created to allow European corporations access to areas where they could operate free of competition from those based in other nations. However, in the wake of World War II, corporate ownership began to become multinational, and corporations were less tied to their nations of origin, a move that continues today. This process undercut an important economic rationale of colonialism.

By December 1960, when the United Nations declared that "all peoples have the right to self determination" and that "immediate steps shall be taken...to transfer all powers to the peoples of [countries that have not yet achieved independence]" (UN Resolution 1514), the process of decolonization was already well underway. At that time, recently decolonized nations included India and Pakistan

(1947), Cambodia (1953), Vietnam (1954), Ghana (1957), Guinea (1958), and many others.

By the late 1970s, almost all colonies held by western European nations had achieved independence. With the formal end of the Soviet Union in 1991 and the collapse of South African apartheid in 1994, almost all areas of the world had some form of home rule. Colonized areas became independent under a variety of circumstances and with many different levels of preparedness. In some, like Ghana, the transition to independence was reasonably orderly, and a sizable (but still inadequate) number of individuals trained as administrators. In others, like Congo, the transition was profoundly violent, and very few colonial subjects had any experience with running government. But although there were great differences among colonies, all came to independence as relatively poor nations in a world that was increasingly divided into the wealthy and the poor rather than the independent and the colonized.

In the half century since most former colonies achieved independence, debate about the nature of that achievement has raged among scholars, politicians, and activists. Some scholars point to the continuing relations of dependence that often characterize former colonies and former colonizing countries. They argue that this *neocolonialism* retained the fundamental structure of the colonial world, but allowed wealthy and powerful corporations an ever greater range in which to operate. Others point to the postcolonial predicament in which many ex-colonies find themselves. Despite formal independence, colonial ways of thinking and understanding remain. Institutions, practices, and conceptual categories do not simply depart with the colonizers. Instead, they may remain as impediments to achieving a stable and prosperous nation.

The European expansion and the era of colonization were historic processes that changed the world from a collection of relatively independent economies and societies to a complex world system. The interconnections among societies have only increased since the end of colonialism. Our world today is characterized not only by enormous disparities in wealth and power but also by an increasingly dense fabric of interwoven technology, finance, communication, and politics. There is no doubt that modernity has spread to virtually all places in the world. This process of extreme globalization certainly interacts with and may replace both neocolonialism and postcolonialism. The world of the future may be a world of a single globalized modernity or, more likely, one of interconnected alternative competing modernities. However, for the foreseeable future, it is likely to be a world of societies that promise enormous hope for their people but face enormous problems and inequities as well. We turn to some of those hopes and problems in the next chapter.

BRINGING IT BACK HOME:
THE LIMITS OF TOLERANCE

One of the impacts of colonialism has been migration from colonized countries to colonizing countries. In Europe, millions of Muslims from the Middle East, North Africa, and South Asia have migrated to Britain, France, Holland, and other nations. This has sometimes resulted in cultural conflict. In Britain, a wave of riots in late 2011 involved many Muslim youths. In France, rioting, mostly by youths of North African origin shook the Paris suburbs in late October 2005, after a police chase led to the electrocution deaths of two boys. In Holland, Theo van Gogh, who made a film critical of the treatment of women in Islam, was assassinated by Mohammed Bouyeri, a Dutch-born Muslim extremist.

Many non-Muslim Europeans associate Islam with backwardness, homophobia, and oppression of women, all values that contrast with the ways Europeans generally like to see themselves. These ideas about Islam, frequently exploited by right-wing political parties (Spiegel 2010), are associated with a sharp rise in anti-Muslim sentiment as well as laws that limit the public face of Islam. In 2009, Switzerland passed a law banning the construction of minarets. In France, laws passed in 2004 and 2011 limiting public displays of religious affiliation were aimed at Muslims wearing veils and full-face coverings (though the laws also cover other religious symbols). The conservative French newspaper *Le Figaro* reports that 43 percent of those they surveyed considered Islam a threat and that support for the laws banning veils and head coverings had risen from 31 percent in 1989 to 63 percent today. Eighty-nine percent support prohibiting the veil at schools (Guénois 2012). Anti-Muslim violence has erupted in several places. The most notorious example thus far is the murder of 92 non-Muslim Norwegians—mostly children—by Anders Breivik, a deeply disturbed individual who said he was motivated by anti-Muslim prejudice. However, the problem is far greater. A reported by the European Muslim Research Centre in Britain concluded that "Muslims in the UK face a specific threat of violence and intimidation from politically motivated attackers and from gangs and individuals who are not aligned to extremist nationalism" (Lambert and Githens-Mazer 2011:33).

The idea that Muslims should assimilate to preexisting European norms dominates much of the conversation on this issue. Some analysts have argued that Muslim immigrants are poorly integrated into European societies and do not wish to adopt European traditions or ideas (for example, Wasif 2011). In fact, the data show little difference between

Muslim and non-Muslim Europeans on many issues. For example, Jackson and Doerschiler (2012:126–127) use large-scale survey techniques to show that Muslim youth in France and Britain are as supportive of European values such as individualism, equality, and secular society as their non-Muslim counterparts, and are not much different from non-Muslims on measures of isolation or alienation. Muslims did riot in Britain in 2011, but most rioters were not Muslims. Half of Dutch Muslims report they "hardly ever" go to religious services (Schmeets 2012). Thus, the issue may be more non-Muslim European attitudes toward Muslims rather than Muslims' failure to accept European values or assimilate to European culture.

The United States and Canada have longer histories of multiculturalism than Europe. Americans and Canadians frequently consider their countries to be nations of immigrant communities. However, it is not clear how tolerant of difference they actually are. For example, in 2010, the voters of Oklahoma, a state with almost no Muslim population, voted to ban Islamic law (a ban later overturned by the courts), and the 2012 Republican Party platform included a line interpreted by many as an obvious reference to banning Sharia (Seitz-Wald 2012).

Muslims comprise about 10 percent of France's population and about 4 percent and 5 percent for Britain and Holland, respectively (Kettani 2010). In the United States, less than one percent of the population is Muslim. How would non-Muslim Americans respond if Muslims made up as high a percentage of the population in the United States as they do in France, Britain, or Holland?

■ YOU DECIDE:

1. Do residents of the countries to which immigrants come have the right to demand that new arrivals adopt specific national customs?
2. Do immigrants have the right to insist that the countries in which they now live allow them practices and customs to which many members of the host culture object?
3. Are there limits to tolerance? What practices, no matter how well accepted they are in foreign cultures, do you think should not be permitted in the United States? What is the rational basis for your decision?

■ CHAPTER SUMMARY

1. To what degree is the current distribution of wealth and power in the world similar to what it was in the 15th century? The world as we see it is the result of historical processes that have moved

wealth and power from one area to another. In the 15th century, the centers of world power lay primarily in the Middle East and Asia. However, Europe was poised on the brink of a great expansion. The rise of today's wealthy nations was connected with the creation of poverty in other places in the world.

2. What were the primary motivations for European expansion? A combination of religious faith, greed, new social arrangements, and new technologies drove European expansion.

3. In what parts of the world were Europeans most successful at capturing and controlling new lands, and why? Europeans were most successful in controlling lands in the Americas because Native Americans lacked resistance to European diseases. As a result, native societies were depopulated and succumbed to European military pressure.

4. What is colonialism, and when were the main eras of European colonialism? Colonialism is the active possession of a foreign territory and the maintenance of political dominance over that territory. Europeans first colonized the Americas in the 16th century. However, elsewhere in the world, European colonization did not happen until the 19th century.

5. What were the key mechanisms Europeans used to make their control of foreign territory pay? Plunder of precious metals, the use of slave labor on monocultural plantations, and the joint stock company were all instrumental in creating wealth for Europeans. Additionally, military and diplomatic maneuvering helped draw wealth from around the world into Europe.

6. Why did Europeans colonize in the 19th century, and how did they justify taking colonial possessions? Europeans colonized because of the collapse of earlier mercantilist firms or to protect their national companies from competition from other Europeans. They wished to increase their wealth and protect their trade. They justified colonialism by calling it a civilizing mission.

7. What methods did Europeans use to try to make colonialism pay? Europeans pressed colonial subjects into forced labor on roads and other projects. They used taxation in colonial money to fund the government and force natives to participate in the European-dominated cash economy. They used education programs to discredit local culture and create a class of people who could help with colonial administration.

8. When did the colonies taken in the 19th century gain their independence, and what key factors were responsible for this? Most colonies gained their independence between the end of World War II and 1965. Civil unrest in the colonies, the emergence of the

United States and the Soviet Union as superpowers, and changes in the structure of international economics played critical roles in the timing of independence.

KEY TERMS

Colonialism	Joint stock company
Colonies	Monoculture plantation
Corvée labor	Pillage
Dutch East India Company	Tirailleurs Senegalais
Heeren XVII	VOC

The women's fashions displayed in this London shop window present a strong contrast with the dress of the female migrants from the Middle East passing by. The photograph illustrates that in the 21st century, large-scale migration is an important aspect of globalization and culture contact. Anthropology, with its emphasis on analyzing culture and culture change, helps us understand these processes.

© David Collingwood/Alamy

CHAPTER 14

CULTURE, CHANGE, AND GLOBALIZATION

LEARNING OBJECTIVES

After you have read this chapter, you will be able to:

△ Give examples of the types and degrees of economic Inequality present in the world today.

△ Compare and contrast the different models of economic development that have been popular in the last half century.

△ Assess the role of multinational corporations in the world, and give examples of the advantages and problems that attend them.

△ Summarize the role and importance of urbanization in the world, and give examples of urbanization in poor nations.

△ Evaluate the significance of population growth, and analyze the effect of government policy and economics in controlling population growth.

△ Discuss some of the key environmental challenges facing the world, and describe the differences between pollution in wealthy and poor nations.

△ Analyze the role that political instability has played in culture change.

△ Examine the relationship of globalization, migration, and refugees.

WEALTH AND POVERTY: GLOBAL PERSPECTIVES

ONSIDER an average family in North America. There probably are four family members with a combined income of more than $50,000. They live in a comfortable house or apartment and have one or two cars. Each child has a separate bedroom. They have numerous consumer goods, mostly manufactured outside North America. They have three meals a day and plenty of snacks. Much of their food is imported. The children are healthy and attend school. They can expect to complete their secondary education, probably go to college, choose among a variety of careers, and live to an average age of 77 years.

On the surface, life seems good for this family, but they have problems as well. The competitive pressures are strong and take their toll on the health of both parents. Rising medical costs, high costs for college education, job insecurity, and debt threaten their way of life. And almost all of the benefits of economic growth over the last 20 years have gone to people far wealthier than them. But on the whole, theirs is an economic status and lifestyle toward which many millions of people throughout the world seem to be aspiring.

Now consider a typical "extended" family in rural Asia. The household likely comprises ten or more people, including parents, children, and other relatives. They have a combined annual income of less than $500. They live in a one-room house as tenant farmers on a large agricultural estate owned by an absentee landlord. The adults and older children work all day on the land. None of the adults can read or write. Of the five school-age children, only two attend school regularly, and they will get only a basic primary education. They often have only one meal a day; this rarely changes and rarely is sufficient to alleviate the children's hunger pangs. The house has no electricity or fresh water supply. They have much sickness but very few medical practitioners. The work is hard, the sun is hot, and the aspirations for a better life are continually being snuffed out.

Shifting to a large city along the coast of South America, we would immediately be struck by the sharp contrast in living conditions among neighborhoods. There is a modern stretch of tall buildings, wide boulevards, and gleaming beaches, but just a few hundred yards away are squalid shanties. It is a typical Saturday evening at an hour when families should be preparing dinner. In the apartment of a wealthy family, a servant sets the table with imported china, high-quality silverware, and fine linen. The family's eldest son is home from his university in North America, and the other two children are on vacation from their boarding schools in France and Switzerland. The father is a medical doctor with a wealthy clientele. Annual vacations abroad, imported luxuries, and fine food and clothing are commonplace amenities for this fortunate family.

And what of a poor family? They live in a dirt-floor hillside shack. The stench of open sewers fills the air. No dinner table is being set; in fact, there is no dinner—only a few scraps of stale bread. The four children spend most of their time on the streets begging, shining shoes, or even trying to steal. They are recent immigrants to the city. The father has had part-time jobs but nothing permanent, and the family income is less than $1,000 a year. The children have been in and out of school many times because they have to help out financially in any way they can. Occasionally, the eldest teenage daughter seems to have some extra money, but no one asks where it comes from or how she obtains it. The contrast between these two South American families is disturbing, though similar inequalities exist in almost any other major city in the world.

Now imagine that you are in eastern Africa, where many small clusters of tiny huts dot a dry and barren land. Each cluster contains a group of extended families, all participating in and sharing the work. They have very little money because the people make and consume most of their food, shelter, and other goods themselves. They have few roads and no schools, hospitals, electricity, or water supply. In many respects, life is as difficult as for the poor family in Latin America.

But roads pass by the village bringing news of the outside world. Before long, exportable tropical fruits will be grown here, which may even end up on the dinner table of the rich South American family. Radios made in Southeast Asia playing music performed by African bands recorded in northern Europe are prized possessions. Although most people don't yet have cell phones, a few villagers use them regularly. Communication links between remote villages and the rest of the world is increasing, a process that will greatly intensify in the future.

These scenarios, adapted from Todaro and Smith's (2003) classic textbook *Economic Development*, dramatically capture some important truths. Although the historical processes described in Chapter 13 have created a global economic network, the world is not a global village. A global village suggests a relatively small place, with easily visited spaces— a place where differences are minimized, a world of screen doors, broad porches, and friendly neighbors. But we live in a world of privilege and exclusion, of rapid change and of shocking inequality. In this globalized world, some areas are hubs that are easy to reach; wealthy and powerful; and in constant communication with each other. Other places are more remote; less in contact with the rest of the world; and only reached with real difficulty. Inequality creates distances beyond those of mere distance. For example, a technology or financial specialist working in Manhattan is likely to have close ties and communicate frequently with colleagues, relatives, and friends living and working thousands of miles away, while having almost no social connections with the urban poor living within sight of their office.

Our contemporary, globalized world is a contradictory place. All around us, we see increasing cultural homogeneity: a can of soda, a CD player, cell phones and Internet access, and fast food chains. At the same time, the world is increasingly divided, with great disparities in both quality and quantity of life. More than 1.2 billion of the world's population lives on less than $1 a day, while a meal for two at a good restaurant in any American city can easily top $100. In the late 1990s, life expectancy in Japan was 81 years; in Malawi or Mozambique in Africa, it was only 37 years. In addition, although many contemporary economic forces in today's world favor cultural homogeneity, people in many places are insisting, sometimes violently, on their right to preserve their cultural identity or to create new identities intentionally separating themselves from the dominant global culture. Globalization results in many challenges, some of which we examine in this chapter.

▨ DEVELOPMENT

Gross national income (GNI): The total value of all goods and services produced in a country.

At the end of colonial rule, many newly independent nations were mired in poverty, uncontrolled urbanization, population growth, expanded immigration and emigration, ecological disaster, war, and political instability. The **gross national income** (GNI) of a nation—the total value of all its production—provides a rough estimate of national prosperity, which shows great worldwide disparities. In 2007, the GNI for the United States was $45,840, but 73 of the 208 nations listed by the World Bank had a per capita GNI of less than $5,000. For 50 of these nations, the figure was less than $2,500. In 2006, about 1 billion people were living on less than $1 a day. In the postcolonial period, during the "Cold War," both the Eastern and Western blocs saw economic development in poor countries as an opportunity to spread their political ideologies and advance their economic systems. Thus, both these political blocs provided financial and military aid to poor nations with the goals of creating political allies and stable trading partners and also to secure sources of raw materials. Additionally, some international agencies, wealthy nation governments, and thousands of private organizations involved in development projects truly hoped to bring a better life to the world's poor. Thus, the end of colonialism did not mean the end of forced cultural change, foreign intervention, or foreign influence. Instead, nations were brought into ever closer contact and the pace of change, both cultural and economic, increased.

Modernization Theory

The model of progress promoted by Western nations from the end of World War II until the 1970s was called **modernization theory**. It assumed that countries were poor because they had underdeveloped, backward economies and were dominated by traditional cultures that opposed the rational thinking demanded by modern society. Modernization theory held that poor countries needed to repeat the historic experience of wealthy countries to become wealthy themselves. Thus, foreign aid from wealthy countries was aimed at building new roads and factories to support rural industrialization; introducing new farming techniques to enable peasants to cultivate cash crops; replacing traditional exchange mechanisms of obligation and reciprocity with a market system; and increasing education to undermine irrational, culturally influenced behavior.

But poor countries were also encouraged to take large loans from governments and banks in wealthy nations. The ability of poor nations to repay these loans was based on expectations of success for the development programs they funded. This kind of development served the interests of both donors in wealthy nations and elites in poor nations. It spread the influence of wealthy nations and made new markets for their products. In poor nations, money from development aid was often used to support an elite lifestyle of exaggerated conspicuous consumption and opened many possibilities for political patronage and corruption. Most of this money did little to improve conditions for ordinary people; indeed in many cases, their poverty increased. Part of the reason for the failure of development was modernization theory itself; it not only ignored the roles that colonialism and exploitation had played in creating wealthy nations, but also ignored the complexities in moving in a single pathway from "tradition to modernity" (see, for example, Besnier 2011 for Tonga, in the Pacific).

Modernization theory: A model of development that predicts that nonindustrial societies will move in the social and technological direction of industrialized nations.

Human Needs Approaches

The failure of most economic development plans in the 1960s, explained by poverty, sickness, hunger, and illiteracy in poor nations, led to the emergence of a new approach to development, specifically, the **basic human needs approach**. Supporters of this approach argued that development could only succeed if people had access to basic necessities, such as education, pure water, and health and sanitation facilities, which were particularly urgent in isolated rural communities. Basic human needs projects continue to play an important role in foreign aid, particularly aid by nongovernmental organizations (NGOs). But human needs projects lost some prominence by the end of the 1980s, first, because although the

Basic human needs approach: Projects aimed at providing access to clean water, education, and health care for the poorest of the world's people.

projects did provide benefits to some communities, they did not create large economic growth, and second, because these projects had high overhead expenses and did not generate very much publicity for their donors. Recipient governments disliked them because they disbursed less money than more traditional modernization projects, and the groups being aided had relatively little political power. Perhaps most importantly, beginning in the 1980s, political changes in both the West and developing countries resulted in yet another approach to development.

Structural Adjustment

When the loans to poor-nation governments for financing modernization failed to produce wealth, these governments found themselves deeply in debt. At the same time, **neoliberalism**, a philosophy that holds that free markets, free trade, the free flow of capital, and minimum government regulation of the economy is the best way to increase economic and social development, was gaining strength in the United States and Europe. Neoliberals opposed state control or support of industries, and supported only the most minimal aid to impoverished individual nations. Those opposed to neoliberalism claimed it only benefitted economic elites and made the poor poorer, both in developing countries and in the United States (Harvey 2005).

Neoliberalism created a new approach to development called **structural adjustment**. Under this regime, before wealthy nations would loan money for development to poorer nations, they demanded that recipients sell off state-owned enterprises, reduce subsidies to local businesses and industries, reduce spending on education, health, and social programs, and open their markets to free trade. Most poor nations protested these policies, but they were often forced to accept them because they were in debt and needed new money to operate their governments or increase their security. This was even, or perhaps especially, the case with countries discovered to be rich in oil and natural gas like Indonesia, Venezuela, Chad, Equatorial Guinea, and Nigeria, in West Africa (Coll 2012).

The evidence indicates that the results of structural adjustment are at best, uneven. For example, a World Bank study of Africa showed that although countries adopting structural adjustment did better than those that did not, the differences were small and probably related more to political than economic factors (World Bank 2005:277). So far, structural adjustment policies have increased inequality within nations, and poverty remains an intractable problem (Greenberg 1997; Kim 2000; SAPRIN 2004).

One important organization in various modernization and development efforts was the **World Bank**. Officially called the International Bank for Reconstruction and Development, the World Bank is an international

Neoliberalism: Political and economic policies that promote free trade, individual initiative, and minimal government regulation of the economy, and oppose state control or subsidy to industries and all but minimal aid to impoverished individuals.

Structural adjustment: A development policy promoted by Western nations, particularly the United States, that requires poor nations to pursue free-market reforms in order to get new loans from the International Monetary Fund and World Bank.

World Bank: Officially called the International Bank for Reconstruction and Development, an international agency that provides technical assistance and loans to promote international trade and economic development, especially to poor nations. The World Bank has often been criticized for interfering in the affairs of these nations.

agency that provides technical assistance and loans to promote international trade and economic development, especially to poor nations. World Bank policy has changed since its creation in 1944, embracing at various times modernization theory, basic human needs projects, and structural adjustment policies. One current focus of the World Bank is poverty reduction in the poorest countries, with an emphasis on investment for economic growth that will uplift the poor.

Like development aid more generally, World Bank efforts have been widely criticized for—among other things—the failure of many of its projects; its current neoliberal emphasis has often increased poverty in poor countries, as conditions for loans insisted on reducing money spent for government social services and raising food prices. Because many World Bank projects have been bad for the environment and for public health, such as its coordination with international oil companies (see Coll 2012), they have been the target of several worldwide protests.

Development Anthropology and the Anthropology of Development

As development projects aimed more directly at improving the welfare of the poor, particularly in rural areas, the involvement of anthropologists increased, as they saw such projects as both desirable and necessary. This resulted in a new specialty: development anthropology. Development anthropologists are trained to act as intermediaries between development organizations and the recipients of aid. With their interest in the local aspects of globalization, their ethnographically based knowledge of remote communities, and their ability to provide cogent analysis and assessment, they make important contributions to development projects. In 1974, the United States Agency for International Development (USAID) employed one full-time anthropologist; by 1980, it employed more than 50 (Escobar 1997). In Haiti, for example, anthropologist and aid worker Timothy Schwartz (2008) focused on the way Haitians actually live, how they spend, and how they actually think about such issues as the family, issues not well understood by NGOs. This lack of understanding resulted in significant wastage and failure in international aid donated to Haiti, including the millions donated in response to the horrific 2010 earthquake.

The World Bank has also employed anthropologists. Its most recently appointed president is Jim Yong Kim, a medical anthropologist who is a global health expert and a cofounder with Paul Farmer of Partners In Health, which focuses on improving health in the poorest nations through HIV/AIDS and tuberculosis reduction (Hodge 2011). Responding to criticism that the World Bank prioritizes Western cultural solutions and marginalizes local cultural approaches to development, Kim emphasizes the anthropologist's view to "amplif[y] the voices of developing countries and draw[s] on the expertise and experience of the people [being] serve[d]" (Lowrey 2012). But although Kim's previous public health projects have saved many lives, he has not generally opposed or called into question the neoliberal economic policies and structures that impede solutions to improving health among the very poorest countries. And herein lies the tension in development anthropology: While engaged anthropologists strongly favor development aid, they note that development may actually reinforce the structures of inequality that create poverty in the first place, and call for programs that empower the oppressed (see Crush 1995; Pigg 2001). This may require a direct and pragmatic engagement with existing structures of power that may not appeal to all anthropologists, and perhaps explains why applied anthropology has not made the impact one would hope for.

There are successes, however: In 2008, anthropologists investigating dam construction in Laos, Turkey, and Uganda documented significant failures in the environmental and social programs that accompanied these projects, which resulted in some substantial changes to the programs (Checker 2009:165). Applied anthropologists help governments and other groups find solutions that are sensitive to local cultural traditions and respond to people's needs and aspirations (Paiement 2007). The poverty, disease, and other problems of the poor nations are social facts, aspects of human culture and human society, and thus can be changed; anthropology can play an important role in this process.

As noted previously in regard to Jim Kim and Paul Farmer's work, one of the more successful anthropological efforts has involved medical anthropologists responding to the AIDS epidemic, which is especially severe in Africa (Timberg and Halperin 2012). Unlike in the West, where AIDS is mainly related to same-sex relationships (Feldman 2009) and infected needles used by heroin addicts, ethnographic research indicates that AIDS in Africa is mainly due to heterosexual relationships (Feldman 2008; Lee and Susser 2008). This requires taking different approaches to the spread of HIV/AIDS, particularly in Africa, for example, with the prevention of AIDS through education, abstinence, and condom use (see Figure 14.1). Sometimes U.S. government aid agencies denigrate anthropological flexibility; medical anthropologist Daniel Halperin's work in

Douglas Feldman

Figure 14.1 Medical anthropologist Douglas Feldman doing field research aimed at HIV/AIDS prevention in Africa through changing normative behavior among Zambian adolescents.

Africa indicates the importance of local solutions that take into primary account the cultural specificities of those that AIDS programs serve.

And in spite of the general failure of many development projects, there are some notable successes: Child mortality before the age of 5 has decreased by 50 percent from a generation ago; life expectancy has increased 20 percent; and literacy has increased 25 percent in the past generation. The Grameen Bank, a grassroots organization founded by the Bangladeshi economist Muhammad Yunus that offers small loans to poor women, has raised the standard of living for millions of the world's poorest people.

▨ MULTINATIONAL CORPORATIONS

Businesses that own enterprises and seek to market their goods and services in more than one nation are known as **multinational corporations** (MNCs). MNCs bring employment opportunities as well as goods and services to people who otherwise would not have them. At the same time, they create major and controversial changes in the natural, economic, social, and political environments. Poor nations are particularly vulnerable to MNCs, many of whom have yearly budgets greater than those of poor-nation governments. For example, in 2005, each of the world's 20 largest MNCs had gross revenues of more than $100 billion, larger than all but 47 of the 208 countries the World Bank tracks. The financial power of these corporations enables them to exert enormous influence on poor nations and makes it extremely difficult for these nations to regulate them. In addition, like all capitalist corporations, the fundamental goal of MNCs is to return wealth to their shareholders, the vast majority of whom live in wealthy nations; thus, most MNC profits in poor nations contribute to the economy of wealthy nations.

Multinational corporation (MNC): A corporation that owns business enterprises or plants in more than one nation.

▨ Sweatshop Labor

The profits of multinational corporations are related to sweatshop production. **Sweatshops** are factories where workers, particularly women and children, are employed for long hours under difficult conditions, at low pay. South and East Asia—a sweatshop belt, which includes China, South Korea, Indonesia, Malaysia, India, and Bangladesh—account for about one-quarter of the global economy (Kristoff and WuDunn 2009). Much sweatshop production is funneled into the United States in the form of cheap consumer goods. In 2004, more than 3,000 factories in 50 nations made the clothing sold at Gap, Old Navy, and Banana Republic, all of which are owned by a single company. A study by the company itself found that between 10 percent and 25 percent of its factories in China, Taiwan, and Saipan use psychological coercion or verbal abuse,

Sweatshop: Generally, a pejorative term for a factory with working conditions that may include low wages, long hours, inadequate ventilation, and physical, mental, or sexual abuse.

and more than 50 percent of the factories in sub-Saharan Africa had inadequate safety practices (Merrick 2004). The issue of sweatshop safety standards was again brought into the spotlight when a textile factory in Bangladesh burned to the ground, killing 112 workers, mainly women and children. Not only had the factory avoided standard safety procedures, but an investigation also showed that many of the midlevel managers actually prevented workers from leaving the building after the fire had started (Manik and Yardley 2012).

In spite of gross exploitation in sweatshops, the alternatives for many of the workers are often worse. Drawn from the ranks of the landless poor, the money these workers earn, however small, is often the main support for their families. Furthermore, historically, although public protests and import restrictions aimed at sweatshops may improve conditions and wages, they may also cause a drop in sales, throwing people out of work and harming the very workers these actions are designed to help (Bhagwati 1996; Brown, Deardorff, and Stern 2003; Maskus 1997).

Sweatshops also are not limited to poor nations; as many as 175,000 people, most of them immigrant women, currently work in sweatshop conditions in the United States (Malveaux 2005). In many cases, sweatshop workers are the victims of labor law violations, and some are victims of human trafficking.

Electronics, Apple, and Foxconn

Many Westerners, including Americans, depend on computers, cell phones, and other electronics, but are unaware of the conditions under which they are made. Foxconn, a company based in Taiwan whose main production facilities are in China but also Mexico and Brazil, assembles about 40 percent of the world's electronics, employing nearly 1.2 million workers under the poorest conditions. Workers log excessive overtime, often laboring seven days a week; they live in crowded dorms—in some cases, living 20 people to a three-room apartment—and work on assembly lines that run 24 hours a day while workers stand, crouch, or sit on backless chairs all day. Some stand for so long that their legs swell and they cannot walk. Employees who arrive late are punished, and workers sometimes have to do two shifts in a row. Even with overtime, a worker earns only about $22 a day (Duhigg and Barboza 2012).

Workers who operate machines that polish iPad cases work in an area where the air is filled with aluminum particles that result from the polishing practice. Although Apple and Foxconn knew about the problem of excessive airborne aluminum dust, nothing was done to eliminate it. In fact, with the iPad newly on sale, demand was very high and the pace of work became frantic. Airborne dust can be explosive, and one day at the Chengdu factory, a series of explosions shook the building, killing 4 and injuring 18.

Although electronics made for many different companies are produced under harsh conditions, Apple, as the world's largest electronic companies, is involved in more of these issues than any other company. Apple outsources 100 percent of its manufacturing, and though it claims to hold the companies with which it does business to the highest safety standards and respect for rights of workers, yearly audits, in fact, show that these patterns are consistently violated (Chen 2012; Duhigg and Greenhouse 2012). Because of Apple's enormous economic power, it can negotiate very low prices from its suppliers. This often means that suppliers cut corners and push their workers harder. Thus far, despite substantial publicity about working conditions, Apple has successfully avoided major consumer resistance, both in the United States and in China (which is Apple's second largest market). It has done so, in part, by deflecting blame from itself to companies like Foxconn that produce its products, though under continuing pressure, especially by the *New York Times* continuing investigations (see Figure 14.2). Apple has agreed to take more action to correct some of the abuses in its production facilities (Bradsher and Duhigg (2012). Multinationals of very popular products like Apple raise questions about how such products can be produced without exploiting workers at a price American, and other Western consumers, will find acceptable. Some multinationals, like Nike, have not only improved working conditions, but are also making commitments of social responsibility to the regions in which they are located.

Figure 14.2 Foxconn, a huge Chinese company that produces electronics for companies such as Apple, has been accused of extreme sweatshop labor abuse. Here, Foxconn workers take part in a "Treasure Your life" rally, after a Foxconn worker's suicide.

Bobby Yip/Reuters

◪ URBANIZATION

In 1950, only about 16 percent of the total population of nonindustrialized nations lived in large cities. By 2000, this figure had reached 40 percent, and by 2008, more than half of the world's population lived in cities. By 2050, the world's urban population is expected to be about 6.4 billion, equal to the world's total population in 2004 (United Nations 2008:3). In 1950, seven of the world's ten largest cities (urban agglomerations) were located in Europe, Russia, Japan, and the United States, with an average population of about 6.7 million people. In 2011, only two cities in these nations made the top ten list: Tokyo and New York. The average population of the world's ten largest cities is now 20.5 million (United Nations 2012). In the future, almost all the urban population growth between now and 2050 is expected to occur in the world's poor nations (United Nations 2008:4). Some of the cities that will result will be truly enormous: By 2025, the population of Dhaka in Bangladesh will be almost 23 million; Lagos, Nigeria will be almost 19 million, and Kinshasa in the Democratic Republic of the Congo will be 14.5 million (United

Figure 14.3 More than half of the world's largest cities are in poor nations. These photographs of Rio de Janeiro, Brazil, depict the enormous contrasts between the lives of Rio's prosperous elite with most of its residents who live in abject poverty in shantytowns (right), with poor sanitation and water supply and a high crime rate.

Nations 2012). They truly will be megacities presenting an enormous challenge in providing basic services to their populations.

Urban growth is significantly affected by rural people who come to cities seeking jobs and other social, material, and cultural advantages. They are forced out of the countryside by high population levels, inability to acquire land, environmental degradation, and, sometimes, violence. When new migrants arrive in urban areas, they often find dismal living conditions. In places such as Bogota, Casablanca, Cairo, and Kolkata (Calcutta), more than half of the urban population lives in slums and squatter settlements (Todaro and Smith 2003). However, in most cases, they also have access to more amenities in these places than in the rural communities they left. As bad as life can be in places like the slums of Mumbai, for example, most people are there because they believe their lives and prospects are better than in the rural villages they left behind.

Urban life can be extremely difficult. Many of the urban poor face hunger, unsafe drinking water, inadequate or practically nonexistent sanitation facilities, substandard shelter, and environments teeming with trash. Disease and early death are rampant in the slums of the world's large cities. Also, the experience of the urban poor is not necessarily characterized by the association and solidarity that characterized, for example, poor immigrant enclaves in 19th-century America. Survival on the margins of the urban environment is often ruthlessly competitive. As Katherine Boo shows in *Behind the Beautiful Forevers* (2012), in-fighting, crime, and violence are common in deeply impoverished urban communities. People struggle for any advantage that might allow them and their children to escape deep poverty. They face laws that protect the interests of the wealthy and powerful and often force them into illegal activities merely to survive. Frequently, police, justice systems, and even religious NGOs do not provide protection and services but rather extort what little money people have. Yet, despite these difficulties, cities continue to grow. This is an index of both the truly deep poverty and desperation that characterizes so much of the rural areas of poor nations and the fervent desire of hundreds of millions of the world's poor for economic advancement. Development projects must provide adequate services, including water, sewage, education, and health care to both their rural and urban populations, however, because unless life chances and opportunities are improved in rural areas, urban development will only draw more migrants who will quickly overwhelm any improvements in services and increased economic opportunities.

▨ POPULATION PRESSURE

The rate of population growth provides a dramatic index of the increasing speed of social change. About 2 million years ago, our remote ancestors numbered perhaps 100,000. By the time the first agricultural

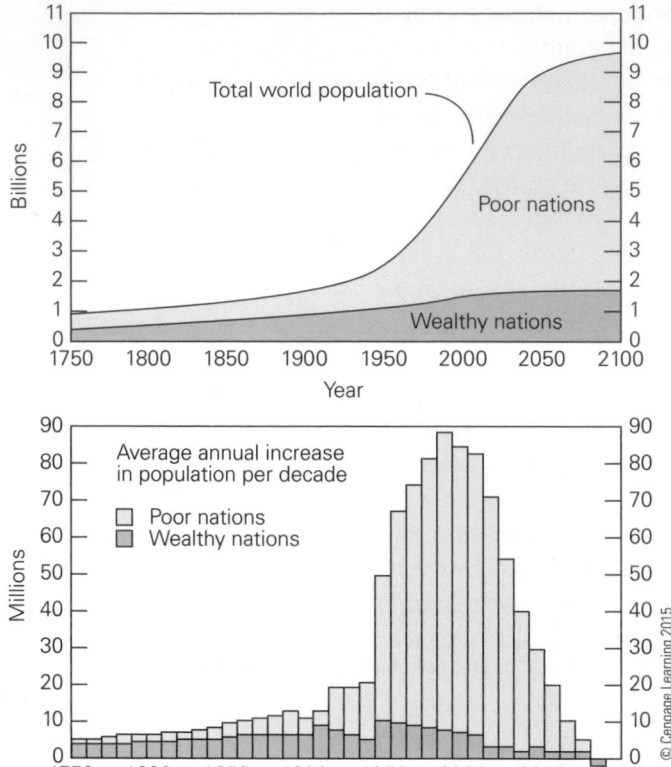

Figure 14.4 If current trends continue, world population will increase to about 10 billion by 2050 before leveling off. Most of this increase will be in poor nations.

societies were developing 10,000 years ago, world population had reached 5 to 10 million. Two thousand years ago, there were about 250 million people in the world. By 1750, this number had tripled to 750 million. Then population growth really began to accelerate. Fifty years later, in 1800, there were 1 billion people; by 1930, there were 2 billion. Since then, world population has tripled, surpassing the 6 billion mark in the summer of 1999 (Erickson 1995; Fetto 1999). In spring 2013, the world population stands at over 7.1 billion. World population continues to increase and is expected to rise to more than 10 billion by 2050 (see Figure 14.4). In the past 50 years, much of the world's population growth has taken place in poor nations; between 1950 and 2000, the population of poor nations rose by some 3 billion, a trend that is expected to continue (Geographical 2005).

In some cases, high population levels mean that the subsistence strategies people have used for years can no longer provide enough food. In parts of East Africa, for example, the amount of arable land per person declined 40 percent between 1965 and 1987 (World Bank 1992). This has resulted in important cultural changes, including land shortage and privatization of land ownership. In Tanzania, for example, in the first half of the 20th century and before, the Waluguru people gained access to land through their lineage, and the lineage head was a powerful figure. Now land must be purchased, and not only has the institution of the lineage head completely disappeared, it is hardly even remembered. As land has become scarce, women in this matrilineal society have tightened their hold over it, weakening the position of men in marriage to the point where many prefer to migrate to the cities to marry. More than 37 percent of women over 20 are now unmarried compared with 15 percent of men (Van Donge 1992).

Population explosion and the search for land and wealth have also pushed people onto land previously occupied only by indigenous groups. For example, between 1955 and 1993, the Agta, a foraging group in the Philippines, was increasingly encroached upon by loggers and migrant farmers. By 1993, the Agta had become landless migrant workers living at the lowest rung of Philippine society (Early and Headland 1998). Although nations like China have succeeded in reducing fertility through extreme population control policies, such as the one-child policy, this so skewed the population in favor of boys that many poor, rural men cannot find brides. This has led to the importation of women from poorer countries such as Myanmar and Vietnam; informal polyandry; the sale of young women; a trade in kidnapped girls; and physical and emotional abuse of women who are virtually captives in their husband's homes.

ENVIRONMENTAL CHALLENGES: POLLUTION

Ironically, even though the world's poor consume only a small fraction of the earth's resources, they also face some of the world's worst problems of pollution and environmental deterioration.

The energy consumption of the United States alone is more than 14 times the energy consumption of the entire African continent (excluding the nation of South Africa) (Harrison and Pearce 2000). Given that consumption creates pollution, one might expect that people in the United States would live in a far dirtier environment than those in Africa. But this is not the case. Consider the city of Bamako, the capital of Mali, on any late afternoon in the dry season. Most streets are unpaved, and automobiles, trucks, carts, bicycles, and foot traffic have been stirring up dust all day. Because most of the city lacks regular trash pickup or sewage, waste from humans and animals has been churned into the air. People are beginning to cook their evening meal. Many, perhaps the majority, of the city's 1.6 million residents cook either on charcoal or wood fires that consume about 1 million tons of wood a year (Cissé 2007), and the smoke from cook fires joins the dust in the air. The combined effect of smoke and dust is like a thick, hot, dry fog. Because most houses are relatively open, lacking glass windows or doors that seal, the dust permeates indoors as well as the outdoors. And Bamako's population suffers. Pollution contributes to respiratory ailments, malaria, many diseases borne by sewage-contaminated water and air, and high childhood mortality.

Figure 14.5 In Indian cities, the growth of industry and motor vehicles has given birth to a new fashion to protect local residents from dust and pollution.

Joan Young Gregg

Compare this with a similarly sized American city, say San Antonio, Texas, a city of about 1.4 million. In San Antonio, most streets are paved, and almost all homes have access to safe, publicly maintained water and sewage systems. Meals are cooked on appliances powered by electricity or gas. There is a huge amount of vehicular traffic, but cars and trucks are equipped with pollution-controlling devices. Although San Antonio is not one of the United State's wealthier cities, its population consumes many times the resources than does the population of Bamako. But almost all of San Antonio's population lives in environments that are healthier and far less polluted than Bamako.

Pollution is closely related to industrialization and globalization. Poor nations, desperate to provide some degree of prosperity to their citizens with limited amounts of capital to invest and limited means of attracting investment from abroad, use less expensive production technologies that are generally more polluting than more expensive, higher-technology processes. Therefore, industry in poor nations tends to be dirtier and more polluting than similar industries in wealthy nations. For example, China has experienced enormous economic growth but has relied extensively on lower-cost, more highly polluting industries, and at least 20 percent of the Chinese population lives in severely polluted areas. Ameliorating this problem by installing adequate pollution control in existing Chinese industries would cost $135 billion (Bremner 2006).

The financial power of multinational corporations may allow them to circumvent national laws designed to control pollution. A good example is oil production in the Niger delta in Nigeria, where gas flaring (the burning off of the natural gas that is a by-product of oil production) releases toxins into the air and releases more carbon dioxide than all the automobiles and other industry in the rest of Africa combined. Gas flaring has been illegal in Nigeria since the 1980s, but continues today because strong and wealthy corporations, using techniques that include bribery and intimidation, are able to ignore or circumvent regulations enacted by the relatively weak government (Adetunji 2006; Walker 2009). In the Niger delta, pollution has created an environmental disaster that has been instrumental in fomenting violence and civil unrest.

Global Warming

Global warming is another important aspect of ecological change caused by human activity (Intergovernmental Panel on Climate Change 2007; Oreskes 2004). Although there are some possible benefits to global warming in places like northern Europe and Russia, where it may extend the growing season through increased rainfall and reduce fuel consumption for heating, most impacts of warming are expected to be largely negative and to fall disproportionately on the poor. Many of the world's poor live in the tropics, where the effects of climate change are expected to be particularly severe. Warming may cut the growing season and reduce crop yields. The intensity of tropical storms is also expected to increase, with devastating effects. Wealthy nations have the resources to respond to climate change: They can build levees to control flooding, move their populations and their industries, and open new land to cultivation. Poor nations simply do not have the means at their disposal to do such things. Where survival is precarious today, climate change is likely to precipitate disaster (Intergovernmental Panel on Climate Change 2007).

◪ POLITICAL INSTABILITY

Political instability has had dire consequences for cultures world-wide. Although violent confrontations often occurred in traditional societies, and Western expansion was accompanied by great loss of life and culture, people in the past hundred years have unleashed more brutality on each other than at any time in earlier human history. Industrialized and wealthy societies are primarily responsible for this savagery, having created the trenches of World War I, the death camps of World War II, nuclear weapons, the Gulag, the demand for the natural resources of Africa.

The era since the end of World War II has been particularly devastating for poor nations. In some, such as French Indochina (later Vietnam), World War II faded into wars of independence that persisted until the 1970s. In many cases, traditional people became involved in networks of warfare that drew them into competition between the great powers. Both the United States and the Soviet Union furnished guerrilla movements, impoverished governments, and rebel armies with vast amounts of weaponry.

Although the end of the Cold War brought relief to some poor nations as wars fueled by great power rivalries such as those in Namibia and El Salvador came to a rapid end, rivalries that had been muted by the Cold War reemerged in new violent forms in other nations. In many places, aid from the United States, the Soviet Union, and other nations supported strong, centralized, and frequently repressive governments. When the Cold War ended, this support diminished, and governments that relied on it often fell apart. Nations such as Yugoslavia, Somalia, Liberia, and Sudan disintegrated as different groups within them fought for wealth, power, and control.

These events in Central Africa, such as Rwanda, Burundi, and the Democratic Republic of the Congo, have been particularly brutal. By the early 2000s, much of Central Africa was engulfed in what was increasingly called Africa's World War. By the late 2000s, this war was believed to have cost over 4 million lives (Prunier 2008), and no end is in sight.

◥◣ Using Anthropology: Helping Refugees

Refugees: People forcibly displaced from their homes either by conflict or persecution.

One by-product of contemporary political conflicts, human rights violations, and genocides, has been the creation of millions of **refugees**, people forcibly displaced from their homes either by conflict or persecution. Since World War II, there have been approximately 16 million refugees worldwide; this figure reached 43 million by 2010. Although we assume wealthier industrialized nations, including the United States, are the most important refugee havens, in fact, 80 percent of refugees are sheltered in poorer countries, such as Pakistan and Iran. Germany is the industrialized nation with the highest refugee population, about 500,000 (Brothers 2011).

Anthropologists are actively involved with helping and advocating for refugee populations, both in the United States and elsewhere. The film, *Well-Founded Fear,* made by anthropologists Michael Camerini and Shari Robertson, highlights the process by which refugees are granted political asylum in the United States if they can prove a "well-founded fear of persecution based on race, religion, nationality, membership in a particular social group, or political opinion." Any foreigner who comes to the United States may apply for political asylum. In 1998, immigration officers who make the decision to approve or deny political asylum applications approved 13,000 of the 41,000 applications they received.

Those seeking refugee status request asylum from the one-child policy in China; the rule that women must be veiled in Algeria; the suppression of political dissent in Romania and Nigeria; the oppression of gays in many countries; refugees fleeing from violence in Haiti and the Congo; and West African women fearful of forced genital mutilation. Iraqis are one of the newest refugee populations in the United States, driven here by the violence resulting from the U.S. invasion of Iraq in March 2003. Unlike the 900,000 Vietnamese refugees accepted in the United States after the Vietnam War, as of early 2009, only 463 Iraqis had been accepted here, with 12,000 slated for ultimate U.S. resettlement, a tiny number compared to the almost 4 million who have become refugees in countries in the Middle East. Many Iraqi refugees have settled in Detroit, where RefugeeWorks, an organization launched by anthropologists, tries to improve their chances for employment.

Another refugee group accepted into the United States, in flight from the civil wars in Sudan, are approximately 25,000 Nuer; even with the creation of the new nation of South Sudan, politically motivated violence continues, creating a disastrous humanitarian crisis (Hutchison 1996; Shandy 2007). More than 60,000 Bhutanese of Nepali ancestry have also become refugees as a result of ethnic cleansing by the king of Bhutan in the 1990s (Bird 2012).

Anthropologist Catherine Besterman, who carried out ethnography in southern Somalia now collaborates and acts as an advocate for the more than 1,000 Somali refugees who have been relocated in Lewiston, Maine, as part of an American resettlement plan for 10,000 Somali Bantu between 2004 and 2006 (Hepner 2011). Besterman teaches at Colby College and designed collaborative projects between Somali refugees and her students, creating videos and digital sites where the Somali talk about their lives and their transition to the United States. Besterman and her students also collaborate in making presentations to dispel anti-Somali and anti-refugee bias in Maine and nationally.

Other anthropologists, like Carole McGranahan (2012a; 2012b; Good 2007) testify for asylum seekers in court. McGranahan, who worked in Nepal, provides expert testimony on the current political conditions in Nepal and the cultural aspects of political conflict, on behalf of Nepalis seeking refuge in the United States. Anthropologist Mike McGovern uses his ethnographic experience in West Africa to write for the public explaining that although it is true that some refugees construct fictional narratives to gain U.S. approval, this comes out of a true desperation to flee the dire poverty and systemic violence in their home countries (2011). Advocating for refugees is one of the important ways anthropology makes a difference in the lives of real people.

MIGRATION

Widespread political, economic, and social instability combined with relatively inexpensive air travel and economic opportunity has led to a boom in international migration, particularly of people from poor nations. Today, an estimated 200 million people, 3 percent of the world's population, live outside of the countries of their birth (Martin 2007). These migrants have enormous influence both on the countries they leave and those where they settle.

When migrants leave, they often make their home communities poorer by depriving these areas of their skills and labor. High-skilled workers can earn many times their local wages through migration. It is difficult to convince people to remain in poor, unstable countries when the salaries paid for their skills may be 30 or more times higher in wealthy nations. This has led to a "brain drain" from poor nations to rich nations.

But migrants' home communities may gain as well: Migrants provide their communities of origin with connections to the rest of the world, creating a broad network of support for community members. These

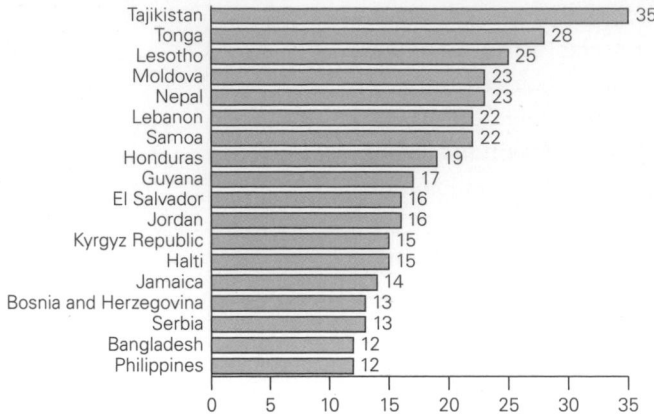

Figure 14.6 Migrant Remittance Graph: Top Remittance-Receiving Countries, 2009.

Source: The International Bank for Reconstruction and Development/The World Bank, http://siteresources.worldbank.org/INTLAC/Resources /Factbook2011-Ebook.pdf, page 14. © Development Prospects Group, World Bank.

connections bring information, ideas, products, and, perhaps most importantly, money. In 2011, the World Bank estimated that migrants sent $483 billion to people in their home countries (see Figure 14.6). Of this sum, $351 billion was sent to poor countries. India alone received $55 billion. By comparison, total U.S. humanitarian aid in 2005 was about $27 billion, almost 30 percent of which was spent in Iraq and Afghanistan (Organization for Economic Cooperation and Development 2007; World Bank 2006). In some nations, remittances from migrants constitute a substantial percentage of the national economy. For example, remittances account for 35 percent of gross domestic product (GDP) in Tajikistan, 25 percent in Lesotho, and 23 percent in Nepal (World Bank 2011).

Migrants also profoundly change the countries in which they arrive, increasing the cultural complexity of the places where they settle, while providing a pool of inexpensive labor that creates large profits for businesses in wealthy countries and low prices for consumers. However, the availability of immigrant labor also suppresses wages in their host countries.

Illegal immigrants are particularly vulnerable to exploitation. Further, although people in host countries may create programs to attract migrants in times of economic prosperity, they frequently turn against migrants in hard economic times, as happened when the world economy faltered in 2008 and 2009. In many cases, wealthy nations began offering immigrants incentives to leave. For example, Spain has offered to pay benefits to immigrants who agree to return home for at least three years (Fuchs 2008). Japan offered Latin American guest workers $3,000 toward a plane ticket to their country of origin to leave Japan on the condition that they never return (Tabuchi 2009). Although not many take these offers, those who stay face increasing discrimination. For example, Vietnamese workers in the Czech Republic increasingly face taunts and are denied admission to restaurants and clubs. In a recent poll, two-thirds of Czechs said that they would not like to have a Vietnamese person as a neighbor. This represents a substantial setback for a community that had been considered successful. Many Vietnamese immigrants speak Czech, own businesses, and have children who are extremely successful in the Czech public school system (Bilefsky 2009).

BRINGING IT BACK HOME:
AMERICA AS A FOREIGN CULTURE

A central contribution of anthropology is to develop an understanding of others, which increases our ability to reflect more deeply on our own culture. Thus, we began our text with the outsider's look at American culture in the classic article on The Nacirema (and see p. 2). With a similar goal, anthropologists Philip DeVita and James Armstrong introduce us to the responses of foreign anthropologists working in the United States, in their collection aptly called *Distant Mirrors: America as a Foreign Culture* (2002).

Perhaps because of their emphasis on individualism, Americans seem more reluctant than others to acknowledge the influence of culture on their behavior and values, believing these to be solely a matter of individual choice; indeed, many deny that there is an American culture (Cerroni Long 2002). Outsiders see it differently. Although recognizing the diversity of the United States, there appears to be a widespread consensus by foreigners on many aspects of the United States as a culture. What outsiders notice about American culture derives partly from contrasts between the United States and their culture of origin, just as our perceptions of others' cultures are derived from our own. The pragmatism, optimism, self-reliance, and voluntarism of Americans are perhaps the most widely noted, and often praised, aspects of American culture, patterns that perhaps derived from our history as both a frontier and an immigrant society.

American egalitarianism is also frequently noted, but some perceptive outsiders see subtle class differences: When the leader of the Russian Moiseyev Folk Dance Company came to the United States in the late 1950s, Sol Hurok, the impresario, asked the troup's leader "What surprised you most on your American tour?" Moiseyev replied, "In America, the workers are fat and the millionaires are thin" (Robinson 1994:355). This relationship between social class and body size still largely holds true in the United States, in contrast not just to Russia, and also to many other cultures; in India, for example, obesity was traditionally viewed as a sign of affluence.

For Asian visitors, the independence of even American toddlers is an eye opener. One anthropologist from the Philippines was amazed that American children choose their own food when the family goes out to eat in a restaurant (Ojeda 2002). A Portuguese anthropologist expressed shock at the independence of American youth: "Is it true," he asked, "that the great ambition of an eighteen-year-old youngster is to leave his

parents' house?" Jay Sokolovsky, an American ethnographer working in a Mexican village, reports that his informants were both puzzled and repelled by the American custom they had heard about, of young children having their own room, with a door they can close! A Russian visitor expressed the view that this American emphasis on freedom and autonomy "destroys families," and that Americans lack the "close . . . relationships that surround a Russian from birth." Unlike in Russia, he emphasized, "instead of spending their 50s and 60s [caring for their grandchildren] American women are busy with their own lives" (Barry 2012). And as we have noted in Chapter 9, even very elderly Americans value their independence greatly. This often means living alone or in a residential institution, without children or other relatives nearby, a situation unheard of in many cultures.

Almost all early visitors from Europe (e.g., deTocqueville 2005; Schama 2010) noted the importance of both independence and conformity in American culture, a contradiction still central in American life. On the one hand, the United States is hailed as a land of freedom of thought, speech, and expression; on the other hand, many Europeans see Americans as politically passive, lacking the activist orientation of their own countries. But this depends on where you come from: Chinese students in American colleges note that Chinese culture "teaches us to be good listeners, American values teach us to be a good speaker" (Levin 2010).

Seeing ourselves through the eyes of others helps moderate our ethnocentrism as an exceptionalist society. ". . . Americans are very patriotic," one visiting anthropologist noted, but they also have "a . . . blinding conviction that their ways are much better than the ways of other people . . . they do not [try] to understand the ways of other peoples. . . ." (Mucha 2002).

Many foreigners express awe at the material abundance of even ordinary Americans, and the desire to improve one's economic status is a main attraction for many immigrants. As one Mexican migrant explains to her son, "I am going to the United States because you can make lots of money there." An El Salvadoran agrees, "If you work hard [in the United States], you can have anything you want" (Chong 2012). And a child from Sudan joining his father was amazed that ". . . he has glass in his windows, a refrigerator, a telephone, running water and I sleep in a bed."

But some see a downside to this material abundance, claiming it results in a "mania" of consumerism, turning Americans into "permanent adolescents" concerned only about materialism and afraid of death and old age. But for people from former Communist nations, with their inferior and scarce consumer goods, extreme consumerism is a positive aspect of American culture. One Albanian migrant considered that she achieved the American Dream when she married a plastic surgeon and acquired her own credit cards. "It's not like Communism," she remarks, "the shopping is better. The sex is worse" (Prose 2011). And a student of mine from Russia once told me "Living in Russia was like a black and white film, living in America is Technicolor."

Foreigners also frequently notice the friendliness and informality of Americans, especially in small towns. An Englishman writes that the first thing he ever heard about Americans was that they all carried guns but that when he actually had direct contact with this "ferocious sounding tribe," he found out they were quite friendly (Dyer 2010). A Polish anthropologist also notes how kind, helpful, and friendly Americans are: "When I make new acquaintances, including the dental hygienist, everyone calls me by my first name" (Mucha 2002). This practice also surprised a Japanese migrant who noted: "Only my mother calls me by my first name." In Japan, except for very close friends, you call people by their last name and add "san," a term of respect (Chong 2012).

American informality spurred an international incident when Gary Locke, the newly appointed American ambassador to China, was photographed carrying his own backpack and luggage while checking in at the airline counter for his flight to his new post and carried his own luggage at the Beijing airport (Wong 2011; LaFraniere 2011). Ambassador Locke's actions, surprised—and pleased—many ordinary Chinese people, but were considered a grave insult by the political elites in China, who often live secret and very privileged lives. American informality seems allied to another American behavior pattern many foreigners note, that of complete strangers telling them the most intimate details of their lives. And a Portuguese anthropologist finds it discomforting that American men at a urinal will chat with strangers—about the weather, football, or even politics (Ramos 2002).

Sometimes, foreigners notice what might seem trivial about American behavior, but in fact, may be based on deeper cultural patterns. A recent Congolese migrant expressed amazement that "in America, people stay with their dogs in the house! In my country you cannot see this," he said. But he was even more amazed that "in the winter I see dogs putting on clothes!" (Chong and Bass 2011). Is there a culture of pets in the United States? Does it have deeper meanings? Some outsiders think so: South African President Jacob Zuma

Joan Young Gregg

In America's pet culture, even dogs get dressed up with Easter Bonnets in the Easter Parade.

recently commented about Westerners, saying that "people who loved dogs more than people had a lack of humanity," and that (black) South African dog owners were trying to "emulate whiteness."

▇ YOU DECIDE:

1. Globalization is an important source of cultural change. How have different aspects of globalization affected both American culture and the idea of American culture as unique?
2. How are the responses of foreigners to the United States shaped by the histories and cultures of the places they come from?
3. Why is it important for Americans to hear how foreigners respond to American culture? If you are a foreigner yourself, what were some of your responses to American culture?

▇ CHAPTER SUMMARY

1. Describe the level of inequality in the world, and explain how it affects wealthy and poor nations differently. Although all nations suffer inequality and poverty, these problems are particularly acute in poor nations, and have a profound effect on many of the people that anthropologists have historically studied.
2. What is development, and what different approaches have been taken to implement it? Development was the idea of creating wealth in poor nations that were considered poor because they had undeveloped economies. In the 1950s and 1960s, modernization approaches to development dominated; by the 1970s, basic human needs approaches emerged. Since the 1980s, structural adjustment programs dominate, focused on enforcing free markets as the means of development.
3. What are multinational corporations (MNCs), and how are they related to poverty? Multinational corporations own business enterprises in more than one nation. They are able to seek the most profitable venues to produce and market goods regardless of national boundaries. Because of their huge annual budgets as well as their mobility, they have gained huge economic and political power. Their Western shareholders benefit most from multinational corporations.
4. What are the major trends and problems associated with urbanization? More than half of the world's population currently lives in cities, a number expected to double in the next 40 years. In the

future, most of the world's largest cities will be in poor countries; providing services to poor people in these cities is beyond the financial capacity of many nations.

5. What are the major problems associated with overpopulation? Overpopulation is an important problem when the rate of economic growth does not keep up with rising populations. But the appropriate level of human population for any area is significantly a political question involving judgments about how best to distribute resources and the necessity for healthy environments.

6. How are problems of environmental pollution different in poor versus wealthy nations? Even though poor nations produce only a small percentage of the world's pollution, environments in poor nations frequently are more polluted than those in rich nations. Global warming negatively affects poor countries because many of these are located in ecologically fragile zones and they have limited financial resources to cope with environmental change.

7. What role does political instability play in globalization, and how is this related to migration and the search for asylum? Political instability, caused by wars of independence, the Cold War, and ethnic rivalries have destroyed cultures and societies, causing a huge increase in global migration and refugees seeking asylum.

8. How has migration changed the relationships between cultures? Very high levels of migration create enormous flows of information and money between nations. Migrants change both the societies they leave and those in which they settle, frequently enriching both. Migrants often face discrimination, alienation, and isolation in the societies where they settle.

KEY TERMS

Basic human needs approach	Refugee
Gross national income (GNI)	Structural adjustment
Modernization theory	Sweatshop
Multinational corporation (MNC)	World Bank
Neoliberalism	

GLOSSARY

achieved status: A social position that a person chooses or achieves on his or her own.

adaptation: A change in the biological structure or lifeways of an individual or population by which it becomes better fitted to survive and reproduce in its environment.

agriculture: A form of food production in which fields are in permanent cultivation using plows, animals, and techniques of soil and water control.

anime: Animation, as in the popular culture of Japan; usually refers to animation of manga, or comic book graphic art.

animism: The notion that all objects, living and nonliving, are imbued with spirits.

anthropological theory: A set of propositions about which aspects of culture are critical, how they should be studied, and what the goal of studying them should be.

anthropology: The scientific and humanistic study of human beings encompassing the evolutionary history of humanity, physical variation among humans, the study of past societies, and the comparative study of current-day human societies and cultures.

antistructure: The socially sanctioned use of behavior that radically violates social norms; frequently found in religious ritual.

applied anthropology: The application of anthropological knowledge to the solution of human problems.

archaeology: The subdiscipline of anthropology that focuses on the study of past cultures based primarily on their material remains.

art: Forms of creative expression that are guided by aesthetic principles and involve imagination, skill, and style.

artifacts (in communications studies): Communication by clothing, jewelry, tattoos, piercings, and other visible body modifications.

ascribed status: A social position into which a person is born.

authority: The ability to cause others to act based on characteristics such as honor, status, knowledge, ability, respect, or the holding of formal public office.

balanced reciprocity: The giving and receiving of goods of nearly equal value with a clear obligation of a return gift within a specified time limit.

band: A small group of people related by blood or marriage, who live together and are loosely associated with a territory in which they forage.

basic human needs approach: Projects aimed at providing access to clean water, education, and health care for the poorest of the world's people.

bhangra: A musical form originating in the folk music of Punjab in northern India and eastern Pakistan that is mixing with British pop music and reggae to become a popular form of world music.

bilateral descent: Both maternal and paternal lines are used as a basis for reckoning descent.

biological (or physical) anthropology: The subdiscipline of anthropology that focuses on the study of people from a biological perspective, primarily on aspects of humankind that are genetically inherited.

bridewealth: Goods presented by the groom's kin to the bride's kin to legitimize a marriage (formerly called "bride-price").

bureaucracy: Administrative hierarchy characterized by specialization of function and fixed rules.

call system: The form of animal communication among nonhuman primates composed of a limited number of sounds that are tied to specific stimuli in the environment.

capital: Productive resources that are used with the primary goal of increasing their owner's financial wealth.

capitalism: An economic system in which people work for wages, land and capital goods are privately owned, and capital is invested for profit.

cargo system: A ritual system common in Central and South America in which wealthy people are required to hold a series of costly ceremonial offices.

caste system: A system of stratification based on birth in which social mobility between castes is not possible.

chiefdom: A society with social ranking in which political integration is achieved through an office of centralized leadership called the chief.

chronemics: The study of the different ways that cultures understand time and use it to communicate.

clan: A unilineal kinship group whose members believe themselves to be descended from a common ancestor but who cannot trace this link through known relatives.

class: A category of people who all have about the same opportunity to obtain economic resources, power, or prestige and who are ranked relative to other categories.

class system: A form of social stratification in which the different strata form a continuum and social mobility is possible.

code-switching: Moving seamlessly and appropriately between two different languages.

cognitive anthropology: A theoretical position in anthropology that focuses on the relationship between the mind and society.

collaborative ethnography: Anthropological work that gives priority to the desires and interests of cultural consultants on the topic, methodology, and written results of fieldwork.

colonialism: The active possession of a foreign territory and the maintenance of political domination over that territory.

colony: A foreign territory under the immediate political control of a nation-state.

communitas: A state of perceived solidarity, equality, and unity among people sharing a religious ritual, often characterized by intense emotion.

comparative linguistics: The science of documenting the relationships between languages and grouping them into language families.

composite (compound) family: An aggregate of nuclear families linked by a common spouse.

conflict theory: A perspective on social stratification that focuses on economic inequality as a source of conflict and change.

consanguinity: Blood ties between people.

consultant/informant/interlocutor/ respondent/partner: A person from whom anthropologists gather data.

contagious magic: The belief that things once in contact with a person or object retain an invisible connection with that person or object.

conventionality: The notion that, in human language, words are only arbitrarily or conventionally connected to the things for which they stand.

corvée labor: Unpaid labor required by a governing authority.

cosmology: A system of beliefs that deals with fundamental questions in the religious and social order.

cross-cousin marriage: Marriage between an individual and the child of his or her mother's brother or father's sister.

cultural anthropology: The study of human thought, behavior, and lifeways that are learned rather than genetically transmitted and that are typical of groups of people.

cultural construction of gender: The idea that gender norms are the result of historical, economic, and political forces acting within each culture.

cultural defense: A legal argument that attempts to mitigate conviction and sentencing in criminal cases by invoking the influence of culture on behavior; mainly used to defend men who assault women in cases of domestic violence.

cultural ecology: A theoretical position in anthropology that focuses on the adaptive dimension of culture.

cultural relativism: The idea that cultures should be analyzed with reference to their own histories and values rather than according to the values of another culture.

culture: The learned behaviors and symbols that allow people to live in groups; the primary means by which humans adapt to their environment; the ways of life characteristic of a particular human society.

culture and personality: A theoretical position in anthropology that held that cultures could best be understood by examining the patterns of child rearing and considering their effect on social institutions and adult lives.

culture shock: Feelings of alienation and helplessness that result from rapid immersion in a new and different culture.

descent: The culturally established affiliation between a child and one or both parents.

diffusion: The spread of cultural elements from one society to another.

displacement: The capacity of all human languages to describe things not happening in the present.

divination: A religious ritual performed to find hidden objects or information.

division of labor: The pattern of apportioning different tasks to different members of a society.

dominant culture: The culture with the greatest wealth and power in a society that consists of many subcultures.

double descent: The tracing of descent through both matrilineal and patrilineal links, each of which is used for different purposes.

dowry: Presentation of goods by the bride's kin to the family of the groom or to the couple.

Dutch East India Company: A joint stock company chartered by the Dutch government to control all Dutch trade in the Indian and Pacific oceans. Also known by its Dutch initials VOC for Verenigde Ostendische Compagnie.

ecological functionalism: A theoretical position in anthropology that focuses on the relationship between environment and society.

economic system: The norms governing production, distribution, and consumption of goods and services within a society.

economics: The study of the ways in which the choices people make combine to determine how their society uses its resources to produce and distribute goods and services.

efficiency (in food production): Yield per person per hour of labor invested.

egalitarian society: A society in which no individual or group has more privileged access to resources, power, or prestige than any other.

elites: The social strata that has differential access to all culturally valued resources, whether power, wealth, or prestige, and possessively protects its control over these resources.

emic (perspective): Examination of societies using concepts, categories, and distinctions that are meaningful to members of those societies.

enculturation: The process of learning to be a member of a particular group.

endogamy: A rule prescribing that a person must marry within a particular group.

ethnicity: Perceived differences in culture, national origin, and historical experience by which groups of people are distinguished from others in the same social environment.

ethnocentrism: (ethnocentric) Judging other cultures from the perspective of one's own culture. The notion that one's own culture is more beautiful, rational, and nearer to perfection than any other.

ethnography: The major research tool of cultural anthropology, including both fieldwork among people in a society and the written results of such fieldwork.

ethnology: The attempt to find general principles or laws that govern cultural phenomena through the comparison of cultures.

ethnoscience: A theoretical position in anthropology that focuses on recording and examining the ways in which members of a culture use language to classify and organize their cognitive world.

etic (perspective): Examination of societies using concepts, categories, and rules derived from science; an outsider's perspective.

exogamy: A rule specifying that a person must marry outside a particular group.

extended family: Family based on blood relations extending over three or more generations.

firm: An institution composed of kin and/or nonkin that is organized primarily for financial gain.

foraging (hunting and gathering): Fishing, hunting, and collecting vegetable food.

functionalism: A theoretical position in anthropology that focuses on finding general laws that identify different elements of society, showing how they relate to each other, and demonstrating their role in maintaining social order.

fundamentalism: A proclamation of reclaimed authority over a sacred tradition that is to be reinstated as an antidote for a society that is believed to have strayed from its cultural moorings.

gender: A cultural construction that makes biological and physical differences into socially meaningful categories.

gender ideology: The totality of ideas about sex, gender, the natures of men and women, including their sexuality, and the relations between the genders.

gender role: The cultural expectations of men and women in a particular society, including the division of labor.

gender stratification: The ways in which gendered activities and attributes are differentially valued and related to the distribution of resources, prestige, and power in a society.

generalized reciprocity: Giving and receiving goods with no immediate or specific return expected.

globalization: The integration of resources, labor, and capital into a global network.

god (deity): A named spirit who is believed to have created or to have control of some aspect of the world.

government: An interrelated set of status roles that become separate from other aspects of social organization, such as kinship, in exercising control over a population.

great vowel shift: A change in the pronunciation of English language that took place between 1400 and 1600.

gross national income (GNI): The total value of all goods and services produced in a country.

haptics: The analysis and study of touch.

Heeren XVII: The Lords Seventeen, members of the board of directors of the Dutch East India Company.

hegemony: The dominance of a political elite based on a close identification between their own goals and those of the larger society.

hijra: An alternative gender role in India conceptualized as neither man nor woman.

historical particularism: A theoretical position in anthropology associated with American anthropologists of the early 20th century that focuses on providing objective descriptions of cultures within their historical and environmental contexts.

holism: In anthropology, an approach that considers the study of culture, history, language, and biology essential to a complete understanding of human society.

horticulture: Production of plants using a simple, nonmechanized technology and where the fertility of gardens and fields is maintained through long periods of fallow.

household: A group of people united by kinship or other links who share a residence and organize production, consumption, and distribution among themselves.

Human Relations Area Files: An ethnographic database that includes cultural descriptions of more than 300 cultures.

imitative magic: The belief that imitating an action in a religious ritual will cause the action to happen in the material world.

incest taboo: A cultural prohibition on sexual relations between relatives.

indigenous peoples: Small-scale societies designated as bands, tribes, or chiefdoms that occupied their land prior to European contact.

industrialism: The process of the mechanization of production.

informant: See *consultant*.

innovation: An object or way of thinking that is based upon but is quantitatively different from existing forms.

interlocutor: See *consultant*.

interpretive anthropology: A theoretical position in anthropology that focuses on using humanistic methods, such as those found in the analysis of literature, to analyze cultures and discover the meanings of culture to its participants.

joint stock company: A firm that is managed by a centralized board of directors but is owned by shareholders.

kinesics: The study of body position, movement, facial expressions, and gaze.

kinship: A culturally defined relationship established on the basis of blood ties or through marriage.

kinship system: The totality of kin relations, kin groups, and terms for classifying kin in a society.

kula ring: A pattern of exchange among trading partners in the South Pacific Islands.

law: A means of social control and dispute management through the systematic application of force by a politically constituted authority.

leadership: The ability to direct an enterprise or action.

leveling mechanism: A practice, value, or form of social organization that evens out wealth within a society.

levirate: The custom whereby a man marries the widow of a deceased brother.

lexicon: The total stock of words in a language.

liminal: The stage of a ritual, particularly a rite of passage, in which one has passed out of an old status but has not yet entered a new one.

lineage: A group of kin whose members trace descent from a known common ancestor.

lineal kin: Blood relations linked through descent, such as ego, ego's mother, ego's grandmother, and ego's daughter.

linguistic anthropology: The study of language and its relation to culture.

magic: A religious ritual believed to produce a mechanical effect by supernatural means.

mana: Religious power or energy that is concentrated in individuals or objects.

manga: Japanese comic book art.

market exchange: An economic system in which goods and services are bought and sold at a money price determined primarily by the forces of supply and demand.

marriage: The customs, rules, and obligations that establish a special relationship between sexually cohabiting adults, between them and any children they take responsibility for, and between the kin of the married couple.

matrilineage: A lineage formed by descent in the female line.

matrilineal descent: A rule that affiliates a person to kin of both sexes related through females only.

mediation: A form of managing disputes that uses the offices of a third party to achieve voluntary agreement between the disputing parties.

messianic: Focusing on the coming of an individual who will usher in a utopian world.

millenarian: Belief that a coming catastrophe will signal the beginning of a new age and the eventual establishment of paradise.

modernization theory: A model of development that predicts that nonindustrial societies will move in the social and technological direction of industrialized nations.

monoculture plantation: An agricultural plantation specializing in the large-scale production of a single crop to be sold on the market.

monogamy: A rule that permits a person to be married to only one spouse at a time.

monotheism: Belief in a single god.

morpheme: The smallest unit of language that has a meaning.

morphology: A system for creating words from sounds.

multiculturalism: The view that cultural diversity is a positive value that should be incorporated into national identity and public policy.

multinational corporation (MNC): A corporation that owns business enterprises or plants in more than one nation.

nation-state: A sovereign, geographically based state that identifies itself as having a distinctive national culture and historical experience.

negative reciprocity: Exchange conducted for the purpose of material advantage or the desire to get something for nothing.

neoliberalism: Political and economic policies that promote free trade, individual initiative, and minimal government regulation of the economy, and to oppose state control or subsidy to industries and all but minimal aid to impoverished individuals.

nomadic pastoralism: A form of pastoralism in which the whole social group (men, women, children) and their animals move in search of pasture.

norms: Shared ideas about the way things ought to be done; rules of behavior that reflect and enforce culture.

organic analogy: The comparison of cultures to living organisms.

parallel-cousin marriage: Marriage between the children of a parent's same-sex siblings (mother's sisters, father's brothers).

participant observation: The fieldwork technique that involves gathering cultural data by observing people's behavior and participating in their lives.

partner: See *consultant*.

pastoralism: A food-getting strategy that depends on the care of domesticated herd animals.

patriarchy: A male-dominated society in which most important public and private power is held by men.

patrilineage: A lineage formed by descent in the male line.

patrilineal descent: A rule that affiliates a person to kin of both sexes related through males only.

peasants: Rural cultivators who produce for the subsistence of their households but are also integrated into larger, complex state societies.

phone: Smallest identifiable unit of sound made by humans and used in any language.

phoneme: The smallest unit of sound that serves to distinguish between meanings of words within a language.

phonology: The sound system of a language.

pillage: To strip an area of money, goods, or raw materials through the threat or use of physical violence.

plasticity: The ability of humans to change their behavior in response to a wide range of environmental and social demands.

political ideology: The shared beliefs and values that legitimize the distribution and use of power in a particular society.

political organization: The patterned ways in which power is legitimately used in a society to regulate behavior, maintain social order, make collective decisions, and deal with social disorder.

polyandry: A rule permitting a woman to have more than one husband at a time.

polygamy: A rule allowing more than one spouse.

polygyny: A rule permitting a man to have more than one wife at a time.

polytheism: Belief in many gods.

population density: The number of people inhabiting a unit of land (usually given as people per square mile or kilometer).

postmodernism: A theoretical position in anthropology that focuses on issues of power and voice. Postmodernists hold that anthropological accounts are partial truths reflecting the backgrounds, training, and social positions of their authors.

potlatch: A form of redistribution involving competitive feasting practiced among Northwest Coast Native Americans.

power: The ability to impose one's will on others.

prayer: Any conversation held with spirits and gods in which people petition, invoke, praise, give thanks, dedicate, supplicate, intercede, confess, repent, and bless.

prestige: Social honor or respect.

priest: One who is formally elected, appointed, or hired to a full-time religious office.

private/public dichotomy: A gender system in which women's status is lowered by their almost exclusive cultural identification with the home and children, whereas men are identified with public, prestigious, economic, and political roles.

productive resources: Material goods, natural resources, or information used to create other goods or information.

productivity (food production): Yield per person per unit of land.

productivity (linguistics): The idea that humans can combine words and sounds into new, meaningful utterances they have never before heard.

proxemics: The study of the cultural use of interpersonal space.

race: A culturally constructed category based on *perceived* physical differences.

racism: The belief that some human populations are superior to others because of inherited, genetically transmitted characteristics.

rank society: A society characterized by institutionalized differences in prestige but no important restrictions on access to basic resources.

rebellion: The attempt of a group within society to force a redistribution of resources and power.

reciprocity: A mutual give-and-take among people of equal status.

redistribution: Exchange in which goods are collected and then distributed to members of a group.

refugees: People forcibly displaced from their homes either by conflict or persecution.

religion: A social institution characterized by sacred stories, symbols, and symbolism; the proposed existence of immeasurable beings, powers, states, places, and qualities; rituals and means of addressing the supernatural; specific practitioners; and change.

respondent: See *consultant*.

revolution: An attempt to overthrow an existing form of political organization and put another type of political structure in its place.

rite of intensification: A ritual structured to reinforce the values and norms of a community and to strengthen group identity.

rite of passage: A ritual that moves an individual from one social status to another.

ritual: A ceremonial act or a repeated stylized gesture used for specific occasions involving the use of religious symbols.

sacred narratives (myths): Stories of historical events, heroes, gods, spirits, and creation that members of a religious tradition hold to be holy and true.

sacrifice: An offering made to increase the efficacy of a prayer or the religious purity of an individual.

Sapir-Whorf hypothesis: The hypothesis that perceptions and understandings of time, space, and matter are conditioned by the structure of a language.

sedentary: Settled, living in one place.

semantics: The subsystem of a language that relates words to meaning.

sex: The biological differences between male and female.

shaman: An individual socially recognized as being able to mediate between the world of humanity and the world of gods or spirits but who is not a recognized official of any religious organization.

social differentiation: The relative access individuals and groups have to basic material resources, wealth, power, and prestige.

social mobility: Movement from one social strata to another.

social stratification: A social hierarchy resulting from the relatively permanent unequal distribution of goods and services in a society.

society: A group of people who depend on one another for survival or well-being as well as the relationships among such people, including their status and roles.

sociolinguistics: The study of the relationship between language and culture and the ways language is used in varying social contexts.

sororate: The custom whereby, when a man's wife dies, her sister is given to him as a wife.

state: A hierarchical, centralized form of political organization in which a central government has a legal monopoly over the use of force.

stratified society: A society characterized by formal, permanent social and economic inequality in which some people are denied access to basic resources.

structural adjustment: A development policy promoted by Western nations, particularly the United States, that requires poor nations to pursue free-market reforms in order to get new loans from the International Monetary Fund and the World Bank.

subculture: A group within a society that shares norms and values significantly different from those of the dominant culture.

subsistence strategies: The pattern of behavior used by a society to obtain food in a particular environment.

sweatshop: Generally, a pejorative term for a factory with working conditions that may include low wages, long hours, inadequate ventilation, and physical, mental, or sexual abuse.

swidden (slash-and-burn) cultivation: A form of cultivation in which a field is cleared by felling the trees and burning the brush.

symbol: Something that stands for something else. Central to language and culture.

symbolic anthropology: A theoretical position in anthropology that focuses on understanding cultures by discovering and analyzing the symbols that are most important to their members.

syncretism: The merging of elements of two or more religious traditions to produce a new religion.

syntax: A system of rules for combining words into meaningful sentences.

Tirailleurs Senegalais: Senegalese riflemen. An army that existed from

1857 to 1960, composed largely of soldiers from French African colonies led by officers from metropolitan France.

totem: An object, an animal species, or a feature of the natural world that is associated with a particular descent group.

transhumant pastoralism: A form of pastoralism in which herd animals are moved regularly throughout the year to different areas as pasture becomes available.

tribe: A culturally distinct population whose members consider themselves descended from the same ancestor.

unilineal descent: Descent group membership based on links through either the maternal or the paternal line, but not both.

universal grammar: A basic set of principles, conditions, and rules that form the foundation of all languages.

values: Shared ideas about what is true, right, and beautiful.

VOC: See Dutch East India Company.

warfare (war): A formally organized and culturally recognized pattern of collective violence directed toward other societies, or between segments within a larger society.

wealth: The accumulation of material resources or access to the means of producing these resources.

witchcraft: The ability to harm others by harboring malevolent thoughts about them; the practice of sorcery.

world art: The contemporary visual arts and cultural performances of non-Western peoples.

World Bank: Officially called the International Bank for Reconstruction and Development, an international agency that provides technical assistance and loans to promote international trade and economic development, especially to poor nations.

world music: World music incorporates different musical styles from cultures throughout the world.

REFERENCES

Abdo, Geneive, 2006. *Mecca and Main Street: Muslim Life in America after 9/11.* New York: Oxford University Press.

Abrahams, Roger D. 1970. *Deep Down in the Jungle.* Chicago: Aldine.

Adam, Karla. 2011. "Occupy Wall Street Protests Go Global." *The Washington Post,* October 15.

Adams, Kathleen M. 1990. "Cultural Commoditization in Tana Toraja, Indonesia." *Cultural Survival Quarterly* 40(1):31–34.

Adams, Kathleen M. 1995. "Making-Up the Toraja? The Appropriation of Tourism, Anthropology, and Museums for Politics in Upland Sulawesi, Indonesia." *Ethnology* 34.143–152.

Adams, Kathleen M. 2006. *Art as Politics. Re-Crafting Identities, Tourism, and Power in Tana Toraja, Indonesia.* Honolulu: University of Hawai'i Press.

Adetunji, Jimoh I. 2006. "Nigeria: An End to Gas Flaring." *E Magazine: The Environmental Magazine* 17(4):38–39.

Agha, Hussein, and Robert Malley. "This is Not a Revolution." *New York Review of Books,* November 8, 2012, pp. 42, 71.

Aker, Jenny C., and Isaac M. Mbiti. 2010. "Mobile Phones and Economic Development in Africa." *Journal of Economic Perspectives* 24(3):207–232.

Akom, A. A. 2008. "Toward an Eco-Pedagogy: Urban Youth Use Digital Media to Combat Environmental Racism." *Anthropology Newsletter,* November, p. 51.

Alexeyeff, Kalissa, and Niko Besnier. 2013. "Gender on the Edge: Identities, Politics, Transformations." In Kalissa Alexeyeff and Niko Besnier (Eds.), *Gender on the Edge: Transgender, Gay, and Other Pacific Islanders.* Honolulu: University of Hawai'i Press.

Ali, Hirsi Ayaan. 2006. *The Caged Virgin: An Emancipation Proclamation for Women and Islam.* New York: Free Press.

Allen, Theodore W. 1997. *The Invention of the White Race* (Vols. 1 and 2). London: Verso.

Allitt, Patrick N. 2002. *Victorian Britain.* Chantilly, VA: Teaching Co.

Alloula, Malek. 1986. *The Colonial Harem* (Myrna Godzich and Wlad Godzich, Trans.). Minneapolis: University of Minnesota Press.

Almond, Gabriel, Emmanuel Sivan, and R. Scott Appleby. 1995. "Fundamentalism: Genus and Species." In E. Marty and R. Scott Appleby (Eds.), *Fundamentalisms Comprehended* (pp. 399–424). Chicago: University of Chicago Press.

Alonso, Ana Maria. 1994. "The Politics of Space, Time and Substance: State Formation, Nationalism, and Ethnicity." In B. Siegel (Ed.), *Annual Review of Anthropology* (vol. 23, pp. 379–405). Stanford, CA: Stanford University Press.

American Anthropological Association. 2007. *American Anthropological Association Executive Board Statement on the Human Terrain System Project.* Available at www.aaanet.org /about/Policies/statements/Human -Terrain-System-Statement.cfm.

American Meat Institute (AMI). 2011. *The United States Meat Industry at a Glance.* Washington DC: American Meat Institute.

Ammon, Paul R., and Mary S. Ammon. 1971. "Effects of Training Black Preschool Children in Vocabulary Versus Sentence Construction." *Journal of Educational Psychology* 62(5):421–426.

Anagnost, Ana. 1989. "Transformations of Gender in Modern China." In S. Morgen (Ed.), *Gender in Anthropology: Critical Reviews for Research and Teaching* (pp. 313–342). Washington DC: American Anthropological Association.

Anderson, Benedict. 1991. *Imagined Communities: Reflections on the Origin and Spread of Nationalism.* New York: Verso.

Anderson, Elijah. 1999. *Code of the Streets.* New York: W.W. Norton.

Archibold, Randal C. 2006. "Border Fence Must Skirt Objections From Arizona Tribe." *New York Times,* September 20, p. A24.

Artz, G., P. Orazem, and D. Otto. 2007. "Measuring the Impact of Meat Packing and Processing Facilities in the Nonmetropolitan Midwest: A Difference-in-Differences Approach." *American Journal of Agricultural Economics* 89(3):557–570.

Babcock, Barbara. 1995. "Marketing Maria: The Tribal Artist in the Age of Mechanical Reproduction." In Brenda Jo Bright and Liza Bakewell (Eds.), *Looking High and Low: Art and Cultural Identity* (pp. 125–150). Tucson: University of Arizona Press.

Bagchi, Amiya Kumar. 2002. "The Other Side of Foreign Investment by Imperial Powers: Transfer of Surplus from Colonies." *Economic and Political Weekly* 37(23):2229–2238.

Bailey, Stanley. 2009. *Legacies of Race: Identities, Attitudes, and Politics in Brazil.* Stanford, Stanford University Press.

Bailey, Stanley R., and Edward E. Telles. 2006. "Multiracial versus Collective Black Categories: Examining Census Classification Debates in Brazil." *Ethnicities* 6(1):74–101.

Bajaj, Vikas, and Ron Nixon. 2006. "Subprime Loans Going from Boon to Housing Bane." *New York Times,* December 6, p. C1.

Baker, Lee D. 2000. "The First Measured Century." By Ben Wattenberg. PBS, July 19.

Balikci, Asen. 1970. *The Netsilik Eskimo.* Prospect Heights, IL: Waveland.

Balter, Michael. 2010. "Anthropologist Brings Worlds Together." *Science* 329 (August 13).

Balter, Michael. 2013. "Timbucktu Manuscripts Apparently Escaped Burning." *ScienceInsider,* January 30. Available at http://news.sciencemag.org/scienceinsider/2013/01/timbuktu-manuscripts-apparently-.html, accessed April 23, 2013.

Banks, Ralph Richard. 2011. *Is Marriage for White People: How the African American Marriage Decline Affects Everyone.* NY: Dutton.

Barfield, Thomas J. 1993. *The Nomadic Alternative.* Englewood Cliffs, NJ: Prentice Hall.

Barker, Randolph, Robert W. Herdt, and Beth Rose. 1985. The Rice Economy of Asia. Washington DC: Resources for the Future.

Barlow, Tom. 2011. "The Most Extravagant Weddings." *Forbes.com.* Available at www.forbes.com/2011/04/06/kate-middleton-prince-william-royal-weddings.html, accessed April 23, 2013.

Barnes-Dean, Virginia Lee. 1989. "Clitoridectomy and Infibulation." *Cultural Survival Quarterly* 9(2):26–30.

Barnett, Homer. 1953. *Innovation: The Basis of Cultural Change.* New York: McGraw-Hill.

Barry, Ellen. 2012. "Moscow Journal: A Hunger for Tales of Life in the American Cul-de-Sac." *New York Times,* December 11, p. A12.

Barth, Fredrik. 1998/1969. *Ethnic Groups and Boundaries: The Social Organization of Culture Difference.* Prospect Heights, IL: Waveland.

Bassani, Ezio, and William Fagg. 1988. *Africa and the Renaissance: Art in Ivory.* New York: Center for African Art.

Basso, Keith. 1979. *Portraits of "The Whitemen."* New York: Cambridge University Press.

Basson, Lauren L. 2008. *White Enough to Be an American? Race Mixing, Indigenous People, and the Boundaries of State and Nation.* Chapel Hill: University of North Carolina Press.

Baumann, Timothy, Andrew Hurley, Valerie Altizer, and Victoria Love. 2011. "Interpreting Uncomfortable History at the Scott Joplin House State Historic Site in St. Louis, Missouri." *The Public Historian* 33(2):37–66.

Bayoumi, Moustafa. 2012. "Fear and Loathing of Islam." *The Nation,* July 2–9.

Behringer, Wolfgang. 2004. *Witches and Witch Hunts: A Global History.* Cambridge, MA: Polity Press.

Bellah, Robert N., Richard Madsen, William M. Sullivan, Ann Swidler, and Steven M. Tipton. 1985. *Habits of the Heart: Individualism and Commitment in American Life.* Berkeley: University of California Press.

Bennett, Andrew. 1997. "Bhangra in Newcastle: Music, Ethnic Identity and the Role of Local Knowledge."

Innovation: The European Journal of Social Sciences 10(1):107–117.

Benzaquén, Adriana S. 2006. *Encounters with Wild Children: Temptation and Disappointment in the Study of Human Nature.* Montreal: McGill-Queen's University Press.

Berdan, Frances F. 1982. *The Aztecs of Central Mexico: An Imperial Society.* New York: Holt, Rinehart, and Winston.

Bereiter, Carl, and Siegfried Engelmann. 1966. *Teaching Disadvantaged Children in Preschool.* Englewood Cliffs: Prentice Hall.

Berlo, Janet C. (Ed.). 1996. *Plains Indian Drawings, 1865–1935: Pages from a Visual History.* New York: Abrams.

Berreman, Gerald D. 1988. "Race, Caste, and Other Invidious Distinctions in Social Stratification." In J. Cole (Ed.), *Anthropology for the Nineties: Introductory Readings* (pp. 485–518). New York: Free Press.

Besnier, Niko. 1996. "Polynesian Gender Liminality through Time and Space." In G. Herdt (Ed.), *Third Sex, Third Gender: Beyond Sexual Dimorphism in Culture and History* (pp. 285–328). New York: Zone.

Besnier, Niko. 2009. *Gossip and the Everyday Production of Politics.* Honolulu, HI: University of Hawai'i Press.

Besnier, Niko 2011. *On the Edge of the Global: Modern Anxieties in a Pacific Island Nation.* Stanford, CA: Stanford University Press.

Besnier, Niko. 2012. "The Athlete's Body and the Global Condition: Tongan Rugby Players in Japan." *American Ethnologist* 39(3):491–510.

Beteille, Andre. 1998. *Society and Politics in India: Essays in a Comparative Perspective.* New Delhi: Oxford India.

Bhagwati, Jagdish. 1996. "The Demand to Reduce Domestic Diversity among Trading Nations." In Jagdish Bhagwati and R. E. Hudec

(Eds.), *Fair Trade and Harmonization.* Cambridge: MIT Press.

Bialostok, Steve. 2009. "Revisiting Class on Campus: Patching the Pipeline." *Anthropology News,* March, p. 43.

Bickerton, Derek. 1998. "Catastrophic Evolution. The Case for a Single Step from Protolanguage to Full Human Language." In James Hurford, M. Studdert-Kennedy, and C. Knight (Eds.), *The Evolutionary Emergence of Language: Social Function and the Origins of Linguistic Form* (pp. 341–358). Cambridge: Cambridge University Press.

Bilefsky, Dan. 2009. "Czechs Cool to Presence of Workers From Asia." *New York Times,* June 7, p. 12.

Bill and Melinda Gates Foundation. n.d. "Who We Are, Foundation Fact Sheet." Available at www .gatesfoundation.org/Who-We -Are/General-Information /Foundation-Factsheet.

Bird, Kai. 2012. "The Enigma of Bhutan." *Nation.* March 26, p. 22.

Bitterli, Urs. 1986. *Cultures in Conflict: Encounters between European and Non-European Cultures, 1432–1800.* Stanford, CA: Stanford University Press.

Bittman, Mark. 2008. "The Meat of the Matter." *The Dallas Morning News,* February 10, 2008.

Blackwood, Evelyn. 1998. *Female Desires: Same-Sex Relations and Transgender Practices across Cultures.* New York: Columbia University Press.

Blumenfield, Tami. 2004. "Walking Marriages." *Anthropology Newsletter* 45(5).

Bodley, John H. 1999. *Victims of Progress* (4th ed.). Mountain View, CA: Mayfield.

Bodley, John H. 2000. *Cultural Anthropology: Tribes, States, and the Global System* (3rd ed.). Mountain View, CA: Mayfield.

Boellstorff, Tom. 2004. "Playing Back the Nation: *Waria,* Indonesian Transvestites." *Cultural Anthropology* 19:159–195.

Bonvillain, Nancy. 1997. *Language, Culture, and Communication* (2nd ed.). Englewood Cliffs, NJ: Prentice Hall.

Boo, Katherine. 2012 *Behind the Beautiful Forevers: Life, Death, and Hope in a Mumbai Undercity.* NY: Random House.

Borgerhoff Mulder, Monique. 1995. "Bridewealth and Its Correlates: Quantifying Changes over Time." *Current Anthropology* 36:573–603.

Borofsky, Robert. 1994. "On the Knowledge and Knowing of Cultural Activities." In R. Borofsky (Ed.), *Assessing Cultural Anthropology* (pp. 331–347). New York: McGraw-Hill.

Borofsky, Robert. 2005. *Yanomami: The Fierce Controversy and What We Might Learn From It.* Berkeley, CA: University of California.

Bourgois, Philippe, and Jeff Schonberg. 2009. *Righteous Dopefiend.* Berkeley: University of California Press.

Bowen, John Richard. 2007. *Why the French Don't Like Headscarves: Islam, the State, and Public Space.* Princeton: Princeton University Press.

Bowerman, M. 1996. "Learning How to Structure Space for Language: A Cross-Linguistic Perspective." In P. Bloom, M. A. Peterson, L. Nadel, and M. F. Garrett (Eds.), *Language and Space* (pp. 385–436). Cambridge, MA: MIT Press.

Bowles, Samuel, Herbert Gintis, and Melissa Osborne Groves (Eds.). 2005. *Unequal Changes: Family Background and Economic Success.* Princeton: Princeton University Press.

Boxer, C. R. 1965. *The Dutch Seaborne Empire 1600–1800.* New York: Knopf.

Boyd-Bowman, Peter. 1975. "A Sample of Sixteenth Century 'Caribbean' Spanish Phonology." In William Milan, John Staczek,

and Juan Zamora (Eds.), *1974 Colloquium on Spanish and Portuguese Linguistics* (pp. 1–11). Washington: Georgetown University Press.

Boynton, Robert S. 2006. "The Plot against Equality." Book review of *The Trouble With Diversity: How We Learned to Love Identity and Ignore Inequality,* by Walter Benn Michaels. *The Nation,* December 25, pp. 23 ff.

Bracken, Christopher. 1997. *The Potlatch Papers: A Colonial Case History.* Chicago: University of Chicago Press.

Bradsher, Keith, and Charles Duhigg. 2012. "Signs of Changes Taking Hold in Electronics Factories in China." *New York Times,* December 27, p. A1.

Brandes, Stanley. 1981. "Like Wounded Stags: Male Sexual Ideology in an Andalusian Town." In S. B. Ortner and H. Whitehead (Eds.), *Sexual Meanings: The Cultural Construction of Gender and Sexuality* (pp. 216–239). Cambridge: Cambridge University Press.

Brandt, Deborah. 2008. *Tangled Routes: Women, Work, and Globalization on the Tomato Trail* (2nd ed.). Lanham: Rowman and Littlefield.

Bremner, Brian. 2006. "What's It Going to Cost to Clean Up China?" *Business Week.* Available at www.businessweek.com /stories/2006-09-26/whats-it-going -to-cost-to-clean-up-china.

Brettell, Caroline B. 2003. *Anthropology and Migration: Essays on Transnationalism, Ethnicity, and Identity.* Walnut Creek, CA: Altamira.

Breusers, Mark. 1999. *On the Move: Mobility, Land Use and Livelihood Practices on the Central Plateau in Burkina Faso.* Münster, Hamburg and London: LIT Verlag.

Briggs, Jean L. 1991. "Expecting the Unexpected: Canadian Inuit Training for an Experimental Lifestyle." *Ethos* 19(3):259–87.

Brothers, Caroline. 2011. "U.N. Reports Steady Rise of Refugees. *New York Times,* June 20, p. A6.

Brown, Drusilla, Alan Deardorff, and Robert Stern. 2003. "The Effects of Multinational Production on Wages and Working Conditions in Developing Countries." National Bureau of Economic Research, Working Paper 9669. Cambridge, MA: National Bureau of Economic Research. Available at www .nber.org/papers/w9669.

Brown, Judith. 1965. "A Cross Cultural Study of Female Initiation Rites." *American Anthropologist* 65:837–855.

Brown, Judith. 1975. "Iroquois Women: An Ethnohistoric Note." In R. R. Reiter (Ed.), *Toward an Anthropology of Women* (pp. 235–251). New York: Monthly Review Press.

Brown, Karen McCarthy. 1991. *Mama Lola: A Vodou Priestess in Brooklyn.* Berkeley, CA: University of California Press.

Brown, Dorothy. 2009. "Two Americas, Two Tax Codes," *New York Times,* March 9, p. A23.

Brown, Patricia Leigh. 2012. "The Problem is Clear: The Water is Filthy." *New York Times,* November 14, p. A15.

Brubaker, Jack. 2012. "Falling Out of the Middle Class: When Bad Breaks Keep Piling Up." Lancaster Online. Available at http://lancasteronline .com/article/local/736404_Falling -out-of-the-middle-class--When -bad-breaks-keep-piling-up .html#ixzz2SX7pnhmp.

Brumfiel, Elizabeth. 1991. "Weaving and Cooking: Women's Production in Aztec Mexico." In J. M. Gero and M. W. Conkey (Eds.), *Engendering Archaeology: Women and Prehistory* (pp. 224–251). Cambridge, MA: Basil Blackwell.

Brumfiel, Elizabeth M. 2006. "Cloth, Gender, Continuity, and Change: Fabricating Unity in Anthropology." *American Anthropologist* 108(4): 862–877.

Bruun, Thilde Bech, Andreas de Neergaard, Deborah Lawrence, and Alan D. Ziegler. 2009. "Environmental Consequences of the Demise in Swidden Cultivation in Southeast Asia: Carbon Storage and Soil Quality." *Human Ecology* 37(3):375–388.

Bryant, Vaughn M. 2003. "Archaeology: Invisible Clues to New World Plant Domestication." *Science* 299(5609):1029–1030.

Burton, John W. 1992. "Representing Africa: Colonial Anthropology Revisited." *Journal of Asian and African Studies* 27:181–201.

Burton, Thomas G. 1993. *Serpent-Handling Believers.* Knoxville, TN: University of Tennessee Press.

Cagan, Jonathan, and Craig M. Vogel. 2002. *Creating Breakthrough Products: Innovation from Product Planning to Program Approval.* Upper Saddle River: Prentice Hall.

Hua, Cai. 2001. *A Society without Fathers or Husbands: The Na of China.* Cambridge, MA: Zone Books.

Calman, Neil, Charmaine Ruddock, Maxine Golub, and Lan Le. 2005. *Separate and Unequal: Medical Apartheid in New York City.* New York: Institute for Urban Family Health.

Canadian Broadcasting Company. 1982. *Ear Pull Hoopla. Broadcast March 21, 1982.* Available at http:// archives.radio-canada.ca/IDC-1 -41-1194-6705/sports/arcticgames /clip4.

Cancian, Frank. 1989. "Economic Behavior in Peasant Communities." In Stuart Plattner (Ed.), *Economic Anthropology* (pp. 127–170). Stanford, CA: Stanford University Press.

Cannon, Walter B. 1942. "The 'Voodoo' Death." *American Anthropologist* 44:169–180.

Carneiro, Robert. 1970. "A Theory of the Origin of the State." *Science* 169:733–738.

Carneiro, Robert. 1981. "The Chiefdom: Precursor of the State." In Grant Jones and Robert Kautz (Eds.), *The Transition to Statehood in the New World* (pp. 37–79). Cambridge: Cambridge University Press.

Carroll, Joseph. 2005. "Who Supports Marijuana Legalization?" *Gallup Poll Tuesday Briefing,* November 1.

Casasanto, Daniel. 2008. "Who's Afraid of the Big Bad Whorf? Crosslinguistic Differences in Temporal Language and Thought." *Language Learning* 58(Suppl. 1):63–79.

Cashdan, Elizabeth. 1989. "Hunters and Gatherers: Economic Behavior in Bands." In S. Plattner (Ed.), *Economic Anthropology* (pp. 21–48). Stanford, CA: Stanford University Press.

Cerroni-Long, E. L. 1993. "Teaching Ethnicity in the USA: An Anthropological Model." *Journal of Ethno-Development* 2(1):106–112.

Cerroni-Long, E. L. 1995. "Introduction." In E. L. Cerroni-Long (Ed.), *Insider Anthropology* (Napa Bulletin, Vol. 16). Washington, DC: American Anthropological Association.

Cerroni-Long, E. L. 2002. "Life and Cultures: The Test of Real Participant Observation." In Philip DeVita and James Armstrong (Eds.), *Distant Mirrors: America as a Foreign Culture* (3rd ed., pp. 148–161). Belmont, CA: Wadsworth/Cengage.

Chagnon, Napoleon. 1997. *Yanomamo* (5th ed.). Fort Worth, TX: Harcourt Brace Jovanovich.

Chagnon, Napoleon A. 2013. *Yanomamo: Legacy* (6th ed.). Belmont, CA: Wadsworth/Cengage.

Chan, Dennis, Valerie Anderson, Yolande Pijnenburg, Jennifer Whitwell, Jo Barnes, Rachael Scahill, John M. Stevens, Frederik Barkhof, Philip Scheltens, Martin Rossor, and Nick C. Fox. 2009. "The Clinical Profile of Right Temporal Lobe Atrophy." *Brain.* 132:1287–1298.

Chance, John K., and William B. Taylor. 1985. "Cofradias and Cargos: An Historical Perspective on the Mesoamerican Civil Religious Hierarchy." *American Ethnologist* 12(1):1–26.

Chance, Norman. 1990. *The Inupiat and Arctic Alaska: An Ethnography of Development.* Fort Worth, TX: Holt, Rinehart and Winston.

Chapman, Mary M. 2008. "Black Workers in Auto Plants Losing Ground." *New York Times*, December 30, p. A1.

Chavez, Leo R. 1998. *Shadowed Lives: Undocumented Immigrants in American Society.* Belmont, CA: Wadsworth.

Checker, Melissa. 2005. *Polluted Promises: Environmental Racism and the Search for Justice in a Southern Town.* New York: New York University Press.

Checker, Melissa. 2009. "Anthropology in the Public Sphere: 2008. Emerging Trends and Significant Impacts." *American Anthropologist* 111(2):162–169.

Chen, Hanqing. 2012. "Interview: Richard Brubaker on Why Apple's Problems Go Beyond Foxconn." *Asia Society.* Available at http://asiasociety.org/blog/asia/interview-richard-brubaker-why-apples-problems-go-beyond-foxconn, accessed June 8, 2012.

Chibnik, Michael. 2005. "Experimental Economics in Anthropology: A Critical Assessment." *American Ethnologist* 32(2):198–209.

Chomsky, Noam. 1965. *Syntactic Structures.* London: Mouton.

Chomsky, Noam. 1975. *The Logical Structure of Linguistic Theory.* New York: Plenum Press.

Chong, Ping. 2012. *Undesirable Elements: Real People, Real Lives, Real Theater.* New York: Theatre Communications Group.

Cissé, Almahady. 2007. "Mali: Wood—The Gift That Can't Keep On Giving." *Inter Press Service (Johannesburg),* April 13. Available at ipsnews.net/news.asp?idnews=37339.

Clark, Lauren, and Ann Kingsolver. n.d. "Briefing Paper on Informed Consent." *AAA Committee on Ethics.* Available at www.aaanet.org/committees/ethics/bp5.htm.

Clemetson, Lynette. 2006. "U.S. Muslims Confront Taboo on Nursing Homes." *New York Times*, June 13, p. A1.

Clendinnen, Inga. 1991. *Aztecs: An Interpretation.* Cambridge: Cambridge University Press.

Cleaveland, A. A., J. Craven, and M. Dadfelser. 1979. *Universals of Culture.* New York: Global Perspectives in Education.

Cohen, Yehudi. 1971. *Man in Adaptation: The Institutional Framework.* Chicago: Aldine.

Cole, Alistair, and Gino Raymond. 2006. *Redefining the French Republic.* Manchester: Manchester University Press.

Coleman, Michael C. 1999. "The Responses of American Indian Children and Irish Children to the School, 1850s–1920s: A Comparative Study in Cross-Cultural Education." *American Indian Quarterly* 23(3/4):83–112.

Coll, Steve. 2012. *Private Empire: ExxonMobil and American Power.* NY: Penguin.

Condon, Richard G., with Julia Ogina and the Holman Elders. 1996. *The Northern Copper Inuit: A History.* Toronto: University of Toronto Press.

Condry, Ian. 2005. "Must-Download TV and Cool Japan." *Anthropology Newsletter* 53 (January).

Conklin, Beth A. 1995. "'Thus Are Our Bodies, Thus Was Our Custom': Mortuary Cannibalism in an Amazonian Society." *American Ethnologist* 22(1):75–101.

Connolly, Bob, and Robin Anderson. 1987. *First Contact: New Guinea's Highlanders Encounter the Outside World.* New York: Penguin.

Conway Long, Don. 1994. "Ethnographies and Masculinities." In Harry Brod and Michael Kaufman (Eds.), *Theorizing Masculinities* (pp. 61–81). Thousand Oaks, CA: Sage.

Coquery-Vidrovitch, Catherine. 1988. *Africa: Endurance and Change South of the Sahara.* Berkeley, CA: University of California Press.

Corbett, Greville G. 2008. "Number of Genders." In Martin Haspelmath, Matthew S. Dryer, David Gil, and Bernard Comrie (Eds.), *The World Atlas of Language Structures Online.* Munich: Max Planck Digital Library, Chapter 30. Available online at wals.info/feature/30, accessed on August 19, 2010.

Costa, LeeRay, and Andrew Matzner. 2007. *Male Bodies, Women's Souls: Personal Narratives of Thailand's Transgendered Youth.* Binghamton, NY: Haworth Press.

Cotter, Holland. 2009. "Putting 'Primitive' to Rest." *New York Times*, June 5, p. C1.

Cotter, Holland. 2012. "Imperiled Legacy." *New York Times*, August 5, p. AR 1.

Covington, Dennis. 1995. *Salvation on Sand Mountain: Snake Handling and Redemption in Southern Appalachia.* Reading, MA: Addison-Wesley.

Crespin, Pamela. 2005. "The Global Transformation of Work." *Anthropology News* 46(3):20–21.

Crush, Jonathan. 1995. *The Power of Development.* New York: Routledge.

Culotta, Elizabeth. 2012. "Turning from War to Peace in Papua New Guinea." *Science* 337(6102):1593–1594.

Cunningham, Lawrence S., John Kelsay, R. Maurice Barineau, and Heather Jo McVoy. 1995. *The Sacred Quest: An Invitation to the Study of Religion* (2nd ed.). Englewood Cliffs, NJ: Prentice Hall.

Curtis, Lewis P. 1968. *Anglo-Saxons and Celts: A Study of Anti-Irish Prejudice in Victorian England.* Bridgeport: University of Bridgeport.

Curtis, Richard, Karen Terry, Meredith Dank, Kirk Dombrowski, and Bilal Kahn. 2008. "The Commercial Sexual Exploitation of Children in New York City. Vol. 1: The CSEC Population in New York City: Size, Characteristics and Needs." Report submitted to the National Institute of Justice, United States Department of Justice.

Dahl, Dick. 2008. "Forensic Linguists Make a Science of Syntax." *Massachusetts Lawyers Weekly,* April 7.

Danaher, Kevin, and Michael Shellenberger (Eds.). 1995. *Fighting for the Soul of Brazil.* New York: Monthly Review Press.

Danfulani, Umar Habila Dadem. 1999. "Exorcising Witchcraft: The Return of the Gods in New Religious Movements on the Jos Plateau and the Benue Regions of Nigeria." *African Affairs* 98(391):167–193.

Daniel, G. Reginald. 2006. *Race and Multiraciality in Brazil and the United States: Converging Paths?* University Park: Pennsylvania State University Press.

Das, Raju. 1998. "The Green Revolution, Agrarian Productivity and Labor." *International Journal of Urban and Regional Research* 22(1):122–135.

Das, Subhamoy. 2009. "Hindus Protest Sony's Hanuman Game." *Subhamoy's Hinduism Blog.* About.com: Hinduism. Available at hinduism.about.com/b/2009/04/22/hindus-protest-sonys-hanuman-game.htm, accessed August 20, 2010.

Daugherty, Mary L. 1976. "Serpent-Handling as Sacrament." *Theology Today* 33:232–243.

Deák, Istvan. 2002. "The Crime of the Century," *New York Review of Books,* September 26, p. 48.

Defoe, Daniel. 1726. *Mere Nature Delineated.* London: T. Warner.

Delcore, Henry D. 2007. "The Racial Distribution of Privilege in a Thai National Park." *Journal of Southeast Asian Studies.* 38(1):83–105.

Demian, Melissa. 2008. "Fictions of Intention in the 'Cultural Defense.'" *American Anthropologist* 110(4):432–442.

DeParle, Jason. 2012. "Two Classes, Divided by 'I Do.': Marriage for Richer; Single Motherhood, for Poorer." *New York Times,* July 15, p. A7.

deTocqueville, Alexis. 2005. *Democracy in America.* Cirencester: The Echo Library.

DeVita, Philip R., and James D. Armstrong, eds. 2002. *Distant Mirrors: America As a Foreign Culture* (3rd ed.). Belmont, CA: Wadsworth/Cengage.

De Vos, George, and Lola Romanucci-Ross. 1995. "Ethnic Identity: A Psychocultural Perspective." In Lola Romanucci-Ross and George A. De Vos (Eds.), *Ethnic Identity: Creation, Conflict, and Accommodation* (3rd ed., pp. 349–380). London: Sage.

Dickson, D. Bruce, Jeffrey Olsen, P. Fred Daum, and Mitchell S. Wachtel. 2005. "Where Do You Go When You Die? A Cross-Cultural Test of the Hypothesis That Infrastructure Predicts Individual Eschatology." *Journal of Anthropological Research* 61(1):53–79.

di Leonardo, Micaela. 1998. *Exotics at Home: Anthropologies, Others, American Modernity.* Chicago: University of Chicago Press.

di Leonardo, Micaela. 2003. "Margaret Mead and the Culture of Forgetting." *American Anthropologist* 105(3):592–595.

Dilger, Hansjorg. 2008. "'We Are All Going to Die': Kinship Belonging, and the Morality of HIV/AIDS-Related Illness and Deaths in Rural Tanzania." *Anthropological Quarterly* 81(1): 207–232.

Diamond, Jared. 1992. "The Arrow of Disease." *Discover* 13(10):64–73.

Diamond, Jared. 1998. *Guns, Germs, and Steel: The Fate of Human Societies.* New York: W.W. Norton.

Divale, William Tulio, and Marvin Harris. 1976. "Population, Warfare and the Male Supremacist Complex." *American Anthropologist* 78:521–538.

Domhoff, G. William. 2013. "Power in America: Wealth, Income, and Power." *Who Rules America?* (blog). Available at www2.ucsc.edu/whorulesamerica/power/wealth.html, accessed on April 23, 2013.

Dominguez Martin, and Pasko Rakic. 2009. "Language Evolution: The Importance of Being Human." *Nature* 462:169–170.

Dozon, Jean-Pierre. 1985. "Les Bété: une creation coloniale." In J. L. Amselle and E. M'bokolo (Eds.), *Au Coeur de l'ethnie* (pp. 49–85). Paris: Editions La Decouverte.

Duhigg, Charles, and David Barboza. 2012. "Pressure, Chinese and Foreign, Drives Changes at Foxconn." *New York Times,* February 20, B1.

Duhigg, Charles, and Steven Greenhouse. 2012. "Electronic Giant Vowing Reforms in China Plant." *New York Times,* March 29, p. 1A.

Duncan, David Ewing. 1995. *Hernando de Soto: A Savage Quest in the Americas.* New York: Crown.

Dunham, S. Ann, Alice G. Dewey, Nancy I. Cooper, and Maya Soetoro-Ng. 2009. *Surviving Against the Odds: Village Industry in Indonesia.* Durham, NC: Duke University Press.

Durkheim, Émile. 1961/1915. *The Elementary Forms of the Religious Life.* New York: Collier.

Durrenberger, E. Paul. 2001. "Explorations of Class and Consciousness in the U.S." *Journal of Anthropological Research* 57(1):41–60.

Durrenberger, E. Paul, and Dimitra Doukas. 2008. "Gospel of Wealth, Gospel of Work: Counterhegemony in the U.S. Working Class." *American Anthropologist* 110(2): 214–224.

Dyer, Geoff. 2010. "My American Friends." *New York Times Book Review*, p. 23.

Earle, Timothy K. 1987. "Chiefdoms in Archaeological and Ethnological Perspective." *Annual Reviews in Anthropology* 16:279–308.

Early, John D., and Thomas N. Headland. 1998. *Population Dynamics of a Philippine Rain Forest People: The San Ildefonso Agta*. Gainesville, FL: University Press of Florida.

Eckert, Penelope. 1989. *Jocks and Burnouts: Social Categories and Identity in the High School*. New York: Teacher's College Press.

Eckert, Penelope. 2000. *Linguistic Variation as Social Practice*. Oxford: Blackwell.

Eckert, Penelope. 2004. "Language and Gender in Adolescence." In Janet Holmes and Miriam Meyerhoff (Eds.), *The Handbook of Language and Gender. Blackwell Reference Online*. Available at http://is.muni.cz /el/1423/podzim2012/SAN230 /um/the_handbook_of_language _and_gender.pdf, accessed May 28, 2010.

Economist, The. 2008. "The Good Consumer." Jan. 17.

Economist, The. 2011 (August 20). "The Flight from Marriage." Available at www.economist.com/node /21526329, accessed June 8, 2012.

Economist, The. 2013 (January 14). "Beijing's Air Pollution: Blackest Day."

Eggan, Fred. 1950. *The Social Organization of Western Pueblos*. Chicago: University of Chicago Press.

El-Feki. 2013. *Sex and the Citadel: Intimate Life in a Changing Arab World*. NY: Pantheon.

Eller, Jack David. 2006. *Violence and Culture: A Cross-Cultural and Interdisciplinary Approach*. Belmont, CA: Wadsworth.

El Saadawi, Nawal. 1980. *The Hidden Face of Eve*. London: Zed Books.

Elkin, A. P. 1967. "The Nature of Australian Totemism." In J. Middleton (Ed.), *Gods and Rituals* (pp. 159–176). Garden City, NY: Natural History Press.

Ember, Carol. 1983. "The Relative Decline in Women's Contribution to Agriculture with Intensification." *American Anthropologist* 85(2): 285–304.

Ember, Carol R., and Melvin Ember. 2005. "Explaining Corporal Punishment of Children: A Cross-Cultural Study." *American Anthropologist* 107(4):609–619.

Ember, Melvin, and Carol R. Ember. 1971. "The Conditions Favoring Matrilocal vs. Patrilocal Residence." *American Anthropologist* 73:571–594.

Engelmann, Siegfried, and Therese Engelmann. 1966. *Give Your Child a Superior Mind: A Program for the Preschool Child*. New York: Simon and Schuster.

Ensminger, Jean. 2002. "Experimental Economics: A Powerful New Method for Theory Testing in Anthropology." In Jean Ensminger (Ed.), *Theory in Economic Anthropology* (pp. 59–78). Walnut Creek: Altamira.

Escobar, Arturo. 1997. "The Making and Unmaking of the Third World through Development." In M. Rahnema and V. Bawtree (Eds.). *The Post-Development Reader* (pp. 263–273). Atlantic Highlands, NJ: Zed Books.

Estioko-Griffin, Agnes. 1986. "Daughters of the Forest." *Natural History* 5:37–42.

Eurostat. 2012. "Total Fertility Rate." Available at http://epp.eurostat .cc.europa.eu/tgm/table.do?tab =table&plugin=1&language =en&pcode=tsdde220, accessed June 8, 2012.

Evans, Peter. 2000. "Fighting Marginalization with Transnational Networks: Counter Hegemonic Globalization." *Contemporary Sociology* 29:230–241.

Evans Pritchard, E. E. 1958/1937. *Witchcraft, Oracles, and Magic among the Azande*. Oxford: Clarendon Press.

Evans-Pritchard, E. E. 1968/1940. *The Nuer*. Oxford: Clarendon Press.

Ewing, Katherine Pratt (Ed.). 2008a. *Being and Belonging: Muslims in the United States since 9/11*. New York: Russell Sage Foundation.

Ewing, Katherine Pratt. 2008b. *Stolen Honor: Stigmatizing Muslim Men in Berlin*. Stanford, CA: Stanford University Press.

Fábrega, Horacio. 1997. *Evolution of Sickness and Healing*. Berkeley, CA: University of California Press.

Fadiman, Anne. 1997. *The Spirit Catches You and You Fall Down: A Hmong Child, Her American Doctors, and the Collision of Two Cultures*. New York: Farrar, Straus, and Giroux.

Fadiman, Anne. 2012. "Lia Lee: A Disabled Life that Changed the Face of Western Medicine." By Joyce Hackel (producer), *The World,* Public Radio International, December 21.

Feinberg, Richard. 1986. "Market Economy and Changing Sex-Roles on a Polynesian Atoll." *Ethnology* 25:271–282.

Feinberg, Richard. 1994. "Contested Worlds: Politics of Culture and the Politics of Anthropology." *Anthropology and Humanism* 19:20–35.

Feldman, Douglas, ed. 2008. *AIDS, Culture and Africa*. Gainesville, FL: University of Florida Press.

Feldman, Douglas A. (Ed.). 2009. *AIDS, Culture, and Gay Men*. Gainesville, FL: University of Florida Press.

Ferguson, R. Brian. 1992. "A Savage Encounter: Western Contact and the Yanomamo War Complex."

In R. B. Ferguson and N. L. Whitehead (Eds.), *War in the Tribal Zone: Expanding States and Indigenous Warfare* (pp. 199–227). Santa Fe, NM: School of American Research Press.

Ferraro, Gary P. 1994. *The Cultural Dimension of International Business* (2nd ed.). Englewood Cliffs, NJ: Prentice-Hall.

Fetto, John. 1999. "Six Billion Served." *American Demographics* June:14.

Flamm, Bruce L. 2002. "Faith Healing by Prayer: Review of Cha, KY, Wirth, DP, Lobo, RA. Does Prayer Influence the Success of In Vitro Fertilization-Embryo Transfer?" *The Scientific Review of Alternative Medicine* 6(1):47–50.

Fletcher, Michael A. 2013. "Ranks of Working Poor Increasing." *Washington Post*, January 15.

Fluehr-Lobban, Carolyn. 2005. "Cultural Relativism and Universal Rights in Islamic Law." *Anthropology News* 46(9):23.

Fondacaro, Steve, and Montgomery McFate. 2008. "In Memoriam— Michael Bhatia." Available at http://humanterrainsystem.army.mil/bhatia.html.

Forbes. 2009a. "NBA Team Valuations #1 Los Angeles Lakers." Available at www.forbes.com/lists/2009/32/basketball-values-09_Los-Angeles-Lakers_320250.html, accessed August 20, 2010.

Forbes. 2009b. "The 400 Richest Americans: #37 Philip Anschutz." Available at www.forbes.com/lists/2009/54/rich-list-09_Philip-Anschutz_DSAK.html, accessed August 20, 2010.

Forbes. 2010. "SportsMoney: Kobe Bryant: King of the Court." Available at blogs.forbes.com/sportsmoney/2010/06/18/kobe-bryant-king-of-the-court, accessed August 20, 2010.

Ford, James D, Barry Smit, and Johanna Wandel. 2006.

"Vulnerability to Climate Change in the Arctic: A case study from Arctic Bay, Canada." *Global Environmental Change* 16:145–60.

Fordham, Signithia. 1999. "Dissin' 'the Standard': Ebonics and Guerrilla Warfare at Capital High." *Anthropology & Education Quarterly* 30(3):272–293.

Foster, Don. 2003. "The Message in the Anthrax." *Vanity Fair,* October.

Foster, Robert J. 1991. "Making National Cultures in the Global Ecumene." *Annual Reviews of Anthropology* 20:235–260.

Fox, Margalit. 2012. "Lia Lee Dies: Life Went on around Her, Redefining Care." *New York Times,* September 14.

Frankenberg, Ruth. 1993. *White Women, Race Matters: The Social Construction of Whiteness.* Minneapolis: University of Minnesota Press.

Freed, David. 2010. "The Wrong Man." *The Atlantic,* May.

Freed, Stanley. 2012. *Anthropology Unmasked: Museums, Science, and Politics in New York City. Vols. I and II.* Wilmington, Ohio: Orange Frazer Press.

Freeland, Chrysia. 2012. "The Self-Destruction of the 1 Percent." *New York Times,* October 14, p. SR 5.

French, Howard W. 2006. "Rush for Wealth in China's Cities Shatters the Ancient Assurance of Care in Old Age." *New York Times,* November 3, p. A8.

French, Jan Hoffman. 2010. "Book review of *Legacies of Race: Identities, Attitudes, and Politics in Brazil.*" American *Anthropologist* 112(3):447.

Freyre, Gilberto. 1946. *The Masters and the Slaves: A Study in the Development of Brazilian Civilization.* New York: Knopf.

Fried, Morton. 1967. *The Evolution of Political Society.* New York: Random House.

Friedheim, William, with Ronald Jackson (Eds.). 1996. *Freedom's*

Unfinished Revolution: An Inquiry into the Civil War and Reconstruction. New York: New Press.

Friedl, Ernestine. 1975. *Women and Men: An Anthropologist's View.* New York: Holt, Rinehart and Winston.

Friedman, Jonathan. 1992. "The Past in the Future: History and the Politics of Identity." *American Anthropologist* 94:837–859.

Fry, Douglas P., and Kaj Bjorkqvist (Eds.). 1997. *Cultural Variation and Conflict Resolution: Alternatives to Violence.* Mahwah, NJ: Erlbaum.

Fuchs, Dale. 2008. "Spain to Pay Immigrants to Leave." *The Guardian,* July 21. Available at www.guardian.co.uk/world/2008/jul/21/spain.

Gardner, Gerald Brosseau. 1949. *High Magic's Aid.* London: Michael Houghton.

Gates, Henry Louis, Jr. 2011. *Black in Latin America.* New York: NYU Press.

Bill and Melinda Gates Foundation. n.d. "Who We Are, Foundation Fact Sheet." Available at www.gatesfoundation.org/Who-We-Are/General-Information/Foundation-Factsheet.

Gaudio, Rudolf Pell. 2009. *Allah Made Us: Sexual Outlaws in an Islamic African City.* West Sussex, UK: Wiley-Blackwell.

Geertz, Clifford. 1973a. "Deep Play: Notes on the Balinese Cockfight." In C. Geertz (Ed.), *The Interpretation of Cultures* (pp. 412–453). New York: Basic Books.

Geertz, Clifford (Ed.). 1973b. *The Interpretation of Cultures.* New York: Basic Books.

Geertz, Clifford. 2008/1973. "Deep Play: Notes on a Balinese Cockfight." In R. Jon McGee and Richard L. Warms (Eds.), *Anthropological Theory: An Introductory History.* Boston: McGraw Hill.

Gell, Alfred. 1993. *Wrapping in Images: Tatooing in Polynesia.* Oxford: Clarendon Press.

Geographical. 2005. "The Fertile Century." *Geographical* 77(3):50–51.

Ghosh, Anjan. 1991. "The Structure of Structure, or Appropriation of Anthropological Theory." *Review* 14(1):55–77.

Gibbs, James L., Jr. 1988. "The Kpelle Moot: A Therapeutic Model for the Informal Settlement of Disputes." In J. B. Cole (Ed.), *Anthropology of the Nineties* (pp. 347–359). New York: Free Press.

Gibbs, W. Wayt. 2002. "Saving Dying Languages." *Scientific American* 287:78–86.

Gibson, Margaret A. 1997. "Ethnicity and School Performance: Complicating the Immigrant/Involuntary Minority Typology." *Anthropology and Education Quarterly* 28(3):431–454.

Gibson, Margaret A., and John Ogbu. 1991. *Minority Status and Schooling: A Comparative Study of Immigrant and Involuntary Minorities.* New York: Garland.

Gilbert, Dennis. 2011. *The American Class Structure in an Age of Growing Inequality* (8th ed.). Thousand Oaks, CA: Pine Forge Press.

Gilbert, Matthew. 2007. "Farewell, Sweet Ice." *The Nation,* May 7, pp. 26–27.

Gilbert, Aubrey L. Terry Regier, Paul Kay, and Richard B. Ivry. 2006. "Whorf Hypothesis is Supported in the Right Visual Field but Not the Left." *PNAS* 103(2):489–494.

Gilmore, David D. 1990. *Manhood in the Making: Cultural Concepts of Masculinity.* New Haven, CT: Yale University Press.

Gilmore, David D. 1996. "Above and Below: Toward a Social Geometry of Gender." *American Anthropologist* 98:54–66.

Glazer, Nathan, and Daniel P. Moynihan. 1970. *Beyond the Melting Pot* (2nd ed.). Cambridge, MA: MIT.

Gmelch, George. 2000. "Baseball Magic." In James Spradley and David McCurdy (Eds.), *Conformity and Conflict* (pp. 322–331). Boston: Allyn and Bacon.

Godelier, Maurice. 1993. "L'Occident, miroir brisé: une evaluation partielle de l'anthropologie sociale assortie de quelques perspectives." *Annales* 48:1183–1207.

Goldschmidt, Walter R. 1986. *The Sebei: A Study in Adaptation.* New York: Holt, Reinhart and Winston.

Goldstein, Donna. 1999. "'Interracial' Sex and Racial Democracy in Brazil: Twin Concepts?" *American Anthropologist* 101:563–578.

Good, Anthony. 2007. *Anthropology and Expertise in the Asylum Courts.* NY: Routlege-Cavendish.

Goodale, J. 1971. *Tiwi Wives.* Seattle, WA: University of Washington Press.

Goody, Jack. 1995. *The Expansive Moment: Anthropology in Britain and Africa 1918–1970.* Cambridge: Cambridge University Press.

Gordon, Peter. 2004. "Numerical Cognition Without Words: Evidence from Amazonia." *Science* 306(5695):496–499.

Gottlieb, Anna. 2002. "Interpreting Gender and Sexuality: Approaches from Cultural Anthropology." In Jeremy MacClancey (Ed.), *Exotic No More: Anthropology on the Front Lines* (pp. 167–189). Chicago: University of Chicago Press.

Graburn, Nelson H. H. (Ed.). 1976. *Ethnic and Tourist Arts: Cultural Expressions from the Fourth World.* Berkeley, CA: University of California Press.

Graham, Laura R. 2006. "Anthropologists Are Obligated to Promote Human Rights and Social Justice: Especially among Vulnerable Communities." *Anthropology News* 47(7):4–5.

Graham, Laura, Alexandra Jaffe, Bonnie Urciuoli, and David Valentine. 2007. "Why Anthropologists Should Oppose English Only Legislation in the U.S." *Anthropology News* 48(1):32–33.

Gramsci, Antonio. 1971. *Selections from the Prison Notebook,* ed. And trans. By Quentin Hoare and Geoffry Nowell Smith. London: Lawrence and Wishart.

Green, Lisa J. 2002. *African American English: A Linguistic Introduction.* Cambridge UK: Cambridge University Press.

Greenberg, James B. 1997. "A Political Ecology of Structural-Adjustment Policies: The Case of the Dominican Republic." *Culture & Agriculture* 19(3):85–93.

Greene, Candace W. 2001. *Silver Horn: Master Illustrator of the Kiowas.* Norman: University of Oklahoma.

Greenhalgh, Susan. 2007. "China's Future With Fewer Females." *China From the Inside.* Washington, DC: Public Broadcasting Service. Available at www.pbs.org/kqed/chinainside/women/population.html.

Greenhouse, Steven. 2013. "Productivity Climbs, but Wages Stagnate." *New York Times,* January 13, p. sr 5.

Grosfoguel, Ramon. 2003. *Colonial Subjects: Puerto Ricans in a Global Perspective.* Berkeley: University of California Press.

Guénois, Jean-Marie. 2012. "L'image de l'islam se dégrade fortement en France." *Le Figaro,* October 24.

Guillermoprieto, Alma. 2006. "A New Bolivia?" *New York Review of Books* 53(13):36.

Gutmann, Matthew C. 1996. *The Meanings of Macho: Being a Man in Mexico City.* Berkeley, CA: University of California Press.

Hacker, Andrew. 2012. "We're More Unequal Than You Think." *New York Review of Books,* February 23, p. 34.

Hacker, Jacob. 2002. *The Divided Welfare State: The Battle over Public and Private Social Benefits in the United States.* New York: Cambridge.

Hadden, Jeffrey K., and Anson Shupe. 1989. "Is There Such a

Thing as Global Fundamentalism?" In Jeffrey K. Hadden and Anson Shupe (Eds.), *Secularization and Fundamentalism Reconsidered* (pp. 109–122). New York: Paragon House.

Haharidge, Dale, photographs by Michael Williamson. 2011. *Someplace Like American: Tales from the New Great Depression.* Berkeley: University of California.

Hale, Sondra. 1989. "The Politics of Gender in the Middle East." In S. Morgen (Ed.), *Gender and Anthropology: Critical Reviews for Research and Teaching* (pp. 246–267). Washington, DC: American Anthropological Association.

Halperin, Rhoda H. 1990. *The Livelihood of Kin: Making Ends Meet "The Kentucky Way."* Austin, TX: University of Texas Press.

Handler, Richard. 1988. *Nationalism and the Politics of Culture in Quebec.* Madison, WI: University of Wisconsin Press.

Hansen, Edward C. 1995. "The Great Bambi War: Tocquevillians versus Keynesians in an Upstate New York County." In J. Schneider and R. Rapp (Eds.), *Articulating Hidden Histories: Exploring the Influence of Eric R. Wolf* (pp. 142–155). Berkeley, CA: University of California Press.

Harrell, Steven. 2002. "Review of *A Society without Fathers or Husbands: The Na of China,* by Cai Hua." *American Anthropologist* 104(3):982–983.

Harries, Patrick. 1987. "The Roots of Ethnicity: Discourse and the Politics of Language Construction in South-East Africa." *African Affairs* 87:25–52.

Harris, Marvin. 1966. "The Cultural Ecology of India's Sacred Cattle." *Current Anthropology* 7:51–66.

Harris, Marvin. 1989. *Our Kind: Who We Are, Where We Came From, Where We Are Going.* New York: Harper Perennial.

Harrison, Faye V. 2009. "The Paradox of Democracy in the New Racial Domain." *Anthropology News,* January, p. 15.

Harrison, Paul, and Fred Pearce. 2000. *AAAS Atlas of Population and Environment,* Victoria Dompka Markham (Ed.). American Association for the Advancement of Science and the University of California Press. Available at atlas .aaas.org/.

Hart, C. W. M. 1967. "Contrasts between Pre-Pubertal and Post-Pubertal Education." In R. Endelman (Ed.), *Personality and Social Life* (pp. 275–290). New York: Random House.

Hart, C. W. M., and Arnold R. Pilling. 1960. *The Tiwi of North Australia.* New York: Holt, Rinehart and Winston.

Hartigan, John. 1997. "Establishing the Fact of Whiteness." *American Anthropologist* 99:495–505.

Harvey, David. 2005. *A Brief History of Neoliberalism.* NY: Oxford University Press.

Haskins, Ron, Julie Isaacs, and Isabel Sawhill. 2008. "Getting Ahead or Losing Ground: Economic Mobility in America." Economic Mobility Project. The Pew Foundation. Available at www .brookings.edu/multimedia /video/2008/0220_mobility _sawhill.aspx.

Hauptman, William. 1985. "Renoir's Master." *EMR* 15:48–66.

Hayden, Brian, and Suzanne Villeneuve. 2011. "A Century of Feasting Studies." *Annual Review of Anthropology* 40:433–449.

Hays, Kelly E. 2011. *Holy Harlots: Femininity, Sexuality, and Black Magic in Brazil.* Berkeley: University of California Press.

Hearn, Maxwell K. 1996. *Splendors of Imperial China: Treasures from the National Palace Museum, Taipei.* New York: Metropolitan Museum of Art.

Hedges, Chris, and Joe Sacco. 2012. *Days of Destruction, Days of Revolt.* New York: Nation Books.

Hepner, Tricia Redeker. 2011. "Collaborative Anthropology Comes to Life: Catherine Besteman and the Somali Bantu Experience." *AA* Vol. 113(2, June):346.

Henrich, Joseph, Robert Boyd, Samuel Bowles, Colin Camerer, Ernst Fehr, and Herbert Gintis. 2004. *Foundations of Human Sociality: Economic Experiments and Ethnographic Evidence from 15 Small-Scale Societies.* Oxford: Oxford University Press.

Herdt, Gilbert H. 1981. *Guardians of the Flutes: Idioms of Masculinity.* New York: McGraw-Hill.

Herdt, Gilbert H. 1987. *The Sambia.* New York: Holt, Rinehart and Winston.

Herdt, Gilbert H. (Ed.). 1996. *Third Sex, Third Gender: Beyond Sexual Dimorphism in Culture and History.* New York: Zone.

Hester, Marianne. 1988. "Who Were the Witches?" *Studies in Sexual Politics* 26–27:1–22.

Higuchi, Takayasu, and Gina Barnes. 1995. "Buddhist Cave Temples in Afghanistan." *World Archaeology* 27(2):282–302.

Hill, Jane H. 1998. "Language, Race, and White Public Space." *American Anthropologist* 100:680–689.

Hinman, Dristen. 2011. "Lost Boys." *The Village Voice* LVI(344):11.

Hitt, Jack. 2012. "Words on Trial: Can Linguistics Solve Crimes that Stump Police?" *The New Yorker,* July 23.

Hobsbawm, Eric, and Terence Ranger (Eds.). 1983. *The Invention of Tradition.* Cambridge: Cambridge University Press.

Hochschild, Adam. 1998. *King Leopold's Ghost.* New York: Houghton Mifflin.

Hochschild, Adam. 2005. "In the Heart of Darkness." *New York Review of Books,* October 6, pp. 39–42.

Hodge, G. Derrick. 2011. "Walking the Line between Accommodation and Transformation: Evaluating the Continuing Career of Jim Yong Kim." *AA*, Vol. 113, no. 1, p. 148.

Hoebel, E. Adamson. 1960. *The Cheyennes: Indians of the Great Plains.* New York: Holt.

Hoebel, E. Adamson. 1974. *The Law of Primitive Man.* New York: Henry Holt.

Hollenberg, K. 2006. "Vascular Action of Cocoa Flavanols in Humans: The Roots of the Story. *Journal of Cardiovascular Pharmacology* 47(suppl 2:s99–102):119–121.

Holthouse, David. 2005. "Arizona Showdown." *Southern Poverty Law Center Intelligence Report,* Summer.

Horowitz, Irving L. (Ed.). 1967. *The Rise and Fall of Project Camelot.* Cambridge, MA: MIT Press.

Horst, Heather A., and Daniel Miller. 2006. *The Cell Phone: An Anthropology of Communication.* New York: Berg.

Howe, James. 2012. "Chocolate and Cardiovascular Health: The Kuna Case Reconsidered." *Gastronomica* 12(1):43–52.

Howell, Signe. 1989. "To Be Angry Is Not to Be Human but to Be Fearful Is: Chewong Concepts of Human Nature." In Signe Howell and Roy Willis (Eds.), *Societies at Peace: Anthropological Perspectives* (pp. 45–59). London: Routledge.

Huber, Brad, William F. Danaher, and William Breedlove. 2011. "New Cross-Cultural Perspectives on Marriage Transactions." *Cross-Cultural Research* 45(4):339–375.

Hughey, Matthew W. 2009. "Cinethetic Racism: White Redemption and Black Stereotypes in 'Magical Negro' Films." *Social Problems* 56(3):543–577.

Human Rights Watch. 2001. *Human Rights in Saudi Arabia: A Deafening Silence.* Available at hrw.org /backgrounder/mena/saudi/.

Human Rights Watch. 2004 "'Political Shari'a'? Human Rights and Islamic Law in Northern Nigeria. *Human Rights Watch* 16(9)A.

Intergovernmental Panel on Climate Change. 2007. "Summary for Policymakers." In Solomon, S., D. Qin, M. Maning, Z. Chen, M. Marquis, K. B. Averyt, M Tignor, and H. L. Miller (Eds.), *Climate Change 2007: The Physical Science Basis. Contributions of Working Group I to the Fourth Assessment Report of the Intergovernmental Panel on Climate Change.* Cambridge: Cambridge University Press.

Investment Company Institute. 2005. *Equity Ownership in America.* Washington, DC: Investment Company Institute.

Isaacman, Allen. 1996. *Cotton Is the Mother of Poverty: Peasants, Work, and Rural Struggle in Colonial Mozambique (1938–1961).* Portsmouth, NH: Heinemann.

Ishemo, Shubi L. 1995. "Cultural Response to Forced Labour and Commodity Production in Portugal's African Colonies." *Social Identities* 1(1):95–110.

Jackson, P. 1999. *Lady Boys, Tom Boys, Rent Boys: Male and Female Homosexualities in Contemporary Thailand.* Binghamton, NY: Haworth Press.

Jackson, Pamela I., and Peter Doerschler. 2012. *Benchmarking Muslim Well-Being in Europe: Reducing Disparities and Polarizations.* Bristol (UK): Policy Press.

Jacobs, Andrew, and Adam Century. 2012. "As China Ages, Beijing Turns to Morality Tales to Spur Filial Devotion." *New York Times,* September 6, p. A11.

Jelly-Schapiro, Joshua. 2009. "The Bob Marley Story." *New York Review of Books,* April, pp. 34–37.

Jennings, Ken. 2013. "Is Your Electric Fan Trying to Kill You?" *Slate.com,* January 22.

Johnstone, Brick, and Bret A. Glass. 2008. "Support for a Neuropsychological Model of Spirituality in Persons with Traumatic Brain Injury." *Zygon* 43(4):861–74.

Jonaitis, Aldona (Ed.). 1991. *Chiefly Feasts: The Enduring Kwakiutl Potlatch.* Seattle. University of Washington Press.

Jones, Maggie. 2012. "Postville, Iowa, Is Up For Grabs." *New York Times,* July 11.

Judt, Tony. 2005. *Postwar: A History of Europe Since 1945.* New York: Penguin.

Kaplan, Flora E. S. (Ed.). 1997. *Queens, Queen Mothers, Priestesses, and Power: Case Studies in African Gender.* New York: New York Academy of the Sciences.

Kapur, Akash. 2012. *India Becoming: A Portrait of Life in Modern India.* NY: Riverhead.

Karkazis, Katrina. 2008. *Fixing Sex: Intersex, Medical Authority, and Lived Experience.* Durham, NC: Duke University Press.

Karlen, Arno. 1995. *Man and Microbes: Disease and Plagues in History and Modern Times.* New York: G. P. Putnam's Sons.

Katrak, Ketu H. 2002. "Changing Traditions: South Asian Americans and Cultural/Communal Politics." *Massachusetts Review* 43(1):75–88.

Kaufman, Stuart. 2001. *Modern Hatreds: The Symbolic Politics of Ethnic War.* New York: Cornell University Press.

Kawano, Satsuki. 2010. *Nature's Embrace: Japan's Aging Urbanites and New Death Rites.* Honolulu: University of Hawai'i Press.

Kelly, Gail P. 1986. "Learning to Be Marginal: Schooling in Interwar French West Africa." *Journal of Asian and African Studies* 21:171–184.

Kelley, Heidi. 1991. "Unwed Mothers and Household Reputation in a Spanish Galician Community." *American Ethnologist.* 18(3):565–580.

Kennedy, Maev. 2011. "Peter the Wild Boy's Condition Revealed

200 Years After His Death." *The Guardian,* March 20.

Kenny, Mary. 2007. *Hidden Heads of Households: Child Labor in Urban Northeast Brazil.* Peterborough, Ontario: Broadview Press.

Kepel, Gilles. 2005. *The Roots of Radical Islam.* London: Saqi.

Kettani, Houssain. 2010. "Muslim Population in Europe: 1950–2020." *International Journal of Environmental Science and Development* 1(2):154–164.

Kilbride, Philip L. 2004. "Plural and Same Sex Marriage." *Anthropology News* 45(5):17.

Kilbride, Philip L. 2006. "African Polygyny: Family Values and Contemporary Changes." In Aaron Podolefsky and Peter J. Brown (Eds.), *Applying Cultural Anthropology: An Introductory Reader* (5th ed., pp. 201–208). Mountain View, CA: Mayfield.

Kilbride, Philip. 2010. "A Cultural and Gender Perspective on Marginal Children on the Streets of Kenya." *Childhood in Africa* 2(1):38–47.

Kluckhohn, Clyde. 1959. "The Philosophy of the Navaho Indians." In M. H. Fried (Ed.) *Readings in Anthropology* (vol. 2). New York: Crowell.

Kim, Jim Yong, Joyce V. Millen, Alec Irwin, and John Gershman. 2000. *Dying for Growth: Global Inequality and the Health of the Poor.* Monroe, ME: Common Courage Press.

Kimmel, Michael. 1996. *Manhood in America: A Cultural History.* NY: Free Press.

Kimmelman, Michael. 2007. "In Marseille, Rap Helps Keep the Peace." *New York Times,* December 19, p. C1.

Klein, Laura F. 1976. "'She's One of Us, You Know': The Public Life of Tlingit Women: Traditional, Historical, and Contemporary Perspectives." *Western Canadian Journal of Anthropology* 6(3):164–183.

Klein, Laura F. 1995. "Mother as Clanswoman: Rank and Gender in Tlingit Society." In L. F. Klein and L. A. Ackerman (Eds.), *Women and Power in Native North America* (pp. 28–45). Norman, OK: University of Oklahoma Press.

Klinenberg, Eric. 2012a. *Going Solo: The Extraordinary Rise and Surprising Appeal of Living Alone.* NY: Penguin.

Klinenberg, Eric. 2012b. "One's a Crowd." *New York Times,* February 5, p. SR4.

Kluckhohn, Clyde. 1959. "The Philosophy of the Navaho Indians." In M. H. Fried (Ed.), *Readings in Anthropology* (Vol. 2). New York: Crowell.

Kluckhohn, Clyde, and Florence Kluckhohn. 1947. "American Culture: Generalized Organization and Class Patterns." In Lyman Bryson, Louis Finkelstein, and R. M. Maciver (Eds.), *Conflicts of Power in Modern Culture: Symposium Conference in Science Philosophy and Religion* (pp. 106–128). New York: Harper.

Kofinas, Gary. 2007. *Subsistence Hunting in a Global Economy.* Available at http://arcticcircle.uconn.edu /NatResources/subsistglobal.html, accessed June 12, 2007.

Kohn, Hans. 1958. "Reflections on Colonialism." In R. Strausz-Hupe and H. W. Hazard (Eds.), *The Idea of Colonialism* (pp. 2–16). New York: Praeger.

Kottak, Conrad P. 1992. *Assault on Paradise: Social Change in a Brazilian Village* (2nd ed.). New York: McGraw-Hill.

Kramer, Sarah. 2011. "Three Generations, One Roof." *New York Times,* September 25, p. MB1.

Krause, J., C. Lalueza-Fox, L. Orlando, W. Enard, R. E. Green, H. A. Burbano, J. J. Hublin, C. Hanni, J. Fortea, M. de la Rasilla, J. Bertranpetit, A. Rosas, and S. Paabo. 2007. "The Derived FOXP2 Variant of Modern Humans was Shared with Neandertals." *Current Biology* 17(21):1908–1912.

Krauss, Michael E. 1992. "The World's Languages in Crisis." *Language* 68(1): 6–10.

Kreider, Rose M., and Renee Ellis. 2011. "Living Arrangements of Children: 2009." Current Population Reports, P70-126. U.S. Census Bureau.

Kristoff, Nicholas, and Sheryl WuDunn. 2000. "The Cheers for Sweatshops." *New York Times,* September 24.

Kristof, Nicholas D., and Sheryl WuDunn. 2009. *Half the Sky: Turning Oppression into Opportunity for Women Worldwide.* New York: Knopf.

Kulick, Don. 1998. *Travesti: Sex, Gender, and Culture among Brazilian Transgendered Prostitutes.* Chicago: University of Chicago Press.

Kumar, G. Stanley Jaya. 1995. *Tribals from Tradition to Transition: A Study of Yanadi Tribes of Andhra Pradesh.* New Delhi: M. D. Publications.

Labov, William. 1972. *Language in the Inner City.* Philadelphia: University of Pennsylvania Press.

Labov, William, Sharon Ash, and Charles Boburg. 2005. *Atlas of North American English: Phonetics, Phonology and Sound Change.* Berlin: Mouton de Gruyter.

LaFraniere, Sharon. 2011. "Chinese Flock to U.S. Envoy, but Leaders Are Ruffled." *New York Times,* November 12, p. A5.

Lamb, Sarah. 2009. *Aging and the Indian Diaspora: Cosmopolitan Families in India and Abroad.* Bloomington, IN: Indiana University Press.

Lambert, Robert, and Jonathan Githens-Mazer. 2011. *Islamophobia and Anti-Muslim Hate Crime: UK Case Studies 2010.* Exeter (UK): University of Exeter, European Muslim Research Center.

Lamphere, Louise (Ed.). 1992. *Structuring Diversity: Ethnographic Perspectives on the New Immigration.* Chicago: University of Chicago Press.

Lamphere, Louise. 2005. "The Domestic Sphere of Women and the Public World of Men: The Strength and Limitations of an Anthropological Dichotomy." In Caroline B. Brettell and Carolyn F. Sargent (Eds.), *Gender in Cross-Cultural Perspective* (4th ed., pp. 86–94). Upper Saddle River, NJ: Pearson/Prentice Hall.

Lapidus, Ira M. 1988. *A History of Islamic Societies.* Cambridge: Cambridge University Press.

Lareau, Annette. 2003. *Unequal Childhoods: Class, Race, and Family Life.* Berkeley, CA: University of California.

Lassiter, Luke Eric. 2004. "Collaborative Ethnography." *AnthroNotes* 25(1):1–9.

Leacock, Eleanor Burke. 1981. *Myths of Male Dominance.* New York: Monthly Review Press.

Leathers, Dale G. 1997. *Successful Nonverbal Communication* (3rd ed.). Boston: Allyn and Bacon.

LeDuff, Charlie. 2006. "Dreams in the Dark at the Drive-Through Window." *New York Times,* November 27, p. A12.

Lee, Richard B. 2000. "Indigenism and Its Discontents: Anthropology and the Small Peoples at the Millennium." Keynote address at the annual meeting of the American Ethnological Society, Tampa, Florida, March 2000.

Lee, Richard B. 2003. *The Dobe Ju/'hoansi* (3rd ed.). Belmont, CA: Wadsworth.

Lee, Richard B., and Ida Susser. 2008. "Confounding Conventional Wisdom: The Ju/'hoansi and HIV/AIDS." In Douglas A. Feldman (Ed.), *AIDS, Culture, and Africa.* Gainesville, FL: University of Florida Press.

Lefever, Harry G. 1996. "When the Saints Go Riding In: Santeria in Cuba and the United States." *Journal for the Scientific Study of Religion* 35:318–330.

Lepowsky, Maria. 1993. *Fruit of the Motherland: Gender in an Egalitarian Society.* New York: Columbia University Press.

Leshkowich, Ann Marie. 2011. "Making Class and Gender: (Market) Socialist Enframing of Traders in Ho Chi Minh City." *American Anthropologist* 113(2):277–290.

Lessinger, Johanna. 2013. "'Love' in the Shadow of the Sewing Machine: A Study of Marriage in the Garment Industry of Chennai, South India." In Shalini Grover, Ravinder Kaur, and Rajni Paltriwalla (Eds.), *Marriage in Globalizing Contexts: Exploring Change and Continuity in South Asia.* Delhi: Orient Blackswan.

Levin, Dan. 2010. "The China Boom." *New York Times,* November 7, p. 16.

Levine, Mark, and Penny Roberts (Eds.). 1999. *The Massacre in History.* New York: Berghahn.

Levine, Mary Ann, and Rita Wright. 1999. "COSWA Corner." *Society for American Archaeology Bulletin* 17(2).

Levinson, David. 1989. "Family Violence in Cross-Cultural Perspective." *Frontiers of Anthropology* (vol. 1). Newbury Park, CA: Sage.

Levinson, David. 1996. *Religion: A Crosscultural Dictionary.* New York: Oxford University Press.

Lévi-Strauss, Claude. 1969/1949. *The Elementary Structures of Kinship.* Boston: Beacon Press.

Lewchuk, Wayne A. 1993. "Men and Monotony: Fraternalism as a Managerial Strategy at the Ford Motor Company." *Journal of Economic History* 53(4):824–856.

Lewis, Herbert S. 2001. "The Passion of Franz Boas." *American Anthropologist* 103(2):447–467.

Lewis, Richard D. 1996. *When Cultures Collide: Managing Successfully across Cultures.* London: Nicholas Brealey.

Lewis, Tom. 1991. *Empire of the Air: The Men Who Made Radio.* New York: Harper Perennial.

Lexington. 2005. "Minding about the Gap." *The Economist,* June 9.

Liebow, Elliot. 1967. *Tally's Corner: A Study of Negro Street Corner Men.* Boston: Little, Brown.

Lindstrom, Lamont. 1993. *Cargo Cult: Strange Stories of Desire from Melanesia and Beyond.* Honolulu, HI: University of Hawaii Press.

Lindquist, Danille Christensen. 2006. "'Locating' the Nation: Football Game Day and American Dreams in Central Ohio." *Journal of American Folklore* 119(4):444–488.

Lipsitz, George 1994. *Dangerous Crossroads: Popular Music, Postmodernism, and the Poetics of Place.* London: Verso.

Lobao, Linda, and Katherine Meyer. 2001. "The Great Agricultural Transition: Crisis, Change, and Social Consequences of Twentieth Century U.S. Farming." *Annual Review of Sociology* 27:103–124

Lockwood, Victoria. 2005. "The Impact of Development on Women: The Interplay of Material Conditions and Gender Ideology." In Caroline B. Brettell and Carolyn F. Sargent (Eds.), *Gender in Cross Cultural Perspective* (4th ed., pp. 500–514). Upper Saddle River, NJ: Prentice Hall.

Los Angeles Times. 2011. "Justin Bieber's Hair Sells for $40.668 on EBay." March 2.

Lovejoy, Paul E. 1983. *Transformations in Slavery: A History of Slavery in Africa.* Cambridge: Cambridge University Press.

Lowrey, Annie. 2012. "U.S. Candidate is Chosen to Lead the World Bank." *New York Times,* April 17.

Luker, Kristin. 1996. *Dubious Conceptions: The Politics of Teenage Pregnancy.* Cambridge, MA: Harvard University Press.

Lutkehaus, Nancy C., and Paul B. Roscoe (Eds.). 1995. *Gender Rituals:*

Female Initiation in Melanesia. New York: Routledge.

Lynch, Marc. 2012. *The Arab Uprising: The Unfinished Revolutions of the New Middle East.* NY: Public Affairs.

Lyon-Callo, Vincent. 2004. *Inequality, Poverty, and Neoliberal Governance: Activist Ethnography in the Homeless Sheltering Industry.* Orchard Park, NY: Broadview Press.

MacCormack, Carol P. Hoffer. 1974. "Madam Yoko: Ruler of the Kpa Mende Confederacy." In Michele Z. Rosaldo and Louise Lamphere (Eds.), *Woman, Culture and Society* (pp. 171–187). Stanford: Stanford University Press.

Mace, Ruth. 2008. "Reproducing in China." *Science* 319(5864):764–766.

Mahdavi, Pardis 2009. *Passionate Uprisings: Iran's Sexual Revolution.* Stanford, CA: Stanford University Press.

Malinowski, Bronislaw. 1929a. "Practical Anthropology." *Africa* 2:22–38.

Malinowski, Bronislaw. 1929b. *The Sexual Life of Savages.* New York: Harcourt, Brace and World.

Malinowski, Bronislaw. 1948. *Magic, Science, and Religion and other Essays.* New York: Free Press.

Malinowski, Bronislaw. 1984/1922. *Argonauts of the Western Pacific.* Prospect Heights, IL: Waveland.

Malveaux, Julianne. 2005. "Sweatshops Aren't History Just Yet." *USA Today,* March 18.

Manji, Irshad. 2003. *The Trouble with Islam: A Wakeup Call for Honesty and Change.* Toronto, Canada: Random House Canada.

Manik, Julfikar Ali, and Jim Yardley. 2012. "Bangladesh Finds Gross Negligence in Factory Fire." *New York Times,* December 18.

Marcus, George E., and Michael M. J. Fischer. 1986. *Anthropology as Culture Critique: An Experimental Moment in the Human Sciences.* Chicago: University of Chicago Press.

Markowitz, Gerald, and David Rosen. 2013. *Lead Wars: The Politics of Science and the Fate of America's Children.* Berkeley, CA: University of California.

Marlowe, Frank W. 2004. "Marital Residence among Foragers." *Current Anthropology* 45(2):277–284.

Marshall, Donald. 1971. "Sexual Behavior on Mangaia." In D. S. Marshall and R. C. Suggs (Eds.), *Human Sexual Behavior: Variations in the Ethnographic Spectrum* (pp. 163–172). New York: Basic Books.

Marshall, Mac. 1979. *Weekend Warriors.* Palo Alto, CA: Mayfield.

Martin, Douglas. 2013. "Nevin S. Scrimshaw, Pioneer Nutritionist, Dies at 95." *New York Times,* February 12.

Martin, Emily. 1987. *The Woman in the Body.* New York: Beacon Press.

Martin, M. K., and Barbara Voorhies. 1975. *Female of the Species.* New York: Columbia University Press.

Martin, Philip. 2007. "Managing Labor Migration in the 21st Century." *City and Society* 19(1):5–18.

Maskus, Keith. 1997. "Should Core Labor Standards be Imposed through International Trade Policy?" World Bank Working Paper 1817. Washington, DC: World Bank. Available at http://elibrary .worldbank.org/content /workingpaper/10.1596/1813-9450 -1817.

Mateu-Gelabert, Pedro, and Howard Lune. 2007. "Street Codes in High School: School as an Educational Deterrent." *City & Community* 6(3):173–191.

Mather, Mark. 2010. "U.S. Children in Single-Mother Families." PRB Data Brief May 2010. Available at www .prb.org/Publications/PolicyBriefs /singlemotherfamilies.aspx, accessed June 11, 2012.

Matsumoto, David, and Tsutomu Kudoh. 1993. "American-Japanese Cultural Differences in Attributions of Personality Based on Smiles."

Journal of Nonverbal Communication 17(4):231–243.

Matthiessen, Peter. 2007. "Alaska: Big Oil and the Whales." *New York Review of Books* November 22:57–64.

Matzner, Andrew. 2001. *'O Au No Keia: Voices from Hawai'i's Mahu and Transgender Communities.* Philadelphia, PA: XLibris.

Mauss, Marcel. 1990/1924. *The Gift: Form and Reason of Exchange in Archaic Societies* (W. D. Halls, Trans.). New York: W.W. Norton.

Mayerowitz, Scott. 2010. "Chelsea Clinton Wedding Price Tag: $2 Million." *ABC News,* July 22. Available at http://abcnews.go.com /Travel/chelsea-clinton-marc -mezvinsky-rhinebeck-wedding -price-tag/story?id=11210739# .UXbV_2wo6Uk, accessed April 23, 2013.

Maybury-Lewis, David. 1997. *Indigenous Peoples, Ethnic Groups, and the State.* Boston: Allyn and Bacon.

McAllester, David. 1954. *Enemy Way Music.* Cambridge, MA: Harvard University Peabody Museum.

McCaskie, T. C. 1995. *State and Society in Pre-Colonial Asante.* Cambridge, UK: Cambridge University Press.

McGee, R. Jon. 1990. *Life, Ritual, and Religion among the Lacandon Maya.* Belmont, CA: Wadsworth.

McGranahan, Carole. 2012a. "An Anthropologist in Political Asylum Court, Part I." *Anthropology News,* March.

McGranahan, Carole. 2012b (April). "Anthropology and the Truths of Political Asylum, Part II." *Anthropology News,* p. 20.

McGovern, Mike. 2011. "Before You Judge, Stand in Her Shoes." *New York Times.* July 6, p. 21.

McIntosh, Peggy. 1999. "White Privilege: Unpacking the Invisible Knapsack." In A. Podolefsky and P. J. Brown (Eds.), *Applying Cultural Anthropology: An Introductory Reader*

(4th ed., pp. 134–137). Mountain View, CA: Mayfield.

Mead, Margaret. 1963/1935. *Sex and Temperament in Three Primitive Societies*. New York: Dell.

Mead, Margaret. 1971/1928. *Coming of Age in Samoa*. New York: Morrow.

Melendez, Edwin. 1993. *Colonial Subjects: Critical Perspectives on Contemporary Puerto Ricans*. Boston: South End Press.

Merrick, Amy. 2004. "Gap Offers Unusual Look at Factory Conditions." *Wall Street Journal*, May 12.

Messenger, John C. 1971. "Sex and Repression in an Irish Folk Community." In D. S. Marshall and R. C. Suggs (Eds.), *Human Sexual Behavior: Variations in the Ethnographic Spectrum* (pp. 3–37). New York: Basic Books.

Messina, Maria. 1988. "Henna Party." *Natural History* 97(9):40.

Meyer, Stephen. 2004. "The Degradation of Work Revisited: Workers and Technology in the American Auto Industry, 1900–2000." *Automobile in American Life and Society*. Available at www.autolife.umd .umich .edu/Labor/L_Overview /L_ Overview3.htm.

Mintz, Sidney W. 1985. *Sweetness and Power: The Place of Sugar in Modern History*. New York: Penguin.

Montagu, Ashley. 1978. *Touching: The Human Significance of the Skin* (2nd ed.). New York: Harper and Row.

Montopoli, Brian. 2011. "Poll: 43 Percent Agree with Views of Occupy Wall Street." *CBS News*, October 25. Available at www.cbsnews.com /8301-503544_162-20125515 -503544/poll-43-percent-agree-with -views-of-occupy-wall-street/, accessed April 23, 2013.

Moore, Sally Falk. 1978. *Law as Process: An Anthropological Approach*. London: Routledge and Kegan Paul.

Moore, Robert. 2011. "If I Actually Talked Like That I'd Pull a Gun on Myself: Accent, Avoidance, and Moral Panic in Irish English." *Anthropological Quarterly* 84(1):41–64.

Morgan, Marcyliena. 2004. "Speech Community." In Alassandro Duranti (Ed.), *A Companion to Linguistic Anthropology* (pp. 3–33). Malden, MA: Blackwell.

Morin, Rich, and Seth Motel. 2012. "A Third of Americans Now Say They Are In the Lower Classes." *Pew Social and Demographic Trends*. Available at www.pewsocialtrends .org/2012/09/10.

Morton, Mark. 2009. "The Shape of Food to Come." *Gastronomica: The Journal of Food and Culture* 9(4):6–7.

Moser, Caroline. 1993. *Gender Planning and Development: Theory, Practice, and Training*. New York: Routledge.

Mshana, Gerry, M. L. Plummer, J. Wamoyi, Z. S. Shigongo, D. A. Ross, and D. Wight. 2006. "She Was Bewitched and Caught an Illness Similar to AIDS: AIDS and Sexually Transmitted Infection Causation Beliefs in Rural Northern Tanzania." *Culture, Health, and Sexuality* 8(1):45–58.

Mucha, Janusz L. 2002. "An Outsider's View of American Culture." In Philip DeVita and James Armstrong, eds., *Distant Mirrors: America as a Foreign Culture* (3rd ed., pp. 37–43). Belmont, CA: Wadsworth/Cengage.

Muhammad, Dedrick. 2008. "Race and Extreme Inequality." The Nation, June 30, p. 26.

Munn, Nancy D. 1990. "Constructing Regional Worlds in Experience: Kula Exchange, Witchcraft and Gawan Local Events." *Man* 25:1–17.

Murdock, George Peter. 1949. *Social Structure*. New York: Free Press.

Murphy, Joseph M. 1989. *Santeria: An African Religion in America*. Boston: Beacon Press.

Murphy, Robert. 1964. "Social Distance and the Veil." *American Anthropologist* 66:1257–1273.

Murphy, Yolanda, and Robert Murphy. 1974. *Women of the Forest*. New York: Columbia University Press.

Mydans, Seth. 2008. "U.S. Deportee Brings Street Dance to Street Boys of Cambodia." *New York Times*, November 30, p. A6.

Myerhoff, Barbara G. 1974. *Peyote Hunt: The Sacred Journey of the Huichol Indians*. Ithaca: Cornell University Press.

Myerhoff, Barbara. 1978. *Number Our Days*. New York: Simon and Schuster.

Myers, Fred. 1986. *Pintupi Country, Pintupi Self: Sentiment, Place, and Politics among Western Desert Aborigines*. Washington, DC: Smithsonian Institution Press.

Myers, Fred R. 2006. "The Unsettled Business of Tradition, Indigenous Being, and Acrylic Painting." In Eric Venbrux, Pamela Sheffield Rosi and Robert L. Welsch (Eds.), *Exploring World Art* (pp. 177–200). Long Grove, IL: Waveland.

Myers, Steven Lee, Andrew C. Revkin, Simon Romero, and Clifford Krauss. 2005. "Old Ways of Life Are Fading as the Arctic Thaws." *New York Times*, October 20, p. A1.

Nader, Laura. 2006. "Human Rights and Moral Imperialism: A Double-Edged Story." *Anthropology News* 47(7):6.

Nagashima, Kenji, and James A. Schellenberg. 1997. "Situational Differences in Intentional Smiling: A Cross-Cultural Exploration." *Journal of Social Psychology* 137:297–301.

Nagengast, Carole. 1994. "Violence, Terror, and the Crisis of the State." In B. J. Siegel (Ed.), *Annual Review of Anthropology* (Vol. 23, pp. 109–136). Stanford, CA: Stanford University Press.

Naimark, Norman. 2001. *Fires of Hatred: Ethnic Cleansing in Twentieth-Century Europe.* Cambridge, MA: Harvard University Press.

Nanda, Serena. 1999. *Neither Man nor Woman: The Hijras of India* (2nd ed.). Belmont, CA: Wadsworth.

Nanda, Serena. 2000a. "Arranging a Marriage in India." In P. R. DeVita (Ed.), *Stumbling Towards Truth: Anthropologists at Work* (pp. 196–204). Prospect Heights, IL: Waveland.

Nanda, Serena. 2000b. *Gender Diversity: Crosscultural Variations.* Prospect Heights, IL: Waveland.

Nanda, Serena. 2005. "South African Museums and the Creation of a New National Identity." *American Anthropologist* 106(2 June):379–384.

Nanda, Serena. 2013. "The Hijras: An Alternative Gender in India." In Elvio Angeloni (Ed.), *Annual Editions, Anthropology* (pp. 102–109). New York: McGraw Hill.

Nanda, Serena, and Joan Young Gregg. 2009. *The Gift of A Bride: A Tale of Anthropology, Matrimony, and Murder.* Lanham (MD): Rowman Altamira.

Nanda, Serena, and Joan Gregg. 2011. *Assisted Dying: An Ethnographic Murder Mystery on Florida's Gold Coast.* Lanham, MD: Rowman Littlefield/Altamira.

Narayan, Kirin. 1993. "How Native Is a 'Native' Anthropologist?" *American Anthropologist* 95:671–686.

Narayanaswami, V. R. 2010. "Linguistics as an Identification Tool." *Livemint,* November 15. Available at www.livemint.com/Opinion/OsefullLDWVtZkNPuXQACN/Linguistics-as-an-identification-tool.html, accessed April 23, 2013.

Nash, June. 1970. *In the Eyes of the Ancestors: Belief and Behavior in a Mayan Community.* New Haven: Yale University Press.

Nash, June. 1986. *Women and Change in Latin America.* South Hadley, MA: Bergin and Garvey.

Nash, June. 1993. "Introduction: Traditional Arts and Changing Markets in Middle America." In June Nash and Helen Safa (Eds.), *Crafts in the World Market* (pp. 1–24). Albany: State University of New York Press.

Nash, June. 1994. "Global Integration and Subsistence Insecurity." *American Anthropologist* 96:7–30.

Nash, Maning. 1961. "The Social Context of Economic Choice in a Small Society." *Man* 219:186–191.

Nayar, Baldev Raj, and T. V. Paul. 2003. *India in the World Order: Searching for Major Power Status.* Cambridge: Cambridge University Press.

Neckerman, Kathryn M. (Ed.). 2004. *Social Inequality.* New York: The Russell Sage Foundation.

Nelson, Edward William. 1983. *The Eskimo About Bering Strait.* Washington: The Smithsonian Institution Press.

Netting, Robert. 1977. *Cultural Ecology.* Menlo Park, CA: Cummings.

Newman, Katherine S. 1999. *Falling from Grace: Downward Mobility in an Age of Affluence* (2nd ed.). Berkeley: University of California.

Newman, Katherine S. 2013. "In the South and West, a Tax on Being Poor." *New York Times,* March 10, p. SR 5.

Newman, Katherine, and Victor Chen. 2007. *The Missing Class: Portraits of the Near Poor in America.* Boston: Beacon.

Newman, Philip L. 1977. "When Technology Fails: Magic and Religion in New Guinea." In James P. Spradley and David W. McCurdy (Eds.), *Conformity and Conflict: Readings in Cultural Anthropology* (3rd ed.). Boston: Little Brown.

Newson, L. 1999. "Disease and Immunity in the Pre-Spanish Philippines." *Social Science and Medicine* 48:1833–1850.

Newton, Michael. 2002. *Savage Girls and Wild Boys: A History of Feral Children.* London: Faber and Faber.

New York Times. 2005. *Class Matters.* New York: *New York Times.*

New York Times. 2009. "Remade in America: The Newest Immigrants and Their Impact." March 15.

Nicolaisen, Ida. 2006. "Anthropology Should Actively Promote Human Rights." *Anthropology News* 47(7):6.[3]

Nisbett, Richard E. 2007. "All Brains are the Same Color." *New York Times,* December 9, Section 4 (Science), p. 11.

Nobles, Melissa. 2000. *Shades of Citizenship: Race and the Census in Modern Politics.* Palo Alto, CA: Stanford University Press.

Norbeck, Edward. 1974. *Religion in Human Life: Anthropological Views.* Prospect Heights, IL: Waveland.

Norgren, Jill, and Serena Nanda. 1996. *American Cultural Pluralism and Law* (2nd ed.). New York: Praeger.

Norgren, Jill, and Serena Nanda. 2006. *American Cultural Pluralism and Law* (3rd ed.). Westport, CT: Praeger.

Offiong, Daniel A. 1983. "Witchcraft among the Ibibio of Nigeria." *African Studies Review* 26:107–124.

Ogbu, John. 1978. "African Bridewealth and Women's Status." *American Ethnologist* 5:241–260.

Ogembo, Justus M. 2001. "Cultural Narratives, Violence and Mother-Son Loyalty: An Exploration into Gusii Personification of Evil." *Ethos* 29(1):3–29.

Ojeda, Amparo B. 2002. "Growing Up American: Doing the Right Thing." In Philip DeVita and James Armstrong, eds., *Distant Mirrors: America as a Foreign Culture* (3rd ed., pp. 44–49). Belmont, CA: Cengage.

O'Kelly, Charlotte G., and Larry S. Carney. 1986. *Women and Men in Society: Cross-Cultural Perspectives on Gender Stratification.* Belmont: Wadsworth.

Oliver, Mary Beth. 2003. "Race and Crime in the Media: Research From a Media Effects Tradition." In A. Valdivia (Ed.), *A Companion to Media Studies* (pp. 421–436). London: Blackwell Publishing.

Oreskes, Naomi. 2004. "The Scientific Consensus on Climate Change." *Science* 306(5702):1686.

Organization for Economic Cooperation and Development. 2007. *United States Donor Information.* Available at www.oecd.org /dataoecd/25/16/43193218.pdf.

Oriard, Michael. 1993. *Reading Football: How the Popular Press Created an American Spectacle.* Chapel Hill: University of North Carolina Press.

Otterbein, Keith F. 2010. "Nobel Peace Prize—Passed Over Again." *General Anthropology: Bulletin of the General Anthropology Division,* Spring, p. 1.

Ottley, Bruce L., and Jean G. Zorn. 1983. "Criminal Law in Papua New Guinea: Code, Custom and the Courts in Conflict." *American Journal of Comparative Law* 31:251–300.

Paiement, Jason J. 2007. "Anthropology and Development." *National Association for the Practice of Anthropology Bulletin* 27(1):196–223.

Palkovich, Anna M. 1994. "Historic Epidemics of the American Pueblos." In C. S. Larsen and G. R. Milner (Eds.), *In the Wake of Contact: Biological Responses to Conquest* (pp. 87–95). New York: Wiley.

Paredes, Anthony J. (Ed.). 2006. "Introduction to In Focus: The Impact of the Hurricanes of 2005 on New Orleans and the Gulf Coast of the United States." *American Anthropologist* 108(4):637–642.

Pareles, Jon. 1996. "A Small World After All. But Is That Good?" *New York Times,* March 24, p. B34.

Patterson, Orlando. 2006. "A Poverty of the Mind." *New York Times,* March 26.

Peacock, Nadine R. 1991. "Rethinking the Sexual Division of Labor: Reproduction and Women's Work among the Efe." In M. di Leonardo (Ed.), *Gender and the Crossroads of Knowledge: Feminist Anthropology in the Postmodern Era* (pp. 339–360). Berkeley, CA: University of California Press.

Peletz, M. 2009. *Gender Pluralism: Southeast Asia Since Early Modern Times.* New York: Routledge.

Peletz, M. 2012. "Gender, Sexuality, and the State in Southeast Asia." *Journal of Asian Studies* 71(4):895–917.

Peoples, James G. 1990. "The Evolution of Complex Stratification in Eastern Micronesia." *Micronesia Suppl.* 2:291–302.

Peregrine, Peter N., Carol R. Ember, and Melvin Ember. 2004. "Universal Patterns in Cultural Evolution: An Empirical Analysis Using Guttman Scaling." *American Anthropologist* 106(1):145–149.

Perez-Pena, Richard. 2012. "Student's Account Has Rape in Spotlight." *New York Times,* October 27, p. A15.

Pew Research Center. 2007. "Muslim Americans: Middle Class and Mostly Mainstream." Available at http://pewsocialtrends .org/2007/05/22/muslim -americans-middle-class-and -mostly-mainstream/, accessed November 15, 2010.

Peyrefitte, Alain. 1992. *The Immobile Empire* (Jon Rothschild, Trans.). New York: Knopf.

Pigg, Stacy Leigh. 2001. "Languages of Sex and AIDS in Nepal: Notes on the Social Production of Commensurability." *Current Anthropology* 16(4):481–541.

Pilkington, Ed. 2010. "South Park Censored after Threat of Fatwa over Muhammad Episode." Guardian.co.uk. Available at www.guardian.co.uk/tv-and -radio/2010/apr/22/south-park -censored-fatwa-muhammad, accessed August 20, 2010.

Pinker, Steven. 1994. *The Language Instinct.* New York: William Morrow.

Pinker, Steven. 2011. *The Better Angels of Our Nature.* New York: Viking.

Pitts, Leonard. 2007. "At Large, Replying to Those E-mails about Vick." *Miami Herald,* September 12.

Plattner, Stuart. 1989. "Marxism." In S. Plattner (Ed.), *Economic Anthropology* (pp. 379–396). Stanford, CA: Stanford University Press.

Polese, Abel. 2008. "'If I Receive It, It Is a gift; If I Demand It, Then It Is a bribe': On the Local Meaning of Economic Transactions in Post-Soviet Ukraine." *Anthropology in Action* 15(3):47–60.

Polyani, Karl. 1944. *The Great Transformation.* New York: Holt, Rinehart and Winston.

Potash, Betty. 1989. "Gender Relations in Sub-Saharan Africa." In S. Morgen (Ed.), *Gender and Anthropology: Critical Reviews for Research and Teaching* (pp. 189–227). Washington, DC: American Anthropological Association.

Powers, Thomas. 2005. The Indians' Own Story." *The New York Review of Books,* April 7, p. 73.

Prah, Kwesi K. 1990. "Anthropologists, Colonial Administrators, and the Lotuko of Eastern Equatoria, Sudan: 1952–1953." *African Journal of Sociology* 3(2):70–86.

Preston, Julia. 2009. "A Slippery Place in the U.S. Work Force." *New York Times,* March 22, p. A1.

Price, Sally. 1989. *Primitive Art in Civilized Places.* Chicago: University of Chicago Press.

Price, Sally. 2007. *Paris Primitive: Jacques Chirac's Museum on the Quai Branly.* Chicago: University of Chicago Press.

Price, David. 2009. "Counterinsurgency's Free Ride." *Counterpunch,* April 7. Accessed June 15, 2012. www.counterpunch.org/2009/04/07 /counterinsurgencys-free-ride/.

Prose, Francine. 2011. *My New American Life.* NY: HarperCollins.

Prunier, Gerard. 2008. *Africa's World War: Congo, the Rwandan Genocide, and the Making of a Continental Catastrophe.* Oxford: Oxford University Press.

Queen, Stuart, and Robert Haberstein. 1974. *The Family in Various Cultures.* New York, NY: J.B. Lippincott Co.

Quinnipiac University. 2012. "American Voters Back Legalized Marijuana, Quinnipiac University National Poll Finds." December 5. Available at www.quinnipiac.edu/institutes --centers/polling-institute/national /release-detail?ReleaseID=1820, accessed April 23, 2013.

Ramos, Francisco Martins. 2002. "My American Glasses." In Philip DeVita and James Armstrong, eds., *Distant Mirrors: America as a Foreign Culture* (3rd ed., pp. 50–58). Belmont, CA: Cengage.

Radcliffe-Brown, A. R. 1965/1952. *Structure and Function in Primitive Society.* New York: Free Press.

Ranco, Darren J. 2006. "Toward a Native Anthropology: Hermeneutics, Hunting Stories, and Theorizing from Within." *Wicazo Sa Review* 21(2):61–78.

Rasmussen Reports. 2010. "87% Say English Should Be U.S. Official Language." *Rasmussen Reports,* May 11. Available at www .rasmussenreports.com/public _content/politics/general _politics/may_2010/87_say _english_should_be_u_s _official_language, accessed August 20, 2010.

Rasmussen, Susan. 2005. "Pastoral Nomadism and Gender: Status, Prestige, Economic Contribution, and Division of Labor among the Tuareg of Niger." In Caroline B. Brettell and Carolyn F. Sargent (Eds.), *Gender in Cross Cultural Perspective* (4th ed., pp. 155–168). Upper Saddle River, NJ: Pearson/Prentice Hall.

Reaney, Patricia. 2012. "Average Cost of U.S. Wedding Hits \$27,021." *Reuters,* March 23.

Reed, Jr., Adolph. 2006. "Undone by Neoliberalism." *The Nation,* September 18, p. 26.

Reichman, Rebecca. 1995. "Brazil's Denial of Race." *NACLA Report on the Americas* 28 (6):35–43.

Rerkasem, Kanok, Deborah Lawrence, Christine Paddoch, Dietrich Schmidt-Vogt, Alan D. Ziegler, and Thilde Bech Bruun. 2009. "Consequences of Swidden Transitions for Crop and Fallow Biodiversity in Southeast Asia." *Human Ecology* 37:347–360.

Renteln, Alison D. 2004. *The Culture Defense.* New York: Oxford.

Rhode, Deborah L. 2010. *The Beauty Bias: The Injustice of Appearance in Life and Law.* NY: Oxford University Press.

Ricklefs, Merle C. 1990. "Balance and Military Innovation in 17th Century Java." *History Today* 40(11):40–47.

Ricklefs, Merle. 1993. *A History of Modern Indonesia Since 1300* (2nd ed.). Houndsmills (UK): Macmillan.

Ringlero, Aleta M. 2008. "Fritz Scholder: The Enigma." *Smithsonian National Museum of the American Indian* (Fall): 16–24.

Robarchek, Clayton A., and Carole J. Robarchek. 1992. "Cultures of War and Peace: A Comparative Study of the Waorani and Semai." In James Silverberg and J. Patrick Gray (Eds.), *Aggression and Peacefulness in Humans and Other Primates* (pp. 189–213). New York: Oxford University Press.

Roberts, Adam and Timothy Garton Ash, eds. 2009. *Civil Resistance and Power Politics: The Experience of Nonviolent Action from Gandhi to the Present.* NY: Oxford University Press.

Roberts, Alan H., D. G. Kewman, L. Mercier, and M. Hovell. 1993. "The

Power of Nonspecific Effects in Healing: Implications for Psychosocial and Biological Treatments." *Clinical Psychology Review* 13:375–391.

Robinson, Harlow. 1994. *The Last Impresario: the Life, Times, and Legacy of Sol Hurok.* New York: Viking.

Rödlach, Alexander. 2006. *Witches, Westerners and HIV: AIDS & Cultures of Blame in Africa.* Walnut Creek CA: Left Coast Press.

Rohde, Douglas, Steve Olson, and Joseph T. Chang. 2004. "Modelling the Recent Common Ancestry of All Living Humans." *Nature* 431: 562–566.

Roland, Edna. 2001. "The Economics of Racism: People of African Descent in Brazil." Paper presented at the International Council on Human Rights Policy Seminar on the Economics of Racism, November 24–25. Geneva, Switzerland.

Romero, Simon. 2012. "Brazil Enacts Affirmative Action Law for Universities." *New York Times,* August 31, p. A4.

Rosaldo, Michelle Z., and Louise Lamphere. 1974. "Introduction." In M. Z. Rosaldo and L. Lamphere (Eds.), *Women, Culture and Society* (pp. 1–16). Stanford, CA: Stanford University Press.

Roscoe, Paul. 2003. "Margaret Mead, Reo Fortune, and Mountain Arapesh Warfare." *American Anthropologist* 105(3):581–591.

Roscoe, Will. 1991. *The Zuni Man-Woman.* Albuquerque: University of New Mexico Press.

Roscoe, Will. 1995. "Strange Craft, Strange History, Strange Folks: Cultural Amnesia and the Case of Lesbian and Gay Studies." *American Anthropologist* 97:448–452.

Rosman, Abraham, and Paula G. Rubel. 1971. *Feasting with Mine Enemy: Rank and Exchange among Northwest Coast Societies.* Prospect Heights, IL: Waveland.

Roybal, Joe. 2007. "Big Beef Buyers." Beef Magazine. Available at http://beefmagazine.com/mag/beef_big_beef_buyers/index. html.

Sacks, Karen Brodkin. 1982. *Sisters and Wives.* Westport, CT: Greenwood.

Sahlins, Marshall. 1961. "The Segmentary Lineage: An Organization of Predatory Expansion." *American Anthropologist* 63:332–345.

Sahlins, Marshall. 1971. "Poor Man, Rich Man, Big Man, Chief." In J. P. Spradley and D. W. McCurdy (Eds.), *Conformity and Conflict* (pp. 362–376). Boston: Little, Brown.

Sahlins, Marshall. 1972. *Stone Age Economics.* Chicago: Aldine.

Salzman, Philip. 1999. *The Anthropology of Real Life: Events in Human Experience.* Prospect Heights, IL: Waveland.

Salzman, Philip C. 2000. *Black Tents of Baluchistan.* Washington, DC: Smithsonian.

Salzmann, Zdenek. 1993. *Language, Culture and Society.* Boulder, CO: Westview Press.

Sanchez-Eppler, Benigno. 1992. "Telling Anthropology: Zora Neale Hurston and Gilberto Freyre Disciplined in Their Field-Home-Work." *American Literary History* 4:464–488.

Sanday, Peggy Reeves. 1981. *Female Power and Male Dominance.* New York: Cambridge University Press.

SAPRIN. 2004. *Structural Adjustment: The SAPRI Report.* London: Zed Books.

Scaglion, Richard. 1981. "Homicide Compensation in Papua New Guinea: Problems and Prospects." In *Law Reform Commission of Papua New Guinea Monograph 1.* New Guinea: Office of Information.

Scammell, G. V. 1989. *The First Imperial Age.* London: HarperCollins Academic.

Schama, Simon. 2010. 'The Unloved American: Two Centuries of Alienating Europe." In *Scribble, Scribble,*

Scribble: Writing on Politics, Ice Cream, Churchill and My Mother. NY: Ecco.

Schensul, Stephen L. 1997. "The Anthropologist in Medicine: Critical Perspectives on Cancer and Street Addicts." *Reviews in Anthropology* 26(1):57–69.

Schepartz, L. A. 1993. "Language and Modern Human Origins." *Yearbook of Physical Anthropology* 36:91–96.

Schildkrout, Enid. 2004. "Inscribing the Body." *Annual Review of Anthropology* 33:319–344.

Schmeets, Hans. 2012. "One in Six Go to Church or Mosque on a Regular Basis." *Statics Netherlands Web Magazine,* December 21.

Schmidt-Vogt, Dietrich, Stephen J. Leisz, Ole Mertz, Andreas Heinimann, Thiha Thiha, Peter Messerli, Michael Epprecht, Pham Van Cu, Vu Kim Chi, Martin Hardiono, and Truong M. Dao. 2009. "An Assessment of Trends in the Extent of Swidden in Southeast Asia." *Human Ecology* 37:269–80.

Schwartz, Stuart B. 1994. *Implicit Understandings: Observing, Reporting, and Reflecting on the Encounters between Europeans and Other Peoples of the Early Modern Era.* Cambridge: Cambridge University Press.

Schwartz, Timothy. 2008. *Travesty in Haiti: A True Account of Christian Missions, Orphanages, Fraud, Food Aid, and Drug Trafficking.* Charleston, SC: Booksurge.

Science. 2012 (January). "News and Analysis" 20: 274–275.

Scott, Elizabeth M. 2001. "Food and Social Relations at Nina Plantation." *American Anthropologist* 103(3):671–691.

Scott, Janny. 2005. "Life at the Top in America Isn't Just Better, It's Longer." *New York Times,* May 16.

Scrimshaw, Nevin S. 2010. "The Origin and Development of INCAP." *Food and Nutrition Bulletin* 31(1):4–8.

Scrimshaw, Susan. 2012. "A 70-Year Marriage." *Timesunion.com,*

Feb 14. Available at http://blog.timesunion.com/scrimshaw/a-70-year-marriage/632/, accessed April 23, 2013.

Seabrook, Jeremy. 1999. *Love in a Different Climate: Men Who Have Sex with Men in India.* Brooklyn, NY: Verso.

Seitz-Wald, Alex. 2012. "GOP Embraces anti-Shariah." Salon.com, August 21. Available at www.salon.com/2012/08/21/gop_embraces_anti_sharia/, accessed April 23, 2013.

Service, Elman. 1962. *Primitive Social Organization.* New York: Random House.

Service, Elman. 1971. *Profiles in Ethnology.* New York: Harper and Row.

Shandy, Dianna J. 2007. *Nuer-American Passages: Globalizing Sudanese Migration.* Gainesville: University Press of Florida.

Sheehan, John. 1982. *The Enchanted Ring: The Untold Story of Penicillin.* Cambridge, MA: MIT Press.

Shepard, Glen H. Jr. 2011 (May). "The Mark and Olly Follies." *Anthropology News.*

Sheriff, Robin E. 2001. *Dreaming Equality: Color, Race and Racism in Urban Brazil.* East Brunswick, NJ: Rutgers University Press. 2001.

Shih, Chuan-Kang. 2001. "Genesis of Marriage among the Moso and Empire-Building in Late Imperial China." *The Journal of Asian Studies* 60(2):381–412.

Shiller, Robert J. 2012. "Spend, Spend, Spend. It's the American Way." *New York Times,* January 15, p. I4.

Silberbauer, George. 1982. "Political Process in G/wi Bands." In Eleanor Leacock and Richard Lee (Eds.), *Politics and History in Band Societies* (pp. 23–35). New York: Cambridge University Press.

Simon, Greg. 2006. "Anger Management: Working through Identity and Objectification in Indonesia."

In Andrew Gardner and David M. Hoffman (Eds.), *Dispatches from the Field: Neophyte Ethnographers in a Changing World* (pp. 105–118). Long Grove, IL: Waveland Press.

Smedley, Audrey. 1998. "'Race' and the Construction of Human Identity." *American Anthropologist* 100:690–702.

Smith, Roberta. 2005. "From a Mushroom Cloud, a Burst of Art Reflecting Japan's Psyche." *New York Times,* April 8, p. E33.

Snajdr, Edward. 2007. "Ethnicizing the Subject: Domestic Violence and the Politics of Primordialism in Kazakhstan." *Journal of the Royal Anthropological Institute (N.S.)* 13:603–620.

SOCPC. 2010. "Standard Occupational Classification." United States Bureau of Labor Statistics. Available at www.bls.gov/soc /major_groups.htm.

Sokolofsky, Jay. 2009. *The Cultural Context of Aging: Worldwide Perspectives,* 3rd ed. Westport, CT: Praeger.

Sokolofsky, Jay. (forthcoming). *Mexico Engages the 21st Century: Never More Campesinos.* Belmont, CA: Cengage.

Southern Baptist Convention. 2006. Resolution 5 of the SBC Meeting, 2006, June 13–14: "On Alcohol Use in America." Available at www.sbc .net/resolutions/amResolution .asp?ID=1156.

Spencer, Kyle. 2012. "For Asians, School Tests are Vital Steppingstones."*New York Times,* October 27, p. A20.

Spener, David. 2009. *Clandestine Crossings: Migrants and Coyotes on the Texas-Mexico Border.* Ithaca, NY: Cornell University Press.

Spiegel. 2010. "The Rise of Europe's Right-Wing Populists." *Spiegel Online,* September 28.

Sponsel, Leslie E. (Ed.). 1995. *Indigenous Peoples and the Future of Amazonia: An Ecological Anthropology of an Endangered World.* Tucson: University of Arizona Press.

Squires, Susan, and Bryan Byrne. 2002. *Creating Breakthrough Ideas: The Collaboration of Anthropologists and Designers in the Product Development Industry.* Westport (CN): Bergin and Garvey.

Stanyon, Roscoe, Marco Sazzini, and Donata Luiselli. 2009. "Timing the First Human Migration into Eastern Asia." *Journal of Biology* 8:18.

Steiner, Christopher B. 1994. *African Art in Transit.* New York: Cambridge University Press.

Steiner, Christopher B. 1995. "The Art of the Trade: On the Creation of Value and Authenticity in the African Art Market." In G. E. Marcus and F. R. Myers (Eds.), *The Traffic in Culture: Refiguring Art and Anthropology* (pp. 151–165). Berkeley, CA: University of California Press.

Steiner, Christopher B. 2002. "Art/ Anthropology/Museums: Revulsions and Revolutions." In Jeremy MacClancy (Ed.), *Exotic No More: Anthropology on the Front Lines* (pp. 400–17). Chicago: University of Chicago Press.

Sterling, Marvin D. 2010. *Babylon East: Performing Dancehall, Roots Reggae, and Rastafari in Japan.* Durham, NC: Duke University Press.

Stern, Pamela R. 1999. "Learning to Be Smart: An Exploration of the Culture of Intelligence in a Canadian Inuit Community." *American Anthropologist* 101:502–514.

Sternberg, Esther. 2002. "Walter B. Cannon and 'Voodoo' Death: A Perspective from 60 Years On." *American Journal of Public Health* 92: 1564–1566.

Stevens, Jr., Phillips. 2006. "Women's Aggressive Use of Genital Power in Africa." *Transcultural Psychiatry* 43(4):592–599.

Stiglitz, Joseph E. 2012. *The Price of Inequality: How Today's Divided Society Endangers Our Future.* New York: W.W. Norton.

Stolberg, Sheryl Gay. 1999. "Black Mother's Mortality Rate is Under Scrutiny." *New York Times,* August 8, p. A1.

Stolcke, Verena. 1995. "Talking Culture: New Boundaries, New Rhetorics of Exclusion in Europe." *Current Anthropology* 36:1–7.

Stone, Glenn Davis. 1998. "Keeping the Home Fires Burning: The Changed Nature of Householding in the Kofyar Homeland." *Human Ecology* 26(2):239–265.

Stone, Linda, and Caroline James. 2005. "Dowry, Bride-Burning, and Female Power in India." In C. B. Brettell and C. F. Sargent (Eds.), *Gender in Cross-Cultural Perspective* (4th ed., pp. 312–320). Upper Saddle River, NJ: Prentice Hall.

Strathern, Marilyn. 1995. *Women in Between: Female Roles in a Male World: Mount Hagen, New Guinea.* Latham, MD: Rowman and Littlefield.

Strauss, Lawrence G. 1991. "Southwestern Europe at the Last Glacial Maximum." *Current Anthropology* 32:189–199.

Strum, Philippa, and Danielle Tarantolo (Eds.). 2003. *Muslims in the United States: Demography, Beliefs, Institutions.* Washington, DC: Woodrow Wilson International Center for Scholars.

Stull, Donald D., and Michael J. Broadway. 2004. *Slaughterhouse Blues: The Meat and Poultry Industry in North America.* Belmont, CA: Wadsworth.

SUCDEN. 2011. "World Sugar Consumptions." Available at www .sucden.com/statistics/4_world -sugar-consumption, accessed April 23, 2013.

Tabuchi, Hiroko. 2009. "Japan Pays Foreign Workers To Go Home." *New York Times,* April 22. Available at www.nytimes.com/2009/04/23

/business/global/23immigrant.html?ref=business.

Tagliabue, John. 2012. "A School's Big Lesson Begins with Dropping Personal Pronouns." *New York Times*, November 14, p. A8.

Tavernise, Sabrina. 2008. "Putting a Dent in a Law against Insulting Turkishness." *New York Times*, January 25, p. A4.

Tavernise, Sabrina. 2012. "For Women Under 30, Most Births Occur Outside Marriage." The *New York Times*, February 17. Available at www.nytimes.com/2012/02/18/us/for-women-under-30-most-births-occur-outside-marriage.html?pagewanted=all&_r=0, accessed October 9, 2012.

Temple University. 2009. "Earliest Evidence of Domesticated Maize Discovered: Dates Back 8,700 Years." *ScienceDaily* 25 (March): 3

Tessman, Irwin, and Jack Tessman. 2000. "Efficacy of Prayer: A Critical Examination of Claims." *Skeptical Inquirer* 24(2):31–33.

Thornton, Lynne. 1994. *Women as Portrayed in Orientalist Painting*. Paris: PocheCouleur.

Thrupkaew, Noy. 2012. "A Misguided Moral Crusade." *New York Times*, September 22, p. SR 1.

Thubron, Colin. 2009. "Madame Butterfly's Brothel." *The New York Review of Books*, June 11, pp. 24–27.

Timberg, Craig, and Daniel Halperin. 2012. *Tinderbox: How the West Sparked the AIDS Epidemic and How the World Can Finally Overcome It*. NY: Penguin.

Todaro, Michael, and Stephen C. Smith. 2003. *Economic Development* (8th ed.). Harlow, UK: Pearson Addison Wesley.

Trachtman, Michael G. 2009. *The Supremes' Greatest Hit, Revised and Updated Edition: The 37 Supreme Court Cases that Most Directly Affect Your Life*. New York: Sterling Publishing.

Traphagan, John W. 1998. "Contesting the Transition to Old Age in Japan." *Ethnology* 37:333–350.

Tsuruta, Kinua. 1989. *The Walls Within: Images of Westerners in Japan and Images of the Japanese Abroad*. Vancouver: Institute of Asian Research.

Turnbull, Colin. 1968. "The Importance of Flux in Two Hunting Societies." In R. B. Lee and I. DeVore (Eds.), *Man the Hunter* (pp. 132–137). Chicago: Aldine.

Turner, Victor. 1967. *The Forest of Symbols: Aspects of Ndembu Ritual*. Ithaca: Cornell University Press.

Turner, Victor. 1969. *The Ritual Process: Structure and Antistructure*. Chicago: Aldine.

UNEP/GRID-Arendal. 2008. "Population Distribution in the Circumpolar Arctic, by Country (Including Indigenous Population)." UNEP/GRID-Arendal Maps and Graphics Library. Available at http://maps.grida.no/go/graphic/population-distribution-in-the-circumpolar-arctic-by-country-including-indigenous-population1, accessed November 1, 2010.

United Nations. 2008. *World Urbanization Prospects. Available at* http://esa.un.org/unup.

United Nations. 2012. "World Urbanization Prospects: The 2011 Revision." United Nations Department of Economic and Social Affairs, Population Division. Available at http://esa.un.org/unpd/wup/index.htm, accessed June 18, 2012.

University of Virginia. 2008. "Choosing and Using Your Major." University Career Services. Available at http://www.career.virginia.edu/students/handouts/choosing_a_major.pdf, accessed on April 24, 2013.

U.S. Bureau of Labor Statistics. 2013. "Employment Projections: Education Pays." Available at www.bls.gof/emp/pe_chart_001.htm, accessed April 24, 2013

U.S. Census Bureau. 2012. "The 2012 Statistical Abstract." *The National Data Book*. Accessed June 18, 2012. Available at www.census.gov/compendia/statab/.

U.S. Department of Agriculture. 2012. "Fruit and Tree Nuts." Economic Research Service. Available at www.ers.usda.gov/topics/crops/fruit-tree-nuts.aspx.

U.S. Department of Agriculture. 2013a. "FSIS Recals." Available at www.fsis.usda.gov/fsis_recalls/Recall_Summary_2012/, accessed April 24, 2013.

U.S. Department of Agriculture. 2013b. "U.S. Food Imports." Economic Research Service. Available at www.ers.usda.gov/data-products/us-food-imports.aspx#25416.

U.S. English. 2012. "Misconceptions about Official English." Available at www.us-english.org/view/15.

U.S. Environmental Protection Agency. N.d. "Pollutants and Sources." Available at www.epa.gov/ttnatw01/pollsour.html, accessed April 24, 2013.

Van Biema, David, and Jeff Chu. 2006. "Does God Want You To Be Rich?" *Time*, September 18.

van Donge, Jan Kees. 1992. "Agricultural Decline in Tanzania: The Case of the Uluguru Mountains." *African Affairs* 91:73–94.

van Gennep, Arnold. 1960/1909. *The Rites of Passage*. Chicago: University of Chicago Press.

Vayda, Andrew P. 1976. *War in Ecological Perspective*. New York: Plenum.

Venbrux, Eric, Pamela Sheffield Rosi, and Robert L. Welsch (Eds.). 2006. *Exploring World Art*. Long Grove, IL: Waveland.

Ventura, Stephanie J. 2009. "Changing Patterns of Nonmarital Childbearing in the United States." *NCHS Data Brief 18* (May).

Verdon, Michel, and Paul Jorion. 1981. "The Hordes of Discord: Australian Aboriginal Social Organization Reconsidered." *Man* 16(1):90–107.

Victor, David A. 1992. *International Business Communication.* New York: Harper Collins.

Vincent, Susan. 1998. "The Family in the Household: Women, Relationships, and Economic History in Peru." *Research in Economic Anthropology* 19:179–187.

Vine, David. 2009. *Island of Shame.* Princeton, NJ. Princeton University Press.

Viswanathan, Gauri. 1988. "Currying Favor: The Politics of British Educational and Cultural Policy in India 1813–1854." *Social Text* 19–20(Fall): 85–104.

Vogel, Susan. 1991. *Africa Explores: 20th Century African Art.* New York: Center for African Art.

Volkman, Toby Alice. 1984. "Great Performances: Toraja Cultural Identity in the 1970s." *American Ethnologist* 11(1):152–168.

Walker, Andrew. 2009. "Nigeria's Gas Profits 'Up in Smoke.'" *BBC News,* Nigeria, January 13. Available at http://news.bbc.co.uk/2/hi/africa/7820384.stm.

Wallerstein, Immanuel. 1995. *Historical Capitalism.* London: Verso.

Walsh, Eileen Rose. 2004. "Desensationalizing the Mosuo." *Anthropology Newsletter* 45(4).

Wang, Jimmy. 2009. "Now Hip-Hop, Too, Is Made in China." *New York Times,* January 24, p. C1.

Warren, Kay B., and Susan C. Bourque. 1989. "Women, Technology, and Development Ideologies: Frameworks and Findings." In S. Morgen (Ed.), *Gender and Anthropology: Critical Reviews for Research and Teaching* (pp. 382–410). Washington, DC: American Anthropological Association.

Wasif, Sehrish. 2011. "European Muslims: Refusal to Integrate the Root of Most Problems." *The Express Tribune,* July 22.

Weiner, Annette B. 1976. *Women of Value, Men of Renown: New Perspectives on Trobriand Exchange.* Austin: University of Texas Press.

Wenzel, George W. 2009. "Canadian Inuit Subsistence and Ecological Instability—If the Climate Changes, Must the Inuit?" *Polar Research* 28:89–99.

White, Benjamin. 1980. "Rural Household Studies in Anthropological Perspective." In H. Binswanger, R. Evenson, C. Florencio, and B. White (Eds.), *Rural Household Studies in Asia* (pp. 3–25). Singapore: Singapore University Press.

White, Geoffrey M. 1997. "Introduction: Public History and National Narrative." *Museum Anthropology* 21(1):3–6.

White, Jenny B. 1994. *Money Makes Us Relatives.* Austin, TX: University of Texas Press.

Whitehead, Harriet. 1981. "The Bow and the Burden Strap: A New Look at Institutionalized Homosexuality in Native North America." In S. B. Ortner and H. Whitehead (Eds.), *Sexual Meanings: The Cultural Construction of Gender and Sexuality* (pp. 80–115). Cambridge: Cambridge University Press.

Whiting, John, Richard Kluckhohn, and Albert Anthony. 1967. "The Function of Male Initiation Ceremonies at Puberty." In R. Endelman (Ed.), *Personality and Social Life* (pp. 294–308). New York: Random House.

Whorf, Benjamin L. 1941. "The Relation of Habitual Thought and Behavior to Language." In Leslie Spier (Ed.), *Language, Culture and Personality* (pp. 75–93). Menasha, WI: Sapir Memorial Publication Fund.

Wiessner, Polly, and Nitze Pupu. 2012. "Toward Peace: Foreign Arms and Indigenous Institutions in a Papua New Guinea Society." *Science* 337(6102): 1651–1654.

Wikan, Unni. 1977. "Man Becomes Woman: Transsexualism in Oman as a Key to Gender Roles." *Man* (new series) 12:304–319.

Wikan, Unni. 2008. *In Honor of Fadime: Murder and Shame.* Chicago: University of Chicago Press.

Wildsmith, Elizabeth, Nicole R. Steward-Streng, and Jennifer Manlove. 2011. "Childbearing Outside of Marriage: Estimates and Trends in the United States." Child Trends Research Brief, 2011–29.

Wilk, Richard (Ed.). 2006. *Fast Food/Slow Food: The Cultural Economy of the Global Food System.* Lanham, MD: Altamira Press.

Williams, Trevor. 1984. *Howard Florey: Penicillin and After.* Oxford: Oxford University Press.

Williams, Walter. 1986. *The Spirit and the Flesh* (2nd ed.). Boston: Beacon Press.

Williams, Walter. 1996. "Amazons of America: Female Gender Variance." In Caroline B. Brettell and Carolyn F. Sargent (Eds.), *Gender in Cross-Cultural Perspective* (2nd ed., pp. 202–213). Upper Saddle River, NJ: Prentice Hall.

Winkelman, Michael. 1996. "Cultural Factors in Criminal Defense Proceedings." *Human Organization* 55:154.

Wolf, Eric R. 1982. *Europe and the People without History.* Berkeley, CA: University of California Press.

Wolff, Edward N. 2010. "Recent Trends in Household Wealth in the United States: Rising Debt and the Middle Class Squeeze an Update to 2007." Levy Economics Institute of Bard College, Working Paper No. 589.

Wong, Edward. 2008. "Factories Shut, China Workers Are Suffering." *New York Times,* November 14, p. A1

Wong, Edward. 2011. "Photo Turns U.S. Envoy Into a Lesson for Chinese." *New York Times,* August 18, p. A14.

Wood, Graeme. 2013. "Anthropology Inc." *The Atlantic* 313(2): 48–56.

Woodburn, James. 1968. "An Introduction to Hadza Ecology." In R. B. Lee and I. DeVore (Eds.), *Man the Hunter* (pp. 49–55). Chicago: Aldine.

Woodburn, James. 1998. "Sharing Is Not a Form of Exchange: An Analysis of Property-Sharing in Immediate Return Hunter-Gatherer Societies." In C. M. Hann (Ed.), *Property Relations: Renewing the Anthropological Tradition* (pp. 48–63). Cambridge: Cambridge University Press.

World Bank. 1992. *Development and the Environment: World Development Report 1992.* New York: Oxford University Press.

World Bank. 2005. *African Development Indicators: From the World Bank Africa Database.* Washington, DC: World Bank.

World Bank. 2006. *Global Economic Prospects. Economic Implications of Remittances and Migration.* Washington, DC: World Bank. Available at econ.worldbank.org/external /default/main?pagePK=6416525 9&theSitePK=469372&piPK=641 65421&menuPK=64166322&entit yID=000112742_20051114174928.

World Bank. 2011. *Migration and Remittances Factbook 2011* (2nd ed.). Washington DC: The World Bank.

World Health Organization. 2004. "Pesticides and Health." Available at www.who.int/mental_health /prevention/suicide/en /PesticidesHealth2.pdf.

World Health Organization. 2008. "Children's Health and the Environment." Available at www.who.int /ceh/capacity/Pesticides.pdf.

Worthman, Carol M. 1995. "Hormones, Sex, and Gender." In William Durham, F. Valentine Daniel, and Bambi Schieffelin (Eds.), *Annual Review of Anthropology* (Vol. 24, pp. 593 618). Stanford, CA: Stanford University Press.

Wrangham, Richard. 2009. *Catching Fire: How Cooking Made Us Human.* New York: Basic Books.

Wright, Stephen. 2008. "Bali Murder: The Story behind the Police Inspector's Evil Plot to Kill His Wife after She Asked for a Divorce." *Mail Online,* January 28. Available at www.dailymail.co.uk /news/article-508046, accessed April 24, 2013.

Yamba, Bawa. 1997. "Cosmologies in Turmoil: Witchfinding and AIDS in Chiawa, Zambia." *Africa* 67(2):200–223.

Yardley, Jim. 2012. "A Village Rape Shatters a Family, and India's Traditional Silence." *New York Times,* October 28, p. A1.

Zeegers, Maurice, Frans van Poppel, Robert Vlietinck, Liesbeth Spruijt, and Harry Ostrer. 2004. "Founder Mutations among the Dutch." *European Journal of Human Genetics* 12:591–600.

Zoepf, Katherine. 2008. "In Booming Gulf, Some Arab Women Find Freedom in the Skies." *New York Times,* December 22, p. A1.

INDEX

The Kandy-Kolored
Tangerine-Flake
Streamline Baby

Picador

———

Farrar, Straus and Giroux
New York

Acknowledgments

The following chapters were first published in *Esquire* Magazine: "Las Vegas (What?) Las Vegas (Can't Hear You! Too Noisy) Las Vegas!!!!," "The Kandy-Kolored Tangerine-Flake Streamline Baby" (under the title, "There Goes [Varoom! Varoom!] That Kandy-Kolored Tangerine-Flake Streamline Baby"), "The Marvelous Mouth," "The Last American Hero" (under the title, "The Last American Hero Is Junior Johnson. Yes!"), and "Purveyor of the Public Life" (under the title, "Public Lives: *Confidential* Magazine; Reflection in Tranquility by the Former Owner, Robert Harrison"); "The New Art Gallery Society" first appeared in *Harper's Bazaar*; all the other essays first appeared in the New York *Herald Tribune*'s Sunday magazine, *New York*. "The Big League Complex" is reprinted from the book, *New York, New York,* © 1964 by the New York *Herald Tribune,* with the permission of the publishers, The Dial Press, Inc.

The drawings for "Teen-age Male Hairdos" first appeared in the Springfield (Mass.) *Sunday Republican,* those for "New York's Beautiful People" first appeared in *Venture* Magazine, and the other drawings first appeared in the New York *Herald Tribune*'s *New York*.

Contents

Introduction

I DON'T MEAN FOR THIS TO SOUND LIKE "I HAD A VISION" OR anything, but there was a specific starting point for practically all of these stories. I wrote them in a fifteen-month period, and the whole thing started with the afternoon I went to a Hot Rod & Custom Car show at the Coliseum in New York. Strange afternoon! I was sent up there to cover the Hot Rod & Custom Car show by the New York *Herald Tribune*, and I brought back exactly the kind of story any of the somnambulistic totem newspapers in America would have come up with. A totem newspaper is the kind people don't really buy to read but just to *have*, physically, because they know it supports their own outlook on life. They're just like the buffalo tongues the Omaha Indians used to carry around or the dog ears the Mahili clan carried around in Bengal. There are two kinds of totem newspapers in the country. One is the symbol of the frightened chair-arm-doilie Vicks Vapo-Rub *Weltanschauung* that lies there in the solar plexus of all good gray burghers. All those nice stories on the first page of the second section about eighty-seven-year-old ladies on Gramercy Park who have one-hundred-and-two-year-old turtles or about the colorful street vendors of Havana. Mommy! This fellow Castro is in there, and revolutions may come and go, but the picturesque poor will endure, padding around in the streets selling their chestnuts and salt pretzels the world over, even in Havana, Cuba, assuring a paradise, after all, full of respect and obeisance, for all us Vicks Vapo-Rub chair-arm-doilie burghers. After all. Or another totem group buys the kind of paper they can put under their arms and have the totem for the tough-but-wholesome outlook, the Mom's Pie view of life. Everybody can go off to the bar and drink a few "brews" and retail some cynical remarks about Zora Folley and how the fight game is these days and round it off, though, with how George Chuvalo has "a lot of heart," which he got, one understands, by eating mom's pie. Anyway, I went to the Hot Rod & Custom Car show and wrote a story that would have suited any of the totem newspapers. All the totem newspapers would regard one of these shows as a sideshow, a panopticon, for creeps and kooks; not even wealthy, eccentric creeps and kooks, which would be all right, but lower-class creeps and nutballs with dermatitic skin and ratty hair. The totem story usually makes what is known as "gentle fun" of this, which is a way of saying, don't worry, these people are nothing.

So I wrote a story about a kid who had built a golden motorcycle, which he called "The Golden Alligator." The seat was made of some kind of gold-painted leather that kept going back, on and on, as long as an alligator's tail, and had scales embossed on it, like an alligator's. The kid had made a whole golden suit for himself, like a space suit, that also looked as if it were covered with scales and he would lie down on his stomach on this long seat, stretched out full length, so that he appeared to be made into the motorcycle or something, and roar around Greenwich Village on Saturday nights, down Macdougal Street, down there in Nut Heaven, looking like a golden alligator on wheels. Nutty! He seemed like a Gentle Nut when I got through. It was a shame I wrote that sort of story, the usual totem story, because I was working for the *Herald Tribune,* and the *Herald Tribune* was the only experimental paper in town, breaking out of the totem formula. The thing was, I knew I had another story all the time, a bona fide story, the real story of the Hot Rod & Custom Car show, but I didn't know what to do with it. It was outside the system of ideas I was used to working with, even though I had been through the whole Ph.D. route at Yale, in American studies and everything.

Here were all these . . . *weird* . . . nutty-looking, crazy baroque custom cars, sitting in little nests of pink angora angel's hair for the purpose of "glamorous" display—but then I got to talking to one of the men who make them, a fellow named Dale Alexander. He was a very serious and soft-spoken man, about thirty, completely serious about the whole thing, in fact, and pretty soon it became clear, as I talked to this man for a while, that he had been living like the *complete artist* for years. He had starved, suffered—the whole thing—so he could sit inside a garage and create these cars which more than 99 per cent of the American people would consider ridiculous, vulgar and lower-class-awful beyond comment almost. He had started off with a garage that fixed banged-up cars and everything, to pay the rent, but gradually he couldn't stand it anymore. Creativity—his own custom car art—became an obsession with him. So he became the complete custom car artist. And he said he wasn't the only one. All the great custom car designers had gone through it. It was the *only way. Holy beasts!* Starving artists! Inspiration! Only instead of garrets, they had these garages.

So I went over to *Esquire* magazine after a while and talked to them about this phenomenon, and they sent me out to California to take a look at the custom car world. Dale Alexander was from Detroit or some place, but the real center of the thing was in California, around Los Angeles. I started talking to a lot of these people, like George Barris and Ed Roth, and seeing what they were doing, and—well, eventually it became the story from which the title of this book was taken, "The Kandy-Kolored Tangerine-Flake Streamline Baby." But at first I couldn't even write the story. I came back to New York and just sat around worrying over the thing. I had a lot of trouble analyzing exactly what I had on my hands. By this time *Esquire* practically had a gun at my head because they had a two-page-wide color picture for the story locked into the printing presses and no story. Finally,

I told Byron Dobell, the managing editor at *Esquire,* that I couldn't pull the thing together. O.K., he tells me, just type out my notes and send them over and he will get somebody else to write it. So about 8 o'clock that night I started typing the notes out in the form of a memorandum that began, "Dear Byron." I started typing away, starting right with the first time I saw any custom cars in California. I just started recording it all, and inside of a couple of hours, typing along like a madman, I could tell that something was beginning to happen. By midnight this memorandum to Byron was twenty pages long and I was still typing like a maniac. About 2 A.M. or something like that I turned on WABC, a radio station that plays rock and roll music all night long, and got a little more manic. I wrapped up the memorandum about 6:15 A.M., and by this time it was 49 pages long. I took it over to *Esquire* as soon as they opened up, about 9:30 A.M. About 4 P.M. I got a call from Byron Dobell. He told me they were striking out the "Dear Byron" at the top of the memorandum and running the rest of it in the magazine. That was the story, "The Kandy-Kolored Tangerine-Flake Streamline Baby."

What had happened was that I started writing down everything I had seen the first place I went in California, this incredible event, a "Teen Fair." The details themselves, when I wrote them down, suddenly made me see what was happening. Here was this incredible combination of form plus money in a place nobody ever thought about finding it, namely, among teen-agers. Practically every style recorded in art history is the result of the same thing—a lot of attention to form, plus the money to make monuments to it. The "classic" English style of Inigo Jones, for example, places like the Covent Garden and the royal banquet hall at Whitehall, were the result of a worship of Italian Palladian grandeur . . . form . . . plus the money that began pouring in under James I and Charles I from colonial possessions. These were the kind of forms, styles, symbols . . . Palladian classicism . . . that influence a whole society. But throughout history, everywhere this kind of thing took place, China, Egypt, France under the Bourbons, every place, it has been something the aris-tocracy has been responsible for. What has happened in the United States since World War II, however, has broken that pattern. The war created money. It made massive infusions of money into every level of society. Suddenly classes of people whose styles of life had been practically invisible had the money to build monuments to their own styles. Among teen-agers, this took the form of custom cars, the Twist, the Jerk, the Monkey, the Shake, rock music generally, stretch pants, decal eyes—and all these things, these teen-age styles of life, like Inigo Jones' classicism, have started having an influence on the life of the whole country. It is not merely teen-agers. In the South, for example, all the proles, peasants, and petty burghers suddenly got enough money to start up their incredible car world. In fifteen years stock car racing has replaced baseball as the number one sport in the South. It doesn't make much difference what happens to baseball or stock-car racing, actually, but this shift, from a fixed land sport, modeled on cricket, to this wild car sport, with standard, or standard-looking, cars that go 180 miles an hour or so—this symbolizes a radical change in the people as a whole. Practically nobody has bothered to see what these changes are all about. People have been looking at the new money since the war in economic terms only. Nobody will even take a look at our incredible new national pastimes, things like stock-car racing, drag racing, demolition derbies, sports that attract five to ten million more spectators than football, baseball, and basketball each year. Part of it is a built-in class bias. The educated classes in this country, as in every country, the people who grow up to control visual and printed communication media, are all plugged into what is, when one gets down to it, an ancient, aristocratic aesthetic. Stock-car racing, custom cars—and, for that matter, the Jerk, the Monkey, rock music—still seem beneath serious consideration, still the preserve of ratty people with ratty hair and dermatitis and corroded thoracic boxes and so forth. Yet all these rancid people are creating new styles all the time and changing the life of the whole country in ways that nobody even seems to bother to record, much less analyze.

A curious example of what is happening is Society, in the sense of High Society, in New York City today. Only it isn't called High Society or even Café Society anymore. Nobody seems to know quite what to call it, but the term that is catching on is Pop Society. This is because socialites in New York today seem to have no natural, aristocratic styles of their own—they are taking all their styles from "pop" groups, which stands for popular, or "vulgar" or "bohemian" groups. They dance the Jerk, the Monkey, the Shake, they listen to rock music, the women wear teenage and even "sub-teen" styles, such as stretch pants and decal eyes, they draw their taste in art, such as "underground" movies and "pop" painting, from various bohos and camp culturati, mainly. New York's "Girl of the Year"—Baby Jane Holzer—is the most incredible socialite in history. Here in this one girl is a living embodiment of almost pure "pop" sensation, a kind of corn-haired essence of the new styles of life. I never had written a story that seemed to touch so many nerves in so many people. Television and the movies all of a sudden went crazy over her, but that was just one side of it. A lot of readers were enraged. They wrote letters to the publisher of the *Herald Tribune*, to the *Herald Tribune* magazine, *New York*, where it appeared, they made phone calls, they would confront me with it in restaurants, all sorts of things—and in all of it I kept noticing the same thing. Nobody ever seemed to be able to put his finger on what he was enraged about. Most of them took the line that the *Herald Tribune* had no business paying that much attention to such a person and such a life as she was leading. Refreshing! Moral Outrage! But it was all based on the idea that Jane Holzer was some kind of freak they didn't like. Jane Holzer—and the Baby Jane syndrome—there's nothing freakish about it. Baby Jane is the hyperversion of a whole new style of life in America. I think she is a very profound symbol. But she is not the super-hyper-version. The super-hyper-version is Las Vegas. I call Las Vegas the Versailles of America, and for specific reasons, Las Vegas happened to be created after the war, with war money, by gangsters. Gangsters happened to be the first uneducated ... but more to the point, unaristocratic, *outside* of the aristocratic tradition ... the first uneducated, prole-petty-burgher Americans to have enough money to build a monument to their style of life. They built it in an isolated spot, Las Vegas, out in the desert, just like Louis XIV, the Sun King, who purposely went outside of Paris, into the countryside, to create a fantastic baroque environment to celebrate his rule. It is no accident that Las Vegas and Versailles are the only two architecturally uniform cities in Western history. The important thing about the building of Las Vegas is not that the builders were gangsters but that they were proles. They celebrated, very early, the new style of life of America—using the money pumped in by the war to show a prole vision ... *Glamor!* ... of style. The usual thing has happened, of course. Because it is prole, it gets ignored, except on the most sensational level. Yet long after Las Vegas' influence as a gambling heaven has gone, Las Vegas' forms and symbols will be influencing American life. That fantastic skyline! Las Vegas' neon sculpture, its fantastic fifteen-story-high display signs, parabolas, boomerangs, rhomboids, trapezoids and all the rest of it, are already the staple design of the American landscape outside of the oldest parts of the oldest cities. They are all over every suburb, every subdivision, every highway ... every *hamlet,* as it were, the new crossroads, spiraling Servicenter signs. They are the new landmarks of America, the new guideposts, the new way Americans get their bearings. And yet what do we know about these signs, these incredible pieces of neon sculpture, and what kind of impact they have on people? Nobody seems to know the first thing about it, not even the men who design them. I hunted out some of the great sign makers of Las Vegas, men who design for the Young Electric Sign Co., and the Federal Sign and Signal Corporation—and marvelous!—they come from completely outside the art history tradition of the design schools of the Eastern universities. I remember talking with this one designer, Ted Blaney, from Federal, their chief designer, in the cocktail lounge of the Dunes Hotel on "The Strip." I showed him a shape, a boomerang shape, that one sees all over Las Vegas, in small signs, huge signs, huge things like the archway entrance to the Desert Inn—it is not an arch, really, but this huge boomerang shape— and I asked him what they, the men who design these things, call it.

Ted was a stocky little guy, very sunburnt, with a pencil mustache and a Texas string tie, the kind that has strings sticking through some kind of silver dollar or something situated at the throat. He talked slowly and he had a way of furling his eyebrows around his nose when he did mental calculations such as figuring out this boomerang shape.

He started at the shape, which he and his brothers in the art have created over and over and over, over, over and over and over in Las Vegas, and finally he said,

"Well, that's what we call—what we sort of call—'free form.' "

Free form! Marvelous! No hung-up old art history words for these guys. America's first unconscious avant-garde! The hell with Mondrian, whoever the hell he is. The hell with Moholy-Nagy, if anybody ever heard of him. Artists for the new age, sculptors for the new style and new money of the . . . Yah! lower orders. The new sensibility—*Baby baby baby where did our love go?*—the new world, submerged so long, invisible, and now arising, slippy, shiny, electric—Super Scuba-man!—out of the vinyl deeps.

part 1

THE NEW
CULTURE-MAKERS

Las Vegas (What?) Las Vegas (Can't hear you! Too noisy) Las Vegas!!!!

HERNIA, HERNIA, HERNIA, HERNIA, HERNIA, HERNIA, HERnia, hernia, hernia, hernia, hernia, hernia, hernia, HERNia; hernia, HERNia, hernia, hernia, hernia, hernia, HERNia, HERNia, HERNia; hernia, hernia, hernia, hernia, hernia, hernia, hernia, eight is the point, the point is eight; hernia, hernia, HERNia; hernia, hernia, hernia, hernia, all right, hernia, hernia, hernia, hernia, hard eight, hernia, hernia, hernia, HERNia, hernia, hernia, hernia, HERNia, hernia, hernia, hernia, HERNia, hernia, hernia, hernia, hernia

"What is all this *hernia hernia* stuff?"

This was Raymond talking to the wavy-haired fellow with the stick, the dealer, at the craps table about 3:45 Sunday morning. The stickman had no idea what this big wiseacre was talking about, but he resented the tone. He gave Raymond that patient arch of the eyebrows known as a Red Hook brush-off, which is supposed to convey some such thought as, I am a very tough but cool guy, as you can tell by the way I carry my eyeballs low in the pouches, and if this wasn't such a high-class joint we would take wiseacres like you out back and beat you into jellied madrilene.

At this point, however, Raymond was immune to subtle looks.

The stickman tried to get the game going again, but every time he would start up his singsong, by easing the words out through the nose, which seems to be the style among craps dealers in Las Vegas—"All right, a new shooter . . . eight is the point, the point is eight" and so on—Raymond would start droning along with him in exactly the same tone of voice, "Hernia, hernia, hernia; hernia, HERNia, HERNia, hernia; hernia, hernia, hernia."

Everybody at the craps table was staring in consternation to think that anybody would try to needle a tough, hip, elite *soldat* like a Las Vegas craps dealer. The gold-lamé odalisques of Los Angeles were staring. The Western sports, fifty-eight-year-old men who wear Texas string ties, were staring. The old babes at the slot machines, holding Dixie Cups full of nickles, were staring at the craps tables, but cranking away the whole time.

Raymond, who is thirty-four years old and works as an engineer in Phoenix, is big but not terrifying. He has the sort of thatchwork hair that grows so low all along the forehead there is no logical place to part it, but he tries anyway. He has a huge, prognathous jaw, but it is as smooth, soft and round as a melon, so that Raymond's total effect is that of an Episcopal divinity student.

The guards were wonderful. They were dressed in cowboy uniforms like Bruce Cabot in *Sundown* and they wore sheriff's stars.

"Mister, is there something we can do for you?"

"The expression is 'Sir,'" said Raymond. "You said 'Mister.' The expression is 'Sir.' How's your old Cosa Nostra?"

Amazingly, the casino guards were easing Raymond out peaceably, without putting a hand on him. I had never seen the fellow before, but possibly because I had been following his progress for the last five minutes, he turned to me and said, "Hey, do you have a car? This wild stuff is starting again."

The gist of it was that he had left his car somewhere and he wanted to ride up the Strip to the Stardust, one of the big hotel-casinos. I am describing this big goof Raymond not because he is a typical Las Vegas tourist, although he has some typical symptoms, but because he is a good example of the marvelous impact Las Vegas has on the senses. Raymond's senses were at a high pitch of excitation, the only trouble being that he was going off his nut. He had been up since Thursday afternoon, and it was now about 3:45 A.M. Sunday. He had an envelope full of pep pills—amphetamine—in his left coat pocket and an envelope full of Equanils—meprobamate—in his right pocket, or were the Equanils in the left and the pep pills in the right? He could tell by looking, but he wasn't going to look anymore. He didn't care to see how many were left.

He had been rolling up and down the incredible electric-sign gauntlet of Las Vegas' Strip, U.S. Route 91, where the neon and the par lamps—bubbling, spiraling, rocketing, and exploding in sunbursts ten stories high out in the middle of the desert—celebrate one-story casinos. He had been gambling and drinking and eating now and again at the buffet tables the casinos keep heaped with food day and night, but mostly hopping himself up with good old amphetamine, cooling himself down with meprobamate, then hooking down more alcohol, until now, after sixty hours, he was slipping into the symptoms of toxic schizophrenia.

He was also enjoying what the prophets of hallucinogen call "consciousness expansion." The man was psychedelic. He was beginning to isolate the components of Las Vegas' unique bombardment of the senses. He was quite right about this *hernia hernia* stuff. Every casino in Las Vegas is, among the other things, a room full of craps tables with dealers who keep up a running singsong that sounds as though they are saying "hernia, hernia,

hernia, hernia, hernia" and so on. There they are day and night, easing a running commentary through their nostrils. What they have to say contains next to no useful instruction. Its underlying message is, We are the initiates, riding the crest of chance. That the accumulated sound comes out "hernia" is merely an unfortunate phonetic coincidence. Actually, it is part of something rare and rather grand: a combination of baroque stimuli that brings to mind the bronze gongs, no larger than a blue plate, that Louis XIV, his ruff collars larded with the lint of the foul Old City of Byzantium, personally hunted out in the bazaars of Asia Minor to provide exotic acoustics for his new palace outside Paris.

The sounds of the craps dealer will be in, let's say, the middle register. In the lower register will be the sound of the old babes at the slot machines. Men play the slots too, of course, but one of the indelible images of Las Vegas is that of the old babes at the row upon row of slot machines. There they are at six o'clock Sunday morning no less than at three o'clock Tuesday afternoon. Some of them pack their old hummocky shanks into Capri pants, but many of them just put on the old print dress, the same one day after day, and the old hob-heeled shoes, looking like they might be going out to buy eggs in Tupelo, Mississippi. They have a Dixie Cup full of nickels or dimes in the left hand and an Iron Boy work glove on the right hand to keep the calluses from getting sore. Every time they pull the handle, the machine makes a sound much like the sound a cash register makes before the bell rings, then the slot pictures start clattering up from left to right, the oranges, lemons, plums, cherries, bells, bars, buckaroos—the figure of a cowboy riding a bucking bronco. The whole sound keeps churning up over and over again in eccentric series all over the place, like one of those random-sound radio symphonies by John Cage. You can hear it at any hour of the day or night all over Las Vegas. You can walk down Fremont Street at dawn and hear it without even walking in a door, that and the spins of the wheels of fortune, a boring and not very popular sort of simplified roulette, as the tabs flap to a stop. As an overtone, or at times simply as a loud sound, comes the babble of the casino crowds, with an occasional shriek from the craps tables, or, anywhere from 4 P.M. to 6 A.M., the sound of brass instruments or electrified string instruments from the cocktail-lounge shows.

The crowd and band sounds are not very extraordinary, of course. But Las Vegas' Muzak is. Muzak pervades Las Vegas from the time you walk into the airport upon landing to the last time you leave the casinos. It is piped out to the swimming pool. It is in the drugstores. It is as if there were a communal fear that someone, somewhere in Las Vegas, was going to be left with a totally vacant minute on his hands.

Las Vegas has succeeded in wiring an entire city with this electronic stimulation, day and night, out in the middle of the desert. In the automobile I rented, the radio could not be turned off, no matter which dial you went after. I drove for days in a happy burble of Action Checkpoint News, "Monkey No. 9," "Donna, Donna, the Prima Donna," and picking-and-singing jingles for the Frontier Bank and the Fremont Hotel.

One can see the magnitude of the achievement. Las Vegas takes what in other American towns is but a quixotic inflammation of the senses for some poor salary mule in the brief interval between the flagstone rambler and the automatic elevator downtown and magnifies it, foliates it, embellishes it into an institution.

For example, Las Vegas is the only town in the world whose skyline is made up neither of buildings, like New York, nor of trees, like Wilbraham, Massachusetts, but signs. One can look at Las Vegas from a mile away on Route 91 and see no buildings, no trees, only signs. But such signs! They tower. They revolve, they oscillate, they soar in shapes before which the existing vocabulary of art history is helpless. I can only attempt to supply names— Boomerang Modern, Palette Curvilinear, Flash Gordon Ming-Alert Spiral, McDonald's Hamburger Parabola, Mint Casino Elliptical, Miami Beach Kidney. Las Vegas' sign makers work so far out beyond the frontiers of conventional studio art that they have no names themselves for the forms they create. Vaughan

Cannon, one of those tall, blond Westerners, the builders of places like Las Vegas and Los Angeles, whose eyes seem to have been bleached by the sun, is in the back shop of the Young Electric Sign Company out on East Charleston Boulevard with Herman Boernge, one of his designers, looking at the model they have prepared for the Lucky Strike Casino sign, and Cannon points to where the sign's two great curving faces meet to form a narrow vertical face and says:

"Well, here we are again—what do we call that?"

"I don't know," says Boernge. "It's sort of a nose effect. Call it a nose."

Okay, a nose, but it rises sixteen stories high above a two-story building. In Las Vegas no farseeing entrepreneur buys a sign to fit a building he owns. He rebuilds the building to support the biggest sign he can get up the money for and, if necessary, changes the name. The Lucky Strike Casino today is the Lucky Casino, which fits better when recorded in sixteen stories of flaming peach and incandescent yellow in the middle of the Mojave Desert. In the Young Electric Sign Co. era signs have become the architecture of Las Vegas, and the most whimsical, Yale-seminar-frenzied devices of the two late geniuses of Baroque Modern, Frank Lloyd Wright and Eero Saarinen, seem rather stuffy business, like a jest at a faculty meeting, compared to it. Men like Boernge, Kermit Wayne, Ben Mitchem and Jack Larsen, formerly an artist for Walt Disney, are the designer-sculptor geniuses of Las Vegas, but their motifs have been carried faithfully throughout the town by lesser men, for gasoline stations, motels, funeral parlors, churches, public buildings, flophouses and sauna baths.

Then there is a stimulus that is both visual and sexual—the Las Vegas buttocks décolletage. This is a form of sexually provocative dress seen more and more in the United States, but avoided like Broadway message-embroidered ("Kiss Me, I'm Cold") underwear in the fashion pages, so that the euphemisms have not been established and I have no choice but clinical terms.

To achieve buttocks décolletage a woman wears bikini-style shorts that cut across the round fatty masses of the buttocks rather than cupping them from below, so that the outer-lower edges of these fatty masses, or "cheeks," are exposed. I am in the cocktail lounge of the Hacienda Hotel, talking to managing director Dick Taylor about the great success his place has had in attracting family and tour groups, and all around me the waitresses are bobbing on their high heels, bare legs and décolletage-bare backsides, set off by pelvis-length lingerie of an uncertain denomination. I stare, but I am new here. At the White Cross Rexall drugstore on the Strip a pregnant brunette walks in off the street wearing black shorts with buttocks décolletage aft and illusion-of-cloth nylon lingerie hanging fore, and not even the old mom's-pie pensioners up near the door are staring. They just crank away at the slot machines. On the streets of Las Vegas, not only the show girls, of which the town has about two hundred fifty, bona fide, in residence, but girls of every sort, including, especially, Las Vegas' little high-school buds, who adorn what locals seeking roots in the sand call "our city of churches and schools," have taken up the chic of wearing buttocks décolletage step-ins under flesh-tight slacks, with the outline of the undergarment showing through fashionably. Others go them one better. They achieve the effect of having been dipped once, briefly, in Helenca stretch nylon. More and more they look like those wonderful old girls out of Flash Gordon who were wrapped just once over in Baghdad pantaloons of clear polyethylene with only Flash Gordon between them and the insane red-eyed assaults of the minions of Ming. It is as if all the hip young suburban gals of America named Lana, Deborah and Sandra, who gather wherever the arc lights shine and the studs steady their coiffures in the plate-glass reflection, have convened in Las Vegas with their bouffant hair above and anatomically stretch-pant-swathed little bottoms below, here on the new American frontier. But exactly!

.   .   .

NONE OF IT WOULD HAVE BEEN POSSIBLE, HOWEVER, WITHOUT one of those historic combinations of nature and art that create an epoch. In this case, the Mojave Desert plus the father of Las Vegas, the late Benjamin "Bugsy" Siegel.

Bugsy was an inspired man. Back in 1944 the city fathers of Las Vegas, their Protestant rectitude alloyed only by the giddy prospect of gambling revenues, were considering the sort of ordinance that would have preserved the town with a kind of Colonial Williamsburg dinkiness in the motif of the Wild West. All new buildings would have to have at least the façade of the sort of place where piano players used to wear garters on their sleeves in Virginia City around 1880. In Las Vegas in 1944, it should be noted, there was nothing more stimulating in the entire town than a Fremont Street bar where the composer of "Deep in the Heart of Texas" held forth and the regulars downed fifteen-cent beer.

Bugsy pulled into Las Vegas in 1945 with several million dollars that, after his assassination, was traced back in the general direction of gangster-financiers. Siegel put up a hotel-casino such as Las Vegas had never seen and called it the Flamingo—all Miami Modern, and the hell with piano players with garters and whatever that was all about. Everybody drove out Route 91 just to gape. Such shapes! Boomerang Modern supports, Palette Curvilinear bars, Hot Shoppe Cantilever roofs and a scalloped swimming pool. Such colors! All the new electrochemical pastels of the Florida littoral: tangerine, broiling magenta, livid pink, incarnadine, fuchsia demure, Congo ruby, methyl green, viridine, aquamarine, phenosafranine, incandescent orange, scarlet-fever purple, cyanic blue, tessellated bronze, hospital-fruit-basket orange. And such signs! Two cylinders rose at either end of the Flamingo—eight stories high and covered from top to bottom with neon rings in the shape of bubbles that fizzed all eight stories up into the desert sky all night long like an illuminated whisky-soda tumbler filled to the brim with pink champagne.

The business history of the Flamingo, on the other hand, was not such a smashing success. For one thing, the gambling operation was losing money at a rate that rather gloriously refuted all the recorded odds of the gaming science. Siegel's backers apparently suspected that he was playing both ends against the middle in collusion with professional gamblers who hung out at the Flamingo as though they had liens on it. What with one thing and another, someone decided by the night of June 20, 1947, that Benny Siegel, lord of the Flamingo, had had it. He was shot to death in Los Angeles.

Yet Siegel's aesthetic, psychological and cultural insights, like Cézanne's, Freud's and Max Weber's, could not die. The Siegel vision and the Siegel aesthetic were already sweeping Las Vegas like gold fever. And there were builders of the West equal to the opportunity. All over Las Vegas the incredible electric pastels were repeated. Overnight the Baroque Modern forms made Las Vegas one of the few architecturally unified cities of the world—the style was Late American Rich—and without the bother and bad humor of a City Council ordinance. No enterprise was too small, too pedestrian or too solemn for The Look. The Supersonic Carwash, the Mercury Jet-away, Gas Vegas Village and Terrible Herbst gasoline stations, the Par-a-Dice Motel, the Palm Mortuary, the Orbit Inn, the Desert Moon, the Blue Onion Drive-In—on it went, like Wildwood, New Jersey, entering Heaven.

The atmosphere of the six-mile-long Strip of hotel-casinos grips even those segments of the population who rarely go near it. Barely twenty-five hundred feet off the Strip, over by the Convention Center, stands Landmark Towers, a shaft thirty stories high, full of apartments, supporting a huge circular structure shaped like a space observation platform, which was to have contained the restaurant and casino. Somewhere along the way Landmark Towers went bankrupt, probably at that point in the last of the many crises when the construction workers *still* insisted on spending half the day flat on their bellies with their heads, tongues and eyeballs hanging over the edge of the tower, looking down into the swimming pool of the Playboy Apartments below, which has a "nudes only" section for show girls whose work calls for a tan all over.

Elsewhere, Las Vegas' beautiful little high-school buds in their buttocks-décolletage stretch pants are back on the foam-rubber upholstery of luxury broughams peeling off the entire chick ensemble long enough to establish the highest venereal-disease rate among high-school students anywhere north of the yaws-rotting shanty jungles of the Eighth Parallel. The Negroes who have done much of the construction work in Las Vegas' sixteen-year boom are off in their ghetto on the west side of town, and some of them are smoking marijuana, eating peyote buttons and taking horse (heroin), which they get from Tijuana, I mean it's simple, baby, right through the mails, and old Raymond, the Phoenix engineer, does not have the high life to himself.

I AM ON THE THIRD FLOOR OF THE CLARK COUNTY COURT house talking to Sheriff Captain Ray Gubser, another of these strong, pale-eyed Western-builder types, who is obligingly explaining to me law enforcement on the Strip, where the problem is not so much the drunks, crooks or roughhousers, but these nuts on pills who don't want to ever go to bed, and they have hallucinations and try to bring down the casinos like Samson. The county has two padded cells for them. They cool down after three or four days and they turn out to be somebody's earnest breadwinner back in Denver or Minneapolis, loaded with the right credentials and pouring soul and apologiae all over the county cops before finally pulling out of never-never land for good by plane. Captain Gubser is telling me about life and eccentric times in Las Vegas, but I am distracted. The captain's office has windows out on the corridor. Coming down the corridor is a covey of girls, skipping and screaming, giggling along, their heads exploding in platinum-and-neon-yellow bouffants or beehives or raspberry-silk scarves, their eyes appliquéd in black like mail-order decals, their breasts aimed up under their jerseys at the angle of anti-aircraft automatic weapons, and, as they swing around the corner toward the elevator, their glutei maximi are bobbing up and down with their pumps in the inevitable buttocks décolletage pressed out against black, beige and incarnadine stretch pants. This is part of the latest shipment of show girls to Las Vegas, seventy in all, for the "Lido de Paris" revue at the Stardust, to be entitled *Bravo!,* replacing the old show, entitled *Voilà.* The girls are in the county courthouse getting their working papers, and fifteen days from now these little glutei maximi and ack-ack breasts with stars pasted on the tips will be swinging out over the slack jaws and cocked-up noses of patrons sitting at stageside at the Stardust. I am still listening to Gubser, but somehow it is a courthouse where mere words are beaten back like old atonal Arturo Toscanini trying to sing along with the NBC Symphony. There he would be, flapping his little toy arms like Tony Galento shadowboxing with fate, bawling away in the face of union musicians who drowned him without a bubble. I sat in on three trials in the courthouse, and it was wonderful, because the courtrooms are all blond-wood modern and look like sets for TV panel discussions on marriage and the teen-ager. What the judge has to say is no less formal and no more fatuous than what judges say everywhere, but inside of forty seconds it is all meaningless because the atmosphere is precisely like a news broadcast over Las Vegas' finest radio station, KORK. The newscast, as it is called, begins with a series of electronic wheeps out on that far edge of sound where only quadrupeds can hear. A voice then announces that this is Action Checkpoint News. "The news—all the news—flows first through Action Checkpoint!—then reaches You! at the speed of Sound!" More electronic wheeps, beeps and lulus, and then an item: "Cuban Premier Fidel Castro nearly drowned yesterday." Urp! Wheep! Lulu! No news a KORK announcer has ever brought to Las Vegas at the speed of sound, or could possibly bring, short of word of the annihilation of Los Angeles, could conceivably compete within the brain with the giddiness of this electronic jollification.

The wheeps, beeps, freeps, electronic lulus, Boomerang Modern and Flash Gordon sunbursts soar on through the night over the billowing hernia-hernia sounds and the old babes at the slots—until it is 7:30 A.M. and I am watching five men at a green-topped card table playing poker. They are sliding their Bee-brand cards into their hands and squinting at the pips with a set to the lips like Conrad Veidt in a tunic collar studying a code message from S.S. headquarters. Big Sid Wyman, the old Big-Time gambler from St. Louis, is there, with his eyes looking like two poached eggs engraved with a road map of West Virginia after all night at the poker table. Sixty-year-old Chicago Tommy Hargan is there with his topknot of white hair pulled back over his little pink skull and a mountain of chips in front of his old caved-in sternum. Sixty-two-year-old Dallas Maxie Welch is there, fat and phlegmatic as an Indian Ocean potentate. Two Los Angeles biggies are there exhaling smoke from candela-green cigars into the gloom. It looks like the perfect vignette of every Big-Time back room, "athletic club," snooker house and floating poker game in the history of the guys-and-dolls lumpen-bourgeoisie. But what is all this? Off to the side, at a rostrum, sits a flawless little creature with bouffant hair and Stridex-pure skin who looks like she is polished each morning with a rotary buffer. Before her on the rostrum is a globe of coffee on a hot coil. Her sole job is to keep the poker players warmed up with coffee. Meantime, numberless uniformed lackeys are cocked and aimed about the edges to bring the five Big Timers whatever else they might desire, cigarettes, drinks, napkins, eyeglass-cleaning tissues, plug-in telephones. All around the poker table, at a respectful distance of ten feet, is a fence with the most delicate golden pickets. Upon it, even at this narcoleptic hour, lean men and women in their best clothes watching the combat of the titans. The scene is the charmed circle of the casino of the Dunes Hotel.

As everyone there knows, or believes, these fabulous men are playing for table stakes of fifteen or twenty thousand dollars. One hundred dollars rides on a chip. Mandibles gape at the progress of the battle. And now Sid Wyman, who is also a vice-president of the Dunes, is at a small escritoire just inside the golden fence signing a stack of vouchers for such sums as $4500, all printed in the heavy Mondrianesque digits of a Burroughs business check-making machine. It is as if America's guys-and-dolls gamblers have somehow been tapped upon the shoulders, knighted, initiated into a new aristocracy.

Las Vegas has become, just as Bugsy Siegel dreamed, the American Monte Carlo—without any of the inevitable upper-class baggage of the Riviera casinos. At Monte Carlo there is still the plush mustiness of the 19th-century noble lions—of Baron Bleichroden, a big winner at roulette who always said, "My dear friends, it is so easy on Black." Of Lord Jersey, who won seventeen maximum bets in a row—on black, as a matter of fact—nodded to the croupier, and said, "Much obliged, old sport, old sport," took his winnings to England, retired to the country and never gambled again in his life. Or of the old Duc de Dinc who said he could win only in the high-toned Club Privé, and who won very heavily one night, saw two Englishmen gaping at his good fortune, threw them every mille-franc note he had in his hands and said, "Here. Englishmen without money are altogether odious." Thousands of Europeans from the lower orders now have the money to go to the Riviera, but they remain under the century-old status pall of the aristocracy. At Monte Carlo there are still Wrong Forks, Deficient Accents, Poor Tailoring, Gauche Displays, Nouveau Richness, Cultural Aridity—concepts unknown in Las Vegas. For the grand debut of Monte Carlo as a resort in 1879 the architect Charles Garnier designed an opera house for the Place du Casino; and Sarah Bernhardt read a symbolic poem. For the debut of Las Vegas as a resort in 1946 Bugsy Siegel hired Abbott and Costello, and there, in a way, you have it all.

.   .   .

I AM IN THE OFFICE OF MAJOR A. RIDDLE—MAJOR IS HIS name—the president of the Dunes Hotel. He combs his hair straight back and wears a heavy gold band on his little finger with a diamond sunk into it. As everywhere else in Las Vegas, someone has turned on the air conditioning to the point where it will be remembered, all right, as Las Vegas–style air conditioning. Riddle has an appointment to see a doctor at 4:30 about a crimp in his neck. His secretary, Maude McBride, has her head down and is rubbing the back of her neck. Lee Fisher, the P.R. man, and I are turning ours from time to time to keep the pivots from freezing up. Riddle is telling me about "the French war" and moving his neck gingerly. The Stardust bought and imported a version of the Lido de Paris spectacular, and the sight of all those sequined giblets pooning around on flamingo legs inflamed the tourists. The Tropicana fought back with the Folies Bergère, the New Frontier installed "Paree Ooh La La," the Hacienda reached for the puppets "Les Poupées de Paris," and the Silver Slipper called in Lili St. Cyr, the stripper, which was going French after a fashion. So the Dunes has bought up the third and last of the great Paris girlie shows, the Casino de Paris. Lee Fisher says, "And we're going to do things they *can't* top. In this town you've got to move ahead in quantum jumps."

Quantum? But exactly! The beauty of the Dunes' Casino de Paris show is that it will be beyond art, beyond dance, beyond spectacle, even beyond the titillations of the winking crotch. The Casino de Paris will be a behemoth piece of American calculus, like Project Mercury.

"This show alone will cost us two and a half million a year to operate and one and a half million to produce," Major A. Riddle is saying. "The costumes alone will be fantastic. There'll be more than five hundred costumes and—well, they'll be fantastic.

"And this machine—by the time we get through expanding the stage, this machine will cost us $250,000."

"Machine?"

"Yes. Sean Kenny is doing the staging. The whole set moves electronically right in front of your eyes. He used to work with this fellow Lloyd Wright."

"Frank Lloyd Wright?"

"Yes. Kenny did the staging for *Blitz*. Did you see it? Fantastic. Well, it's all done electronically. They built this machine for us in Glasgow, Scotland, and it's being shipped here right now. It moves all over the place and creates smoke and special effects. We'll have everything. You can stage a bombardment with it. You'll think the whole theatre is blowing up.

"You'll have to program it. They had to use the same mechanism that's in the Skybolt Missile to build it. It's called a 'Celson' or something like that. That's how complicated this thing is. They have to have the same thing as the Skybolt Missile."

As Riddle speaks, one gets a wonderful picture of sex riding the crest of the future. Whole tableaux of bare-bottomed Cosmonaughties will be hurtling around the Casino de Paris Room of the Dunes Hotel at fantastic speed in elliptical orbits, a flash of the sequined giblets here, a blur of the black-rimmed decal eyes there, a wink of the crotch here and there, until, with one vast Project Climax for our times, Sean Kenny, who used to work with this fellow Frank Lloyd Wright, presses the red button and the whole yahooing harem, shrieking ooh-la-la amid the din, exits in a mushroom cloud.

THE ALLURE IS MOST IRRESISTIBLE NOT TO THE YOUNG BUT the old. No one in Las Vegas will admit it—it is not the modern, glamorous notion—but Las Vegas is a resort for old people. In those last years, before the tissue deteriorates and the wires of the cerebral cortex hang in the skull like a clump of dried seaweed, they are seeking liberation.

At eight o'clock Sunday morning it is another almost boringly sunny day in the desert, and Clara and Abby, both about sixty, and their husbands, Earl, sixty-three, and Ernest, sixty-four, come squinting out of the Mint Casino onto Fremont Street.

"I don't know what's wrong with me," Abby says. "Those last three drinks, I couldn't even feel them. It was just like drinking fizz. You know what I mean?"

"Hey," says Ernest, "how about that place back 'ere? We ain't been back 'ere. Come on."

The others are standing there on the corner, squinting and looking doubtful. Abby and Clara have both entered old babe-hood. They have that fleshy, humped-over shape across the back of the shoulders. Their torsos are hunched up into fat little loaves supported by bony, atrophied leg stems sticking up into their hummocky hips. Their hair has been fried and dyed into improbable designs.

"You know what I mean? After a while it just gives me gas," says Abby. "I don't even feel it."

"Did you see me over there?" says Earl. "I was just going along, nice and easy, not too much, just riding along real nice. You know? And then, boy, I don't know what happened to me. First thing I know I'm laying down fifty dollars...."

Abby lets out a great belch. Clara giggles.

"Gives me gas," Abby says mechanically.

"Hey, how about that place back 'ere?" says Ernest.

"... Just nice and easy as you please...."

"... get me all fizzed up...."

"Aw, come on...."

And there at eight o'clock Sunday morning stand four old parties from Albuquerque, New Mexico, up all night, squinting at the sun, belching from a surfeit of tall drinks at eight o'clock Sunday morning, and—marvelous!—there is no one around to snigger at what an old babe with decaying haunches looks like in Capri pants with her heels jacked up on decorated wedges.

"Where do we *come* from?" Clara said to me, speaking for the first time since I approached them on Fremont Street. "He wants to know where we come from I think it's past your bedtime, sweets."

"Climb the stairs and go to bed," said Abby.

Laughter all around.

"Climb the stairs" was Abby's finest line. At present there are almost no stairs to climb in Las Vegas. Avalon homes are soon to go up, advertising "Two-Story Homes!" as though this were an incredibly lavish and exotic concept. As I talked to Clara, Abby, Earl and Ernest, it came out that "climb the stairs" was a phrase they brought along to Albuquerque with them from Marshalltown, Iowa, those many years ago, along with a lot of other baggage, such as the entire cupboard of Protestant taboos against drinking, lusting, gambling, staying out late, getting up late, loafing, idling, lollygagging around the streets and wearing Capri pants—all designed to deny a person short-term pleasures so he will center his energies on bigger, long-term goals.

"We was in 'ere"—the Mint—"a couple of hours ago, and that old boy was playing the guitar, you know, 'Walk right in, set right down,' and I kept hearing an old song I haven't heard for twenty years. It has this little boy and his folks keep telling him it's late and he has to go to bed. He keeps saying, 'Don't make me go to bed and I'll be good.' Am I *good,* Earl? Am I *good?*"

The liberated cortex in all its glory is none other than the old babes at the slot machines. Some of them are tourists whose husbands said, *Here is fifty bucks, go play the slot machines,* while they themselves went off to more complex pleasures. But most of these old babes are part of the permanent landscape of Las Vegas. In they go to the Golden Nugget or the Mint, with their Social Security check or their pension check from the Ohio telephone company, cash it at the casino cashier's, pull out the Dixie Cup and the Iron Boy work glove, disappear down a row of slots and get on with it. I remember particularly talking to another Abby—a widow, sixty-two years old, built short and up from the bottom like a fire hydrant. After living alone for twelve years in

Canton, Ohio, she had moved out to Las Vegas to live with her daughter and her husband, who worked for the Army.

"They were wonderful about it," she said. "Perfect hypocrites. She kept saying, you know, 'Mother, we'd be delighted to have you, only we don't think you'll *like* it. It's practically a fron*tier* town,' she says. 'It's so garish,' she says. So I said, I told her, 'Well, if you'd rather I didn't come . . .' 'Oh, no!' she says. I wish I could have heard what her husband was saying. He calls me 'Mother.' '*Mother,*' he says. Well, once I was here, they figured, well, I *might* make a good baby-sitter and dishwasher and duster and mopper. The children are nasty little things. So one day I was in town for something or other and I just played a slot machine. It's fun—I can't describe it to you. I suppose I lose. I lose a little. And *they* have fits about it. 'For God's sake, Grandmother,' and so forth. They always say '*Grand*mother' when I am supposed to 'act my age' or crawl through a crack in the floor. Well, I'll tell you, the slot machines are a *whole lot* better than sitting in that little house all day. They kind of get you; I can't explain it."

The childlike megalomania of gambling is, of course, from the same cloth as the megalomania of the town. And, as the children of the liberated cortex, the old guys and babes are running up and down the Strip around the clock like everybody else. It is not by chance that much of the entertainment in Las Vegas, especially the second-stringers who perform in the cocktail lounges, will recall for an aging man what was glamorous twenty-five years ago when he had neither the money nor the freedom of spirit to indulge himself in it. In the big theatre–dining room at the Desert Inn, The Painted Desert Room, Eddie Fisher's act is on and he is saying cozily to a florid guy at a table right next to the stage, "Manny, you know you shouldn'a sat this close—you know you're in for it now, Manny, baby," while Manny beams with fright. But in the cocktail lounge, where the idea is chiefly just to keep the razzle-dazzle going, there is Hugh Farr, one of the stars of another era in the West, composer of two of the five Western songs the Library of Congress has taped for posterity, "Cool Water" and "Tumbling Tumbleweed," when he played the violin for the Sons of the Pioneers. And now around the eyes he looks like an aging Chinese savant, but he is wearing a white tuxedo and powder-blue leather boots and playing his sad old Western violin with an electric cord plugged in it for a group called The Country Gentlemen. And there is Ben Blue, looking like a waxwork exhibit of vaudeville, doffing his straw skimmer to reveal the sculptural qualities of his skull. And down at the Flamingo cocktail lounge—Ella Fitzgerald is in the main room—there is Harry James, looking old and pudgy in one of those toy Italian-style show-biz suits. And the Ink Spots are at the New Frontier and Louis Prima is at the Sahara, and the old parties are seeing it all, roaring through the dawn into the next day, until the sun seems like a par lamp fading in and out. The casinos, the bars, the liquor stores are open every minute of every day, like a sempiternal wading pool for the childhood ego. ". . . Don't make me go to bed . . ."

FINALLY THE CASUALTIES START PILING UP. I AM IN THE MANager's office of a hotel on the Strip. A man and his wife, each about sixty, are in there, raging. Someone got into their room and stole seventy dollars from her purse, and they want the hotel to make it up to them. The man pops up and down from a chair and ricochets back and forth across the room, flailing his great pig's-knuckle elbows about.

"What kind of security you call that? Walk right in the goddern room and just help themselves. And where do you think I found your security man? Back around the corner reading a goddern detective magazine!"

He had scored a point there, but he was wearing a striped polo shirt with a hip Hollywood solid-color collar, and she had on Capri pants, and hooked across their wrinkly old faces they both had rimless, wraparound French sunglasses of the sort young-punk heroes in *nouvelle vague* movies wear, and it was impossible to give any earnest contemplation to a word they said. They seemed to have the great shiny popeyes of a praying mantis.

"Listen, Mister," she is saying, "I don't care about the seventy bucks. I'd lose seventy bucks at your craps table and I wouldn't think nothing of it. I'd play seventy bucks just like that, and it wouldn't mean nothing. I wouldn't regret it. But when they can just walk in—and you don't give a damn—for Christ's sake!"

They are both zeroing in on the manager with their great insect corneas. The manager is a cool number in a white-on-white shirt and silver tie.

"This happened three days ago. Why didn't you tell us about it then?"

"Well, I was gonna be a nice guy about it. Seventy dollars," he said, as if it would be difficult for the brain to grasp a sum much smaller. "But then I found your man back there reading a goddern detective magazine. *True Detectives* it was. Had a picture on the front of some floozie with one leg up on a chair and her garter showing. Looked like a god-derned athlete's-foot ad. Boy, I went into a slow burn. But when I am burned up, I am *burned up!* You get me, Mister? There he was, reading the god-derned *True Detectives.*"

"Any decent hotel would have insurance," she says.

The manager says, "I don't know a hotel in the world that offers insurance against theft."

"Hold on, Mister," he says, "are you calling my wife a liar? You just get smart, and I'm gonna pop you one! I'll pop you one right now if you call my wife a liar."

At this point the manager lowers his head to one side and looks up at the old guy from under his eyebrows with a version of the Red Hook brush-off, and the old guy begins to cool off.

But others are beyond cooling off. Hornette Reilly, a buttery-hipped whore from New York City, is lying in bed with a bald-headed guy from some place who has skin like oatmeal. He is asleep or passed out or something. Hornette is relating all this to the doctor over the Princess telephone by the bed.

"Look," she says, "I'm breaking up. I can't tell you how much I've drunk. About a bottle of brandy since four o'clock, I'm not kidding. I'm in bed with a guy. Right this minute. I'm talking on the telephone to you and this slob is lying here like an animal. He's all fat and his skin looks like oatmeal—what's happening to me? I'm going to take some more pills. I'm not kidding, I'm breaking up. I'm going to kill myself. You've got to put me in Rose de Lima. I'm breaking up, and I don't even know what's happening to me."

"So naturally you want to go to Rose de Lima."

"Well, yeah."

"You can come by the office, but I'm not sending you to Rose de Lima."

"Doctor, I'm not kidding."

"I don't doubt that you're sick, old girl, but I'm not sending you to Rose de Lima to sober up."

The girls do not want to go to the County Hospital. They want to go to Rose de Lima, where the psychiatric cases receive milieu therapy. The patients dress in street clothes, socialize and play games with the staff, eat well and relax in the sun, all paid for by the State. One of the folk heroines of the Las Vegas floozies, apparently, is the call girl who last year was spending Monday through Friday at Rose de Lima and "turning out," as they call it, Saturdays and Sundays on the Strip, to the tune of $200 to $300 a weekend. She looks upon herself not as a whore, or even a call girl, but as a lady of assignation. When some guy comes to the Strip and unveils the little art-nouveau curves in his psyche and calls for two girls to perform arts upon one another, this one consents to be the passive member of the team only. A Rose de Lima girl, she draws the line.

At the County Hospital the psychiatric ward is latched, bolted, wired up and jammed with patients who are edging along the walls in the inner hall, the only place they have to take a walk other than the courtyard.

A big brunette with the remnants of a beehive hairdo and decal eyes and an obvious pregnancy is the liveliest of the lot. She is making eyes at everyone who walks in. She also nods gaily toward vacant places along the wall.

"Mrs.———is refusing medication," a nurse tells one of the psychiatrists. "She won't even open her mouth."

Presently the woman, in a white hospital tunic, is led up the hall. She looks about fifty, but she has extraordinary lines on her face.

"Welcome home," says Dr.———.

"This is not my home," she says.

"Well, as I told you before, it has to be for the time being."

"Listen, you didn't analyze me."

"Oh, yes. Two psychiatrists examined you—all over again."

"You mean that time in jail."

"Exactly."

"You can't tell anything from that. I was excited. I had been out on the Strip, and then all that stupid—"

Three-fourths of the 640 patients who clustered into the ward last year were casualties of the Strip or the Strip milieu of Las Vegas, the psychiatrist tells me. He is a bright and energetic man in a shawl-collared black silk suit with brass buttons.

"I'm not even her doctor," he says. "I don't know her case. There's nothing I can do for her."

Here, securely out of sight in this little warren, are all those who have taken the loop-the-loop and could not stand the centripety. Some, like Raymond, who has been rocketing for days on pills and liquor, who has gone without sleep to the point of anoxia, might pull out of the toxic reaction in two or three days, or eight or ten. Others have conflicts to add to the chemical wackiness. A man who has thrown all his cash to the flabby homunculus who sits at every craps table stuffing the take down an almost hidden chute so it won't pile up in front of the customers' eyes; a man who has sold the family car for next to nothing at a car lot advertising "Cash for your car—*right now*" and then thrown that to the homunculus, too, but also still has the family waiting guiltlessly, guilelessly back home; well, he has troubles.

"... After I came here and began doing personal studies," the doctor is saying, "I recognized extreme aggressiveness continually. It's not merely what Las Vegas can do to a person, it's the type of person it attracts. Gambling is a very aggressive pastime, and Las Vegas attracts aggressive people. They have an amazing capacity to louse up a normal situation."

The girl, probably a looker in more favorable moments, is pressed face into the wall, cutting glances at the doctor. The nurse tells her something and she puts her face in her hands, convulsing but not making a sound. She retreats to her room, and then the sounds come shrieking out. The doctor rushes back. Other patients are sticking their heads out of their rooms along the hall.

"The young girl?" a quiet guy says to a nurse. "The young girl," he says to somebody in the room.

But the big brunette just keeps rolling her decal eyes.

Out in the courtyard—all bare sand—the light is a kind of light-bulb twilight. An old babe is rocking herself back and forth on a straight chair and putting one hand out in front from time to time and pulling it in toward her bosom.

It seems clear enough to me. "A slot machine?" I say to the nurse, but she says there is no telling.

"... and yet the same aggressive types are necessary to build a frontier town, and Las Vegas is a frontier town, certainly by any psychological standard," Dr.——is saying. "They'll undertake anything and they'll accomplish it. The building here has been incredible. They don't seem to care what they're up against, so they do it."

I go out to the parking lot in back of the County Hospital and it doesn't take a second; as soon as I turn on the motor I'm swinging again with Action Checkpoint News, "Monkey No. 9," "Donna, Donna, the Prima Donna," and friendly picking and swinging for the Fremont Hotel and Frontier Federal. Me and my big white car are sailing down the Strip and the Boomerang Modern, Palette Curvilinear, Flash Gordon Ming-Alert Spiral, McDonald's Hamburger Parabola, Mint Casino Elliptical and Miami Beach Kidney sunbursts are exploding in the Young Electric Sign Company's Grand Gallery for all the sun kings. At the airport there was that bad interval between the rental-car stall and the terminal entrance, but once through the automatic door the Muzak came bubbling up with "Song of India." On the upper level around the ramps the slots were cranking away. They are placed like "traps," a word Las Vegas picked up from golf. And an old guy is walking up the ramp, just off the plane from Denver, with a huge plastic bag of clothes slung over the left shoulder and a two-suiter suitcase in his right hand. He has to put the suitcase down on the floor and jostle the plastic bag all up around his neck to keep it from falling, but he manages to dig into his pocket for a couple of coins and get going on the slot machines. All seems right, but walking out to my plane I sense that something is missing. Then I recall sitting in the cocktail lounge of the Dunes at 3 P.M. with Jack Heskett, district manager of the Federal Sign and Signal Corporation, and Marty Steinman, the sales manager, and Ted Blaney, a designer. They are telling me about the sign they are building for the Dunes to put up at the airport. It will be five thousand square feet of free-standing sign, done in flaming-lake red on burning-desert gold. The d—the D—alone in the word Dunes, written in Cyrillic modern, will be practically two stories high. An inset plexiglas display, the largest revolving, trivision plexiglas sign in the world, will turn and show first the Dunes, with its twenty-two-story addition, then the seahorse swimming pool, then the new golf course. The scimitar curves of the sign will soar to a huge roaring diamond at the very top. "You'll be able to see it from an airplane fifteen miles away," says Jack Heskett. "Fifty miles," says Lee Fisher. And it will be sixty-five feet up in the air—because the thing was, somebody was out at the airport and they noticed there was only one display to be topped. That was that shaft about sixty feet high with the lit-up globe and the beacon lights, which is to say, the control tower. Hell, you can only see that forty miles away. But exactly!

chapter 2

Clean Fun at Riverhead

THE INSPIRATION FOR THE DEMOLITION DERBY CAME TO Lawrence Mendelsohn one night in 1958 when he was nothing but a spare-ribbed twenty-eight-year-old stock-car driver halfway through his 10th lap around the Islip, L.I., Speedway and taking a curve too wide. A lubberly young man with a Chicago boxcar haircut came up on the inside in a 1949 Ford and caromed him 12 rows up into the grandstand, but Lawrence Mendelsohn and his entire car did not hit one spectator.

"That was what got me," he said, "I remember I was hanging upside down from my seat belt like a side of Jersey bacon and wondering why no one was sitting where I hit. 'Lousy promotion,' I said to myself.

"Not only that, but everybody who *was* in the stands forgot about the race and came running over to look at me gift-wrapped upside down in a fresh pile of junk."

At that moment occurred the transformation of Lawrence Mendelsohn, racing driver, into Lawrence Mendelsohn, promoter, and, a few transactions later, owner of the Islip Speedway, where he kept seeing more of this same underside of stock-car racing that everyone in the industry avoids putting into words. Namely, that for every purist who comes to see the fine points of the race, such as who is going to win, there are probably five waiting for the wrecks to which stock-car racing is so gloriously prone.

The pack will be going into a curve when suddenly two cars, three cars, four cars tangle, spinning and splattering all over each other and the retaining walls, upside down, right side up, inside out and in pieces, with the seams bursting open and discs, rods, wires and gasoline spewing out and yards of sheet metal shearing off like Reynolds Wrap and crumpling into the most baroque shapes, after which an ash-blue smoke starts seeping up from the ruins and a thrill begins to spread over the stands like Newburg sauce.

So why put up with the monotony between crashes?

Such, in brief, is the early history of what is culturally the most important sport ever originated in the United States, a sport that ranks with the gladiatorial games of Rome as a piece of national symbolism. Lawrence Mendelsohn had a vision of an automobile sport that would be all crashes. Not two cars, not three cars, not four cars, but 100 cars would be out in an arena doing nothing but smashing each other into shrapnel. The car that outrammed and outdodged all the rest, the last car that could still move amid the smoking heap, would take the prize money.

So at 8:15 at night at the Riverhead Raceway, just west of Riverhead, L.I., on Route 25, amid the quaint tranquility of the duck and turkey farm flatlands of eastern Long Island, Lawrence Mendelsohn stood up on the back of a flat truck in his red neon warmup jacket and lectured his 100 drivers on the rules and niceties of the new game, the "demolition derby." And so at 8:30 the first 25 cars moved out onto the raceway's quarter-mile stock-car track. There was not enough room for 100 cars to mangle each other. Lawrence Mendelsohn's dream would require four heats. Now the 25 cars were placed at intervals all about the circumference of the track, making flatulent revving noises, all headed not around the track but toward a point in the center of the infield.

Then the entire crowd, about 4,000, started chanting a countdown, "Ten, nine, eight, seven, six, five, four, three, two," but it was impossible to hear the rest, because right after "two" half the crowd went into a strange whinnying wail. The starter's flag went up, and the 25 cars took off, roaring into second gear with no mufflers, all headed toward that same point in the center of the infield, converging nose on nose.

The effect was exactly what one expects that many simultaneous crashes to produce: the unmistakable tympany of automobiles colliding and cheap-gauge sheet metal buckling; front ends folding together at the same cockeyed angles police photographs of night-time wreck scenes capture so well on grainy paper; smoke pouring from under the hoods and hanging over the infield like a howitzer cloud; a few of the surviving cars lurching eccentrically on bent axles. At last, after four heats, there were only two cars moving through the junk, a 1953 Chrysler and a 1958 Cadillac. In the Chrysler a small fascia of muscles named Spider Ligon, who smoked a cigar while he drove, had the Cadillac cornered up against a guard rail in front of the main grandstand. He dispatched it by swinging around and backing full throttle through the left side of its grille and radiator.

By now the crowd was quite beside itself. Spectators broke through a gate in the retaining screen. Some rushed to Spider Ligon's car, hoisted him to their shoulders and marched off the field, howling. Others clambered over the stricken cars of the defeated, enjoying the details of their ruin, and howling. The good, full cry of triumph and annihilation rose from Riverhead Raceway, and the demolition derby was over.

That was the 154th demolition derby in two years. Since Lawrence Mendelsohn staged the first one at Islip Speedway in 1961, they have been held throughout the United States at the rate of one every five days, resulting in the destruction of about 15,000 cars. The figures alone indicate a gluttonous appetite for the sport. Sports writers, of course, have managed to ignore demolition derbies even more successfully than they have ignored stock-car racing and drag racing. All in all, the new automobile sports have shown that the sports pages, which on the surface appear to hum with life and earthiness, are at bottom pillars of gentility. This drag racing and demolition derbies and things, well, there are too many kids in it with sideburns, tight Levi's and winkle-picker boots.

Yet the demolition derbies keep growing on word-of-mouth publicity. The "nationals" were held last month at Langhorne, Pa., with 50 cars in the finals, and demolition derby fans everywhere know that Don McTavish, of Dover, Mass., is the new world's champion. About 1,250,000 spectators have come to the 154 contests held so far. More than 75 per cent of the derbies have drawn full houses.

The nature of their appeal is clear enough. Since the onset of the Christian era, i.e., since about 500 A.D., no game has come along to fill the gap left by the abolition of the purest of all sports, gladiatorial combat. As late as 300 A.D. these bloody duels, usually between men but sometimes between women and dwarfs, were enormously popular not only in Rome but throughout the Roman Empire. Since then no game, not even boxing, has successfully acted out the underlying motifs of most sport, that is, aggression and destruction.

Boxing, of course, is an aggressive sport, but one contestant has actually destroyed the other in a relatively small percentage of matches. Other games are progressively more sublimated forms of sport. Often, as in the case of football, they are encrusted with oddments of passive theology and metaphysics to the effect that the real purpose of the game is to foster character, teamwork, stamina, physical fitness and the ability to "give-and-take."

But not even those wonderful clergymen who pray in behalf of Congress, expressway ribbon-cuttings, urban renewal projects and testimonial dinners for ethnic aldermen would pray for a demolition derby. The demolition derby is, pure and simple, a form of gladiatorial combat for our times.

As hand-to-hand combat has gradually disappeared from our civilization, even in wartime, and competition has become more and more sophisticated and abstract, Americans have turned to the automobile to satisfy their love of direct aggression. The mild-mannered man who turns into a bear behind the wheel of a car—i.e., who finds in the power of the automobile a vehicle for the release of his inhibitions—is part of American folklore. Among teen-agers the automobile has become the symbol, and in part the physical means, of triumph over family and community restrictions. Seventy-five per cent of all car thefts in the United States are by teen-agers out for "joy rides."

The symbolic meaning of the automobile tones down but by no means vanishes in adulthood. Police traffic investigators have long been convinced that far more accidents are purposeful crashes by belligerent drivers than they could ever prove. One of the heroes of the era was the Middle Eastern diplomat who rammed a magazine writer's car from behind in the Kalorama embassy district of Washington two years ago. When the American bellowed out the window at him, he backed up and smashed his car again. When the fellow leaped out of his car to pick a fight, he backed up and smashed his car a third time, then drove off. He was recalled home for having "gone native."

The unabashed, undisguised, quite purposeful sense of destruction of the demolition derby is its unique contribution. The aggression, the battering, the ruination are there to be enjoyed. The crowd at a demolition derby seldom gasps and often laughs. It enjoys the same full-throated participation as Romans at the Colosseum. After each trial or heat at a demolition derby, two drivers go into the finals. One is the driver whose car was still going at the end. The other is the driver the crowd selects from among the 24 vanquished on the basis of his courage, showmanship or simply the awesomeness of his crashes. The numbers of the cars are read over loudspeakers, and the crowd chooses one with its cheers. By the same token, the crowd may force a driver out of competition if he appears cowardly or merely cunning. This is the sort of driver who drifts around the edge of the battle avoiding crashes with the hope that the other cars will eliminate one another. The umpire waves a yellow flag at him and he must crash into someone within 30 seconds or run the risk of being booed off the field in dishonor and disgrace.

The frank relish of the crowd is nothing, however, compared to the kick the contestants get out of the game. It costs a man an average of $50 to retrieve a car from a junk yard and get it running for a derby. He will only get his money back—$50—for winning a heat. The chance of being smashed up in the madhouse first 30 seconds of a round are so great, even the best of drivers faces long odds in his shot at the $500 first prize. None of that matters to them.

Tommy Fox, who is nineteen, said he entered the demolition derby because, "You know, it's fun. I like it. You know what I mean?" What was fun about it? Tommy Fox had a way of speaking that was much like the early Marlon Brando. Much of what he had to say came from the trapezii, which he rolled quite a bit, and the forehead, which he cocked, and the eyebrows, which he could bring together expressively from time to time. "Well," he said, "you know, like when you hit 'em, and all that. It's fun."

Tommy Fox had a lot of fun in the first heat. Nobody was bashing around quite like he was in his old green Hudson. He did not win, chiefly because he took too many chances, but the crowd voted him into the finals as the best showman.

"I got my brother," said Tommy. "I came in from the side and he didn't even see me."

His brother is Don Fox, thirty-two, who owns the junk yard where they both got their cars. Don likes to hit them, too, only he likes it almost too much. Don drives with such abandon, smashing into the first car he can get a shot at and leaving himself wide open, he does not stand much chance of finishing the first three minutes.

For years now sociologists have been calling upon one another to undertake a serious study of America's "car culture." No small part of it is the way the automobile has, for one very large segment of the population, become the focus of the same sort of quasi-religious dedication as art is currently for another large segment of a higher social order. Tommy Fox is unemployed, Don Fox runs a junk yard, Spider Ligon is a maintenance man for Brookhaven National Laboratory, but to categorize them as such is getting no closer to the truth than to have categorized William Faulkner in 1926 as a clerk at Lord & Taylor, although he was.

Tommy Fox, Don Fox and Spider Ligon are acolytes of the car culture, an often esoteric world of arts and sciences that came into its own after World War II and now has believers of two generations. Charlie Turbush, thirty-five, and his son, Buddy, seventeen, were two more contestants, and by no stretch of the imagination can they be characterized as bizarre figures or cultists of the death wish. As for the dangers of driving in a demolition derby, they are quite real by all physical laws. The drivers are protected only by crash helmets, seat belts and the fact that all glass, interior handles, knobs and fixtures have been removed. Yet Lawrence Mendelsohn claims that there have been no serious injuries in 154 demolition derbies and now gets his insurance at a rate below that of stock-car racing.

The sport's future may depend in part on word getting around about its relative safety. Already it is beginning to draw contestants here and there from social levels that could give the demolition derby the cachet of respectability. In eastern derbies so far two doctors and three young men of more than passable connections in eastern society have entered under whimsical *noms de combat* and emerged neither scarred nor victorious. Bull fighting had to win the same social combat.

All of which brings to mind that fine afternoon when some high-born Roman women were out in Nero's box at the Colosseum watching this sexy Thracian carve an ugly little Samnite up into prime cuts, and one said, darling, she had an inspiration, and Nero, needless to say, was all for it. Thus began the new vogue of Roman socialites fighting as gladiators themselves, for kicks. By the second century A.D. even the Emperor Commodus was out there with a tiger's head as a helmet hacking away at some poor dazed fall guy. He did a lot for the sport. Arenas sprang up all over the empire like shopping center bowling alleys.

The future of the demolition derby, then, stretches out over the face of America. The sport draws no lines of gender, and post-debs may reach Lawrence Mendelsohn at his office in Deer Park.

The Fifth Beatle

JOHN, PAUL, GEORGE, RINGO AND — MURRAY THE K! — THE fifth Beatle! Does anybody out there really under*stand* what it *means* that Murray the K is the Fifth Beatle? Does anybody comprehend what something like that *took*? Does anybody comprehend what a victory it was to become George the Beatle's roommate in the hotel in Miami and do things like tape record conversations with George during those magic bloomings of the soul just before a man goes to sleep and bring back to the kids the sound of a pure universe with nothing but George, Murray the K and Fedders Miami air-conditioning in it? No; practically nobody out there comprehends. Not even Murray the K's fellow disc jockey William B. Williams, of WNEW, who likes singers like Frank Sinatra, all that corny nostalgia of the New Jersey roadhouses, and says, "I like Murray, but if that's what he has to do to make a buck, he can have it."

You can imagine how Murray the K feels! He not only makes a buck, he makes about $150,000 a year, he is the king of the Hysterical Disc Jockeys, and people *still* look at him and think he is some kind of amok gnome. Do they know what's happening? Here in the studio, close up, inside the glass panels, amid the microphone grilles, cue sheets and commercials in capital letters, Murray the K sits on the edge of his seat, a solidly built man, thirty-eight years old, with the normal adult worried look on his face, looking through the glass at an engineer in a sport shirt. Granted, there are Murray the K's clothes. He has on a Stingy Brim straw hat, a shirt with wide lavender stripes on it, a pair of black pants so tight they have to have three-inch Chinese slits on the sides at the bottom so they will fit over the gussets of his boots. Murray the K has 62 outfits like this, elf boots, Russian hats, flipnik jerseys, but isn't that part of it? Murray the K is sitting on the vinyl upholstery on the edge of a chair, which makes it tip forward, and his legs are pumping up and down, but all the time he has to be thinking. He has to concentrate under all these layers of noise, such as the Barbasol commercial.

"Men, listen as we rub a microphone against an ordinary beard . . ."

What comes out of the speaker is a sound like a garbage man dragging a can up the cellar stairs of the Union Square Automat.

". . . and now listen to the Barbasol sound . . ."

This sounds like an otter turned loose in a bin full of immies. And through the whole thing, while all these odd sounds come over the speaker, Murray the K has to sit there in a glass box in the techni-blue of the fluorescent lights and think ahead. He presses down the lever on the intercom box and says to the engineer, "Give me Ringo and me—'You're what's happening.'" Then he wheels around to where Earl, from a British record magazine, is sitting, right behind him in the studio, and Earl gets his word in:

"Look, Murray, when can we sit down and talk?"

"Wait a minute," says Murray, "I got a whole tumultuous opening here and I don't know whether I'm coming or going. I can't do a show tonight—look at those commercials!"

"You sound like you've got troubles!"

Murray the K eyes the Englishman for a second and then says, "Yeah, I've got troubles and I'm creating troubles."

"What do you mean?"

Old Barbasol is scraping and rumbling away overhead.

"The Animals," says Murray.

"Murray!" says the Englishman. "The Animals are *very big!*"

"Yeah, but they're trying to do me in," says Murray.

What a sixth sense the man has! In the very same moment the red light is going on, before he can even see it, Murray is wheeling around, putting his face up to the microphone, starting his legs pumping and throwing body English into his delivery—and out comes the incredible cascade of words:

"All right, baby, that's Barbasol, baby, and this is the boss sound, 1010 WINS in New York, and that's what's happening, babe, John, Paul, George, Ringo and yours truly, Murray the K, the Fifth Beatle, seven minutes before seven o'clock, Beatle time, Beyezeatle Teyezime, and you ask Ringo what's happening, baby——"

All this starts out in a Southern accent ground out from way back in the throat like a Bible Way preacher and then turns into hippodrome circuit showbiz, and all the while Murray the K is wrenching his body this way and that and the words are barreling out on top of one another, piling up hysteria until he points at the engineer and—pow—the tape of Ringo and him is on, and the voice of Murray the K is heard shouting;

"What's happening, baby?"

And the curious black-water adenoid of Ringo Starr the Beatle is heard shouting:

"You're what's happening, baby!"

And Murray shouts, "You're happening, too, baby!"

And Ringo shouts, "O.K., we're both happening, baby!"

And—what is happening?

What is happening is radio in the modern age. It is a curious thing, psychologically. Radio is back strong after its early losses to television, but in an altogether different form. The radio is now something people listen to while they are doing something else. They're getting dressed in the morning, driving to work, sorting mail, painting a building, working in a manhole and listening to the radio. Then comes nightfall, and all the adults in New York and New Jersey and Long Island and Connecticut, like everywhere else, are stroked out, catatonic, in front of the television set. The kids, however, are more active. They are outside, all over the place, tooling around in automobiles, lollygagging around with transistors plugged into their skulls, listening to the radio. Listening is not exactly the word. They use the radio as a background, the aural prop for whatever kind of life they want to imagine they're leading. They don't want any messages at all, they want an atmosphere. Half the time, as soon as they get a message—namely, a commercial or a news spot—they start turning the dial, looking for the atmosphere they lost. So there are all those kids out there somewhere, roaming all over the dial, looking for something that will hook not the minds, but the psyche.

That was the problem for which Murray the K, at Station WINS, was the solution. Given the problem, this man was a genius. He was probably the original hysterical disc jockey and in any case he was the first big hysterical disc jockey. Murray the K doesn't operate on Aristotelian logic. He operates on symbolic logic. He builds up an atmosphere of breathless jollification, comic hysteria, and turns it up to a pitch so high it can hypnotize kids and keep them frozen to WINS through the commercials and everything else. The name Murray the K itself is an example of what he does. His real name is Murray Kaufman, but who cares if they're listening to somebody named Murray Kaufman? Murray the K is different. It doesn't mean anything, but it signifies something, a kind of nutty hipsterism. Symbolic logic. He does the same thing with sound effects. The sound effects come on cartridges. He can ask the engineer for No. 39 and wham, when he gives the signal, the biggest crash in the history of the world comes over the air. There are freight trains, cavalry charges, the screams of men plunging down an abyss, nutty macaw laughter from the jungle, anything, and it all goes off like rockets in an on-going lunacy, all spliced together only by the hysterical apostrophes—"All right, baby!"—of Murray the K.

For a while, after discovering hysteria and symbolic logic, Murray the K was murdering the competition. His rating was 29, he says, against 9 for the next best disc jockey in New York. Other stations were slow to copy the new technique because— well, it was too damned nutty. It sounded kind of *demented* or something. But they got over that, and pretty soon two stations, WABC and WMCA, had set up teams of disc jockeys who were working the rock and roll and hysteria gimmick practically around the clock. WABC called its group the All Americans and WMCA called theirs the Good Guys. Some of them, like Bruce Morrow of WABC, "Cousin Brucie" he is called, could even keep up with Murray the K in sheer pace. It got wild on the airways. There was a great manic competition going on, shrieks, giggles, falsettos, heaving buffoonery, laughing gargles, high school beat talk, shouts, gasps, sighs, yuks, loony laughs, nonsense rhymes, puns, crazy accents, anything that came spinning off the mind. And by last February 7, Murray the K was losing. He was behind both the All Americans and the Good Guys in the ratings.

"For one thing," says Murray the K, "I was boxed in. The station made some changes in the format and there was a half-hour news bloc in front of me and a talk show behind me."

Sure, Murray the K may have been boxed in, but a lot of times radio stations don't show much appreciation for the esoterica of disc jockey competition, just as nobody else out there does. Murray the K had put in four years at WINS, which was some kind of a record, but historically that doesn't mean much. There are about 25,000 or more disc jockeys in the country, and the turnover is ferocious; they are all the time quitting or getting fired, and about 95 per cent of them, employed or unemployed, have their jaws open and their eyes set on the 16 big disc jockey jobs in New York, the minimum expectation here being $20,000 a year for a no-talent disc jockey who works regularly.

Actually, Murray the K has done a great deal to diversify his work. About half his income comes from things like pop music shows he puts on at the Fox Theater in Brooklyn, his personal appearances at places like Freedomland, the Murray the K T shirts he sells, the record albums he "hosts," such as "Murray the K's Golden Gassers" and "Murray the K and Jackie the K's Golden Gassers." Jackie is his wife. Jackie's father, Hilary Hayes, runs Murray the K's office over at Station WINS, upstairs in a two-story building on Central Park West right where it hits Columbus Circle. And one of the finer points of Hilary Hayes' approach is that Murray the K is not merely WINS' outstanding disc jockey, he is a showman and personality in his own right. Hayes is a white-haired man who sits up there in the office at a desk underneath a poster reading, "Kongratulations to Murray the K, You're What's Happening, Baby." On the other side of the desk are a bunch of girls, volunteers, who answer Murray the K's mail, 150 or so letters a day. The girls being volunteers, there are always a lot of new girls, and he has to keep going over the instructions for answering the letters.

"Now remember," he tells them, "end the note with 'Murray sends his love' before 'Sincerely,' and remember to say, 'Listen to the boss show'—don't name it, if they don't know which it is, too bad. Also, remember, we're not happy because they listen to WINS—we're just happy they listen to Murray the K. If he was on any other station, we'd be just as happy."

The truth is, however, that for Murray the K, like every other disc jockey, all of it would evaporate, the T shirts, the albums, everything, if he ever found himself without a top radio show. That was what he had to think over when the All Americans and the Good Guys made their big surge. And then came February 7, 1964, the day of the biggest coup in Murray the K's life.

That was the day the Beatles first arrived in the United States, out at Kennedy Airport. The scene out there was the expected madhouse, 4,000 kids ricocheting all over the place, hurling themselves at plate glass to try to break through into the customs area when the Beatles got off the plane and came through, things like that. Every newspaper, television station, network, all the wire services, all the radio stations, everybody who could get somebody out there was covering it, and they were all angling for something exclusive. At WINS they had been trying to figure out which of their regular news reporters to send out to Kennedy to do a live broadcast of the Beatles' arrival, and they couldn't think of anybody suitable, and then Joel Chaseman, the station's manager, got the idea of why not send Murray the K.

The trouble was, the press was only going to get one shot at the Beatles, and that was when they were led into a steaming little press room and put up on a platform with literally about a hundred reporters, photographers and interviewers packed into the room around them in overcoats, it being February. To make it worse, all the photographers were yelling at once, and it was bedlam generally, but this was Murray the K's finest hour. Murray the K must have looked odd even to the Beatles. Here he was with a straw hat on in February, hunched up practically in a ball at the foot of the platform, looking up at them with his best manic look on and sticking a stick microphone up to about the level of their knees. Murray the K was copping an interview. The photographers were supposed to have first crack at the Beatles, but Murray the K was copping an interview by shooting questions up to them from somewhere in the general area of their feet, so they could answer into the microphone at their knees. Some photographer would be yelling something like, "Hey, how about you guys getting in a little closer there!" but all the time Murray the K would be singling out one Beatle like George Harrison and saying something like, "Hey, George, baby, hey, hey, George, George, baby, yeah, hey down here, how did this reception compare with the reception you got in Stockholm, baby?" Murray knew their whole history. And George, a literal-minded boy, would look down and see this odd friendly face under a straw hat and say, "Well, we were worried at first. Everywhere else we couldn't hear the plane for the screams, you know. But here we could hear the screams but we could also hear the planes—you know?—it worried us. It didn't seem big, you know, sort-of-thing."

All right! Cuba, de Gaulle, unilateral disarmament, Lyndon B. Johnson, South Viet Nam, it wasn't the sweep of history, but in the league of disc jockeys covering the first moments the Beatles set foot on the earth of America, it was a historic scoop. The whole press conference went that way. Even after the questions started from everybody, Murray the K kept copping exclusive interviews. Some reporter would yell out a question like, "What do you think of Beethoven?" John Lennon, the Beatle, would answer most of these random questions, saying things like, "Beethoven? He's crazy, especially the poems," and all the while Murray the K would be sticking the stick microphone up and asking, say, Ringo Starr, something like, "Ringo, what's the first thing you want to see in New York?" and Ringo would look down and see this odd little character balled up at his feet and say, "Oh, I dunno, some of the historic buildings, like the Peppermint Lounge." Finally somebody in the back, some reporter, yelled out, "Hey, somebody tell Murray the K to cut out the crap!" So Paul McCartney, the Beatle, stepped forward and looked down at Murray the K and said, "Murray the K, cut out the crap!" Paradise! "Crazy, Paul, baby," Murray the K said into the microphone, "You're what's happening, Paul, baby, and remember, you heard it first on 1010 WINS!" Cut out the crap! From Paul himself! This was the perfect note, for by now it seemed like this was Murray the K's press conference and the rest of these hundred or so guys around here were just some kind of a chorus. Murray the K's fortunes started skyrocketing from that very moment.

Somehow, the next night, it was Murray the K who was taking the Beatles twisting at the Peppermint Lounge and from then on he was the Beatles' guide, Boswell, buffer, playmate throughout their American tour, and he even went to England with them. Maybe it was his magic hat, he doesn't know, he had never had any communication with the Beatles at all before the moment he turned up stationed at their feet at Kennedy. "It was involuntary," says Murray, not necessarily choosing the precise word. By the end of a week there were reporters who were getting mad because to get anything out of the Beatles they had to go through Murray the K, and who the hell was he anyway. In Miami, Murray the K roomed with one of the Beatles, George Harrison, and there and everywhere else Murray the K was making tape recordings a mile a minute. He had all the Beatles, one by one, saying anything he wanted into the tape recorder—plugs for WINS, plugs for Murray the K, plugs for the "Swinging Soiree," which is the name of his nightly show from 6:30 to 10.

The impact of all this was great for Murray the K. Every station, practically every disc jockey in town, was trying to capitalize on the Beatles, who were probably the biggest single popular music phenomenon ever. WABC, for example, was calling itself WABeatleC, and so forth, but nobody could match Murray the K. He was the Fifth Beatle!

Susan Tyrer, a seventeen-year-old girl, is now sitting in Murray the K's studio. She is up there for something called the "Miss Swinging Soiree" contest, and there are 25 finalists, none of whom seems to have the faintest notion of what happens if she wins. Susan tells how it was with her: "I started listening to Murray the K when he started getting popular, you know, with the Beatles and the English groups." Murray the K also plays a lot of the other English groups, such as the Dave Clark Five and The Animals, groups like that. "Murray the K—well, you know," says Susan, "like, he's what's happening!"

So Murray the K's rating shot back up, and now his program is almost entirely Murray the K and the Beatles. He not only plays Beatle records all the time, the whole show sort of moves in the medium of the Beatles.

One evening there is a story in the newspapers that Ringo Starr, the Beatle, is going to get married.

"I'm here to deny, baby," Murray the K says into the microphone, "I mean I'm here to deny that Ringo's marrying anyone. You know if he was you'd hear it first on the boss show, 1010 WINS, New York. And now, baby, listen, baby, it's the Beyezeatlesingbooees!"

Murray the K even has tapes denying Beatle marriages. He'll say something like, "Paul, baby, we're glad you called us about that marriage bit, baby." And Paul says, "Well, Murray, I was glad to get it cleared up sort-of-thing."

He runs in Beatle dialogues all night long. Sometimes they have a wacky jumpy quality about them, something on the order of Murray the K saying, "Hey, Paul, baby, what's happening, baby?"

"I dunno, Murray, everything's happening sort-of-thing."

"Paul, somebody asked me to ask you—I mean, they asked me, some of your fans, they asked me to ask you, so I'm going to go ahead and ask you, What is your favorite color?"

"Well, uh, it's kind of, you know, black."

"Black."

"Yeah, you know, black. John is going to jump off the ladder now."

There is a sound of applause.

"They applaud," says Paul. "Sounds like a cricket match."

"You're what's happening, Paul, baby!"

Symbolic logic, baby! Who cares what's happening? The Beatles are there, and Murray the K is in there with them, tight.

One minute he feels like he is a showman who is playing the role of "Murray the K" at this particular stage in his career, which is a way of saying that Murray the K is not the real him. Then the next minute he has a very jealous regard for his Murray the K role and all the unique skills that have gone into it. The symbol of his pride about this is his hat. He keeps his straw hat on all the time when he is being Murray the K and he is ready to fight over it. One time he was MC'ing a show at the Fox Theater in Brooklyn and some singer, one of the parade of them that come and go, got playful and grabbed Murray the K's hat off his head and threw it out into the audience. Murray the K blew up. He made the fellow stop everything, right in the middle of the show, and go out in the audience, out among a lot of screaming kids, and retrieve the hat. There was something about the look in his eyes, and the fellow didn't have to think twice about whether he was going to obey or not. He just went after the hat.

The same goes for the music he plays, which is generally called rock and roll, a term that Murray the K considers out of date. He argues that it is *the* popular music now, not just a teen-age deviation, just as swing was the popular music of the 1930's. He really blows up when someone like William B. Williams starts panning rock and roll as infra dig, such as the way Williams used to introduce the Beatles' first hit record, "I Want to Hold Your Hand," as "I Want to Hold My Nose" and just play 12 seconds of it. The same people, says Murray the K, will then start going on and on about Glenn Miller, Tommy Dorsey, Artie Shaw and all that bunch as if they were classics, all those mushy woodwinds, mushy ballads, all that stupid roadhouse glamor of the "Big Band" and some aging smoothie leading the band with a moon face and his hair combed straight back. The Glenn Miller business really gets him. Pop music today has a vitality and an intricacy that Glenn Miller couldn't have come up with in a hundred years.

"When I hear people start going about Glenn Miller," says Murray the K, "well, that's too much."

Ironically, rock and roll, or whatever you want to call what the hysterical disc jockeys play, is very much in vogue now among intellectuals in New York and Paris and London. They revere it like primitive art. They play the Shirelles, the Jelly Beans, the Beach Boys, Shirley Ellis, Dionne Warwick, Johnny Rivers, musicians like that, on the record player at parties. Jazz, especially jazz as played by people like Miles Davis and Thelonious Monk, is considered a hopelessly bourgeois taste, the kind you might expect from a Williams College boy with a lie-down crewcut on a big weekend in New York.

Yet the vogue has never included the disc jockeys themselves, although you hear some of them, Murray the K and Cousin Brucie, particularly, mentioned as sort of pop art phenomena. So the disc jockeys themselves remain about the only people who appreciate the art. Does anybody truly realize what it amounted to when Murray the K took over the Beatles?

"When the Beatles came here," he says, "I believed that this was the test. This was the biggest thing in the history of popular music. Presley was never this big, neither was Sinatra. The fact that I was able to be associated with the Beatles the way I was, living with them, having George as my roommate—well, it caused such jealousy as I have never seen in my life."

Murray the K stands up and paces around in his gusseted boots. When he says something with conviction, his southern accent breaks through. He was born in Virginia.

"But I'm not riding on the Beatles' coat tails," he says. "Actually, I think the Beatles are going to last a lot longer than everybody believes. I think they are natural wits and comedians, they're the coolest, they're too much, they're the greatest. But I'm not riding the Beatles' coat tails, and if they go, I'm going to be ready for the next person who comes along.

"I've done everything you have to do in this business, I've made every move you have to make, I've put cash on the line, and I came out a winner, and now I want everything that goes with it, all the goodies and all the respect, because I earned it."

Murray the K winds up his show a couple of minutes before 10 o'clock, and as soon as he leaves his glass cubicle, in walks a young man wearing a crease-top hat, of the genre known as the Madison Avenue crash helmet, and carrying an attaché case. He looks like an account executive on the 5:25. He sits at a table studying a script. His name is Pete Myers. Suddenly he leans into the microphone and says, "It's 10 P M. and now, from Sponge Rubber Hall—it's Mad Daddy."

Down on the street, on Central Park West, three girls are waiting to get Murray the K's autograph as he comes out the door. One of them is squeezed into a pair of short shorts that come up to about her ilial crest. Coming down over her left breast she has a row of buttons. The top one says, "We Love the Beatles." The next one says, "We Love Ringo," the next one, "We Love Paul," the next, "We Love John," the next, "We Love George," and the next—well, the next one, the bottom one, is kind of rough in execution. It is made of paper wrapped around an old button with the letters penciled on, saying, "We Love Murray the K." But so what? The letters are big, and her little mary poppins tremble honestly.

The Peppermint Lounge
Revisited

ALL RIGHT, GIRLS, INTO YOUR STRETCH NYLON DENIMS! You know the ones—the ones that look like they were designed by some leering, knuckle-rubbing old tailor with a case of workbench back who spent five years, like Da Vinci, studying nothing but the ischia, the gemelli and the glutei maximi. Next, hoist up those bras, up to the angle of a Nike missile launcher. Then get into the cable-knit mohair sweaters, the ones that fluff out like a cat by a project heating duct. And then unroll the rollers and explode the hair a couple of feet up in the air into bouffants, beehives and Passaic pompadours. Stroke in the black makeup all around the eyelids, so that the eyes look as though Chester Gould, who does Dick Tracy, drew them on. And then put those patient curls in your lips and tell Mother—you have to spell it out for her like a kid—that yes, you're going out with some of your girlfriends, and no, you don't know where you're going, and yes, you won't be out late, and for God's sake, like don't panic all the time, and then, with an I-give-up groan, tell her that "for God's sake" is *not* cursing.

At least that is the way it always seemed, as if some invisible force were out there. It was as though all these girls, all these flaming little Jersey Teen-agers, had their transistors plugged into their skulls and were taking orders, simultaneously, from somebody like the Ringleader Deejay.

Simultaneously, all over Plainfield, Scotch Plains, Ridgefield, Union City, Weehawken, Elizabeth, Hoboken and all the stretches of the Jersey asphalt, there they went, the Jersey Teen-agers, out of the house, off to New York, every week, for the on-going Jersey Teen-agers' weekend rebellion.

They headed off up Front Street if it was, say, Plainfield, and caught the Somerset Line bus at the stop across the street from the Public Service building around 7:30 P.M. Their bouffant heads would be bouncing up and down like dandelions until the bus hit the Turnpike and those crazy blue lights out there on the toothpaste factories started streaming by. They went through the Lincoln Tunnel, up the spiral ramps into the Port Authority Terminal and disembarked at some platform with an incredible number like 155. One hundred and fifty-five bus platforms; this was New York.

The first time people in Manhattan noticed the Jersey Teen-agers was when they would come bobbing out of the Port Authority and move into Times Square. No one ever really figured out what they were up to. They were generally written off as Times Square punks. Besides the bouffant babies in their stretch pants, furry sweaters and Dick Tracy eyes, there would be the boys in Presley, Big Bopper, Tony Curtis and Chicago boxcar hairdos. They would be steadying their hairdos in the reflections in the plate glass of clothing stores on 42nd Street that featured Nehru coats, Stingy-Brim hats, tab-collar shirts and winkle-picker elf boots. No one ever seemed to notice how maniacally serious they were about their hairdos, their flesh-tight pants, puffy sweaters, about the way they walked, idled, ogled or acted cool; in short, how serious they were about anything that had to do with form and each other. They had a Jersey Teen-age netherworld going in the middle of Manhattan. Their presence may not have been understood, but it was not ignored. There were nightspots that catered to them with rock and roll music. And when the Jersey Teen-agers started dancing in Times Square nightspots, they were serious about that, too. The Lindy, which was the name the kids had for what an older generation called jitterbugging, was already out. The kids were doing a dance called the Mashed Potatoes and another called the Puppet. Curiously, they were like the dances at a Lebanese maharajan. There was a lot of hip movement, but the boy and girl never touched. Then a new variation caught on, the Twist. There would be the Jersey Teen-agers, every weekend, doing the Mashed Potatoes, the Puppet and the Twist, studying each other's legs and feet through the entire number, never smiling, serious as always about form. One of these places was the Wagon Wheel. Another one was the Peppermint Lounge, 128 West 45th Street, half a block east of Times Square.

THE PEPPERMINT LOUNGE! YOU KNOW ABOUT THE PEPPER-mint Lounge. One week in October, 1961, a few socialites, riding hard under the crop of a couple of New York columnists, discovered the Peppermint Lounge and by the next week all of Jet Set New York was discovering the Twist, after the manner of the first 900 decorators who ever laid hands on an African mask. Greta Garbo, Elsa Maxwell, Countess Bernadotte, Noël Coward, Tennessee Williams and the Duke of Bedford—everybody was there, and the hindmost were laying fives, tens and twenty-dollar bills on cops, doormen and a couple of sets of maître d's to get within sight of the bandstand and a dance floor the size of somebody's kitchen. By November, Joey Dee, twenty-two, the bandleader at the Peppermint Lounge, was playing the Twist at the $100-a-plate Party of the Year at the Metropolitan Museum of Art.

That, of course, was two years ago. Everybody knows what has happened to the Jet Set in that time, for the Jet Set is always with us. But whatever became of the Jersey Teen-agers and the Peppermint Lounge?

Marlene Klaire, leader of the club's Twist chorus line, is standing in the hall off the dressing rooms in back, talking about the kind of fall it has been for her. Marlene is a short, lithe, gorgeous brunette. It is right after the second show, and she has on her Twist chorus satin, a pair of net stockings, Cleopatra eye makeup and a Passaic pompadour that brings her up to about six feet four. Yes, there is an institution now called the Twist chorus line, tended by a couple of choreographers named Wakefield Poole and Tom Roba. Marlene arrived at the Peppermint Lounge two years ago via the Jersey Teen-age route, but now her life is full of institutions.

"The Waddle," Marlene is saying, "is one of the dances we were demonstrating the other night over at Sacred Heart. You get in two straight lines sort of like, you know, the Hully Gully."

"Sacred Heart?"

"The Catholic Church. We weren't *in* the church, really, it was the auditorium. They let us wear our costumes. They were all adults there. We were teaching them the Waddle, the Dog, the Monkey—the Monkey is probably the most popular right now."

Well, all that was with the young adults at Sacred Heart. And then there was the night the educational program took her and the girls over to the Plaza Hotel for the Bourbon Ball, where they showed the Society people the Waddle, the Dog, the Monkey, the Mashed Potatoes and the Slop.

"The Society people loved it," Marlene is saying, "but the Mashed Potatoes is hard for some of them, and—"

Marlene came to New York over the Jersey Teen-age route way back in 1961 when the Peppermint Lounge was first getting hot. She was from Trenton, and then she had a job as a secretary in Newark, but then one night she came rolling into the Port Authority like everybody else and headed for the Peppermint Lounge. She worked her way up fast. First she got a job as a waitress, then she got one of the jobs dancing between shows, in street clothes, which is to say, something like stretch pants and a mohair sweater, to encourage customers to come up and dance. Marlene could really dance, and she got a job in the first Twist chorus line.

Now, two years later, the Jet Set has moved on from the Peppermint Lounge, but the Jersey Teen-age cycle is continuing. Inside the club the Younger Brothers and the Epics are on the bandstand, and Janet Gail and Misty More and Louis and Ronnie are in street clothes, dancing between shows, and customers are packed in around them, bouncing. A few leggy kids in red satin shorts, waitresses, are standing around the sides miming the Monkey with their hips, shuffling to themselves. And out in the center nine girls from Jersey, all with exploding hair and Dick Tracy eyes, have a table and watch the dancing with that same old dead-serious look. Nobody is doing the Twist anymore. Everybody is doing something like the Monkey, in which you make some motions with your arms like you're climbing the bars of your cage, or the T-Bird, in which there is some complicated business with the hands about opening the front door and going inside and mixing a cocktail. Every now and then Larry Cope, who is one of the Younger Brothers, will introduce a pure Twist number, but he has to use a historical preface, sort of like they do at Roseland or some place when they say, well, now we're going to have a good old-fashioned waltz.

The Jersey Teen-age set has no trouble getting into the place now, although there are always a lot of tourists, especially on the weekends, who have heard of the Twist and the Peppermint Lounge.

"—and we had a lot of little kids in here Saturday, showing them the dances. They were, you know, little kids, four to ten years old, something like that. They catch on pretty fast, or at least they see us, you know, shaking around, and they do that. And then sometimes we get women's groups. They're going to a show or something, and they then drop in here."

On the one hand Marlene sees a limitless future for the Twist as an institution. She figures the tourists coming to the World's Fair will add years to its life, and already she and the dancers are working on an act for the Fair called "Twisting Around the World," in which they will start off doing a native dance from some country when somebody shouts out "Twist!" in the native tongue, which usually comes out "Tweest!" and then the native dance becomes the native twist. Marlene had another idea, which was "Twisting Into Outer Space," but it looks like it will be "Around the World."

In another sense, however, Marlene does not associate the Twist with the future at all. Marlene's goal! Marlene's goal is ... Marlene's answer should reassure a whole generation of Jersey mothers about where the Jersey Teen-age rebellion is heading, it and all its bouffant babies, nylon stretch denims, Dick Tracy eyes, Nehru coats and Monkey dancers.

Out in the club the Epics, with four electric instruments going, are playing "Doing the Dog," and Misty is doing the Dog, and Janet is doing the Mashed Potatoes, and Jerri Miller is doing the Monkey, with a few baroque emendations, but Marlene reflects a moment, as if upon her busy round of work with the churches, the benefit balls, the women's groups and the youth.

"Well," she says, "I'd like to teach dancing, in my own house, you know, the way it was when I took lessons from my teacher. Or maybe be a psychologist. I used to want to, and I may still do that. Anyway, I don't want to live in New York. I want some place more like where we used to live in New Jersey. I don't like living here. There aren't any trees."

The First Tycoon
of Teen

ALL THESE RAINDROPS ARE *HIGH* OR SOMETHING. THEY
don't roll down the window, they come straight back, toward
the tail, wobbling, like all those Mr. Cool snow heads walking on mattresses. The plane is taxiing out toward the runway to
take off, and this stupid infarcted water wobbles, sideways, across
the window. Phil Spector, twenty-three years old, the rock and
roll magnate, producer of Philles Records, America's first teen-
age tycoon, watches . . . this watery pathology. . . . It is *sick, fatal.*
He tightens his seat belt over his bowels. . . . A hum rises inside
the plane, a shot of air comes shooting through the vent over
somebody's seat, some ass turns on a cone of light, there is a sign
stuck out by the runway, a mad, cryptic, insane instruction to the
pilot—Runway 4, Are Cylinder Lap Mainside DOWN?—and
beyond, disoriented crop rows of sulphur blue lights, like the
lights on top of a New Jersey toothpaste factory, only spreading
on and on in sulphur blue rows over Los Angeles County. It is . . .
disoriented. Schizoid raindrops. The plane breaks in two on

takeoff and everybody in the front half comes rushing toward Phil Spector in a gush of bodies in a thick orange—*napalm!* No, it happens aloft; there is a long rip in the side of the plane, it just rips, he can see the top ripping, folding back in sick curds, like a sick Dalí egg, and Phil Spector goes sailing through the rip, dark, freezing. And the engine, it is *reedy—*

MISS!

A stewardess is walking back to the back to buckle herself in for the takeoff. The plane is moving, the jets are revving. Under a Lifebuoy blue skirt, her fireproof legs are clicking out of her Pinki-Kini-Panty Fantasy—

"Miss!" says Phil Spector.

"Yes?"

"I, like I have to get off the plane."

She stops there beside his seat with her legs bent slightly, at a 25-degree angle to her ischium. She laughs with her mouth, yes yes, but there is no no in her eyes, you little bearded creep, you are not very funny. Her face ... congeals ... she looks at his suede jerkin. She says,

"Sir?"

"I, you know, I have to get off," says Phil Spector, "I don't want to *fly* on this plane. Let me—" but she will never figure out about the raindrops. She is standing there hoping this is a joke. "—uh, I'm not putting you on, I'm not putting you down, I'm not anything, all I want is—you know?—just open the door and let me off. I'll walk back. The rest—everybody—I mean, go ahead, *fly.*"

"Sir, we're already in a pattern. There are seven aircraft, seven jet aircraft, behind us waiting for the runway—"

By this time Phil Spector's Hollywood friends, in this nutball music business—there is one of them beside him and a couple of them behind him, they are craning around.

"Phil! What's wrong, baby!"

Phil turns around and says in his soft and slightly broken voice: "Man, this plane's not going to make it."

They all look around, they all look like frozen custard in the seat lights.

"You know?" Phil says. "It's not making it."

They all look around, the goddamned *noise* is roaring off the wings, and Phil sits there in that kind of doldrum fury he lives in, his beard, his hair, his suede. O.K., we're in a pattern, seven jets. But this guy Phil Spector has just produced *eight straight hit records*—you know? Eight hits! This kid is practically a baby, twenty-three years old, f'r chrissake, and he has made two million dollars, clear. The first teen-age business magnate—living teen tycoon. Like he is programmed into the Whole Life Bit— you know? He does A & R for Daddy God, he's *lucky*—you know?—and if he's getting off—

So the big chap behind with the moon head and the little Seventh Avenue toy black hat says,

"Yeah, we wanna get off. There's something wiggy or something about this plane."

"Yeah!"

"Yeah!"

The stewardess is looking around, and here is her life being drowned by this little guy—he has a Fu Manchu beard sticking out in front of his hair, his wispy locks are combed back, coming down in back over his shoulders in a kind of pageboy, like Bishop McCullough's, the heir to Daddy Grace. He has on a suede leather shirt, jerkin style. Somebody's cone of light lies in Miami saffron pools on his Italian pants. He looks like—what kind of—

All this commotion. Yeah, says Phil Spector's pals. It's wiggy. Off this flying cretin. Phil Spector broods over the raindrops. The stewardess runs for the cabin.

So they stop the plane, they break up the whole pattern, they knock out everybody's schedule, they turn the plane around, take everybody off. They check Phil Spector's luggage for—*bombs*. Look at this *beatnik's* hair in *back* there, and they stare at Son of

Bop in a leather jerkin, ten men in alumicron suits bombarding him with corporate hate rays. But his pals keep up this strange upbeat talk:

"Phil, baby, you saved my life!"

"Phil, if you say it's wiggy, it's wiggy."

"You done it again, Phil, babes, you done it again!"

"... *You* say it's wiggy, Phil? *I* say it's wiggy ..."

"... I hurts, too, D'Artagnan, baby, right here, same as you ..."

"... wiggy ..."

"... baby ..."

"SO," SAYS PHIL SPECTOR, "THEY GROUNDED ME. THEY TOOK away my credit cards, they suspended the pilot, I don't know."

Spector is sitting in a little cream room in his office suite at 440 East 62nd Street with his back to a window that is practically on top of the East Side Drive. Twenty-three years old—he has a complex of corporations known as Phil Spector Productions. One of them is Mother Bertha Productions, named after his mother, Bertha. She works for his office in Los Angeles, but only because she wants to. The main organization is Philles Records. Spector has produced 21 "single" Philles records since October, 1962—and sold more than 13 million copies. All rock and roll. His most recent big hit, "Walking in the Rain," by the Ronettes, went as high as No. 20 on the *Cashbox* chart and has sold more than 250,000 copies. His latest record, "You've Lost That Lovin' Feelin'," by the Righteous Brothers, rose from the 70's to No. 37 with a "bullet" beside it—meaning "going up fast." He has pro-duced seven albums. The first teen-age tycoon! He is leaning back in the chair. He has on his suede jerkin, his Italian pants, a pair of pointy British boots with Cuban heels. His hair hangs down to his shoulders in back. The beard is shaved off, however.

Danny Davis, his promotion man, is talking on the phone in the inner office. A fellow sits across from Spector with his legs crossed and a huge chocolate brown Borsalino hat over his bent knee, like he was just trying it on. He says,

"Phil, why do you do—"

"I'm moving the whole thing to California," says Phil Spector. "I can't stand flying anymore."

"—why do you do these things?"

Spector—without his beard, Spector has a small chin, a small head, his face looks at first like all those little kids with bad hair and reedy voices from the Bronx, where he was born. But—an *ordinary* Phil Spector? Phil Spector has the only pure American voice. He was brought up not in the Bronx, but California. It meanders, quietly, shaking, through his doldrum fury, out to somewhere beyond cynical, beyond cool, beyond teen-age world-weary. It is thin, broken and soft. He is only twenty-three years old, for godsake, the first millionaire businessman to rise up out of the teen-age netherworld, king of the rock and roll record producers—

Spector jumps out of the chair.

"Wait a minute," he says. "Just a minute. They're making deals in here."

Spector walks into the inner office, gingerly, like a cowboy, because of the way the English boots lift him up off the floor. He is slight, five feet seven, 130 pounds. His hair shakes faintly behind. It is a big room, like a living room, all beige except for nine gold-plated rock and roll records on the wall, some of Phil Spector's "goldies," one million sales each. "He's a Rebel," by the Crystals, "Zip-a-dee-doo-dah," by Bob B. Soxx and the Blue Jeans, "Be My Baby," by the Ronettes, "Da Do Ron Ron," "Then He Kissed Me," "Uptown," "He's Sure the Boy I Love," all by the Crystals, "Wait Til My Baby Gets Home," by Darlene Love. And beige walls, beige telephones all over the place, a beige upright piano, beige paintings, beige tables, with Danny Davis crowding over a beige desk, talking on the telephone.

"Sure, Sal," says Danny, "I'll ask Phil. Maybe we can work something out on that."

Spector starts motioning thumbs down.

"Just a minute, Sal." Danny puts his hand over the mouthpiece and says,

"We *need* this guy, Phil. He's the biggest distributor out there. He wants the one thousand guarantee."

Phil's hands go up like he is lifting a slaughtered lamb up on top of an ice box.

"I don't care. I'm not interested in the money, I've got millions of dollars of money, I don't care who needs this animal. I'm interested in selling records, O.K.? Why should I give him a guarantee? He orders the records, I guarantee I'll buy a thousand back from him if he can't sell them; he sells them, then after the record dies, he buys up 500 cut rate from somebody, sends them back and cries for his money. Why should we have to be eating his singles later?"

Danny takes his hand away and says into the mouthpiece:

"Look, Sal, there's one thing I forgot. Phil says this record he can't give the guarantee. But you don't have anything to worry about . . . I know what I said, but Phil says . . . look, Sal, don't worry, 'Walking in the Rain,' this is a tremendous record, tremendous, a very big record . . . What? . . . I'm not reading off a paper, Sal . . . Wait a minute, Sal—"

"Who needs these animals?" Phil Spector tells Danny.

"Look, Sal," Danny says, "this man never made a bad record in his life. You tell me one. Nothing but hits."

"Tell him to go to hell," says Spector.

"Sal—"

"Who needs these animals!" says Spector, so loud this time that Danny cups his hand around the receiver and puts his mouth down close.

"Nothing, Sal," says Danny, "that was somebody came in."

"Joan," says Phil, and a girl, Joan Berg, comes in out of another room. "Will you turn the lights off?" he says.

She turns the lights off, and now in the middle of the day the offices of Philles Records and Mother Bertha Productions are all dark except for the light from Danny Davis' lamp. Danny crowds into the pool of light, hunched over the phone, talking to Sal.

Phil puts his fingers between his eyes and wraps his eyebrows around them.

"Phil, it's dark in here," says the fellow with the large hat. "Why do you do these things?"

"I'm paying a doctor $600 a week to find out," says Phil, without looking up.

He sits there in the dark, his fingers buried between his eyes. Just over his head one can make out a painting. The painting is kind of came-with-the-frame surrealist. It shows a single musical note, a half note, suspended over what looks like the desert outside Las Vegas. Danny has to sit there huddled in his own pool of light talking to this animal on the telephone.

"This is a primitive country," says Phil Spector. "I was at Shepheard's, the discotheque, and these guys start saying these things. It's unbelievable. These people are animals."

"What kind of things, Phil?"

"I don't know. They look at, you know, my hair—my wife and I are dancing, and, I mean, it's unbelievable, I feel somebody yanking on my hair in the back. I turn around, and here's this guy, a grown man, and he is saying these unbelievable things to me. So I tell him, like this, 'I'm going to tell you this one time, that's all—don't ever try that again.' And the guy—it's unbelievable—he shoves me with the heel of his hand and I go sprawling back into a table—"

—Spector pauses—

"—I mean, I've studied karate for years. I could literally *kill* a guy like that. You know? Size means nothing. A couple of these—" he cocks his elbow in the gloom and brings up the flat of his forearm—"but what am I going to do, start a fight every time I go out? Why should I even have to listen to anything from these animals? I find this country very condemning. I don't have this kind of trouble in Europe. The people of America are just not born with culture."

Not born with culture! If only David Susskind and William B. Williams could hear that. Susskind invited Phil Spector to the *Open End* television program one evening "to talk about the record business." Suddenly Susskind and "William B.," station WNEW's old-nostalgia disc jockey, were condemning Spector as some kind of sharpie poisoning American culture, rotting the minds of Youth and so forth. That was how it all hit Spector. It was as if he were some kind of old short-armed fatty in the Brill Building, the music center on Broadway, with a spread-collar shirt and a bald olive skull with strands of black hair pulled up over it from above one ear. There was something very ironic about that. Spector is the one record producer who wouldn't go near Broadway. His setup is practically out in the East River, up by the Rockefeller Institute. The Rockefeller Institute, for godsake. Susskind and Williams kept throwing Spector's songs at him—"He's a Rebel," "Da Do Ron Ron," "Be My Baby," "Fine Fine Boy," "Breakin' Up"—as if he were astutely conning millions of the cretins out there with this stuff. Spector didn't know exactly what to tell them. He *likes* the music he produces. He writes it himself. He is something new, the first teen-age millionaire, the first boy to become a millionaire within America's teenage netherworld. It was never a simple question of him taking a look at the rock and roll universe from the outside and exploiting it. He stayed within it himself. He *liked* the music.

SPECTOR, WHILE STILL IN HIS TEENS, SEEMED TO COMPREHEND the prole vitality of rock and roll that has made it the kind of darling holy beast of intellectuals in the United States, England and France. Intellectuals, generally, no longer take jazz seriously. Monk, Mingus, Ferguson—it has all been left to little executive trainees with their first apartment and a mahogany

African mask from the free-port shop in Haiti—let me *tell* you!—and a hi-fi. But rock and roll! Poor old arteriosclerotic lawyers with pocky layers of fat over their ribs are out there right now twisting with obscene clumsiness to rock and roll. Their wives wear stretch pants to the seafood shoppe. A style of life! There have been teen-agers who have made a million dollars before, but invariably they are entertainers, they are steered by older people, such as the good Colonel Tom Parker steers Elvis Presley. But Phil Spector is the bona-fide Genius of Teen. Every baroque period has a flowering genius who rises up as the most glorious expression of its style of life—in latter-day Rome, the Emperor Commodus; in Renaissance Italy, Benvenuto Cellini; in late Augustan England, the Earl of Chesterfield; in the sal volatile Victorian age, Dante Gabriel Rossetti; in late-fancy neo-Greek Federal America, Thomas Jefferson; and in Teen America Phil Spector is the bona fide Genius of Teen. In point of fact, he had turned twenty-one when he made his first clear million. But it was as a teen-ager, working within the teen-age milieu, starting at the age of seventeen, that Phil Spector developed into a great American business man, the greatest of the independent rock and roll record producers. Spector's mother, Bertha, took him from the Bronx to California when he was nine. California! Teen Heaven! By the time he was sixteen he was playing jazz guitar with some group. Then he got interested in rock and roll, which he does not call rock and roll but "pop blues." That is because—well, that is a complicated subject. Anyway, Phil Spector likes this music. He genuinely likes it. He is not a short-armed fatty hustling nutball fads.

"I get a little angry when people say it's bad music," Spector tells the man with the brown hat. "This music has a spontaneity that doesn't exist in any other kind of music, and it's what is here now. It's unfair to classify it as rock and roll and condemn it. It has limited chord changes, and people are always saying the words are banal and why doesn't anybody write lyrics like Cole Porter anymore, but we don't have any presidents like Lincoln anymore, either. You know? Actually, it's more like the blues. It's pop blues. I feel it's very American. It's very *today*. It's what people respond to today. It's not just the kids. I hear cab drivers, everybody, listening to it."

And Susskind sits there on his show reading one of Spector's songs out loud, no music, just reading the words, from the Top Sixty or whatever it is, "Fine Fine Boy," to show how banal rock and roll is. The song just keeps repeating "He's a fine fine boy." So Spector starts drumming on the big coffee table there with the flat of his hands in time to Susskind's voice and says, "What you're missing is the beat." Blam blam.

Everybody is getting a little sore with Susskind reading these simple lyrics and Spector blamming away on the coffee table. Finally, Spector says the hell with it and, being more ... hip ... than Susskind or William B. Williams, starts cutting them up. He starts asking Williams how many times he plays Verdi on his show—Monteverdi?—D. Scarlatti?—A. Scarlatti?—that's good music, why don't you play that, you keep saying you play only good music, I don't hear you playing that. Williams doesn't know what to say. Spector tells Susskind he didn't come on the show to listen to somebody tell him he was corrupting the Youth of America—he could be home making money. Susskind—well, ah, all right, Phil. Everybody is testy.

Making money. Yes! At the age of seventeen Spector wrote a rock and roll song called "To Know Him Is To Love Him." He took the title off his father's tombstone. That was what his mother had had engraved on his father's tombstone out in Beth David cemetery in Elmont, L.I. He doesn't say much about his father, just that he was "average lower middle class." Spector wrote the song, sang it and played the guitar in the recording with a group called the Teddy Bears. He made $20,000 on that record, but somebody ran off with $17,000 of it, and, well, no use going into that. Then he was going to UCLA, but he couldn't afford it and became a court reporter, one of the people who sit at the shorthand machine, taking down testimony. He decided to

come to New York and get a job as an interpreter at the UN. His
mother had taught him French. But he got to New York, and the
night before the interview, he fell in with some musicians and
never got there. The hell with stenography. He wrote another hit
that year, "Spanish Harlem." *There is a rose in Spanish Ha-a-a-a-
a-ar-a-lem.* And then—only nineteen—he became head of A & R,
artists and repertoire, for Atlantic Records. By 1961 he was a
free-lance producer, producing records for the companies, working with Connie Francis, Elvis Presley, Ray Peterson, the Paris
Sisters. All this time, Spector would write a song and run all
phases of making records: get the artists, direct the recording ses-
sions, everything. Spector could work with these hairy goslin
kids who make these records because he was a kid himself, in one
sense. God knows what the music business biggies thought of
Phil Spector—he already wore his hair like Salvador Dalí did at
that age or like an old mezzotint of Mozart at the Academy or
something. And he was somehow *one of them,* the natives, the
kids who sang and responded to this . . . music. Phil Spector
could get in one of those studios with the heron microphones, a
representative of the adult world that makes money from
records, and it became all one thing—the kids comprehended
him.

Spector had an ideal, Archie Bleyer. Bleyer was a band leader
who founded a record company, Cadence Records. Spector
formed a partnership with two other people in 1961, then bought
them out and went on his own as Philles Records in October of
1962. His first big hit was "He's a Rebel," by the Crystals. Spector had a system. The big record companies put out records like
buckshot, 10, maybe 15 rock and roll records a month, and if one
of them catches on, they can make money. Spector's system is to
put them out one at a time and pour everything into each one.
Spector does the whole thing. He writes the words and the music, scouts and signs up the talent. He takes them out to a recording studio in Los Angeles and runs the recording session himself.
He puts them through hours and days of recording to get the two

or three minutes he wants. Two or three minutes out of the whole struggle. He handles the control dials like an electronic maestro, tuning various instruments or sounds up, down, out, every which way, using things like two pianos, a harpsichord and three guitars on one record; then re-recording the whole thing with esoteric dubbing and over-dubbing effects—reinforcing instruments or voices—coming out with what is known throughout the industry as "the Spector sound."

The only thing he doesn't keep control of is the actual manufacture, the pressing, of the records and the distribution. The only people around to give him any trouble all this time are the distributors—cigar-chewing fatties . . . and—well, to be honest, there is a lot that gives Phil Spector trouble, and not so much any kind of or any group of people as much as his . . . status. A Teenage Tycoon! It is too wacked out. He is betwixt and between. He identifies with the teen-age netherworld, he defends it, but he is already too mature for it. As a millionaire, a business genius, living in a penthouse 22 stories up over the East River, with his wife, Annette, who is twenty, a student at Hunter College, and with a four-room suite downstairs on the ground floor as his office, and a limousine, and a chauffeur, and a bodyguard, and a staff, Danny and Joan Berg and everybody, and a doorman who directs people to Mr. Spector's office—well, that makes Phil Spector *one of them,* the universe of arteriosclerotic, hypocritical, cigar-chewing, hopeless, larded adults, infarcted vultures, one meets in the music business. And so here in the dark is a twenty-three-year-old man with a Shelley visage, a suede shirt, a kind of page-boy bob and winkle-picker boots, the symbol of the one, sitting in the dark in this great beige office, the symbol of the other, in the middle of the day, in the dark, tamping his frontal lobes with his fingers in the gloom.

One of the beige phones rings and Danny answers. Then he presses the "hold" button and tells Phil Spector, "It's the Rolling Stones, they just got in."

Spector comes alive with that. He gets up on his ginger toes and goes to the telephone. He is lively and he spins on the balls of his feet a little as he stands by the phone.

"Hello, Andrew," he says. He is talking with Andrew Oldham, the manager of the Rolling Stones. And then he puts on a Cockney accent. "Are you all in?" he says.

The Rolling Stones; all right. The Rolling Stones, English group, and Andrew Oldham, are like him. They grew up in the teen-age netherworld and made it, and they all want to have it all, too, the kids' style of life and the adult's . . . money . . . and not cop out on one side or the other, larded and arteriosclerotic. God! Phil Spector's British trip! That was where suddenly he had it all.

Phil Spector is here! The British have the ability to look at all sorts of rebel baddies and alienated thin young fellows and say coo and absorb them like a great soggy lukewarm, mother's poultice. The Beatles, Beatlemania, rock and roll, suddenly it is all absorbed into the center of things as if it could have been there all along if it only asked. Phil Spector arrives at London Airport and, Santa Barranza, there are photographers all over the place, for him, Phil Spector, and the next morning he is all over the center fold of the *London Daily Mirror,* the biggest newspaper in the Western World, five million circulation: "The 23-year-old American rock and roll magnate." He is in the magazines as the "U.S. Recording Tycoon." Invitations go out to come to the receptions to meet "America's outstanding hit maker, Phil Spector." And then he lands back at Idlewild and waiting are, yes, the same bunch of cheese-breath cabbies, and he takes a cab on back to 440 E. 62nd St. and goes into his beige world, the phones are ringing and it is all the same, the same—

"Cigar-smoking sharpies," says Phil Spector. He is in a livelier mood after the talk with Andrew Oldham. "They're a bunch of cigar-smoking sharpies in record distribution. They've all been in the business for years and they resent you if you're young. That's one reason so many kids go broke in this business. They're always starting new record companies, or they used to, the business is very soft right now, they start a company and pour all their money into a record, and it can be successful and they're still broke, because these characters don't even pay you until you've had three or four hit records in a row. They order the records and sell them and don't pay you. They don't pay you because they know they don't have to. You start yelling for the money and they tell you, 'Whattya mean, I have all these records coming back from the retailers and what about my right to return records, and blah-blah.' What are you going to do? Sue twenty guys in twenty different courts in the United States?

"They look at everything as a product. They don't care about the work and sweat you put into a record. They respect me now because I keep turning out hits, and after that they become sort of honest . . . in their own decayed way."

Where does a man find friends, comrades, anything, in a world like that? They resent his youth. They resent his success. But it is no better with the kids. He is so much more mature and more . . . eminent . . . they all want to form "the father thing" with him. Or else they want to fawn over him, cousin him, cajole, fall down before him, whistle, shout, stomp, bang him on the head, anything to get his attention and get "the break," just one chance. Or one more chance. Spector can't go near the Brill Building, the center of the music business, because the place is crawling with kids with winkle-picker shoes cracking in the folds, who made one hit record five years ago and still can't realize that they are now, forever, in oblivion. They crawl all over the place the way the small-time balding fatty promoters and managers used to in the days when A. J. Liebling wrote about the place as the Jollity Building. Phil Spector steps onto an elevator in the Brill Building, the elevator is packed, and suddenly he feels this arm hooking through his in the most hideously cozy way and a mouth is closing in on his ear and saying, "Phil, baby, wait'll you hear this one: 'Ooh-oom-bah-ay,'" and Phil Spector is imprisoned there with the elevator inching up, "vah ump nooby poon fang ooh-ooh ayub bah-ay—you dig that, Phil? You dig that, don't you, Phil? Phil, babes!" He walks down the hall and kids sneak up behind him and clip songs, music, lyrics into his coat pocket. He finds the stuff in there, all this ratty paper, when he gets home. Or he is leaving the Brill Building and he feels a great whack on the back of his head and wheels around and there are four kids in the singing stance, their heads angled in together, saying, "Just one bar, Phil—Say wohna love boo-uh ayyay bubby—" while the guy on the end sings bass with his chin mashed into a pulpy squash down over his collar bone, *beh-ungggh, beh-ungggh.*

STATUS! WHAT IS HIS STATUS? HE PRODUCES "ROCK AND ROLL," and, therefore, he is not a serious person, and he won't join the Young Presidents or whatever the hell kind of organization jaycee geniuses would join for their own good.

"Phil," says the man with the hat, "why don't you hire a press agent, a P.R. man—"

Phil is tamping his frontal lobes in the gloom. Danny Davis is hunched up in the little pool of light on his desk. Danny is doing his level best for Phil.

"Jack? Danny Davis ... Yeah ... No, I'm with Phil Spector now ... Right! It's the best move I ever made. You know Phil ... I'm in the best shape of my career ... Jack, I just want to tell you we've got—"

"A press agent?" Phil says to the man in the hat. "In the first place, I couldn't stand to hear what he'd say about me."

"——Got two tremendous records going, Jack, 'Walking in the Rain,' the Ronettes, and—"

"In the second place," Phil says, "there's no way my image can be bought."

"——And 'You've Lost That Lovin' Feelin' '" by the Righteous Brothers," says Danny. "... Right, Jack ... I appreciate that, Jack ..."

"The only thing I could do—you know what I'd like to do? I'd like to do a recording session in the office of *Life* or *Esquire* or

Time, and then they could see it. That's the only chance I've got. Because I'm dealing in rock and roll, I'm, like I'm not a bona-fide human being—"

". . . Absolutely! . . . If there's anything we can do for you on this end, Jack, let us know. O.K.? Great, Jack . . ."

". . . and I even have trouble with people who should never say *any*thing. I go over to Gristede's to get a quart of milk or something and the woman at the cash register has to start in. So I tell her, 'There's a war in Viet Nam, they've fired Khrushchev, the Republican party is falling to pieces, the Ku Klux Klan is running around loose, and you're worrying about my hair . . .' "

America's first teen-age tycoon, a business genius, a musical genius—and it is as if he were still on the corner on Hoffman Street in the Bronx when the big kids come by in hideous fraternity, the way these people act. What is he now? Who is he in this weird country? Danny talks in the phone in the little pool of light, Joan is typing up whatever it is, Phil is tamping his frontal lobes.

ANOTHER AIRPLANE! IT LEVELS OFF, AND THE MAN IN THE seat by the window, next to Phil Spector, lights a cigarette, pure as virgin snow. Phil Spector sits there with his kind of page-boy bob pressed down in back and a checked shirt and tight black pants. The man with the cigarette keeps working himself up to something. Finally, he says, "If you don't mind me asking—have I seen you on television or something? What's your name, I mean, if you don't mind me asking?" Phil Spector presses back into the seat but his head won't disappear. Then he says, "I'm Goddard Lieberson."

"Gottfried Lieberman?"

Marvelous! Reassuring! Nobody ever heard of Goddard Lieberson, either. Who the hell is Goddard Lieberson! He is the president of Columbia Records, all those nice straight cookie jar "tunes" William B. Williams would go for, very big—and who the hell knows who he is?

"I'm the president of Columbia Records."

The man sucks on his cigarette a moment. A skinny ash, all limp, hangs out.

"Well—you must be kind of young."

Phil Spector lies back. Then he says,

"I was only kidding. I'm Chubby Checker. That's who I really am."

"Chubby Checker?"

Who the hell is Chubby Checker? Yes! Who the hell has *any-body* ever heard of? It's like the last time when he said he was Paul Desmond. Who the hell is Paul Desmond? Or Peter Sellers' cousin. Or Monsieur Fouquet, of the de Gaulle underground. Or . . . who the hell is *anybody*? Phil Spector tamps his frontal lobes and closes his eyes and holds his breath. As long as he holds his breath, it will not rain, there will be no raindrops, no schizoid water wobbling, sideways, straight back, it will be an even, even, even, even, even, even, even world.

The Kandy-Kolored
Tangerine-Flake
Streamline Baby

THE FIRST GOOD LOOK I HAD AT CUSTOMIZED CARS WAS AT an event called a "Teen Fair," held in Burbank, a suburb of Los Angeles beyond Hollywood. This was a wild place to be taking a look at art objects—eventually, I should say, you have to reach the conclusion that these customized cars *are* art objects, at least if you use the standards applied in a civilized society. But I will get to that in a moment. Anyway, about noon you drive up to a place that looks like an outdoor amusement park, and there are three serious-looking kids, like the cafeteria committee in high school, taking tickets, but the scene inside is quite mad. Inside, two things hit you. The first is a huge platform a good seven feet off the ground with a hully-gully band—everything is electrified, the bass, the guitars, the saxophones—and then behind the band, on the platform, about two hundred kids are doing frantic dances called the hully-gully, the bird, and the shampoo. As I said, it's noontime. The dances the kids are doing are very jerky. The boys and girls don't touch, not even with their hands.

They just ricochet around. Then you notice that all the girls are dressed exactly alike. They have bouffant hairdos—all of them—and slacks that are, well, skin-tight does not get the idea across; it's more the conformation than how tight the slacks are. It's as if some lecherous old tailor with a gluteus-maximus fixation designed them, striation by striation. About the time you've managed to focus on this, you notice that out in the middle of the park is a huge, perfectly round swimming pool; really rather enormous. And there is a Chris-Craft cabin cruiser in the pool, going around and around, sending up big waves, with more of these bouffant babies bunched in the back of it. In the water, suspended like plankton, are kids in scuba-diving outfits; others are tooling around underwater, breathing through a snorkel. And all over the place are booths, put up by shoe companies and guitar companies and God knows who else, and there are kids dancing in all of them—dancing the bird, the hully-gully, and the shampoo—with the music of the hully-gully band piped all over the park through loudspeakers.

All this time, Tex Smith, from *Hot Rod Magazine,* who brought me over to the place, is trying to lead me to the customized-car exhibit—"Tom, I want you to see this car that Bill Cushenberry built, The Silhouette"—which is to say, here are two hundred kids ricocheting over a platform at high noon, and a speedy little boat barreling around and around and around in a round swimming pool, and I seem to be the only person who is distracted. The customized-car exhibit turns out to be the Ford Custom Car Caravan, which Ford is sending all over the country. At first, with the noise and peripheral motion and the inchoate leching you are liable to be doing, what with bouffant nymphets rocketing all over the place, these customized cars do not strike you as anything very special. Obviously they *are* very special, but the first thing you think of is the usual—you know, that the kids who own these cars are probably skinny little hoods who wear T shirts and carry their cigarette packs by winding them around in the T shirt up near the shoulder.

But after a while, I was glad I had seen the cars in this natural setting, which was, after all, a kind of Plato's Republic for teenagers. Because if you watched anything at this fair very long, you kept noticing the same thing. These kids are absolutely maniacal about form. They are practically religious about it. For example, the dancers: none of them ever smiled. They stared at each other's legs and feet, concentrating. The dances had no grace about them at all, they were more in the nature of a hoedown, but everybody was concentrating to do them exactly *right*. And the bouffant kids all had form, wild form, but form with rigid standards, one gathers. Even the boys. Their dress was prosaic—Levi's, Slim Jims, sport shirts, T shirts, polo shirts—but the form was consistent: a stove-pipe silhouette. And they all had the same hairstyle: some wore it long, some short, but none of them had a part; all that hair was brushed back straight from the hairline. I went by one of the guitar booths, and there was a little kid in there, about thirteen, playing the hell out of an electric guitar. The kid was named Cranston something or other. He looked like he ought to be named Kermet or Herschel; all his genes were kind of horribly Okie. Cranston was playing away and a big crowd was watching. But Cranston was slouched back with his spine bent like a sapling up against a table, looking gloriously bored. At thirteen, this kid was being fanatically cool. They all were. They were all wonderful slaves to form. They have created their own style of life, and they are much more authoritarian about enforcing it than are adults. Not only that, but today these kids—especially in California—have *money*, which, needless to say, is why all these shoe merchants and guitar sellers and the Ford Motor Company were at a Teen Fair in the first place. I don't mind observing that it is this same combination—money plus slavish devotion to form—that accounts for Versailles or St. Mark's Square. Naturally, most of the artifacts that these kids' money-plus-form produce are of a pretty ghastly order. But so was most of the paraphernalia that developed in England during the Regency. I mean, most of it was on the order of starched cravats. A man could walk into Beau Brummel's house at 11 A.M., and here would come the butler with a tray of wilted linen. "These were some of our failures," he confides. But then Brummel comes downstairs wearing one perfect starched cravat. Like one perfect iris, the flower of Mayfair civilization. But the Regency period did see some tremendous formal architecture. And the kids' formal society has also brought at least one substantial thing to a formal development of a high order—the customized cars. I don't have to dwell on the point that cars mean more to these kids than architecture did in Europe's great formal century, say, 1750 to 1850. They are freedom, style, sex, power, motion, color—everything is right there.

Things have been going on in the development of the kids' formal attitude toward cars since 1945, things of great sophistication that adults have not been even remotely aware of, mainly because the kids are so inarticulate about it, especially the ones most hipped on the subject. They are not from the levels of society that produce children who write sensitive analytical prose at age seventeen, or if they do, they soon fall into the hands of English instructors who put them onto Hemingway or a lot of goddamn-and-hungry-breast writers. If they ever write about a highway again, it's a rain-slicked highway and the sound of the automobiles passing over it is like the sound of tearing silk, not that one household in ten thousand has heard the sound of tearing silk since 1945.

Anyway, we are back at the Teen Fair and I am talking to Tex Smith and to Don Beebe, a portly young guy with a white sport shirt and Cuban sunglasses. As they tell me about the Ford Custom Car Caravan, I can see that Ford has begun to comprehend this teen-age style of life and its potential. The way Ford appears to figure it is this: Thousands of kids are getting hold of cars and either hopping them up for speed or customizing them to some extent, usually a little of both. Before they get married they pour *all* their money into this. If Ford can get them hooked on Fords now, after the kids are married they'll buy new Fords. Even the kids who aren't full-time car nuts themselves will be influenced by which car is considered "boss." They use that word a lot, "boss." The kids used to consider Ford the hot car, but then, from 1955 to 1962, Chevrolet became the favorite. They had big engines and were easy to hop up, the styling was simple, and the kids could customize them easily. In 1959, and more so in 1960, Plymouth became a hot car, too. In 1961 and 1962, it was all Chevrolet and Plymouth. Now Ford is making a big push. A lot of the professional hot-rod and custom-car people, adults, will tell you that now Ford is the hot car, but you have to discount some of it, because Ford is laying money on everybody right and left, in one form or another. In the Custom Car Caravan, all the cars have been fashioned out of Ford bodies except the ones that are completely handmade, like the aforementioned Silhouette.

Anyway, Don Beebe is saying, over a loudspeaker, "I hate to break up that dancing, but let's have a little drag racing." He has a phonograph hooked up to the loudspeaker, and he puts on a record, produced by Riverside Records, of drag-strip sounds, mainly dragsters blasting off and squealing from the starting line. Well, he doesn't really break up the dancing, but a hundred kids come over, when they hear the drag-strip sounds, to where Beebe has a slot-racing stand. Slot racing is a model-train-type game in which two model drag racers, each about five inches long, powered by electricity, run down a model drag strip. Beebe takes a microphone and announces that Dick Dale, the singer, is here, and anybody who will race Dick at the slot-racing stand will get one of his records. Dick Dale is pretty popular among the kids out here because he sings a lot of "surfing" songs. The surfers—surfboard riders—are a cult much admired by all the kids. They have their own argot, with adjectives like "hang ten," meaning the best there is. They also go in for one particular brand of customizing: they take old wood-bodied station wagons, which they call "woodies," and fix them up for riding, sleeping and hauling surfing equipment for their weekends at the beach. The surfers also get a hell of a bang out of slot racing for some reason, so with Dick Dale slot racing at the Teen Fair, you have about three areas of the arcane teen world all rolled into one.

Dick Dale, rigged out in Byronic shirt and blue cashmere V-neck sweater and wraparound sunglasses, singer's mufti U.S.A., has one cord with a starter button, while a bouffant nymphet from Newport named Sherma, Sherma of the Capri pants, has the other one. Don Beebe flashes a starting light and Sherma lets out a cry, not a thrilled cry, just nerves, and a model 1963 Ford and a model dragster go running down the slot board, which is about chest high. The slot board is said to be one-twenty-fifth the actual size of a drag strip, which somehow reminds you of those incredible stamp-size pictures in the dictionary with the notation that this is one-hundredth the size of a real elephant. A hundred kids were packed in around the slot racers and did not find it incredible. That is, they were interested in who would win, Dick Dale or Sherma. I'm sure they had no trouble magnifying the slot racers twenty-five times to the size of the full-blown, esoteric world of hot rods and custom cars.

I MET GEORGE BARRIS, ONE OF THE CELEBRITIES OF THE custom-car world, at the Teen Fair. Barris is the biggest name in customizing. He is a good example of a kid who grew up completely absorbed in this teen-age world of cars, who pursued the pure flame and its forms with such devotion that he emerged an artist. It was like Tiepolo emerging from the studios of Venice, where the rounded Grecian haunches of the murals on the Palladian domes hung in the atmosphere like clouds. Except that Barris emerged from the auto-body shops of Los Angeles.

Barris invited me out to his studio—only he would never think of calling it that, he calls it Kustom City—at 10811 Riverside Drive in North Hollywood. If there is a river within a thousand miles of Riverside Drive, I saw no sign of it. It's like every place else out there: endless scorched boulevards lined with one-story stores, shops, bowling alleys, skating rinks, tacos drive-ins, all of them shaped not like rectangles but like trapezoids, from the way the roofs slant up from the back and the plate-glass fronts slant out as if they're going to pitch forward on the sidewalk and throw up. The signs are great, too. They all stand free on poles outside. They have horribly slick dog-legged shapes that I call boomerang modern. As for Kustom City—Barris grew up at the time when it was considered sharp to change all the C's to K's. He also sells Kandy Lac to paint cars Kandy Kolors with, and I know that sibilant C in City must have bothered the hell out of him at some point. It's interesting, I think, that he still calls the place Kustom City, and still sells Kandy Kolors, because he is an intelligent person. What it means is, he is absolutely untouched by the big amoeba god of Anglo-European sophistication that gets you in the East. You know how it is in the East. One day you notice that the boss's button-down shirt has this sweet percale roll to it, while your own was obviously slapped together by some mass-production graph keepers who are saving an eighth of inch of cloth per shirt, twelve inches per bolt or the like, and this starts eating at you.

Barris, whose family is Greek, is a solid little guy, five feet seven, thirty-seven years old, and he looks just like Picasso. When he's working, which is most of the time, he wears a heavy white T-style shirt, faded off-white pants cut full with pleats in the manner of Picasso walking along in the wind on a bluff at Rapallo, and crepe-sole slipper-style shoes, also off-white. Picasso, I should add, means nothing to Barris, although he knows who he is. It's just that to Barris and the customizers there is no one great universe of form and design called Art. Yet that's the universe he's in. He's not building cars, he's creating forms.

Barris starts taking me through Kustom City, and the place looks like any other body shop at first, but pretty soon you realize you're in a *gallery*. This place is full of cars such as you have never seen before. Half of them will never touch the road. They're put on trucks and trailers and carted all over the country to be exhibited at hot-rod and custom-car shows. They'll run, if it comes to that—they're full of big, powerful, hopped-up chrome-plated motors, because all that speed and power, and all that lovely apparatus, has tremendous emotional meaning to everybody in customizing. But it's like one of these Picasso or Miró rugs. You don't walk on the damn things. You hang them on the wall. It's the same thing with Barris' cars. In effect, they're sculpture.

For example, there is an incredible object he built called the XPAK-400 air car. The customizers love all that X jazz. It runs on a cushion of air, which is beside the point, because it's a pure piece of curvilinear abstract sculpture. If Brancusi is any good, then this thing belongs on a pedestal, too. There is not a straight line in it, and only one true circle, and those countless planes, and tremendous baroque fins, and yet all in all it's a rigid little piece of solid geometrical harmony. As a matter of fact, Brancusi and Barris both developed out of a design concept that we can call Streamlined Modern or Thirties Curvilinear—via utterly different roads, of course—and Barris and most other custom artists are carrying this idea of the abstract curve, which is very tough to handle, on and on and on at a time when your conventional designers—from architects to the guys who lay out magazines—are all Mondrian. Even the young Detroit car stylists are all Mondrian. Only the aircraft designers have done anything more with the Streamline, and they have only because they're forced to by physics, and so on. I want to return to that subject in a minute, but first I want to tell you about another car Barris was showing me.

This was stuck back in a storeroom. Barris wasn't interested in it any more since he did it nine years ago. But this car—this old car, as far as Barris was concerned—was like a dream prefiguration of a very hot sports car, the Quantum, that Saab has come out with this year after a couple of years of consultation with all sorts of aerodynamic experts and advance-guard designers. They're beautiful cars—Saab's and Barris'. They're the same body, practically—with this lovely topology rolling down over the tunneled headlights, with the whole hood curving down very low to the ground in front. I told Barris about the similarity, but he just shrugged; he is quite used to some manufacturer coming up with one of his cars five or six years later.

Anyway, Barris and I were walking around the side of Kustom City, through the parking lot, when I saw an Avanti, the new Studebaker sports model, very expensive. This one had paper mock-ups added to the front and the rear, and so I asked Barris about it. That wasn't much, he said; starting with the paper mock-ups, it brought the hood out a foot with a chic slope to it. He was doing the same sort of thing in the back to eliminate that kind of loaf-of-bread look. It really makes the car. Barris doesn't regard this as a very major project. It may end up in something like a kit you can buy, similar to the old Continental kits, to rig up front and back.

If Barris and the customizers hadn't been buried in the alien and suspect underworld of California youth, I don't think they would seem at all unusual by now. But they've had access to almost nothing but the hot-rod press. They're like Easter Islanders. Suddenly you come upon the astonishing objects, and then you have to figure out how they got there and why they're there.

If you study the work of Barris or Cushenberry, the aforementioned Silhouette, or Ed Roth or Darryl Starbird, can you beat that name?, I think you come up with a fragment of art history. Somewhere back in the thirties, designers, automobile designers among them, came up with the idea of the Streamline. It sounded "functional," and on an airplane it is functional, but on a car it's not, unless you're making a Bonneville speed run. Actually, it's baroque. The Streamline is baroque abstract or baroque modern or whatever you want to call it. Well, about the time the Streamline got going—in the thirties, you may recall, we had curved buildings, like the showpieces later, at the World's Fair—in came the Bauhaus movement, which was blown-up Mondrian, really. Before you knew it, everything was Mondrian—the

Kleenex box: Mondrian; the format of the cover of *Life* Magazine: Mondrian; those bled-to-the-edge photograph layouts in *Paris-Match*: Mondrian. Even automobiles: Mondrian. They call Detroit automobiles streamlined, but they're not. If you don't believe it, look down from an airplane at all the cars parked on a shopping-center apron, and except that all the colors are pastel instead of primary, what have you got? A Mondrian painting. The Mondrian principle, those straight edges, is very tight, very Apollonian. The Streamline principle, which really has no function, which curves around and swoops and flows just for the thrill of it, is very free Dionysian. For reasons I don't have to labor over, the kids preferred the Dionysian. And since Detroit blew the thing, the Dionysian principle in cars was left to people in the teen-age netherworld, like George Barris.

Barris was living in Sacramento when he started customizing cars in 1940. As the plot develops, you have the old story of the creative child, the break from the mold of the parents, the garret struggle, the bohemian life, the first success, the accolade of the esoteric following, and finally the money starts pouring in. With this difference: We're out on old Easter Island, in the buried netherworld of teen-age Californians, and those objects, those cars, they have to do with the gods and the spirit and a lot of mystic stuff in the community.

Barris told me his folks were Greeks who owned a restaurant, and "they wanted me to be a restaurant man, like every other typical Greek, I guess," he said. But Barris, even at ten, was wild about cars, carving streamlined cars out of balsa wood. After a few years, he got a car of his own, a 1925 Buick, then a 1932 Ford. Barris established many of the formal conventions of customizing himself. Early in the game he had clients, other kids who paid him to customize their cars. In 1943 he moved to Los Angeles and landed in the middle of the tremendous teen-age culture that developed there during the war. Family life was dislocated, as the phrase goes, but the money was pouring in, and the kids began to work up their own style of life—as they've been doing ever since—and to establish those fanatic forms and conventions I was talking about earlier. Right at the heart of it, of course, was the automobile. Cars were hard to come by, what with the war, so the kids were raiding junkyards for parts, which led to custom-built cars, mostly roadsters by the very nature of it, and also to a lot of radical, hopped-up engines. All teen-age car nuts had elements of both in their work—customizing and hot-rodding, form and power—but tended to concentrate on one or the other. Barris—and Ed Roth later told me it was the same with him—naturally gravitated toward customizing. In high school, and later for a brief time at Sacramento College and the Los Angeles Art Center, he was taking what he described to me as mechanical drawing, shop, and free art.

I liked this term "free art." In Barris' world at the time, and now for that matter, there was no such thing as great big old fructuous Art. There was mechanical drawing and then there was free art, which did not mean that it was liberating in any way, but rather that it was footloose and free and not going anywhere in particular. The kind of art that appealed to Barris, and meant something to the people he hung around with, was the automobile.

Barris gets a wonderful reflective grin on his face when he starts talking about the old days—1944 to 1948. He was a hot-rodder when hot-rodders were hot-rodders, that's the kind of look he gets. They all do. The professional hot-rodders—such as the Petersen magazine syndicate (*Hot Rod Magazine* and many others) and the National Hot Rod Association—have gone to great lengths to obliterate the memory of the gamey hot-rod days, and they try to give everybody in the field transfusions of Halazone so that the public will look at the hot-rodders as nice boys with short-sleeved sport shirts just back from the laundry and a chemistry set, such an interesting hobby.

In point of fact, Barris told me, it was a lurid time. Everybody would meet in drive-ins, the most famous of them being the Piccadilly out near Sepulveda Boulevard. It was a hell of a show, all the weird-looking roadsters and custom cars, with very loud varoom-varoom motors. By this time Barris had a '36 Ford roadster with many exotic features.

"I had just come from Sacramento, and I wasn't supposed to know anything. I was a tourist, but my car was wilder than anything around. I remember one night this kid comes up with a roadster with no door handles. It looked real sharp, but he had to kick the door from the inside to open it. You should have seen the look on his face when he saw mine—I had the same thing, only with electric buttons."

The real action, though, was the drag racing, which was quite, but quite, illegal.

"We'd all be at the Piccadilly or some place, and guys would start challenging each other. You know, a guy goes up to another guy's car and looks it up and down like it has gangrene or something, and he says: 'You wanna *go?*' Or, if it was a real grudge match for some reason, he'd say, 'You wanna go for pink slips?' The registrations on the cars were pink; in other words, the winner got the other guy's car.

"Well, as soon as a few guys had challenged each other, everybody would ride out onto this stretch of Sepulveda Boulevard or the old divided highway, in Compton, and the guys would start dragging, one car on one side of the center line, the other car on the other. Go a quarter of a mile. It was wild. Some nights there'd be a thousand kids lining the road to watch, boys and girls, all sitting on the sides of their cars with the lights shining across the highway."

But George, what happened if some ordinary motorist happened to be coming down the highway at this point?

"Oh, we'd block off the highway at each end, and if some guy wanted to get through anyway, we'd tell him, 'Well, Mister, there are going to be two cars coming down both sides of the road pretty fast in a minute, and you can go through if you want to, but you'll just have to take your best shot.'

"They always turned around, of course, and after a while the cops would come. Then you *really* saw something. Everybody jumped in their cars and took off, in every direction. Some guys would head right across a field. Of course, all our cars were so hopped up, the cops could never catch anybody.

"Then one night we got raided at the Piccadilly. It was one Friday night. The cops came in and just started loading everybody in the wagons. I was sitting in a car with a cop who was off duty—he was a hot-rodder himself—or they would have picked me up, too. Saturday night everybody came back to the Piccadilly to talk about what happened the night before, and the cops came back again and picked up three hundred fifty that night. That pretty well ended the Piccadilly."

From the very moment he was on his own in Los Angeles, when he was about eighteen, Barris never did anything but customize cars. He never took any other kind of job. At first he worked in a body shop that took him on because so many kids were coming by wanting this and that done to their cars, and the boss really didn't know how to do it, because it was all esoteric teen-age stuff. Barris was making next to nothing at first, but he never remembers feeling hard up, nor does any kid out there today I talked to. They have a magic economy or something. Anyway, in 1945 Barris opened his own shop on Compton Avenue, in Los Angeles, doing nothing but customizing. There was that much demand for it. It was no sweat, he said; pretty soon he was making better than $100 a week.

Most of the work he was doing then was modifying Detroit cars—chopping and channeling. Chopping is lowering the top of the car, bringing it nearer to the hood line. Channeling is lowering the body itself down between the wheels. Also, they'd usually strip off all the chrome and the door handles and cover up the wheel openings in the back. At that time, the look the kids liked was to have the body lowered in the back and slightly jacked up in the front, although today it's just the opposite. The front windshield in those days was divided by a post, and so chopping the top gave the car a very sinister appearance. The front windshield always looked like a couple of narrow, slitty little eyes. And I think this, more than anything else, diverted everybody from what Barris and the others were really doing. Hot-rodders had a terrible reputation at that time, and no line was ever drawn between hot-rodders and custom-car owners, because, in truth, they were speed maniacs, too.

This was Barris' chopped-and-channeled Mercury period. Mercurys were his favorite. All the kids knew the Barris styling and he was getting a lot of business. What he was really doing, in a formal sense, was trying to achieve the kind of streamlining that Detroit, for all intents and purposes, had abandoned. When modified, some of the old Mercurys were more streamlined than any standard model that Detroit has put out to this day. Many of the coupes he modified had a very sleek slope to the back window that has been picked up just this year in the "fastback" look of the Rivieras, Sting Rays, and a few other cars.

At this point Barris and the other customizers didn't really have enough capital to do many completely original cars, but they were getting more and more radical in modifying Detroit cars. They were doing things Detroit didn't do until years later—tailfins, bubbletops, twin headlights, concealed headlights, "Frenched" headlights, the low-slung body itself. They lifted some twenty designs from him alone. One, for example, is the way cars now have the exhaust pipes exit through the rear bumper or fender. Another is the bullet-shaped, or breast-shaped if you'd rather, front bumpers on the Cadillac.

Barris says "lifted," because some are exact down to the most minute details. Three years ago when he was in Detroit, Barris met a lot of car designers and, "I was amazed," he told me. "They could tell me about cars I built in 1945. They knew all about the four-door '48 Studebaker I restyled. I chopped the top and dropped the hood and it ended up a pretty good-looking car. And the bubbletop I built in 1954—they knew all about it. And all this time we thought they frowned on us."

Even today—dealing with movie stars and auto manufacturers and all sorts of people on the outside— I think Barris, and certainly the others, still feel psychologically a part of the alien teenage netherworld in which they grew up. All that while they were carrying the torch for the Dionysian Streamline. They were America's modern baroque designers—and, oddly enough, "serious" designers, Anglo-European-steeped designers, are just coming around to it. Take Saarinen, especially in something like his T.W.A. terminal at Kennedy. The man in his last years came around to baroque modern.

It's interesting that the customizers, like sports-car fans, have always wanted cars minus most of the chrome—but for different ideals. The sports-car owner thinks chrome trim interferes with the "classic" look of his car. In other words, he wants to simplify the thing. The customizer thinks chrome interferes with something else—the luxurious baroque Streamline. The sports-car people snigger at tailfins. The customizers love them and, looked at from a baroque standard of beauty, they are really not so trashy at all. They are an inspiration, if you will, a wonderful fantasy extension of the curved line, and since the car in America is half fantasy anyway, a kind of baroque extension of the ego, you can build up a good argument for them.

Getting back to Easter Island, here were Barris and the others with their blowtorches and hard-rubber mallets, creating their baroque sculpture, cut off from the rest of the world and publicized almost solely via the teen-age grapevine. Barris was making a fairly good living, but others were starving at this thing. The pattern was always the same: a guy would open a body shop and take on enough hack collision work to pay the rent so that he could slam the door shut at 2 P.M. and get in there and do his custom jobs, and pretty soon the guy got so he couldn't even face *any* collision work. Dealing with all those crusty old arteriosclerotic bastards takes up all your *time,* man, and so they're trying to make a living doing nothing but custom work, and they are starving.

The situation is a lot like that today, except that customizing is beginning to be rationalized, in the sense Max Weber used that word. This rationalization, or efficient exploitation, began in the late forties when an $80-a-week movie writer named Robert Petersen noticed all the kids pouring money into cars in a little world they had created for themselves, and he decided to exploit it by starting *Hot Rod Magazine,* which clicked right away and led to a whole chain of hot-rod and custom-car magazines. Petersen, by the way, now has a pot of money and drives Maseratis and other high-status-level sports cars of the Apollonian sort, not the Dionysian custom kind. Which is kind of a shame, because he has the money to commission something really incredible.

Up to that time the only custom-car show in the country was a wild event Barris used to put on bereft of any sort of midwifery by forty-two-year-old promoters with Windsor-knot ties who usually run low-cost productions. This car show was utterly within the teen-age netherworld, with no advertising or coverage of any sort. It took place each spring—during the high-school Easter vacations—when all the kids, as they still do, would converge on the beach at Balboa for their beer-drinking-*Fasching* rites, or whatever the Germans call it. Barris would rent the parking lot of a service station on a corner for a week, and kids from all over California would come with their customized cars. First there would be a parade; the cars, about a hundred fifty of them, would drive all through the streets of Balboa, and the kids would line the sidewalks to watch them; then they'd drive back to the lot and park and be on exhibit for the week.

Barris still goes off to Balboa and places like that. He likes that scene. Last year at Pacific Ocean Park he noticed all these bouffant babies and got the idea of spraying all those great puffed-up dandelion heads with fluorescent water colors, the same Kandy Kolors he uses on the cars. Barris took out an air gun, the girls all lined up and gave him fifty cents per, and he sprayed them with these weird, brilliant color combinations all afternoon until he ran out of colors. Each girl would go skipping and screaming away out onto the sidewalks and the beaches. Barris told me, "It was great that night to take one of the rides, like the Bubble Ride, and look down and see all those fluorescent colors. The kids were bopping [dancing] and running around."

The Bubble is a ride that swings out over the ocean. It is supposed to be like a satellite in orbit.

"But the fellows sky-diving got the best look as they came down by parachute."

In 1948 Petersen put on the first custom-car show in the Los Angeles armory, and this brought customizing out into the open a little. A wild-looking Buick Barris had remodeled was one of the hits of the show, and he was on his way, too.

At some point in the fifties a lot of Hollywood people discovered Barris and the customizers. It was somewhat the way the literary set had discovered the puppeteer Tony Sarg during the thirties and deified him in a very arty, in-groupy way, only I think in the case of Hollywood and Barris there was something a lot more in-the-grain about it. The people who end up in Hollywood are mostly Dionysian sorts and they feel alien and resentful when confronted with the Anglo-European ethos. They're a little slow to note the difference between top-sides and sneakers, but they appreciate Cuban sunglasses.

In his showroom at Kustom City, down past the XPAK-4oo air car, Barris has a corner practically papered with photographs of cars he has customized or handmade for Hollywood people: Harry Karl, Jayne Mansfield, Elvis Presley, Liberace, and even celebrities from the outside like Barry Goldwater (a Jaguar with a lot of airplane-style dials on the dashboard) and quite a few others. In fact, he built most of the wild cars that show-business people come up with for publicity purposes. He did the "diamond-dust" paint job on the Bobby Darin Dream Car, which was designed and built by Andy DiDia of Detroit. That car is an example par excellence of baroque streamlining, by the way. It was badly panned when pictures of it were first published, mainly because it looked like Darin was again forcing his ego on the world. But as baroque modern sculpture—again, given the fantasy quotient in cars to begin with—it is pretty good stuff.

As the hot-rod and custom-car-show idea began catching on, and there are really quite a few big ones now, including one at the Coliseum up at Columbus Circle last year, it became like the culture boom in the other arts. The big names, particularly Barris and Roth but also Starbird, began to make a lot of money in the same thing Picasso has made a lot of money in: reproductions. Barris' creations are reproduced by AMT Models as model cars. Roth's are reproduced by Revel. The way people have taken to these models makes it clearer still that what we have here is no longer a car but a design object, an *objet,* as they say.

Of course, it's not an unencumbered art form like oil painting or most conventional modern sculpture. It carries a lot of mental baggage with it, plain old mechanical craftsmanship, the connotations of speed and power and the aforementioned mystique that the teen-age netherworld brings to cars. What you have is something more like sculpture in the era of Benvenuto Cellini, when sculpture was always more tied up with religion and architecture. In a lot of other ways it's like the Renaissance, too. Young customizers have come to Barris' shop, for example, like apprentices coming to the feet of the master. Barris said there were eleven young guys in Los Angeles right now who had worked for him and then gone out on their own, and he doesn't seem to begrudge them that.

"But they take on too much work," he told me. "They want a name, fast, and they take on a lot of work, which they do for practically nothing, just to get a name. They're usually undercapitalized to begin with, and they take on too much work, and then they can't deliver and they go bankrupt."

There's another side to this, too. You have the kid from the small town in the Midwest who's like the kid from Keokuk who wants to go to New York and live in the Village and be an artist and the like—he means, you know, things around home are but *hopelessly,* totally square; home and all that goes with it. Only the kid from the Midwest who wants to be a custom-car artist goes to Los Angeles to do it. He does pretty much the same thing. He lives a kind of suburban bohemian life and takes odd jobs and spends the rest of his time at the feet of somebody like Barris, working on cars.

I ran into a kid like that at Barris'. We were going through his place, back into his interiors—car interiors—department, and we came upon Ronny Camp. Ronny is twenty-two, but he looks about eighteen because he has teen-age posture. Ronny is, in fact, a bright and sensitive kid with an artistic eye, but at first glance he seems always to have his feet propped up on a table or something so you can't walk past, and you have to kind of bat them down, and he then screws up his mouth and withdraws his eyeballs to the optic chiasma and glares at you with his red sulk. That was the misleading first impression.

Ronny was crazy over automobiles and nobody in his hometown, Lafayette, Indiana, knew anything about customizing. So one day Ronny packs up and tells the folks, This is it, I'm striking out for hip territory, Los Angeles, where a customizing artist is an artist. He had no idea where he was going, you understand, all he knew was that he was going to Barris' shop and make it from there. So off he goes in his 1960 Chevrolet.

Ronny got a job at a service station and poured every spare cent into getting the car customized at Barris'. His car was right there while we were talking, a fact I was very aware of, because he never looked at me. He never took his eyes off that car. It's what is called semi-custom. Nothing has been done to it to give it a really sculptural quality, but a lot of streamlining details have been added. The main thing you notice is the color—tangerine flake. This paint—one of Barris' Kandy Kolor concoctions—makes the car look like it has been encrusted with chips of some kind of semi-precious ossified tangerine, all coated with a half-inch of clear lacquer. There used to be very scholarly and abstruse studies of color and color symbolism around the turn of the century, and theorists concluded that preferences for certain colors were closely associated with rebelliousness, and these are the very same colors many of the kids go for—purple, carnal yellow, various violets and lavenders and fuchsias and many other of these Kandy Kolors.

After he got his car fixed up, Ronny made a triumphal progress back home. He won the trophy in his class at the national hot-rod and custom-car show in Indianapolis, and he came tooling into Lafayette, Indiana, and down the main street in his tangerine-flake 1960 Chevrolet. It was like Ezra Pound going back to Hamilton, New York, with his Bollingen plaque and saying, Here I am, Hamilton, New York. The way Ronny and Barris tell it, the homecoming was a big success—all the kids thought Ronny was all right, after all, and he made a big hit at home. I can't believe the part about home. I mean, I can't really believe Ronny made a hit with a tangerine-flake Chevrolet. But I like to conjecture about his parents. I don't know anything about them, really. All I know is, *I* would have had a hell of a lump in my throat if I had seen Ronny coming up to the front door in his tangerine-flake car, bursting so flush and vertical with triumph that no one would ever think of him as a child of the red sulk— Ronny, all the way back from California with his grail.

ALONG ABOUT 1957, BARRIS STARTED HEARING FROM THE DE- troit auto manufacturers.

"One day," he said, "I was working in the shop—we were over in Lynwood then—and Chuck Jordan from Cadillac walked in. He just walked in and said he was from Cadillac. I thought he meant the local agency. We had done this Cadillac for Liberace, the interior had his songs, all the notes, done in black and white Moroccan leather, and I thought he wanted to see something about that. But he said he was from the Cadillac styling center in Detroit and they were interested in our colors. Chuck—he's up there pretty good at Cadillac now, I think—said he had read some articles about our colors, so I mixed up some samples for him. I had developed a translucent paint, using six different ingredients, and it had a lot of brilliance and depth. That was what interested them. In this paint you look through a clear surface into the color, which is very brilliant. Anyway, this was the first time we had any idea they even knew who we were."

Since then Barris has made a lot of trips to Detroit. The auto companies, mainly GM and Ford, pump him for ideas about what the kids are going for. He tells them what's wrong with their cars, mainly that they aren't streamlined and sexy enough.

"But, as they told me, they have to design a car they can sell to the farmer in Kansas as well as the hot dog in Hollywood."

For that reason—the inevitable compromise—the customizers do not dream of working as stylists for the Detroit companies, although they deal with them more and more. It would be like René Magritte or somebody going on the payroll of Continental Can to do great ideas of Western man. This is an old story in art, of course, genius vs. the organization. But the customizers don't think of corporate bureaucracy quite the way your conventional artist does, whether he be William Gropper or Larry Rivers, namely, as a lot of small-minded Babbitts, venal enemies of culture, etc. They just think of the big companies as part of that vast mass of *adult* America, sclerotic from years of just being too old, whose rules and ideas weigh down upon Youth like a vast, bloated sac. Both Barris and Roth have met Detroit's Young Stylists, and seem to look upon them as monks from another country. The Young Stylists are designers Detroit recruits from the art schools and sets up in a room with clay and styluses and tells to go to it—start carving models, dream cars, new ideas. Roth especially cannot conceive of anyone having any valid concepts about cars who hasn't come out of the teen-age netherworld. And maybe he's right. While the Young Stylists sit in a north-lit studio smoothing out little Mondrian solids, Barris and Roth carry on in the Dionysian loop-the-loop of streamlined baroque modern.

I've mentioned Ed Roth several times in the course of this without really telling you about him. And I want to, because he, more than any other of the customizers, has kept alive the spirit of alienation and rebellion that is so important to the teen-age ethos that customizing grew up in. He's also the most colorful, and the most intellectual, and the most capricious. Also the most cynical. He's the Salvador Dalí of the movement—a surrealist in his designs, a showman by temperament, a prankster. Roth is really too bright to stay within the ethos, but he stays in it with a spirit of luxurious obstinacy. Any style of life is going to produce its celebrities if it sticks to its rigid standards, but in the East a talented guy would most likely be drawn into the Establishment in one way or another. That's not so inevitable in California.

I had been told that Roth was a surly guy who never bathed and was hard to get along with, but from the moment I first talked to him on the telephone he was an easy guy and very articulate. His studio—and he calls it a studio, by the way—is out in Maywood, on the other side of the city from North Hollywood, in what looked to me like a much older and more rundown section. When I walked up, Roth was out on the apron of his place doing complicated drawings and lettering on somebody's ice-cream truck with an airbrush. I knew right away it was Roth from pictures I had seen of him; he has a beatnik-style beard. "Ed Roth?" I said. He said yeah and we started talking and so forth. A little while later we were sitting in a diner having a couple of sandwiches and Roth, who was wearing a shortsleeved T shirt, pointed to this huge tattoo on his left arm that says "Roth" in the lettering style with big serifs that he uses as his signature. "I had that done a couple of years ago because guys keep coming up to me saying, 'Are you Ed Roth?'"

Roth is a big, powerful guy, about six feet four, two hundred seventy pounds, thirty-one years old. He has a constant sort of court attendant named Dirty Doug, a skinny little guy who blew in from out of nowhere, sort of like Ronny Camp over at Barris'. Dirty Doug has a job sweeping up in a steel mill, but what he obviously lives for is the work he does around Roth's. Roth seems to have a lot of sympathy for the Ronny Camp–Dirty Doug syndrome and keeps him around as a permanent fixture. At Roth's behest, apparently, Dirty Doug has dropped his last name, Kinney, altogether, and refers to himself as Dirty Doug—not Doug. The relationship between Roth and Dirty Doug—which is sort of Quixote and Sancho Panza, Holmes and Watson, Lone Ranger and Tonto, Raffles and Bunny—is part of the folklore of the hot-rod and custom-car kids. It even crops up in the hot-rod comic books, which are an interesting phenomenon in themselves. Dirty Doug, in this folklore, is every rejected outcast little kid in the alien netherworld, and Roth is the understanding, if rather overly pranksterish, protective giant or Robin Hood—you know, a good-bad giant, not part of the Establishment.

Dirty Doug drove up in one of his two Cadillacs one Saturday afternoon while I was at Roth's, and he had just gone through another experience of rejection. The police had hounded him out of Newport. He has two Cadillacs, he said, because one is always in the shop. Dirty Doug's cars, like most customizers', are always in the process of becoming. The streaks of "primer" paint on the Cadillac he was driving at the time had led to his rejection in Newport. He had driven to Newport for the weekend. "All the cops have to do is see paint like that and already you're 'one of those hot-rodders,'" he said. "They practically followed me down the street and gave me a ticket every twenty-five feet. I was going to stay the whole weekend, but I came on back."

At custom-car shows, kids are always asking Roth, "Where's Dirty Doug?" and if Dirty Doug couldn't make it for some reason, Roth will recruit any kid around who knows the pitch and install him as Dirty Doug, just to keep the fans happy.

Thus Roth protects the image of Dirty Doug even when the guy's not around, and I think it becomes a very important piece of mythology. The thing is, Roth is not buying the act of the National Hot Rod Association, which for its own reasons, not necessarily the kids' reasons, is trying to assimilate the hot-rod ethos into conventional America. It wants to make all the kids look like candidates for the Peace Corps or something.

The heart of the contretemps between the NHRA Establishment and Roth can be illustrated in their slightly different approach to drag racing on the streets. The Establishment tries to eliminate the practice altogether and restricts drag racing to certified drag strips and, furthermore, lets the people know about that. They encourage the hot-rod clubs to help out little old ladies whose cars are stuck in the snow and then hand them a card reading something like, "You have just been assisted by a member of the Blue Bolt Hot Rod Club, an organization of car enthusiasts dedicated to promoting safety on our highways."

Roth's motto is: "Hell, if a guy wants to go, let him *go*."

Roth's designs are utterly baroque. His air car—the Rotar—is not nearly as good a piece of design as Barris', but his beatnik Bandit is one of the great *objets* of customizing. It's a very Rabelaisian *tour de force*—a twenty-first-century version of a '32 Ford hot-rod roadster. And Roth's new car, the Mysterion, which he was working on when I was out there, is another *tour de force,* this time in the hottest new concept in customizing, asymmetrical design. Asymmetrical design, I gather, has grown out of the fact that the driver sits on one side of the car, not in the middle, thereby giving a car an eccentric motif to begin with. In Roth's Mysterion—a bubbletop coupe powered by two 406-horsepower Thunderbird motors—a thick metal arm sweeps up to the left from the front bumper level, as from the six to the three on a clock, and at the top of it is an elliptical shape housing a bank of three headlights. No headlights on the right side at all; just a small clearance light to orient the oncoming driver. This big arm, by the way, comes up in a spherical geometrical arc, not a flat plane. Balancing this, as far as the design goes, is an arm that comes up over the back of the bubbletop on the right side, like from the nine to the twelve on a clock, also in a spherical arc, if you can picture all this. Anyway, this car takes the Streamline and the abstract curve and baroque curvilinear one step further, and I wouldn't be surprised to see it inspiring Detroit designs in the years to come.

Roth is a brilliant designer, but as I was saying, his conduct and his attitude dilute the Halazone with which the Establishment is trying to transfuse the whole field. For one thing, Roth, a rather thorough-going bohemian, kept turning up at the car shows in a T shirt. That was what he wore at the big National Show at the New York Coliseum, for example. Roth also insists on sleeping in a car or station wagon while on the road, even though he is making a lot of money now and could travel first class. Things came to a head early this year when Roth was out in Terre Haute, Indiana, for a show. At night Roth would just drive his car out in a cornfield, lie back on the front seat, stick his feet out the window and go to sleep. One morning some kid came by and saw him and took a picture while Roth was still sleeping and sent it to the model company Roth has a contract with, Revel, with a note saying, "Dear Sirs: Here is a picture of the man you say on your boxes is the King of the Customizers." The way Roth tells it, it must have been an extraordinarily good camera, because he says, with considerable pride, "There were a bunch of flies flying around my feet, and this picture showed all of them."

Revel asked Roth if he wouldn't sort of spruce up a little bit for the image and all that, and so Roth entered into a kind of reverse rebellion. He bought a full set of tails, silk hat, boiled shirt, cuff links, studs, the whole apparatus, for $215, also a monocle, and now he comes to all the shows like that. "I bow and kiss all the girls' hands," he told me. "The guys get pretty teed off about that, but what can they do? I'm being a perfect gentleman."

To keep things going at the shows, where he gets $1000 to $2000 per appearance—he's that much of a drawing card—Roth creates and builds one new car a year. This is the Dalí pattern, too. Dalí usually turns out one huge and (if that's possible any more) shocking painting each year or so and ships it on over to New York, where they install it in Carstairs or hire a hall if the thing is too big, and Dalí books in at the St. Regis and appears on television wearing a rhinoceros horn on his forehead. The new car each year also keeps Roth's model-car deal going. But most of Roth's income right now is the heavy business he does in Weirdo and Monster shirts. Roth is very handy with the airbrush—has a very sure hand—and one day at a car show he got the idea of drawing a grotesque cartoon on some guy's sweat shirt with the airbrush, and that started the Weirdo shirts. The typical Weirdo shirt is in a vein of draftsmanship you might call Mad Magazine Bosch, very slickly done for something so grotesque, and will show a guy who looks like Frankenstein, the big square steam-shovel jaw and all, only he has a wacky leer on his face, at the wheel of a hot-rod roadster, and usually he has a round object up in the air in his right hand that looks like it is attached to the dashboard by a cord. This, it turns out, is the gearshift. It doesn't look like a gearshift to me, but every kid knows immediately what it is.

"Kids *love* dragging a car," Roth told me. "I mean they really love it. And what they love the most is when they shift from low to second. They get so they can practically *feel* the r.p.m.'s. They can shift without hardly hitting the clutch at all."

These shirts always have a big caption, and usually something rebellious or at least alienated, something like "MOTHER IS WRONG" or "BORN TO LOSE."

"A teen-ager always has resentment to adult authority," Roth told me. "These shirts are like a tattoo, only it's a tattoo they can take off if they want to."

I gather Roth doesn't look back on his own childhood with any great relish. Apparently his father was pretty strict and never took any abiding interest in Roth's creative flights, which were mostly in the direction of cars, like Barris'.

"You've got to be real careful when you raise a kid," Roth told me several times. "You've got to spend time with him. If he's working on something, building something, you've got to work with him." Roth's early career was almost exactly like Barris', the hot rods, the drive-ins, the drag racing, the college (East Los Angeles Junior College and UCLA), taking mechanical drawing, the chopped and channeled '32 Ford (a big favorite with all the hot-rodders), purple paint, finally the first custom shop, one stall in a ten-stall body shop.

"They threw me out of there," Roth said, "because I painted a can of Lucky Lager beer on the wall with an airbrush. I mean, it was a perfect can of Lucky Lager beer, all the details, the highlights, the seals, the small print, the whole thing. Somehow this can of Lucky Lager beer really bugged the guy who owned the place. Here was this can of Lucky Lager beer on *his* wall."

The Establishment can't take this side of Roth, just as no Establishment could accommodate Dadaists for very long. Beatniks more easily than Dadaists. The trick has always been to absorb them somehow. So far Roth has resisted absorption.

"We were the real gangsters of the hot-rod field," Roth said. "They keep telling us we have a rotten attitude. We have a different attitude, but that doesn't make us rotten."

Several times, though, Roth would chuckle over something, usually some particularly good gesture he had made, like the Lucky Lager, and say, "I am a real rotten guy."

Roth pointed out, with some insight, I think, that the kids have a revealing vocabulary. They use the words "rotten," "bad" and "tough" in a very fey, ironic way. Often a particularly baroque and sleek custom car will be called a "big, bad Merc" (for Mercury) or something like that. In this case "bad" means "good," but it also retains some of the original meaning of "bad." The kids know that to adults, like their own parents, this car is going to look sinister and somehow like an assault on their style of life. Which it is. It's rebellion, which the parents don't go for—"bad," which the kids *do* go for, "bad" meaning "good."

Roth said that Detroit is beginning to understand that there are just a hell of a lot of these bad kids in the United States and that they are growing up. "And they want a better car. They don't want an old man's car."

Roth has had pretty much the same experience as Barris with the motor companies. He has been taken to Detroit and feted and offered a job as a designer and a consultant. But he never took it seriously.

"I met a lot of the young designers," said Roth. "They were nice guys and they know a lot about design, but none of them has actually done a car. They're just up there working away on those clay models."

I think this was more than the craftsman's scorn of the designer who never actually does the work, like some of the conventional sculptors today who have never chiseled a piece of stone or cast anything. I think it was more that the young Detroit stylists came to the automobile strictly from art school and the abstract world of design—rather than via the teen-age mystique of the automobile and the teen-age ethos of rebellion. This status-group feeling is very important to Roth, and to Barris, for that matter, because it was only because of the existence of this status group—and this style of life—that custom-car sculpture developed at all.

With the Custom Car Caravan on the road—it has already reached Freedomland—the manufacturers may be well on the way to routinizing the charisma, as Max Weber used to say, which is to say, bringing the whole field into a nice, safe, vinyl-glamorous marketable ball of polyethylene. It's probably already happening. The customizers will end up like those poor bastards in Haiti, the artists, who got too much, too soon, from Selden Rodman and the other folk-doters on the subject of primitive genius, so they're all down there at this moment carving African masks out of mahogany—what I mean is, they never *had* an African mask in Haiti before Selden Rodman got there.

I think Roth has a premonition that something like that is liable to happen, although it will happen to him last, if at all. I couldn't help but get a kick out of what Roth told me about his new house. We had been talking about how much money he was making, and he told me how his taxable income was only about

$6200 in 1959, but might hit $15,000 this year, maybe more, and he mentioned he was building a new house for his wife and five kids down at Newport, near the beach. I immediately asked him for details, hoping to hear about an utterly baroque piece of streamlined architecture.

"No, this is going to be my wife's house, the way she wants it, nothing way out; I mean, she has to do the home scene." He has also given her a huge white Cadillac, by the way, unadorned except for his signature—"Roth"—with those big serifs, on the side. I saw the thing, it's huge, and in the back seat were his children, very sweet-looking kids, all drawing away on drawing pads.

But I think Roth was a little embarrassed that he had disappointed me on the house, because he told me his idea of the perfect house—which turned out to be a kind of ironic parable:

"This house would have this big, round living room with a dome over it, you know? Right in the middle of the living room would be a huge television set on a swivel so you could turn it and see it from wherever you are in the room. And you have this huge easy chair for yourself, you know the kind that you can lean back to about ninety-three different positions and it vibrates and massages your back and all that, and this chair is on tracks, like a railroad yard.

"You can take one track into the kitchen, which just shoots off one side of the living room, and you can ride backward if you want to and watch the television all the time, and of course in the meantime you've pressed a lot of buttons so your TV dinner is cooking in the kitchen and all you have to do is go and take it out of the oven.

"Then you can roll right back into the living room, and if somebody rings the doorbell you don't move at all. You just press a button on this big automatic console you have by your chair and the front door opens, and you just yell for the guy to come in, and you can keep watching television.

"At night, if you want to go to bed, you take another track into the bedroom, which shoots off on another side, and you just kind of roll out of the chair into the sack. On the ceiling above your bed you have another TV set, so you can watch all night."

Roth is given, apparently, to spinning out long Jean Shepherd stories like this with a very straight face, and he told me all of this very seriously. I guess I didn't look like I was taking it very seriously, because he said, "I have a TV set over the bed in my house right now—you can ask my wife."

I met his wife, but I didn't ask her. The funny thing is, I did find myself taking the story seriously. To me it was a sort of parable of the Bad Guys, and the Custom Sculpture. The Bad Guys built themselves a little world and got onto something good and then the Establishment, all sorts of Establishments, began closing in, with a lot of cajolery, thievery and hypnosis, and in the end, thrown into a vinyl Petri dish, the only way left to tell the whole bunch of them where to head in was to draw them a huge asinine picture of themselves, which they were sure to like. After all, Roth's dream house is nothing more than his set of boiled shirt and tails expanded into a whole universe. And he is not really very hopeful about that either.